The Salvation Army
School For Officers' Training
Library
Chicago, Illinois

The Life of Our Lord
Upon the Earth

232.9
AND
Christ — Life of
Jesus — New Testament
1954

651

36065700173801

The Life of Our Lord
Upon the Earth

CONSIDERED IN ITS
HISTORICAL, CHRONOLOGICAL, AND GEOGRAPHICAL
RELATIONS

BY
SAMUEL J. ANDREWS

BIOGRAPHICAL INTRODUCTION BY
Dr. Wilbur M. Smith

ZONDERVAN PUBLISHING HOUSE
Grand Rapids, Michigan

THE LIFE OF OUR LORD was
first published in 1862, when Andrews
was 45 years of age, undergoing complete revision for the edition of
1891, the edition from which this
classic reprint was made.

1954 Edition

Printed in the U. S. A.

TABLE OF CONTENTS.

1651

BIOGRAPHICAL INTRODUCTION

by Wilbur M. Smith

This volume on the life of Christ by Samuel J. Andrews has the unique distinction of being the only permanently important, scholarly life of the Lord Jesus Christ ever produced by an American theologian. The life of the author of such a work cannot then help but be a subject worth studying—and yet, very few of our generation, or even of this half-century could truthfully say that they know much of a definite nature about him. To understand the ministry and literary productions of Samuel J. Andrews, it will be necessary to consider briefly the origin and influence of a movement which, though rarely heard of today, created a great deal of discussion a century ago, and won to itself a very loyal group of devotees at the time of our author's prime — the Catholic Apostolic Church.

Not many fathers have had as many as three sons whose achievements entitle them to notice in the *Dictionary of American Biography,* but this was true of the father of Samuel J. Andrews. Seven children were born to the Rev. William Andrews, sixth in descent from the immigrant William Andrews, who arrived in America in 1635, and his wife Sarah Parkhill. Four of these men attained fame in American theological and educational circles. William Watson Andrews (1810-1897) graduated from Yale University in 1831, and remained throughout his life an intimate friend of Dr. Noah Porter (1811-1892), the president of Yale College. He served as a Congregational minister in the parish of Kent, Connecticut, until identifying himself with the Catholic Apostolic Church in 1844. (His son, Dr. Charles McLean Andrews [1863-1943] became one of the outstanding historians in America, Farnam Professor of American History at Yale University from 1910 to 1931, and author of such famous works as the *Historical Development of Modern Europe,* and *The Colonial Period of*

1

American History.)   Edward Warren Andrews was the first
pastor of the Broadway Tabernacle, New York, beginning
in 1841, the church which was later made famous by the ministry of Dr. Charles E. Jefferson.   Israel Ward Andrews
(1815-1888) was identified with Marietta College for fifty
years, becoming in 1855 both its Professor of Political Science
and its President; the latter office he held with distinction for
thirty years.   Among other volumes, President Andrews wrote
A Manual of the Constitution of the United States (1874),
used extensively as a textbook for many years.

Samuel J. Andrews was born July 31, 1817, and lived to be
almost ninety years of age, his death occurring on October 11,
1906.   He graduated from Williams College in 1839 (the
phenomena often observed in the colonial era of our colleges,
when some young men were graduated from Harvard before
they were eighteen years of age, had passed by the time our
author entered his collegiate life), and was admitted to the
Connecticut Bar in 1842.   Two years later, he was admitted
to the Ohio Bar, and later to the Bar of New York, after
which, for a short period, he practiced law in New York City.
His whole bent, however, was toward theology, and he began
serious theological study at Lane Theological Seminary in
Cincinnati, Ohio.   Mr. Andrews was licensed to preach in
1846, and was ordained pastor of the Congregational Church
in Scantic, East Windsor, Connecticut in 1848, from which
charge he was dismissed after seven years because of the failure of his voice.   This was his only pastorate in the Congregational denomination.   For several years he was in charge of
the Department of Philosophy at Trinity College—a period in
his life about which I have been able to discover nothing
of value.

It will be necessary for us now to turn to the Islands from
which, two centuries before, the founder of the Andrews
family in this land had sailed for America, to consider one of
the strangest ecclesiastical movements of the 19th century.
In the late 1820's, there became apparent in Scotland a deep
longing on the part of some for a new manifestation of the
Spirit of God.   Among those who were bringing new life
to this age, whatever may have been the soundness of his
views, was Dr. McLeod Campbell, author of a work on the

atonement that was to cause a veritable flood of literature in repudiation and defense. In the group of those deeply moved by all this was a Mr. A. J. Scott, who insisted that the spiritual gifts of the early church, such as prophesying and speaking in tongues, would appear at the close of the age, as a sign of the near approach of the second advent of Christ. In this crisis, a woman of devout character, Mary Campbell, of Fernicarry, was miraculously healed of consumption, or so those near-by claimed, causing a writer in *Frazer's Magazine* to declare, "By this young woman it was that God not many months after would restore the gift of speaking with tongues and prophesying to the Church." This was followed by other miraculous cures, and an outburst of speaking in tongues.

Among those who were profoundly influenced by this movement was the gifted Edward Irving (1792-1834), a personal friend of Thomas Carlyle and Jane Welsh, whose ministry in London can be compared only to the sudden appearance of a blinding meteor. Irving's earlier ministry at Regent Square drew vast audiences from every level of British society, but soon the continual speaking in tongues, accompanied by shrieks and all sorts of physical manifestations in the congregation, which Irving failed to control, or repudiate, led to the alienation of many, and to his ultimate expulsion from the Presbyterian Church in Scotland, of which he had been a member (for some time serving as assistant to the great Thomas Chalmers in Glasgow). This movement, oddly enough, developed into something closely akin to Romanism, with definite emphasis upon apostolic succession, the sacraments, an elaborate ritual, etc.

Irving and others believed that the original order of apostles should now be restored, though it was not until after his own death that the apostolic company of twelve was completed. They insisted on the importance of the headship of Christ over all the Church, a display of all the gifts originally bestowed by the Holy Spirit, including tongues and healing, and had a deep conviction that the return of Christ was near.

Irving himself was carried away with prophetic studies to which he had been introduced in the private conferences on prophecy held in the home of the famous banker and Christian layman, Henry Drummond (in no way related to the later

Christian leader bearing that name, active at times in the great revivals of D. L. Moody). The time of the second coming of Christ was dogmatically set for 1868, the theory being put forth that the vials of the Apocalypse began to be poured out in 1793, and that the last one would be poured out seventy-five years later. Irving himself did not always hold to this particular date, for in 1831, preaching at Doncaster, he declared that within three and one-half years believers would be caught up to be with the Lord, and the world would be delivered over to judgment.

Returning to our own shores, it is important to note that William Watson Andrews, upon his graduation from Yale in 1831, had his attention drawn, even then, to these peculiar manifestations in Scotland and in the so-called Irvingite movement. In 1845 he crossed the ocean to visit the leaders of the Catholic Apostolic Church, the ritual and doctrine of which was then fully developed. Deeply impressed by what he observed, in 1849 he united with the Catholic Apostolic Church in this country, coming under the influence of two notable Canadian apostles, George Ryerson, the "angel" of the Toronto church, and W. L. MacKenzie. Together with his brother Samuel J. Andrews and John S. Davenport, he took up residence in Hartford, Connecticut, where the congregation was soon large enough to require the erection of a church building. This, in 1896, was located opposite Hartford Theological Seminary, but "as the site was needed by the city for other purposes, that building was demolished and the present modern and attractive one was erected in a residential part." In 1855, Samuel J. Andrews followed his brother into this communion.

The brilliance, the noble character, and the prominence of the Andrews brothers elicited from their friends long letters of protest, pleading with them to refrain from going along with this strange and wrongly-called apostolic movement. Dr. Noah Porter himself wrote to William Andrews, then in England: "The delusion, if you allow me to call it such, is of no ordinary kind. It is adapted to men of a high order. It is altogether aloof from and above the vulgar taste and cannot be agreeable to any but to those who by culture and refinement rise high enough to appreciate its visions and to be interested in its promises. The same is true of Swedenborgianism and all the forms of fanciful Christianity. I cannot but regard its first assumption as one most violent and unwarranted—I mean the assumption of the need or desirableness of a Church—one in any visible sense."

In the "Statement of Faith" of this group, prepared by W. W. Andrews for Schaff's work on the creeds, it is said, "The restoration of the primitive gifts and ministeries . . . is to prepare for the next stage of God's actings. The immediate and special work of the Apostles is to gather and make ready a company of first fruits described (Revelation 7:1-8) as sealed with the seal of the living God." The Catholic Apostolic Church dared to say that, "The two apostolates at the beginning and end of the dispensation (that is, the original twelve apostles appointed by Christ and the twelve apostles appointed by this church) form the company of the four and twenty elders who sit on thrones around the throne of the Great King (Revelation 4:12), partakers of His dominion and associated with Him in His work of judgment and rule." However, nine of these twelve apostles died before 1876, and the vacancies were never filled; as said previously, the last of the twelve died in 1901.

There can be only one conclusion drawn from these facts, and that is, these godly men were deceived in their conception of their relationship to the Church of Christ. It would seem that none of the Andrews brothers ever leaned toward speaking in tongues. The author of this volume never, in all of his writings, set dates for the Lord's return, and in his three principal works he makes no reference whatever to the Catholic Apostolic Church. Though he was a member of this body, I cannot find any indication that he allowed its teachings to pervert or becloud his interpretation of the Word of God as set forth in his major writings. I believe that nothing more is now said in this rapidly decreasing group about an apostolic college.

We may frankly say that no literature came out of the Irvingite movement in England of any lasting importance, with one exception. The flood of pamphlets defending or condemning speaking in tongues is now of no value, except to those specializing in the history of charismatic manifestations, and Edward Irving's own writings, *Babylon and Infidelity Fore-*

doomed of God (1826), and, *Expositions of the Book of
Revelation* (1831, 4 vols.) contain so many fantastic interpretations, especially the latter, that they cannot even be
considered as worthy of being listed in the more valuable
works on the Apocalypse published in the 19th century. The
one exception referred to is the periodical, *The Morning
Watch,* which does contain some studies of prophetic subjects
that are still worth reading.

In America, however, three leaders of the Catholic Apostolic
Church produced a number of volumes and essays that were
quite free from the delusions of the English group: John
Davenport wrote a notable volume on *The Parousia of Christ*
(1876) : William Watson Andrews, in addition to a number
of pamphlets and larger works, did the article on the Catholic Apostolic Church for the first volume of Schaff's *Creeds
of Christendom,* and also, on the same subject, for the second
volume of McClintock and Strong: *Cyclopedia of Biblical,
Theological and Ecclesiastical Literature.* But the one man
of this entire movement who produced works of *permanent*
value, unobscured by fanciful views of church order, or by
date-setting, was the author of the volume to which this
biographical sketch forms a preface. His two more significant
works are in different areas of Biblical teaching, and are
recognized at once as pre-eminent in their respective fields
of investigation. Let us consider the later and lesser-known
volume first and then go on to some concluding words about
this great life of Christ.

In 1890, Mr. Andrews issued the most profound study of
Antichrist and the apostasy of the last days that ever came
from the pen of an American Biblical scholar. This was signi-
ficantly entitled, *Christianity and Anti-Christianity in Their
Final Conflict*; the second edition, published in 1898, embraced
nearly four hundred pages. The four major divisions of the
book will in part indicate the richness of its contents: Part I:
The Teachings of the Scriptures Respecting the Antichrist;
Part II: The Falling Away of the Church; Part III: Tendencies
in Our Day Preparing the Way of the Antichrist; Part IV: The
Reign of the Antichrist. The third part is divided into seven
chapters, the titles of which will give one a further concept of

the scope of Andrews' study: Modern Pantheistic Philosophy
—Modern Philosophy and the New Christianity—Deification
of Humanity—Tendencies of Modern Biblical Criticism—
Tendencies of Modern Science—Tendencies of Modern Literature and the Periodical Press—Christian Socialism and the
Kingdom of God. Every tendency of modern thought toward
the close of the 19th century unfolded in these pages is to be
seen manifested in the middle of this century with even greater
power and more universal influence than Andrews was discerning sixty years ago. One might say that he was a true prophet
of God, fulfilling in his study that gift of the Spirit referred
to by the Apostle Paul in the phrase, "discerning the spirits."

Our author had mastered the writings of the major poets,
scientists, philosophers and theologians of the entire 19th
century, those of Germany, France, Britain and America.
Innumerable events and movements occuring since his death
confirm the insight of almost every page in this volume. He
did not live to see the coming of communism, but his deep
study of the true significance of socialism reads almost as an
inspired utterance. Among other things, Andrews foresaw
the union of Europe, and devoted a number of pages to the
subject.

All who had the privilege of knowing Dr. James M. Gray,
for many years Dean, and then President, of the Moody Bible
Institute, would immediately agree that he was not a person
given to making rash statements. He was a wide reader, and
wrote a number of books himself. It was not often that he
vigorously suggested that some book outside of the Bible was
absolutely indispensable. Concerning Andrews' work, however, which he persuaded the Moody Press to reprint many
years ago, Dr. Gray used the following words which, to my
knowledge, he never allowed himself to use in reference to
any other work:

> After the Bible, a concordance, a Bible dictionary and, per-
> haps, an all-round work like Angus' *Bible Hand-Book*, the next
> book I would recommend as indispensable for the library of
> the pastor, missionary or Christian worker of today is *Chris-
> tianity and Anti-Christianity in Their Final Conflict* by Rev.
> Samuel J. Andrews. As to its scholarship it is only necessary to
> know that the author is he who wrote *The Life of Our Lord,*

which is recognized as the best history of Christ from the chronological standpoint ever published . . .

Originally put out by a New York publisher some years ago, the book commanded so high a price, that, although passing through more than one edition, the larger Christian public never became acquainted with it. And therefore the Bible Institute Colportage Association, at my solicitation, has now obtained the right to bring out a further printing of it, at a more popular figure. It is not a commercial venture on their part, but a Christian philanthropy.

Pastors, missionaries, Sunday-school teachers and social workers, bear with me if I say, *you must read this book.* By Divine grace, I have a large acquaintance among you, wherever the Gospel is preached, and I appeal to you, by whatever spiritual tie unites us, to become acquainted with what this prophet of the twentieth century has to teach.

The full title of Andrews' volume is *The Life of Our Lord Upon the Earth, Considered in Its Historical, Chronological, and Geographical Relations,* which exactly defines the nature of this work. (The English edition of 1884 carried the title, *The Bible Student's Life of Our Lord.*) It was first published in 1862, when Andrews was forty-five years of age, undergoing complete revision for the edition of 1891. It is interesting to note the type of men whose aid Andrews was able to command: Professor A. T. Perry, himself the author of a harmony, constructed the invaluable Synopsis at the beginning of this volume. Proof was read by Professor A. C. Zenos, later to enter a brilliant career of teaching at McCormick Theological Seminary in Chicago, but at this time Professor of New Testament Exegesis at Hartford Theological Seminary. Andrews also gave extensive credit for valuable assistance to Dr. Samuel Hart (1845-1917) then Professor of Latin at Trinity College and later the Professor of Doctrinal Theology and the Prayer Book at Berkeley Divinity School, and to Dr. John H. Barbour (1854-1900), Professor of New Testament Literature and Interpretation in the Berkeley Divinity School. Particularly interesting is his expression of indebtedness "to my younger friends Mr. E. E. Nourse and Mr. C. Hazen," who were at that time "theological students," but were destined to hold high places in theological education in the decades to follow. It is Nourse who contributes the interesting appendix on the Gospel miracles, listing 57 events of a supernatural nature occurring during the life of our Lord. Dr. Edward E.

Nourse (1863-1929) was an instructor in the Hartford Theological Seminary from 1898-1905, and author of a number of important books. Some years later, Professor Nourse, together with Zenos and others, edited the *Standard Dictionary of the Bible,* appearing in 1909, and then, the much larger work published in 1926, *The New Standard Dictionary of the Bible.* It seems a little unfair that when these men constructed a bibliography for the article, "Jesus Christ," in their dictionary, they should have wholly ignored this epochal work by Andrews.

In coming now to a brief consideration of this volume itself, may I repeat the statement which begins this sketch, namely, that the life of Christ by Samuel J. Andrews is the only truly great life of our Lord, resulting from a long, thorough study of the most comprehensive presentations of the chronological, geographical and historical problems of the gospels, that has been produced in this country, although the first edition of this book was issued nearly one hundred years ago. Germany gave us the great lives of Christ by Lange and Neander, not to mention more liberal works, and Britain contributed in the last half of the 19th century those notable works by Geikie, Farrar and Edersheim, and later, David Smith; but for some reason our own country has never produced, since Andrews, any work covering every aspect of the life of Christ that could be called epochal. Our scholars have issued important works on the birth of Christ; including Machen's monumental *The Virgin Birth of Christ;* Votaw has given us one of the greatest studies of the Sermon on the Mount ever done; there have been a few scattered works on the Resurrection of Christ, though none to compare with those published in England; and the best harmonies of the Gospels in our language have originated on this side of the water, especially those by Stevens and Burton, A. T. Robertson, and the more recent one, by A. C. Wieand. It is true that we have had books devoted exclusively to the life of Christ by American writers such as Fahling, Wood, Henry Ward Beecher and Lyman Abbott, but none of them can compare in scholarly worthiness with Andrews.

An enormous amount of material on the life of Christ appeared in Germany, France, England and America in the forty years that elapsed between the first and last edition of Andrews' work, but he kept abreast of all of it. One is surprised to find references to the earlier works of Sir William Ramsay, in this last edition, as well as to the writings of such men as Sanday, Stalker, and Zahn, and even to the great *Dictionary of the Bible* edited by James Hastings. The author of this volume approached the study of the Gospels with a conviction which one seldom finds stated in a modern scholarly life of Christ, and though it appears in the Preface also, I would like to include it here, knowing that many never read a Preface: "There is no fact more important to be kept clearly in mind in these studies than this, that Jesus was very man no less than very God. While recognizing the supernatural elements in the evangelical narratives wherever they exist, we are not so to introduce them as to make these narratives the records of a life neither human nor divine. His life on earth was in the highest sense a human one, and it is this fact that gives us the key to the Gospels as real historical records . . . In Him, as the Everlasting One, not in the Gospel records, Christianity lives. In the light of His present glory how trivial does much of the modern gospel criticism appear . . . Upon all who believe that Jesus is the son of the virgin, very God and very man, now exalted to the right hand of the Father and having all power in heaven and in earth, the boldness with which a few critics attack the truthfulness of the Gospels and find them full of legends and mistakes, will produce little effect. They will read the past in the light of the present, the earthly in the light of the heavenly, and find good ground for belief that the coming years will but confirm and illumine the records of His earthly life and add to their deep significance."

In his *Christianity and Anti-Christianity,* Andrews gives expression to a conviction regarding the earthly life of our Lord which should be included here:

> It need not be said that a knowledge of the earthly life of the Lord is necessary to understand aright His present heavenly life; but as every later stage in a Divine work illustrates and confirms the earlier so is it here. The life on earth gave the basis for the life in heaven, but the continuity of the two must be proved by the last; and from the present we look back,

and judge the past. Thus the Gospels can be rightly read only in the light of the Lord's present heavenly life. If this life be denied or ignored, the Lord's words recorded in them become in many points unintelligible, the true significance of His works is not seen. Criticism, however learned and acute, seeing only the earthly life cannot comprehend it, or enter into the largeness of its meaning as the initial stage of a work which embraces the whole redemptive age. As the full-grown oak shows what was hidden in the acorn, so is it the Heavenly Man who fully reveals the powers hidden in the Babe of Bethlehem, and only partially manifested in the Man of Galilee. The living man is always his own witness that he lives; and the Lord in heaven will be His own witness, unless hindered, as at Nazareth, by the unbelief of His people.

This work by Andrews met with universal praise on both sides of the Atlantic. Dr. Marcus Dods, in his preface to the first volume of the English translation of Lange's great *Life of Christ* went out of his way to say of even the first edition of Andrews' volume: "In this unassuming volume the various opinions of the best authorities are brought together, sifted, arranged, compared and weighed; while the author's own opinion, though never asserted with arrogance or parade, is always worthy of consideration. Indeed, this work is indispensable to any one who intends a thorough study of the subject, but yet has not access to the authorities themselves, or has not leisure to use them. And so extensive is the literature of the mere external aspects of this Life, that it will still be but a few who can dispense with such a handbook as this. The accuracy of his references, and impartiality of his citations, as well as the fairness and candour of his own judgments, inspire us with confidence in the author."

In the finest Harmony of the Gospels to be published in the last sixty years, Stevens and Burton refer, in their preface of 1893, to only two contemporary volumes, in the following words: "Our greatest debt to contemporary works of similar purposes with our own is first, to the Harmony of Edward Robinson, and next, to the Life of our Lord by Samuel J. Andrews, a work into which has gone a lifetime of scholarly research, and to which all students of the Life of Christ are under large obligation."

As a further illustration of the high regard which British

scholars had for this work, I quote here a paragraph review of a later edition of the volume, appearing in *The Expository Times* for 1892 (Vol. III, p. 284):

> The old edition of Andrews' *Life of Our Lord Upon the Earth,* which has got to be known in this country by the title, "The Bible Student's Life of our Lord," has long been recognized as far ahead of all books written to guide us to a better understanding of the Gospels. Writers of lives of Christ, like Dr. Stalker, unhesitatingly place it first of all their authorities. We know at least one painstaking student who confesses to putting Andrews always beside his Bible when he goes from home: "It gives you so much, it saves you so much; and it is so rarely at fault.'
>
> But the old Andrews' will not do any more. The new is better. The new is as much better as the old was better than its rivals. Many of us owe most of all we have about the history, chronology, and geography of the Gospels to our studies in the book as it used to be, and we cannot but envy those who have now to begin upon this fuller, clearer, and more accurate edition. It has been not only revised and brought down to date; the whole book has been worked over slowly, carefully, with every new monogram and magazine article at command, involving a labour greater than the original writing of it, but producing a result more valuable than if this had been its first production. The identity of the old is preserved, but it is a new book. Many matters both exegetical and archaeological are still unsettled, but he who would know what has been done towards their settlement will find it here. One thing is puzzling—why, in a land where degrees are said to be sown broadcast, the author of a work like this should still be plain Samuel Andrews.

In the realization that this work is being reprinted, there is for me only one regret. I somehow feel that the Modern Protestant Church, and especially its New Testament scholars, can hardly escape the justice of the charge of dilatoriness, perhaps even lack of interest, in preparing during this last half-century a new, monumental, worthy life of our Saviour, the Lord Jesus Christ. Why should the Roman Catholic Church produce four magnificent lives of Christ, abreast of the latest scholarship, during this period when the Protestant Church has produced none? The statement of Professor Hunter of Aberdeen, in a recent article on "The Life of Christ in the Twentieth Century" (*Expository Times,* February, 1950, p. 132), is perhaps more true than many of his readers realized—

"There is nothing our world needs more than a fresh and truer vision of the Life of lives." Would that the republication of Andrews' work, pre-eminent for his day, should lead some young man qualified for the task to consecrate his next ten years to giving us a new life of Christ that would be for this era of the Christian Church what Andrews' work was for his generation.

Pasadena, California   WILBUR M. SMITH

Note: In addition to the writings of Samuel J. Andrews, which I have had in my library and used constantly for years, the following works have been of assistance in the writing of this biographical preface:

W. W. Andrews: "The Catholic Apostolic Church," in *Bibliotheca Sacra,* Vol. XXIII, January, 1866, pp. 108-159.

Philip Schaff: *The Creeds of Christendom.* New York, 1905. Vol. I, pp. 905-915.

Samuel J. Andrews: *William Watson Andrews: a Religious Biography.* New York, 1910.

Andrew Landale Drummond: *Edward Irving and His Circle.* London, n.d.

P. E. Shaw: *The Catholic Apostolic Church, Sometimes Called Irvingite—a Historical Study.* New York, 1946. This volume is the result of years of study; originally presented, I believe, as a thesis for a doctorate degree. It is the only thorough modern examination of the Irvingite movement.

Dictionary of American Biography, Volume I.

E. H. Klotsche: *Christion Symbolics.* Rev. ed., Burlington, Iowa, 1929. pp. 327-331. Valuable for its discussion of the division of the Catholic Apostolic Church in Germany.

I am also deeply indebted to Miss Elizabeth DeW. Root, Reference Librarian, and Dr. H. A. Gleason, Jr., Librarian, of the Case Memorial Library of the Hartford Seminary Foundation, for important data; and to the Hartford Public Library for supplying me with photostatic copies of obituary notices of Dr. Samuel J. Andrews.

PREFACE.

THIS book was published in 1862. That it has continued in request for so many years, shows at least that it meets a want not otherwise adequately met. It has seemed to me, therefore, little less than a duty carefully to revise it, and to make it, so far as I am able to do, more worthy of the favor it has received.

In this revision the character of the book has not been changed. It deals with the life of the Lord on the earth in its chronological, topographical, and historical relations only. As was said in the original preface : "It does not design to enter into any questions respecting the authorship of the Gospels, the time when written, or their relations to each other. Nor does it discuss the point of their inspiration, but assumes that they are genuine historical documents, and true statements of facts ; and deals with them as such. Nor does it attempt to explain the Lord's discourses or parables, or to discuss questions of mere archæology or verbal criticism." Of course disputed readings, when bearing on the special objects of our enquiries, have been considered, and for comparison with the *textus receptus* the text of Tischendorf and that of Westcott and Hort have been used, with occasional reference to the readings preferred by Meyer, Alford, Keil, and others. Whenever the translation in the Revised Version seemed to give light, it has been

(v)

quoted. No reference is made to any Greek manu
scripts, as unnecessary to those who use the Greek
Testament, and useless to those who do not.

I am not at all confident that I have always kept
within the limits which my purpose prescribes. The
line between the historical and the archæological is
not always plain, and doubtless some readers will seek
here information which properly belongs to commentaries and Bible dictionaries.

The last thirty years have added much to our
knowledge of the Holy Land, especially through the
explorations of the Palestine Exploration Fund Society
and the English Ordnance Surveys. Of these constant
use has been made. But it remains true that with all
the recent investigations, the sites of many places
mentioned in the Gospels are almost as undetermined
as ever. This may be said of Bethabara, Bethsaida,
Ænon, Capernaum, Cana, Emmaus, Golgotha—all are
still in dispute. If those who have made the topography of the Gospels their special study were agreed as
to results, we could readily accept them ; but as the
most diligent and learned explorers differ, we are
forced to take to our help the statements of others
more or less competent — geographers and travellers
— and so arrive at a probable conclusion. Not a few
may think some of the topographical discussions un-
necessarily long, and ask of what real importance is
it whether Capernaum was one side of the Sea of
Galilee or the other, whether the Lord was transfigured
at Tabor or at Hermon ? Renan asks : " How does it
concern us that Jesus was born in such or such a village, that he had such or such ancestors, that he suffered on such or such a day of the holy week ? " We

answer that these particulars are not unimportant in
the life of Jesus, for they prove the reality of His
earthly history. Time and place are essential parts of
the great fact of the Incarnation. The Son of God,
in becoming man, must be born at a certain period of
the world's history, in a certain portion of its territory,
and stand in well-defined relations to certain of its
inhabitants. Such limitations belong to the very es-
sense of His humanity. These outward facts the
Evangelists do not overlook. It is true that they do
not enter into any great minuteness of detail. Of the
external events of the Lord's life for many years we
know very little. Yet they do not neglect those relations of time and place which are necessary to convince us of the reality of His earthly existence, and to
give us a distinct picture of His labors.

Again, if the elements of time and place are
stricken from the Gospels, the Lord's life ceases to be
a truly human and intelligible one; He becomes only
a wandering Voice. The more fully we know the outward circumstances of His life, and His relations to
those around him, the more do His words gain in significance, and attest His discernment and wisdom.
Thus it is of importance to know, so far as we are
able, both the times and the places of His utterances;
and the labor spent in this study is not idle, but will
yield rich reward.

The present book differs from the original in putting the longer discussions into small type. This is a
gain as to space, and also permits those who are not
interested in them to pass them by. In this I have
had regard to those — Sunday-school teachers and
others who are intelligent students of the Gospels, but

not scholars — who wish results rather than processes.
For them, what is said in the headings and the larger
type will generally suffice. But there are others, edu
cated laymen and theological students — perhaps I
may venture to add clergymen — who wish to have
some full statement of the latest phases of the questions discussed, and references to the chief modern
writers upon them; and for them these statements are
made. They are not exhaustive, much is not said that
might have been said; but they present the means for
inquirers to carry their investigations further.

In regard to references to other books and writers,
a few words may be said. The grounds on which they
are made are these: To enable the reader to verify
the statements of his author; to furnish him the
means of further pursuing his inquiries; to show by
enumeration of names where the weight of authority
lies; and incidentally to indicate if any writer of importance has been neglected. We may err here either
on the side of excess or defect; perhaps many will
think I have erred in the former way. But those who
know how much time is wasted in hunting for passages where references are scanty, will pardon me.

I think it right for me to say, that very rarely is
any reference made at second-hand. That I have not
always hit a writer's meaning is very likely, and there
will certainly be some mistakes, clerical or other; but
I hope that in general the references will be found
accurate. That I refer for the most part only to the
more recent writers, lies in the purpose of the book to
notice the latest results of criticism and investigation. Of course, some notice has been taken of the
older and prominent writers in this department, as

Lightfoot, Lardner, Reland, but the list of books added will show that chief attention has been given to the most recent authors.

Meyer and others often speak disparagingly of "harmonistic expedients," and of forcing the differing narratives of the Evangelists into harmony with one another. But is there any consistent history which is not the result of harmonistic expedients? The discordant statements of credible but independent witnesses are studied and compared, that from them a full and harmonious record may be made. This is true also in its measure of every biography. Why is not the same rule to be applied to the Gospels? If there are found in them statements of facts directly contradictory, truth demands that we frankly acknowledge them ; but if discrepancies only are found, it is perfectly warrantable that we attempt to reconcile them by probable suppositions.

That all will find the solutions of alleged discrepancies and contradictions here given satisfactory, is not to be expected. Nor will the chronological order, or topographical results, be received by all. But it is a great point gained, to be able to see just what the amount of the discrepancy or contradiction, if it really exists, is. Those readers who have been accustomed to hear, through skeptical critics, of the numerous errors and mistakes of the Evangelists, will be surprised to learn how few are the points of real difficulty, and how often these are exaggerated by the misunderstanding of the critic himself. There are not a few commentators who adopt the rigid literalism of Osiander, not like him to defend the credibility of the Gospel narrative, but to destroy it.

There are certain portions of the Gospels whose genuineness is questioned, as Mark xvi. 9-20, John xxi. In regard to the first, which is bracketed by Westcott and Hort, but retained in the Revised Version, it is here accepted as true, but as possibly added at a later period. It is marked as an appendix. In regard to the second, it is accepted as genuine. The account of the adulterous woman, John vii. 53-viii. 11, is bracketed in the Revised Version (bracketed also by Westcott and Hort, and transposed). Its omission does not affect the general narrative.

I repeat what was said in the early Preface : "It will not be expected that I should present, upon a subject discussed for so many centuries by the best minds of the Church, anything distinctively new. Still, I trust that some points have been set in clearer light, and that the general arrangement will facilitate the inquiries of those who seek to know as much as is possible of the external history of the Lord's works and words, that they may the better penetrate into their spiritual meaning. I have given considerable prominence to the great divisions of His work, first in Judæa, and then in Galilee, and to the character of His last journey to Jerusalem, and to the accounts of the resurrection and of His acts after it, both as explaining some peculiarities in the synoptical Gospels, and as showing that His work was carried on under true historic conditions. There is no fact more important to be kept clearly in mind in these studies than this, that Jesus was very man no less than very God. While recognizing the supernatural elements in the evangelic narratives wherever they exist, we are not so to introduce them as to make these narratives the records of a life neither human nor divine. The Lord, in all his words and works, in His conduct toward the Jews, and His repeated efforts to make them hear and receive Him, acted as man, under those laws which God at the beginning established to guide human action. His life on earth was in the highest sense a human one, and it is this fact that gives us the key to the Gospels as real historic records."

I am happy here to acknowledge my obligations to several friends who have taken an interest in this revision, and have helped me in various ways : to Professor E. C. Richardson, former Librarian of the Hartford Theological Seminary, (now of Princeton,) for the free use of its books; also to the present Librarian, Professor A. T. Perry—himself the author of a Harmony—to whom I owe the Synopsis at the begining of this book; and to Professor A. C. Zenos for corrections of proof. To my old friends, Dr. Samuel Hart of Trinity College, and Professor John H. Barbour of the Berkeley Divinity School, I am indebted for most valuable assistance, not only in the reading of the proof, and in critical suggestions, but for some original contributions which are acknowledged in their proper places. I would add my thanks also to my younger friends, Mr. E. E. Nourse and Mr. C. Hazen, theological students, for their aid ; a useful paper by Mr. N. will be found in the Appendix.

I cannot conclude this Preface without expressing my hope that this attempt to set forth the main events in the Lord's life on earth will always be read in the light of the great fact that He "who was dead is alive again forevermore." His life on earth and His labors here were but the initial stage of His work ; and if

questions arise in regard to them which we are not
able to answer, these are of very little importance
when we remember that He IS. In Him, as the Ever-
living One, not in the Gospel records, Christianity
lives. In the light of His present glory how trivial
does much of the modern Gospel criticism appear!
In studying His earthly life we have always need to
keep in mind the Apostle's words: "Though we
have known Christ after the flesh, yet now henceforth know we Him no more." Our communion is
with Him as the immortal and glorified Lord.

Again, after so many years, and with a deeper sense
of its truth, I say: "How poor and unworthy of Him,
the external aspects of whose earthly life I have endeavored in some points to portray, my labors are,
none can feel more deeply than myself. I can only
pray that His blessing — the blessing that changed
the water into wine — may go with this book, and
make it, in some measure, useful to His children."

HARTFORD, CONN., Aug. 1, 1891.

PREFACE TO REVISED EDITION

SINCE the last revision of this book several lives of Christ have appeared, and a number of monographs and articles bearing on the subjects here specially treated of; I have therefore added these, so far as known to me, in an addendum to the former list of authors and books, mentioning particularly those presenting anything distinctively new.

With the development of the modern critical methods and their application to the Gospels, the belief in their unity has been much affected; and the diversity of judgments as to the events of the Lord's life and their order largely increased.

Aside from questions as to the text and the authorship and time of composition, there is emphasized by many the uncertainty whether we have the Lord's words as He spake them or as modified by the Evangelists, thus leaving the reader to put into the Lord's mouth what he thinks He might or ought to have said.

The absence of any authoritative standard of judgment, leaving the critic free to bring all points, even those which have long been regarded as settled, before his bar, and to reject all statements which do not commend themselves to him, necessarily leads to confusion, and often to contradictory conclusions. This is seen especially in the field of chronology. There is no agreement as to the length of the Lord's public ministry, or as to the data on which a sure judgment can rest. One affirms that no Gospel follows a chronological order; another selects a single Gospel, and to its order all the rest are forced to conform; and another finds that a later Evangelist corrects the errors of an earlier. Not a few deny that it is possible to harmonize by any corrections the conflicting statements.

It seems to be accepted as a postulate of much recent criticism, that each Evangelist, not being critically trained, must be more or less wrong, and that it is the business of the critic to set him right.

To this we may add that the most advanced critics, denying to the Lord any Divine commission, get rid of His miracles, and reduce His words to their minimum of meaning.

The general result upon the reader of this liberty to pick and choose, and the consequent diversity of judgments, is that anything like certainty as to many events in the Lord's life, and their order, is unobtainable; and this uncertainty extends also to His teachings.*

Thus the New Testament becomes like the vineyard of the prophet, "the hedge taken away, the wall

---

* We are told by the editors of the "Encyclopædia Biblica," now in process of publication, and the latest representative of the most advanced criticism, that "unfortunately the literary and historical criticism of the New Testament is by no means so far advanced as that of the Old ; for a real history of the movement of religious life and thought in the New Testament period we shall have to wait. As we are unable to check the evangelistic statements, we can treat them only as hypotheses." All the lives of Jesus hitherto written are thus hypothetical; the certainty is to come with the era of "philosophically purified thought."

broken down, so that all who pass by the way do pluck her."

A single remark may be made here. It is obvious that our understanding of the life of any one—of his words and works—must be conditioned by the sphere of that life and its purpose. If Jesus was the Son of God, who was made man that He might be the Saviour of the world, His life, like His person, must have had a wholly distinctive character, and His words and works must be interpreted in accordance with it.

To reduce that life to the level of a mere human life, makes any right interpretation of it impossible. As His person, so His words and works were unique.

In reading much of the recent criticism the Christian believer will first ask as to the belief of the critic; for if the critic believes Jesus to have been a mere man, even if prophetically inspired, his standard of judgment as regards the Gospel records must be far unlike his who believes Him to have been the Incarnate Son.

Upon all who believe that Jesus is the Son of the Virgin, very God and very man, now exalted to the right hand of the Father, and having all power in heaven and in earth, the boldness with which not a few critics attack the truthfulness of the Gospels, and find them full of legends and mistakes, will produce little effect. They will read the past in the light of the present, the earthly in the light of the heavenly, and find good ground for belief that the coming years will but confirm and illumine the records of His earthly life, and add to their deep significance.

Several of the more recent writers upon the chronology of the public ministry of the Lord reduce the time to two years and a half. This is done by making the Judæan ministry of very brief duration. But when we consider the great importance of this period of National trial, ending in the rejection of Him as the Messiah, it is plain that it demanded a considerable interval of time in order that He might fully testify to His Messianic claims, and that the rulers and people in His rejection might act with full knowledge of the character of their action.

I wish to add my thanks to Professor E. E. Nourse, of the Hartford Theological Seminary, for his valuable aid.

HARTFORD, CONN.
April 20, 1900.

LIST OF AUTHORS REFERRED TO.

In the first edition of this book a list was given of the authors referred to, and the titles of their works. To the original list I add the more recent writers, indicating them by an asterisk. I have for the sake of brevity referred rather to names than to titles, except in cases of two or more books by the same writer, when the titles are given.

*ABBOTT, LYMAN, Jesus of Nazareth. New York, 1869.
*ALDRICH, J. K., The Day of Our Saviour's Crucifixion. Boston, 1882.
ALEXANDER, J. A., Commentary upon Matthew and Mark. New York. 1858-1861.
ALFORD, H., The Greek Testament, vol. I., containing the Four Gospels. New York, 1859.

BAEDEKER, K., Palestine and Syria. A Handbook. Leipzig, 1876.
BARCLAY, J. T., City of the Great King. Philadelphia, 1858.
*BARTLETT, S. C., From Egypt to Palestine. New York, 1879.
*BÄUMLEIN, W., Commentar ü. d. Evangelium des Johannes. Stuttgart, 1863.
BAUMGARTEN, M., Die Geschichte Jesu. Braunschweig, 1859.
*BEECHER, H. W., The Life of Jesus, the Christ. New York, 1871.
*BEYSCHLAG, W., Leben Jesu. Halle, 1887.
BLEEK, F., Beiträge zur Evangelien Kritik. Berlin, 1846.
        "   Synoptische Erklärung der drei ersten Evangelien. Leipzig, 1862.
BLOOMFIELD, S. T., Greek Testament with English Notes. Boston, 1837.
*BOVET, F., Egypt and Palestine. Stuttgart, 1863. Trans.
BROWNE, H., Ordo Sæclorum. London, 1844.
BUCHER, J., Das Leben Jesu Christi. Stuttgart, 1859.
*   "   Die Chronologie des Neuen Testamentes. Augsburg, 1865.

*CASPARI, C. E., Chronological and Geographical Introduction to the Life of Christ. Trans. Edinburgh, 1876.

CLINTON, HENRY F., Fasti Romani. Oxford, 1845-1850.
*COHEN, J., Les Deicides. Paris, 1864.
*COLANI, T., Jesus Christ. Strasbourg, 1864.
*CONDER, F. R. and C. R., Handbook of the Bible. London, 1882.
*CONDER, C. R., Tent Work in Palestine. New York, 1878.

*DAWSON, J. W., Egypt and Syria. London, 1885.
DE COSTA, I., The Four Witnesses. New York, 1855.
*DE PRESSENSÉ, E., Jesus Christ: His Times, Life, and Work.
  Trans. New York, 1868.
DE SAULCY, Dead Sea and Bible Lands, Trans. London, 1854.
*DERENBOURG, J., Histoire de la Palestine. Paris, 1867.
*DOLLINGER, J. J., Christenthum und Kirche. Regensburg, 1868.

EBRARD, J. H. A., Wissenschaftliche Kritik der Evangelischen
  Geschichte. Erlangen, 1850. Dritte Auflage, 1868.
*EDERSHEIM, A., The Life and Times of Jesus the Messiah, 5th ed.,
  New York.
*   "   The Temple and its Ministers. American Edition.
*   "   Sketches of Jewish Social Life.   "   "
ELLICOTT, C. J., Historical Lectures on the Life of Our Lord. Lon-
  don, 1860.
EWALD, H., Drei ersten Evangelien. Göttingen, 1850.
      "   Die Alterthümer des Volkes Israel. Göttingen, 1854.
      "   Geschichte Christus und seiner Zeit. Göttingen, 1857.

FAIRBAIRN, P., Hermeneutical Manual. Philadelphia, 1859.
*FARRAR, F. W., The Life of Christ. Illustrated. London, 1874.
FRIEDLIEB, J. H., Archäologie der Leidensgeschichte. Bonn, 1843.
      "   "   Geschichte des Lebens Jesu Christi. Breslau,
        1855.
*   "   "   Das Leben Jesu Christi. Münster, 1887.
*   "   "   Quatuor Evangelia Sacra in Harmoniam Redacta.
        Ratisbon, 1869.
FULLER, J. M., Harmony of the Four Gospels. London, 1888.

GAMS, Johannes der Täufer. Tübingen, 1853.
*GARDINER, F., Harmony of the Four Gospels. Andover, 1885.
*GEIKIE, C., Life and Words of Christ. New York, 1880.
*GERLACH, H., Die Römischen Statthalter in Syrien und Judæa.
  Berlin, 1865.
*GRENVILLE, H., Chronological Synopsis of the Four Gospels. Lon-
  don, 1866.
GREENLEAF, S., Testimony of the Evangelists. Boston, 1846.

GRESWELL, E., Dissertations upon the Principles of an Harmony of the Gospels. Oxford, 1837.
" Harmonia Evangelica. 1855.

HACKETT, H. B., Illustrations of Scripture. Boston, 1857.
*HANNA, W., Life of Our Lord. New York, 1873.
*HAUSRATH, A., Neutestamentliche Zeitgeschichte. Erster Theil. Heidelberg, 1868.
*HENDERSON, A., Palestine. Edinburgh.
HOFMANN, R., Das Leben Jesu nach den Apokryphen. Leipzig, 1851.
HUG, J. L., Introduction to New Testament. Trans. Andover, 1836.

IDELER, C., Handbuch der Mathematischen und Technischen Chronologie. Berlin, 1825-1826.
*IMMER, A., Hermeneutics. Trans. Andover, 1877.
ITINERA Hierosolymitana, Tobler et Molonier. Geneva, 1879.

JARVIS, S. F., A Chronological Introduction to the History of the Church. New York, 1845.
JONES, J., Notes on Scripture. Philadelphia, 1861.

*KEIM, T., Jesu von Nazara. Zürich, 1872.
KITTO, J., Life of Our Lord. New York, 1853.
KRAFFT, C. H. A., Chronologie und Harmonie der vier Evangelien. Erlangen, 1848.

LANGE, J. P., Leben Jesu. Heidelberg, 1847.
" " Bibel Werk: Matthäus, Markus, Johannes. Bielefeld, 1857-1860.
" " Life of Christ. Trans. Edinburgh, 1872.
*LANGEN, J., Die letzten Lebenstage Jesu. Freiburg, 1864.
" Das Judenthum in Palästina zur Zeit Christi. 1866.
*LAURENT, J. M., Neutestamentliche Studien. Gotha, 1866.
*LIPSIUS, R. A., Die Apokryphen Apostelgeschichten. Braunschweig, 1884.
LEWIN, THOMAS, Jerusalem. London, 1861.
* " " Fasti Sacri. London, 1865.
*LEWIS, T. H., The Holy Places of Jerusalem. London, 1888.
LICHTENSTEIN, F. W. J., Lebensgeschichte des Herrn. Erlangen, 1856.
LYNCH, W. F., Exploration of the Jordan and Dead Sea. Philadelphia, 1849.

*McCLELLAN, J. B., The New Testament, vol. I. London, 1875.

*Merrill, S., Galilee in Time of Christ. 1881.
*   "   East of the Jordan. New York, 1881.
Messiah, The. London, 1861.
Meyer, H. A. W., Commentar. Die Evangelien. Göttingen, 1855-1858.
Mill, W. H., The Mythical Interpretation of the Gospels. Cambridge, 1861.
Milman, H. H., History of Christianity. New York, 1841.
Morison, J. H., Notes on Matthew. Boston, 1860.
*Morrison, W. D., The Jews under Roman Rule. New York, 1890.
*Mommsen, P., Provinces of the Roman Empire. Trans. 1887.

Neander, A., The Life of Jesus Christ. Trans. New York, 1848.
*Nebe, A., Das Leidensgeschichte. Wiesbaden, 1881.
*   "   Das Auferstehungsgeschichte, 1881-1882.
*Neubauer, A., La Geographie du Talmud. Paris, 1868.
Newcome, Bishop, Harmony of the Gospels, edited by Robinson. Andover, 1834.
*Norris, J. P., Key to the Gospel Narratives. London, 1887.
Norton, A., Translation of the Gospels with Notes. Boston, 1856.

Oosterzee, J. J., Bibel Werk: Lukas. Bielefeld, 1859.
Osborne, H. S., Palestine, Past and Present. Philadelphia, 1859.
Owen, J. J., Commentaries on Matthew, Mark, and Luke. New York, 1858-1861.

Patritius, F. X., De Evangeliis: Friburgi, 1853.
Paulus, H. E. G., Das Leben Jesu. Heidelberg, 1828.
    "   "   Exegetisches Handbuch, über die drei ersten Evangelien. Heidelberg, 1842.
*Perry, A. T., Harmony of the Gospels. Boston, 1890.
Porter, J. L., Handbook for Syria and Palestine. London, 1858.
*Pound, W., The Story of the Gospels, vol. II. London, 1869.
*Pieritz, G. W., The Gospels from the Rabbinical Point of View. London, 1873.

*Quandt, L., Chronologische-geographische Beiträge. Gutersloh, 1872.

Raumer, Karl von, Palästina. Leipzig, 1850.
Riggenbach, C. J., Leben Jesu. Basel, 1858.
Ritter, Carl, Die Erdkunde von Asien. Band viii. 15er u. 16er Theile.

ROBINSON, E., Biblical Researches in Syria and Palestine. Boston, 1856. 3 vols.
" Harmony of the Gospels. Boston, 1845.
* " Harmony with additional Notes by M. B. Riddle. Boston, 1885.

*SALMON, G., Historical Introduction to the Books of the New Testament. London, 1886.
*SCHAFF, P , Through Bible Lands. New York, 1880.
SCHAFFTER, A., Der ächte Lage des Heiligen Grabes. Berne, 1849.
*SCHNECKENBURGER, M., Vorlesungen über Neutestamentliche Zeitgeschichte. Frankfurt am Main, 1862.
*SCHÜRER, E., The Jewish People in the Time of Jesus Christ. Trans. Edinburgh, 1890.
SCHWARTZ, J., Geography of Palestine. Philadelphia, 1850.
*SCRYMGEOUR, W., Lessons on the Life of Jesus. Edinburgh, 1888.
SEPP, J. N., Das Leben Jesu. Regensburg, 1853–1862.
* " Jerusalem and das Heilige Land. Schaffhausen, 1863.
* " Kritische Beiträge zum Leben Jesu. München, 1890.
*SEVIN, H., Chronologie des Lebens Jesu. Tubingen, 1874.
STANLEY, A. P., Sinai and Palestine. New York, 1857.
*STALKER, J., The Life of Jesus Christ. Edinburgh, 1880.
*STAPFER, E., Palestine in the Time of Christ. Trans. New York.
*STEINMEYER, F. L., History of the Passion and Resurrection of our Lord. Trans. 1879.
STEWART, R. W., Tent and Khan. Edinburgh, 1857.
STIER, R., The Words of the Lord Jesus. Trans. Edinburgh, 1855.
STRONG, JAMES, Greek Harmony of the Gospels. New York, 1854.
STROUD, W., Physical Cause of the Death of Christ. London, 1847.
" Greek Harmony of the Gospels. 1853.

THIERSCH, H. W. J., Versuch für die Kritik N. T. Erlangen, 1845.
THILO, J. C., Codex Apocryphus, vol. I. Leipsic, 1832.
THOLUCK, Commentary on St. John. Trans. Philadelphia, 1859.
THOMSON, W. M., Land and Book. New York, 1859.
* " " The Land and the Book. New edition, 3 vols. New York.
TISCHENDORF, C., Synopsis Evangelica. Lipsiæ, 1854. New Ed. 1878.
TOBLER, T., Bethlehem. Gallen u. Berne, 1849.
" Golgotha. Seine Kirchen u. Kloster. Berne, 1851.
" Die Siloahquelle u. der Oëlberg. St. Gallen, 1852.
" Topographie von Jerusalem. Berlin, 1853.

TOBLER, T., Denkblätter aus Jerusalem. Constanz, 1856.
"   Dritte Wanderung nach Palästina. Gotha, 1859.
TOWNSEND, G., The New Testament, arranged in Historical and Chronological Order. Revised by T. W. Coit. Boston, 1837.
*TRENCH, Archbishop, Studies in the Gospels. New York, 1867.
*TRISTRAM, H., Bible Places. London, 1874.
*   "   Land of Israel. London.

*UPHAM, F. W., The Wise Men. New York, 1871.
*   "   Thoughts on the Holy Gospels. New York, 1881.

VAN DER VELDE, C. W. M., Journey through Syria and Palestine. Trans. Edinburgh, 1854.
"   "   "   Memoir to accompany Map of the Holy Land. Gotha, 1858.
*VAN LENNEP, H., Bible Lands. New York, 1875.
*VALLINGS, J. F., Jesus Christ, the Divine Man. New York.
*VOLKMAR, G., Jesus Nazarenus: Zürich, 1882.
*VIGOUROUX, F., Le Nouveau Testament. Paris, 1890.

*WEISS, B., The Life of Christ. Trans. Edinburgh, 1884.
*WEITBRECHT, G., Das Leben Jesu. Stuttgart, 1881.
WESTCOTT, B. F., Introduction to Study of the Gospels. London, 1860.
WICHELHAUS, J., Geschichte des Leidens Jesu Christi. Halle, 1855.
WIESELER, K., Synopse der vier Evangelien. Hamburg, 1843.
*   "   Beiträge zur richtigen Wurdigung der Evangelien. Gotha, 1869.
WILLIAMS, G., The Holy City. London, 1849.
WILLIAMS, I., Narrative of Our Lord's Nativity. London, 1844.
WILSON, J., Lands of the Bible. Edinburgh, 1847.
WINER, G. B., Grammatik des Neutestamentlichen Sprachidioms. Leipzig, 1855. Trans. Andover, 1889.
*WOOLSEY, T. D., Historical Credibility of Luke ii. 1-5. New Englander, 1869.
*   "   Year of Christ's Birth. Bibliotheca Sacra, 1870.
WRIGHT, T., Early Travels in Palestine. London, 1848.

*ZOECKLER, O., The Cross of Christ. Trans. London, 1877.
*ZUMPT, A. W., Das Geburtsjahr Christi. Leipzig, 1869.

Frequent references are made to the valuable articles in the Cyclopædias and Bible Dictionaries.

Encyklopädie für Protestantische Theologie und Kirche, von Herzog, Hamburg, 1854-1862.   Neue Auflage, Leipzig, 1877-1888.

Kirchen Lexicon, oder Encyklopädie der Katholische Theologie, von Wetzer und Welte, Friburg, 1847-1857.

Realwörterbuch von G. W. Winer, Leipzig, 1847.

Encyclopédie des Sciences Religeuses. Lichtenberger.   Paris, 1881.

Real-Encyclopädie für Bibel und Talmud.   J. Hamburger, 1884.

Bibel Lexicon, von Schenkel.   1869-1875.

Handwörterbuch des Biblischen Alterthums, von Riehm, Bielefeld, 1884.

Schaff-Herzog, Encyclopædia.   New York.   1883.

Cyclopædia of Biblical, Theological, and Ecclesiastical Literature, McClintock & Strong.   New York, 1874.

Imperial Bible Dict.   Fairbairn.   London, 1866.

Kitto's Cyclopædia, edited by Alexander.   1862.

Smith's Dict. of the Bible.   London, 1863.

American Revised Ed.   Boston, 1879.

Publications of the Palestine Exploration Fund :

Recovery of Jerusalem.   New York, 1871.

Our Work in Palestine.   New York, 1873.

Twenty-one Years Work in the Holy Land.   London, 1886.

Quarterly Statements, 1869-91.

Survey of Western Palestine, 1881-83.

Bible Educator, edited by E. H. Plumptre.

Picturesque Palestine.   New York, 1878-81.

Zeitschrift des Deutschen Palästina Verein.   1879-1891.

The recent Commentaries of Keil, Godet, Lindsay, Milligan and Moulton, Westcott, Luthardt, Rice, Watkins, Riddle, Plumptre, Schaff, Lutteroth; and Monographs of Schürer, Roth, Röpe, Rosch, Müller, Payne, Merrill, Woolsey, Stevens, and others.

Most of the abbreviations of names and titles are obvious.   We give a few which seem to need explanation.

Grimm's Greek Lexicon translated and revised by Dr. Thayer — T. G. Lex.

Commentary on John, by Dr. Milligan and Dr. Moulton — M. and M.

Greek New Testament, by Westcott and Hort — W. and H.

Authorized Version — A. V.

Revised Version — R. V.

ADDENDUM

BESANT, W., and PALMER, G. H., Jerusalem, fourth edition, enlarged. 1899.

BRIGGS, CHARLES, Messiah of the Gospels. New York, 1898.

BUTLER'S Bible Work, vol. V., New Testament. New York, 1894.

DIDON, Rev. Father, Jesus Christ. From the French. 2 vols., Philadelphia, 1897.

FOUARD, ABBÉ CONSTANTINE, The Christ, the Son of God. From the French. London, 1890.

FULLERTON, K., The Critical and Chronological Table of the Gospels. 1898.

GILBERT, GEORGE H., The Student's Life of Jesus. Chicago, 1896.

GODET, F., Introduction to the New Testament, 2d Part. Trans.

HODGE, R. M., Historical Atlas and Chronology of the Life of Jesus Christ. Nashville, 1899.

HOLTZMANN, Neuetestamentliche Zeitgeschichte. Freiburg, 1895.

INNES, A. T., The Trial of Jesus Christ. Edinburgh, 1899.

"LAYMAN" (R. Bird), Jesus, the Carpenter of Nazareth. London, 1892.

MAC COUN, T., The Holy Land in Geography and History. 2 vols., 1897.

MATHEWS, SHALER, History of New Testament Times in Palestine. New York, 1899.

PHELPS, ELIZABETH S., The Story of Jesus Christ. Boston, 1899.

RAMSAY, WILLIAM M., Was Christ Born at Bethlehem? New York, 1898.

RHEIS, RUSH, The Life of Jesus of Nazareth. New York, 1900.

RIGGS, J. S., A History of the Jewish People; Maccabæan and Roman Periods. New York, 1900.

ROGERS, A. K., Life and Teachings of Jesus. New York, 1895.

SANDAY, W., Article, Jesus Christ, in Hastings' Bible Dictionary. New York, 1899.

SELL, H. T., Bible Studies by Periods. Part V. 1899.

SMITH, G. A., Historical Geography of the Holy Land. New York, 1895.

Socin, A (Baedeker, Handbook of Palestine). 1898.

Stalker, J., The Trial and Death of Jesus Christ. New York, 1894.

Stapfer, Edmund, Life of Jesus, 3 parts. From the French. New York, 1896.

Stevens, W. A., and Burton, E. D., Harmony of the Gospels for Historical Study. Boston, 1894.

Stewart, R. L., The Land of Israel. 1899.

Thomas, Margaret, Two Years in Palestine and Syria. London, 1900.

Turner, C. H., Article, Chronology of the New Testament, in Hastings' Bible Dictionary. New York, 1899.

Von Soden, Prof., Article, Chronology of the New Testament, in Encyclopædia Biblica. London, 1899.

Walker, N. L., Jesus Christ and His Surroundings. 1899.

Wallace, E. S., Jerusalem the Holy. New York, 1898.

Wright, A., Some New Testament Problems. London, 1898.

Zahn, T., Einleitung in das Neue Testament, vol. II., Excursus 2. Leipzig, 1899.

Bible Dictionaries.

Davis, J. A., A Dictionary of the Bible. Philadelphia, 1898.

Encyclopædia Biblica. Editors, Cheyne and Black. Vol. I. London, 1899.

Hastings, J., Bible Dictionary, vols. I. and II. New York, 1899.

Smith, William, Dictionary of the Bible, second edition, vol. I. London, 1893.

Baedeker's Palestine and Syria. 1898.

Periodicals.

Biblical World, vol. 1890-1900.

Expositor, vol. 1890-1900.

Quarterly Statements, vol. 1890-1899.

HISTORY

The book of Prof. Ramsay, "Was Christ Born at Bethlehem?" deserves special mention because it gives a new datum for our historical investigations.

Prof. Ramsay affirms that Luke in his statement on the taxing, ii. 1-4, was acquainted with a system of periodic enrolments in

Syria, and probably in the East generally, and was not speaking
at random. A very brief outline of Prof. Ramsay's discussion will
be given here.

Prof. Ramsay translates the words, Luke ii. 2, "that all the
world should be taxed," to mean the Roman world, including the
dependent kingdoms, as that of Herod. The later clause, "should
be taxed" or enrolled, affirms that "Augustus now ordered enrolments to be regularly made," not the taking of a single census.
Luke's statement will therefore read: "This was the first enrolment"—the first in a series of enrolments, and the only one with
which he was here concerned. It was in force in Syria, and was
periodic. This first census he distinguishes from that in Acts v.
37, by the use of the article applied to the last, "The census," *i.e.*,
that taken about 7 A. D., when Judæa had become part of the province of Syria, and which was to serve as the basis of taxation.

The light cast upon this matter comes from Egypt through the
discovery that periodic enrolments for the purpose of numbering
the people were made under the Roman rule. "The census was
carried on by Roman officials, and formed part of the Imperial system of administration." The same Greek term, ἀπογραφὴ, is used
in the Egyptian documents. Prof. Ramsay thinks that Augustus
was "the originator of a new system in Egypt of periodic enrolments by households, developing some previously existing system
of numbering the population." This, like our own census, is to be
distinguished from an enrolment for the purpose of taxation, such
as was made by Quirinius 7 A. D. Both existed in Egypt, but only
the first, the enrolment as a basis for the enumeration of the total
population, corresponds to that mentioned by Luke, and such an
enumeration was general throughout the Roman Empire. That the
cycle of enrolments was in force as early as 20 A. D., is shown by
the recently found papyri.

A second point is the relation of the taxing to Cyrenius (Quirinius). Luke says, "It was first made when Cyrenius was Governor
of Syria." Here Prof. Ramsay adds little to our knowledge. His
conclusion is that he was twice Governor of Syria, the second term
6–9 A. D., and under him at this time was the taxing, Acts v. 37.
Was he Governor earlier? He was administrator of Syria, 5–2 B. C.
But in what capacity? Not as administering the internal and civil
affairs, for this was done by Saturninus and Varus, 7 B. C., but as
having direction of foreign affairs and command of the armies.
He was a special lieutenant of Augustus, and conducted the war
against the Homonadenses whilst Varus administrated the ordinary
affairs. Thus at the time of the first enrolment Varus was the

civil governor and Quirinius the military commander, the *legatus
Augusti pro prœtore.*

But the question arises : Would Luke speak of him as "governing"
Syria if his office was that of military commander? Prof. Ramsay
thinks he would, and cites some historical analogies. Luke might
well have spoken of him as the Egemon, or Governor.

We have still to note the bearings of this historical investigation
on the chronology of the Lord's life.

The enrolment being periodic, having a cycle of fourteen years;
He was born when the first enrolment of the series was being made
in Palestine; another followed after fourteen years. Prof. Ramsay
makes the first periodic year to be that of 9–8 B. C., the actual
enumeration beginning after it was ended, or during the year 8–7
B. C. But this first enrolment was delayed in Herod's kingdom, and
made in late summer of 7–6 B. C. The Lord, therefore, was born
6 B. C., though possibly as late as 5 B. C.

His ministry began at the age of thirty in the latter half of 25
A. D. The fifteenth year of Tiberius is to be counted from the time
that he became the colleague of Augustus, 11–12 A. D.

In regard to birth at Bethlehem, Prof. Ramsay says : " To go
personally to the enrolment was regarded as substantiating a claim
to a true Hebrew origin and family." The "all" of Luke—"all
went to be taxed"—means all true Hebrews.

The time of the enrolment was fixed by law, and he concludes
that His birth was between August and October, since the pasturing
of the flocks was only during the hot season and not in the winter.

THE TRIAL OF JESUS CHRIST. A legal monograph by A. Taylor
Innes, Advocate, Edinburgh, 1899.

The points discussed in this monograph concern the relation in
which the two trials of Jesus, that before Caiaphas and that before
Pilate, stood to one another, their conformity with Hebrew and
Roman law respectively, and the righteousness of each.

Other subordinate questions are discussed : whether His arrest
and subsequent examination were legal; whether there were two
trials, one before Annas and one later before Caiaphas; whether the
forms of Hebrew and Roman law were observed; and whether the
Jews had power to put to death.

His judgment as to the Hebrew trial is that the arrest and subsequent examination, and the sentence—a sentence which described
a claim to be the Fulfiller of the hope of Israel as blasphemy—had
neither the form nor the fairness of a judicial trial.

There is no reason to think that the Council missed the fact that

Jesus claimed to be their King, though they deeply misunderstood the nature of His kingdom.

Of the trial before Pilate, Mr. Innes says : " When Pilate sent Jesus to the cross it was as claiming to be a King, and on the original charge of acting *adversus majestatem populi Romani.* The judgment was legal, though the unjust judge did not believe in it. . . . The claim of Jesus was truly inconsistent with the claim of the State, which Cæsar represented. . . . In both trials the judges were unjust, and the trial was unfair ; yet in both the right issue was substantially raised. . . . Jesus died because in the ecclesiastical council He claimed to be the Son of God and the Messiah of Israel, and because before the world-wide Roman tribunal He claimed to be Christ the King."

CHRONOLOGY

DATE OF LORD'S BIRTH.

7 or 6 B. C.   Turner, Sanday.
6 or 5   "   Ramsay, S. Matthews.
5   "   Didon, Fouard, Gilbert.
4   " or earlier.   Holtzmann, Von Soden.

DATE OF BAPTISM.

25   A. D.   Ramsay.
26–27   "   Turner, Sanday.
27   "   Didon, Fouard, Hodge.
28–29   "   Von Soden.

DATE OF LORD'S DEATH.

29 A. D.   Ramsay, Wright, S. Matthews, Sanday, Gilbert.
30   "   Didon, Fouard, Stapfer, Von Soden, Hodge.

DAY OF CRUCIFIXION.

Friday, 14th Nisan, March 18th, 29 A. D.   Wright, Turner.
Friday, 15th Nisan, April 7th, 30 A. D.   Didon.

Fouard says that the Lord partook of the paschal supper twenty-four hours before the legal time, or on the 13th Nisan.

Sanday finds a contradiction between John and the Synoptists which he cannot now explain in relation to the paschal meal, and also as to the time of the day occupied by the crucifixion.

DURATION OF MINISTRY.

1 year, 2 Passovers. Von Soden.

2 years and more, 3 Passovers. Turner, Sanday, Wright, Gilbert, S. Matthews.

3 years and more, 4 Passovers. Didon, Fouard, Ramsay, Hodge.

DIVISIONS OF LORD'S MINISTRY.

SANDAY. Preliminary period, from winter, 26 A. D., to a little after Passover, 27 A. D. 1. Active period, from Pentecost, 27 A.D., to Passover, 28 A. D. 2. Middle period, from Passover to Tabernacles, 28 A. D. 3. From Tabernacles to Passover, 29 A. D. 4. The Messianic crisis, six days before Passover, 29 A. D., to Pentecost.

DIDON. 1. Ministry in Judæa, from baptism, 27 A. D., to John's imprisonment early in 28 A. D. 2. Galilæan ministry, from Passover, 28 A. D., to Tabernacles, 29 A. D. 3. Peræan ministry, from Tabernacles, 29 A. D., to last Passover, 30 A. D.

STEVENS and BURTON. 1. From the coming of the Baptist to the cleansing of the temple. 2. Early Judæan ministry to the return to Galilee. 3. Galilæan ministry, three periods in: *a.* To the choosing of the twelve. *b.* To the withdrawal into northern Galilee. *c.* To the final departure for Jerusalem. 4. Peræan ministry. 5. Passion week.

FOUARD. 1. Judæan ministry from baptism to the imprisonment of the Baptist, from January to December, A. D. 27. 2. Galilæan ministry, to feast of Dedication, December, 29 A. D. 3. Peraean ministry, from Dedication to last Passover, 30 A. D. Jesus at Jerusalem, Passovers, 28 and 29 A. D.

GILBERT. Twelve months of the public ministry spent in Judæa and Jerusalem and nine in Galilee. The Galilæan ministry divided into two parts.

GEOGRAPHY

As to the places mentioned in the Lord's life little new can be said, and the same want of agreement already noted continues to prevail.

BETHPHAGE and BETHANY. Schick, Qt. Statement, with map, April, 1897.

BETHABAREH. The ford opposite Jericho, so Didon, Fouard, Stewart; "quite uncertain," G. A. Smith; near Bethshan, MacCoun.

BETHSAIDA. Two of this name, one in Galilee, a mile north of Khan Minyeh, so Stewart, Ewing, Fouard, Didon ; only one, Bethsaida Julias, G. A. Smith, Socin.

CANA. The traditional site, Fouard, Ewing, Stewart, MacCoun ; undecided, G. A. Smith.

CAPERNAUM. Tell Hum, Didon ; Khan Minyeh, G. A. Smith ; undecided, MacCoun.

CHORAZIN. Tell Hum, G. A. Smith ; Ain et Tin, Fouard.

DECAPOLIS. See G. A. Smith.

EMMAUS. Kulonieh, Fouard ; Nicopolis (Amwas), Didon ; Kubeibeh, Socin ; Conder, uncertain.

SYCHAR. El Asker, G. A. Smith, MacCoun.

THE HOLY SEPULCHRE.

No new knowledge as to the course of the second wall has been gained by excavation, but the recent excavations of Dr. Bliss on the southern slopes of Mounts Zion and Ophel have an indirect bearing on the site of the Sepulchre. He has found that the south wall of the city was placed much further south than it now is, and included a large area now without the wall. It was upon these hills stretching down into the valleys of Hinnom and Jehoshaphat that the city was first built, and here was gathered the greater part of its population. It was not till the population overflowed the north wall that the second wall was built northward, and this took in only so much territory as then needed to be protected.

The points in question are as to the dates of the south wall of Dr. Bliss, and of the second wall. If the south wall extended so far southward when the second wall was built, as his excavations show, it was not necessary that this last wall should extend far to the north. It was intended only as a defence to those living northward of the original north wall—only a suburb. It may therefore well have excluded the site of the Holy Sepulchre.

It is said by Dr. Bliss (Quarterly Statement, 1895): "The wall occupied the extreme southern position, which is just the position of our wall. Our line is identical with that of the Jewish kings and of Herod, for in their various epochs the city obtained its maximum growth on the south ; and if Hadrian's wall occupied a different line it would have been inside rather than outside this line, contracting not enlarging the city." With this wall extending so far southward, it was not necessary that the second wall should extend far north, since it was intended only as a defence to those living in the northern suburb. The site of the present Sepulchre may, therefore, have been without this second wall, and the course of this wall as defensive have been determined chiefly by the nature of the ground. That the city far outgrew the second wall is shown by the later erection of the third wall by Agrippa; but though a large population may at the time of the crucifixion have lived without the second wall, the site of the Holy Sepulchre may also have been without it.

The objection to the present site, drawn from the small area of the city, is thus at least partially set aside.

There seems to be an increasing number who accept the claims of Skull Hill—the hill beyond the Damascus gate—to be the place of the Lord's crucifixion and of His Sepulchre, though no new evidence in its favor has been presented. So Stewart, MacCoun, Wallace, Thurston in Journal Bib. Lit., 1900. Contra, Quarterly Rev., July, London, 1899.

It is admitted that the tomb shown there is not the garden Sepulchre.

OUTLINE HARMONY OF THE GOSPELS AND CHRONOLOGICAL INDEX.

PART I.—From the Annunciation to Zacharias to the Baptism of Jesus.

DATE.	PLACE.	EVENT.	PAGE.	MATTHEW.	MARK.	LUKE.	JOHN.
		Introduction of Evangelists,			i. 1	i. 1-4	i. 1-18
		Genealogies,	52	i. 1-17		iii. 23-38	
Oct. B. C. 6,	Jerusalem,	Annunciation to Zacharias,	53			i. 5-22	
		Elizabeth conceives a son and lives in retirement,	54			i. 23-25	
Mar.-Apr. B. C. 5	Nazareth,	Annunciation to Mary,	55			i. 26-38	
	Judæa,	Visit of Mary to Elizabeth (Magnificat),	68			i. 39-56	
	Nazareth,	Annunciation to Joseph,	70	i. 18-25			
June,	Judæa,	Birth of John the Baptist (Benedictus),	70			i. 57-80	
Dec.,	Bethlehem,	Joseph and Mary go to Bethlehem to be taxed,	71			ii. 1-5	
	"	Birth of Jesus,	82			ii. 6-7	
	"	The Angel and the Shepherds,	87			ii. 8-20	
Jan., B. C. 4,		Circumcision of Jesus,	89			ii. 21	
Feb.,	Jerusalem,	Presentation of Jesus,	89			ii. 22-38	
	Bethlehem,	Visit of the Wise Men,	93	ii. 1-12			
	Egypt,	Flight into Egypt,	98	ii. 13-15			
	Bethlehem,	Slaughter of the Innocents,	100	ii. 16-18			
May,	Nazareth,	Return to Nazareth and sojourn there,	102	ii. 19-23		ii. 39, 40	
Apr. 8, A.D. 8,	Jerusalem,	Jesus at twelve years of age attends the Passover,	108			ii. 41-52	

PART II.—From the Baptism of Jesus to the First Passover of His Ministry.

DATE.	PLACE.	EVENT.	PAGE.	MATTHEW.	MARK.	LUKE.	JOHN.
A. D. 26. Summer,	Judæa,	Preaching of John the Baptist,	137	iii. 1-12	i. 2-8	iii. 1-18	
A. D. 27. Jan.,	The Jordan,	Baptism of Jesus,	137	iii. 13-17	i. 9-11	iii. 21-23	
Jan.—Feb.,	Desert of Judæa,	Temptation of Jesus,	154	iv. 1-11	i. 12, 13	iv. 1-13	
Feb.,	Bethany beyond Jordan,	Deputation of Priests and Levites to the Baptist,	155				i. 19-28
		Witness of John the Baptist,	156				i. 29-34
	"	The first Disciples,	158				i. 35-51
	Galilee,	Wedding at Cana,	160				ii. 1-12

PART III.—The Judæan Ministry.

DATE.	PLACE.	EVENT.	PAGE.	MATTHEW.	MARK.	LUKE.	JOHN.
A. D. 27.							
April 11-17,	Jerusalem,	*Passover.* Jesus cleanses the Temple,	169				ii. 13-25
		Discourse with Nicodemus,	170				iii. 1-21
	Judæa,	Jesus baptizes in Judæa,	171				iii. 22-24
Dec.,		Further testimony of John the Baptist,	178				iii. 25-36
		Jesus departs into Galilee,	178				iv. 1-3
	Sychar,	Discourse with woman of Samaria,	182				iv. 4-42
	Galilee,	Jesus comes into Galilee,	186				iv. 43-45
	Cana, Capern'm,	Healing of the nobleman's son,	187				iv. 46-54
A. D. 28.							
Mar. 30-Apr. 5	Jerusalem,	A few weeks spent by Jesus in retirement,	188				
		Passover. Healing of man at Pool of Bethesda,	189				v. 1-47

PART IV.—From the Imprisonment to the Death of John the Baptist.

DATE.	PLACE.	EVENT.	PAGE.	MATTHEW.	MARK.	LUKE.	JOHN.
April,	Galilee,	Jesus goes into Galilee after arrest of John,	215	iv. 12	i. 14, 15	{ iii. 19, 20; iv. 14, 15. }	
	Nazareth,	Jesus rejected at Nazareth,	218			iv. 16-30	
April—May,	Capernaum,	Jesus takes up His abode at Capernaum,	221	iv. 13-17		iv. 31	
	"	Calling of Disciples,	245	iv. 18-22	i. 16-20	v. 1-11	
	Galilee,	Healing of demoniac in Synagogue,	248		i. 21-28	iv. 31-37	
	"	Healing of Peter's wife's mother, and many others,	249	viii. 14-17	i. 29-34	iv. 38-41	
May,		Ministry in Galilee,	249	iv. 23, 24	i. 35-39	iv. 42-44	
Early Summer,	Capernaum,	Healing of a leper,	250	viii. 2-4	i. 40-45	v. 12-16	
	"	Healing of a paralytic,	252	ix. 2-8	ii. 1-12	v. 17-26	
	Near Capern'm,	Calling of Levi (Matthew),	254	ix. 9	ii. 13, 14	v. 27, 28	
	Galilee,	Disciples pluck corn on the Sabbath,	255	xii. 1-8	ii. 23-28	vi. 1-5	
	"	Healing of withered hand on the Sabbath,	259	xii. 9-14	iii. 1-6	vi. 6-11	
	Near Capern'm,	Jesus withdraws to seashore,	265	xii. 15-21	iii. 7-12		
Summer,	"	Choosing of the Twelve,	266		iii. 13-19	vi. 12-16	
	Capernaum,	Sermon on the Mount,	269	iv. 25-viii. 1		vi. 17-49	
	Nain,	Healing of the Centurion's servant,	274	viii. 5-13		vii. 1-10	
	Galilee,	Raising of widow's son at Nain,	276			vii. 11-17	
Autumn,		John sends his disciples to Jesus,	279	xi. 2-19		vii. 18-35	
		Anointing by a woman in house of Simon,	281			vii. 36-50	
		Jesus preaches in the cities of Galilee,	281			viii. 1-3	
	Capernaum,	Healing of a blind and dumb possessed man,	286	xii. 22, 23			
	"	Pharisees blaspheme and seek a sign,	289	xii. 24-45	iii. 22-30		

PART VI.—The last Journey from Galilee, and the Peræan Ministry, to the arrival at Bethany.

DATE.	PLACE.	EVENT.	PAGE.	MATTHEW.	MARK.	LUKE.	JOHN.
A. D. 29.							
Nov.–Dec.,...	Galilee,	Final departure from Galilee,	385 / 385	xix. 1...	x. 1...	ix. 51...	
	Samaria,	Jesus rejected in Samaria,	386			ix. 52-56.	
	Galilee,	The half-hearted disciple,	386			ix. 61, 62.	
	Peræa,	The Seventy sent forth,	380			x. 1-16...	
	"	Jesus follows, teaching,	387	xix. 2...	x. 1...		
	"	Return of the Seventy,	389			x. 17-24...	
	"	Parable of the Good Samaritan,	383 / 387	xi. 25-30.		x. 25-37.	
	"	Disciples taught how to pray,	389			xi. 1-13.	
	"	Healing of a blind and dumb possessed man,	390			xi. 14...	
	"	Blasphemy of Pharisees. Discourse,	391	xii. 22-23.	iii. 22, 30.	xi. 15-36.	
	"	Feast at Pharisee's house. Woes upon Pharisees,	391	xii. 24-45.		xi. 37-54.	
	"	Discourse. Parable of Rich Fool,	392			xii. 1-59.	
	"	Parable of the Barren Fig-tree,	393			xiii. 2-9.	
	"	Healing of infirm woman on the Sabbath,	394			xiii. 10-17.	
	"	Parables of the Mustard Seed and the Leaven,	395			xiii. 18-21.	
	"	Jesus goes teaching and journeying towards Jerusalem. Is warned against Herod,	395			xiii. 22-35.	
Dec. 20-27,...	Bethany,	Jesus visits Mary and Martha,	397			x. 38-42...	
	Jerusalem,	Feast of Dedication. Discourses,	398				x. 22-30.
	"	Jews attempt to stone him,	400				x. 31-39.
A. D. 30.							
January,.....	Bethany beyond Jordan,	Jesus retires beyond Jordan,	401				x. 40-42.
	Peræa,	Dines with a Pharisee. Heals a man with dropsy,...	402			xiv. 1-14.	
	"	Parable of the Great Supper,	403			xiv. 15-24.	
	"	What is required of true disciples,	403			xiv. 25-35.	
	"	Parables of Lost Sheep, and Lost Piece of Silver,	404			xv. 1-10.	
	"	Parable of the Prodigal Son,	404			xv. 11-32.	
	"	Parable of the Unjust Steward,	404			xvi. 1-13.	
	"	Pharisees reproved. Parable of the Rich Man and Lazarus,	404			xvi. 14-31.	
	"	Jesus instructs the Disciples,	404			xvii. 1-10.	
Jan.–Feb.,....	Bethany,	Raising of Lazarus,	405				xi. 1-46.

PART VII.—From the arrival at Bethany to the Resurrection.

PART VII.—From the arrival at Bethany to the Resurrection.—(Continued.)

DATE.	PLACE.	EVENT.	PAGE.	MATTHEW.	MARK.	LUKE.	JOHN.
A. D. 30.	Jerusalem	Plotting of rulers. Bargain of Judas,	446	{ xxvi. 1-5, xxvi. 14-16	{ xiv. 1, 2, xiv. 10, 11		xxii. 1-6	
Wed., Apr. 5,	Bethany	Jesus seeks retirement,	450				
Thur., Apr. 6,	Jerusalem	Preparation for the Passover,	451	xxvi. 17-19	xiv. 12-16	xxii. 7-13	
"	"	Arrival at the upper room,	451	xxvi. 20	xiv. 17	xxii. 14	
"	"	Strife for precedence,	483			xxii. 24-30	
"	"	Jesus washes the feet of his disciples,	482				xiii. 1-20
"	"	The Paschal Supper,	484				
"	"	Jesus declares the betrayer. Judas goes out,	486	xxvi. 21-25	xiv. 18-21	xxii. 21-23	xiii. 21-35
"	"	Institution of the Lord's Supper,	488	xxvi. 26-29	xiv. 22-25	xxii. 19-20	1Cor. xi.23-25
"	"	Jesus foretells the fall of Peter,	494			xxii. 31-38	xiii. 36-38
"	"	Farewell Discourse of Jesus,	496				xiv. xv. xvi.
"	"	Intercessory Prayer of Jesus,	496				xvii. 1-26
	Mt. of Olives,	Jesus goes forth. Peter's confidence,	497	xxvi. 30-35	xiv. 26-31	xxii. 39	xviii. 1-3
	"	The agony in the garden of Gethsemane,	497	xxvi. 36-46	xiv. 32-42	xxii. 40-46	
	"	The betrayal,	503	xxvi. 47-50	xiv. 43-45	xxii. 47, 48	xviii. 4-9
	"	The arrest,	504	xxvi. 50-56	xiv. 46-52	xxii. 49-53	xviii. 10-12
Midnight, Fri., Apr. 7, 1-5 A.M.	Jerusalem	Jesus led to Annas, then to Caiaphas,	505				xviii. 13-15
	"	Jesus before Caiaphas,	510	xxvi. 57, 58	xiv. 53-54	xxii. 54, 55	xviii. 19-24
	"	Jesus before the Sanhedrin,	510	xxvi. 59-66	xiv. 55-64		
	"	Denials of Peter,	516	xxvi. 69-75	xiv. 66-72	xxii. 56-62	{ xviii. 15-18, xviii. 25-27 }
	"	Jesus mocked by his enemies. Jesus condemned for blasphemy,	522	xxvi. 67, 68	xiv. 65	{ xxii. 63-65 }	
5-6 A.M.,	"	Meeting of the Sanhedrin. Jesus condemned for	522	xxvii. 1, 2	xv. 1	{ xxii. 66-71, xxiii. 1 }	
	"	Death of Judas,	524	xxvii. 3-10	[Acts i. 18, 19]		
	"	Jesus before Pilate; charged with sedition,	529	xxvii. 11-14	xv. 2-5	xxiii. 2-5	xviii. 28-38
	"	Jesus sent to Herod,	533			xxiii. 6-12	xviii. 38-40
	"	Pilate seeks to release Jesus. Jews demand Barabbas,	534	xxvii. 15-23	xv. 6-14	xxiii. 13-23	
	"	Jesus condemned, scourged, and mocked by soldiers,	538	xxvii. 26-30	xv. 15-19	xxiii. 24, 25	xix. 1-3
	"	Pilate again seeks to release Jesus,	539	xxvii. 24, 25			xix. 4-16
9 A.M.,	"	Jesus is led away to be crucified,	545	{ xxvii. 31-34, xxvii. 38 }	xv. 20-23	xxiii. 26-32	xix. 16-18
	"	The superscription,	553	xxvii. 37	xv. 25, 27, 28	xxiii. 38	xix. 19-22
	"	First word from the cross ("Father, forgive them"),	553		xv. 26	xxiii. 33, 34	
	"	Soldiers cast lots for his garments,	554	xxvii. 35, 36	xv. 24	xxiii. 34	xix. 23, 24

			Matt.	Mark	Luke	John
Jerusalem	Jews mock at Jesus on the cross	555	xxvii. 39–44	xv. 29–32	xxiii. 35–37	
"	Second word (The penitent thief)	556			xxiii. 39–43	
"	Third word ("Woman, behold thy son")	556				xix. 25–27
12 m., "	Darkness covers the land	557	xxvii. 45	xv. 33	xxiii. 44–45	
"	Fourth word (Cry of distress to God)	559	xxvii. 46, 47	xv. 34, 35		
"	Fifth word ("I thirst")	559	xxvii. 48, 49	xv. 36		xix. 28, 29
"	Sixth word ("It is finished")	560				xix. 30
"	Seventh word ("Into thy hands," etc.)	560			xxiii. 46	
3 p. m., "	Jesus dies. Veil rent. Earthquake	561	xxvii. 50–56	xv. 37–41	xxiii. 45, 46–49	xix. 30
"	Jesus is pierced with a spear in the side	563				xix. 31–37
3–6 p. m., "	The burial. The watch at the Sepulchre	569	xxvii. 57–66	xv. 42–47	xxiii. 50–56	xix. 38–42

PART VIII.—From the Resurrection to the Ascension.

			Matt.	Mark	Luke	John
Sun., Apr. 9, Jerusalem	The morning of the Resurrection	586	xxviii. 2–4		xxiv. 1, 2	
"	Women come to the Sepulchre	597	xxviii. 1	xvi. 1–4		xx. 1
"	Mary Magdalene calls Peter and John	602				xx. 2
"	The women at the Sepulchre	599	xxviii. 5–8	xvi. 5–8	xxiv. 3–8	
"	Peter and John go to the Sepulchre	603			xxiv. 12	xx. 3–10
"	Jesus appears to Mary Magdalene	603		xvi. 9–11		xx. 11–18
"	He appears to the women	604	xxviii. 9, 10		xxiv. 9–11	
"	The guard report to the priests	612	xxviii. 11–15			
Emmaus	Jesus appears to two on the way to Emmaus	614		xvi. 12, 13	xxiv. 13–35	
Jerusalem	He appears to Peter	622		[1 Cor. xv. 5]	[1 Cor. xv. 5]	
"	He appears to the apostles except Thomas	620		xvi. 14	xxiv. 36–48	xx. 19–23
"	He appears to the other apostles with Thomas	623				xx. 24–29
Sun., Apr. 16, Sea of Galilee	He appears to seven in Galilee	625				xxi. 1–23
April..., Galilee	He appears to a multitude. The great commission	628	xxviii. 16–20	xvi. 15–18		[1 Cor. xv. 6]
April—May...	He appears to James	627	[1 Cor. xv. 7]			
Jerusalem	He appears to all the Apostles	630	[Acts i. 1–8]		xxiv. 49	
Thur., May 18, Bethany	The Ascension	631	[Acts i. 9–12]	xvi. 19	xxiv. 50–53	
"	Conclusions of Mark and John	...		xvi. 20		{ xx. 30, 31. / xxi. 24, 25. }

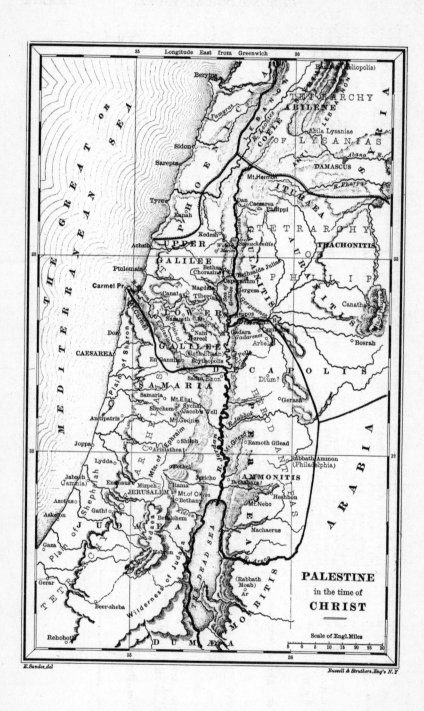

PALESTINE

in the time of

CHRIST

Scale of Engl. Miles

E. Sandoz, del.

Russell & Struthers, Eng's N.Y.

CHRONOLOGICAL ESSAY.

[In the following essay and throughout this work the dates are given according to the æra beginning with the building of Rome, or *ab urbe condita;* more briefly, U. C. Reckoning backward from Christ, the year 1 of Rome corresponded to the year 753 B.C. The year of Rome corresponding to the year 1 of the Christian æra was 754. Hence, to obtain the year of Rome after Christ, we must add to 753 the number in question: thus the year 30 A.D. would correspond to 753+30, or 783. If we would obtain the year of Rome before Christ, we must subtract the number in question from 754: thus, if Herod died four years before the Christian æra, or 4 B.C., 754—4 would give 750 of Rome. Always, if not expressly stated to the contrary, the year of Rome is to be understood.]

I. DATE OF THE LORD'S BIRTH.

Datum 1.— We take as our starting point in this inquiry the statement of Matthew (ii. 1–9) that Jesus was born before the death of Herod the Great. We must, therefore, first ascertain when Herod died. According to Josephus,[1] "he died the fifth day after he had caused Antipater to be slain, having reigned since he caused Antigonus to be slain, thirty-four years, but since he had been declared king by the Romans, thirty-seven." He was so declared king in 714. This would bring his death in the year from 1st Nisan 750 to 1st Nisan 751, according to Jewish computation, at the age of seventy.

But the date of his death may be more definitely fixed. Josephus relates[2] that he executed the insurgents, Matthias and his companions, on the night of an eclipse of the moon. This eclipse took place, as has been ascertained by astronomical calculations,[3] on the night of the 12th and 13th March, 750; yet he was dead before the 5th of April, for the Passover of that year fell upon the 12th April, and Josephus states[4] that before this feast his son and successor, Archelaus, observed the usual seven days' mourning for the dead. His death

---

[1] Antiq., xvii. 8. 1. [2] Antiq., xvii. 6. 4.
[3] Ideler, Handbuch Chronologie, ii. 391. [4] Antiq., xvii. 8. 4.

(1)

must therefore be placed between the 13th March and 4th April, 750. We may take the 1st of April as an approximate date.[1]

How long before Herod's death was the Lord born? The Evangelists Matthew and Luke relate certain events that occurred between His birth and Herod's death, — His circumcision upon the eighth day, the presentation at the Temple on the fortieth, the visit of the Magi, the flight into Egypt, the murder of the Innocents. Whatever view may be taken as to the order of these events, they can scarcely have occupied less than two months. This would bring His birth into January, or February at latest, 750.

Datum 2.— Having thus reached a fixed period in one direction, and ascertained that His birth cannot be placed later than the beginning of 750, let us consider the data that limit the period upon the other side. And the first of these we find in the statement of Luke (ii. 1–6) that He was born after the edict of Augustus that all the world should be taxed. In obedience to this edict His parents went to Bethlehem to be taxed, and there He was born.

Let us inquire what chronological aid this statement gives us. Two questions may be asked: When did this decree go forth? When did it go into effect in Judæa? We here pass by the many historical points connected with this edict and its execution, as these will be examined later.

1.   When did this decree go forth? It is known from Suetonius and from the Ancyranian monument that Augustus three times instituted a census, in 726, 746, and 767. Of these, the second only needs to be considered.[2] Is this to be identified with that in Luke? Do the two stand in any known relation to each other? It would seem not, since that in Luke embraced the whole empire, and the census of 746, as also those of 726 and 767, was confined to the Italians or Romans, and seems not to have extended to the provinces, and thus was a *census civium* (Usher, x. 458; Greswell, i. 536, and 422; Zumpt, Sevin). Woolsey says (Bib. Sacra, 1870, p. 297): "There is no evidence that these censuses extended beyond Italy, or included any beside Roman citizens." (This, however, is doubted by many, — Browne, 45; Friedlieb, 53; Sepp, i. 141. See Ewald, v. 141.) All we can say is, that this census in 746 was about the same time as the taxing in Luke, but cannot be identified with it, and, therefore, gives in this inquiry no definite chronological datum.[3]

---

[1] Almost all chronologists agree in putting Herod's death in 750. So Browne, Sepp, Wieseler, Ammer, Ewald, Winer, Meyer, Sevin, Schürer, Zumpt, Woolsey, Keim; 749, Jarvis; 750 or 751, Clinton; 751, Greswell, Pound, Quandt; 752, Caspari.

[2] Zumpt (209) accepts the year 727 as that in which this decree went forth, and its execution as beginning in the provinces in 744.

[3] As to these censuses all falling on Sabbatic years, see Caspari, 37; also Quandt, 7.

In this matter we have no help from contemporary historians, since none mention the decree. Nor do we gain much help from Luke's statement that the decree went out "in those days." Strictly construed, this must be understood of the time embracing the events related in his first chapter — a period of a year and a half or two years. But the phrase is often taken in a larger sense (Matt. ii. 1; Acts v. 26), and may be understood as equivalent to "about this time." Assuming it to have been a general census, we have, therefore, no certain knowledge how long the interval was before it was carried into effect in Judæa.

2. Can it be ascertained from any data when this edict went into effect in Judæa? If so, it must be through those who executed it — the governors of Syria — by knowing the times of their administrations. And here we have two sources of information, St. Luke and Tertullian; let us examine the statement of Tertullian first. According to him (Adv. Marc. iv. 19, about 207 A. D.), the census at the birth of Christ was taken by Sentius Saturninus. *Sed et census constat actos sub Augusto tunc in Judæa per Sent. Saturninum, apud quos genus ejus inquirere potestis.*

But has this statement any historical value? Some have questioned it, but it is received by many modern scholars (Zumpt, Lewin, Friedlieb, Browne, McClellan). Woolsey says: "This information is historical, and justly regarded by the best scholars as of the highest importance."

When, then, was Saturninus governor? He is often mentioned by Josephus (Antiq., xvi. 10. 8; xvi. 11. 3; xvii. 1. 1. War, i. 27. 2; i. 29. 3). There is general agreement that his administration ended in the summer of 748, when he was succeeded by Varus (Greswell, in 750); but there is difference of opinion as to its beginning, — most say, in 746 (so Ideler, Sevin; Zumpt, in 745). If we accept Tertullian's statement, the execution of the decree must have been begun by Saturninus before the end of 748. We may suppose the following order of events. Early in his governorship, 746–748, Saturninus is directed by the Emperor to carry out the decree in Judæa, and this he did, or began to do. If the enrollment (Luke ii. 31) was by him, the Lord was born in 747 or 748; and each of these dates is accepted by many. (For 747 Ideler, Jarvis, Sepp, Patritius, Alford; for 748 Kepler, Lewin.)

But if the execution of the edict was only begun and not completed under Saturninus, the Lord may have been born under his successor, Varus, — the governor from the summer of 748 to the summer of 750. As he was governor at the death of Herod in April,

750, the Lord, if not born under Saturninus, 746–748, was certainly born under Varus, and probably in 749.

We now turn to the statement of Luke (ii. 2), "This taxing was first made when Cyrenius was governor of Syria." This statement is susceptible of various interpretations, which will be hereafter examined. But it is to be noted that it does not say that the Lord was born during his governorship; only that the decree was executed, or was in process of execution, at the time of His birth. Cyrenius or Quirinius (R. V.), if he were twice governor, probably succeeded Varus in the summer of 750, and certainly after Herod's death, and therefore after the Lord's birth. Our knowledge of the length of his administration, supposing him to have followed Varus as governor, gives us no help in our chronological inquiry. The point whether Saturninus and Quirinius may not have been commissioners extraordinary, or Saturninus governor and Quirinius such commissioner, and both have conducted the census, will be considered later.

From Tertullian, then, we learn only that the Lord was born subsequent to the year 746. From Luke we can draw no chronological conclusion, since the relation of Quirinius to the first stage of the execution of the decree is uncertain.

Datum 3.— The statement of Luke (iii. 23), "And Jesus Himself began to be about thirty years of age," is rendered in the R. V. "And Jesus Himself, when He began to teach, was about thirty years of age." Most modern scholars accept the latter rendering. (Wieseler, Beiträge, 165, "He was in the beginning "—*i. e.*, the time immediately after His baptism— "about thirty years old.") It is said by Godet: "The expression 'He began' can only refer in this passage to the entrance of Jesus upon His Messianic work." And Woolsey says: "This explanation is far preferable to any other."

If rendered "He began to be about thirty," it must be understood as saying that He was about, but not quite, thirty. (So Lightfoot, Greswell, Bloomfield.) Greswell affirms that this was the universal interpretation of the words by the Greek fathers. (But see Patritius, iii. 388; as to the chronological conclusions drawn by them, see Zumpt, 243.)

Taking the meaning to be "Jesus was about thirty when He began His ministry," and we may count His baptism as its beginning, we ask, How great latitude shall be given to the expression "about thirty"? According to some, it is to be understood as a round or indefinite number, embracing any age between twenty-five and thirty-five. But when we consider how short was the Lord's ministry, this is in the highest degree improbable. According to others, it permits a latitude of two or three years. (So Ammer, Alford, Sevin. Browne says, "any age between twenty-six and thirty-two"; Keil, "He may have been thirty-two"; Lewin, "age thirty-three and upwards.") But even the latitude of a year is hardly justified by Luke's use of language.[1] The more natural construction is that the Lord was some months or part of a year more or less than thirty. (So Meyer, Alford, Norton, DeWette, Wies., Tisch., Rob. Edersheim says, "either a little more or a little less than that exact number. He was not just thirty, nor twenty-nine, nor thirty-one.") Still it cannot be positively affirmed that the Evangelist does not use it in a larger sense.

The argument that He was thirty at this time, because the priests at this age began their ministry,[2] has little force. The law (Num. iv. 3) has reference only to Levites, and the age when the priests began to serve is not known.[3] Besides, Jesus was not a priest, although the Baptist was.

Datum 4. — If we assume that the Lord was about thirty at the beginning of His ministry, we must, to make this datum useful in our present inquiry, ascertain in what year this ministry began. This, it is said, we are able to do through the words spoken by the Jews at Jerusalem in reply to His parable respecting the temple of His body (John ii. 20): "Then said the Jews, Forty and six years was this temple in building, and wilt thou rear it up in three days?" (So R.V. By some, as by Lightfoot, it is rendered "Forty and six years hath this temple been in building." So Gres., Norton, Bloom.) This implies that it was not at this date completed; and we know from other sources that it was not; this building, or rather rebuilding, of the temple being begun by Herod in the eighteenth year of his reign, or during the year from Nisan 734 to Nisan 735. (Jos., Antiq., xv. 11. 1.) The forty-sixth year following was from Nisan 780 to Nisan 781. But from what point of time are the forty-six years to be reckoned? Up to this time, to the Passover when the words were spoken, the work of rebuilding, which began in the autumn, had continued, and was not yet ended. But is the forty-sixth year to be taken as current, or as completed? If the latter, the Passover was that of 781. (So Wieseler, Meyer, Weiss, Tisch., Schürer, Lange, Godet.) If the former, it was that of 780. (So Lardner, Licht., Friedlieb, Edersheim, McClellan, Woolsey. The temple was finished later under Agrippa. (Jos., Antiq., xx. 9. 7, in 817 Godet, in 818 Meyer.)

If, however, this statement is understood as by Tholuck; "In forty and six years was this temple," all that is yet finished, "built,"

---

[1] We give for comparison all the passages where ὡσεί is used by him in connection with numerals: Gospel, i. 56; ix. 14; ix. 28; xxii. 59; xxiii. 44; Acts of Apostles, ii. 41; iv ʒ; v. 36; x. 3; xix. 7.

[2] So Lightfoot, Jarvis.   [3] Winer, ii. 769.

it loses all its chronological value. "We may suppose," he remarks, "that at this time, probably after the completion of some main part of the edifice, a cessation in the building had taken place." But in this case, as it is impossible to tell when this cessation began, we cannot say how long the forty-six years had been completed.

There is still another view of this passage founded on the rendering of ναός as opposed to ἱερόν, and meaning "the sanctuary"; not the whole temple, but the holy and most holy places. Taking this view, Quandt (16) refers the statement to the period of the rebuilding under Zerubbabel, after the return from Babylon. But this has few advocates.

All, therefore, that this statement respecting the time occupied in the rebuilding of the temple, gives us, is the strong probability that the Lord's first Passover was that of 780 or 781. The former has most in its favor. Edersheim (i. 375) remarks "that if a Jew had calculated the time at the Passover 781, he would not have said forty-six but forty-seven years was the temple in building." The Passover of 780 fell upon the ninth of April. If then He was about thirty at this time, but not a year more or less, His birth would be about 750. His baptism was a few weeks earlier than the Passover, for there intervened the temptation of forty days, His return to Jordan, His visit to Cana and to Capernaum, and His journey to Jerusalem. Allowing two or three months for all this, His baptism was in the last of 779, or beginning of 780. If we suppose Him to have been just thirty at His baptism, His birth must be placed in the last of 749, or beginning of 750. If, then, for reasons already given, we cannot interpret "about thirty" as a wholly indefinite expression, but must understand it as meaning that He was some months more or less than thirty, we cannot place His birth earlier than the middle of 749.

Datum 5.— Still another datum is the visit of the Magi. This, as we learn from Matthew (ch. ii.), was before the death of Herod, and so before April, 750. How long an interval elapsed between their coming and his death, is matter of inference. Their arrival at Jerusalem cannot, however, well be placed later than February, 750. At this time Herod was there (Matt. ii. 1-7), but at the eclipse of the moon,[1] March 12-13, he was at Jericho, where he subsequently died. If, then, the Magi came in February, the Lord's birth must have taken place some time earlier, as early at least as the beginning of 750.

The cause of the coming of the Magi to Jerusalem was the appearing of a star, which in some way, whether by astrology, or tradition,

---

[1] Josephus, Antiq., xvii. 6. 4.

or by direct divine revelation, they knew to indicate the birth of the King of the Jews. If this star were a real star, subject to the ordinary laws which rule the heavenly bodies, and the time of its appearing could be determined astronomically, we should find in it a most valuable chronological aid. But many regard it as wholly supernatural, a luminous body like a star specially prepared by God for this end; and others as a new star, that, after shining awhile in the heavens, totally disappeared; and others still, as a comet.[1] If either of these suppositions be correct, it gives us no chronological datum. But a considerable number of modern commentators are inclined to regard it as a conjunction of planets, and its time thus capable of determination. This hypothesis was first advanced by Kepler, whose attention was turned to the matter by a similar conjunction at the close of 1603, A.D. In December of that year, Saturn and Jupiter were in conjunction, and to them in the spring following Mars was added. In the autumn of 1604, a new star of distinguished brilliancy appeared, which, however, soon began to fade, and finally, at the end of 1605, vanished from sight. His attention thus aroused, Kepler found by computation that during the year 747 of Rome, the planets Jupiter and Saturn three times came into conjunction. These computations, according to the latest corrections, show these conjunctions to have taken place on May 29th, October 1st, and December 5th, of that year, all in the sign of Pisces. At the first conjunction they were only one degree removed, in the two latter were so near that both planets appeared to a weak eye as one. In the spring of 748 to these conjunctions Mars was added, and from some Chinese astronomical records it has been affirmed that a comet was visible from February to April, 749, and again in April, 750. (Ideler, Handbuch Chronologie, ii. 456; Wieseler, Syn., 67; Zumpt, 302.)

Several difficult questions meet us here. Are these planetary conjunctions to be regarded as the star seen by the Magi? "We have seen His star in the east." That the word ἀστήρ originally meant a single star is admitted, and was distinguished from ἀστρόν, but this distinction was lost later. McClellan affirms (400) that "the word cannot in any case be a conjunction of stars," and Meyer that "this star was certainly not a constellation." (So Trench, but not so positively, Star, 29; and Ellicott.) But Edersheim (i. 204, note 2) quotes Schleusner (Lex. in N. T.) to prove that ἀστήρ may be used of constellations, meteors, and comets: *omne designare quod aliquem splendorem habet et emittit.* Alexander *in loco* says: "Star is in Greek

---

[1] Winer, ii. 523. Trench, Star of the Wise Men, 28. Spanheim, Dubia Evangelica, Pars Secunda.

applied to any luminary in the heavens, whether fixed star, planet, comet, or meteor. . . . It may denote the conjunction itself, or the appearance of a new star." Ebrard (283), however, attempts to show upon astrological grounds that the star cannot have been a fixed star, because these do not change their places; nor could it have been a comet, since comets, though portents, cannot astrologically indicate a definite event, as the birth of a king; nor can it have been a new star, since no previous knowledge of it existed, and could have no astrological value. It must, therefore, have been one of the planets. But as the appearing of a single unrelated planet would have in astrology no significance, it must have been a conjunction of planets.

But if it be admitted that the term may have so large a meaning as to embrace the heavenly bodies in general and their conjunctions, yet the mention of "His star" seems plainly to refer to the prophecy (Numb. xxiv. 17): "There shall come forth a star out of Jacob," a prediction to which the Jews in the Lord's day gave a Messianic interpretation. The idea of a conjunction of planets being the star, seems thus excluded.[1]

But would any conjunction of planets answer to the statements of Matthew respecting this star? If so, they must have been so near together as to appear as one. This is said by Ideler. But, on the other hand, Rev. Prof. Pritchard (Smith's Bible Dict., i. 1072) denies that the two planets were so near together as to appear as one. He finds, and his calculations have been verified and confirmed at Greenwich, "that this conjunction was not on November 12th, but on December 5th, and that, even with Ideler's somewhat strange postulate of an observer with weak eyes, the planets could never have appeared as one star, for they never approached each other within double the apparent diameter of the moon." Even if for a short time the two planets appeared as a single star, this would hardly answer to the accounts which Matthew gives of its movements.

If, then, we reject the view that a conjunction of planets was the star of the Magi, was it a new one? This was held by Augustine and many of the ancients, meaning, however, not merely a newly-appearing, but a newly-created star (Münter, Das Stern, 9; Trench, Star, 28). That it was a new star, following the conjunctions, was held also by the astronomer Kepler. He was led to this conclusion the more readily that some thirty years before his day there appeared

---

[1] It is a remark of Lewin (878), that rumors of the coming Messiah, occasioned by the vision of Zacharias and the birth of John the Baptist, had spread from Jerusalem to the Jews of the East, and thus led the Magi to watch the heavens. This is very improbable.

a very remarkable star, which is thus described by Grant (Hist. of Phys. Ast., 539): "It was first seen by Tycho Brahe on the evening of the 11th of November, 1572. It then surpassed in lustre the brightest of the fixed stars, and was even more brilliant than the planet Jupiter. . . . It almost rivalled Venus, and, like that planet, was seen by some persons even in the daytime. During the remaining part of November it continued to shine with undiminished lustre, but it subsequently began to decline, until at length, in the month of March, 1574, it ceased to be visible." Another new star appeared in 1604, and was seen by Kepler himself, who describes it "as surpassing in brightness stars of the first magnitude, as well as the planets Mars, Saturn, and Jupiter, all of which were in its vicinity." Like the star of 1572, it began to decline soon after its appearance, and finally ceased to be visible between October, 1605, and February, 1606. Grant adds, that "phenomena of a similar kind have subsequently been observed, but have not exhibited such remarkable features as the two stars just mentioned." But if the star of the Magi was a new star, as held by Kepler and many since, has its appearance any chronological value? Clearly it has not, unless we can connect it in point of time with the conjunctions of 747, whose times we know. This was done by Kepler, whose attention was turned to the matter by the similar conjunctions in 1603 and 1604. The new star of which mention has been made, appeared in October of this year, 1604. Kepler, having ascertained that like conjunctions took place in 747, inferred that a new star may then have appeared following the conjunctions — the star of the Magi. If this were so, and at a like interval of time, its appearance would have been in 748, and thus would give us a chronological datum.

But other questions would here arise. Did the new star indicate to the Magi the actual birth of the Lord, or the announcement to the Virgin of His birth? (Luke ii. 31.) Or did it merely indicate, like the conjunction of which Abarbanel speaks as occurring three years before the birth of Moses, that the time of His birth was approaching? (Wieseler, Beiträge, 153, affirms that it was a common Jewish belief that these conjunctions preceded the birth two or three years, but this statement seems to rest on no sufficient authority.) We cannot answer these questions. If a new star, like that in Kepler's day, appeared to the Magi, and if it followed at a like interval after the conjunctions, then only some valid chronological inferences might be drawn from it.

If confidence may be given to the Chinese records, a new star was visible in February and March, 749, and again in April, 750.

1*

Pingré says there were two comets, — one in 749, and one in 750. Wieseler, assuming that there was but one, argues that this star or comet was the star of the Magi, and that when it appeared they began their journey. He thus obtains a definite date, and infers that the Lord was born early in 750. It is plain that this has little chronological value.

But another view of this star has been taken by many, — that it was not one of the heavenly orbs, but some extraordinary luminous appearance like a star, which, having served its purpose in guiding the Magi to Bethlehem, vanished forever. (Many of the early fathers ascribed the movements of this supernatural body to angelic activity, — see a Lapide *in loco;* a view which Chemnitz favors, and as confirmatory refers to the angel and to the glory of the Lord shining around the shepherds.) In favor of this view is the statement (Matthew ii. 9) that the star went before them and stood over where the child was. It is observed by Mill (305, note) that "this, literally interpreted, cannot possibly be understood of any star so called, but of a meteoric body moving in the region of the terrene atmosphere." And this seems to be the meaning of Augustine in calling it a new star whose purpose — *ministerium officii* — was fulfilled when it led them to the house of the infant Lord. On the other hand, many deny any mention in the narrative of a miraculous star. (So Weiss.)

But if this be accepted, we must still bring this luminous appearance into some relations of time with the conjunctions whose date we know, or, as regards our present inquiry, we gain nothing. But of such relations we are ignorant. We can only say that, if later than the conjunctions, it must have appeared sometime during or after December, 747.

Most recent writers take the view that these conjunctions, though they were not the star itself, were of importance in awaking the attention of the Magi, who were students of the heavens, and thus preparing them to watch for some more positive sign. This they found in the star appearing later, whether that star may have been a transient one, such as seen by Kepler, or a comet, or a meteor, or a luminous body specially prepared for this end. In this case, the conjunctions defined the earliest period of the Lord's birth, and as we have the other terminus — the death of Herod — His birth must be placed in the interval 747–750.

Datum 6. — Many have found a more definite chronological datum in the statement of Matthew (ii. 16), that Herod, after the departure of the Magi, slew all the children of Bethlehem "from two years old and under, according to the time which he had diligently inquired of the wise men." The inference is drawn that the appearing of the star must have been two years before their arrival in Jerusalem. (So Münter and many.) There are too many uncertain elements here to make this datum of the two years of much value. What was the star? What event did the star denote? Was it prophetic, foretelling the Lord's birth? In this case it may have appeared one, or two, or more years before the nativity. Did it follow the birth? If so, by what interval? It is by no means certain what the Magi understood it to denote, though more probably the birth. Nor do we know that Herod had the same understanding as they. But if he believed that it appeared at the time of the Lord's birth, did he ascertain how soon after its appearing they began their journey; and how long they were on the way? He may have done so, but as he counted on their return to him from Bethlehem with definite information as to the child they had seen, it was not necessary that he should do this. All that we can say is, that unable to obtain from them personally the information he sought, he meant to be sure that the infant should not escape him, and to this end orders that all the children within the limits in any way indicated by the star, should be killed.[1]

Datum 7.— Still another datum on which some rely, is the existence of general peace throughout the world at the Lord's birth. This peace is supposed to have been foretold by the prophets, and its realization announced by the angels in their song on the night of the nativity (Luke ii. 14), "Glory to God in the highest, and on earth peace, good will toward men." With this is joined the closing of the temple of Janus by Augustus, the sign of peace throughout the Roman Empire. It is known that this temple was twice closed by him, in 725, in 729, and probably also a third time, though the year is not certainly determined. "We know no more concerning it than this: that 744 *sub finem*, it was intended to have taken place, but was delayed a little longer by some unimportant commotions among the Daci and Dalmatæ."[2] In the absence of exact information, we can say no more than that there was a period of general tranquillity throughout the Roman world for five or six years, or probably from

---

[1] Greswell, ii. 135, would understand by children of two years those of thirteen months only. All older than this were exempt. But this is doubtful, and is unnecessary. Browne, Ordo Sæclorum, 52, explains Herod's order from the fact the star appeared two years before the nativity.

[2] Greswell, i. 469. See Patritius, iii. 165. According to Sepp and Browne, it was closed from 746–752; to Ammer and Greswell, from 748 or 749–752 or 753; to Jarvis, from 746–758. Wieseler makes the order to shut it to have issued in 743, but its execution to have been delayed till 752.

746 to 752, during which period the Lord was born. We cannot, without building on conjecture, reach any more exact result.[1]

To sum up the results of our inquiries, we find that the birth of the Lord was not later than April, 750, and probably not later than January. The time in this direction is limited by the death of Herod in April of that year, and the events immediately preceding it. On the other hand, if we give to the conjunction of planets in 747 as connected with the visit of the Magi, any chronological value, we cannot put His birth earlier than that year. Again, if we understand the statement of Tertullian, that the enrollment which brought Joseph and Mary to Bethlehem was under Saturninus as governor, He may have been born in 746 or 747 or 748. But if the enrollment was under Varus, He may have been born in 749 or in the first half of 750. And as He was about thirty years of age at the beginning of His ministry, and the date of His first Passover after its beginning was 780, we reach the year 749. We have thus to choose between the years 747, 748, 749, and the beginning of 750. The probabilities are in favor of 749, and in our further examinations we shall assume this as the year of His birth.

We give the opinions of some of the older and of the more modern chronologists and commentators:

For the year 747, Sanclemente, Wurm, Ideler, Münter, Sepp, Jarvis, Alford, Patritius, Ebrard, Zumpt, Keim; 748, Kepler, Lewin; 749, Petavius, Usher, Norris, Tillemont, Lichtenstein, Ammer, Friedlieb, Bucher, Browne, Godet, McClellan; 750, Bengel, Wieseler, Greswell, Ellicott, Pressensé, Thomson; for 751, Keil, Quandt; 752, Caspari, Reiss; Lardner hesitates between 748 and 749; so Robinson, "not later than the autumn of 749, perhaps a year earlier"; so Beyschlag, Schenkel; Pound, "August 749–August 750." Clinton finds the earliest possible date the autumn of 748, the latest that of 750; Woolsey, undecided.

TIME OF THE YEAR.

Datum 1. — We proceed to inquire in what part of the year the Lord was born. The only direct datum which the Gospels give us is found in the statement of Luke (i. 5), that Zacharias "was of the course of Abia." It is known that the priests were divided into twenty-four classes, each of which officiated at the temple in its turn for a week.[2] This order, originally established by David, was broken

---

[1] For recent discussions leading to the same general conclusion, see Woolsey in Bib. Sacra, 1870, 322; Zumpt, 232; others, as Sepp, i. 132, attach more chronological importance to it.

[2] 1 Chron., xxiv. 1–19; Lightfoot, ix. 44.

up by the captivity. The four classes that returned from Babylon were divided anew by Ezra into twenty-four, to which the old names were given. Another interruption was made by the invasion of Antiochus, but the old order was restored by the Maccabees. Of these courses that of Jehoiarib was the first, that of Abia the eighth. We need, therefore, only to know a definite time at which any one of the courses was officiating to be able to trace the succession. Such a datum we find in the Talmudical statements, supported by Josephus,[1] that at the destruction of the temple by Titus on the 5th August, 823, the first class had just entered on its course. Its period of service was from the evening of the 4th August, which was the Sabbath, to the evening of the following Sabbath, on the 11th August. We can now easily compute backward, and ascertain at what time in any given year each class was officiating.

If now we take the year 749 as the probable year of Christ's birth, the appearance of the angel to Zacharias announcing John's birth must be placed in 748. In this year we find by computation that the course of Abia, or the eighth course, officiated from the 17-23d April, and again from the 3-9th October.[2] At each of these periods, therefore, was Zacharias at Jerusalem. If the annunciation of the angel was made to him during the former, the birth of John may be placed near the beginning of 749, and the Lord's birth about six months later, or near the middle of 749; if the annunciation was made during the latter, John's birth was near the middle of 749, and the Lord's birth near its end.

The fact that we do not know how soon after the completion of the ministry of Zacharias the conception of John is to be placed, prevents any very exact statement of dates. Luke (i. 24) uses only the general expression "after those days his wife Elisabeth conceived." Yet the tenor of the narrative leads us to believe that it was soon after his return to his home, and may be placed in either of the months April or October, 748. Counting onward fifteen months we reach June and December, 749, in one of which the Lord's birth is to be placed. The Greek church celebrates it on the 23d September. (Tillemont, i. 145, note.)

It is a very obvious objection to the chronological value of these conclusions, that if we take another year we reach other results. As said by Godet: "Everything depends upon our knowledge of the year of the Lord's birth." Thus Lewin (109), taking 748 as the year

---

[1] War, vi. 4. 5.

[2] So Wieseler. 143; Licht., 76; Friedlieb, 80; Browne, 85. Greswell, i. 434, Sept. 30 — Oct. 7. Edersheim, i, 135.

of the Nativity, finds that in 747 the course of Abia was on duty from the 16th to the 20th May, and if we place the conception of John the Baptist about the end of May, he was born in February, 748, and the Lord about the first of August of the same year. Upon this datum that Zacharias was of the course of Abia, Edersheim places some reliance, but is not sure (ii. 705). McClellan, 391, relies on it with much confidence as proving that the Nativity was about December 25, 749. If we find reason on other grounds to put the Nativity in 749, the argument from the course of Abia helps to confirm it.

Datum 2. — In choosing between these months — June and December — some weight is to be given to the statement of Luke (ii. 8) that in the night when the Lord was born shepherds were in the field keeping watch over their flock. Does not this rather point to the summer than to the winter, to June than to December? To answer this we must make some inquiries respecting the climate of Judæa. Travelers in Palestine differ widely in their meteorological accounts, nor is this to be wondered at, as the seasons vary greatly in different years, and each traveler can speak only of what falls under his own personal observation. Instead, therefore, of trying to reach some general conclusions from such isolated accounts, we shall take the statements of those who, having resided some time in Jerusalem, give us the results of their observations for several successive years. And we note first the statements of Schwartz[1] and Barclay.[2]

The year is divided into two seasons, summer and winter, or the dry and the wet. The winter rains begin to fall in the latter part of October or beginning of November. The most rainy month is February. During the months of December, January, February, and March, there is no entire cessation of rain for any long interval; "yet an interregnum of several weeks' dry weather generally occurs between the middle of December and the middle of February, somewhat distinguishing the former rains of the season from the latter."[3] "The average monthly temperature during four years from 1851 was, for November, 63.8°; December, 54.5°; January, 49.4°; February, 54.4°; March, 55.7°."[4] "The temperature of Palestine averages during the winter 50° to 53$\frac{1}{4}$°."[5] Of the month of December the following account is given: "The earth fully clothed with rich verdure. Wheat and barley still sown, also various kinds of pulse. Sugar-cane in market. Cauliflowers, cabbages, radishes, lettuce, lentils, etc. Ploughing still continues at intervals."[6] "Temperature same as

---

[1] Descriptive Geography of Palestine, 325–331.
[2] City of the Great King, 414–429.   [3] Barclay.
[4] Barclay.   [5] Schwartz.   [6] Barclay.

preceding month. The sowing of grain in the field has already commenced. Although the oranges and kindred fruit have been long since ripe, they continue to mature on the trees till toward April and May."[1] February is the coldest part of the year, and fires are used by the Frank population, though little by the natives, and snow and ice are occasionally seen.

These statements are confirmed, in general, by the latest and best authorities.[2] From these we select the observations of Dr. Chaplin made at Jerusalem for a period of twenty-one years, from 1861–1882. (Qt. St. 1883, p. 8, ff.) Speaking of the rainy season, he says there are three times of rain: 1. The early rain, beginning in October and extending to the middle of December; 2. the copious winter rain, from the middle of December to the middle of March; 3. the latter or spring rain, from the middle of March to May. The mean duration of the rainy season is 188 days; of the dry, 177. For the three winter months, December, January, and February, the average number of rainy days was as follows: December, 9.04; January, 10.18; February, 10.43. "During the rainy season rain falls on one or more days, and is followed on one or more days by fine weather; and, therefore, these days of the winter and early spring months are some of the most enjoyable that the climate of Palestine affords."[3] As to the temperature of these years, his observations give a mean of 62.8°; in February, the coldest month, 47.9°; in August, 76.1°. The lowest temperature for these twenty years was, in January, 25° Fahr. In fourteen of these years was snow, in eight none. In December the highest temperature, 73°; the lowest, 36°. On the 20th of December, 1879, snow fell to the depth of seventeen inches. But, from 1861–82, snow fell only three times in December (Table 12). In Jerusalem frost generally occurs on five or six nights in the course of the winter, but it is rare for ice to remain through the day, except in cold situations, and sheltered from the sun.

It should be said that Dr. Chaplin took his observations in a garden within the city; and he remarks: "It is no doubt often much cooler on the hills eastward."

Although these observations have special reference to Jerusalem, they apply equally well to Bethlehem, the climate of which is not unlike that of Jerusalem, though, according to Tobler, somewhat milder. On the 10th of February, 1887, snow was lying on the higher mountains beyond Bethlehem, and there were heavy frosts for several nights in Jerusalem (Qt. St., April, 1887).

---

[1] Schwartz.

[2] Winer, ii. 691; Raumer, 77; Robinson, ii. 428; Tobler, Denkblätter, iii., etc.

[3] As to the rainfall in Palestine, see Rice in Journ. Bib. Lit. & Ex., June, 1886.

There seems, then, so far as climate is concerned, no good ground to affirm that shepherds could not have been pasturing their flocks in the field during the month of December. As we have seen, Barclay states that in this month the earth is fully clothed with rich verdure, and there is generally an interval of dry weather between the middle of December and the middle of February. Schubert[1] says that the period about Christmas is often one of the loveliest periods of the whole year. Tobler says, the weather about Christmas is favorable to the feeding of flocks, and often most beautiful. "On the 27th December, 1845, we had very agreeable weather."[2] It is during this month that the wind begins to blow from the south or southwest, which, according to Schwartz, "brings rain and betokens warm weather," and thus hastens forward vegetation.

Unless, then, the climate of Judæa has become in the lapse of years much warmer than of old, the flocks may have been feeding in the fields of Bethlehem in the month of December. But, according to Arago,[3] there has been no important change for the last three thousand and three hundred years. Nor do the incidental notices of Scripture conflict with this. The Lord's words, "Pray that your flight be not in the winter," are easily understood when we remember that winter is the rainy season, and most unfavorable for journeying. That a fire was made at a much later period of the year (John xviii. 18) is plainly an exceptional case, and for this reason mentioned. "Strong, and at times cold winds prevail in April."[4]

There remains to be noticed a saying of the Talmudists, that the flocks were taken to the fields in March and brought home in November. But this had reference to those pastures that were found in the wilderness far away from the cities or villages, and were resorted to by the shepherds during the summer months. "The spring coming on, they drove their beasts into wildernesses or champaign grounds, where they fed them the whole summer. The winter coming on, they betook themselves home again with the flocks and herds."[5]

Edersheim (i. 187, note) refers to another Rabbinic authority, which says that the flocks, fed in the wilderness, remained there all the year round. The inference, therefore, drawn by many, that this flock being kept through the night in the field, it could not have been so late as December, is without ground. And, if the flock was near Bethlehem, having been brought in from the wilderness, it would show that this was after November, and in one of the winter months.

---

[1] Quoted by Wieseler, 148.
[2] So Ritter, Theil, xvi. 480.
[3] In Winer, ii. 692.
[4] Schwartz.
[5] Lightfoot, on Luke ii. 8.

The question is raised by Edersheim, whether this flock was an ordinary one, and the shepherds ordinary shepherds; or, one reserved for temple sacrifices, and the shepherds its keepers? If the last, the presence of the flock at Bethlehem gives in itself no indication of the time of the year. The point will be considered when the birth of the Lord is spoken of in its historical relations.

If, then, we have to choose between the months of December and June, the balance of probabilities is in favor of the former. As the spring rains cease in April, the whole country soon becomes dry and barren. Of May, Barclay (423) remarks: "Vegetation having attained its maximum, now begins rapidly to decline for want of rain;" and of June, "Herbage becoming parched, the nomad Arabs begin to move northward with their flocks."

As the early tradition of the Church designated this month as the time of the Lord's birth, it has been generally accepted, but not universally. Lightfoot makes it to have been in September; Newcome, in October; Paulus, in March; Wieseler, in February; Lichtenstein, in June; Greswell, in April; Clinton, in spring; Lardner and Robinson, in autumn; Strong and Lewin, in August; Quandt, in May.

DAY OF THE MONTH.

If we accept the month of December, the day of the month still remains undetermined. If we place the ministry of Zacharias in Jerusalem from the 3d to 9th October, 748, and the conception of John soon after, the sixth month of Elisabeth (Luke i. 36) would extend from the middle of March to the middle of April. During this period was the annunciation to Mary, and the Lord's birth must then be placed between the middle of December, 749, and the middle of January, 750. A more definite result we cannot reach, except we receive the traditional date of the 25th of December. The origin and value of this tradition we proceed to consider.

It is now generally granted that the day of the nativity was not observed as a feast in any part of the Church, east or west, till some time in the fourth century.[1] If any day had been earlier fixed upon as the Lord's birthday, it was not commemorated by any religious rites, nor is it mentioned by any writers. The observance of the 25th December is ascribed to Julius, Bishop of Rome, A.D. 337–352. It is mentioned as observed under his successor, Liberius, A.D. 352–366.

---

[1] So Clinton. "Not only was the day unknown, but for 300 years after the ascension no day was set apart for the commemoration of the birth of Christ." Binterim, Denkwürdigkeiten, v. 1. 328, asserts that the feast was celebrated much earlier, but his proofs are not convincing.

In the Eastern Church till this time, the 6th January had been observed as the day of the Lord's baptism, and had been regarded also as the day of His birth, it being inferred from Luke iii. 23, that He was just thirty when baptized. It was only by degrees that a distinction began to be made between the date of His birth and that of His baptism, and that each began to be observed upon different days. Chrysostom[1] states that it was only within ten years that the 25th December had been made known to them by the Western Church as the day of His nativity, but asserts that through the public records of the taxing (Luke ii. 1-4) preserved at Rome, it had long been known to the Christians of that city. From this time, about the end of the fourth century, this day was commemorated as the birthday both in the east and west. The ground of its non-observance for so long a time is explained by the fact that in His birth He humbled Himself, and His glory was hidden. Those acts of God were commemorated in which His glory was revealed. The first of these was the visit of the Magi and their adoration; the second, the descent of the Holy Ghost at His baptism, and the voice from heaven; the third, the exhibition of His power in changing the water into wine. It is certain that down to the middle of the fourth century, the Orientals, if they commemorated the birthday at all, commemorated it with the Epiphany on the 6th January. (Binterim, v. 1. 530.)

Thus we have in favor of the 25th December, the fact that the Eastern Churches were induced to adopt it, and to transfer to it the feast which they had before observed upon the 6th of January. We can scarce think this done without some good chronological grounds, real or supposed. But we do not know what these grounds were. Some[2] ascribe great importance to the statements of Justin Martyr, Tertullian, and Chrysostom, that in the public archives at Rome a registry existed of the census under Augustus, by which the Lord's birthday was conclusively established. Jarvis supposes Tertullian to give the very words of the enrollment as he found them in the Roman archives, in which Mary is mentioned as the mother of Jesus — *Maria ex qua nascitur Christus.* Thus the day being proved by the register at Rome, the knowledge of it gradually spread to the Eastern Churches. But most chronologists have regarded these statements as of little value.[3]

---

[1] Antioch, A. D. 386.   [2] So Jarvis, 370 and 537.

[3] See Kingsley in New Englander, April, 1847, who says that they are not referred to by Baronius, or Pagi, or Causabon, or relied on by Usher or Newcome. "In the time of Julius Caesar it [the vernal equinox] corresponded to the 25th of March, in the sixteenth century it had retrograded to the 11th. By suppressing ten days in the calendar, Gregory [in 1582] restored the equinox to the 21st of March, the day on which it fell at the time of the Council of Nice in 325," Dr. Barnard in Johnson's Cyclopedia, Art. Calendar.

The fact that the tradition, which placed the Lord's birth on the 25th December, also placed the birth of John Baptist on the 24th June preceding, the annunciation to the virgin on the 25th March, and the day of Elisabeth's conception on the 24th September, or on the four cardinal points of the year, has led many to suppose that these periods were selected with reference to their astronomical significance, rather than as the real dates of these events.   It strengthens this supposition that so many of the Christian festivals were placed upon days remarkable in the Julian calendar.   Noting these facts, Sir Isaac Newton [1] inferred that "these days were fixed in the first Christian calendars by mathematicians at pleasure, without regard to tradition, and that the Christians afterward took up what they found in the calendars."   More probable is the supposition that these dates were in part selected as the times of Christian feasts, in order to serve as a counterpoise to the corresponding heathen festivals, and in part because of their typical meaning.   It does not appear that the feast of the nativity can be directly connected with any heathen festival, for the connection between this day and the *dies natalis solis invicti*, cannot be proved; but as the winter solstice, its bearings are often typically interpreted by the fathers.[2]   Thus the words of John Baptist spoken of Christ (John iii. 30), "He must increase but I must decrease," are applied to the fact that, at John's birth in June 24th, or the summer solstice, the days began to decrease in length, but at Christ's birth, December 25th, the days began to increase. Thus Augustine [3]: *Hodie natus est Johannes, quo incipiunt decrescere dies — eo die natus Christus, quo crescere.*

While such typical applications naturally tend to beget doubts whether the dates so connected with the great astronomical epochs of of the year have any historic foundation, yet on the other hand it should be borne in mind that if the 25th December were actually the Lord's birthday, the events preceding it, the conception of John, the annunciation to Mary, and the birth of John, must have taken place nearly at the times which tradition has assigned.   And it deserves to be considered, that the hour of His birth, who is Lord of all, was not matter of accident, but divinely appointed.   What season of the year might be most fitting to so great an event, or whether, astronomically viewed, the winter solstice has any such fitness, are questions not necessary to be answered here.   It is at least not unreasona-

---

[1] Observations upon Daniel and Apoc.

[2] Sepp, i. 200. Caspari, 71. "In the first Christian centuries the 25th December was looked upon as the day of the winter solstice."

[3] Homil., 3.

ble to believe, that the sun in its course may typify Him who is the Sun of righteousness, and the year in its seasons foreshadow the epochs of His life.

The strongest argument against the 25th December, if the birth be put in 749, is that it leaves too little space for the events that occurred before Herod's death. This death was about the 1st of April, 750; we thus have a little more than three months. In this period were the visit of the Magi, the presentation at the Temple, the flight into Egypt; how soon after Herod's death was the return from Egypt, is to be later considered. If, according to general tradition, the Magi came on the 6th January or 13th day after the Lord's birth, and the presentation was on the 40th, or early in February, He went down into Egypt about two months before Herod's death. Those who put the coming of the Magi on the 6th January, the flight into Egypt immediately after, and the presentation upon the return after Herod's death, gain another month. If, however, we follow the order of most modern harmonists, and put the visit of the Magi after the presentation on the 40th day, the time of the sojourn in Egypt up to Herod's death was a little less than two months.

Those who put the Lord's birth in 747 or 748, make the period spent in Egypt much longer — some three years, some two, some one, some six months. Those who put the birth later than the 25th December, 749, and Herod's death in April, 750, make the sojourn but three to four weeks, or less; Wieseler and Ellicott only about a fortnight. There is nothing in Matthew's narration, or the circumstances of the case, that makes it probable He was there more than a few weeks. There does not, therefore, appear any good reason why all the events he narrates may not have taken place between the 25th December and the following 1st of April.

Our inquiries lead us, then, to these general results. We find it most probable that the Lord was born near the end of the year 749. At this period all the chronological statements of the Evangelists seem most readily to center and harmonize. In favor of December, the last month of that year, as much may be said as in favor of any other, and this aside from the testimony of tradition. As to the day, little that is definite can be said. The 25th of this month lies open to the suspicion of being selected on other than historic grounds, yet it is not inconsistent with any data we have, and has the voice of tradition in its favor. Still, in regard to all these conclusions, it must be remembered that many elements of uncertainty enter into the computations, and that any positive statements are impossible. All who have attempted the task, will say with Bynaeus: *Frustra hic omnem operam consumi.* It is well said by Spanheim: *Sed cum hac de re altum apud Evangelistas sit silentium, nec Apostolicæ Ecclesiæ vel sanctionem, vel praxin legamus, causæ nihil est, cur temere definiamus quod solide definiri non potest.*

II. DATE OF THE LORD'S BAPTISM.

We have seen that the Lord was about thirty years old when He began His ministry; and as this followed immediately upon His baptism, He was about thirty when He was baptized. If born, as we have supposed, at the end of 749, His baptism may be put in 779, or in 780. The only data we have to determine the time are, the year of the Passover, which followed His baptism (John ii. 13); and the statement of Luke, that John began his ministry in the fifteenth year of Tiberius Caesar (Luke iii. 1). The other data here given by Luke are too general to be of value in this inquiry.

Datum 1.—The Lord's first Passover. This we have seen to be that of 780. His baptism was some time before this, how long depends upon the time necessary for the intervening events. After the baptism was the temptation of forty days, the return to the Jordan, and the gathering of His first disciples, His visit to Cana, His sojourn at Capernaum, and His journey up to the Passover, which fell this year on the 9th April. All this, we may say, would occupy about two or three months. (Chronicon Paschale 76 days, Friedlieb 87, Greswell 64.) Counting backward from the Passover, we may then put the baptism at the end of 779, or very early in 780.

Datum 2.—The fifteenth year of Tiberius. Before asking to what year of the Lord's life this would bring us, we must ask what is meant by the statement, that "the word of God came to John in the wilderness"? (Luke iii. 1.) The obvious meaning is, that he then began his ministry; but because of chronological difficulties, of which we shall soon speak, it has been referred to other events affecting directly the Lord Himself and His ministry. Three interpretations have had their advocates.

1. Sanclemente regards the statements of Luke (iii. 1, 2) as a general heading of his theme—the sufferings and death of Christ. He attempts to show (as cited by Wieseler, 196, note) that the fifteenth year of Tiberius "*non ad initium ministerii Joannis, non ad baptismum a Christo in Jordane susceptum, sed ad ipsius passionis et crucifixionis tempus ipso evangelista duce atque interprete esse referendum.*"

Browne (92), who makes the Lord's ministry to have lasted but little more than a year, adopted this explanation in a modified form. "The heading of St. Luke's third chapter contains the date, not of the mission of St. John the Baptist, but of the year of our Lord's ministry, especially in reference to the great events with which it closed." But this interpretation is accepted by few, and is manifestly a makeshift.

2. That the imprisonment of the Baptist was the event chiefly meant, and therewith the beginning of the Lord's ministry. (Matt. iv. 12.) This was advocated by Wieseler (Synopsis, 196), taking the same ground as Sanclemente, that Luke's chronological statement was a general heading for all that followed. (In his Beiträge, 177, he has since given up this view.) It was accepted by Ellicott (104, note). "The fifteenth year of Tiberius coincides not with the first appearance, but with the captivity of John." That it was early so understood, is said to be shown by Eusebius (iii. 24) when he says, that the Synoptists "only wrote the deeds of our Lord for one year after the imprisonment of John the Baptist, and intimated this in the very beginning of their history."

3. That the event referred to is the Lord's baptism. This is advocated by Zumpt (247), who, however, includes in this the Baptist's ministry, whose beginning is not defined by any single act, but which culminated in the baptism of Jesus; and for this reason, Luke gives this chronological datum. (So Caspari, 110, who says it was not the commencement of John's ministry, but a later call.) If the Lord was baptized very soon after John's ministry began, the fifteenth year of Tiberius might include both events.

But it is better to keep to the obvious sense of the words, and we therefore conclude, in common with the great body of chronologists and commentators, that Luke designs to refer the fifteenth year of Tiberius to the beginning of the Baptist's ministry. How long that ministry may have preceded the Lord's baptism, is to be later considered.

We must now turn to the second point — from what period is the fifteenth year of Tiberius to be reckoned? Tiberius was the step-son of the emperor Augustus, and was formally adopted by him in 757. After filling several high stations in the civil and military service, he was associated with him in the general administration of the empire in 764 or 765. Upon the death of Augustus, on the 19th of August, 767, he became sole ruler. Thus there are two periods from which his rule or administration may be reckoned: that when he was associated with Augustus, and that when he began to rule alone. To which of these periods does Luke refer? If to the former, the fifteenth year of his government was that of 779–780; if the latter, of 781–782. If we accept the latter date, and John began his ministry in August, the baptism of Jesus must be put in 782.

But we have seen that the Lord was about thirty when He was baptized; and as John had been active some time before, to this the period, longer or shorter, of his activity, must be added. Let us then say that John began his work in August or September, 781, and that the Lord was baptized some three months later, or near the beginning of 782. But we have accepted, on grounds already given, His baptism as before the Passover, 780, and have thus a discrepancy of two years. Again, we have placed His birth at the end of 749; add to this thirty years, His age at His baptism, and we reach ¶79 or 780, and thus again there is a discrepancy of two years. If born in 748 or 747, He was now, in 782, thirty-four or thirty-five, which presents a still greater difficulty.

We find here the ground of the perplexity of the early Christian chronologists and commentators. Counting the fifteenth of Tiberius from the death of Augustus, they reached the year from August, 781 to August, 782, as the first of the Lord's ministry, and He was then about thirty years of age. (If Luke counted, after the Jewish method, from Nisan to Nisan, this would make little difference, since from Nisan to August is only five months.) It was, therefore, necessary that they should put the birth of the Lord as late as possible, and it was very generally placed in 752 in order that He might be about thirty at His baptism.

The importance of this date, and the many difficulties connected with it, demand that we give to it a more particular examination. Three points claim our attention. First. The fact of Tiberius' association with Augustus in the government of the empire. This fact is beyond all doubt. The direct evidence is found in Tacitus, Suetonius, and Paterculus, and there are incidental allusions to it in several other writers.[1] Tacitus says[2] "that on him every honor was accumulated; he was adopted by Augustus for his son, assumed colleague in the empire, and presented to the several armies." He relates also that Tiberius, in reply to the request of the Senate to take the government, said that "Augustus only was capable of so mighty a charge, that for himself, having been called by him to a participation of his cares, he had learned by experience how difficult to bear, and how subject to fortune was the burden of the general administration "— *regendi cuncta*. In like manner, Suetonius[3] says that "Augustus ordered that Tiberius should be named as his colleague."— *collegam*.

---

[1] See Lardner, i. 355.

[2] Ann., i. 3. See also i. 7. "*Nam Tiberius cuncta per consules incipiebat, tanquam vetere republica et ambiguus imperandi. Ne edictum quidem, quo patres in curiam, vocabat, nisi tribuniciae potestatis praescriptione possit sub Augusto acceptae.*"

[3] August., 97.

suum Tiberium nuncupare jussit. He mentions also a law promul‑ gated by the consuls that "Tiberius, jointly with Augustus, should rule in the provinces and also take the census,"— *ut provincias cum Augusto communiter administraret, simulque censum ageret.* Paterculus (103), alluding to his adoption by Augustus, represents himself as unable to describe the joy of that day; the great concourse of all ranks of the people, and their hopes and prayers. He mentions also the triumph due him because of his victories in Pannonia and Dalmatia, and which was celebrated with great magnificence, after the Senate and people of Rome, on a request being made by his father that he might be invested with authority equal to his own — *ut aequum ei jus in omnibus provinciis exercitibusque esset, quam erat ipsi,* —had passed a decree to that effect. Paterculus adds, as his own comment, that it would have been unreasonable if he could not have ruled what he had secured.

Thus the fact is abundantly established that Augustus did for‑ mally associate Tiberius with himself in the rule of the empire. At his request, a decree to this effect was passed by the Senate and peo‑ ple. Nor was Tiberius a colleague in name merely. Augustus, very aged, and now sinking under bodily infirmities, was almost wholly under the control of his wife, the mother of Tiberius, while the latter was in the prime of life, active and energetic. In the very nature of the case, Tiberius, from the time of his colleagueship the recognized successor to the imperial throne, must have been a con‑ spicuous and influential person, and, we may perhaps say, the emperor *de facto,* although the name and prestige remained with Augustus till his death. That upon this event he did not openly and immediately act as emperor, but paid court to the Senate as if the Republic still existed, and as if he were irresolute about assuming the sovereign rule, is attributable to the peculiar political circumstances of the times, and also to his haughty temper, that chose rather to ascribe his elevation to the voice of the people than to the intrigues of his mother, and to the favor of a weak, superannuated old man.

Second. When was Tiberius thus made colleague with Augustus? Most chronologists agree in placing the decree of the Senate, already alluded to, near the end of 764 or beginning of 765.[1] We may accept this as the true date. Taking, then, the year 765, from Jan‑ uary to January, as the first of Tiberius, the fifteenth is the year 779, from January to January. Some time, then, in 779, is the beginning of John's ministry to be placed.

Third. Is it probable that Luke would compute the reign of Tibe‑

---

[1] So Gres., Wiesel., Licht., Rob., Sepp.

rius from his colleagueship? It is admitted that the Roman historians, Tacitus, Suetonius, Dio Cassius, compute it from the death of
Augustus, and that they should do so is easily explainable, since the
death of an emperor after the order of imperial succession had been
once established, formed a marked epoch from which to count the
reign of his successor, and was an event interesting all parts of the
empire. and universally known.   But notwithstanding this, other
methods of computation, as by consulships, continued in use for many
years.   (See Wies., Beiträge, 186.)   It seems to be unquestionable that
a two-\old computation took place in case of some of the later emperors.   A coin exists bearing the inscription, " In the eleventh holy
year of the government of the emperor Titus."   As he lived only two
years after his father's death, the other nine years must refer to his joint
rule with his father.   But Luke, writing not a political but a religious
history, and to whose purpose the succession of the emperors was of
no moment, could well speak of Tiberius as *de facto* the ruler at the
time and in the region of which he speaks.   He was not ignorant
that there were two modes of computing Herod's reign, and the
reigns of his sons; and whether he thought of the sole rule of Tiberius, or of his co-regency, would in all likelihood have been determined
by the fact of his residence at Rome or in a province.   As a provincial,
he would naturally see in Tiberius the acting head of the empire.

It is said also that there is no proof that this mode of computation
was known to any of the Fathers.   Clemens of Alexandria does, however, mention that according to one mode of computing Tiberius reigned
twenty-two years, which, if it be not a numerical error, as regarded
by Zumpt, 284, indicates a two-fold beginning of his reign.   Whether
the Fathers in general were ignorant that the reign of Tiberius might
be reckoned from his co-regency, is doubtful.   Lardner reasons that
they must have known it, because as they almost universally placed
the crucifixion in the fifteenth year, they must have seen how inconsistent it was with Luke's statement, who placed the beginning of
John's ministry in that year.

In regard to Josephus, it has been said that he refers to the colleagueship when he states (Antiq., xviii. 4. 6.) that "Tiberius died
after he himself had held the government twenty-two years —
σχὼν αὐτὸς τὴν ἀρχήν.   The most obvious construction of this phrase
is that which refers it to his sole administration in contradistinction
to his colleagueship.   (Hofmann in Licht., 129.)

It is only justice to any historian that he should be interpreted so
as to be consistent with himself, if possible.   And he has a higher
claim to this if he shows himself in general, as Luke undoubtedly

2

does, to be painstaking, accurate, and well-informed. Of the chronological data given by Luke we must take some leading one as regulative, with which he clearly intended the rest to be in harmony. If we take the datum of the fifteenth year of Tiberius, as beginning at the death of Augustus, and make it the chronological norm, we cannot bring his other data into harmony with it. He is inconsistent with himself, if not self-contradictory. But if we count the fifteenth year from his co-regency, all his statements are consistent. As it is certainly possible, not to say very probable, that he counted from this period, the presumption is that he did so, and we find additional proof of this in the peculiar position of public affairs.

It is to be noted here that the time of Augustus and Tiberius was a transition period in the government, and that neither the principles nor the forms of imperial succession were yet established. It is said by Merivale (His., iii. 335) that Julius Caesar permitted the senate to decree that his imperatorial title should descend to the adopted heir, but Octavius had carefully abstained from claiming it in virtue of his descent. Though he became at last absolute ruler, yet he ruled under republican names and forms, and "warily declined any of the recognized designations of sovereign rule." Thus the time of his sovereignty is dated from several periods. (Clinton, Fasti, iii. 276. For the gradual growth of his power, see Merivale, iii. 342.) Merivale seems to place it in 731, when he accepted the *potestas tribunitia*, and remarks that "this power was justly considered the keystone of the whole imperial edifice. From this period Augustus may deserve the title of emperor."

With regard to the imperial succession, it is said by Mommsen (ii. 2. 1040) that "a Roman emperor could not designate his successor. The day of the death of one is not the day of the succession of the other; who should succeed him is to be determined after he is dead. This sprung from the old republican usages, for the empire was a republic with a monarchical head. It was from this fact that a co-regency was of so much importance, no rules of succession being established. A co-regency was the mode of designating a successor, and at first under Augustus conveyed a large degree of power. A co-regent was not the equal of a *princeps*, for there could be but one prince." (But see Wieseler, Beiträge, 178, who says that Tiberius was called *princeps* two years before the death of Augustus.) The conferring of the tribunitial power upon Tiberius was, says Merivale, "universally regarded as a virtual introduction to the first place in the empire; and the pro-consulate throughout the provinces, decreed him later by the senate, would hardly admit of any other interpretation than that the son was thereby formally associated in the empire with his father." (iv. 280, Zumpt, 295, note.)

We cannot, without doing St. Luke great injustice as a historian, suppose him to have been ignorant of a fact so public and notorious as that of the association of Tiberius with Augustus in the empire, much less of his actual rule in the east; and there is no good reason why, if knowing it, he should not have taken it as an epoch from which to reckon. If the Italians dated his reign from the emperor's death, that naturally followed from the fact that the imperial authority of Tiberius during his colleagueship was little felt in Italy, his administration being confined to the provinces. But it gives a good reason why those in the provinces, especially of Asia Minor and Syria, should reckon from the time when he became, in regard to them, the acting emperor. It is said by Woolsey (Bib. Sac., 1870, 333) that at Rome, "as the government became established, and imperial power began to be looked on as a unity, the accession of an emperor on the death of his predecessor soon furnished a convenient and uniform date. Nor was it of much significance to the Romans that the man next to the emperor received an accession of dignity or authority. But in the provinces it was otherwise. Investment with proconsular power, for instance, might affect their welfare, and be a matter of interest to them, when it was not so in the central city. Hence such computations might readily spring up into use in the east, as we know it to have been true in regard to the reign of Augustus." One such reckoning, departing from the ordinary date, is found on Egyptian coins, which count the years of Tiberius from 4 A.D., when he was adopted by Augustus, and invested with the tribunicial power for five years. If Egypt counted his years from the time of his adoption, and of his acquisition of tribunicial power, with much more reason might this be an era to those who were deeply affected by it. (See Wieseler, Beiträge, 189.) The cases in all eastern countries where the sons of kings were associated with their fathers in the kingdom, were so common, that the double reckoning of their reigns could not have been anything unusual. Indeed, the epoch from which to date a reign is often perplexing, and brings no little confusion into chronology. Greswell (i. 336) ascribes the Evangelist's statement to "that scrupulous regard to truth which we should have a right to expect from an inspired historian. He could not deliberately call that year the thirteenth of Tiberius which he knew to be really his fifteenth."

Whether, as has been said, Luke, by the choice of the word "reign," ἡγεμονία rather than μοναρχία or βασιλεία, designed to indicate this, is uncertain, but the word is certainly applicable to a government administered by more than one person. (See Zumpt, 296.) Wieseler (Beiträge, 195) asserts that the term "Caesar," in the formula Τιβερίου Καίσαρος, is not to be taken as a family name, but as an expression of dignity, and to be translated, "In the fifteenth year of the reign of Tiberius as Caesar";[1] and that this, in connection with the use of ἡγεμονία instead of μοναρχία, leaves no doubt that the co-regency of Tiberius is to be understood.

(As to coins and the inferences to be drawn from them, see Wieseler, Beiträge, 190. He accepts as genuine one of Antioch on which Tiberius, before the death of Augustus, is called Σεβαστός — Augustus; contra, Sevin, Keil.)

These considerations will, we trust, exculpate the Evangelist from all charges of historical inaccuracy. It is plain that he might reckon the years of Tiberius' reign from that time, when, by his father's desire and the solemnly expressed will of the Senate and people, he entered upon the exercise of imperial power. But whether, in point of fact, Luke thus computes, continues to be matter of dispute.[2]

To sum up our investigations upon this point, we find three solutions proposed of the chronological difficulties which the statements of Luke present. First, That the fifteenth year of Tiberius is to be reckoned from the death of Augustus, and extends from August, 781, to August, 782, and that in this year the Baptist, whose labors began some time previous, was imprisoned, but the Lord's ministry began in 780, before this imprisonment, and when He was about thirty years of age. Second, That the fifteenth year is to be reckoned from the death of Augustus, but that the statement, that the Lord was then about thirty years of age, is to be taken in a large sense, and that He may have been of any age from thirty to thirty-five when He began His labors. Third, That the fifteenth year is to be reckoned from the year when Tiberius was associated with Augustus in the empire, and is, therefore, the year 779. In this case the language, "He was about thirty," may be strictly taken, and the statement, "the word of God came unto John," may be referred to the beginning of his ministry.

Of these solutions, the last seems to have most in its favor; and

---

[1] See Winer, Gram., 138, trans.

[2] In favor of the computation from the colleagueship, Usher, Bengel, Lardner, Jarvis, Greswell, Lichtenstein, Sepp, Friedlieb, Bucher, Patritius, Edersheim, Zumpt, Woolsey, Weiss; from the sole reign of Tiberius, Lightfoot, Meyer, Ebrard, Tischendorf, Ewald, Browne, Ellicott, Ammer, Keil, Sevin, Wieseler, Quandt. Clinton says, "We are compelled to conclude that St. Luke computed the years of Tiberius in a peculiar manner."

we shall assume that during the year 779, or the fifteenth year of Tiberius reckoned from his colleagueship with Augustus, John began to preach and baptize.

We have next to inquire in what period of the year his labors began.

Datum 1. — From the fact that the Levites were not allowed to enter upon their full service till the age of thirty (Numb. iv. 3), it has been generally supposed, although there is no express law to that effect, that the priests began their labors at the same age. At this period the body and mind were deemed to have reached their full vigor. Hence, it has been inferred that John must have reached the age of thirty ere he began his ministry. If this inference be correct, he began to preach during the summer of 779, his birth having taken place, as we have seen, in the summer of 749. We may, then, conclude that he entered upon his work near the middle of 779, when he was about thirty. If so, he began to preach and baptize about July or a little later. How long his labors had continued before Jesus came to him to be baptized, we can but conjecture.[1] That, however, he had been active for a considerable period, is apparent from the statements by the Synoptists respecting "the multitudes that came out to him from Jerusalem, and all Judæa, and all the region round about Jordan" (Matt. iii. 5; Mark i. 5; Luke iii. 7). Some months at least must have elapsed ere his fame could have spread so widely, and so many have been drawn to him. And if we suppose that the larger part of these crowds received the rite of baptism at his hands, a still longer period is required. A body of disciples, as distinguished from the multitudes, had already gathered around him (Acts xiii. 24). If we add to this, that at Christ's baptism, his work seemed to have reached its highest point, and thenceforward began to decline, we cannot well estimate this period as less than some months in duration. As John was born six months before the Lord, some have said that his ministry began six months earlier (Weiss, Lewin).

On the other hand, there are some considerations that prevent us from much enlarging this period. The general belief of the Jews that the coming of the Messiah was near, and their earnest desire for it, would naturally turn their attention to John as soon as he appeared in public. His ascetic life, his energetic speech, his boldness of reproof, and the whole character of his teachings, were adapted to pro-

---

[1] Caspari, 117, one month; Meyer, a very short time; and Sepp, that he began his ministry on the day of atonement, October — the beginning of a new era of years. Döllinger and others think that he preached some months before he began to baptize.

duce an immediate and powerful impression upon the people at large.
And the frequent gathering of the inhabitants from all parts of the
land at the feasts, would serve rapidly to diffuse the tidings that a
new prophet had arisen. But as such a phenomenon as this preacher
in the wilderness could not long escape the notice of the Pharisees
and the ecclesiastical rulers at Jerusalem, so it could not long remain
unquestioned. So soon as his popularity became wide-spread, and
multitudes began to receive baptism at his hands, they would seek to
know who he was, and by what authority he instituted this new rite.
But, as appears from John (i. 19–28), no such formal inquiry was
made by the Pharisees of the Baptist till after the baptism of Jesus.
Hence we may infer that his ministry had not yet continued any very
long period.

We may also add that John's message, " Repent ye, for the kingdom of heaven is at hand," was plain and easily understood. He was
no teacher of abstract doctrines, but a herald of the Messiah, and his
words took immediate hold of men's hearts. Thus his mission could
be speedily fulfilled.

In view of the above considerations, we conclude that John's ministry, including a period of preaching before his baptism began, may
have continued about six months, when the Lord came to be baptized.[1] If he was already thirty when he began his work, and his
birth be placed in June, 749, six months before that of the Lord, he
began in July, 779, to preach in the wilderness. If about six months
elapsed ere the Lord came to him at the Jordan, His baptism was
near the beginning of 780. It confirms us in this result, that two or
three months must have elapsed from the baptism of Jesus to the first
Passover (John ii. 13). We rest, then, in the conclusion, that Jesus
was baptized December, 779, or January, 780.

In the absence of all other data, we must here consider the tradition that puts His baptism on the 6th of January. It has already
appeared in our inquiries into the date of our Lord's nativity, that
both His birth and baptism, and also the adoration of the Magi, were
originally commemorated on the same day, and that this day was the
6th of January. This feast was called the feast of the Epiphany,
ἐπιφάνεια (Titus ii. 13), and commemorated His manifestation to the
world. It is uncertain how early the western church distinguished
the birth from the other events and commemorated it on another day.
That the primary reference of the Epiphany was to the baptism is
very probable, and that the baptism continued for a long time
to be the more important of the two, appears from the old Roman

---

[1] So Lightfoot, Newcome, and many.

Ordo, where it is said, *quod secunda Nativitas Christi — Epiphania — tot illustrata mysteriis, honoratior est quam prima.* (But see article "Christmas," in Dict. of Christian Antiquities, Smith and Cheetham. The writer says: "The western church, so far as we can trace the matter back, seems to have kept the two festivals of the Epiphany and Nativity always distinct.") After the Roman church had established the feast of the Nativity upon the 25th December, it still continued to observe the 6th January in commemoration of the adoration of the Magi and of the baptism, giving, however, more prominence to the former than to the latter.[1] The Greek Church, on the contrary, after it began to observe the 25th December as the day of the nativity, transferred to it also the adoration of the Magi, and commemorated only the baptism on the 6th January. Thus both the Roman and Greek Churches now agree in the observance of this day as that of the Lord's baptism.

If we now proceed to ask, on what grounds this day was selected as that of the baptism, we obtain no very satisfactory answer. The feast of the Epiphany seems to have been originally commemorative of the baptism as the time when the Lord was first manifested openly as the Son of God (Matt. iii. 16–17); and as He was supposed, through a too literal interpretation of Luke (iii. 23), to have been just thirty years of age, the day of the baptism was also that of the birth. The same feast, therefore, might well embrace both events. Afterward, other events, coming under the same general idea of manifestation, were included in the commemoration; the adoration of the Magi, the first miracle at Cana of Galilee, where "He manifested forth His glory," and, later still, the miraculous feeding of the five thousand.[2] As all these events could not have taken place on the same day of the year, it becomes doubtful whether any of them can be referred to the 6th of January. The observance of this day as that of the baptism, is first mentioned by Clemens of Alexandria, as existing amongst the Gnostic Basilidians of that city.[3] Some have thought that, as the Egyptians celebrated at this time the feast *Inventio Osiridis*, the Basilidians adopted both the feast and the date from them. But, aside from other objections to this Egyptian origin,[4] it is most improbable that the church at large would have borrowed any feast from the Gnostics. We may rather, with Neander,[5] suppose it to have originated with the churches in Palestine or Syria. If so, the selection of the 6th January may rest upon some good basis. There

---

[1] See Missale Romanum, in Epiphania Domini.
[2] See Dorner. Christologie, i. 284.   [3] Guericke. Archäologie, 201.
[4] See Wieseler. 136.   [5] Ch. Hist., i. 302.

can be no question that the baptism, the *secunda nativitas*, was commemorated before the nativity itself. Beyond the simple fact that the Epiphany was put on this day, we have no knowledge. Sepp (i. 243), though in general a defender of tradition, here rejects it, and Jarvis (467), at the close of his investigations into the matter, simply says that, as there is no testimony against it, there is no impropriety in considering the 6th January as the true date.[1]

But there is an objection to the month of January drawn from the climate of Palestine in the two particulars of rain and cold, that deserves to be considered. It is said that such multitudes could not have gathered to John in the mid-winter, nor could the rite of baptism then have been performed in the cold and swollen Jordan.[2] We must then examine more closely the climatic peculiarities of Judæa in these respects.

In the inquiry into the date of the Lord's birth, we have already had occasion to speak of the general character of the seasons. That during the winter, or rainy season, after heavy rains the traveling is difficult and fatiguing, all travelers testify.[3] But the rains are not constant. Beginning in October or November they fall gradually and at intervals, but become more copious and frequent in December, January, and February, and continue into March and April. It is stated by Barclay, that nine-tenths of all the rain falls in December, January, February, and March. In January, there are gushes of rain and sometimes snow, but in the southern parts of the land the sky clears up and there are often fine days.[4] The rain comes mostly out of the west, or west-northwest, and continues from two to six days in succession, but falls chiefly at night. Then the wind turns to the east, and several days of fine weather follow. The whole period from October to March is one continuous rainy season, during which the roads become muddy, slippery, and full of holes; but when the rain ceases, the mud quickly dries up, and the roads become hard,[5] though never smooth.

If, as we have supposed, John began to preach in the summer, perhaps in July, there is nothing in these statements to lead us to suppose that he suspended his labors when the rainy season began. During the intervals of clear weather, at least, the people continued to gather to him. Besides, we cannot tell what was the character of this

---

[1] So Bucher, Friedlieb, Browne, Edersheim, McClellan. "About the last half of January," Greswell. In December or January, Lichtenstein. "In Tisri, about the feast of Tabernacles." Lightfoot. In November, Usher. In Spring, Clinton. The 7th of October Sepp. Beginning of December, Patritius. In February, Lewin.

[2] So Robinson, Sepp.   [3] Thomson. i. 329.

[4] Winer. ii. 692.   [5] Herzog's Encyc., xi. 23.

particular season. According to Thomson (i. 129), the climate is "extremely variable and uncertain. I have seen the rains begin early in November and end in February, but they are sometimes delayed until January and prolonged into May." We cannot, in a climate so changeable, undertake to say that John might not without any serious obstruction continue to preach and baptize throughout the whole rainy season. Greswell (i. 372) finds it specially fitting that he should commence his ministry at a time when water was so abundant, and affirms that "in Judæa the winter season would be no impediment to the reception of baptism." So far as regards the valley of the Jordan, he is in this justified by the statements of travelers. This valley lies so low that the cold of winter can scarce be said to be felt there at all. Especially is this true of the lower part of it, where John baptized. Lying twelve or thirteen hundred feet below the level of the Mediterranean Sea, it has a tropical climate. Josephus,[1] speaking of the plain of Jericho, says: "So mild is the climate, that the inhabitants are dressed in linen when the other parts of Judæa are covered with snow." Robinson also (i. 533), writing in May, speaks in like terms: "The climate of Jericho is excessively hot. In traversing the short distance of five or six hours between Jerusalem and Jericho, the traveler passes from a pure and temperate atmosphere into the sultry heat of an Egyptian climate." Porter describes the air as being "like the blast of a furnace." Weiss thinks that because of the heat, John could not have fulfilled his ministry in the Jordan valley in the summer. (So Wies., Beiträge, 187.)

It appears, then, that the mere chilliness of the water of the Jordan running through this deep hot valley, where snow or ice is never found, cannot be so great as to prevent baptism, even in midwinter, except, perhaps, in some very rare instances. Nor is this river usually at its highest stage till April or May. As it was in Joshua's time so is it now. "Jordan overfloweth all his banks all the time of harvest" (Josh. iii. 15), or, as explained by Robinson, was full up to all its banks, "ran with full banks, or brimful." "Then, as now, the harvest occurred during April and early in May, the barley preceding the wheat harvest by two or three weeks. Then, as now, there was a slight annual rise of the river, which caused it to flow at this season with full banks, and sometimes to spread its waters even over the immediate banks of its channel where they are lowest, so as in some places to fill the low tract covered with trees and vegetation along its sides."[2] Thomson (ii. 453) speaks to the same effect, and explains why the overflow of this river should be so late in the season as

---

War, iv. 8, 3.   [2] Robinson, i. 540.

2*

March or April after the rains are all over. This explanation he finds in the fact that its waters come from great permanent springs lying on the southern declivities of Hermon, and which are not at all affected by the early winter rains. "It requires the heavy and long-continued storms of mid-winter before they are moved in the least; and it is not till toward the close of winter that the melting snows of Hermon and Lebanon, with the heavy rains of the season, have penetrated through the mighty masses of these mountains, and filled to overflowing their hidden chambers and vast reservoirs, that the streams gush forth in their full volume. The Huleh, marsh and lake, is filled, and then Gennesaret rises and pours its accumulated waters into the swelling Jordan about the first of March."

That there should be occasional floods in this river after long-continued rains, before the time of harvest, and during the rainy season, is to be expected, and will serve to explain the statements of those travelers who found it swollen during the autumn and early winter. Thus Seetzen[1] states that in consequence of a storm accompanied with high cold winds, he was compelled to remain from the 8th to the 14th January on the bank before he was able to cross. Sepp (i. 240), who bathed in it on the 6th January, 1846, found the current swift and the water cold. But such occasional floods do not affect the general rule, that during the winter the water remains at its ordinary level, and begins to rise toward March, and is highest at the time of harvest. "All rivers that are fed by melting snows are fuller between March and September than between September and March, but the exact time of their increase varies with the time when the snows melt."[2]

From what has been said, it follows that so far as the climate is concerned, and the overflowing of the Jordan, no reason exists why John may not have been baptizing in midwinter. That baptisms at this season of the year actually took place in later times, we learn from the testimony of Felix Fabri.[3] He says that the cloisters of St. John on the banks of the river at the time of the Abbot Zozima were inhabited by many monks, who about the time of Epiphany — the 6th January — kept high festival there. The Abbot of Bethlehem, the Patriarch of Jerusalem, with many monks and clergy, walked down to the river in solemn procession, and after a cross had been dipped in the waters, all the sick through their baptism were healed, and many miracles wrought in behalf of the pious. So in the time of Antonius Martyr and Willibaldus, "the annual throng of pilgrims

---

[1] Cited in Ritter, Theil, xv. 517.   [2] Smith's Bib. Dict., i. 1128.
[3] Cited in Ritter, Theil, xv. 539.

to bathe in the Jordan took place at the Epiphany." [1] It is therefore perfectly credible that John may have baptized many, and with others the Lord, in the month of January.

We may now sum up the results of our inquiry. The first Passover after the Lord's baptism was that of 780, and fell upon the 9th April. The baptism preceded this Passover some two or three months, and so probably fell in the month of January of that year. John's ministry began soon after he was thirty years of age, or about July, 779. Allowing that his labors had continued six months before the Lord was baptized, we reach in this way also the month of January, 780. Tradition has selected the 6th of this month as the day of the baptism, but we have no positive proof that the tradition is well or ill-founded. The climatic peculiarities of the country offer no valid objections to this date. Although there is good reason to believe that in December or January Jesus was baptized, yet the day of the month is very uncertain.

III. DATE OF THE LORD'S DEATH.

This point is so closely connected with the length of His ministry that we shall consider the two together.

Datum 1. — Let us first ask in what years the crucifixion might have taken place ? The latest year is defined by the administration of Pontius Pilate under whom the Lord was crucified. He was governor of Judæa from the middle of 779 to 789; the Lord's death, then, could not have been later than the year 789. But, supposing Him to have been baptized in 782, the latest possible period, as we have seen, His ministry, if prolonged to 789, would have continued six or seven years, which no one asserts. Assuming, as most agree, that His ministry was not more than three or four years, His death could not have been later than 786. We have, thus, the years 780-786, in some one of which the crucifixion must be put.

Having the *termini*, what shall guide us in the choice of the year ? The first and most important *datum* is one which astronomy gives us. The day on which the Lord was crucified was Friday, as appears from the Evangelists. Joseph went to Pilate to obtain the body of Jesus "when the even was come, because it was the Preparation, that is, the day before the Sabbath" (Mark xv. 42; Luke xxiii. 54; John xix. 42). That this Sabbath was the regular weekly Sabbath appears from all the Synoptists (Matt. xxviii. 1; Mark xvi. 1; Luke xxiii. 56). Jesus was crucified on Friday, and buried the

---

[1] Robinson, i. 546. Early Travels, 17.

same day, was in the grave over the Sabbath, and rose on the morn-ing of the first day of the week.

Thus, most agree that the crucifixion was on Friday, in the month Nisan (Ex. xii., ff.), but it is in dispute whether this was the fourteenth or fifteenth of that month. If we assume here, for the moment, that the Lord died on Friday, the fifteenth Nisan, — a point to be fully considered later, — the question before us is, whether there is any year, within the possible range of dates, in which the fifteenth day of Nisan fell on Friday.

[1] "Two matters in which the Jewish method of computation dif-fered from ours must be distinctly borne in mind: first, that the Jewish day extended from sunset to sunset, and that, therefore, the fifteenth day of Nisan began at sunset on the fourteenth day and in-cluded what we should call the evening of the fourteenth day; and, in like manner, the sixth day of the week (Friday) began at sunset on the fifth day (Thursday) and included what we should call the evening of Thursday; and, secondly, that the Jewish month did not begin on the day of the conjunction of the moon with the sun (the astronomical new moon), but on the day when the new moon was first visible in the sky. It follows from this last statement that the fifteenth day of Nisan was not necessarily the day of the astronomical full moon, and that no special observation was made to determine it; it was simply two weeks after the day when the new moon was first seen, or supposed to be seen, in the heavens.

The time of a lunation, that is to say, the interval between two new moons, is not far from twenty-nine and one-half days. A lunar month, according to the time of the new moon's appearance, consists of either twenty-nine or thirty days. To determine when the new month should begin, we are told that the Sanhedrim held a session on the day following the twenty-ninth day of each month. If credible witnesses appeared and testified that they had seen the moon on the preceding evening, the Sanhedrim made proclamation that the month had ended, having been a "deficient" month of twenty-nine days, and the new month was reckoned from the preceding sunset. If, however, there was no satisfactory testimony that the new moon had been seen, it was proclaimed that the new month would begin at the following sunset, the day of the Sanhedrim's session being the thirtieth and last day of a "full" month; and no further watch was kept for the new moon. [Edersheim, *The Temple, etc.*, pp. 169, sqq.; Stapfer's *Palestine in the time of Christ* (trans.), p. 195.]

It may be noted that in the modern Jewish calendar the beginning

---

[1] For the following discussion we are indebted to Prof. Hart of Trinity College.

of the months is determined beforehand by astronomical calculation, and that the month Nisan is not allowed to begin on the second, the fourth, or the sixth day of the week. But it is quite certain that there was no such limitation in the time of Christ. [Caspari, *Introduction to the Life of Christ* (trans.), p. 195.]

Now, when the fifteenth day of Nisan fell on Friday, that is to say, when it began at sunset on Thursday, the first day of Nisan must also have begun at sunset on Thursday; and, therefore, either the new moon which determined the beginning of Nisan must have been seen on Thursday evening, or else the preceding month must have been adjudged to have thirty days, and the month must have begun without any observation of the moon. This latter supposition, depending upon the state of the weather and on other uncertainties, does not appear to have been considered by writers on the subject. Passing this by, the question recurs, whether there is any year, within the possible range of years within which the Lord's Passion must have occurred, when, the sky being clear, the new moon could have been seen by watchful observers on the evening, as we should call it, of Thursday.

Dr. Salmon (*Introduction to the New Testament*, ed. 2, pp. 266–267), giving a table of the time of the astronomical new moon for each year from A. U. C. 780 to 789 (A. D. 27 to 36) inclusive, and adding the day when, in his judgment, the moon was first visible, comes to the conclusion that there is but one of these years, namely, the year 787, when the new moon could possibly have been first seen on a Thursday evening; and in that year he thinks it very doubtful whether it could have been thus seen. He holds that the Passion was on a Friday, but that it was on the fourteenth of Nisan, the day before the Passover; and, being of the opinion that the year 783 was the probable year, he finds his views as to the day and the year corroborated by the date of the moon's first visibility, which he gives as Friday, March 24th. This would make the fifteenth day of Nisan to have begun at sunset on Friday, April 7th.

Dr. Salmon's great eminence as a mathematician, no less than as a theologian, makes one hesitate to criticise his conclusions; but it seems that they may be fairly questioned on grounds suggested by Caspari (*op. cit.*, pp. 14, sqq.), who, nevertheless, agrees with Dr. Salmon as to the day of the Passion. In the year 783 the moon was in conjunction with the sun at about eight o'clock P. M. of Wednesday, March 22d, according to our reckoning. It is generally thought necessary to allow some thirty hours after conjunction, or the time of the astronomical new moon, before one can expect to see the moon in the heavens; and if thirty hours were required at this time, the moon could not have been seen on Thursday evening, and the month could not have begun till sunset on Friday.

But it is by no means certain that the moon could not have been seen by skilled observers — and such there were at Jerusalem, engaged in watching for the faintest crescent which should show that the moon had changed — on Thursday evening. The sun would set at about six o'clock; the moon, then twenty-two hours old, would be nearly an hour behind it; and it certainly is not impossible, under favorable circumstances, to see the moon when between twenty-two and twenty-four hours old. Kepler informs us that at Seville, on the 13th day of March, 1553, the new moon was seen about midday at a distance of ten degrees from the sun, that is to say at less than twenty hours after conjunction. "The whole city," says he, "saw it and bore witness." (Kepler's *opera*, ed. Frisch, ii. 699, vi. 488.) He also says (vi. 488) that the moon is sometimes seen, both old and new, on the same day, and he thus interprets (erroneously) the Greeks phrase, ἕνη καὶ νέα. Caspari, who refers to the phenomenon at Seville, tells us (p. 15) that Americus Vespuccius once saw the moon on the day of the conjunction, and — which is more pertinent to the present purpose — he gives (p. 14) Jewish authority for the statement that, under given circumstances, the moon may be seen fourteen hours after conjunction. It seems quite possible, therefore, that in the year 783, the watchers at Jerusalem may have seen the moon on the evening of Thursday, March 23d, and that therefore the first and the fifteenth days of Nisan in that year may have began with sunset on Thursday and ended with sunset on Friday. And in such an argument as this, the proof of possibility is all that can be required.

In the year 780, the time of the moon's conjunction was also eight P. M. on a Wednesday (March 26th). It is possible, therefore, that in this year the Lord might have suffered on the first day of the Passover being a Friday. But we have other reasons for placing the Passion in the year 783.

It must not be forgotten that it is possible that the beginning of the month in which the Lord suffered was not determined by observation of the moon. The uncertainties which must be caused in almost any climate by clouds or by disturbed states of the atmosphere, are such as to make purely astronomical calculations somewhat unsatisfactory. Yet, on the-view which is here maintained, the month began early, rather earlier than might have been expected; and it seems, therefore, almost certain that the opening of the Passover-month was proclaimed on the evidence of witnesses who declared that on the evening following the fifth day of the week, or, as they would have said, on the evening beginning the sixth day of the week, they had seen a faint streak of light in the west with perhaps the outline of the moon's orb.   If we have reasonable proof that, as was assumed at the beginning, the Lord's Passion was on a Friday, which was the fifteenth day of Nisan, and if it is quite possible, without the assumption of any very extraordinary phenomenon, that the fifteenth day of Nisan fell on a Friday in the year 783, to which year other indications point, we need not hesitate to fix upon that year (A. U. C. 783, or A. D. 30) as the year of the Passion and the Resurrection.

It may be added that the tables given by Browne (*Ordo Saeclorum,* p. 55) are of little value for our purpose, as they are based on astronomical computations of the time of full moon, as if the Jews determined in that way the place of the first day of the Passover.   But it is interesting to note that, according to these tables, in the year 783 the moon came to the full about two hours before the midnight which ended our sixth day of April, or belonged to the Jewish seventh day of April, which was Friday.

The error made by Wieseler, who forgot that the Jewish day began with sunset, has been corrected both by Caspari and by Salmon (*opp. citt.*)   But Wieseler also assumed that the new moon, which determined the beginning of Nisan in 783, could not have been seen until Friday evening, an assumption which we have seen to be untenable.   The two errors correct each other; and we can agree with Wieseler's conclusion that the year 783 was the year of the Passion."

Let us see how far this result reached by Prof. Hart will harmonize with those already obtained.   If the Lord was born in 749, or beginning of 750, He would have been in April, 783, about 33 years old. If He was baptized in the beginning of 780, He was about thirty when He began His work, and His ministry continued about three years.

If the data given by the Evangelists were sufficient to determine the length of His ministry, then, by adding it to the year of His baptism, we easily define the year of His death; but the data are not sufficient.   It has already been shown that about three months intervened between His baptism and the Passover following; which was probably that of 780, the first of His ministry (John ii. 13).   Two other Passovers are mentioned by this Evangelist (John vi. 4, and xi. 56), the latter being the last Passover.   If there were but three Passovers during His ministry, it was only of two years and some months duration.   But John speaks of a feast (v. 1) which he does not name, and which many regard as a Passover; if so, there would be four Passovers, and His ministry extend a little over three years.

The point as to this unnamed feast will be fully discussed in its place. Assuming here that it was a Passover, we reach the result, that His ministry, computing from His baptism in 780, continued about three years and three months.

Datum 2. — Some have thought to find a chronological datum in the fact of the darkening of the sun at the time of the Lord's crucifixion. As this was upon the 14th or 15th of Nisan, and so at the time of a full moon, it could not have been an eclipse. But as mention is made of an eclipse which occurred near this time, some of the fathers and some moderns have sought to establish a connection between the two events. Phlegon, of Tralles, who died about 155 A.D., and who wrote some historical works, of which only a few fragments remain, relates that, in the fourth year of the 202 Olympiad, or from July, 785 to 786, a great eclipse of the sun took place, greater than any that had ever been known, so that at the sixth hour it was very dark and the stars appeared. There was also a great earthquake in Bithynia, and a great part of Nice was destroyed.[1] This statement presents several apparent points of resemblance to those of the Evangelists, but a brief examination shows that it cannot refer to the darkness at the crucifixion. Phlegon speaks of an eclipse; had he meant an extraordinary or supernatural darkness, as said by Sepp, he could scarcely have failed distinctly to mention it. The time also of this eclipse is uncertain, for some of those who have reported his statement refer it to the fourth, and some to the second year of the 202d Olympiad, or to the fourth year of the 201st.[2] But the astronomer Wurm has computed that only one eclipse took place in this Olympiad, and that in November 24, 782.[3] It seems, therefore, that Phlegon has himself erred in the date, or that he wrote the first year of this Olympiad, which has been changed into the fourth. As it is not mentioned at all by most of the early fathers, it seems that they must have regarded it as an ordinary eclipse, and therefore without any special relation to the crucifixion.[4] Most moderns agree that it is of no chronological value.[5]

Datum 3. — Some have found ground for a chronological inference as to the time of the Lord's death, in the assertion of the Pharisees before Pilate (John xviii. 31), "It is not lawful for us to put any man to death." Lightfoot (on Matt. xxvi. 3) gives, as a correct tradition of the Talmudists, "Forty years before the Temple was destroyed, judgment in capital causes was taken away from Israel." It is gen-

---

[1] For some little differences in the version, see Jarvis, 420.

[2] See Ammer, 41; Wieseler, 387.   [3] Winer, 2. 482.   [4] See Jarvis, 427.

[5] Winer, Lichtenstein, Meyer, Jarvis, Greswell. Sepp would prove from it that the crucifixion was in 782; Ammer, that it was in 786.

erally agreed that the Temple was destroyed in August, 823. Com-puting backward **forty years**, we reach 783 as the year when the Jews lost the power of inflicting capital punishments. Hence it follows, that if Christ had been tried by them before the year 783, they would have had the power of punishing Him with death, according to their own laws. His crucifixion, therefore, could not have been earlier than this year.

As we have no knowledge how this judgment in capital cases was lost to the Jews, whether by the act of the Romans, or, as Lightfoot supposes, by their own remissness, we cannot tell how strictly the "forty years" is to be taken. They may be used indefinitely, forty being here, as often, a round number. Little stress in this uncertainty can be laid upon this result.[1]

Datum 4. — Some find in the parable of the barren fig-tree (Luke xiii. 6–9), an allusion to the length of the Lord's ministry: "Behold these three years I come seeking fruit on this fig-tree and find none."[2] It certainly cannot be without meaning that three years are mentioned. This is ascribed by some to the fact that so many years must pass after planting before the tree can bear fruit.[3] But the language shows that fruit is sought, not after, but during the three years. Some refer it to the whole period of grace before Christ.[4] But why designate it as three years? Perhaps some three epochs in Jewish history may be meant, although it is not clear what they are. It is not, however, improbable that Christ's ministry is referred to. If we suppose it to have been spoken late in 782, His ministry beginning in 780, this was the third year, and He was not crucified till 783. But it cannot be said that the tree was actually cut down after the expiration of the one year of grace. As a chronological datum, the mention of the three years has little value.[5]

Datum 5. — From early times, many have found a prophetic announcement of the length of the Lord's ministry in the words of Daniel, ix. 27, — " And He shall confirm the covenant with many for one week, and in the midst of the week He shall cause the sacrifice and the oblation to cease." Of the fathers, Browne says (77), " Others, comparatively late writers, were led by their interpretation of Daniel's prophecy to assign it a term of three and a half years." This interpretation has, all along to the present day, had advocates. Thus Lightfoot (iii. 39), " He had now three years and a half to live, and to be a public minister of the Gospel, as the Angel Gabriel had

---

[1] Schürer, ii. 1. 188, says the date is worthless. Eders., ii. 254.
[2] So Bèngel, Hengstenberg, Wieseler, Alford. [3] So Bloomfield.
[4] So Grotius, McKnight. [5] So Meyer, Trench, Keil, Godet.

told that in half of the last seven of the years then named He should confirm the covenant." It is said by Browne: "It seems also to have been commonly believed by the ancients that the last week of the seventy includes the *prædicatio Domini* to the Jews for three and a half years before, and the same length of time after the Passion." Greswell (iv. 406) maintains the same interpretation. Vitringa, with whom Hengstenberg agrees (Christology, iii. 163), says: "His death was undoubtedly to happen in the middle of the last hebdomad, after the seven and sixty-two weeks had already come to an end."

Without denying that the prophecy has reference to the Messiah, it is questionable whether it is to be so pressed as to furnish a proof that the Lord's public work continued just three and a half years. The number of interpretations that have been proposed is very great, and there is far from being even now unanimity of opinion. Thus Lightfoot makes the Lord's own ministry to have been three and a half years; Sepp, twelve hundred and ninety days; Greswell adds to three years of the Lord's ministry half a year of the Baptist; Browne, to one year of the Lord's ministry two and a half years of the Baptist. We cannot, under these circumstances, attach much chronological importance to it.— *Obscurum non probatur per obscurius.*

Computations as to the year when the seventy weeks ended, as bearing on the time of the Lord's death, can be but little relied on, and need not be considered here.

Datum 6.— Several recent attempts have been made to determine the year of the Lord's death by the death of the Baptist. It is said with great positiveness that the statements of Josephus show that John's death, and therefore the Lord's death, must have been much later than is generally supposed. (So Keim, Volkmar, Sevin.) We must, therefore, examine these statements to determine their chronological value. They refer to two points, the relations of Herod Antipas to Aretas, and his relations to John Baptist (Antiq. xviii. 5, 1).

The substance of Josephus' statement upon the first point is that Herod A. married the daughter of Aretas, an Arabian king, and that he lived with her a long time; but on a journey to Rome he visited his half-brother Herod, living as a private person, and fell in love with his wife Herodias; and she agreed to become his wife if he would divorce the daughter of Aretas. The latter, hearing of the agreement, persuaded Herod to send her to Machaerus, a fortress on the east coast of the Dead Sea, and on the borders of the territories of Herod and Aretas, and then subject to her father; and from this point, aided by his officers, she went on to his own capital. This treatment of his daughter stirred up Aretas, who also had other causes of dissatisfaction, and after a time hostilities began which ended with the total defeat of Herod A. After this defeat he sought aid from the emperor Tiberius, who sent orders to Vitellius, Governor of Syria, to punish Aretas; but the speedy death of the emperor put a stop to further proceedings.

Upon the second point — John's imprisonment and death — Josephus says that some of the Jews thought the destruction of Herod's army a just punishment for his crime in putting the Baptist to death. He gives as the cause of Herod's treatment of him his fear that John might use his great power over the people to incite them to rebellion, and therefore sent him a prisoner to Machaerus, where he was put to death.

Let us now examine these statements of Josephus and find what light they cast on the date of the Baptist's imprisonment and death. In the Gospels we have the following order of events, but without any definite dates; the marriage of Herod A. and Herodias, the rebuke by John, the anger of Herod, John's imprisonment, his death through the enmity of Herodias. We know only that John was beheaded before the Passover (John vi. 4), which was probably that of 782.

Let us note the order of Keim and Sevin, derived as they think from Josephus — the imprisonment of John at Machaerus, because Herod A. feared he would stir up the people to insurrection, his death, Herod's divorce of his wife, and his marriage with Herodias, in the same year, 786; the death of Jesus was a year later. (Sevin, in 787; Keim, in 788.)

Let us prove this order. Its basis is the assumption that Josephus narrates events chronologically, and having mentioned the death of Herod P. in 786 or 787, the twentieth year of Tiberius, and in the next chapter the war of Herod A. and Aretas, the inference is drawn that the marriage of Herod and Herodias was after the death of Herod P. and after the imprisonment of John. The statements of the Evangelists that he was executed because of the rebuke of their marriage, and his death as due to her enmity, are rejected as wholly unhistorical. The basis of all this, that Josephus has narrated events in their chronological order, is pure assumption. In many instances he departs from it, and the formula with which he begins chapter five, "About this time," is very indefinite. (As to the chronological order of Josephus in general, see Ewald, v. 50.) As against so late a date of the marriage of Herod A. and Herodias are their ages. She must have been some forty-three or four, and he much older; a time of life when it is not likely that he would have been so transported by passion as to incur the anger of his people by ε marriage forbidden in the law, and the dangerous enmity of his father-in-law Aretas.

Have we any other data in Josephus to determine the time of this marriage? One much urged by Sevin is, that the divorce of his daughter was the cause of the war between Aretas and Herod A., which ended in Herod's defeat; this defeat was probably in 789, a little before the death of Tiberius in March, 790. The inference is, that Herod was married to Herodias one, two, or three years earlier. Of course all depends here on the fact whether these hostilities and Herod's defeat were immediately after the divorce. Two circumstances make against this: 1. That Aretas had been at enmity with Herod because of boundary disputes some time before the divorce. 2. That both kings were so under the domination of Rome that they could not make war upon one another at their pleasure. Wieseler conjectures that not till the Parthian war, when the Romans were occupied by more important matters, did they find a fit opportunity to begin their contest. (Ewald puts this defeat in 787.)

Another datum in Josephus on which great weight is placed is, that Aretas at the time of the divorce was in possession of the fortress Machaerus, where John was beheaded. It is said that Herod could not have sent John there, after the divorce of his wife, and marriage with Herodias. If he sent him there before, he must have been in friendship with Aretas, and the statement of the Evangelists, that John was in prison because he rebuked that marriage, is thus shown to be erroneous. That the statement of Josephus presents a historical difficulty, all admit. But it especially concerns those who rely on him, since the Evangelists do not say where John was imprisoned and beheaded, and some deny that Machaerus was the place of his death. But admitting that Josephus is right, how came Aretas in possession of Machaerus? and what kind of possession had he? That it was a most important fortress is said by Josephus (War, vii. 6. 1), who gives a brief history of it. This fortress, as a chief defense of Perea, must have been included in that province when Herod was made its Tetrarch. It is certain that it was not captured from him afterwards by Aretas, nor is it likely that Herod gave it up voluntarily into his hands. Even if their relations were friendly up to the time of the marriage of Herod A. with Herodias, yet we cannot believe that Herod would give up the strongest, and in some respects the most important, fortress of his dominions, to an ally who might at any time become an enemy.

The question then arises, what kind of control Aretas may have had at Machaerus at the time of his daughter's flight thither? The statement of Josephus is that Machaerus was "then tributary to her father." τότε πατρὶ αὐτῆς ὑποτελῇ. Is this equivalent to saying that it was garrisoned by his soldiers, and that both the fortress and the city were under his authority as a part of his dominion? It is scarcely credible that this could have been the case, and, if it were, how did Herod regain possession of it? That after the divorce of his daughter Aretas would voluntarily have restored it, is incredible; and if it had been recovered forcibly by Herod, Josephus would have made some mention of it. (This point is discussed by Sevin, 93, who feels the difficulty to be so great that he can solve it only by supposing that Herod borrowed a dungeon from Aretas in which to imprison the Baptist, and that this was before Herod's agreement with Herodias.)

The true solution of the question is probably to be found in the fact that, during their period of friendship, Machaerus, as a border city, may have been a common meeting place for the subjects of both kings, and that Aretas may have had by Herod's gift some claims for tribute from the citizens, and have had military officials there for this purpose. We have seen that Josephus speaks of the distinction between the city and fortress; the latter being a rocky eminence very high, and the city lying below it. Tristam (Land of Moab, 272), who in 1872 carefully examined the site, speaks of the ruins of the town as distinguished from the fortress, " They covered perhaps a larger area than any site we had yet visited; . . .   and cover in solid mass more than a square mile of ground." He found the remains of a temple devoted to the Sun-God, from which he infers that there must have been a large population who were either Greeks or Syrians. Separated from the town by a narrow and deep valley was the fortress on the top of a conical hill. The citadel was on the summit of the cone which is the apex of a long flat ridge. " The whole of the ridge appears to have been one extensive fortress, the key of which was the keep on the top of the cone."

We may, then, accept the view (in substance, that of Gerlach, Keil, and others; contra, Schürer) that the citizens of Machaerus paid tribute, on grounds which we cannot explain, to Aretas who had military officials there, while the fortress itself which commanded the town was in the hands of Herod. The order of events may have been something like this: The daughter of Aretas, Herod's wife, early heard of her husband's agreement with Herodias; and, without revealing to him her knowledge, desired him to send her to Machaerus, where she knew she would find officials of her father who would forward her on her way to him. It would seem from the narrative of Josephus that the real difficulty was to get from Machaerus into

Arabia. But she arranged the matter beforehand; and, apparently without making any stop at Machaerus, went on to her father. It is obvious that, if the town and fortress had been in the hands of Aretas, there was no necessity of her hastening away from Machaerus, as she evidently did, to a place where Herod could not follow her.

If this be the right solution of the matter, the chronological difficulty, arising from the possession of Machaerus by Aretas, disappears. Had he possessed it at the time of the divorce of his daughter, and later, we should be compelled to put the imprisonment of the Baptist either before the divorce or several years later, and thus contradict the Evangelist's account. But, if the fortress of Machaerus was all the time in the possession of Herod, he could have imprisoned the Baptist there at his pleasure, whatever fiscal claims Aretas may have had on the city. Some say, (Wies., Beiträge, 13,) that Augustus ordered Aretas to deliver up the fortress to Herod about 782, but of this there is no proof, and the silence of Josephus makes it improbable. Schürer (239) supposes that it came into Herod's hands soon after the flight of his wife, but why Aretas should deliver it up does not appear; Keim (i. 622), that Herod took it from Aretas by force.

Can we get light from any other source as to the time of the marriage of Herod with Herodias? Attempts have been made to fix the time of that journey to Rome when he met Herodias. (Gres., iii. 417; Wies. Syn., 241, and Beiträge, 13; Licht., 181.) But no satisfactory result is thus reached. (So Schürer.)

But, if we knew the year of the marriage, we cannot tell how long an interval may have passed before the reproof of Herod A. by John. It is often said that it must have been very soon, while the popular mind was most stirred up (So Winer, Gres.), but this, by no means, follows. The marriage may have preceded the ministry of John by a considerable interval, and that which he denounced was not merely the marriage act, but the continuance of the marriage relation. When and where he met Herod and rebuked him, we do not know. As regards the defeat of Herod by Aretas, which the Jews thought a just judgment of God upon him for the death of the Baptist, we cannot infer that it was immediately after John's death. An interval of eight or ten years would not be so long that the connection of the two events would be forgotten. Keim says, one or two years.

Nor do we get any light from the knowledge of the time when Herod P. was married to Salome, daughter of Herodias. (Josep. Antiq., xviii. 5. 4.) If he died about the beginning of 787, she may have been married to him two or three years before his death. Her age at this time is unknown, but computations founded on the probable year of her birth make her age to have been about twenty. She is called by the Evangelist (Matt. xiv. 11) a damsel — κοράσιον, — which implies that she was not more than twelve or fifteen at the "Baptist's" death. (As to the average age of females at marriage, Gres., iii. 415.)

To sum up what we learn from Josephus in this matter of the time of John's death, he gives us two dates, — the death of Herod Philip in 787, and, inferentially, the defeat of Herod A. in 789. Neither of these dates helps us in our chronological inquiry. We do not learn from him when Herod A. went to Rome, when he married Herodias, when he was reproved by the Baptist, when the latter was imprisoned, or when he was beheaded. All inferences as to the date of the Lord's death from the death of John, are without basis. The historical difficulty as to the possession of Machaerus by Aretas is one which our present knowledge does not enable us to solve.

If Josephus does not help us in this inquiry as to the time of John's death, what other data have we?

The chief one is the statement, in John vi. 4, that a Passover took place a little after the feeding of the five thousand. "And the Passover, a feast of the Jews, was nigh." This Passover, the third of our Lord's ministry, was, as we have seen, that of 782, and fell on the 17th of April, and the death of John was a few days before this; the exact interval we cannot tell, as we do not know how long his death preceded the feeding of the five thousand, nor how long this feeding preceded the Passover. If John was beheaded at Machaerus, some days must have elapsed ere his disciples could bury his body, and come to inform Jesus. So far as this datum goes, we may place his death in the latter part of March or the beginning of April, 782.

Wieseler and others have attempted to reach a more definite result from the statements of Matthew (xiv. 6) and Mark (vi. 21) that Herod gave order for the death of John at a feast held by him. "And when Herod's birthday came," etc. The word translated birth-day — γενέσια — found only in this passage, is generally understood in its later usage as meaning a birthday festival or celebration. (See T. G. Lex. *sub voce.* So Rob., Meyer, Ols., Alex., Keil, Bleek, Farrar.)

If it be so used here by the Evangelists, it gives us no chronological datum, since we do not know the time of Herod's birth. But Wieseler (Syn. 292) would understand it of the feast kept in honor of his accession to the throne, and in this way obtain a known date, — the 8th Nisan or 11th April, 782, as the day of John's execution.

Greswell (iii. 425), who also supposes that Herod was celebrating his accession on the grounds that "the day of a king's accession was both considered and celebrated as his birthday," and that the magnifi cence of his entertainment (Mark vi. 21) shows that he was com- memorating more than his birthday, reaches the result that John was put to death about the feast of Tabernacles, September 22, 781. (With Wieseler, in the meaning of γενέσια, agrees Elli., 195; Ebrard; Eders., i. 672, note; Caspari, undetermined.)

It is obvious that this datum does not give us any certainty as to the time of John's death.[1]

We conclude that this enquiry as to the time of the Baptist's death leads to no sure results, and, therefore does not help us as to our main enquiry, the time of the Lord's death. (The other questions which arise respecting the imprisonment and death of John, will be con- sidered in their place.)

From this survey of the several data respecting the time of the Lord's death, we conclude that none lead us to positive results. If it were certain that the Friday on which He was crucified was the 15th of Nisan, there would be strong probability, if not absolute cer- tainty, that the year was that of 783. If, however, it was the 14th of Nisan, as many affirm, this datum fails us, and we have to choose between the years 780 and 786. The computations based upon the darkening of the sun at His crucifixion, upon the loss of power to inflict capital punishment by the Jews, upon the parable of the barren fig-tree, upon the prophetic half-week of Daniel, and upon tradition, are all inconclusive. It is rather by a comparison of the sev- eral chronological sections in the gospels with one another, and with the results of astronomical calculations, that we reach the well-grounded conclusions that the Lord died at the Passover in the year 783. The day of the crucifixion, whether the 14th or 15th Nisan of that year, will be the subject of examination when His death is spoken of.

Into the mazes of patristic chronology we are not called to enter, still a brief survey of early opinions will not be without its value. (See the very full investigations of Patritius iii., Diss. 19; Greswell i. 438 ; Zumpt, Geburtsyahr, 3 ff.) We find three distinct views prev- alent. First, that which makes the Lord's ministry to have continued one year, and the whole length of His life about thirty years. This view first comes to our notice among the Valentinians, who put the Lord's death the twelfth month after His baptism. Among the orthodox,

---

[1] John's death is variously placed by harmonists in the years 778–786.

Clemens of Alexandria (†220) is the earliest defender of this view. It is placed mainly upon Scriptural grounds, much stress being laid upon Isaiah lxi. 2, quoted by the Lord (Luke iv. 19), its advocates understanding "the acceptable year" to be the one year of His ministry. Others refer to Exodus xii. 5. *Haec omnium vetustissima opinio*, says Scaliger. Among those who adopted it in substance, were Tertullian, Origen, Lactanius, and perhaps Augustine; although Tertullian is by no means consistent in his statements, Origen seems to have changed his opinion, and Augustine is doubtful.

Second. That which makes His age at His death to have been between forty and fifty, but leaves the length of the ministry undetermined. Of this, Irenæus (†202) was the first defender, although it appears from Augustine that there were others later that held it. In proof, two passages in John's Gospel were cited (viii. 57 and ii. 20). From the former it was inferred that He was more than forty, and from the latter that He was just forty-six, as the temple of His body had been so long in building. Irenæus, arguing against the Valentinians, shows from the mention of three Passovers by this Evangelist, that the Lord's ministry was more than a year, but how long he does not determine.

Third. That which makes His ministry to have continued from two to four years, and His whole life from thirty-two to thirty-four years. Of this view Eusebius (Hist. i. 10, "not four entire years"), Epiphanius, and Jerome were the earliest representatives.

The early fathers were not wholly unaware of the uncertainty of their chronology, and several of them state that they had not the data for a conclusive judgment. Irenæus says: "We cannot be *ignorant* how greatly all the fathers differ among themselves, as well concerning the year of the Passion as the day." Again: "Concerning the time of the Passion, the diversities of opinion are infinite." Augustine says, that except the fact that He was about thirty at His baptism, all else is obscure and uncertain. Tertullian, as we have said, is inconsistent with himself, and now makes His ministry to have continued one year, and now three; now puts His baptism in the fifteenth year of Tiberius, and now in the twelfth. Some began early to put His death in the sixteenth, others in the seventeenth or eighteenth, and finally in the nineteenth of Tiberius.

One point, however, in patristic chronology may here be noticed, the early and general belief that the Lord was crucified in 782. It is well known that almost all the fathers of the first three centuries, particularly the Latins, accepted this date (Ideler ii. 412). Greswell remarks (i. 439): "I am persuaded that during the first two centuries

2

no Christian doubted of the fact that our Lord suffered in the fifteenth or sixteenth year of Tiberius." This date, 782, is first mentioned by Tertullian (†243), who says: "The Lord suffered under Tiberius Caesar, C. R. Geminus and C. F. Geminus being consuls, on the eighth day before the calends of April " (25 March). On what grounds does this statement rest? Is it on a wrong interpretation of Luke's word (iii. 1) that the fifteenth year of Tiberius (August, 781–782) is to be understood as the year of the Saviour's death? This is inexplicable, since if He died March 25, 782, His ministry continued only some six or seven months; which is received by none. And if He died in the sixteenth year of Tiberius, as some fathers said, His ministry was but little more than a year. They must have seen this brief duration of His public life to be in direct contradiction with the statements of the Evangelist John, who mentions at least three Passovers, making His ministry to continue, at the shortest, two years.

On what grounds Tertullian connects His death with the consulship of the Gemini, we do not know, but probably because they were consuls in the fifteenth year of Tiberius. In this case we get no chronological aid. The statement that Pilate, like all the procurators, was accustomed to send to Rome an account of his proceedings, and sent an account of the Lord's trial and crucifixion— *ea omnia super Christo Pilatus Caesari, tunc Tiberio, nuntiavit* — which was open to inspection in the Roman archives, and known to Tertullian; though not in itself improbable, is generally questioned. (It is maintained by Greswell, i. 440; Brown, 72; and Müller, *Pontius Pilate*, Stuttgart, 1888. See Tisch., *Pilati circa Christum Judicio*, 1855.) Aside from this, was there any independent tradition as to this date? It is affirmed by some that the church at Jerusalem had thus preserved a knowledge of the year, but there is no sufficient proof of this. It seems unlikely that all the conclusions of the early fathers rested solely on a misunderstanding of Luke's statement. Three solutions of the difficulty are proposed by Ideler: 1. That the Lord's ministry continued only a year. 2. That Luke (iii. 1) designates the time of John's death. 3. That Luke computes the fifteenth year of Tiberius from his co-regency. This last solution makes the Evangelist wholly consistent with himself, but was he so understood by the fathers?

We add a brief survey of opinions as to the length of his ministry. The first is that which limits His ministry to a single year, or a year and some months. As has been said, this was a very early opinion in the church. This early opinion has been recently defended by Browne in his *Ordo Saeclorum* (p. 92), who finds only two Passovers in John. On the other hand, Lewin finds five, and a ministry of four years. MacKnight supposes that the Lord's public work may have been prolonged more than five years complete.[1] "Nay, it may have been several years longer, on the supposition that there were Passovers in His ministry, of which there is neither direct mention made, nor any trace to be found in the history."

Rejecting the extremes of either case, our choice must lie between a ministry embracing three, and one embracing four Passovers; sometimes called the Tripaschal and Quadripaschal theories. The former has many advocates, but labors under many difficulties, which will be pointed out as we proceed. (Among its advocates are Wieseler, Godet, Pressensé, Ellicott, Caspari, Döllinger, Tischendorf, Farrar, and others.) On both internal and external grounds we are led to choose the latter, and to give to His ministry a duration of a little more than three years. Placing His death in April, 783, His public life, if it be dated from the purgation of the Temple, continued just three years, if from His baptism, three years and about three months, or from January, 780, to April, 783.

It will be noted that many of those who put the Lord's death in 783, hold to a two years' ministry, making the first Passover (John ii. 13) that of 781.

We accept, then, as probable conclusions, that the Lord was born December, 749; baptized January, 780; crucified April 7, 783; length of ministry, three years and three months. That the 25th December and 6th January were the days of the nativity and baptism, rests wholly upon tradition.

For comparison, we add the various dates of the Lord's death, which have found recent advocates: 781, Jarvis; 782, Browne, Sepp, Clinton, Patritius, Ideler, Zumpt; 783, Wieseler, Friedlieb, Greswell, Tischendorf, Bucher, Ellicott, Thompson, Riggenbach, Lichtenstein, Caspari, McClellan, Edersheim, Godet; 784, Hales, Paulus; 786, Ebrard, Ammer, Ewald.

---

[1] Harmony, Preliminary Obs.

We give for convenience the years of Rome from 745 to 795, with the corresponding years B. C. and A. C.

Year of Rome.	Year B. C.	Year of Rome.	Year A. C.	Year of Rome.	Year A. C.	Year of Rome.	Year A. C.
745	9	757	4	770	17	783	30
746	8	758	5	771	18	784	31
747	7	759	6	772	19	785	32
748	6	760	7	773	20	786	33
749	5	761	8	774	21	787	34
750	4	762	9	775	22	788	35
751	3	763	10	776	23	789	36
752	2	764	11	777	24	790	37
753	1	755	12	778	25	791	38
	A.C.	766	13	779	26	792	39
754	1	767	14	780	27	793	40
755	2	768	15	781	28	794	41
756	3	769	16	782	29	795	42

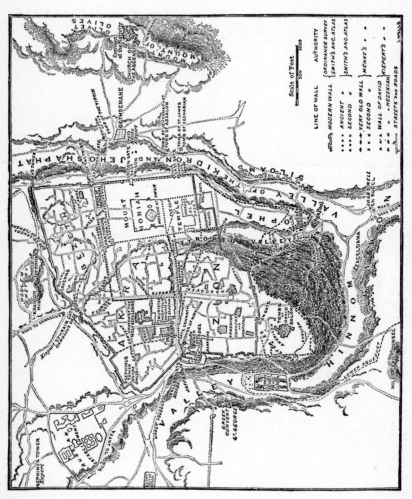

MAP OF JERUSALEM.

THE LIFE OF OUR LORD.

PART I.

FROM THE ANNUNCIATION TO ZACHARIAS TO THE BAPTISM OF
JESUS; OR, FROM OCTOBER, 748, TO JANUARY, 780.   6 B. C.—
27 A. D.

3–9 OCTOBER, 748.   6 B. C.

Near the end of the reign of Herod the Great, King of   LUKE i. 5–22.
Judæa, an angel was sent by God to Zacharias, an aged priest
of the course of Abia, whilst ministering in the Holy Place, to
announce to him the birth of a son, who should be the forerunner of the Messiah.

THE chronological value of this statement has been already
considered in the essay on the date of the Lord's birth.

Some of the fathers supposed that Zacharias was the high
priest, and that the services in which he was engaged were
those of the great day of atonement, upon the 10th of Tisri.[1]
But there is no ground for this. Zacharias is called only a
priest, not high-priest, and was a member of one of the twenty-
four courses; which the high-priest was not.   He was also
chosen by lot to burn incense upon the golden altar in the Holy
Place ; but the high-priest's duties upon this day, as at other
times, were prescribed by law, and could not be given him by
lot.   Besides, the latter must reside at Jerusalem, but the
residence of Zacharias was in some neighboring city.[2]   According to Edersheim (i. 135), it was the morning service, and this
was the first time in his life in which he had offered incense.
(See *Temple Service*, 129.)

---

[1] So Chrysostom, Ambrose; see Williams' Nativ., 23; Maldonatus, *in loco*.
[2] Greswell, i. 382; Patritius, iii. 8.

OCTOBER, 748 — MARCH, 749.   6–5 B. C.

Returning, after his course had completed its ministry, to   LUKE i. 23–25,
his own house in the hill-country of Judah, his wife Elisabeth conceived a son and spent the five months following in
retirement.

The home of Zacharias was "a city of Judah" in "the hill-
country," or mountainous region of Judah (Luke i. 39, 65).
But, as the name of the city is not mentioned, several cities
have contended for the honor of John's birthplace. Many have
supposed Hebron to be meant, a city very ancient and very
conspicuous in early Jewish history.[1] A Jewish tradition also
gives this as John's birthplace.[2] The objection of Caspari (55)
that Hebron was in the territory of Idumæa, and no priestly
family would dwell there, is not important. Aside from this,
its claims rest chiefly upon the fact that it was a priestly city,
and upon the form of expression in Joshua (xx. 7; xxi. 11),
where it is described as being "in the mountain" and "in the
hill-country of Judah."

Some have contended for Jutta, the Juttah of Joshua (xv. 55),
regarding Juda, 'Ιούδα, (i. 39) as an erroneous writing of Jutta, 'Ιούθα,
or 'Ιούτα. This view, first suggested by Reland (870), although
wholly unsupported by any manuscript authority, has found many
advocates.[3] The modern Jutta is described by Robinson (iii. 206),
who saw it from a distance, as "having the appearance of a large
Mohammedan town on a low eminence, with trees around." It is
about five miles south of Hebron, and was one of the priestly cities
(Josh. xxi. 16). But, granting the identity of the Juttah of Joshua
with the modern city, this adds nothing to the proof that it was
John's birthplace; and the fact that there is no tradition of that
kind amongst the inhabitants, nor any local memorials, seems to make
strongly against it. Keil reads it: "a city of the tribe of Judah."

Those who made Zacharias to be high priest, and so necessarily
resident near the temple, supposed Jerusalem to be the city meant,
but this has now no advocates.

An ancient tradition designates a small village about four miles
west of Jerusalem as the home of Zacharias.[4] It is now called by
the natives Ain Karim, and is thus described by Porter (i. 233):

---

[1] So Baronius, Lightfoot, Ewald, Sepp, Weiss, Geikie, Farrar, Sevin,
[2] Winer, i. 586.   [3] Ritter, Raumer, Robinson, Patritius.
[4] See Early Travels, 287 and 461.

"Ain Karim is a flourishing village, situated on the left bank of Wady Beit Hanina. In the midst of it, on a kind of platform, stands the Franciscan convent of St. John in the Desert. The church is large and handsome, and includes the site of the house of Zacharias, where St. John Baptist was born. It is in a kind of grotto like all the other holy places, and is profusely ornamented with marble, bas-reliefs, and paintings. In the center of the pavement is a slab with the inscription, *Hic Praecursor Domini natus est.* About a mile distant is the place known to the Latins by the name of the *Visitation.* It is situated on the slope of a hill, where Zacharias had a country house. Tradition says that the Virgin Mary, on her visit, first went to Elisabeth's village residence; but, not finding her there, proceeded to that in the country, where accordingly took place the interview related in Luke i. 39–55. The spot is marked by the ruins of a chapel, said to have been built by Helena. About one mile farther is the grotto of St. John, containing a little fountain, beside which the place is shown where he was accustomed to rest." (See also Pic. Pal., 204.)

Ain Karim has found a recent supporter of its traditionary claim in Thomson, who finds no reason "why the home of the Baptist should be lost any more than the site of Bethlehem or Bethany or Nazareth or Cana." (Cen. Pal., 57.) Tobler, however, traces these traditional claims of Ain Karim only to the beginning of the sixteenth century. According to Raumer, a still older tradition designated Beth Zacharias as the place of John's birth. Caspari advocates Khirbet el Yehud in Wady Bittir. See Baed., 276. The point is in itself of very little importance. We need not infer, as some have done (so Meyer), from the Evangelist's silence, that he was ignorant where Zacharias lived, but only that he did not think it important to mention it.

That Elisabeth left her own house, and went to some obscure dwelling, where she might be hidden from all observation for a time, is not improbable; yet the text is consistent with the supposition that, continuing at home, she withdrew herself from the eyes of visitors.

MARCH — APRIL, 749.　5 B. C.

In the sixth month of Elisabeth's conception, the angel LUKE i. 26–38. of the Lord was sent to Nazareth, a city in Galilee, to a virgin named Mary, who was betrothed to a man named Joseph, of MATT. i. 20. the house of David, to announce to her that she should be the mother of the Messiah.

The most important point that meets us here is the relation of Mary to the house of David. Was she of that royal family? But before we consider it, let us sum up what is known, either from the Gospels or from tradition, of the personal history of Joseph and of Mary.

Joseph is distinctly declared by Matthew to have been of the house of David through Solomon, and his genealogical register, going back to Abraham, is given (Matt. i. 1–17). In his dream the angel addresses him as "the son of David" (verse 20). So by Luke (i. 27) he is said to be of "the house of David" (also ii. 4). He was thus of royal descent, though occupying a humble position in society. His calling was that of a τέκτων, or carpenter, or, as the word may mean, any worker in wood.[1] He was generally believed by the early Church to have been an old man at the time he was espoused to Mary, and is so represented in the earliest paintings of the Holy Family.[2] In later pictures he is represented as younger, and from thirty to fifty years of age. According to Epiphanius, he was more than eighty; while in the Apocryphal Gospel, *Historia Josephi*,[3] he is said to have been ninety, and his age 111 years at the time of his death. It is not improbable that he may have been considerably older than Mary, as, though alive twelve years after Christ's birth (Luke ii. 42), his name is not afterward mentioned; a circumstance most easily accounted for upon the supposition that he was dead before the Lord began His ministry. Some have inferred from Luke's words (ii. 51), that He was subject unto His parents, that Joseph lived till He had reached manhood. Tradition also relates of him that he was a widower, and the father of four sons and two daughters. This point of a prior marriage will be considered when we come to inquire who were the Lord's brethren.

Of Mary, the Gospels give us even less information than of Joseph. In Matthew, her name only is mentioned, and no allusion is made to her family or lineage. In Luke, she is simply spoken of as a virgin; and only incidentally is it mentioned that Elisabeth, the wife of Zacharias, was her "cousin," or relative,

---

[1] Thilo, Codex Apoc., 368, note.   [2] Jameson, Legends of the Madonna.
[3] Thilo, Codex Apoc., 361, note; Hofmann, 62.

συγγενής (i. 36), "a blood relation on her mother's side" (Eders. i. 149), in R. V. "kinswoman." Some have inferred from this that Mary, like Elisabeth, was of the tribe of Levi ; but her mother may have been of this tribe, or the mother of Elisabeth of the tribe of Judah.[1] But the silence of the Gospels is amply compensated by the fullness of tradition.[2] We thus learn that she was the daughter of Joachim (Eliachim or Eli) and of Anna, her father being of Nazareth, and her mother of Bethlehem. They seem, however, to have resided at Jerusalem, as the Church of St. Anne is said to have been built over the grotto which was the birthplace of the Virgin.[3] Yet another tradition makes them to have resided at Seffurieh, a village a few miles north o Nazareth.[4] Many fables are related of the miracles heralding her birth, of her education at Jerusalem in the Temple, of her vow of perpetual virginity, and of her marriage to Joseph.[5] That she was young at the time of her marriage, we may infer from the fact that females were married in the East at a very early age, generally from fourteen to seventeen, and often earlier.[6] The Apocryphal Gospels make her to have been, some twelve, and some fourteen, when betrothed to Joseph. The latter was more generally received in later times, though a few theologians make her to have been twenty-four or twenty-five when Jesus was born, *ut perfecta mater perfectum filium gigneret.*[7] No allusion is made in any of the Evangelists to her parents, or to any brothers, but Mary, the wife of Cleophas, is spoken of as her sister (John xix. 25), though this relationship, as we shall hereafter see, has been called in question.

From the statements of Luke (i. 26 ; ii. 4), we naturally infer that both Joseph and Mary resided at Nazareth at the time of the Annunciation. But some have maintained (see Meyer) that this is inconsistent with the statements of Matthew (ii. 22, 23), which show that he then dwelt at Bethlehem. But there is no real discrepancy. None of the Evangelists tells us

---

[1] (See Bleek *in loco;* a Lapide, Luke iii. 23, says that Matthan had two daughters, Soba and Anna, and a son Jacob. Soba was mother of Elisabeth, the mother of the Baptist, and of Anna, mother of the Virgin Mary.)

[2] Hofmann, 5.   [3] Robinsou, i. 233.   [4] Robinson, ii. 346.

[5] See Apocryphal Gospels, Baronius, Sepp. In W. and W. Kirchen Lex. vi. 815, these are rejected as unworthy of credence and without papal sanction.

[6] Greswell, i. 398.   [7] Hofmann, 52.

3*

where Joseph lived before he was espoused to Mary. Matthew, relating the circumstances connected with the birth of Christ (i. 18–25), makes no allusion to the place where they occurred. He does not mention Nazareth or Bethlehem. Afterward, in connection with the visit of the Magi (ii. 1), he speaks of Bethlehem as His birthplace, and we may infer that Joseph intended to return thither from Egypt after Herod's death. But the direction of the angel to him was to return to "the land of Israel," and probably he came first to Judæa, but by divine direction he was made to change his purpose, and go and dwell at Nazareth. All this proves nothing respecting his previous residence at Bethlehem. Matthew relates only the fact that the child was born there; Luke tells us how it happened that this was His birthplace. Matthew implies that it was Joseph's purpose to return there from Egypt, but unable to do so he went to Nazareth ; why to this obscure village, unless it had been his former residence, does not appear. Luke states only that leaving Bethlehem he went to Nazareth. The only ground for supposing that Joseph had formerly resided in Bethlehem[1] is found in his purpose to return thither; but this is easily explained as springing from the desire to rear the child of David's line in David's city. That he had no possessions there is apparent from Luke's statement respecting the circumstances of Mary's confinement. The only interest that Matthew takes in Nazareth or Bethlehem is from the connection in which these two cities stand to the Messianic prophecies (ii. 5–6, 23). In itself it was of no moment to him where either Joseph or Mary had lived before the birth of Jesus, nor indeed after it, except so far as their residence was His.

We now turn to the question of the Davidic descent of Mary. If we set aside for the present the genealogical table in Luke (iii. 23–38) as of doubtful reference, there is no express declaration that she was of the house of David. The supposition that Luke i. 27, refers to her, though formerly defended by many, and lately by Wieseler,[2] is very doubtful.[3] Some have supposed that

---

[1] See Upham, "Thoughts on the Holy Gospels," p. 215.
[2] Stud. u. Krit. 1845; Beiträge, 143; so Keil.
[3] Against it, Bengel, Meyer, Patritius, Alford, Fairbairn, Godet.

she went with Joseph to Bethlehem at the time of the taxing (Luke ii. 5), because she, like him, was a descendant of David.[1] This journey, however, may be explained, as will soon appear, on other grounds.[2] This silence respecting Mary, contrasted with the prominence given to the Davidic descent of Joseph, has led many to suppose that the Evangelists attached no importance to her lineage, but only to her conjugal relation to him. As his wife she became a true member of David's family. Her child belonged to him according to the principle which lay at the foundation of marriage amongst the Jews, that what was born of the wife belonged to the husband. As it had no human father, and as he adopted it, it became in fact his, and inherited whatever rights or privileges belonged to Davidic descent. Since, then, through His legal relationship to Joseph, Jesus could truly be said to be of the house and lineage of David, it was wholly unimportant to specify the family of Mary.[3] That she was, however, in fact of David's line, is maintained by most who regard the fact as in itself unimportant, or not proved.[4]

When we compare the very remarkable declarations of the prophets respecting the Messiah, as the son of David, with their historical fulfilment as recorded by the Evangelists, it may at first appear that they refer to Him rather as the adopted and legal son of Joseph than as the son of Mary. Had His descent through His mother been regarded as the true fulfilment of the prophetic predictions, and of the covenant with David, would the Evangelists have passed it by without distinct mention? We might therefore infer from their silence respecting Mary's relation to David, that they regard her royal lineage as not essential to the fulfilment of prophecy. Joseph had a good title to the throne, and Jesus as his son stood in his stead, the rightful Heir of all the Covenant promises.[5]

---

[1] So Robinson's Harmony, 186; Mill, 209: " The words distinctly indicate that Mary accompanied Joseph for the purpose of being enrolled herself."

[2] Patritius finds in Mary's supposed vow of perpetual virginity a proof that she was an heiress, and married to Joseph as a kinsman.

[3] So lately Da Costa, Fairbairn.

[4] A legal proof is given by Upham (203). He affirms that Mary's marriage with a descendant of David proves her Davidic descent, since as a prince he could intermarry only with a princess. So Patritius.

[5] So Da Costa, who supposes Mary to have been of the tribe of Levi. See contra Spanheim, Dubia Evangelica, i. 128, against Antonius, who defends this view. See also an able paper on this side in Bibliotheca Sacra of April, 1861, by G. McClelland.

The question of the Davidic descent of Mary thus regarded becomes one of secondary interest, as no promise of God is made dependent upon it. But if we take higher ground and seek more than a legal relationship, there is good reason to believe that she was of the royal family, and that thus Jesus was in every sense the son of David. Peter at Pentecost (Acts ii. 30) declared that in Him was fulfilled the oath which God sware to David, "that of the fruit of his loins according to the flesh He would raise up Christ to sit on his throne." This language, taken in connection with the phraseology of the original promise (2 Sam. vii. 12), "I will set up thy seed after thee which shall proceed out of thy bowels," seems to point to Jesus as his lineal descendant. The words of Paul readily bear the same interpretation (Acts xiii. 23): "Of this man's seed hath God according to His promise raised unto Israel a Saviour, Jesus." Again, he says (Rom. i. 3); "Which was made of the seed of David according to the flesh." (See also Isaiah xi. 1; 2 Tim. ii. 8; Heb. vii. 14; Rev. xxii. 16.) In the words of the angel to her (Luke i. 32), "the Lord God shall give unto Him the throne of His father David," it is intimated that as her son He was son of David, and so heir to the throne. (See also Luke i. 69.) That one should sit on the throne of David did not make him in any real sense a son of David.

The prominence given by Matthew to the Davidic descent of Joseph, and his silence respecting the family of Mary, finds a ready explanation in the peculiarities of his Gospel as designed for the Jews. Its very first sentence gives the clue to its right understanding: "The book of the generation of Jesus Christ, the son of David, the son of Abraham." He aims to show that Jesus is the heir of the two great Jewish covenants, that with Abraham and that with David. To this end he must establish first, that Joseph, Jesus' legal father, was of David's house, and so a lawful heir of the dignity promised in the covenant ; second, that Jesus stood in such relation to Joseph as Himself to have legal claim to all promises belonging to the latter. He therefore brings prominently forward in the beginning of his Gospel the fact that Joseph was of royal lineage, and cites his genealogical register in proof. To have said that Mary was of the house of David, and to have cited her genealogy, would have availed nothing, as it was a rule of the Rabbins, and one univer- sally recognized, that "the descent on the father's side only shall be called a descent ; the descent by the mother is not called any descent."[1]   He could not therefore speak of Jesus as son of Mary, even had it been generally known that she was of David's line, for as such He had no royal rights.   It was only as the son of Joseph that He could be the heir of the covenants. Matthew must therefore bring forth clearly the legal relation in which Jesus stood to Joseph as his adopted son, but for his pur- pose it was wholly unimportant who his mother was.   Hence he says very little of Mary, mentioning only her name, and without any explanatory remarks except respecting her relation as a be- trothed virgin, but says much of Joseph.   His silence, therefore, so easily explained from the character of his Gospel, respecting Mary's lineage, proves nothing against her Davidic descent.

In our examination of this point it should be remembered that from the earliest period the testimony of the Church has been that Mary was of David's family.[2]   This was a matter of fact about which the Apostles and early Christians could not well have been ignorant ; and it is difficult to see how such a belief, if not well founded, could have become so early and uni- versally prevalent.

The allusion (Luke i. 36) to kinship between Mary and Elisabeth determines nothing respecting the tribe of the former, as the term used denotes simply kindred or relationship, without defining its degree.   As all the tribes might intermarry, Mary might have been of the tribe of Judah, though Elisabeth was of the tribe of Levi.   It was early said that the Lord was both of kingly and priestly descent, by Joseph on the one side and Mary on the other.[3]   But this has no foundation.

Thus we find sufficient grounds aside from the genealogical table of Luke to regard Jesus as the son of David through His mother.   Yet the question, to whom does this table refer, is one of no little interest, as well as difficulty, and worthy of our care- ful examination.

---

[1] Da Costa, 474.   [2] Meyer on Matthew, i. 17.
[3] Testamentum xii. Patriarchum, in Lardner, ii. 330. Hofmann, 7.

The fact that there should be two genealogies of Jesus given is in itself a remarkable and perplexing one, and the most obvious explanation is that presented by the peculiar circumstances of His birth. As the legal son of Joseph, the genealogy of His father must be given; as the son of Mary and without any earthly father, her lineage becomes His. Yet in point of fact this explanation in early times found few or no advocates; the general opinion being that both tables were those of Joseph.[1] But how could the same person have two such differing lines of ancestors? Three chief modes of reconciling them have been presented: by the law of adoption; by the law of Levirate marriages; and by plurality of names. The common answer is that which combines the first and third of these modes, and which refers the table of Matthew to the legal successors of the throne of David, and that of Luke to Joseph's paternal ancestors.[2] The former gives those who were the legal heirs to the kingdom. The line of Solomon failed in Jechonias (Jer. xxii. 30), and the right of succession then passed over to the line of Nathan in the person of Salathiel. From Joseph, a younger son of Judah, or Abiud of that line, Joseph, the husband of Mary, traced his descent. The family of the elder son becoming extinct, Matthan, Joseph's grandfather, became the heir. This Matthan had two sons, Jacob and Heli. The elder Jacob had no son, but probably a daughter, the Virgin Mary. The younger Heli had a son Joseph, who thus became both heir to his uncle and to the throne. Thus Mary and Joseph were first cousins, and the genealogical tables have equal reference to both.

Both tables were referred to Joseph by Africanus (220 A.D.), whose solution of their difficulties by the law of Levirate marriages is given by Eusebius (i. 7). It supposes that Melchi and Matthan, Joseph's grandfathers in the two genealogies, the one being of the family of Nathan, the other of the family of Solomon, had married successively the same woman, Estha, by whom the former had Eli, and the latter Jacob. Eli and Jacob were thus brothers uterine, though by their fathers of different families. Eli married and died childless, and Jacob according to the Jewish law married his widow, and had by her a son Joseph, who was in the eye of the law the son of the deceased Eli. According to Jewish custom the pedigree is recorded following both descents, the legal and the natural, that of Eli given by Luke in the line of Nathan, and that of Jacob given by Matthew in the line of Solomon.[3]

---

[1] Mill, 196, says: " We find no tradition more clear, more perpetual and universal."

[2] So Hervey in Smith's Bible Dictionary, 666. McClellan, 417, reverses this order; Matthew gives the natural lineage; Luke the legal.

[3] Some, in later times, reversed this, making Joseph the natural son of Eli and legal son of Jacob.

It deserves to be noticed that Africanus affirms that his account is not an idle conjecture, nor incapable of proof, but came from the relatives of the Lord, who "gloried in the idea of preserving the memory of their noble extraction." Whether his statement respecting the destruction of the Jewish family registers by Herod is historically true has been often doubted.[1] Of this mode of solution by reference to the ancient law of Levirate marriages, Lightfoot says (on Luke iii. 23); "There is neither word, nor reason, nor indeed any foundation at all."[2]

But while the early Church generally ascribed both tables to Joseph, many since the Reformation have strenuously maintained that Luke gives the genealogy of Mary. And this view has not a little in its favor. It is not improbable that the tables given by Matthew and Luke are to be regarded as copies of family registers to which they had access, and which they give as they found them. It is said that there is no reason to believe that they were guided by the Spirit to make any corrections, for only as exact copies would the Jews deem them of validity.[3] This must be taken with some limitations. It, however, would not forbid the insertion of an explanatory clause not affecting the order of the descent. Looking at the table in Luke (iii. 23), the first point is as to the right reading; two things are in dispute: 1. The position of "son."—υἱός. 2. The presence or absence of the article. In the received Greek text the reading is: ὢν, ὡς ἐνομίζετο, υἱὸς Ἰωσήφ, "being (as was supposed) the son of Joseph." The reading of Tisch. and W. and H. is: ὢν υἱός, ὡς ἐνομίζετο, Ἰωσήφ, "being the son (as was supposed) of Joseph." R. V. The article τοῦ is omitted before Ἰωσήφ, and Joseph is therefore not the first name of the series, but Heli. It is said by Godet, "The absence of the article puts the name outside the genealogical series properly so called." On what antecedent does Heli depend, upon "son" or "Joseph?" "Being son, as was supposed, of Joseph who was the son of Heli," or, "Being son, as was supposed, but falsely, of Joseph, and in fact of Heli." As Luke had stated in full the manner of the Lord's birth, no reader could fail to understand him that Jesus was not the son of Joseph, as was supposed, but of Heli.

To determine the construction of this clause, let us consider the general scope of Luke's Gospel. If, like Matthew, it was his purpose to found Christ's Messianic claims upon His legal relationship to Joseph, he would, like him, give Joseph's genealogical table. But such does not seem to have been his purpose. Had he designed to

---

[1] So Hervey in Smith's Bible Dictionary, 663; contra, Sepp, ii. 106. See Hamburger. ii. 393.　　　[2] See, however, Mill, 201.　　　[3] So Morrison.

set forth Jesus as the Messiah he would in some way have designated
the covenants with Abraham and David, which were the basis of all
Messianic hopes.   But no allusion is made to these covenants, nor
any prominence given to Abraham, or David, and the genealogy is
continued upward to Adam.   We do not therefore find grounds for
believing that Luke had in view, like Matthew, the proof that Jesus
as the legal son of Joseph was the promised Messiah.   What then is
his purpose?   It is one in conformity with the general scope of his
Gospel, which was designed for Gentiles, and takes little note of the
special relations of the Jews to God.   After giving a full narrative of
the Lord's miraculous conception and birth, and a brief mention of
His baptism, as preparatory to His public ministry, he proceeds to
give His genealogy on that side only on which it could be really
given, that of His mother.   Through her He was made man, and
through her should His descent from Adam be traced.

If upon these grounds we assume that Luke gives the genealogy of
Mary, let us note the force of his explanatory statement.   Why does
he insert the clause, "being the son (as was supposed) of Joseph"?
Is it that, being about to give Joseph's genealogy as the legal father
of Jesus, he thinks it necessary to insert a declaration that he was not
His true father?   This in view of the previous narrative seems superfluous, for he had already shown Him to be the Son of God.   And it
is plainly incongruous to assert that He was not the son of Joseph,
and then proceed to give Joseph's genealogy, unless he would make
prominent His legal sonship, which, as we have seen, he has not done.
If, however, we suppose that he designs to give the Lord's descent
through His mother, the bearing of the parenthetical clause is
obvious.   By the Jews at large he was regarded as the son of Joseph,
and some explanation therefore was necessary why, contrary to all
usage, the mother's, not the father's, genealogy should be given.
This explanation is made in the statement that He was supposed to be
son of Joseph.   "Jesus, generally but erroneously supposed to be son
of Joseph, was the son of Eli, of Matthan, of Levi," etc.   That Mary's
own name is not mentioned makes no difficulty, since the mention of
female names was contrary to usage in such tables, and as she had
already been distinctly mentioned as His mother, there was no danger
of misapprehension.   Her name being omitted, Jesus must be brought
into immediate connection with her father, His grandfather.   That
He is called son, not grandson, is unimportant, the former term being
often used to express the more distant relationship.   That it is not
strictly used throughout the table is apparent from verse 38, where
Adam is called the son of God.   That Eli is not expressly said to be

Mary's father is not essential, since the form of the table implies the degree of relationship.[1]

Some, who regard the table in Luke as that of Mary, and Eli as her father, suppose that Joseph is brought into it as his son-in-law or adopted son.[2] If it be admitted that this degree of relationship may be thus expressed, it is doubtful whether it would, without express mention, find place in a table in which only the direct line of descent is given. Jesus, having no earthly father, may well be called the son of Eli, although strictly grandson, from the necessity of the case, but the same reason does not hold in the case of Joseph.[3]

We conclude that the two tables given by Matthew and Luke are to be regarded as those of Joseph and of Mary, and are in beautiful harmony with the scope of their respective Gospels. Through that of Matthew, Jesus is shown to be the heir of David as the legal son of Joseph; through that of Luke, to be of David's seed according to the flesh by His birth of Mary. The former, beginning with Abraham, the father of the chosen people, descends through David the king, to Christ the royal heir, in whom all the national covenants should be ful-filled ; the latter, beginning with the second Adam, the eternally begotten Son of God, ascends to the first Adam, the son of God by creation. Each Evangelist gives His genealogy in that aspect which best suits his special purpose; to the one He is the Messiah of the Jews, to the other the Saviour of the world.[4]

Our purpose does not lead us to consider further the special features of these genealogies. Regarding them as copies of family registers, documents for whose accuracy in every point the Evangelists are not responsible, any real or seeming dis-crepancies do not affect their credibility, unless disproving the fundamental fact of Christ's descent from Abraham and David.

---

[1] That the Jews so regarded him is shown by Lightfoot on Luke iii. 23; Sepp, ii. 8.

[2] Robinson's Harmony, 185 ; Alexander.

[3] As to the use of " son " to express the relation of " grandson," see Keil, *in loco*.

[4] The opinions of modern scholars upon this point are about equally divided. Among those who regard Luke's table as that of Mary, not of Joseph, are: Newcome, Robinson, Greswell, Lange, Wieseler, Riggenbach, Auberlen, Ebrard, Krafft, Bloomfield, Alexander, Oosterzee, Godet, Keil, Riddle, Weiss, who says that to refer Luke's table to Joseph " is exegetically impossible " ; contra, Alford, Meyer, Winer, Bleek, Fairbairn, Da Costa, Friedlieb, Patritius, Mill, Ellicott, Westcott, McClellan, Farrar, Sabbatier, Edersheim, " more likely." Pressensé thinks there are " contradictions now insoluble."

But in this fact both tables agree, and any minor inaccuracies, if there be such, are unimportant.[1]

That Joseph was the legal heir to the throne of David, his relation to Jesus, the promised Messiah, sufficiently shows. Whether he and Mary were the only surviving descendants of David we have no positive data to decide, but it is not probable; for, if they had been the sole survivors, this very fact, which could not have been unknown, must have made them conspicuous. Hegesippus[2] makes mention of the grandchildren of Judas, the brother of the Lord, who were brought before Domitian, as being of David's race. Not improbably there were many in more or less distant affinity to this royal family. It has been supposed by some that the residence of Joseph and Mary, so far from their ancestral seat, in despised Galilee, and in one of its most obscure villages, is to be explained by the fact that they were generally known to be of David's line, and so exposed to the jealousy of Herod.[3] But of this there is no proof. It is rather to be explained as a sign of the fallen state of that once royal house. Its members were now amongst the humblest of the people, too humble to arouse the jealousy of the Idumæan usurper. We do not learn that in the course of his reign he took any precautionary measures against any of the descendants of David, looking upon them as claimants of the throne. They seem to have sunk wholly out of public sight. Yet, on the other hand, the expectation that the Messiah should spring from the house of David was strong and general.[4] How can these facts be reconciled? If the people were really looking for a Messiah descended from that family, must not all who were known to be members of it have occupied a large space in public attention?

Perhaps the following may be the just solution of the difficulty. The promise made to David and his house respecting

---

[1] Those who wish to see the questions respecting the divisions in Matthew's tables, his abridgments and omissions, and the relations of his table to that of Luke, will find all points fully treated by Mill, 147. See also Ebrard, 188, and the Dubia Evangelica of Spanheim, Pars Prima.

[2] In Eusebius, iii. 20.   [3] So Bucher.

[4] According to Mill (285), it was with the view to obviate this national expectation that Herod, two years before his death, imposed an oath of fidelity to Caesar and himself. This is hardly warranted by the language of Josephus.

the throne of Israel was not absolute. (2 Sam. vii. 12, etc.) Its fulfilment was to depend upon the condition of obedience. Yet, if the condition failed, the promise was not withdrawn. His descendants were not reduced to the rank of private citizens, but its fulfilment was suspended, and their kingly claims were in abeyance. After the return from the captivity of Babylon, the house of David, at first prominent in Zerubbabel, fell more and more into obscurity. Other families began to be more prominent. At last the Maccabees, through their wisdom and valor, won the highest place, and became the acknowledged heads of the nation — both the civil and ecclesiastical chiefs. After their decay the family of Herod, through Roman favor, became dominant. During these 400 years no one of David's lineage seems to have been conspicuous, or in any way to have drawn to himself public attention; and probably little faith existed among the people at large that the divine promise would have any fulfilment in that house. But the Messianic hopes of the Jews had, during the wars of the Maccabees and under the usurpation of Herod, been constantly gaining in depth and strength. (Edersheim, i. 62.) Everywhere they began to turn to their Scriptures, and to read them with new earnestness and faith. And as the expectation of the Messiah became and more prevalent, it was naturally connected with the promise to David, and we know that the Lord was addressed often as "Son of David." (See John vii. 42.) Yet among his descendants there was no one to whom public attention was turned as in any way likely to fulfil their hopes. Hence, while a general belief existed that the Messiah should be of that family, its individual members continued to live in obscurity. And, as it was also firmly believed that Elijah the prophet must personally come as the forerunner of the Messiah, this belief would naturally prevent any special attention being turned to them till the prophet actually appeared. Thus Joseph, the carpenter of Nazareth, might have been known by some to be of David's line, and even the legal claimant of the throne, and yet live un-honored and unnoticed.

Nazareth and its geographical position will hereafter be more particularly spoken of. It is disputed where Mary was

when the angel visited her to announce the Lord's birth.[1] The
Greek Church affirms that she was not at her own house when
he came, but had gone to the fountain of the village, and that he
found her there.[2] Over this fountain, the source of the present
one, to which its waters are conducted by a stone aqueduct, the
Greeks have built a church which is called the Church of the
Annunciation. The Latins affirm that the angel found her in a
grotto, over which stood the house that was carried in the thirteenth century by angels, first to Dalmatia, and thence to Italy,
where it still remains.[3] The exact places in this grotto where
the angel and the virgin stood during their interview are marked
out by two pillars. Over this grotto now stands a church,
which is said to be, after that of the Holy Sepulchre, the most
beautiful in Syria.[4] Tradition also points out the workshop of
Joseph, now a Latin chapel. The time of Gabriel's appearance
was, according to Bengel (*in loco*), at evening, *vesperi, ut probabile est.* (See Dan. ix. 21.)

MARCH — APRIL, 749. 5 B. C.

Immediately after the visit of the angel Mary left Nazareth, LUKE i. 39-56.
and went to the home of Zacharias in the hill-country of Judah,
and remained there about three months.

It has been supposed that Mary remained at Nazareth several weeks before visiting Elisabeth, and that during this period
the events related by Matthew (i. 18–25) occurred.[5] But with
this, Luke's statement (i. 39), that "she went with haste into the
hill-country," is inconsistent ; for going with haste cannot refer
merely to the rapidity of the journey after it was begun, but to
the fact that she made no delay in commencing it. Hug refers
to a traditionary law that virgins should not travel, and that
therefore Joseph must previously have taken her home as his
wife. Alford says that "as a betrothed virgin she could not
travel," but cites no authority. But if any such law were at this
time in force, which is very doubtful, Mary may have journeyed

---

[1] See Hofmann, 74.   [2] See Protevangelium Jacobi, ch. ii.; Baed., 362.
[3] See Baronius, who affirms that no one should doubt respecting the reality of this
miracle. In refutation, Stanley, 439.
[4] Porter, ii. 361; Stewart, 445.   [5] Ebrard, Alford.

in company with friends, or under the special protection of a servant, or with a body of neighbors going up to the Passover. That no unmarried female could journey even to visit her friends is incredible. "The incidental mention of women and children in the great assemblies gathered around Jesus is true to Oriental life, strange as it may appear to those who read so much about female seclusion in the East. In the great gatherings of this day, at funerals, weddings, feasts, and fairs, women and children often constitute the largest portion of the assemblies." [1] Ebrard's supposition (222) that Mary continued at Nazareth till certain suspicious women, the *pronubœ*, informed Joseph of her condition, and that then God made known to him what had occurred, has nothing in its favor. As little basis has the supposition that she told Joseph of the visit of the angel.[2] The narrative plainly implies that Mary, without communicating to him, or any one else, what had taken place, departed immediately to seek Elisabeth.[3] That under the peculiar circumstances in which she was placed she should greatly desire to see Elisabeth, was natural, and it is most improbable that she should wait several weeks. The whole narrative shows that neither Elisabeth nor Mary rashly forestalled God's action by premature revelation. Both, full of faith, waited in quietness and silence till He should reveal in His own way what He had done. Perhaps the expression (Luke i. 56), "she returned to her own house," εἰς τὸν οἶκον αὐτῆς, may imply that she had not yet been taken to the house of Joseph.

The distance from Nazareth to Jerusalem is about eighty miles,[4] and if Zacharias lived at Hebron, seventeen miles south of Jerusalem, the whole journey would occupy four or five days. Several routes were open to Mary. The most direct was by Nain and Endor, and through Samaria and southward by Bethel. If for any cause Samaria was to be avoided, the Jordan could be crossed near Scythopolis, and the way followed through Peræa along its eastern bank. This was the common route with the Jews in their journeyings to the feast, if they wished spe-

[1] Thomson, ii. 84.   [2] So Lange.

[3] So Tischendorf, Robinson, Lichtenstein, Edersheim.

[4] Kitto, Sepp, 80-90 Roman miles; others, more.

cially to avoid Samaria. Still a third way was by Dor on the
sea-coast, passing through Lydda, and thence over the mountains
of Ephraim.

JUNE, 749. 5 B. C.

A little before the birth of John, Mary returns to Nazareth ;
Joseph, seeing her condition, is minded to put her away priv- MATT. i. 18-25.
ily, but is commanded by God, through an angel, to take her
home as his wife, for that which is conceived in her is of the
Holy Ghost. He obeys the word, and takes Mary as his wife.
Elisabeth gives birth to a son, who is circumcised on the eighth LUKE i. 57-80.
day, and named John in obedience to angelic direction.

Whether Mary left Elisabeth before or after John's birth, is
not expressly stated, but the most natural construction of the
narrative is that it was before.[1]

The interval that had elapsed between the Annunciation and
Mary's return from Judæa, was sufficient to make manifest to
Joseph her condition. That she at this time informed him of
the visit of the angel, and of the divine promise, is not said in
so many words, but is plainly implied. The position in which
Joseph was now placed was one of great perplexity ; and as a
just man who desired to mete out to every one that which was
his due, he was, on the one hand, unwilling to take her under
such imputation of immorality, yet, on the other hand, unwilling
to condemn her where there was a possibility of innocence. He
therefore determined to put her away privately, which he could
lawfully do, and so avoid the necessity of exposing her to public disgrace, or of inflicting upon her severe punishment.
While yet in doubt as to his proper course, the angel of the
Lord, in a dream, confirmed the statement of Mary, and directed
him to call her son by the name of Jesus, as the future Saviour
of His people. Agreeably to the divine commandment, Joseph
took Mary at once to his own house as his wife.

While these things were taking place in Galilee, John was
born in Judæa, and was circumcised at the legal time. It was
customary to join the giving of the name with the performance
of this rite. This custom seems to have originated in the fact
that Abraham's name was changed at the time he was circum-

---

[1] So Keil, McClellan, Pressensé; contra, Godet.

cised (Gen. xvii. 23). The name John, given the Baptist by the angel, is of importance, as showing the purpose of God in his ministry. It means "the Grace of Jehovah," or, "one whom Jehovah bestows," and indicated that God was about to begin an economy of grace, in distinction from the economy of the law. His ministry, like that of Jesus, was for mercy, not for judgment.

DECEMBER, 749. 5 B. C.

In consequence of an edict that all the world should be
taxed, Joseph and Mary leave Nazareth to go to Bethlehem,   LUKE ii. 1-5.
the city of David, to be taxed there.

The chronological and other questions connected with this taxing are undoubtedly among the most perplexing which meet us in the whole Gospel narrative. The former have been already considered, but the latter demand a careful examination. Before we proceed to consider them, let us note the character of the Evangelist's statements, and his general purpose.

Turning to Luke's words (ii. 1–3), we find that he speaks in very brief and comprehensive terms. An edict had been issued by the Emperor Cæsar Augustus, "that all the world should be taxed ; and this taxing was first made when Cyrenius was governor of Syria." In obedience to this edict, all went to be taxed, each into his own city. This is all the information the Evangelist gives. He does not say when this edict was issued, nor what were its peculiar features, nor give any account of its execution, except in Judæa. Its only apparent value to him, and the only cause that leads him to mention it, is that it was the occasion that brought Joseph and Mary to Bethlehem. He therefore speaks of it only in the most general way, and we cannot learn from him whether it was a mere enrollment of persons, or also a census of property; whether it was carried on by governors of provinces, or by special commissions; whether it was executed at once, or after a lapse of time, or in various provinces at various times. He is concerned only with its immediate relations to the birth of Jesus at Bethlehem, and does not mention even the manner of its execution in Judæa, whether by Herod and his officers. in obedience to imperial direction, or by a special commissioner from Rome, or by the governor of some adjoining province. The manner of its execution had no interest for him. Its more important and long disputed historical points we now proceed to examine.

In our examination of this subject we shall consider: 1st. The nature and extent of this taxing; 2d. The proof that it actually took place; 3d. Its connection with Cyrenius.

I. Nature and extent of this taxing.

The word (ἀπογραφή), rendered "taxing" A. V., "enrollment" R. V., is defined as "an enrollment on the public record of persons together with their property and income, as the basis of a valuation ἀποτίμησις, i. e., how much tax should be levied upon each one" (T. G. Lex.). This would seem to distinguish the enrollment or registration of persons from the subsequent valuation of property; a distinction, indeed, which lies in the nature of the case. It may, however, be questioned whether this definition is not too narrow. The term seems often to have been applied to registrations of persons for other purposes than taxation, as to ascertain the number of inhabitants in a given province, how many men were fit to be soldiers, and for other statistical ends (Zumpt, 95). But that Luke uses it here with reference to taxation, we may believe, since the Jews were free from military service; and we see no good reason why Joseph and Mary should go to Bethlehem simply to be numbered as citizens. The opposite view is taken by Greswell (i. 541): "The census at the nativity paid no regard to the value of property. . . Joseph and Mary went to Bethlehem, not because they possessed any property there, but because they belonged to the house and family of David." It was an enrollment *per capita*. So Weiss (*Leben Jesu*, i. 250), holds that the edict does not refer to a valuation for the purpose of taxation, but was an administrative measure commanding a general enumeration of the people. It is said by Zumpt, 96, "the word 'taxing' has no exact meaning; it sometimes includes an estimate of property and sometimes not." On the other hand, it is held by Meyer that the words "should be taxed" or "enrolled" must be regarded as a direct registration into the tax list.

In looking at the taxing as a whole, there seem to be three successive acts clearly distinguishable: 1. That of registration or enrollment, an act done by an official, but demanding the personal presence of those whom he registered, or of their legal representatives. (ἀπογράφεσθαι, "to get oneself registered"). 2. Preparation by an official of the tax lists, based upon the registration, and called ἀπογραφαί, *tabulæ censorinæ ;* these were preserved till the next census. 3. The collection of the taxes as assessed upon the lists. Some interval of time must have elapsed between each of these several acts, and it may have been a considerable one. It is probable that, as their names were enrolled, the amount of their property and income was stated by them as the basis of the subsequent assessment.

That Luke elsewhere uses the word ἀπογραφή, "in the days of the taxing" (Acts v. 37), as embracing all these several steps, is probable, for it was apparently the collection of the tax that incited the rebellion. (Jos. Antiq., xviii. 1. 1.) But it does not follow that he so uses it here. Joseph and Mary were registered at Bethlehem, but does this imply that all the successive steps were taken while they were there — the tax list completed, and the taxes paid? It is greatly improbable that anything more than the registration of the name and the amount of taxable property then took place.

To whom did this enrollment apply? Luke says that "all the world should be taxed" — πᾶσαν τὴν οἰκουμένην. This is the phrase generally applied to the Roman empire — orbis terrarum — and must be so understood here, and not limited, as some have said, to the province of Judæa. (Lardner, i. 267; Lewin, 109. But Wieseler confines it to the provinces, since Italy was not subject to taxation.)

We conclude, then, that this edict ordering an enrollment had as its ultimate end taxation, and that its operation was to extend through the whole Roman empire.

II. The proof as to its execution, the manner and time. It is not necessary here to discuss the manner of the Roman census. It is admitted that Roman citizens distinctively so called, whether in Italy or elsewhere, were not subject to direct taxation. We are concerned only with the provinces.[1]

Let us note, first, the antecedent probability of such an edict. That Augustus, now become absolute master of a kingdom composed of many heterogeneous and discordant provinces, should attempt to bring them all under some equable and uniform system of government, is only what we should expect of one who had in an eminent degree the large and comprehensive mind of a statesman, and in this he only carried out the measures begun by Julius Cæsar, whose general policy he adopted. The intrinsic difficulties were very great, and he must proceed cautiously and slowly. It is very unlikely that he would disregard the peculiarities of the several provinces, and carry out everywhere at the same time and under all circumstances the same modes of taxation. The end to be reached was a general and uniform system, but he was far too wise a man to hasten matters

---

[1] The more recent discussions of this question are by Zumpt, Geburtsjahr, 90, ff.; Wieseler, Beiträge, 16; Woolsey, Bib. Sacra, 1870, 294.

4

prematurely, or to force disagreeable measures upon his disaffected provinces. (It is said by Woolsey, New Englander, 706, 1869, "a settled plan was pursued, which looked toward a complete estimate of property and population for the Roman world.")

If, then, the statement of Luke that Augustus made a decree that all the world should be taxed, be taken in its larger sense as a declaration of his fixed policy to establish a uniform system of taxation throughout the empire, probably including Italy, it has abundant confirmation. But if Luke's language be taken literally, and the note of time 'in these days" (ii. 1) be limited to the events spoken of in chapter I, — perhaps a period of one or two years, — we must confess that we have no other proof of it than his statement. But there is nothing intrinsically improbable in it, if we do not press his words so far as to make him assert that this enrollment was carried out everywhere in the same manner and at the same time. He is interested only in showing the application of this edict to Judæa as determining the place of the Lord's birth. (But see Steinmeyer, 40.)

That Augustus three times held a census has been already mentioned in the discussion respecting the time of the Lord's birth, but that any of them embraced the provinces is in dispute; the weight of authority seems to be against it. It is also in dispute whether in all these there was both an enumeration of Roman citizens and a census of property.

It is objected to the statement of Luke that no mention is made of an edict by the Roman historians. (Lardner, i. 267. See Wieseler, Beiträge, 51.) But in the history of Dio Cassius there is a great gap from 747–757, — the very period in which Luke states this taxing to have been held. Suetonius is very brief, as also Tacitus. The argument, therefore, from the silence of contemporary writers, is of little force, and, if pushed to its extreme, would compel us to believe that no important event took place in the long reign of Augustus, of which the few historians, whose works remain to us in whole or in part, have not made specific mention. It has often been remarked how little attention historians of that time gave to the most important measures of civil administration in comparison with military affairs, and even in comparison with things of a momentary popular interest, as games, public buildings, and the like. Zumpt (148) gives an illustration in Dio Cassius, who mentions some of the edifices built by Agrippa, but does not mention his map of the world, of incomparably greater importance.

But, if there is no direct historical mention of the edict, there is much strong incidental evidence of it.

1. That there was a geometrical survey of the empire, which, if not commenced by Augustus but by Julius Cæsar just before his death, was continued by him. (Wies., Syn., 81, Beiträge, 55; Sepp, i. 135; Zumpt, 130; Woolsey, N. Eng., 704.) Of the Roman chorographic maps, Merivale (iv. 426) says: "The labors of a quarter of a century produced, no doubt, a complete registration of the size, the figure, and other natural features of every province, district, and estate throughout the empire." But this survey, if carried out in the provinces under Augustus, which is denied by some, was not accompanied by a census; it can be regarded only as preparatory to one, and in the interest of a better taxation.

2. The *Breviarium imperii.* We know from Tacitus (Annal, i. xi.) that Augustus had a little book, which he had written out with his own hand, and which contained accounts of the numbers of soldiers, of the taxes, imposts, and the like: *Opes publicae continebantur. Quantum civium, sociorumque, in armis; quas classes, regna, provincae tributa, aut vectigalia et necessitates et largitones, quae cuncta sua manu perscripserat Augustus.* This *Breviarium imperii* is mentioned also by Suetonius and Dio Cassius, and must have been based upon government examinations of all parts of the empire. According to Prideaux, it was probably something of the same kind as the Doomsday Book of William the Conqueror. This much, at least, is fairly to be inferred from these labors of Augustus, that he had made an examination of the provinces of the empire as to their resources and capacities, and with reference to their respective contributions in men and money for the support of the government. Weiss remarks that if Augustus procured memoranda estimating the population, the number capable of bearing arms, the extent to which the whole country, including allies, was available for revenue, this involved throughout the empire just such estimates of the people as this in Luke. But that he then ordered a general census is not shown.

3. Into the statements of individuals of later time which affirm or imply a general census, we cannot here enter. One of the most important of these is Cassiodorus (6th century.) It is said by him that in the days of Augustus there was a census of the Roman world — *orbis Romanus;* that there were measurements of the lands for taxable purposes; and that the records of these measurements had been preserved, and were still to be seen. To this statement many give credit.[1] But others think that Cassiodorus only repeats in part the account of Luke, and cannot be considered as an independent witness. (So Mommsen quoted by Zumpt. Woolsey says, Bib. Sacra, 300: "We cannot receive it with full confidence.")

---

[1] Zumpt, 149, Wies. Beiträge, 53.

A statement made by some unknown writer is found in Suidas (Lex. s. v. ἀπογραφή) to the effect that Augustus sent forth throughout the empire twenty men of distinction, who made censuses of both persons and property, and apparently established some rules of taxation.   This statement is received as substantially true by many (Zumpt, 155; Wies., Beiträge, 153; Woolsey, McClellan; *contra,* Schürer, Sevin).

4. Historical evidence of several provincial censuses. As Rome extended its conquests, each new province was made to pay tribute, but usually it was collected after the old local manner.   Thus there was great diversity of usage, and necessarily much inequality and complaint.   Augustus, whose aim was to consolidate the empire and centralize his authority, seems early to have determined to equalize the pecuniary burdens, and establish some general fiscal system, perhaps with the intent ultimately to establish in Italy, also, direct taxation; but if so, it was not carried out.   (Zumpt (159) dates this determination as early as 27 B. C.) It was at this time that a division of the provinces into imperial and senatorial took place, and that Augustus began to carry out his purpose to introduce into his provinces some uniformity of taxation; whether it then embraced any of the senatorial provinces, we do not know.   But the condition of a province, whether long conquered, well settled, and peaceful, or a new conquest, and so disaffected and restless, would affect both the time and manner of his action.   Hence we are not to look for the same measures in all the provinces, and, in point of fact, we find them very unequal.

Into details respecting these provincial censuses it is impossible here to enter.   Schürer (270) admits that in Augustus' time most of the provinces were taxed.   We can only refer to some of the recent writers who have fully discussed them.   (See Wies., Beiträge, 60 ff.; Zumpt, 164 ff.; Woolsey, briefly in New Englander, 1869, 710; Schürer.)

To the objection that an enrollment under Herod would then have caused an insurrection, it may be said that there was a very serious insurrection just after his death, and before his will was confirmed by Augustus.   Josephus (Antiq., xvii. 10) says: " The whole nation was in tumult," and plainly thinks the rebellion at this time of much more consequence than that which followed the taxing in 760.   He, however, does not mention this enrollment, and leaves his readers at some loss to know why such an insurrection should then have broken out.

III. The connection of this enrollment with Quirinius.[1]

But before this point is examined, we must ask, what is the right rendering of Luke's words (ii. 2)? In *Textus Receptus* the article is inserted: αὕτη ἡ ἀπογραφή. In W. and H. the text is αὕτη ἀπογραφὴ πρώτη ἐγένετο ἡγεμονεύοντος τῆς Συρίας Κυρηνίου. In A. V. "This taxing was first made when Cyrenius (Quirinius) was governor of Syria." In R. V., "This was the first enrollment made when Quirinius was governor of Syria." Both translations are ambiguous.

The point whether this verse is to be regarded as a parenthesis, is for us not very important. It is parenthetical in the A. V. and in the translations of Norton and Noyes, and in the Greek of W. and H., but not in the R. V. or in most versions. The objection to regarding is as a parenthesis is, that, so taken, verse 3d must be read: "All the citizens of the Roman empire went to be taxed, every one into his own city." If the second verse be wholly omitted, the continuity of the statement would not be broken; but with it, the application of the decree may be limited to a given country and time.

The more important renderings of this verse are the following:

1. This first taxing was made — carried into effect — when Q. was governor of Syria.

2. This taxing was first made — carried into effect — when Q., etc.

3. This taxing itself, αὐτή for αὕτη, i. e., its last stage, as distinct from the earlier, was first made by Q.

4. This taxing was before, or earlier than, the governorship of Q.

5. This was the first taxing under Q. as distinguished from a second, either (*a*) under him (So Meyer, Zumpt); or (*b*) under another official who is not mentioned (so Woolsey).

6. This taxing was first made when Q. was acting officially in Syria, either (*a*) as one of two governors, or (*b*) as a special census agent.

To determine the right rendering of Luke's words is the province of exegesis, and it is evident that till the exegetes are agreed much uncertainty must enter into our historical inquiries.

We will assume that rendering to be correct which affirms that this was the first taxing or enrollment under Quirinius as distinguished from a second under him. But for several of the other renderings may be cited names of very high authority.

---

[1] All points connected with Quirinius have been most thoroughly discussed by Zumpt: first, in his essay, *de Syria Romanorum Provincia.* in the second volume of his *Comment. Epigr., ad Antiq. Rom. pertinent.*, Berol., 1854; second, in his *Das Geburtsjahr Christi*, 1869, 20–89. They are also discussed by Wieseler, Beiträge, 1869, 16–107; by Woolsey, New Englander, 1869, 682; by Schürer, art. Cyrenius in Riehm; Winer, art. Quirinius.

We now inquire, what knowledge have we of Quirinius? What we know is chiefly derived from Tacitus (Annals, iii. 48). He was of low origin, a bold soldier, and attained a consulship under Augustus in 742, and was afterward proconsul in the province of Africa. After this he conquered the Homonadenses, a rude people living in Cilicia, and obtained a triumph. He was subsequently made rector to Caius Caesar when the latter was appointed governor of Armenia. At what time, and in what capacity, did he carry on the war against the Homonadenses? There is no question that it was between 747 and 753, for in the last year he was made rector to C. Caesar, and this was after the war. In what capacity did he carry it on? This was thoroughly examined by Zumpt, who reached the conclusion that he was then acting as governor of Syria, having succeeded Varus in 750, and continued in this office till 753. In the fact of this governorship, Mommsen, Schürer, and Woolsey agree with Zumpt.

Taking, then, the fact as sufficiently established, can we reach any more definite result as to the time of this governorship? Zumpt gives the following list of Syrian governors:

748–750,	6–4 B. C.,	P. Q. Varus.
750–753,	4–1 "	P. S. Quirinius.
753–757,	1 B. C.–3 A. C.,	M. Lollius.
757–758,	3–4 "	C. M. Censorinus.
758–760,	4–6 "	L. V. Saturninus.
760–765,	6–11 "	P. S. Quirinius.

With the accuracy of this list, in general, we are not concerned; our present inquiry is only as to the length of the first administration of Quirinius. That he succeeded Varus in 750 is accepted by Schürer and others. He is not, indeed, mentioned by Josephus, but of what took place during the rule of Archelaus, 750–760, this historian says very little, nor does he mention the name of any Syrian governor after Varus till Quirinius in 760. We have thus a period from the end of the administration of Varus, probably in summer of 750, to 760, when Archelaus was deposed, about which we know very little.

Comparing this list of Zumpt's with that of Schürer (I. i. 350 ff.), we find some chronological differences. The following is the order of Schürer:

748–750,	6–4 B. C.,	P. Q. Varus.
751–752 ?	3–2 "	P. S. Quirinius.
753–757,	1 B. C.–4 A. C.,	C. Caesar.
757–758,	4–5 A. C.,	L. V. Saturninus.
759–	6 "	P. S. Quirinius.

Schürer thinks that as Caesar had proconsular authority, there were during his administration no governors in Syria. This is said also by Woolsey (New Englander, 691). Gerlach (34) does not insert Quirinius in his list of Syrian governors, regarding him as *legatus Caesaris proconsulari potestate*, and as such taking the census.

If, then, we accept, as historically proved, that Quirinius was governor of Syria either from 750–753 or from 751–752, of what importance is this fact ?

As we have seen in the chronological discussion, the Lord was born about the end of 749, and before the administration of Quirinius began; and, therefore, the enrollment which brought the Lord's parents to Bethlehem could not have been under him as governor of Syria, but was under some preceding governor. Why, then, does Luke mention the name of Q. in connection with this enrollment ? Two explanations are given: First, that the decree was issued, and the preparations for the census begun under Saturninus, 746–8, or under Varus, 748–50, but the census was continued and finished under Quirinius. (See Zumpt, 219.) In this view of the matter there is nothing intrinsically improbable. The census taken as a whole might be referred to Saturninus who began it, or Quirinius who finished it.

It will be kept in mind that Luke does not affirm that Q. was governor at the time of the Lord's birth ; he affirms a decree of Augustus, and that He was born after the decree began to be executed in Judæa. It is evident that if the execution of the decree, from the first stage to the last, took place under one Syrian governorship, then He was born under it; but if the execution embraced a longer period, He might have been born under an earlier administration. The enrollment might have been begun by one, and been continued by a second, and finished by a third; the mention of Q. is no proof that the Lord was born under his administration. The point is as to the execution of the decree, whether begun or completed under any one governor.

The second explanation is by those who think that Quirinius, in carrying on the first census, was not governor of Syria, but acted in some other official capacity, perhaps as procurator or fiscal governor of Syria. (So McClel., 398.) In this case he may have been connected with the census from the first. Or he may have been an extraordinary commissioner acting under Saturninus or Varus, or jointly with them, or perhaps as their official superior: or as governor of Syria at the same time with Varus.

We can readily see that if the initial steps of the taxing had been

taken under Varus, 748–750, and that under him just at the close of
his administration Joseph and Mary were enrolled, and the final steps
were taken under the governorship of Quirinius, Luke might well
mention the name of Q. only.

We come now to the much disputed question, whether the statement of Luke as to the application of this policy to Judæa at this
time is to be received? The objection is vigorously urged that
Herod was a *rex socius* — an allied king, and that all taxes in his
dominion must, therefore, have been levied by himself. (As to the
position of a *rex socius*, see Schürer, I. i. 1. 449.) But it is difficult to
see how Herod was entitled, in fact, to be called a *rex socius*, since the
term means one allied, in commercial language, a partner, and *socii*,
the nations in alliance with Rome. Herod was wholly the creature
of Augustus; originally set as king, not as having any hereditary
claims, or being even of Jewish descent, but because he could be a
useful instrument in the hands of the Romans. He was hated of the
Jews both as an alien and as of a cruel and despotic nature, and he
held the throne only through the fear which the Roman support inspired. It was never a question with Augustus what Herod wished,
but what his own interests demanded. Josephus mentions many
instances, showing how far he was subjected all his reign to the
emperor and to his representatives, the governors of Syria. (Wies.,
Syn., 96, Beiträge, 79.) A clear proof of this is seen in the fact that
the Jews were forced to take the oath of allegiance to Augustus as
well as to Herod. (Joseph., Antiq., xvii. 2. 4.)

To say, then, that Augustus would, from regard to any royal
rights of Herod, make him an exception, and not carry out his
general policy of taxation in his dominions, is to make the Roman
ruler a constitutional monarch of the modern type, and to attribute
to him a softness of disposition which is indicated by no other acts
of his public life. And there may have been special reasons why,
before the death of Herod, known to be near his end, and his
sons quarreling about the succession, Augustus should have had this
enrollment made; for he must have foreseen the probability, if he
had not already formed the determination, that his kingdom should
speedily be made a Roman province. (As to taxation in allied states,
see Zumpt, 183, Schürer, I. i. 451 note.)

Winer (ii. 399) seems to be wholly in the right in saying, that
there was nothing in the political relations of Herod that would have
prevented Augustus from applying the decree to his territories. In
the *Breviarium Imperii* mention is made of the *regna et socii*, showing that they were included in the new policy of Augustus.

Nor was the payment of tribute to the Romans a thing to which the Jews were unaccustomed. They had been from the time of Pompey treated as a conquered people rather than as allies. When first brought into subjection by him, very heavy exactions were made, and later by Crassus. (Joseph., Antiq., xiv. 4. 5.) It needs only a careful persual of the decrees of Caesar and the Senate (Joseph., xiv. 10. 2–6) to see that the Romans looked upon Judæa as a conquered province which had only such rights as they chose to confirm. (Joseph., War, ii. 16; Wies., Beiträge, 69 etc., and Stud. u. Krit., 1875, 536.)

Whether the Jews under Herod paid regular taxes to the Romans is in dispute. A distinction is doubtless to be taken between tribute and tax. It is admitted that Herod paid tribute to Antony, but denied by Schürer that he paid taxes to Augustus. But it is said by Wieseler (Beiträge, 98) that a poll tax was imposed by Julius Caesar as early as 707, and continued to be enforced. (As to taxes in general, see Winer, i. 5; Woolsey, Bib. Sacra, 309; and the Bible Dictionaries.) Zumpt (201) affirms that the first registration at the Lord's birth was of persons, and that this was a new thing, as the Jews had probably at this time paid no capitation tax; but the second registration, after the deposition of Archelaus, was of property, and conducted after the Roman manner. It is said by Schürer (Riehm, s. v. Cyrenius) that Palestine was an independent kingdom, put, indeed, under the supervision of the governor of Syria, but not under the immediate administration of the Roman officials. The last point may be admitted, and the fact remain that Herod was himself little more than a Roman official, having a certain liberty of action, but in no true sense of the term an independent king. Whether under him capitation and land taxes had been paid to the Romans does not materially affect the point that Augustus, near the close of Herod's life, may have ordered an enrollment to be taken in his dominions. It would be a matter of course that as time went on, and Roman institutions found more and more entrance, the system of taxation in the provinces would take on it more and more of Roman modes.

We conclude upon this much-disputed matter of the taxing, that we have not sufficient material, aside from Luke's statements, for a decisive judgment either as to its nature or as to the connection of Quirinius with it. But it may be said that as our historical knowledge has been enlarged by new investigations, the accuracy of the Evangelist has been rather confirmed than weakened. It is evident that the last word as to these questions has not yet been spoken.

4*

If Joseph and Mary went to Bethlehem to be enrolled in the tax list, does it show that they, one or both, had property there? It is said by Luke that "all went to be taxed, every one to his own city"; his own, not necessarily as having been born there, or as having possessions there, but as the original family seat—*forum originis.* The ground on which Joseph went, was that "he was of the house and lineage of David." Woolsey (Bib. Sacra, 715) thinks there is "no proof that, after the return from captivity, lands reverted to particular tribes or families." It is only conjecture whether Joseph owned any land at Bethlehem. But it is not improbable, as said by him, that "the principle of the tribe and lineage should be followed in the operations of the census." And Roman usage seems to confirm this, if we give credit to Edersheim (i. 183, who refers to Huschke). "According to the Roman law, all country people went to be registered in their own city, meaning thereby the town to which the village or place where they were born was attached." (As to the distinction in this respect between Roman and Jewish usages, Zumpt, 194.) It has been said that Mary was the owner of land there, but there is no evidence whatever of it. It may be that the capitation tax, which was probably levied upon all alike, male and female, may have made it necessary for her to go with Joseph, but this is not certain (so Zumpt, 204); probably she was moved by other considerations.

DECEMBER, 749.   5 B. C.

Upon the arrival of Joseph and Mary at Bethelem, they could   LUKE ii. 6-7.
find no room at the inn, and took refuge in a stable where the
babe was born, and laid in the manger.

The village of Bethlehem, "house of bread," lies about five miles south of Jerusalem on the way to Hebron. There was another city or village of this name in Zebulon (Josh. xix. 15), whence this is called, to distinguish it, Bethlehem-Judah. It is not mentioned in the catalogues of the cities of Judah. In Genesis (xlviii. 7) it is called Ephrath, and in Micah (v. 2) Ephratah—an epithet given it because of its fruitfulness. It appears in Scripture chiefly in connection with the house of David, and seems never to have been a place of much importance. "The Jews are very silent of this city; nor do I remember that I have read anything in them concerning it besides those things which are produced out of the Old Testament" (Lightfoot). Micah speaks of it as little amongst the thousands of Judah. It was here that the fields of Boaz lay, in which Ruth gleaned (Ruth ii. 4); and here the son of Obed was born. Hither came Samuel, and anointed the youthful David to be the successor of Saul. That the Messiah should be born here was expressly declared by the prophet Micah (v. 2); and the Jews seem to have had no question as to his meaning, nor ever to have doubted the literal fulfillment of the prophecy. (Matt. ii. 6 ; John vii. 42)

Bethlehem lies on the eastern brow of a ridge that runs from east to west, a mile in length, and is surrounded by hills. From the highest point of the ridge — 2,537 feet — there is an extensive view toward the south and east, in the direction of Jericho, the Dead Sea, and the mountains of Moab beyond. There are deep valleys both on the south and north ; that on the north stretches toward Jerusalem, and in it olives, figs, almond-groves, and vineyards are found. The village has one street, broad, but not thickly built. The present inhabitants are chiefly occupied in the manufacture of holy trinkets and relics, beads, crosses, etc., for the pilgrims who visit Jerusalem. There are no Jews living here, and it is said that a Protestant church and hospice are soon to be built.

The exact spot where the Lord was born has been the subject of earnest investigation and of zealous controversy. All the information upon this point that the Scriptures give, is contained in the words of Luke, that when Joseph and Mary arrived at Bethlehem, they could find no place at the inn, or khan, κατάλυμα,[1] and that when Jesus was born, she was compelled to put the new-born babe in a manger, φάτνη. From this statement some have inferred that the manger was in a stall connected with the inn itself ;[2] but this is hardly consistent with other features of the narrative. That the place in which she took refuge was a stall, or room where cattle were lodged, may fairly be inferred from the mention of a manger. Keil supposes that some friendly hosts received them, and gave them the stable, then empty, the cattle being in the fields.

The place now shown as the Lord's birthplace is a cave southeast from the town, and covered by the Latin convent.

---

[1] This is understood by Geikie to be " a guest-chamber," as in Mark xiv. 14; but see T. G. Lex., and Edersheim, i. 185.

[2] Wilson, Lands of the Bible, i. 392 ; Kitto, Life of Christ, 62 ; Farrar.

The tradition that connects this cave with His birth is very ancient.[1] Robinson (ii. 416) speaks of it as "reaching back at least to the middle of the second century." Justin Martyr (150 A. D.) mentions it ; as also Origen about a hundred years later. Queen Helena erected a church over it (325 A. D.). Here came Jerome (368 A. D.), and dwelt for many years. So far then as early tradition can authenticate a place, this seems well authenticated.[2] Edersheim says, "the best authenticated of all local traditions." So Farrar, Ellicott. Yet there are objections which have led many to deny the truth of the tradition.[3] The point then demands some further examination.

The objection, that Luke says nothing of a cave, is not important. His purpose is simply to show the humble and friendless state of the infant child, and this is done by the mention of the circumstances that there was no room for His parents in the inn, and that when He was born He was laid in a manger. Any other particulars were, for his purpose, unnecessary.

A more important objection is that drawn from the fact, that tradition makes caves or grottoes to be the sites of so many remarkable events. That, as was long ago said by Maundrell, "wherever you go, you find almost everything represented as done under ground," naturally awakens our incredulity. Yet, on the other hand, they could not have been so generally selected for such sites, unless there were some grounds of fitness in the selection. The Scriptures, Josephus, and all travellers speak of the numerous caves that are found throughout Palestine. They were used for dwellings, for fortresses and places of refuge, for cisterns, for prisons, and for sepulchres. Travellers used them as inns, robbers as dens, herdsmen as stalls, husbandmen as granaries. Many of these caves were very large. One is mentioned (Judges xx. 47) large enough for six hundred men. Bonar,[4] in reference to the cave of Adullam, says "you might spend days in exploring these vast apartments, for the whole mountain seems excavated, or, rather, honey-combed." Pococke speaks of one large enough for thirty thousand men.

These caves, so numerous in the light limestone formation of Judæa, and easily wrought into any shape, and always dry, were naturally thus applied to many uses. We need not be surprised to find them connected with many remarkable events and hallowed by

---

[1] See Thilo, Codex Apoc., i. 381, note.
[2] See a full statement of the evidence in Patritius, iii. 293.
[3] So Ritter, Robinson.   [4] Land of Promise. 246.

sacred associations. The traditions that connect them with the history of Jesus are neither to be indiscriminately received, nor indiscriminately rejected. Whether a particular event did, or did not, take place in a grotto is to be judged of according to its intrinsic probability, and the amount of evidence. While no unprejudiced person will be disposed to put the site of the Annunciation to Mary, or of the Agony, or of the Ascension, in a cave, yet all recognize the cave as a fitting place for the sepulchre. Whether a cave (either isolated or part of a house) was, or not, the birthplace of the Lord, must be judged of by its own merits.

Thus looking upon this tradition, we find no sufficient reason why it should be wholly rejected. Probably there is some measure of truth in it. It is indeed hard to believe that the present artificial cave, so deep down and inaccessible, could ever have been used as a stall for cattle. Perhaps the fact may be that the cave, in its original shape, was connected with a house, forming its rear apartment, and used as a stable. (So Tristram.) To this house went Joseph and Mary, when they could find no room at the inn, and when the child was born, it was laid in the manger as the most convenient place. Arculf (A. D. 700),[1] describing the cave as it was in his day, says : "At the extreme eastern angle (of the ridge) there is a sort of natural half-cave, the outer part of which is said to have been the place of our Lord's birth ; the inside is called our Lord's manger. The whole of this cave is covered within with precious marble." Willibald (A. D. 722) says : "The place where Christ was born was once a cave under the earth, but it is now a square house cut in the rock, and the earth is dug up and thrown from it all around, and a church is now built above it." Thus the small cave that originally existed in the rear of the dwelling, and was used as a stable, has been gradually converted into its present shape.

This view of the matter is defended by Thomson (ii. 533): "It is not impossible, to say the least, but that the apartment in which our Saviour was born was in fact a cave. I have seen many such, consisting of one or more rooms in front of, and including a cavern where the cattle were kept. It is my impression that the birth actually took place in an ordinary house of some common peasant, and that the babe was laid in one of the mangers, such as are still found in the dwellings of the farmers of this region. That house may have stood where the convent does now, and some sort of a cave, either natural or made by digging the earth away for building and for the roofs of houses, may have been directly below, or even in-

---

[1] Early Travels, 6.

cluded within its court." Elsewhere (ii. 98) he thus speaks of the manger, which he identifies with the "*crib*" — φάτνη — mentioned by Isaiah (i. 3): "It is common to find two sides of the one room, where the native farmer resides with his cattle, fitted up with these mangers, and the remainder elevated about two feet higher for the accommodation of the family. The mangers are built of small stones and mortar in the shape of a box, or rather of a kneading-trough, and when cleaned up and white-washed, as they often are in summer, they do very well to lay little babes in. Indeed, our own children have slept there in our rude summer retreats on the mountains."

We may then conclude that tradition has not, in this case, erred. The site of the Lord's birthplace must long have been remembered by the shepherds (Luke ii. 16), and been generally known in the region round. But the present condition of the cave is doubtless very unlike its original condition. It has been greatly enlarged and deepened, and space made in various directions for the various accessory grottoes and sepulchres which are now shown. In this way all the statements of Luke can be easily reconciled with the tradition. Here was the cave in the rear of the house, and used for cattle. In a manger, as the most ready and fitting place, the babe was laid. Hither came the shepherds to pay their adorations. (Whether Joseph and Mary were still here when the Magi came, some weeks later, is not certain; perhaps they had removed to some house — Matt. ii. 11 — though this may have been that connected with the cave.) These remarkable events would not easily pass from men's memories, and some knowledge of the spot where they occurred could not well have escaped the early disciples.

The church that now stands over the cave of the nativity was built by the Emperor Justinian upon the site of that built by the Empress Helena, A. D. 330.[1] Adjoining it are the Latin, Greek, and Armenian convents, whose monks have a common interest in it for purposes of worship. It is now much dilapidated, though, as the oldest Christian church in the world, it continues to possess great architectural interest.[2] The cave of the nativity is 38 feet long by 11 wide, and a silver star in a marble slab at the eastern end marks the precise spot where the

---

[1] Tobler's Bethlehem, 104.

[2] For a plan of it and the crypt, see Baed., 246 ; Tristram, B. P., 74

Lord was born.   Here is the inscription : *Hic de virgine Maria Jesus Christus natus est.*   Silver lamps are always burning around, and an altar stands near, which is used in turn by the monks of the convents.   The manger in which the Lord was laid was taken to Rome by Pope Sixtus V., and placed in the church of St. Maria Maggiore, but its place is supplied by a marble one.   A few feet opposite, an altar marks the spot where the Magi stood. The walls are covered with silken hangings.

The usual exaggeration of tradition may be seen in the many apocryphal sites gathered around the central one.   In adjoining grottoes are shown the chapel of Joseph and the chapel of the Innocents, where the children murdered by Herod were buried.   A stone is also shown that marks the spot where, in the firmament above, the star stood still that guided the Magi in their journey.   Of more interest to the Christian scholar is the cave, now converted into a chapel, where Jerome lived, studied, and prayed (386-420 A. D.).   It is said by Stanley (436), that during the invasion of Ibrahim Pasha the Arabs took possession of the convent, and found by the removal of the marbles, etc., with which it was encased, that the grotto of the nativity was an ancient sepulchre.   If this were so, it is highly improbable that Joseph and Mary would have entered it.   But the statement needs confirmation.   (See *contra*, Farrar.)

That the Lord was born very soon after their arrival at Bethlehem, may be fairly inferred from the fact that "there was no room for them in the inn."

December, 749.   5 B. C.

The same night upon which He was born, an Angel of the Luke ii. 8-20. Lord appeared to some shepherds, who were keeping watch over their flocks, and announced to them His birth.   Leaving their flocks, they hastened to Bethlehem to see the child, and finding Him, returned, praising God.

The bearing of the fact that the shepherds were in the field watching their flocks, upon the date of the Lord's birth, has been already examined.

The residence of the shepherds is not mentioned, nor do we know the place where they were keeping watch.   It appears to have been in the vicinity of Bethlehem, and yet some little dis-

tance removed.   There is now, a mile or more east from the
convent, a plain in which is a little village called the Village of
the Shepherds.   Not far from this village is pointed out the
field where, it is said, they were feeding their flocks, and here is
shown a grotto, called the Grotto of the Shepherds.   In this
field a church was built by the Empress Helena.   In its neighborhood stood formerly a cloister, but now only ruins of a
church or cloister are to be found.   It is mentioned by Bernard,
A. D. 867.[1]   "One mile from Bethlehem is the monastery of the
holy shepherds to whom the angel appeared at our Lord's nativity."   About half a mile north from the church Migdal
Eder, or "Tower of the flock," is said to have stood.   (See *Itinera
Hierosolymitana.*   Sepp. i, 212.)   Tradition makes the number
of shepherds three or four, and gives their names.[2]

It is said by Edersheim (i. 186), that it was a firm belief of
the Jews, that the Messiah should be revealed from Migdal Eder,
"the tower of the flock" (Gen. xxxv. 21).   "This Migdal Eder
was not the watch-tower of the ordinary flocks which pastured
on the barren sheep ground beyond Bethlehem, but lay close to
the town, on the road to Jerusalem.   A passage in the Mishnah
leads to the conclusion that the flocks that pastured there were
destined for temple sacrifices ; and, accordingly, that the shepherds who watched over them were not ordinary shepherds."
He calls attention to the fact that shepherds were under the ban
of Rabbinism because of their calling, which necessarily kept
them away from the temple services, and prevented them from
a strict observance of the law ; and cites the Mishnah to show that
the keeping of flocks, except those for the temple, was forbidden
throughout the land of Israel, except in the wilderness.   (See
Wies., Beiträge, 172.)

But did not those flocks fed in the wilderness return in the
winter months to the villages ?   This is said by Lightfoot on
Rabbinic authority, but Edersheim finds, on like higher authority, that the wilderness flocks remained in the open all the year
round ; the other flocks pastured near the towns were destined
for temple sacrifice.   (See Eders., *Sketches of Jewish life*, 80.)

---

[1] Early Travels, 29.   [2] Hofmann, 107 ; Maldonatus, 2.
[3] See Thilo, Codex Apoc., i. 385, note.

If this be so, and the flock at Bethlehem was for the temple, its shepherds cannot be regarded as ordinary shepherds. From their place as keepers of the sacrificial flocks, they must have been often at the temple, and in constant intercourse with the Levites and priests. The manifestation of the angels to them would thus be very early known to all those at the temple. Every argument against the Lord's birth in December, drawn from the fact that the shepherds were then in the field, thus loses its force.

JANUARY — FEBRUARY, 750.   4 B. C.

Upon the eighth day following His birth, the Lord was cir- LUKE ii. 21. cumcised, and the name Jesus given Him.   Forty days after the birth, Mary presented herself with the child at the Temple in LUKE ii. 22–38. accordance with the law, and after the presentation returned again to Bethlehem.

The order of events following Christ's birth to the time He went to reside at Nazareth, is much disputed. The chief point of controversy is respecting the time of the visit of the Magi. If this can be determined, the other events may be easily arranged.

An early and current tradition placed the coming of the Magi on the 6th of January, or on the 13th day after His birth.[1] In that case, supposing that the star announced His birth, and that they left soon after its appearing, they were only some ten days on their journey. This day was early celebrated as the feast of the Epiphany, or the manifestation of Christ, and originally had reference to the visit of the Magi, and to His baptism; and later, to His first miracle. It is now observed both in the Greek and Roman Churches with reference to the two former events, of which the adoration of the Magi is made most prominent. This is also the case in the English and American Episcopal Churches. But the tradition did not command universal assent. Eusebius and Epiphanius, reasoning from Matt. ii. 16, put the coming of the Magi two years after His birth. And others have thought the 6th of January selected for convenience, rather than as having any direct chronological connection with the event.

---

[1] See Thilo, Codex Apoc., 1. 385, note.

The apocryphal gospel of the birth of Mary puts their coming on the forty-second day, or after the presentation, but some copies on the thirteenth.[1]

If we now ask the grounds upon which, aside from this tradition, the coming of the wise men is placed so soon after the birth, and before the presentation in the Temple, the more important are these: first, that the words τοῦ δὲ Ἰησοῦ γεννηθέντος, "now when Jesus was born" (Matt. ii. 1), imply that the one event speedily followed the other, the participle being in the aorist and not in the perfect ; second, that directly after the presentation, Jesus went with His parents to Nazareth (Luke ii. 39), and that therefore the presentation must have been preceded by their visit; third, that at the coming of the Magi, Herod first heard of the birth of Jesus, but if the presentation at the Temple had previously taken place, he must have heard of it, as it had been made public by Anna (Luke ii. 38).   But none of these reasons is decisive.   There is nothing, as asserted, in the use of γεννηθέντος, "now when Jesus was born," that proves that they came as soon as He was born, or that an interval of two months may not have elapsed.[2]   The opinion of many of the fathers that they found Him still in the manger, or stall, *in spelunca illa qua natus est,* may be true, if the manger was in a cave in the rear of the house. (See Matt. ii. 11.)   The statement of Luke, that "when they had performed all things according to the law of the Lord, they returned into Galilee, to their own city Nazareth," has often been interpreted as affirming that they went directly from the Temple to Nazareth without any return to Bethlehem.[3]   But this interpretation is arbitrary.   It is apparent that Luke does not design to give a full history of Christ's infancy.   He says nothing of the Magi, of the murder of the children, of the flight into Egypt.   Whatever may have been the motive of this omission, which Alford, in common with many German critics, ascribes to ignorance, nothing can be inferred from it to the impugning of Luke's accuracy.   His statement respecting the return to Galilee is general, and does not imply any strict chronological connection.   Elsewhere in Luke like

---

[1] Hofmann, 126.   [2] See Gal. iv. 29, and Meyer, *in loco.*
[3] So early. Chrysostom: and now. A. Clarke and Meyer.

instances occur, as in iv. 14, where Jesus is said to have "returned in the power of the Spirit into Galilee," whence it would
appear that this return followed immediately upon the temptation; yet we know that an interval of many months must have
elapsed. It is the fact that His childhood was passed at Nazareth, which Luke brings prominently forward, not the precise
time when He went thither, which was unimportant. It is not
inconsistent with his language that His parents should have returned to Bethlehem from the Temple, an afternoon walk of two
hours, and have gone thence to Nazareth by way of Egypt, though
had we this gospel alone, we could not infer this. Besides, it is
apparent from Matthew's narrative (ii. 22–3), that Joseph did
not design upon his return from Egypt to go to Galilee, and
went thither only by express divine direction. Plainly he looked
upon Bethlehem, not Nazareth, as the proper home of the child
who should be the heir of David.[1] And finally the fact that
Anna "spoke of Him to all them that looked for redemption in
Jerusalem," by no means shows that her words came to the ears
of Herod. The number of those who shared the faith of
Simeon and Anna was doubtless few, and the birth of Jesus was
not an event which they would blazon abroad before the Pharisees
and Herod.

Those who thus place the visit of the Magi before the purifi
cation of Mary and the presentation of Jesus, are by no means
agreed as to the time of the latter events. If the visit of the
Magi was on the thirteenth day after His birth, and the murder
of the children and the flight into Egypt took place immediately
after, the purification must have been delayed till the return, and
so in any event after the legal time on the fortieth day.[2] To
avoid this, some suppose that, although the suspicions of Herod
had been aroused by the inquiries of the Magi, yet he took no
active measures for the destruction of the child, till the rumor of
what had taken place at the Temple at the time of the presentation (Luke ii. 27–38) reaching his ears, stirred him up to give
immediate orders for the murder of the children.[3] Others still,
making the departure to Nazareth to have immediately followed

---

[1] See Wieseler, 154.   [2] Friedlieb, Bucher.
[3] Augustine, Sepp, Alford.

the purification, are compelled to make Nazareth, not Bethlehem, the starting point of the flight into Egypt.[1]

The obvious difficulties connected with this traditional view of the coming of the wise men on the thirteenth day after the Lord's birth, have led most in modern times to put it after the purification on the fortieth day. Some, holding that Jesus went immediately after that event to Nazareth, suppose that after a short sojourn there He returned to Bethlehem, and there was found by the wise men.[2] But most who put the purifica- tion upon the fortieth day, make the visit of the Magi to have shortly followed, and prior to any departure to Nazareth.[3] And this order seems best to harmonize the scripture narratives. The language of Luke ii. 22, compared with verse 21, plainly intimates that, as the circumcision took place on the eighth, or legal day, so did the presentation on the fortieth. The feast of the Purifi- cation is observed by both Eastern and Western churches on the 2d of February. Till this day, the mother was regarded as un- clean and was to abide at home, and it is therefore very improbable that the adoration of the Magi, and especially the flight into Egypt, should have previously taken place Doubt- less, in case of necessity, all the legal requisitions could have been set aside, but this necessity is not proved in this case to have existed. That the purification was after the return from Egypt, is inconsistent with Matthew's statements (ii. 22), that after Joseph had heard that Archelaus was reigning in Judæa, he was afraid to go thither. If, then, he dared not even enter the king's territory, how much less would he dare to go to Jeru- salem, and enter publicly into the temple. The conjecture of some,[4] that Archelaus was then absent at Rome, is wholly with- out historic proof.

That Matthew puts the flight into Egypt in immediate con- nection with the departure of the Magi (ii. 13), is plain.[5] No interval could have elapsed after their departure, for it is said,

---

[1] Maldonatus.

[2] Epiphanius, and now Jarvis, and Patritius.

[3] Robinson, Tischendorf, Wieseler, Lichtenstein, Pressensé.

[4] So Hug.

[5] Alford. Ellicott says: "Probably on the same night that the Magi arrived." From the fact that they "were warned of God in a dream," it may, however, be inferred that the dream of Joseph was the night following.

verse 14, that he "took the young child and His mother by night, and departed into Egypt." He went so soon as the angel appeared to him, apparently the same night. We cannot then place the history of the purification after their departure, and before the flight into Egypt, as is done by Calvin and many. Nor could Herod, after his jealousy had been aroused by the inquiries of the Magi after the new-born King of the Jews, have waited quietly several weeks, till the events of the purification awakened his attention anew. He, doubtless, acted here with that decision that characterized all his movements, and seeing himself mocked by the wise men, took instant measures for the destruction of the child.

The fact that Mary offered the offering of the poor (Luke ii. 24), may be mentioned as incidentally confirming this view; for if she had received previously the gifts of the Magi, particularly the gold, we may suppose that she would have used it to provide a better offering.

We thus trace a threefold adoration of Christ: 1st, that of the shepherds; 2d, that of Simeon and Anna; 3d, that of the Magi; or a twofold adoration of the Jews, and then the adoration of the heathen.

FEBRUARY, 750.   4 B. C.

Soon after the presentation, came the wise men from the **MATT. ii. 1–12.** East to worship the new-born King of the Jews. This visit excited the suspicions of Herod, who made diligent inquiries of them, but being warned of God in a dream that they should not return to him, they departed to their own country another way.

The time of the appearing of the star which led the Magi to seek Jesus has been already considered; and in the preceding remarks the reasons have been given why their coming should be placed after the purification of the fortieth day. It is not said whence the Magi came, except ἀπὸ ἀνατολῶν, "from the east." Some questions respecting their country, the nature of Magism, and its relation to astrology, will be briefly considered.

A distinction has been taken between the singular, ἀνατολή, and the plural, ἀνατολαί; the former meaning "the east," the quarter of the sun's rising, the latter, "the eastern regions." (See T. G. Lex. *sub voce.*) Upham says (*The Wise Men*, New York, 1871) that by the singular term is meant "the East." by the plural, "the far East." As Assyria was to the Jews "the North," so Babylonia was "the East," and Persia beyond Babylonia "the far East." The Magi coming from the east, ἀπὸ ἀνατολῶν, Vul. *ab orientibus*, he thinks to have been Persians. This was an early and current opinion. But a more ancient and general belief was that they came from Arabia, and this on several grounds: it was near to Judæa, and its inhabitants were known to be, at least in part, descended from Abraham; the gifts brought by them were native to that country; the Psalmist (lxxii. 10) also had predicted that the kings of Seba and Sheba should offer gifts.[1] Some have thought of Babylonia as the country of the Magi, of the northern parts of Mesopotamia, and of Parthia. The suggestion that they were Jews had no probability; their question, "Where is the king of the Jews?" would be put only by one not a Jew.

The question from whence they came, is not answered by their name, Magi, since Magism seems to have been widely spread. It is in dispute where was the home of the Magian religion. Herodotus (i. 40) speaks of the Magi as a Median tribe; but they existed as a priestly order long before. It is said by Rawlinson[2] that this form of religion was developed, under circumstances unknown to us, among the earlier inhabitants of Cappadocia, Armenia, and the Zagros mountain range, and was essentially worship of the elements. When the followers of Zoroaster, spreading southwestward from their original seat in Central Asia, came into contact with Magism, there was a partial fusion of religious beliefs and rites. This seems first to have taken place in Media, and the Magi became the priest-class of the Median nation, and were later accepted as such by the Persians. To the same effect are the statements of Rogazin. (*The Story of Media, Babylonia, and Persia*, New York, 1888.) The Magi were originally the native priesthood of that mountain region subsequently occupied by the Medes, and known as Western Eran. After the Aryans came, there was a fusion of the two religions, followed by a fusion of the two priesthoods; and the Magi became the national priestly class of Media. They appear as a powerful and separate body, possessing large territories, with cities of their own. They continued to be the sacerdotal order in Persia to its fall, and also under the Parthian rule; and, it is said, continue to be the priestly class even to this day.

By some, however, Babylonia is regarded as the home of Magism, because of its essential likeness to Babylonian Chaldaism. It is said

---

[1] Patritins, B., 111, 315; Mill, 308, note.
[2] The Religions of the Ancient World, New York, 1883, p. 97.

by Rawlinson [1] that a distinction was taken between the terms, Babylonian and Chaldean; the former being the ethnic appellation of the
inhabitants at large, the latter of a small but learned section. (See
in Daniel ii. 2. Some find five classes of Babylonian Magi mentioned
by this prophet.) From Babylonia Chaldaism spread to the Assyrians,
and thence to the Medians, and later to the Persians. The question
is not important for us. [2]

If Chaldaism and Magism were in substance the same, this readily
accounts for its wide diffusion.

The name of Magi was at first one of honor, but lost in later times
its better meaning, and became among the Greeks and Romans the
general designation of all who made pretensions to supernatural
knowledge — the interpreters of dreams, and of astronomical phenomena, false prophets, sorcerers, conjurers, and of all dealers in the
black arts. This process of deterioration can readily be understood.
(In this lower sense it is used in the Acts xiii. 6, 8. Elymas — *the
magus*, ὁ μάγος, "the sorcerer." The Vulgate retains magus.) Some
of the fathers, and later Lightfoot, say that the term is used here,
as elsewhere, by Matthew in its bad sense. (Trench, Star, 8.)
But there is general agreement that the term in Matthew, if translated at all, is well translated by "wise men." Doubtless, they
were astrologers; but astrology is not without some elements of
truth, for amongst other purposes served by "the lights in the
firmament" is that of "signs." (Genesis i. 14.)

Their knowledge of astrology was the means used by God to
teach them of the birth of his Son. The star was to them what
Augustin calls it, *magnifica lingua coeli*, speaking to them by its appearance of a new divine act in which all the world, Gentiles, no
less than Jews, had the deepest interest. [3]

That the star seen by the Magi was recognized by them as the star
of the king of the Jews — " His star " — shows that they must have
had some previous knowledge of Him. This knowledge they may
have obtained from traditions of the early prophecy of Balaam (Num.
xxiv. 17) of " a star out of Jacob," pointing to a king hereafter to
arise; or from the prophecies of Daniel; or from the known
Messianic expectations of the Jews in their captivity; or from personal
intercourse with the Jews then dwelling in the East, of whom there
were many and widely scattered; or, finally, from immediate divine
revelation. Of the prophecies of Daniel, from the peculiar relation in

---

[1] Egypt and Babylon, N. York, 1885, p. 43.
[2] Jer. xxxix. 3-13; Riehm, *sub voce*; Herzog, 2 auf. s. v.
[3] For a full discussion of the significance of stellar signs, see Sepp, i. 147, etc.

which he stood to the wise men of Babylon, and from his long residence there, extending over the reign of four kings, and his prominent official position, they could scarcely have been ignorant.

That a general expectation pervaded the East at this time that a king would arise in Judæa to rule the world, seems well authenticated.[1] It is, however, asserted by Gieseler that the Roman historians copied Josephus; and Edersheim (i. 203) says: "There is no historical evidence that there was among the nations any wide-spread expectancy of the Messiah in Palestine." But if such an expectation existed, all agree that it must originally have been derived from the Jews. Aside, then, from any immediate supernatural revelation, we may infer that the Magi were in a position to interpret the appearing of the star as connected with the fulfilment of Jewish prophecy respecting the Messiah, and thus to speak of it as "His star." If the statement often made that the Gentile astrologers divided the zodiac into parts, each of which denoted a particular country, and that the sign Pisces denoted Judæa, the conjunction of planets in this sign would at once have marked out this country as the place of present interest. But we have seen no satisfactory proof that at the time of the Lord's birth Judæa was astrologically designated by this sign. The statement of Abarbanel (1597 A. D.) as to a much later belief is hardly sufficient, but it is accepted by many.[2]

Some minor points remain yet to be noticed. Did this star, seen by the Magi "in the east," or, as rendered by many, "at its rising" (so Meyer, *in loco*), go before them on their way to Jerusalem to serve as a guide? If so, was it visible by day, or did they travel only by night? Was it visible to all, or to them only? Some understand "the time of the appearing star"—τοῦ φαινομένου ἀστέρος—to show a constant appearance (Wieseler, Beiträge, 149). But clearly Herod asked the time of its first appearing.

It is generally assumed that the star was seen by the Magi all the way till they reached Jerusalem, and then disappeared for a time, and again reappeared to guide them to Bethlehem. This is not said in the narrative. Its first appearing was to tell them of the Messiah's birth; His relations to the Jews, we may believe, they already knew; the way to Judæa was so well known to them, that they needed not a celestial guide. (See Speaker's

---

[1] Suetonius Ves., c. 4, *vetus et constans opinio;* Tacitus, Hist., v. 13; Josephus, War. vi. 5, 4.

[2] So Sepp, i. 158; Wieseler, Beiträge, 154. Abarbanel says that Jesus was born under Mars, and therefore His blood was upon His own head.

Com.)   It was its reappearance at Jerusalem after so long a disappearance, that filled them with great joy.

It is often said that the Magi addressed their enquiry, " Where
is He that is born King of the Jews? " to Herod, as the official
head of the nation. (So Edersheim.)   This may be so, but it is
not said by the Evangelist; but if they did not, their arrival and
its purpose would soon have come to his knowledge.

Was the gathering of the chief priests and scribes of the
people (verse 4), a meeting of the Sanhedrin?   This is often
said on the ground of Matthew's words, that Herod "gathered all the chief priests and scribes of the people."   But it is
denied by others on the ground that "the elders" are not mentioned, who were a constituent part of the Sanhedrin.   Meyer
says that he gathered " all the theologians because it was a theological question."   The language of Matthew does not affirm an
official meeting, but only that Herod gathered all those of whom
he might best obtain an answer to his question ; and these, doubtless, were those most famed for their knowledge of the Scriptures, and probably, most or all of them were members of the
Sanhedrin.   Edersheim says: "all the high priests, past and
present, and all the learned Rabbis."

Where did the Magi find the infant King ?   It has been
taken for granted that they found Him at Bethlehem, and this
has always been the traditional belief.   But it has been questioned by some, cited by Patritius, who present the view that
Joseph and Mary went immediately after the presentation to
their former home in Nazareth; and that the Magi found them
there.   This seems in accordance with Luke's statement (ii. 39):
" When they had performed all things according to the law of
the Lord, they returned into Galilee to their own city Nazareth."
And there is in this nothing intrinsically improbable.   The
question of the Magi was, " Where is He ?" and although they
were sent by Herod to Bethlehem as the prophetic birthplace of
the Messiah, the star may have directed them to Nazareth, and
here they may have paid Him their adoration, His parents being
in their own house.   If so, it was from Nazareth that Joseph
and Mary went down to Egypt; and the Magi did not return to
Jerusalem, but went to their own country another way, perhaps
by way of Damascus.

5

But the question naturally arises, Why should Herod slay the children in Bethlehem, if the Magi did not go there? Why not follow them to Nazareth, and there slay the Child they worshipped? A strong, perhaps decisive, objection to this view is, that no tradition of the visit of the Magi to Nazareth has been preserved; tradition is constant that they went to Bethlehem.

Many traditions have been current in the Church respecting these Magi.[1] They were said to be three in number, either from their gifts, or because regarded as representatives of the three divisions — Hamites, Shemites, and Japhetites. They were kings, one of Arabia, one of Godolia or Saba, and one of Tharsis ; their names, Melchior, Balthasar, Caspar; they were baptized by St. Thomas, their bones were gathered by St. Helena, and buried at St. Sophia in Constantinople, and were finally removed to Cologne, where they now lie.[2] The belief that they were kings might easily arise from the fact already spoken of that they, as a class, had large territorial possessions. Mill (310) speaks of them " as not improbably toparchs or provincial governors, as well as priests." They are often called priest-kings.

If the Magi came from beyond the Euphrates, they probably came by way of Damascus, and thence to Jerusalem. In returning, they may have gone south of the Dead Sea to Petræa, and thence have crossed the Euphrates.

FEBRUARY — MAY, 750. 4 B. C.

Immediately after their departure, Joseph, warned by God MATT. ii. 13-15. in a dream, takes Jesus and Mary and goes down into Egypt.
Herod, as soon as he finds himself mocked by the wise men, MATT. ii. 16-18. gives orders that all the children in Bethlehem of two years and under be slain. Joseph, with Jesus and Mary, remains in MATT. ii. 19-23. Egypt till he hears, through an angelic messenger, of Herod's death. He designs to return to Judæa, but is directed by God LUKE ii. 39-40. to go to Nazareth, where the Lord remains during His childhood and youth.

The time of the sojourn in Egypt was not probably of long duration, although extended by some of the early writers to

---

[1] Hofmann, 120.
[2] Hildesheim, die Legende von den heiligen drei Königen; Hertzog Encyc., ii. 503. For a full discussion of all these traditions, see Spanheim, Dubia Evangelica, ii. 271, and Patritius iii 318

several years. In the Gospel of the Infancy it is stated at three years ; in the History of Joseph, at one year; in Tatian's Harmony, at seven years; by Epiphanius, at two years. Athanasius makes Jesus four years old when He came from Egypt; Baronius, eight years. In modern times, those who put the Lord's birth one or more years before Herod's death, prolong correspondingly the sojourn in Egypt, some one, some two, some three years.[1] But if His birth be placed late in 749, some months before Herod's death in April, 750, as we place it, His return from Egypt must have been in the early summer of 750. Lardner (i. 358), after Kepler, has attempted to show from the expression of the angel (Matt. ii. 20), " they are dead that sought the young child's life," that Antipater, Herod's son, was included with Herod; and as he had been at enmity with his father for nearly a year, that the attempt upon His life and the murder of the Innocents must have been before this enmity, and at least a year before Herod's death. But this is doing violence to the expression.[2]

Joseph was to remain in Egypt till God should send him word, and this word was sent apparently so soon as Herod died. Considering how numerous were the Jews in Egypt, and the constant communication between the two countries, the news of Herod's death must soon have reached him in the ordinary way; but it was first made known to him by the angel, and no long interval, therefore, could have elapsed. That he made no delay but hastened his return, is implied in the fact that he did not know that Archelaus was Herod's successor till he came to the land of Israel. We infer, then, that the return was in the summer of 750, after a sojourn of three or four months.[3]

Tradition marks out the route which Joseph took into Egypt to have been by way of Hebron, Gaza, and the desert ; which, as the most direct way, is very likely the true one. At Hebron

---

[1] Patritius, Sepp, Jarvis, Geikie.

[2] See Trench, Star, 107; Meyer *in loco*.

[3] According to Greswell, seven months; Lichtenstein, four to five weeks; Wieseler, and Ellicott, two to three weeks. Patritius, iii. 403, argues that the return was during the little interval when Archelaus ruled as king, or from the death of his father to his departure to Rome, whither he went to obtain the confirmation of Herod's will. This would make it to have been early in April, 750. It may, however, be doubted whether the expression of Matthew, ii. 22, that " Archelaus did reign," is not pressed too far.

is still pointed out upon a hill the spot where the family rested at night, and a similar one at Gaza. Probably near a fortnight was occupied in the journey. The traditional place of their sojourn in Egypt is the village Metariyeh, not far from the city of Heliopolis on the way toward Cairo. An old sycamore is still shown as that under which they rested in their journey, or, according to present Coptic traditions, the successor of that, and near by is a fountain in which the child was bathed.[1] It is probable that many Jews dwelt at this time in the neighborhood of Heliopolis, which may explain the choice of a village in its vicinity as their place of refuge. Another tradition, however, makes them to have left Metariyeh, and to have dwelt at Memphis. The temple built by Onias about 150 B. C. at Leontopolis still continued to be a much-frequented place of worship to the Egyptian Jews, of whom Lightfoot says, "there was an infinite number at this time."

From the nearness of Bethlehem to Jerusalem, Herod doubtless learned very early after the departure of the Magi, that they had deceived him, and that through them he could not discover the new-born child. But as he had already diligently inquired of them what time the star appeared, he thought to accomplish his purpose by ordering that all the male children from two years old and under, in Bethlehem and its environs, should be put to death. The truth of the narrative has been often questioned, and on various grounds. The only important objection, however, is that springing from the silence of Josephus, who, it is said, must have mentioned an event so peculiar and cruel.[2] The common answer to this, that among the many insane and fiendish acts of cruelty that marked the last days of Herod, this might be easily overlooked, is amply sufficient.[3] The expression, "from two years old and under," is ambiguous. According to Campbell, "only those beginning the second year are included." Greswell also limits it to the age of thirteen months. If it be thus confined, the number of the children murdered is much' diminished. But under any circumstances, it could not have been large. Sepp, supposing the whole num-

---

[1] Chester, Qt. St., July 1880. Kitto, Life of Christ, 130.
[2] Meyer, *in loco.* [3] Winer, i. 483.

ber of inhabitants of Bethlehem and its coasts to be 5,000, would make the male children of this age about ninety; but this is a large estimate. Townsend, making the inhabitants to be 2,000, makes 50 children to have been slain. Some would reduce the number to ten or fifteen.[1] Voltaire, after an old Greek tradition, would make it 14,000. In peaceful times, such an act as this, even if executed, as this probably was, in secrecy, would have excited general indignation when it became known; but now the Jewish people had so long "supped with horrors," and were so engrossed in the many perils that threatened their national existence, that this passed by comparatively unnoticed. Such a deed — from a man, of whom Josephus says that "he was brutish and a stranger to all humanity," who had murdered his wife and his own children, and who wished, in his dying rage, to destroy all the chief men of his kingdom, that there might be a general mourning at his funeral — could have awak-ened no surprise. It was wholly in keeping with his reckless and savage character, but one, and by no means the greatest, of his crimes. It is therefore possible that it may never have come to the knowledge of the Jewish historian, writing so many years after the event.

If, however, Josephus was aware of this atrocity, it by no means follows that he would have mentioned it. With the rea-sons for his silence we are not particularly concerned. It may be, as some say,[2] that he purposely avoided everything that drew attention to the Messianic hopes of his people; or, as others,[3] that " he could not mention it without giving the Christian cause a great advantage." But whatever his motives, his silence cannot invalidate the statement of Matthew, except with those who will not credit an Evangelist unless corrobo-rated by some Jewish or heathen author.

There are some[4] who think that the sedition of Judas and Matthias [5] occurred at this very time, and was connected with the visit of the Magi. The inquiries of these strangers for the King of the Jews aroused into immediate activity the fiery Zealots, and a report of the king's death finding credence, they

---

[1] Winer, i. 483; Morrison; Farrar, Edersheim, say twenty at most.
[2] Lichtenstein, 97.   [3] Lardner, i. 351.
[4] Lardner, i. 348; Münter.   [5] Josephus, Antiq., xvi. 6. 3 and 4.

attacked at noon-day the golden eagle he had placed over the temple gate. About forty of them being arrested, were burned with fire. Exasperated at this bold sedition, and aware of the cause, the king gave orders for the slaughter of the children at Bethlehem. Of the two acts of this tragedy, Matthew relates only that with which he was concerned, that which took place at Bethlehem; and Josephus, that which concerned the general history of affairs. The silence of the one is no disproof of the other.

The objection of Hase and Meyer, that this murder of the children was both superfluous and unwise, may be very true, but does not affect the historic truth of the event. The silence of heathen historians respecting it is wholly unimportant. Judæa did not hold so high a place in their estimation that they should trouble themselves about its internal history, so little intelligible to a stranger. Herod's name is occasionally mentioned by them in connection with Roman matters, and there is in one a brief allusion to the trial and death of his sons, but nothing more. The well-known jest of Augustus, preserved by Macrobius,[1] might be cited if it could be shown that he had borrowed nothing from Christian sources. He says: "When Augustus had heard that among the children under two years old, *intra bimatum*, which Herod had commanded to be slain in Syria, his own son had been killed, he said 'it is better to be Herod's swine than his son.'" The expression, "two years old," points too directly to Matthew to allow us to suppose that it had an independent origin, although the words of Augustus may be literally given. Most agree that it is of no historical value.[2]

It would be strange, indeed, that while oriental history is full of such deeds of cruelty which are believed upon the authority of a single writer, the statement of the Evangelist should be disbelieved, though confirmed by all that we know of the character of the chief actor, and of the history of the times. A like rule applied to general history would leave not a few of its pages empty.

When directed to go into Egypt, Joseph was not told to

---

[1] Sat., ii. 2.

[2] So Lardner, Meyer, Trench, Alford. See, however, Mill, 294; Ellicott, 78, note 2.

what place he should return (Matt. ii. 13), nor afterward, when directed to return, was the place designated (verse 20). It is plain, however, that he did not design to return to Nazareth. He evidently regarded Bethlehem, the city of David, the proper place in which to rear the son of David. He naturally supposed that He who was of the tribe of Judah, should dwell in the land of Judah, the most religious, most sacred part of Palestine; and, as the promised Messiah, should be brought as near as possible to the theocratic centre, where He might have frequent intercourse with the priests and rabbins, and be educated under the very shadow of the temple. Only through a special command of God, was he led to return with Jesus to Galilee; and that he made his abode in the upland city of Nazareth, can only be explained by the fact, of which Matthew is wholly silent, that this had been his earlier residence as related by Luke.

How diverse the opinions of harmonists have been, in regard to the order of events of the Lord's infancy, will appear by a comparison of their several arrangements. These may be thus classified: I. That put the coming of the Magi before the fortieth day, the legal time of the Purification.

Sepp. Coming of the Magi on thirteenth day. Purification on fortieth day. Flight into Egypt, and sojourn there two years. Return to Galilee.

Chemnitz. Coming of the Magi just before the Purification. Purification on fortieth day. Flight into Egypt, and sojourn there four years. Return into Galilee.

II. That put the coming of the Magi after the Purification. Here we distinguish two classes. (a) That put the Purification at the legal time on the fortieth day.

Epiphanius. Purification on fortieth day. Departure to Nazareth, and sojourn there two years. Return to Bethlehem. Coming of Magi. Flight into Egypt, and sojourn there three years. Return to Galilee.

Lightfoot. Purification on fortieth day. Return to Bethlehem, and sojourn there till two years of age. Coming of Magi. Flight into Egypt, and sojourn there three or four months. Return to Galilee.

Wieseler. Purification on fortieth day. Coming of Magi.

Flight into Egypt, and sojourn there two or three weeks. Return to Galilee.

(b) That put the Purification after the legal time, and after the return from Egypt.

Friedlieb. Coming of Magi on the thirteenth. Flight into Egypt, and sojourn there three or four months. Return to Judæa. Purification. Departure to Nazareth.

Caspari. Coming of Magi. Flight into Egypt, and sojourn there three or four weeks. Return to Bethlehem. Purification. Departure to Nazareth.

That the coming of the Magi was placed on the 6th of January, the thirteenth from His birth, the same day that was celebrated as that of His baptism, has been already spoken of in speaking of the feast of the Epiphany.

That the Magi did not come till after the Purification, rests on several grounds: 1st, that Mary gave the offering of the poor, a thing not likely after she had received the gifts of the Magi; 2d, that Herod would not wait after their departure some weeks before slaying the children at Bethlehem ; 3d, that Matthew and Luke are to be reconciled. That the Purification was not delayed appears from Luke ii. 22. On these and other grounds, almost all harmonists put the coming of the Magi after the Purification. Those who put the birth of the Lord in 747 or 748, and the death of Herod in 750, must make the sojourn in Egypt proportionately long.

RESIDENCE IN NAZARETH. — In the city of Nazareth the Lord spent the larger part of his earthly life; it is called " His own **x**ountry," πατρίς (Matt. xiii. 54, and elsewhere), and He is constantly called Jesus of Nazareth; it therefore deserves our special notice. His residence here being brought by Matthew into direct connection with the Old Testament prophecy, the etymology of the name has been much discussed.[1] By many it is derived from *netser,* the Hebrew for sprout or twig, either because of so many thickets upon the adjoining hills, or because the village itself was small and feeble like a tender twig.[2] So Jesus is called (Isaiah xi. 1) a Branch. Others derive it from *notser,* that which guards

---

[1] See Meyer, *in loco*   [2] Winer, ii. 142; Hengst. Christology, ii. 109; T. G. Lex.

or keeps; hence, Nazareth, the protecting city.[1]　Others still
derive it from *nezer*, to separate.[2]　Jerome interpreted it as meaning a flower: *Ibimus ad Nazareth, et juxta interpretationem nominis
ejus, florem videbimus Galilæae;* referring, as would appear from
his language elsewhere, to Jesus as the Branch or Flower from the
root of Jesse.　It is noticeable that travellers speak of the great
quantity of flowers now seen there.[3]　The present name in
Arabic is En Nâsirah.

Nazareth lies in a small valley of Lower Galilee, a little
north of the great plain of Esdraelon, from which it is reached
by very rocky and precipitous paths.　Its elevation above the
plain is estimated to be from 300 to 350 feet.　Bonar (398)
speaks of the main road "as little better than a succession of
rocky slopes or ledges, rugged with holes and stones.　Yet this
was the old road to Nazareth.　There could be no other from
this side, so that one travelling from the south must have taken
it."　The valley runs northeast and southwest, and is about a
mile long and a quarter of a mile broad.　Around it rise many
small hills of no great height, the highest being on the west or
southwest.　They are of limestone, and give to the scenery a
grayish tint, and are covered thickly with shrubs and trees.
"The white rocks all around Nazareth give it a peculiar aspect.
It appears dry and tame, and this effect is increased by the trees
being powdered over with dust during the summer season.　The
heat was very great, and the gleam from the rocks painful to the
eye."[4]　"The upper ridges of the hills were, as is usual in this
worn-out land, gray and bare, but the lower slopes and dells and
hollows were green, sprinkled not scantily with the olive, the fig,
the prickly pear, and the karub ; while in the gardens the usual
oriental fruit trees showed themselves."[5]

The village itself lies on the western side of the valley upon
the side of the hill.　The houses are, in general, of stone, and

---

[1] See Riggenbach, Stud. u. Krit., 1855; Edersheim, i. 145, "Watch " or "watchers " ;
Merrill (Galilee, 29), "The guarded or watched," and connects it with the high hill
above it and watching over it.

[2] Lightfoot and Bengel, *in loco.*

[3] Stanley, 359.　The subject is discussed by Mill, 335.　Keim calls it Nazara.　So in the
Greek text, Matt. iv. 13, Luke iv. 16, W. and H., against Keim.　See Riehm, *sub voce.*

[4] Mission of Inquiry, 306.　　　　　　　　　　　[5] Bonar.

more substantially built than most of the towns of the region,
and from their whiteness it has been called "the white city"; [1] the
streets or lanes are, however, narrow and filthy. Porter
(ii. 359) speaks of it as "built on the side of the highest hill;
on the north the side of the hill is steep, and where it joins
the plain is seamed by three or four ravines; and on the
lower declivities of the ridges between them stands the
village of Nazareth. This, therefore, is 'the hill whereon the
city was built' (Luke iv. 29). The houses in some places seem
to cling to the sides of the precipices, in others they nestle in
glens, and in others again they stand boldly out overlooking the
valley." The present number of inhabitants is variously estimated, [2] and is said to be increasing.

Nazareth is not mentioned in the Old Testament, nor by Josephus,
from which we may conclude that it was a place of no importance.
But this conclusion would not be just, if we receive the statement of Neubauer (189), resting on a doubtful rabbinical authority,
that it was a gathering place for the priests who went up from that
region for the service of the temple. This is accepted by Edersheim
(i. 147): "Nazareth was one of the great centers of Jewish temple-
life. . . . The priests of the course which was to be on duty
always gathered in certain towns, whence they went up in company to
Jerusalem." If this was the case, the frequent presence of these
priests, and the interest thereby excited in the temple service, must
have been an important element in the religious character of the
child Jesus.

The general belief that Nazareth was a lonely, out-of-the-way
place, having very little connection with the outer world, and its
citizens, therefore, uncivilized and rude, is also strongly combated
by Edersheim, who says that the lower caravan route from Acre to
Damascus — the *via maris* — led through Nazareth, and therefore "it
was not a stagnant pool of rustic seclusion. Men of all nations,
busy with another life than that of Israel, would appear in its streets."
Merrill takes the same view, and gives the distances to certain other

---

[1] Although not named in the Talmud, Schwartz (178) thinks it was known under
another name: "I have ascertained that the town of Nazareth was called Laban — The
White Town — from the color of the soil, and stones, and houses." This is accepted by
Hamburger, ii. 854. Baedeker speaks of "its dazzling white walls," *i. e.*, of the houses.

[2] The Turkish officials assert that it amounts to 10,000, while others fix the number at
5,000 to 6,000; more than half are Christians. Baed., 359. The population in our Lord's day
is variously estimated from 5,000 to 15,000; Merrill, more; but there seems to be no valid
data for an estimate so large.

cities, thus showing that its inhabitants had that stimulus which comes from easy and frequent intercourse with other and larger communities.

Although so intimately connected with the life of Jesus, and therefore so prominent in the Gospels, it is not mentioned by any Christian writer prior to Eusebius in the fourth century, nor does it seem to have been visited by pilgrims till the sixth.[1] After this time it became one of the most famous among the holy places.   In the seventh century two churches are mentioned, one on the site of Joseph's house, and the other on the site of the house where Gabriel appeared to Mary.[2] During the Crusades it was made the seat of a bishopric. It was destroyed about A. D. 1200 by the Saracens, and for 300 or 400 years seems to have been inhabited chiefly by Mohammedans, and very little visited by pilgrims.[3] One of the churches was rebuilt in 1620 by the Franciscans, who added to it a cloister.   Nazareth has been for many years the seat of a Greek titular bishop.

All travellers agree in praising the extent and beauty of the prospect from the top of the hill northwest of Nazareth, 1,788 feet above the sea.   It is surmounted by the tomb of a Mohammedan saint, and is about 400 or 500 feet above the valley.[4] To the north is seen the wide plain of el Buttauf, running from east to west, having Cana of Galilee upon its northern, and Sepphoris upon its southern border, and beyond it rise in parallel ridges the hills, one behind another, to the heights of Safed.   To the northeast Hermon is seen, and eastward the ranges of Bashan beyond the Sea of Galilee, while Tabor lies between it and the sea.   To the southeast stretch Little Hermon and Gilboa in parallel lines.   On the south lies the great plain of Esdraelon, bounded southward by the hills of Samaria and the long line of Carmel.   Over the broken ridges that join Carmel to Samaria, is seen the Mediterranean far to the southwest, and the eye following the summits westward reaches the high promontory where Carmel ends upon the shore: from this point is seen the unbroken expanse of water many miles to the north.   This view is said by Porter (ii. 263) to be the richest, and perhaps also the most extensive, which one gets in all Palestine, and to surpass that from Tabor.[5]

That Nazareth, from some cause, had, at the time when the Lord resided in it, an evil name, appears plainly from John i

---

[1] Robinson, ii. 341.   [2] Arculf, Early Travels, 9.
[3] Early Travels, 46 and 298.
[4] So Robinson, ii. 333, note. Schubert makes it 700 or 800 feet above Nazareth.
[5] See Robinson, ii. 336; Stanley, 357.

46.[1] The objection of Nathanael was not merely that it was in Galilee, and that the Messiah could not come out of Galilee (John vii. 41), but he refers specially to Nazareth. Nor was it that it was a little village, for so was Bethlehem; and whenever designated in the Gospels, it is always called a city. The obvious import is, that Nazareth was in ill-repute throughout the province, and of this Nathanael, who was from Cana, but a little way distant, was well aware. This is confirmed by the revengeful and cruel treatment of the Lord when he first preached to the inhabitants (Luke iv. 28, 29).

APRIL 8, 761. A. D. 8.

From Nazareth, at the age of twelve, the Lord goes up for LUKE ii. 41-52. the first time to Jerusalem to keep the Passover. After the departure of His parents He remained behind to converse with the doctors, and was found in the temple three days after by them. Returning to Nazareth, He dwelt there in retirement till the time came that He should enter upon His public work.

Supposing the Lord to have been born in 749, the year when He went up with His parents to the Passover was 761, and the feast began on the 8th of April. His presence at the Passover, at the age of twelve, was in accordance with Jewish custom. At that age, the Jewish boys began to be instructed in the law, to be subject to the fasts, and to attend regularly the feasts, and were called the sons of the Law.[2] This, however, is called in question by Greswell (i. 396), who asserts that boys did not become subject to ordinances till they had reached the age of fourteen years, and that the purpose for which Jesus was now taken up was not to celebrate the Passover, but to be "made a disciple of the Law, and to undergo a ceremony, something like to our confirmation." He sees in this the explanation of the Lord's presence in the midst of the doctors.[3] It is not probable that up to this time Jesus had accompanied His parents to Jerusalem to any of the festivals. Of all that passed between Him

---

[1] See Kitto, Life of Christ, 27. Merrill "denies that there is any disparagement in the words. So also Godet, *in loco*, who says; "There is nothing in history to prove that it was a place of worse fame or less esteemed than any other village of Galilee."

[2] Meyer *in loco*; Sepp, ii. 172.

[3] But see Edersheim, Sketches of Jewish life, 120.

and the rabbis, a full account may be found in the Apocryphal Gospel of the Infancy.[1] It needs no proof that on this occasion He was not taking upon Himself the part of a teacher, nor asking questions for disputation, but was seeking to learn the truth from those who were appointed of God to be the teachers of the Law.   Where He was sitting with the doctors is uncertain. Lightfoot (*in loco*) says: "There were three courts of judicature in the temple, and also a synagogue," but does not say where He was found.   "There is nothing absurd in it if we should suppose Christ gotten into the very Sanhedrin itself." Edersheim denies that there was such a temple-synagogue, and affirms that, during the feasts, the members of the Sanhedrin sat on the *Chel* or terrace, to hear and answer questions, and that there Jesus found them. He infers that this was during the feast, and not after it (ii. App. x.).

The three days that elapsed before His parents found Jesus, may be thus computed: the first, that of their departure from Jerusalem; second, the day of their return; third, the day when He was found; or, if we exclude the day of departure — first, the day of their return; second, the day of search in Jerusalem; third, the day when He was found. Some, with much less probability, count three days from the day of their return. That He might very easily be separated from them without any culpable carelessness on their part, appears from the great multitudes that were present and the confusion that would necessarily prevail at such a time. Tradition makes Beer or El Bireh to have been the place where His parents spent the first night, and where they missed their son. "The place where Christ was first missed by His parents is commonly shown at this day to travellers, by the name of Beer, but ten miles from the city."[2] Edersheim says, Sichem, if the direct road north through Samaria was taken. As is well known, the first day's journey of a company of eastern travellers is always short. "On that day it is not customary to go more than six or eight miles, and the tents are pitched for the first night's encampment almost within sight of the place from which the journey commences."[3]   That,

---

[1] See Hofmann, 259.   [2] Lightfoot.
[3] Hackett, Scrip. Ill., 12.

leaving Jerusalem in the afternoon with the crowd of Galilæan pilgrims, Mary and Joseph should have lost sight of Jesus for three or four hours, and yet not have felt any alarm, supposing Him to have been somewhere in the company, presents no difficulty.[1]

The Lord now disappears from our sight and does not reappear for many years. We are simply told He went with His parents to Nazareth, and was subject unto them.

How the eighteen years of His life passed at Nazareth were spent, we have no means of determining. The Evangelists have maintained upon this point entire silence. It is most probable that He was taught His father Joseph's trade, according to the settled custom of the Jews to bring up their sons to some trade or art.[2]   This is very plainly taught in the question of the inhabitants of Nazareth, "Is not this the carpenter?" which, as Alford remarks, "signifies that the Lord had *actually worked* at the trade of His reputed father." Justin Martyr (100–150 A. D.) says that Christ being regarded as a worker in wood, "did make, while among men, ploughs and yokes, thus setting before them symbols of righteousness, and teaching an active life."[3] That this was His occupation seems to have been generally believed by the early fathers. Some, in later times, thinking bodily labor derogatory to him, made this time of retirement at Nazareth to have been spent in contemplation and prayer. The traditions that He made a journey to Persia to visit the Magi, or to Egypt to visit her sages, need no notice.[4]

Of the means for the mental and spiritual education of the child Jesus, we have only a general knowledge. It is doubtless true, as said by Edersheim (i. 230), that "from the first days of its existence a religious atmosphere surrounded the child of Jewish parents." Besides the influences of the home and the teaching of the father and mother, there were the synagogue, the school, and the feasts. For the first years the Bible was the text-book, and later the traditional law. It is a point in question whether Joseph possessed a copy of the old Testament in whole

---

[1] As to the more distinguished rabbis whom the Lord may have met at this time see Sepp, ii. 178.

[2] See Lightfoot on Mark vi. 3.   [3] See contra Mosheim. Com.. i. 85

[4] See Hofmann, 264.

or in part; or if he did not, did Jesus during his youth have regular access to one? This is a question that cannot be positively answered. It is said by some that the cost of a whole copy, or even of a part, was so great that a poor man could not possess it. But others, as Edersheim, affirm that every devout Jew could have at least some part of the Scriptures, and if Joseph had not, Jesus could have found a copy in the school for Bible study.

We may believe that in Him the words of the Psalmist found their perfect fulfillment (Ps. i. 2.): "His delight is in the law of the Lord; and in His law doth he meditate day and night." But there is no reason to believe that during all these years He ever took upon himself the work of a teacher. The time for this had not come. He was silent till God by the voice of the Baptist called Him forth. (See Mark vi. 2 ff.)

THE LORD'S BRETHREN.

It is an interesting inquiry, and one that may properly be considered here, Who constituted the household of Joseph and Mary at Nazareth? Was Jesus the only child in the family circle; or, if there were other children, in what relation did they stand to Him? Mention is several times made by the Evangelists of His brothers and sisters. Who were they? This question has been in dispute from very early times, and many elaborate essays have been written upon it; but opinions are as much at variance now as ever. Credner (*Einleitung in das N. T.*, 570) makes an apt quotation from Bacon: " *Citius emerget veritas ex errore quam ex confusione.*" Its impartial discussion has been hindered by dogmatic considerations connected with the perpetual virginity of the Lord's mother, with Church polity, and with the canonicity of non-Apostolic epistles. Passing by these for the present, and avoiding, so far as possible, mere conjectures, let us attempt to bring the matter in its more important bearings fairly before us.

Let us first sum up what we know from the New Testament of the brothers and sisters of the Lord. They are mentioned in Matthew xii. 46–50, xiii. 55–56; Mark iii. 31, vi. 3; Luke viii. 19; John ii. 12, vii. 3; Acts i. 14; 1 Cor. ix. 5; and St. Paul speaks of a James the Lord's brother (Galatians i. 19). Of the brothers, there seem to have been four, whose names are given by Matthew xiii. 55: James, Joses, Simon, and Judas; in the Revised Version, James, Joseph, Simon, and Judas (see Mark vi. 3). Both Evangelists mention the sisters, but neither the number nor the names are given. From the language of the Nazarenes (Matthew xiii. 56), "His sisters, are they not all with us?" there must have been at least two, probably more, and apparently married, and resident at Nazareth. (Woolsey, "at least three"; Mill, four.) These brothers and sisters are not mentioned at all till after the Lord began His ministry, and are first mentioned as going with His mother and Himself to Capernaum (John ii. 12). It is in dispute whether any were believers in His Messianic claims, at least till the very end of His ministry (John vii. 3–10). Most say that they were made believers through His resurrection, as they immediately after appear in company with the Apostles (Acts i. 14).

In all the references to the Lord's brethren several things are noticeable: first, that they are always called brothers and sisters, ἀδελφοί, ἀδελφάι; not cousins, ἀνέψιοι, or kinsmen, συγγενεῖς; second, that their relationship is always defined with reference to Him, not to Joseph or to Mary; they are always called His brothers and sisters, not sons and daughters of Mary; third, that they always appear in connection with Mary (except in John vii. 3) as if her children, members of her household, and under her direction.

We may thus classify the several theories respecting them: first, that they were His own brothers and sisters, the children of Joseph and Mary; second, that they were the children of Joseph by a former marriage, and so His step-brothers and sisters; third, that they were children of a sister of His mother, and so His cousins german — consobrini. Some make them His cousins on His father's side, not on the mother's — patrueles; and some, His cousins on both sides. These three theories are sometimes called from the names of their original or chief advocates, the Helvidian, the Epiphanian, and the Hieronymian.[1] It is the last theory, as most generally held, which we will first examine.

1. *Hieronymian Theory.* — In a question involving so many intricate details, we will begin our inquiry by asking, What blood relatives had the Lord's parents? There are two sources of information, the New Testament and tradition. From the first we learn very little of Joseph. Aside from the genealogical tables, nothing is said of his relatives or of his history. In the table (Matthew i. 16) his father's name is given as Jacob, the son of Matthan; in Luke (iii. 23), if we accept this as the genealogy of Joseph, it is Heli. Nothing is said as to his age at the time of his marriage to Mary, or as to any former marriage.

Of Mary's relatives, the New Testament gives us very slight information. She is called a "cousin" of Elisabeth — συγγενίς — R. V.,

---

[1] See Bp. Lightfoot, Com. on Galatians, Dissertation II. 242.

" Kinswoman " (Luke i. 36).   We know that she had a sister only by
incidental mention (John xix. 25): " Now there stood by the cross of
Jesus His mother, and His mother's sister, Mary the *wife* of Cleophas,
and Mary Magdalene." (In W. and H. Tisch. for Cleophas is read
Clopas: So R. V.)   The relation of Mary to Clopas is undetermined,
Μαρία ἡ τοῦ Κλωπᾶ.   Examining this passage, two questions arise,
one of punctuation, and one of relationship.   Are there three women
mentioned here, or four?   If three, we have, first, the Lord's
mother; second, Mary her sister, who is called the *wife* of Cleophas;
and third, Mary Magdalene.   If four, we have, first, the Lord's
mother; second, her sister, name not mentioned; third, Mary *wife* of
Cleophas; and fourth, Mary Magdalene.[1]

If we assume that there were four, and that the Virgin's sister was
not Mary of Clopas, who was she?   It is said by some that she was
Salome the wife of Zebedee, and mother of the two apostles, James
and John. (So Wies., M. and M., Eders., Dwight.)   Tradition has
been busy with Salome, as with Joseph and Mary.   According to one
report accepted by a Lapide, she was the daughter of Alphæus and
Mary, and older than her brothers, James and Joses, and, of course,
the Lord's relative in the same degree.   Her two sons were thus much
younger than their uncles, James and Joses.   According to another
report she was the daughter of Alphæus by a former marriage.   (For
other accounts, see Winer, *sub voce*.)

If this were so, her sons were the Lord's relatives; and some find
a proof of this in the request of their mother for the two highest
places in His Kingdom (Matt. xx. 20).   But this may be explained
by the high estimation in which they stood in His eyes.   If they had
been His cousins — blood relatives — some trace of it would be found
in early tradition, but there is none.   If she was not Salome, we
have no knowledge whatsoever of this sister of the Virgin.

Assuming for the present, that the sister of the Virgin, using the
term sister in its ordinary sense, was Mary, that she was the wife of
Clopas, and identifying Clopas with Alphæus, had they any children?   This we can ascertain only by a minute comparison of names
and relationships, and this our space does not permit.   Let us then
admit that Alphæus and Mary had two sons, James and Joses, and
perhaps two more, Judas and Simeon, though this is much disputed,

---

[1] As to the point whether three or four women, modern opinions are much divided.
In favor of three: Neander, A. Norton, Stier, Mill, Bleek, Ebrard, Ellicott, Godet, Pres-
sensé, Caspari, McClellan, and all Roman Catholic writers. In favor of four: Lucke,
Wieseler, Ewald, Meyer, Schaff, Riggenbach, Luthardt, Edersheim, Weiss, Woolsey,
Westcott, Dwight. In the Syrian version we read: " His mother, His mother's sister,
and Mary of Cleophas, and Mary Magdalene." (Murdock's Trans.)

and the proof is not strong; and some daughters. Can we identify
them with the brothers and sisters of the Lord? Here, three points
are to be considered: 1st, the actual degree of relationship; 2d, the
fact that the Lord and His brethren made one household; 3d, the
use of the terms brother and sister, as denoting the relationship.

1. It is obvious that if our Lord had any cousins in the true sense
—blood relatives—it must have been on the mother's side. The
children of Alphæus, admitting him to have been the brother of
Joseph, the husband of Mary, were not relatives of this degree unless
his wife was a blood relative of the Virgin. If the two were sisters,
then only their children were cousins.

But it is said by many Roman Catholic writers that the Virgin
had no sister; she was the only child of her parents.[1] The term
"sister" (John xix. 25) is therefore equivalent only to "kinswoman"
or "relative." But a relative of what degree? Here, all is uncertainty, and we cannot affirm that, on His mother's side, the Lord had
any blood relatives. a Lapide quotes Baronius as affirming that the
Virgin had three female relatives — *tres ponit Marias sorores, id est
tonsobrinas B. Viginis* — one the wife of Alphæus, one the wife of
Cleophas, and one the wife of Zebedee. How these three Maries were
related to the Virgin and to one another, we are not told.

We now ask in what relationship Alphæus stood to Joseph and
Mary? It is said by Hegesippus (Euseb. iii. 11), that Joseph and
Alphæus were brothers, and this is regarded by many as trustworthy;[2]
but others understand this as meaning that they were brothers-in-law,
having married sisters. But admitting their brotherhood, the children
of Alphæus were not, therefore, the Lord's cousins, although nephews
and nieces of Joseph. If, indeed, Joseph and the Virgin were
cousins, she being, as some say, the eldest daughter of his father's
brother, then Alphæus was also her cousin, and his children the
Lord's cousins in the second degree.

The many uncertainties we find as to the relationship of these several parties make any conclusions of little value. Had the Virgin a
sister? Was she the "Mary of Clopas"? In what relation did she
stand to Clopas — as wife, or mother, or daughter? Was Clopas the
the same as Alphæus? Is he to be identified with the Alphæus,
the father of Levi? Was he the brother of Joseph? What children had
he? To these and other questions we can give no positive answers.
If the Virgin had no sister, but had a female relative of an unknown
degree, who had children, these were only kinsmen of Jesus in an
indefinite sense. We do not know what the actual degree of con-

---

[1] Welte u. Weltzer, Kirchen Lex., 6, 837; Hofmann, 5; Friedlieb, 330.
[2] Bleek, Godet, Edersheim, Bp. Lightfoot.

sanguinity between the Lord and the children of Alphæus was, or whether there was any.

2. Let us consider the fact, that the Lord and His brethren made one household under the care of the Virgin. If these were the children of Alphæus and Mary, it implies that one parent, at least, was dead. Some say that, Alphæus dying early, Joseph took his widow and her children into his own house, perhaps adopted them as his own;[1] others, that, Joseph dying first, Alphæus took the Virgin and Jesus to his house; and others, that, Alphæus dying without children, Joseph married the widow according to the law of the levirate marriage. (On the various and discordant views of the fathers, see a Lapide on Matt. xiii. 55.) It is plain that all these are merely conjectures, and do not sufficiently account for the fact that the Lord's brothers always appear as under the immediate care of the Virgin, no mention being made of their own parents. If it were proved that Alphæus died first, and that Joseph took his children and adopted them, and himself died later before the Lord began His public ministry, and that the two widows and their children made one family; it is very improbable that the other Mary should never be spoken of even by those who, as the Nazarenes, were well acquainted with their domestic relations. We must, therefore, conjecture, that she also was dead.

3. The use of the terms denoting the relationship. If there was any consanguinity, there is no proof of it closer than that of cousins of the second degree. Why, then, do the Evangelists call them "brothers and sisters"? The advocates of this theory affirm that these terms are used in the indefinite sense of "relatives" and "kinsmen," not in their primary and usual sense. But if this be the meaning of the Evangelists, why do they not use the more indefinite terms? It is obvious that when Jesus is called the "son" of Joseph, or Joseph is called his "father," the relation is not that which the terms usually express, and this from necessity; it is not so when called "the son of Mary." If the Lord had cousins-german, there is no reason why they should not be so called, the Greek tongue having a special word for that relation. If St. Paul (Col. iv. 10) spoke of "Marcus, sister's son to Barnabas," (in R. V., "the cousin of Barnabas,") why was it not used here where it would be wholly appropriate? The reply that the Jews had no special word to express this relationship, and therefore used the word brother to express it,[2] is not wholly accurate. Brother in Hebrew, in its first and proper sense, applies to those who

---

[1] So Döllinger, 104; Schegg; Matt. xii. 46.

[2] So Maldonatus, Matt. xii. 46; *Solitos consobrinos et cognatos fratres appellari.*

have the same parents, or one parent in common; it defines that degree of blood relationship, but it does not define other degrees, as that of cousin. When used of others, not brothers and sisters, it affirms some relationship which may be of blood or alliance or friendship, the nature of which must be learned from other sources.[1] When the Nazarenes asked: "Are not His brethren James, and Joses, and Simon, and Judas ? And His sisters, are they not all with us ?" they either expressed a definite relationship such as the words mean, or one wholly indefinite. We cannot doubt that they meant to express more than the fact of some undefined relationship. They do not ask, Are not these His kinsmen and kinswomen ? They speak of brothers and sisters; had they meant cousins, the nephews and nieces of Joseph, they would have expressed it in some other way.

It is clearly better to hold to the primary meaning of these terms, unless compelled to depart from it. If we regard them as equivalent to relatives, we cannot tell what degree of relationship in any given case is intended, but must learn this in some other way. Most translations of the Gospels render them in the definite sense. So the Vulgate, Luther, Weizsäcker, and English versions. But Norton, in his translation of the Gospels, uses the terms, "kinsmen," "He and His mother and His kinsmen," "His kinsmen said to Him," "And His kinsmen James and Joses . . . and His kinswomen." If we depart from the primary meaning, this is doubtless the best rendering as expressing the fact of kinship, but leaving undecided its degree. The burden of proof lies upon those who affirm that the terms, "brothers and sisters," are used by the Evangelists in the indefinite sense of "relatives or kinsmen." This proof is supposed to be found in the language of St. Paul (Gal. i. 19), where he speaks of a James as "the Lord's brother." It is said that this is James the Apostle, the son of Alphæus; and as the children of Alphæus were His cousins in the first or second degree, we may infer that all of them are called by the Evangelists His brothers and sisters.

We meet here with many perplexing questions, but the central point is, whether there were two or three Jameses. We know that there were two, James the son of Zebedee and James the son of Alphæus, both of the Twelve (Mark iii. 17 ff.). Was there a third ? This is denied by those whose theory we are now examining. They affirm that James the Lord's brother and James the son of Alphæus were one and the same person. Without entering into details, we must hold that the two are not to be identified. It is not clearly shown that St. Paul calls the Lord's brother an apostle. After speaking of seeing St. Peter

---

[1] See Laurent, *Neutestamentliche Studien*, 156.

at Jerusalem, St. Paul says: "But others of the apostles saw I
none save James, the Lord's brother." (R. V. margin, "but only.")
Does he mean, "I saw no other of the apostles save James?" If
so, James is included among the apostles. But the words may be
rendered: "I saw none other of the apostles, but I saw James, the
Lord's brother." Thus rendered, James is brought into contrast with
the apostles, and excluded from them.[1] But if included among them,
is the word "apostle" used here in its narrower or larger sense? If this
James was the son of Alphæus, he was one of the Twelve; and those,
therefore, who think that he is here called an apostle only in the larger
sense, exclude him from the Twelve, and so deny him to be the son of
Alphæus,[2] and thus make three Jameses.

It should here be noted that those who identify James the son of
Alphæus and James the Lord's brother, make one or more of the other
sons to be apostles. This is said of Judas. Mill says: "James and
Jude are found to be of the Twelve, and Simon has been by many
not improbably thought identical with Simon Zelotes of the same
number."[3]

But here we meet the difficulty that only six months before the Lord's
death it is said by John vii. 5: "For neither did His brethren believe
on Him"; and yet two, if not three of these brethren, it is claimed, (a
third, Simon, if not an apostle, is said to have been one of the Seventy,)
were apostles, and had been living with Him as such, and sent out by
Him on a special mission. It is not satisfactory to say that they had
only a little faith, or had temporarily lost their faith; the Evangelist's
words clearly affirm that up to this time His brethren had not
believed on Him, and did not count themselves as His disciples, as thus
distinguished; nor do the narratives distinguish between them as part
believers and part unbelievers. We are bound to include them all in
one class or the other. So in Acts i. 14 and 1 Cor. ix. 5 we cannot
distinguish between them and say that two are to be counted among
the apostles.

We conclude, then, that James the Lord's brother cannot be
identified with James the son of Alphæus; and, therefore, the relationship of cousin fails to be sustained, and with this the identity
of his children with the brethren of the Lord is unproved. Who

---

[1] As to the grammatical construction, see Winer, Gram.; Ellicott, 97, note 2; Bp.
Lightfoot, *in loco*. In favor of the construction excluding him from the apostles, Grotius,
Credner, Bleek, Schaff, Thiersch, Laurent, McClellan, and many; on the other, the Roman
Catholics commentators in general, and Meyer, Lichtenstein, Pressensé, Bp. Light-
foot, Ellicott.

[2] So Ellicott, Bp. Lightfoot, and many.

[3] So, as regards James and Judas, Döllinger, 104; Friedlieb, 333; a Lapide.

James was and what place he held in the Church, are points that will soon meet us.

2. *The Epiphanian Theory.*— But if the brethren of the Lord were not the children of Alphæus and Mary, who were they? We turn for an answer to the second theory mentioned before, that they were the children of Joseph by an earlier marriage. On what ground can such a marriage be affirmed? The New Testament gives us no hint of it, and we know of it only from early tradition. The first notice of it is in some apocryphal gospels, written probably in the first part of the second century. In them we are told that Joseph had several sons and daughters before his marriage with the Virgin, being then an old man.[1] Have these statements a basis of fact, " a genuine apostolic tradition," or are they, as Jerome called them, "*deliramenta apocryphorum*"? There is certainly nothing intrinsically improbable in them, and they may easily be separated from the legends in which they are imbedded, and we know that they were received very early by many of the fathers, both Greek and Latin,[2] and are accepted to this day by the Greek Church, and by many Protestants. All that we can now do, is to see whether, assuming their truth, they harmonize with and explain the gospel narrative.

It is obvious at once, that some of the difficulties we have found in the examination of the former theory are removed. If Joseph had sons and daughters by a former wife, we can understand the use of the terms "the Lord's brothers and sisters" by the Nazarenes. Knowing that he had been twice married, and ignorant of the mystery of the Incarnation, they would not hesitate to call the children of the first wife the Lord's brothers and sisters. Very few among us at the present day would speak of children so related as half-brothers, unless there were some special reason for making the distinction.

In this case, all of Joseph's children must have been older than Jesus, and some of them much older, and this may help to explain their treatment of Him when they thought Him becoming too zealous or enthusiastic in His work (Mark iii. 21–31; see Mill, 223), and in general, their unbelief in His Messianic claims. It is probable, that James, who is generally thought to have been the eldest of the sons,

---

[1] In the "History of Joseph," ch. ii., the names of his children by his first wife are given — Judas, Justin, Jacobus, and Simon; and daughters, Anna and Lydia. See Hofmann, 4.

[2] Maldonatus says, Matt. xii. 46, *In qua opinione omnes paene auctores Graeci fuerunt . . Ex Latinis, Hilarius et Ambrosius.* See also the catena of references to the fathers in Bp. Lightfoot, 259.

was at this time between forty and fifty years of age, for he must have been some fifteen years old at the birth of Jesus. Naturally, they would all be disposed to look down upon Him as so much younger, and to give less credence to His divine mission. Persons of such maturity, and of fixed modes of belief, would not so readily accept His claims and teachings as brothers and sisters younger than Himself. The same feeling may have arisen here as in the case of Joseph and his brethren (Gen. xxxvii. 8 ff.), and given a keener edge to the proverb: "A prophet is not without honor except in his own house."

If they were His elder brothers, we can also better understand their special position among the disciples after they believed on Him, and the high estimation in which they were held by the churches; we can also, in this way, best explain the official position and influence of James, and the fact that he was the accepted representative of the Jewish Christians. It was to him, in all probability, that the Lord appeared after His resurrection (1 Cor. xv. 7), and perhaps through his testimony, all his brothers became believers, and were with the Apostles before the day of Pentecost (Acts i. 14); and it was of him that Eusebius speaks (Ch. Hist., ii. 25) as the first Bishop of the Church at Jerusalem. He was called the " just," and was a strict observer of the law, and the chief official representative of the Jewish Christian part of the Church (Acts xv. 13; xxi. 18). His age, his personal character, and his position, made him very conspicuous and influential; and if to this we add his relationship to the Lord, we can understand why he should be classed among "the pillars," and his name be put before those of Cephas and John (Gal. ii. 9). We can also understand why Judas should designate himself in his epistle only as "the brother of James," the less known by the better known.

The Lord's brethren seem to have been distinguished, for a time, both from the Apostles and the believers in general, as if forming a special class (1 Cor. ix. 5). Probably one ground of this distinction lay in the respect felt for those who, for so many years, had stood in such close communion with the Holy One; and possibly, also, their Davidic descent.

But in this identification of the children of Joseph with the Lord's brethren, there are some difficulties. If Joseph had sons older than Jesus, had they not the legal claim to the throne of David? If the claim of the Lord rested on His legal right as the adopted son of Joseph (see a Lapide on Matt. i. 16; Mill, 210), had not His elder brother, James, a prior title? But if His title came through His mother, as is implied in the angel's words, "The Lord God shall give unto Him the throne of His father David," the difficulty is removed. (So Bengel: *Ipsa erat heres partis suae, et jus regni David-icae in Jesum transmittebat.*)

Again, as the children of Joseph were all older than Jesus, it is not easy to explain their continued presence with His mother; it is natural to suppose that they were already, at the beginning of His ministry, married men, and residents in some town in Galilee, whether in Nazareth or in its vicinity. It may be said that they were with her only on special occasions and when summoned by her, but the impression is made that they constituted one household.

Again, it may surprise us, that the two families of Joseph and Alphæus should have so many sons of the same name, but this is to be explained by the poverty of names at that time, and so the constant repetition of a few. But that three or four cousins should have the same name is not so remarkable as that the same name should be given to two sisters.[1]

3. *Helvidian Theory.*— But if neither of the views already presented is accepted by us, if the Lord's brethren were neither His half brothers nor His cousins, they must have been His brothers in the full sense — the children of Joseph and Mary. This view has the great advantage that it takes the words "brother" and "sister" in their natural sense. Passing by, for the present, the question of Mary's perpetual virginity, and assuming that these were her children, how do we thus meet the conditions of the narrative?

As they were, at least, six in number, and all younger than the Lord, He must have been, after Joseph's death, the head of the family, and its responsibilities would devolve upon Him. (So Eders. i. 250.) It is obvious that, in this position, He would have great influence in moulding the character of the younger children; and this makes it more difficult to see why they should not earlier have accepted His teaching and mission. It may be said, indeed, that their attitude was not one of hostility, but rather of doubt; and that their domestic familiarity with Him was a hindrance to a right appreciation of His work. On the other hand, their youth best explains their presence with their mother; and the sons still may have made one family, although the eldest at the death of Jesus was probably about thirty years of age. Still, there is another difficulty: if her own sons were then living, it is not easy to see why the Lord at His death should have committed her to the care of John (John xix. 26). This

---

[1] According to Smith, Bible Dict. i. 231, Josephus mentions 21 Simons, 17 Joses, and 16 Judes; and in the New Testament, mention is made of 12 Simons, and of nearly as many Josephs or Joses. Bp. Lightfoot, 255.

objection would also apply, though not with equal force, if they were her step-sons. But in our ignorance of the circumstances we cannot draw any positive inferences from this act of the Lord. It may be that He foresaw that she would have with John a life of greater peace and quiet than with her children, whether her own or those of Joseph; and that he could not only better supply her bodily wants, but also better comfort and strengthen her in the peculiar spiritual trials through which she would be called to pass.

But this view, that Mary had other children than Jesus, is summarily rejected by a very large part of the church, on the ground of her perpetual virginity. This is either an article of faith, as with the Greeks and Romans — *Semper mansisse virginem, dogma est fidei,* — or a matter of feeling. It is expressed in the Lutheran symbols, and in the Helvetic Confession the Lord is spoken of as *natus ex Maria semper virgine.* A large number of Protestant writers in all the religious bodies strongly maintain the perpetual virginity. Pearson[1] says that the Church of God in all ages has maintained that she continued in the same virginity.[2] But into the history of opinions, this is not the place to enter; each of the respective theories we have considered presents its claims to be the primitive belief of the Church. The views of the early fathers are very clearly, and it would seem, fairly, presented by Bp. Lightfoot, 260 ff., who himself holds the Epiphanian account to have the highest claim to the sanction of tradition. Of the Hieronymian solution, he says: "There is not the slightest indication that it ever occurred to any individual, or sect, or church, until it was put forward by Jerome himself." It is said by Thiersch (Versuch., 361, 431), that the Epiphanian view is the only tradition that existed during the second and third centuries, and was the ruling one till the time of Jerome. This father, writing against Helvidius, first gave currency to the solution that they were the cousins of the Lord, and hence is called by Baronius its *fortissimus adstipulator vel potius auctor.* On the other hand, for the defense of Jerome, see Mill, 242 ff.

The early belief in the perpetual virginity of Mary may perhaps be explained as springing in part from a desire to separate Christ, as widely as possible, from other men. He had no brothers or sisters; His mother had no other child. Thus, not only in His essential personality, but in the outward circumstances of His life, a broad line of distinction was to be drawn between Him and all beside. To suppose that He had brothers according to the flesh was to degrade

---

[1] Upon the Creed, Art. iii.
[2] So Mill, 272 ff., who gives the opinions of the chief English divines.

6

Him by bringing Him into too close relationship with weak and sinful men. The special honor paid to Him would naturally cause high honor to be paid to His mother. To this was added the admiration of celibacy springing from Gnostic principles, that began very early to prevail. Both His parents were thought to be honored by being presented to the world as virgins. Occasionally from time to time, and especially for a few years past, the tendency has manifested itself to bring more distinctly forward the humanity of Christ, and to give prominence to the truth expressed by the Apostle (Heb. ii. 11): "For both He that sanctifieth and they who are sanctified, are all of one." Not to remove Him from the pale of human sympathies, but to bring Him in as many points as possible into contact with the experiences of human life, has seemed to many best to correspond to the historical statements of the Gospel, and the doctrinal statements of the Epistles. Hence, perhaps, there is now felt less reluctance to regard Him as having been in the truest sense a member of the family, having brothers and sisters bound to him by ties of blood, and as a partaker of the common lot in all the relationships of life which were possible to Him, that thus "He might be touched with a feeling of our infirmities."

Leaving all theological considerations on one side, the more natural and obvious interpretation of the language of the Evangelists leads to the belief that the Lord's brothers and sisters were such in the ordinary meaning of the words. In the case of another no hesitation could be felt. (But for the right interpretation of their statements, particularly Matt. i. 25 and Luke ii. 7, we must refer to the commentators.)

It has been well remarked by Alexander (on Mark vi. 3) "that multitudes of Protestant divines and others, independently of all creeds and confessions, have believed, or rather felt, that the selection of a woman to be the mother of the Lord carries with it, as a necessary implication, that no other could sustain the same relation to her; and that the selection of a virgin still more necessarily implied that she was to continue so. After all, it is not so much a matter of reason or of faith as of taste and sensibility; but these exert a potent influence on all interpretation, and the same repugnance, whether rational or merely sentimental, which led fathers and reformers to deny that Christ had brothers in the ordinary sense, is likely to produce the same effect on multitudes forever, or until the question has received some unequivocal solution." The words of Calvin on Matt. i. 25 deserve to be kept in mind: *Certe nemo unquam hac de re questionem movebit nisi curiosus; nemo vero pertinaciter insistet nisi contentiosus rixator.*

We may thus classify the more recent writers. 1. That His brethren were the Lord's cousins is held by the Roman commentators and harmonists; So Patritius, Sepp, Bucher, Friedlieb. So also, by many Protestants: Olshausen, Lange, Lichtenstein, Mill, Ellicott, Keil, Wordsworth, Norton.

2. That they were the sons of Joseph by an earlier marriage, is held by the Greeks in general. So also by Thiersch, Westcott, Bp. Lightfoot, Salmon.

3. That they were the sons of Joseph and Mary is held by the large majority of Protestants. So Neander, Greswell, Meyer, Winer, Alford, Wieseler, Stier, Schaff, Ewald, Edersheim, Farrar, Godet, Weiss, Caspari, Beyschlag.

See, upon this subject, *Das Verhältniss des Jacobus, Bruders des Herrn, zu Jacobus Alphäi, von Philipp Schaf,* 1842, Stier. Der Brief Juda; Wieseler, in Stud. u. Krit. 1842; Mill, Mythical Interpretation, 219; Bp. Lightfoot, Galatians, Diss. ii., "The Brethren of the Lord," 241; Greswell, ii. 108; Lichtenstein, 100. See also the several Bible Dictionaries: Winer, i. 525; Smith, i. 231 and 920; Riehm, 663; Herzog, vi. 409; Schenkel, i. 482; McClintock and Strong.

PART II.

THE DIVISIONS OF THE LORD'S MINISTRY.

In order to understand the scope of the Lord's ministry in its external aspects, as narrated by the Evangelists, it is necessary to keep in mind certain great facts that gave it form and character. We shall thus be prepared to understand the significance of particular events, and to assign them their proper places in the history.

First, The Lord came to a nation in covenant with God — His elect people. He had chosen for them a land in which they might dwell apart from the nations, and in a wonderful manner had given them possession of it. He had given them laws and institutions, which, rightly used, should secure their highest national well-being. He had established His temple in their chief city, in which He revealed Himself in the Visible Glory, and which was appointed to be "a house of prayer for all nations." How highly they had been honored and blessed of God is seen from His words (Exod. xix. 5–6): "If ye will obey my voice indeed, and keep my Covenant, then ye shall be to me a peculiar treasure above all people, and ye shall be unto me a kingdom of priests and a holy nation." And from among them should the great Deliverer, the Seed of the woman, come. The Messiah should reign at Jerusalem, and from thence establish justice and judgment throughout the earth. He was to be of the tribe of Judah, of the family of David, and His birthplace at Bethlehem; and many other things respecting Him had been foretold by the prophets.

To a people thus in covenant with God, and awaiting the Messiah, Christ came. There was a general expectation that the long-promised King was about to come, and a general desire for His coming. The appearing of the Baptist, and his message, gave a new impulse to the common feeling, and doubtless, in the minds of many, changed what had been but an indefinite expectation into an assured hope. But how should the nation discern the Messiah when He came? Would there be such wonderful signs attending His birth that it would at once be known? or would His infancy and youth be passed in obscurity? How would His public career begin? What would be His acts as Messiah? Here was a large field for differences of opinion among the people, according to differences in spiritual character and discernment. But the great part of the nation, including most of the ecclesiastical rulers and teachers, seems to have had no doubt that He was to appear primarily, not as a religious reformer, but as a political leader and warrior, and that one of His first Messianic acts would be to cast off the Roman yoke and set the nation free. This done, He would proceed to restore the Mosaic institutions to their primitive purity, and fulfill the prediction that "out of Zion should go forth the law, and the word of the Lord from Jerusalem."

It is apparent that, thus mistaking the character and work of the Messiah, the very intensity of their desire for His coming would but the more certainly insure His rejection. They had formed conceptions of Him which Jesus could not realize. Their ideal Christ was not the Christ of the prophets. To be at once received by them, Jesus must act in a manner corresponding to their preconceived opinions, and thus fulfill their expectations. But this He could not do, since these expectations were based upon misconceptions of their own moral needs, and of God's purpose. They felt deeply their political servitude, but were unconscious of the spiritual bondage into which they had fallen. They knew not how utterly unprepared they were for the coming of their Deliverer, and that His first work would be to teach them what God demanded of them as His covenant people. Hence it was that Jesus could not openly assume the name of Messiah, because it had become the exponent of so many false hopes, and would have gathered around Him a body of followers moved more by political than spiritual impulses.

Second, the will of God that the Jews should receive His Son. Here, indeed, we meet the same problem that we meet everywhere in human history — the foreknowledge and purpose of God, and the freedom and responsibility of man. According to the eternal purpose of God, Christ was "the Lamb slain from the foundation of the world," and without the shedding of blood is no remission of sin. "Known unto God are all His works from the beginning of the world." But the Jews knew not of this purpose, although, as we now see, it was not dimly intimated in their sacrificial rites. The Jews knew not, nor would God have them know, that they would crucify their Messiah. They had not learned this from their prophets. The Baptist said nothing of His death; Jesus Himself, till near the close of His ministry, made no distinct mention of it; the Apostles, down to the week of His Passion, did not comprehend it. When therefore, Jesus presented Himself to the nation as the Messiah it acted without knowledge of the secret counsel of God, and with entire freedom. He desired that His people should receive Him. All that God had done for them from the days of Abraham, was with the intent that they should be a people ready for the Lord at His coming. The end of all the institutions He gave them, was so to develop faith and holiness in them that they should discern and receive His Son. And Jesus, during His ministry, gave them every possible proof of His divine mission, and reproved and warned and besought them, that He might save them from the guilt of His rejection; yet all in vain. "He came unto His own, and His own received Him not." How touching are His farewell words to Jerusalem (Matt. xxiii. 37): "How often would I have gathered thy children together, even as a hen gathereth her chickens under her wings, and ye would not."

Third, as the covenant of God with the Jews was a national one, so must also Christ's acceptance or rejection be. From the beginning of their history, God had dealt with the people as a corporate body. Their blessings were national blessings, their punishments national punishments. All their institutions, ecclesiastical and civil, were so devised as to deepen the feeling of national unity — one high priest, one temple, one altar, one royal family, one central city. What was done by the heads of the nation was regarded as the act of all, and involving common responsibility. Only in this way could the purpose of God, in their election to be His peculiar people, be carried out. Hence, in this greatest and highest act, the acceptance or rejection of His Son, the act must be a national one. It must be done in the name of the whole people by those who acted as their rightful representatives. If those who sat in Moses' seat should discern and receive Him, the way for the further prosecution of His work was at once opened, and under His Divine instruction the nation might be purified and made ready for the glorious kingdom, so often sung by the psalmists and foretold by the prophets. But if, on the other hand, He was rejected by the nation acting through its lawfully constituted heads, this national crime must be followed by national punishment. Individuals might be saved amid the general overthrow, but the people, as such, failing to fulfill God's purpose in their election, must be scattered abroad, and a new people be gathered out of all nations.

It was under the conditions imposed by these great historic facts that the Lord began His ministry among the Jews. He came to a people in covenant with God; a people that God desired to save, and that must, as a people, accept or reject Him. All the details that are given us of that ministry by the Evangelists must, therefore, be viewed in the light of these facts.

The first event that meets us in the evangelic narrative is the mission of John the Baptist, the forerunner of the Messiah. Had the chosen people been faithful to their covenant, no such work of preparation for their Messiah would have been necessary. As they were not faithful, God must prepare His way by announcing to them what He was about to do, and by calling them to repentance. John's work was threefold.

First, he was to announce that the kingdom of God was at hand, and the Messiah about to appear. In this announcement he especially displayed his prophetic character. To him it had been revealed that God would now fulfill His promises, and send the Redeemer of Israel.

Second, he was to bring the nation to repentance, and "make ready a people prepared for the Lord." Here he especially manifested himself as a preacher of righteousness. Of this righteousness the law was the standard, and by the law must the nation be judged. Hence, John was a preacher of the law. The burden of his message was, " Repent, for the kingdom of God is at hand." As a wicked, disobedient people, they were not ready for that kingdom. True, they were " Abraham's children," and "sons of the kingdom," but this did not suffice. They had broken the holy Covenant, they had not hearkened to God's voice, and He had punished them terribly in His anger in the destruction of their city and temple by the Babylonians, and their long subsequent bondage to the heathen nations. The Baptist came to awaken them to a sense of their guilt, to make them see how by their unbelief and sin they had frustrated the grace of God, and thus to move them to repentance. Comparing the promises of God with their fulfillment, they might see how little He had been able to bestow upon them, how little they had answered to the end for which He chose them. How glorious the promises, how melancholy the history ! Their national independence was gone; the covenant with the house of David was suspended, and the royal family had sunk into obscurity. Their high priest was appointed by the Roman governor for political ends, and was a mere tool in his hands; the priesthood, as a body, was venal and proud; the voice of prophecy had long been unheard, and for the teachings of inspiration were substituted the sophisms and wranglings of the rabbis; the law was made, in many of its vital points, of none effect by traditions; the nation was divided into contending sects; a large party, and that comprising some of the most rich, able, and influential, were infidels, open or secret; others, aspiring after a higher piety than the observance of the law could give, wholly ceased to observe it, and withdrew into the wilderness to follow some self-devised ascetic practices; still more were bigots in their reverence for the letter of the law, but wholly ignorant of its spirit, and bitter and intolerant toward all whom they had the power to oppress. The people at large still continued to glory in their theocratic institutions, in their temple,

6*

in their priesthood, and deemed themselves the only true wor-
shippers of God in the world.   They were unmindful that almost
everything that had constituted the peculiar glory of the theocracy
was lost by sin; that the Visible Glory that dwelt between the
cherubim had departed; that there was no more response by the
Urim and Thummim; that the ark, with its attendant memorials,
was no more to be found in the Holy of Holies; that all those
supernatural interpositions that had marked their early history
had ceased; in short, that the whole nation "was turned aside
like a deceitful bow."

To the anointed eye of the Baptist the unpreparedness of the
nation for the Messiah was apparent.   He saw how in it was
fulfilled the language of Isaiah: "The whole head is sick, and
the whole heart faint.   From the sole of the foot even unto the
head, there is no soundness in it, but wounds, and bruises, and
putrefying sores"; and he would, if it were possible, awake the
people to a sense of their real spiritual condition.   Unless this
were done, they could not receive the Messiah, and His coming
could be only to their condemnation and destruction.   Deliverance was possible only when, like their fathers in Egypt, they
became conscious of their bondage, and began to sigh and cry
for deliverance (Exod. ii. 23).

To awaken in the hearts of the Jews a deeper sense of their
sins and of the need of cleansing, John began his work of preaching and baptizing. He taught that this baptism was only preparatory, a baptism of repentance ; and that the higher baptism
of the Spirit they must still receive at the hands of the Messiah
Himself, who was speedily to come.   All whom he baptized
came confessing their sins   Thus, the extent of his baptism was
an index how general was the repentance of the people, and on
their repentance rested all further preparation for the Messiah.

Third, John was to point out the Messiah personally to the
nation, when He should appear.   This was the culminating
point of his ministry, and would naturally come near the close
of the preparatory work.

Let us, now, survey for a moment the Baptist's ministry as
narrated by the Evangelists, and see how far its purpose was
accomplished. First, he aroused general attention to the fact

that the Messiah was at hand.   Second, his preaching brought great numbers to repentance.   Multitudes from every part of the land came to his baptism.   But of these it is probable that many did not understand the significance of the rite, or truly repent of their sins.   Perhaps with comparatively few was the baptism with water a true preparation for the baptism with the Holy Ghost. And it is to be specially noted that those thus coming to John to be baptized were mostly, if not exclusively, of the common people, and not of the priests, or Levites, or members of the hierarchical party.   Many of the Pharisees and Sadducees came to be spectators of the rite, but only with hostile intent; or if some received baptism at his hands, we find few or no traces of them in the subsequent history (Matt. iii 7; Luke vii. 29–30). In the hearts of those who sat in Moses' seat, the spiritual rulers and guides of the nation, no permanent sense of sin was awakened, and they could not submit to a baptism of which they felt no need.   To all his exhortations they had the ready and, as they deemed, sufficient reply, "We have Abraham to our father."   Thus John did not effect national repentance.   The highest proof of this is seen in the Deputation that was sent him from Jerusalem to ask him who he was, and by what authority he acted (John i. 19–27).   It is plain from the narrative that he was wholly unable to satisfy the Jewish leaders that he was divinely commissioned, or that his baptism had any validity.   It followed, of course, that they paid no heed to his prophetic or personal testimony to the Messiah.

As his chief official act, he pointed out Jesus in person to the nation represented in the Deputation that came to him from Jerusalem as the Messiah.   He whom he had foretold was come.   Henceforth they must see and hear Him.

Turning now to the ministry of the Lord, let us consider it in its relations to that of the Baptist, and as under those historic conditions that have been already mentioned.   Having been publicly witnessed to by the Baptist, His first work was to present Himself to the Jews as their Messiah, in whom the covenants of God with Abraham and David should find their fulfillment, and all the predictions of the prophets be accomplished.   He did not, indeed, assert in so many words that He was the Messiah, but left them to infer from His words and works who He was. They must now seek Him out, and learn from His own lips what were his Messianic claims, as did the two disciples at Bethabara. Of His Divine Mission He must give proof, first and chiefly, by His words, which should show Him to be sent of God, an inspired teacher and prophet; and second, by His works, which should show Him to be the Power of God. All the scriptural expectations created by the announcement of John were to be realized in Him. As the elders of the people gathered themselves together unto Moses (Exod. iv. 29), and co-operated with him in the work of their deliverance, so now must the priests and Levites, and all who by God's appointment held any office among the people, be co-workers with Jesus. In this way only was it possible that the promises of the Covenant could take effect, and the predictions of the prophets be fulfilled. Thus presenting Himself to the people, and especially to its ecclesiastical rulers, and having shown by the evidence of His own works and words, corresponding to the testimony of the Baptist, that He was the Messiah, He must await the action of the nation.

The obstacles that stood in the way of His acceptance are obvious. The nation was morally unprepared for Him. While so many were looking for Him, few were looking for Him in such a guise. To say nothing of the obscurity in which He had hitherto lived, and of His supposed birth at Nazareth, His present conduct in no degree corresponded to their expectations. His first public manifestation of Himself in the cleansing of the temple displeased the priests, for it was a sharp rebuke to them. Nor did He make friends with the Pharisees, who doubtless believed that, when the Messiah appeared, He would first of all seek them out, and make an alliance with them; but they saw no such movement on His part, and those who for a time might have been friendly to Him, soon turned away. The common people judged Him more favorably. His wisdom and eloquence could not be questioned, nor the fact that He wrought miracles; but all this did not suffice. He might be a teacher sent from God, or a prophet, but the Messiah must be much more than this. He might perhaps be, as John declared himself to be, a forerunner of the Messiah. A few, mostly or wholly from the ranks of John's disciples, at once received Him as the Messiah, but, as afterward appeared, with most imperfect conceptions of His person and work; the people at large, and their rulers, discerned Him not. It is plain, from the account of Nicodemus (John iii. 1–2), that the presentation of Himself at Jerusalem, and His words and works there, had called forth no response from the ecclesiastical leaders. Even now their incredulity was shown in a demand for a sign, which He would not give.

Whatever hostility had manifested itself at this His first public appearing in Jerusalem, still there was hope that it might be removed by greater knowledge of His character and work. The Lord, therefore, still remaining in the province of Judæa, and thus directly under the eyes of the priests, and where they might easily visit Him, begins the work of baptizing. Many gather around Him, and receive baptism at the hands of His disciples. But it does not appear that any of the Pharisees, or of the higher and more influential classes, were among them, and still less any of the rulers. After a summer thus spent, His enemies endeavoring to sow dissensions between His disciples and those of John, He gives up His baptismal work, and retires into Galilee. Nearly a year had now passed since He had been pointed out as the Messiah to the nation, and yet very few had received Him as such ; and all who bore rule, or certainly most of them, manifested an increasing hostility. He had found no general, much less a national, reception.

After a few weeks spent in seclusion in Galilee, Jesus goes up the second time to Jerusalem to a feast, and heals the impotent man at the pool of Bethesda (John v.). The charge is at once made against Him that He had broken the Sabbath by this work of healing, and His defense, based upon His Divine Sonship, so offended the ruling party that His life was in danger. This open manifestation of hostility marks the first great turning-point in the Lord's ministry. It was now apparent that the rulers at Jerusalem would neither listen to His words, nor be convinced by His works. So far from recognizing in Him the Messiah, His acts were violations of the law, and His defense blasphemy. Henceforth, they stood to Him in an attitude of avowed hostility, and waited only for a sufficient pretext to arrest Him and put Him to death.   How far in this they represented the sentiment of the people at large, it is impossible for us to say, but it appears from the subsequent history, that although many came to Christ's baptism, yet He had not at any time a large body of adherents in Judæa.   So far as appears, the people there acquiesced in the decision of their rulers.

Forced to flee from Jerusalem, the Lord goes into Galilee. And now the second stage of His ministry begins.   His work in Galilee seems to have had a twofold purpose.   It was first directed to the gathering of disciples, such as hearing His words felt their truth, and seeing His works recognized in them a Divine power.   To Him, the true Light, all who loved the light would come.   Thus He gathered around Him the most receptive, the most spiritually minded from every rank and class, and teaching them, as they were able to hear, the mysteries of His Person and of His kingdom, prepared them to be His witnesses unto the nation.   Through the testimony of a body of faithful disciples, the rulers at Jerusalem might yet be led to hearken to His words, and their own faith be quickened by the faith of others, and thus the nation be saved.   But if this were in vain, and neither the words of the Baptist, nor the teachings of Jesus Himself and His works, nor the testimony of the disciples, could convince them, these disciples would still serve as the foundation of that new and universal church which God would build if the Jews rejected His Son.   If, because of unbelief, the natural branches should be broken off and the heathen be grafted in, the Lord had those prepared in that body of followers who could serve Him as the builders and rulers of the new household of God.

Thus the gathering of disciples, while, on the one hand, it looked toward the acknowledgment by the nation of Christ's Messianic claims, and regarded such acknowledgment as still possible, yet, on the other, looked forward to the hour when He, whom the Jewish builders rejected, should be the corner-stone of a church, in whose blessings Jews and Gentiles should alike participate   Of this future service, the disciples themselves knew nothing, nor could they till Christ had ascended.   For the present, He would teach them such truth as immediately concerned Himself, His Person, and His work.   He must deliver them from the false and narrow notions in which they had been educated by their rabbis, and, so far as they had ears to hear, open to them the purpose of God as revealed in the Law and the Prophets.

Into the details of the Lord's work in Galilee, this is not the place to enter. Suffice it to say that He gathered many disciples, and that His fame spread throughout all the land. But the favor which was showed Him in Galilee did not propitiate His enemies at Jerusalem.   They very early sent spies to watch His movements, and in concert with the Pharisees, who were found in greater or less numbers in all the villages, they organized a systematic opposition to the progress of His work.   Everything was done to poison the mind of the people against Him as a transgressor of the law, and even as in alliance with evil spirits.   The fact that a large number believed in Him as the Messiah, was so far from proving to the ecclesiastical authorities the reality of His Messiahship, that it only stimulated them to new efforts for His destruction.   Thus, more and more, the hope that the nation, as represented in its rulers, could be brought to receive Him, faded away.   He sent forth the Twelve as His witnesses, but they were not heard.   His journey to the feast of Tabernacles and His reception at Jerusalem, showed in the plainest way that their hostility was undiminished (John, chs. vii.-x.). It was apparent to Him that the "Kingdom of God must be taken from them and given to a nation bringing forth the fruits thereof," and as preparatory to this, He began to teach His disciples of His approaching death, resurrection, ascension, and coming again.

The false conceptions entertained by the Jews respecting the person and work of the Messiah had to this time prevented the Lord from publicly assuming this title and proclaiming Himself the Son of David and rightful King of Israel.   He spoke of Himself habitually as the Son of Man.   But, as it became evident that His death was determined upon, He will not permit the nation to commit so great sin without the distinct knowledge of His Messiahship.   They shall not reject Him as a simple prophet, or as a forerunner of the Messiah, but as the Messiah Himself. In the third or last stage of His ministry, therefore, we shall find His Messianic claims made prominent, both in His own teachings and in the testimony of His disciples, who, to the number of seventy, were sent two and two before Him as He journeyed to Jerusalem. In this city only could He die, for this was the "the City of the Great King," and His death could not be by lawless violence, or in secret, but must be in the most public manner, and by a solemn and judicial act; and here He must announce Himself as the true King, the Son of David, the long-promised Deliverer. This He did when He entered the city, fulfilling the prophetic word, "Behold, thy King cometh, sitting on an ass's colt." He accepted, as rightfully belonging to Him, the homage of the multitude, who spread their garments and branches of palm trees in the way, and cried, "Hosanna to the Son of David." "Blessed is the King of Israel that cometh in the name of the Lord."

Thus, in the Lord's public life, we seem to find three stages distinctly marked. The first is that period extending from the first Passover (John ii. 13) to the feast when the impotent man was healed (John v. 1), and embracing about a year. It began with the purgation of the Temple, and ended with the attempt of the Jews to kill Him because He made Himself equal with God. During this time, His labors were confined mainly to Judæa. Near the close of this period, we may place the imprisonment of the Baptist. The second stage is that period following His return to Galilee immediately after the feast, and embraces the whole duration of His ministry there, or about a year and six months. This period may be divided into two, of which the death of the Baptist will serve as the dividing line. The third stage begins with His final departure from Galilee, and ends with His death at Jerusalem, and embraces five or six months. The peculiarities of these several stages of ministry will be noticed more in detail as each shall come before us.

If we put the beginning of the Lord's public ministry at the Passover when He cleansed the temple (John ii. 14), we have, between His baptism and this Passover, a period of about three months, in which the following events occurred: the baptism;

the temptation; John's witness to the Deputation; the departure of Jesus with some disciples to Cana; His first miracle; He goes down to Capernaum; He goes up to Jerusalem to the feast. This period may be regarded as preparatory to His manifestations of Himself at Jerusalem.

FROM THE BAPTISM OF JESUS TO THE FIRST PASSOVER OF HIS MINISTRY; OR FROM JANUARY TO APRIL, 780, 27 A. D.

In the fifteenth year of the reign of Tiberius Caesar, John LUKE iii. 1–18.
enters upon his work of preaching and baptizing. The peo- MATT. iii. 1–17.
ple throng to him from all parts of the land, whom he bap- MARK i. 4–11.
tizes, and to whom he bears witness of the coming Messiah.
After his ministry had continued several months, Jesus comes JOHN i. 32–34.
from Nazareth to the Jordan, and is baptized, and immedi- LUKE iii. 21–22.
ately the Holy Spirit descends upon Him.

The chronological questions connected with this date have been already discussed in the essay upon the time of the Lord's baptism. The only points that now demand our attention are those relating to the tetrarchy of Lysanias and to the respective offices of Annas and Caiaphas.

In connection with Lysanias and the tetrarchy of Abilene, we meet with some historical difficulties. It was formerly said by some critics that Luke had fallen into error, and referred to a Lysanias, who, according to Josephus, had long before died, as contemporary with Pilate and Antipas and Philip. The accuracy of the Evangelist is now generally admitted,[1] but a careful comparison of his statements with those of Josephus will show us why the name of a ruler is mentioned who did not rule in Palestine, or stand in any apparent connection with the Gospel history.

Let us sum up what we know of the elder Lysanias and his territories. He was the son of a Ptolemy, king of Chalchis or Chalcis, a city lying in Coelesyria, northwest of Damascus, and identified by Robinson with the present Anjar, where considerable ruins still exist (Josephus, War, i. 13. 1). Of the extent of his kingdom or the names of its provinces we have little knowledge. Lichtenstein (132) infers from a comparison of the statements of Josephus that, besides Chalcis, the kingdom embraced Trachonitis, Ituræa, and Batanæa (Wies., Beiträge, 199 ff.). This Lysanias succeeded to his father's throne, 714, was put to death by Antony at the instigation of Cleopatra about 720, and a part of his dominions given to her (Joseph., Antiq., xv. 4. 1). It is not clear what was done by Antony

---

[1] See Meyer *in loco*.   Schürer, I. ii. 338.

with the residue, but after his death it may have been restored by the Romans to the children of Lysanias, since it is said by Josephus (Antiq., xv. 10. 1) that one Zenodorus, — a relative and ruling over Trachonitis — farmed what was called "the house — οἰκία — of Lysanias"; but whether in the interests of that family or of the Romans, is not said. It seems clear that in this grant to Zenodorus Abila and its territory was not included; although, as lying between Chalcis and Damascus, it formerly belonged to the kingdom of Lysanias. (See Joseph., Antiq., xiii. 16. 3). Did Abila, after Antony's death, come under Herod's rule? This is said by Zumpt (298, note), who distinguishes between the city Abila and the province Abilene. But if so, it was not given by Herod to his sons; the view of others is more probable, that it was given again to the family of Lysanias.

The original dominions of Herod were much enlarged by gradual additions. From Zenodorus Augustus took away his principality of Trachonitis, and gave it to Herod; and after the death of Zenodorus he gave to him the region between Trachonitis and Galilee, and Paneas and the country around. (Joseph., Antiq., xv. 10. 3). In the division of Herod's territories among his sons (Joseph., Antiq., xvii. 8. 1), to Philip was given Gaulanitis, Trachonitis, and Paneas; but this tetrarchy was not co-extensive with the kingdom of the earlier Lysanias; the northern part of the latter must either have been under the immediate rule of the Romans, or under some tributary prince.

The existence of a tetrarchy under a Lysanias is several times mentioned by Josephus (Antiq., xviii. 6. 10; xix. 5. 1). The emperor Caligula, on his accession in 790, gave to Agrippa I., grandson of Herod the Great, the tetrarchy of Philip and the tetrarchy of Lysanias, the last probably now having no prince. When Claudius four years later became emperor, he confirmed the gift, and added to his territories all that his grandfather Herod had possessed — Judæa and Samaria; and out of his own territories he gave him Abila of Lysanias and all that lay at Mt. Libanus. To the same effect Josephus says (War, ii. 11. 5) that Claudius gave Agrippa the whole of his paternal dominions, and the district given by Augustus to Herod, Trachonitis and Auranitis, with the addition of another principality styled the kingdom of Lysanias. On his brother Herod he bestowed the kingdom of Chalcis.

The question before us is, does Josephus here refer to the kingdom of the elder Lysanias who died about 720, some twenty years before, or to a principality then existing, and under the rule of a Lysanias? There can hardly be a doubt that the last view is the true one. Of this Lysanias and his principality we have no direct information. It may have been that Abila with its territory, and perhaps also Chalcis, had remained under the family of Lysanias, or been restored to it after Antony's death; if it had then passed into the hands of Herod, it had been given up, after his death, to a Lysanias, probably a descendant of the earlier king. There is no good ground for identifying the original heritage of Lysanias with the tetrarchy spoken of by Josephus. The objection that historians make no mention of any Lysanias but the first, assumes the theory to be proved; and the other assumption, that Abilene, having once belonged to the kingdom of Lysanias, should ever after be called "Abilene of Lysanias," is most improbable, especially if we take it into account how rapidly those little kingdoms and principalities arose and passed away. Besides, why should Josephus speak of the "tetrarchy" of Lysanias if he referred to the older kingdom ?

After the death of Agrippa (797) his dominion was reduced to a Roman province, and annexed to Syria (Antiq., xix. 9. 2), but in 811 Claudius gave to his son, Agrippa II., the tetrarchy of Philip, with Abila, which had been in the tetrarchy of Lysanias. (Antiq., xx. 7. 1.) Thus for the second time this tetrarchy became a part of the Jewish territory; of its subsequent history nothing certain is known.

We find, thus, good ground to believe that at the time of which Luke speaks — the fifteenth year of Tiberius — there was a principality of Abilene of which a Lysanias was prince, and that the Evangelist, so far from being in error, shows himself well informed as to the political divisions of that earlier period. (In this agree, with some slight differences, such high historical authorities as Winer, Ewald, Zumpt, Wieseler, Schürer; of the commentators and harmonists, Meyer, Keil, Bleek, Lewin, Greswell, Godet; *contra*, Keim, Sevin.

Abila, from which the province of Abilene took its own name, is identified in Baedeker (490) with the village of Suk Wady Barada, on the river Barada, a few miles northwest of Damascus. The name is popularly derived from Abel, and tradition points out a hill where he was slain by Cain. This Abila is to be distinguished from the Abila of the Decapolis, southeast of the sea of Galilee. (For the last, see Qt. St., July, 1889.)

We can now see clearly the reason why Luke should have mentioned the fact, having apparently so little connection with Gospel history, that at the time when the Baptist appeared, this tetrarchy was under the rule of Lysanias. It was an allusion to a former well-known political division that had now ceased to exist, and was to his readers as distinct a mark of time as his mention of the tetrarchy of

Antipas or of Philip. This statement respecting Lysanias shows, when carefully examined, the accuracy of the Evangelist's information of the political history of his times, and should teach us to rely upon it even when unconfirmed by contemporaneous writers.[1]

Having mentioned the civil rulers, Luke proceeds to mention the ecclesiastical. "Annas and Caiaphas were the high-priests." "In the high-priesthood of Annas and Caiaphas," R. V.;[2] (see Acts iv. 6, "Annas the high priest, and Caiaphas.") Let us, therefore, consider the personal and official relations of these two men to each other.

Annas was made high-priest by Quirinius, the Roman governor of Syria, in 760, but was deposed by Gratus in 767 or 768. He was succeeded in office by Ismael, by his own son Eleazar, by Simon, and then by his son-in-law, Joseph Caiaphas. (John xviii. 13.)[3] The latter was appointed 778, and held the office till 790. Schürer (in Riehm) thinks him to have been appointed much earlier, in 771. Afterward, several other sons of Annas became high-priests, and one of them, named Ananus, was in power when James, brother of the Lord, was slain.[4]

It thus appears that, although Annas had been high-priest, yet Caiaphas was actually such when the Baptist appeared, and that he continued in office during all the public life of Christ. According to the Mosaic institutions there could be but one high-priest at a time. The office was hereditary, and was held for life. As was to be expected after the Jews had fallen under bondage to the heathen nations, the high-priests, though nominally independent, became tools in the hands of their masters, and this high dignity was transferred from one to another, both by Herod, who appointed seven, and by the Roman governors afterwards, as their political interests demanded. Hence, there were often living at the same time a number who had filled this office, and been deposed. Probably other ex-high-priests besides Annas were now living, who were upon that ground, equally well entitled as himself to the name. That he should be distinctively so called in the passage before us, does not then seem sufficiently explained by the fact that he had been high-priest some years before,

---

[1] See, in reference to this point, Wieseler, 174; Lichtenstein, 130; Winer, i. 7; Robinson, iii. 482; that Luke mentions this tetrarchy because it had once been a part of the holy land, or to show "the political dissolution into which the theocracy had fallen,"—so Godet, Lewin, is not apparent.

[2] The reading, ἐπὶ ἀρχιερέως Ἄννα καὶ Καϊάφα, is now generally accepted. Tisch., W. and H.

[3] Matt. xxvi. 3; John xi. 49.

[4] Euseb. ii. 23. For list of high-priests, see Schürer ii. 1. 197.

and that he still retained the title among the people at large. Some ascribe the prominence given him to the fact that he stood high in popular estimation, and still exerted great influence; or that, as father-in-law of Caiaphas, he continued to direct public matters. Against this it may be said that Luke would scarcely have mentioned him in connection with the emperor, the governor, the tetrarchs, and the high-priest, unless he also was filling some high official position.

If, then, we conclude that Annas is not mentioned merely as an influential private person who had once been high-priest, what office did he fill? The word ἀρχιερεύς, high-priest, does not decide it, as it is itself of indefinite signification. It is applied in the New Testament to three classes of persons: first and properly, to the high-priest in office; second, to all who had filled the office; third, to their families, "the kindred of the high-priest" (Acts iv. 6). As to its use in Josephus, see Schürer, i. 204. This writer, in Stud. u. Krit., 1872, classifies opinions under two heads, and discusses the questions, what political position had the high-priest under Roman rule, and what the position of those who had been high-priests. As Annas was not the high-priest in office, did he fulfill any of its functions? Browne (71, note) thinks there may have been an interval of some months between the deposal of Simon and the elevation of Caiaphas, when Annas may have acted as high-priest. Hug (followed by Friedlieb)[1] supposes both Annas and Caiaphas to have held office at the same time, and to have officiated as high-priests in turn, one at one feast, and the other at the next; or, more probably, one during one year, and the other during the next. For this supposition there is no good ground, and it implies a tenure of office inconsistent with facts.[2] Others, therefore, make Annas to have been the *Nasi*, or president of the Sanhedrin; others, as Schürer, affirm, that this office was always filled by the high-priest; others make him the vice-president, the office of president belonging to the high-priest; others still suppose that he was the *sagan* or *vicarius* of the high-priest, "in his absence to oversee, or in his presence to assist in the oversight of the affairs of the temple and the service of the priests."[3] "The vicar of the high-priest, the next in dignity to him, and the vice-president of the Sanhedrin."[4] But the existence of such a deputy is doubtful;[5] and if Annas was the vicar of Caiaphas, why is he mentioned before him? Wieseler says that Annas was the head — *Nasi* — of the Sanhedrin, and Caiaphas of the temple

---

[1] Archäologie, 73. For like earlier opinions, see Nebe, Leidensgeschichte, 205.

[2] Josephus, Antiq., xviii. 2. 2.

[3] Lightfoot, ix. 38.   [4] Greswell, iii. 200.   [5] Winer, i. 507.

priests (Beiträge, 205); Caspari, that Annas having been high-priest
and *Nasi*, continued to fill the latter office.   Some, finally, as Alford,
referring to the fact that the Law directed the office to be held during
life, suppose that Luke speaks of Annas as the lawful high-priest,
one who, having held it, could not be legally deposed.   Meyer
thinks the Evangelist to have been ignorant who was the real high-
priest, and that therefore he erroneously ascribes this title to Annas.
Schürer (ii. 1) thinks that there is some inaccuracy in the Evangelist's
statements.

It seems from the manner in which Annas is mentioned, not only
by Luke but by John, that he did in fact hold some high official
position, and this probably in connection with the Sanhedrin, perhaps
as occasional president (so Keil).   It is said by Edersheim, i. 264:
"Deprived of the Pontificate, he still continued to preside over the
Sanhedrin."   This point will be further examined when we consider the part he took in the trial of the Lord.   That, in times of
such general confusion, when the laws of Moses respecting the high-
priesthood were very little regarded, and offices became important
according to the political capacity of those that filled them, the exact
relations of Annas and Caiaphas to each other can be determined, is
not to be expected.   A like difficulty seems to exist in explaining the
relations of Ananus and Jesus, mentioned by Josephus (War, iv. 3. 9).

We may, at this point, properly consider the political and other
changes from the Lord's birth to the beginning of his ministry (750
to 780) a period of about thirty years.   This period was not so full of
political excitement as that preceding it under Herod's rule, yet was
by no means uneventful.

Herod the Great left four sons who are mentioned by the Evangelists: Archelaus and Antipas, sons of Malthace; Philip (the Tetrarch,
Luke iii. 1), son of Cleopatra; and Herod (called Philip, Matt.
xiv. 3), son of Mariamne, the daughter of the high-priest Simon.
(Some disputed points in regard to this Herod will be later considered.   Joseph., War, i. 28. 4.) Herod, by his last will, divided his
dominions among the three — Archelaus, Antipas, and Philip — subject, however, to the approval of Augustus. (Joseph., Antiq., xvii. 8.
1.)   Augustus confirmed it in substance, but gave to Archelaus only
one-half of his father's dominions — Idumæa, Judæa, Samaria — with
the title of Ethnarch; and the other half he divided between Antipas
and Philip, giving to the former Galilee and Peræa, and to the latter Batanæa, Auranitis, Trachonitis, and a part of the domains of
Zenodorus. (Antiq., xvii. 11. 4.)

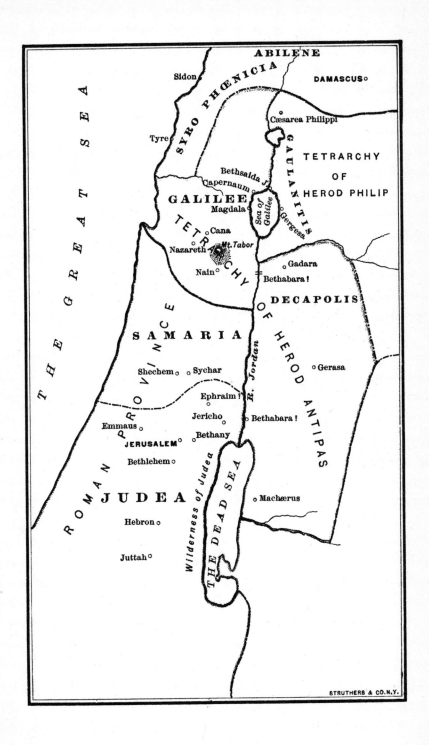

Archelaus, who from the first was hated by the Jews, and who treated them with great cruelty, was in the tenth year of his reign accused by them before the Emperor, who deposed him and banished him to Gaul. Judæa was then — 760 — united to Syria, and put under the authority of the Syrian governor, but under the more immediate rule of a procurator sent from Rome. (Joseph., War, ii. 8. 1.) Morrison, 121, says that "Augustus decided to form the territories of Archelaus into an independent province of the second rank."

Thus Judæa became a Roman province in the Lord's early youth, and continued such till after His death. Five procurators followed one another, the last being Pontius Pilate (779–789), their usual residence being at Cæsarea, not in Jerusalem. When at Jerusalem at the feasts, they occupied the palace of Herod (Schürer and many, but others, the tower of Antonia). Under the first governor of Syria after Judæa was annexed to it, Cyrenius, took place the taxing mentioned in Acts v. 37, (Antiq., xvii. 1. 11), when Judas, the Galilaean or Gaulonite, made an insurrection which terminated in his defeat and death, 760. This insurrection was probably confined to Judæa, since the taxing (Acts v. 37) took effect there only, and not in Galilee then under the rule of Antipas. After the suppression of this insurrection, there seems to have been comparative peace in Judæa until the administration of Pilate, of which we shall speak later.

Herod Antipas (Herod Antipas is never called Antipas in the Gospels, only Herod; Philip is called Philip only) began to reign over Galilee and Peræa in 750, and reigned till he was deposed in 792. Under his administration, Galilee and Peræa were in comparative quiet. Like his father, he was fond of building. He made Sepphoris, lying only four or five miles from Nazareth, the metropolis of the country, and fortified it. He also built anew Livias or Julias, the old Betharamtha, on the north end of the Dead Sea; and later, he built Tiberias on the Sea of Galilee. (Joseph., Antiq., xxiii. 2. 1; Life, vii. 81; War, i. 3. 4.)

Herod Philip is generally regarded as the best of the Herods, and ruled peacefully till his death, 787. He built Cæsarea Philippi (Matt. xvi. 13), and also enlarged the village Bethsaida on the east bank of the lake. Here he built a mausoleum, in which he was buried. The larger part of the people of his tetrarchy were heathen of various races.

As in Palestine there was but little change after Judæa became a Roman province, so in the Roman Empire at large there was nothing affecting Jewish affairs; the death of Augustus, 767, and the succession of Tiberius making no change in the general political administration.

But if the times after the suppression of the insurrection of Judas were comparatively uneventful, the minds of the Jews were by no means at rest. The death of Judas and dispersion of his followers did by no means extinguish the theocratic idea which controlled them. More and more it became the popular belief, that, as the covenant people of God, their duty to their Divine King forbade submission to the Roman Emperor. As His elect, they might confidently count on His help in a contest with Rome, and they might hopefully look for the fulfillment of His promise to send the Messiah, who would be their leader. This smouldering fire slowly extended, becoming more and more intense, but did not burst into a flame till a few years after the death of the Lord. An observant eye could, however, see that the theocratic idea was pervading more and more the masses of the people, and that a struggle with Roman domination must soon come, a struggle unto death.

But besides the more advanced who were watching to cast off the Roman yoke at the first moment, the conception of the Theocracy, the making the will of God supreme, undoubtedly strengthened itself among the great party of the Pharisees. This was seen in the importance attached to the observance of the law, even in its minutest details. As the expression of the Divine will, it must be obeyed, even to the loss of property and life. Of this punctilious observance there are many examples in the Evangelists, but the most striking illustration is seen in the refusal for a time of the Jewish warriors to fight on the Sabbath, even in self-defense. (Joseph., Antiq., xii. 6. 2.)

But, curiously enough, with many of the Pharisees, on the other hand, this high regard for the law made them indifferent to their political bondage. The observance of the law, they said, was the one great thing, and this observance being possible under the Roman yoke, there was no sufficient ground for rebelling.

The Herodians, who supported the pretensions of the Herods to reign, were few in number, but of considerable political importance. It is said by Tertullian, (Praescrip. 45,) that they claimed Herod to be the Christ: *Christum Herodem esse dixerunt.*

There was also a more important body, both in numbers, in rank, and in wealth, embracing the chief priests and their families, and many members of the Sanhedrin, who, for the most part, cared little for the Pharisaic traditions; and if they believed in any special covenant relation of the Jews to God, were little influenced by any Messianic hopes. These, for the most part, found it for their personal advantage to uphold the Roman authority, and discountenanced anything that tended to cause an insurrection (John xi. 47, ff.). To these may be added the very few who, seeing in their subjection to Rome a just punishment of the national sins, refused to take into their own hands the work of liberation, but waited patiently for the liberating hand of God.

Such, in brief, being the political and religious condition of the land, and so great the divisions of sentiment among the people, we see that there was much when the Lord began His ministry to agitate and excite the popular mind. It was no period of mental stagnation, or of religious repose. Doubtless, all thoughtful men saw that the political quiet then existing could not long continue. The antagonisms of every kind were every day becoming more plain, more pronounced. And what shall we say of the Lord during these years? Was He not from His youth up a careful and deeply interested observer of these tendencies? Did He not watch all that passed, and compare events with the revealed purpose of God; and especially with the prophecies respecting the Messiah and His kingdom? We cannot doubt this. He was well acquainted with the current Messianic conceptions and the popular expectations, and saw clearly how deeply rooted was the hatred of the Roman yoke; nor was the worthlessness of the Herods hidden from Him. Sepphoris, the chief city of Galilee, was close by Nazareth; and even if He never entered it, which is scarcely possible, He must have known what was going on at the court of Herod Antipas — the semi-heathenish vices and luxury that there prevailed. And He must have seen, in His yearly visits to the feast, how the temple of God was defiled by the covetousness and unholiness of many of the priests; and have discerned the hollowness of much of the current Pharisaic piety. Yet here and there He would discern not a few meek and poor in spirit, who were hungering and thirsting after righteousness, fearing God, and striving to walk in all His commandments and ordinances blameless.

The year during which John began his ministry was probably a Sabbatic year (Ex. xxiii. 11. According to Wieseler, Syn., 204, such a year was that from Tisri 779 to Tisri 780. Lewin, 60, reckons from Nisan to Nisan, but most agree with Wieseler. So Eders., McClellan. See Hamburger, i. 866. Greswell, ii. 235, makes 780–781 a Sabbatic year. He admits, however, that the received principles of the modern Jewish reckoning would require him to place it a year earlier.) If this year was then observed by the Jews according to its original intent, it was a most appropriate time for the Baptist to begin

7

his labors, the people having no burdensome agricultural tasks
to occupy them, and being thus at liberty to attend upon his
instructions.[1] It is said by Edersheim (*The Temple*, 160), that
"the Sabbatic year was strictly observed by the Jews in the
Lord's day."

It is not improbable that John may have begun his labors
as a preacher of the kingdom some time before he began to
baptize. Some instruction as to the nature of the rite, and some
exhortation to convince of its necessity, would naturally precede
its administration. It is said by Pressensé that the Baptist came
forth from the desert already attended by a band of hearers.
His preaching need not have been confined to the banks of the
Jordan, but may have begun in the wilderness, nor after he
began to baptize, did he remain in one place only (Luke iii. 3).
From the expression in Mark i. 4, "John did baptize in the
wilderness," some have inferred that he baptized before he
came to the Jordan. But the Jordan was included in the well
known designation "the wilderness." This desert, called in Matt
iii. 1 "the wilderness of Judæa," and which is mentioned in
Judges i. 16, seems to have comprised all the region between the
mountains of Judæa on the one side and the Dead Sea and
the lower parts of the Jordan on the other. According to
some, this wilderness of Judæa stretched along on the west side
of the Jordan from the end of the Dead Sea to Scythopolis.

The place where John baptized was Bethabara, or Bethany, on the
east side of Jordan (John i. 28). Two questions here arise: Where
was Bethabara? Was Jesus baptized there? But, first, we must
inquire as to the text. It is generally admitted that the most ancient
reading was Bethany, and that Bethabara found its way into the
text through Origen, who was told that there was a Bethabara on the
Jordan, but no Bethany. It has been suggested that the Bethabara
meant by Origen might have been the Beth-barah in Judges (vii. 24);
and some suppose that at different times the same place may have
had both names, or that one was the name of a district, and the
other of the village or ferry.[2]

[1] Ewald, Alterthümer, 414. As to the refusal of the Jews to fight on Sabbatic years,
see Joseph., Antiq., xiii. 8. 1. Caesar exempted them from tribute on the seventh year.
Joseph., Antiq., xiv. 10. 6. See Hamburger, i. 886.

[2] Accepting Bethany, are Tisch., W. and H. R. V.; *contra*, Stanley, 304, note. Βηθαβαρά
"house of crossing," "ferry house: Βηθανία "house of misery." See T. G. Lex.,
sub voce. But, according to some, *domus navis* or *domus transitus* — "a house of a
ship" or "of passage."

Assuming that Bethany is the right reading, where was it ? That the village of that name near Jerusalem is not meant, needs not be said; and there is no place of that name on the Jordan, east or west. In the absence of any mention of such a village, efforts have been made to find it in the province of Batanæa, on the east of Jordan. But some say that the province itself is meant. This province is mentioned by Josephus (Antiq., xviii. 4. 6; War, ii. 6. 3) as a part of Herod Philip's dominions. But where was Batanæa ? Raumer (405), supporting himself on the statement of Josephus (War, iii. 3. 5) that Gamalitis and Gaulanitis and Batanæa and Trachonitis belonged to Judæa, argues that there was a Judæa beyond Jordan (Josh. xix. 34: "Judah at Jordan toward the sunrising"), and that this extended from the source of the Jordan down to the middle or lower end of Galilee (see his map). Caspari (89), citing Raumer, accepts his reasoning, and finds a Judæa east of the Jordan within the limits of the ancient Gaulanitis, the modern Jaulan; and here, he says, we are to look for Bethany, the place of John's baptism. (See Conder, in Qt. St., 1877, 284). It was, according to him, in the large plain of El Batihah, on the northeastern side of the lake, the site now known as Et Tell, where Robinson and others place Bethsaida Julias. It was this "Judæa beyond Jordan" which is mentioned (Matt. xix. 1), and where Jesus went after the Feast of Dedication (John x. 40. See Caspari's map). But Conder (H. B., 315), thinks it pretty clear that Batanæa was a district southeast of the Sea of Galilee, and probably extended westward to the Jordan, and southward to Pella. And here, on the east bank of Jordan, we are to find Bethany or Bethabara, and here, a little north of Pella, he places it upon his map. On the other hand, Porter (H. B., 499) identifies Batanæa with a district east of the Lejah, and north of the range of Jebel Hauran, the old name being still retained among the natives. If this was its position, Bethania was far away from the Jordan. (See Bible Dic., *sub voce:* Riehm, art. Bashan.)

Thus it appears that we reach no definite result as to the site of Bethany by seeking it as a village in the province of Batanæa, or by identifying it with the province, since the position and limits of this province are in doubt.

No satisfactory result being obtained in this way, let us ask what we learn from the Gospels as to the places of John's baptism. Mention is made in them of two, Bethabara and Ænon. (The site of the latter will be considered later.) That John may have baptized at different points along the river, is not in itself improbable. The words of Luke iii. 3, "He came into all the country about Jordan, preaching the baptism of repentance," may be understood as embracing all the places of his activity, earlier and later. Such change of place has nothing against it.

It is intrinsically probable that the Baptist would seek a place for his baptism at or near some ford of the Jordan; and the narrative leads us to suppose that his baptismal work began in lower Peræa, not far from Jericho, since here was a convenient place for the people to gather from Judæa and Jerusalem, and also from Galilee (Keim, i. 494). Two chief roads lead from Jericho to the east of the river, — that to Heshbon southeast, and that to Ramoth Gilead northeast. If we choose between the fords on these two roads, it could not well have been the lower, as the depth of the water is too great, and it would have been too far south for those coming from Galilee; we must, therefore, take the upper ford opposite Beth-Nimrah — now Beit-Nimrim — where was an ancient ferry, and where recently a bridge has been built. Of course, crossing the river is possible in many places when the water is low, but John would naturally select a spot on some great line of travel, and so easily accessible to all. We think there can be little doubt that he began his baptism on the lower Jordan at a point near Jerusalem.

What light do we get upon this from tradition? As Joshua and the people crossed the Jordan "right against Jericho" (Joshua iii. 16), it was natural that the early Christians should put the Lord's baptism at the same place. This feeling is seen much later in Lightfoot, who says: "There is reason to believe that John was baptizing in the very place where the Israelites passed over, and that our Lord was baptized in the spot where the Ark rested on the bed of the river." But even if the places, as is probable, were not far apart, any identification of them is, of course, impossible. Tristram (B. P., 103) thinks that as "the principal ford was in ancient times opposite Beth-Nimrah, the passage under Joshua probably took place here, and here also Elijah probably passed " (2 Kings ii. 8). How early the Christian disciples began to baptize at the lower fords near Jericho we do not certainly know. It may have been as early as the second century. Jerome speaks of many that went there to be baptized — *plurimi e fratribus ibi renasci cupientes vitali gurgite baptizantur*. Antonius in the sixth century speaks of a wooden cross in the middle of the stream; and Arculf (700 A. D.) says: "A wooden cross stands in the Jordan on the spot where our Lord was baptized. A stone bridge raised on arches reaches from the bank of the river to the cross where people bathe. A little church stands on the brink of the water on the spot where our Lord is said to have laid his clothes when he entered the river. On the higher ground is a large monastery of monks and a church dedicated to St. John. (Early Travels, viii.) Willibald also, a little later, speaks "of a cross as standing in the middle of the river where is a small depth of water, and a rope is extended to it over the Jordan. At the feast of the Epiphany the infirm and sick come hither, and, holding by the rope, dip in the water." These accounts would seem to intim-ate that this was not a ford or place of regular crossing.

There are now the ruins of several monasteries on the west bank near Jericho. That known as the Jews' castle — Kusr El Yehudi — and which, according to Robinson (i. 445), existed before Justinian (518 A. D.), is believed to be that which was dedicated to St. John the Baptist. These ruins are about eight miles north from the Dead Sea, and a mile north of the confluence of the Wady Kelt. On the south side of the Kelt is the Haglah ford, and this was regarded in earlier times by both Greeks and Latins as the place of the Lord's baptism; but now they have their distinct bathing places some miles apart; that of the Greeks, near the Jews' castle, that of the Latins below, but Robinson and Thomson and others say that the Greeks bathed lower down. "The Greek pilgrims bathe at a spot where there is a vacant clearing down to the water's edge; the Latins' sacred place is higher up near the ruins of an old convent." (Pict. Pal., 165.) McGarvey (342) puts the Greek bathing place about four miles north of the Dead Sea near to the Helu ford, and here, he thinks, Jesus was baptized. He speaks of the ford opposite Jericho as an admirable place for bathing. (Baed., 266; N. Test. map of the P. E. F. See Lynch, 255; Ritter, Theil, xv. 536.)

But both the time and place of the pilgrim baptisms have been changed. Till the sixteenth century the pilgrims baptized at the Epiphany — the sixth of January, — after this at Easter; now the Greek pilgrims on the Monday after Easter. It is uncertain how early the Greeks and Latins began to have separate bathing places.

But if it be admitted that the Lord was baptized, as most hold, on the lower Jordan near Jericho, perhaps at the ford opposite Beit-Nimrim, this does not identify it with Bethabara or Bethany, for the Baptist may have changed the place of his baptism before the Lord returned from the temptation. There are three views that may be taken of the matter: 1. That Bethabara was near Jericho, and that He was baptized there, and that He found John still there on return-ing from the wilderness. 2. That Bethabara was higher up on the Jordan, perhaps at the ford Damieh, or still higher at Succoth, or higher still near Bethshean, or at Abarah, or even above the entrance of the river into the Sea of Galilee; and that from this point He departed into the wilderness. Both these views assume that Bethabara, wherever it may have been, was the place of His baptism, and that to it He returned after His temptation. 3. That Bethabara was not His baptismal place; He was baptized, perhaps, near Jericho, and thence went into the wilderness; but before He returned from the temptation, John had left that place and gone to Bethabara, and that Jesus went to him there.

1. The first of these views, that Bethabara was on the lower Jordan near Jericho, is that most generally held; the chief objection brought against it is, that the distance from it to Cana of Galilee is too great. It is said that the Lord must have gone from there to Cana in one day, which He could not have done. (See John i. 43; ii. 1. So Caspari, Conder, and others.) But as we shall see in our examination of the passage, there is no good ground to say that the journey was made in one day.

2. The second of these views, that Bethabara was higher up on the Jordan, has often been presented. Thomson thinks that to put Bethabara at the ford of Damieh some twenty miles above Jericho is not too far north to accord with the narrative. Merrill (198) speaks of a good ferry here, and on the east bank a Bethabara or "house belonging to the ford." According to Stanley, it was the ford near Succoth, which is some ten miles above Damieh. (Gen. xxxiii. 17; Judges viii. 4, 5.) Caspari puts it on the east side of the Jordan just above its entrance into the Sea of Galilee.

3. The third view, that the Lord was baptized near Jericho, but that John soon after moved up the river to Bethabara or Bethany, and was there when Jesus returned from the wilderness, was long since presented by Lightfoot. He says: "Let us place the Bethabara we are seeking for on the further side of Jordan in the Scythopolitan Country." But he holds that Jesus was not baptized here. His baptism was at "at the passage at Jericho," and after this John baptized at the passage at Scythopolis. On his map of Canaan, Bethabara is put on the east side, between the Sea of Galilee and Lake Merom. Conder (Qt. St., 1878, 120) takes the same general view, holding that the Lord's baptism was near Jericho, but that John soon after went some fifty miles higher up the river, and baptized at a ford which now bears the name Abarah, and is a little above Beisan or Scythopolis. With Conder Edersheim (i. 278) agrees, and thinks that the Baptist at this point had reached the most northern point of his mission journey. From this ford to Nazareth is little more than twenty miles.

There is nothing which enables us to say positively that John, after the baptism of Jesus and during the period of the forty days of the temptation, did not leave the neighborhood of Jericho and go higher up the river, but there is nothing in the narrative to indicate this; and the language, "where John was — ἦν — at the first baptizing" (John x. 40, R. V.), rather implies permanence; "He was employed in baptizing" (Meyer). But that he may have baptized at different points along the river is very probable, and is intimated by "first," his later baptismal work having been carried on in other places. McGarvey (515), who made particular examinations as to this point, found many places where John might have baptized at ordinary stages of the water; and Conder speaks of some forty fords which he visited. The words of Luke (iii. 3), "He came into all the country about Jordan," are understood by Ebrard (313) to embrace all the places of John's baptismal labors, earlier and later. Ffoulkes (Smith's B. D., i. 1127) supposes John to have baptized at three distinct fords of the Jordan: first, at the lower ford near Jericho, to which the people of Judæa and Jerusalem would naturally come; second, higher up the river at Bethabara, to which the people of Galilee and the northern parts of the land came, and where Jesus was baptized; third, still higher up at Ænon, a ford less frequented, but where was abundance of water. (Of Ænon we shall speak later.)

Was Bethabara the place where John began to baptize? This has been inferred from John x. 40: "The Lord went away again beyond Jordan to the place where John at first baptized." "Where John was at the first baptizing " (R. V.). This is read by Meyer: "Where John was when he baptized for the first time"; i. e., he began his baptism there. If this be the right understanding of the words, Bethabara was in or near the wilderness of Judæa, and this would disprove the assertion that the site of Bethabara could have been above the Sea of Galilee, or a little way below.

The time of baptism in the Jordan, as affected by the rain and heat, has already been considered in the chronological discussion. We may notice here an objection of Caspari's (112) to John's baptizing in the lower Jordan, on the ground that it was unclean for purposes of lustration, and that he would have incurred the censure of the Pharisees and Sanhedrists. But this rests on very slender Rabinnical authority, and is not even mentioned by Hamburger or Neubauer in their articles on the Jordan. It is said by others that the Jordan takes its name only after it leaves the Sea of Galilee. (See Neubauer, 30.) Reland (273) notices the distinction of major and minor Jordan, and makes Lake Merom the point of divison.

The recognition of Jesus as the Messiah when He came to be baptized, is to be explained, not by the fact of prior acquaintance, for such acquaintance is by no means certain,[1] but by the immediate revelation of God, and through an appointed sign. John knew the nature of his own mission as the herald of the Messiah, but he did not know who the Messiah was, or when He would appear. The mark by which he should recognize Him was one to be given at a fitting time, the supernatural descent of the Spirit upon Him (John i. 33). How far John may have had knowledge of the events connected with Jesus' birth, or been brought into personal intercourse with Him, does not appear (Ebrard, 258). Assuming such knowledge on the ground of the intimacy of the two mothers, Elisabeth and Mary, the words of the Baptist (John i. 31), "I knew Him not," are said by some to be in contradiction to the statements in Luke i. 26 ff. If these mothers were so closely brought together, they ask, must not their children, as they grew up, have known through them of one another, and of the supernatural actings of God, and of the prophetic words spoken of them? Thus, Alford says: "From the nature of John's relationship to the Lord, it follows that John could not but know those events which had accompanied His birth." And would they not only have had friendly relations but also personal acquaintance? (Such acquaintance is affirmed by some, Hales, Townsend; *contra*, Ebrard, 319.) But we are to remember here that the purposes of God in these children, as made known to their parents, were something far too high and sacred to be made known by them to others without His direction. He who is admitted to the divine counsels knows that God has a fitting time for speech and a time for silence; and that those whom He takes to be workers together with Him must wait His bidding. What Zacharias and Elisabeth may have told John of the wondrous events connected with his birth, and of his calling to be the forerunner of the Messiah, we do not know; but there is every reason to believe that they said nothing. They knew that he must be prepared for his work by the spirit of God teaching him, and that the knowledge of his future mission could not be prematurely given

[1] Ewald, v. 162; Ellicott, 107, note; Eders., i. 282.

him. This is also true of the Lord. We are told that "His mother kept these things, and pondered them in her heart." It was not hers to make His heavenly descent known even to Himself, nor to anticipate God in His revelation of Him to men by untimely disclosures, but to give Him such an education in the ways of God as was possible for her, and to wait quietly till the Holy Spirit should awaken in Him the consciousness of His mission, and indicate that the time for His Messianic work had come.

It is not, therefore, necessary to believe that either Jesus or John knew of the high calling of the other, or even that they had any personal acquaintance. Their homes were far removed, one dwelling in Galilee, and one in Southern Judæa. They may have met, but we have no proof of it. We, therefore, find no contradiction between John's words (Matt. iii. 14), "I have need to be baptized of Thee, and comest Thou to me?" and his words (John i. 34), "I saw, and bare record that this is the Son of God." The knowledge that John had of Jesus before His baptism was not as the Messiah, but as a holy man, and one not to be classed among those whom he came to call to repentance. This knowledge of Him he may have obtained by a previous knowledge of His holy life, by the absence of any confession of personal sin at His baptism, or by a spiritual perception of His holy character given him at the time. (Pressensé, 221, "By a divine intuition.") After His baptism, when John saw the Spirit descending upon Him — the divinely appointed sign, — he "bare record that this is the Son of God."

We may well believe that when Jesus came to be baptized, His whole appearance, His demeanor and language, so manifested His exalted character to the discerning eye of the Baptist illumined by the Spirit, that he had an immediate presentiment who He was, and could say to Him: "I have need to be baptized of Thee." Such supernatural discernment of character was sometimes given to the old prophets. So Samuel discerned the future king in Saul, and afterward in David. (1 Sam. ix. 17; xvi. 12. Compare also Luke i. 41, when John, yet a babe in his mother's womb, leaps for joy at the salutation of the Virgin Mary.) Still it was not till John had seen the appointed sign,

7*

the descent of the Spirit, that he could bear witness to Jesus as the Messiah.[1]

The placing of the Lord's baptism, not at the beginning but during or at the end of His Judæan ministry,[2] is wholly arbitrary.

Some have inferred from Luke iii. 21, that the descent of the Spirit was in the presence of the multitude, and visible to all.[3] But we should rather say, with Edersheim, that Jesus and John were alone, or, if not alone, that the vision was to John only. It was a sign peculiar to him, for he was to bear witness to others who should receive his witness. And thus he says (John i. 32–34), "I saw the Spirit" — "And I saw, and bare record that this is the Son of God." Others were to believe, not because they saw, but because he bare record.

JANUARY — FEBRUARY, 780. A. D. 27.

Immediately after His baptism Jesus is led by the Spirit MATT. iv. 1–11. into the wilderness to be tempted of the devil, and continues MARK i. 12, 13. there forty days. After the temptations are ended He re- LUKE iv. 1–13. turns to the Jordan. Just before His return, John is JOHN i. 19–28. visited by a Deputation of priests and Levites from Jerusalem, to inquire who he is, and by what authority he baptizes. In reply, he announces himself as the forerunner of the Messiah. The next day he sees Jesus coming to him, and bears witness to Him as the Lamb of God. The day following JOHN i. 29–37. he repeats this testimony to his disciples. Two of them fol- low Him to His home, and, joined by others soon after, go with Him to Galilee.   JOHN i. 38–51.

Whether the Baptist remained during the forty days of the temptation in the same place where the Lord was baptized, is in question, and has already been spoken of.

Matthew and Luke differ in the order of the three tempta- tions; but on internal grounds, which cannot here be given, that of Matthew is to be preferred.[4]

That Jesus returned at once from the wilderness to the Jor- dan is apparent from the whole order of the narrative. Wiese- ler, however (258), makes a period of 5–7 months to have inter-

---

[1] Meyer, *in loco*; Ebrard, 259.   [2] So Pilkington and Whiston.
[3] So Meyer.
[4] As to the relation of the fast to the temptations, see Greswell, ii. 206; Williams, Nativ., 244.

vened, during which nothing respecting Him is narrated. This is in the highest degree improbable.

The Synoptists do not mention the visit of the Deputation to the Baptist, nor does John mention the temptation, but it is generally agreed that the latter preceded the former.

The temptation seems to have followed immediately upon the baptism. The place of the Lord's temptation was in the wilderness of Judæa already spoken of, and cannot be more particularly desig-nated. Tradition points to a high mountain a little west of Jericho, overlooking the plain of the Jordan and beyond, as "the exceeding high mountain" from which the tempter showed the Lord all the kingdoms of the world. This mountain, in allusion to the forty days' fast, was called the Quarantana. Thomson says that "the side facing the plain is as perpendicular, and apparently as high, as the rock of Gibraltar, and upon the very summit are still visible the ruins of an ancient convent." Robinson speaks of it as "a perpendi-cular wall of rock, 1,200 or 1,500 feet above the plain." He does not think the name or tradition to be older than the crusades, the mountain being first mentioned by Saewulf about 1100 A. D., and its name a hundred years later. The place of the temptation was probably not very far distant from the place of His baptism; and those who put this higher up on the Jordan near the Sea of Galilee, must find the wilderness on the east or southeast of the sea. (See Ellicott, 106; Greswell, ii. 202; Edersheim, i. 300, note.) Stanley makes the scene of the temptation to have been on the eastern side of the Jordan among the "desert hills whence Moses had seen the view of all the kingdoms of Palestine"; Sepp also puts it on the eastern shores of the Dead Sea. But there is greater fitness if we find it on the western shores of that sea. As said by Pressensé (230): "Those denuded rocks, that reddened soil scorched by a burning sun, that sulphurous sea stretching like a shroud over the accursed cities, all this land of death, mute and motionless as the grave, formed a fitting scene for the decisive conflict for the Man of Sorrows."

The reputation of the Baptist seems now to have reached its culminating point, and attracted the attention of the Pharisees and ecclesiastical rulers at Jerusalem. So popular a religious reformer could no longer be left unnoticed; and accordingly, acting probably in an official manner as the Sanhedrin,[1] they

---

[1] So Meyer, Wieseler, Godet; *contra*, M. and M., Eders. Tholuck remarks that the Sanhedrin was "under special obligation to prevent the appearing of false prophets."

sent a Deputation of priests and Levites to ask him certain questions. As he denied that he was "the Christ," or "Elias," or "that prophet," his answers gave them no sufficient ground of accusation against him, however much they might have sought it. The next day he saw Jesus, apparently now returning from the temptation, and for the first time pointed Him out as He that should come after him, the Lamb of God, and the Baptizer with the Holy Ghost. This he could not have done till after the baptism, for after it was the sign given, and immediately after the descent of the Spirit Jesus departed into the wilderness. This was, therefore, the first opportunity of the Baptist to testify to Him personally as the Christ. His testimony to Jesus was, up to this time, general. He knew that one should come after him, but who, or when, he could not say; and this is the character of his witness, as given in the Synoptists. But after the baptism he could bear a definite witness. He had seen and recognized the Messiah by the divinely appointed sign, and could say, This is the man, He is come, He is personally present before you.

Let us consider the order of events. Two points are in dispute: Had the Lord been baptized and tempted at the time of the coming of the Deputation? Had He returned from the wilderness to the Jordan before their coming? Almost all put the baptism and the temptation before they came; but a few invert this order, on the ground that John's words (verse 27), "He coming after me, is preferred before me," must refer to the revelation of Jesus to John, including the testimony at His baptism; and this, therefore, must be put between verses 27–29. The Deputation came in the morning, and Jesus was baptized in the evening of the same day, and on the next day John bore his testimony to the people (verse 29 f. See Bäumlein, *in loco*). But the grounds on which this is affirmed are insufficient.

The second question is not so easily answered. Some say that the Lord returned to the Jordan before the Deputation came, on the ground that John's words (verse 26) "There standeth one among you whom ye know not," ("In the midst of you standeth one," R. V.) imply that, He was then among those who were listening to John's answer. "There He stood unknown and unrecognized amidst the throng." (M. and M., Godet, and others.) But it may be taken in a general sense to mean: He has already appeared; He is among you, the Jewish people. (So apparently, Meyer, Tholuck.)

This is a point which cannot be positively decided. The order of events may have been in one of the two following ways: 1. Baptism of Jesus. 2. His departure to the wilderness, temptation, and return. 3. Visit of the Deputation. 4. John's witness to it of Jesus (verses 19–27). In this case the question arises, Did Jesus hear this testimony, standing unknown among those there gathered ?

1. Baptism. 2. Departure into the wilderness, and temptation. 3. Coming of the Deputation, and John's testimony to it. 4. Return of Jesus on the next day.

The Baptist seems to have borne three distinct testimonies on three successive days: 1 (verses 19–27). To the Deputation ; whether this was in public and heard by all we do not know. 2 (verses 29–34). To whom this testimony was borne we are not told, some say, to the Deputation; some, to the miscellaneous crowd of the baptized; some, to a small circle of disciples. If it was to the Deputation, they must have taken note of the person of Jesus, and so been able to recognize Him again when He appeared to cleanse the temple.[1] 3 (verses 35–36). To the two disciples.

The question here arises, How was the Lord's baptism in point of time related to that of John's Galilæan disciples, Andrew, Simon, John ? Were they baptized before Him or after ? It is commonly supposed, before; if so, they must have been with John a considerable period ; and this would indicate that they took some part in his baptismal work. This is the view of Pressensé (218) that "they aided him in his ministry, and baptized the multitudes with him." It seems, however, not improbable that the Lord was baptized before them, and that they came to John afterward, during His absence in the wilderness. This finds some support in the fact that in the mention of the parts of the land from which people came to John's baptism, Galilee is not included. Matthew says (iii. 5), " Then went out to him Jerusalem and all Judæa, and all the region round about Jordan." Mark (i. 5), " All the land of Judæa and they of Jerusalem." Luke does not say from whence they came, but of the place of his ministry (iii. 3): "He came into all the country about Jordan." This silence about Galilee does not seem to be accidental. May it not indicate that the Lord was the first, or among the first, who came from that province ? and that His baptism was before that of John's Galilæan disciples? If so, the order of events would be as follows: Jesus comes and is baptized, and departs into the wilderness; Andrew, Peter, and others come from Galilee, and are baptized during

---

[1] As to the view of Origen that there were three different missions from Jerusalem, distinguished in verses 19, 21, 25, see Williams' *Nativity*, 264.

His absence; upon His return John points Him out to them, and they follow Him.

One of the two disciples to whom John pointed out Jesus as the "Lamb of God," was Andrew, and there is no doubt that the other was the Evangelist John himself; though with the reserve that characterizes him, he does not mention here or elsewhere in his gospel, his own name, or that of his brother, or of his mother.

"It was about the tenth hour" that the two disciples went with Jesus to His abode (verse 39). If we adopt the Jewish computation, which divides the period from sunrise to sunset into twelve hours, the tenth hour would be that from 3–4 P. M. (Winer, ii. 560). This, however, would leave but a brief space for their interview, and seems inconsistent with the statement that "they abode with Him that day." Some, therefore, refer this to the time when Andrew brought his brother Simon to Jesus (Licht., 153). All the day had the two disciples been with Him, and did not leave Him till the tenth hour. Others say, that the two going to Him late in the afternoon remained with Him during the night and the next day (Lightfoot). Many, not satisfied with these explanations, prefer the Roman computation from midnight, according to which the tenth hour would be from 9–10 A. M., and thus the disciples had the whole day for their interview. As the notes of time in John are important, his mode of computing the hours must be considered.

The beginning of a day may be counted from different points, from sunrise, from sunset, from noon, from midnight. The Jews computed their day from sunset to sunset, or from evening to evening — νυχθήμερον, — night-day, — and this period was divided into night, from sunset to sunrise, and day, from sunrise to sunset. (John xi. 9; Matthew xx. 3–6.) The Babylonians are said to have computed from sunrise to sunrise, and the Romans from midnight to midnight, as do we. Did the Jews in the Lord's day use this Roman mode? As is obvious, much confusion arises from the indefiniteness of terms. The term "day," when applied to mark the period of one revolution of the earth on its axis, is sufficiently definite, since a certain fixed point must be taken — sunrise, or noon, or other — as the beginning of the revolution. But the division of this day into twenty-four hours is artificial, and is said to have been taken by the Jews from the Babylonians during their captivity.

Besides this day of 24 hours there is the natural day from sunrise to sunset, which, being variable, the hours into which it is divided are correspondingly variable, the shortest being 49, and the longest 71 minutes in that latitude.

Having thus one term applied both to the period of 24 hours and to the period from sunrise to sunset, and the last being divided into 12 hours of variable length, confusion may easily arise as to the exact time of events.   The natural day regarded as the time of light is the time for human labor; but this period is not strictly defined by the moment of sunrise and sunset so that labor must then begin and then cease. In common usage, the term day would not be thus exactly defined, but would embrace the time of labor, be it longer or shorter.   Another element also comes in, which adds to the indefiniteness of the term. We connect night not only with darkness, but with sleep, and the day may be supposed to continue till the usual hour of sleep comes.

In the case before us, "the disciples went to Jesus about the tenth hour, and abode with Him that day."   If we accept the Jewish reckoning, that this tenth hour was from three to four in the afternoon, it does not, therefore, follow that they left Him just at sundown, when the day ended; they may have remained much later, and thus have had three or four hours for their interview.

The point is of interest only as regards John's gospel, as it is admitted that the Synoptists use the Jewish computation, and important here mainly as bearing on the time of the crucifixion (John xix. 14).   It is not easy to decide with any positiveness.   Those who advocate Roman time find that this best suits the various passages in which the hours are specified by this Evangelist.   (See the following: iv. 6, 52; xi. 9; xix. 1, 4, which will each be examined in their order.) It is said by Wieseler (Syn. 410 f.) that at Ephesus where John lived and wrote, the Roman mode of computation was in use.[1]   (So M. and M., *in loco*; McClellan, 741; but this is questioned by some.   See Farrar.)

Greswell (ii. 216) admits that the Jewish and Roman modes of computation were alike, the Romans reckoning the civil day from sunrise to sunset, but supposes John to have used the modern counting of the hours — from midnight to noon, and noon to midnight. (See, as to Roman usage, Becker's Gallus, 315; Pauly, Real Encyc., ii. 1017; Wies., Beiträge, 252.)

The finding of Simon (verse 41) by his brother Andrew, and his coming to Jesus, was upon the same day spoken of (verse 35). It is probable, from the form of expression, "He first findeth his own brother Simon," that as Andrew brought his brother Simon to the Lord, so John also brought his brother James.[2]

---

[1] For the Roman computation, Ewald, 248, note 2 ; Westcott, Eders., i. 346, note 5 : M. and M., Ebrard, 339 ; Tholuck; for the Jewish, Meyer, Rob., Godet, Alford, Caspari, Watkins, McClellan, Farrar.

[2] Meyer, Lichtenstein.

But Alford explains it as "implying that both disciples went together to seek Simon, but that Andrew found him first."

The next day (verse 43) Jesus departs to Galilee. There seems no good reason to doubt that He was accompanied by Simon and Andrew and John, who had recognized in Him the Messiah. Some, however, suppose that they remained with the Baptist, and did not join Jesus till a much later period.[1] This is intrinsically improbable. Whether Philip was called by the Lord before His departure, or upon His way, is doubtful.[2] Nor is it certain that the calling of Philip was founded upon a previous acquaintance with the Lord, though the term "find" implies this; it may have been through the agency of Simon and Andrew, who were of the same city (verse 44). Philip now brings to the Lord another disciple. Where he found Nathanael is not said, but most probably upon the journey.

FEBRUARY — APRIL, 780. A. D. 27.

Going to Cana of Galilee, the Lord at a marriage feast JOHN ii. 1-11. there changes water into wine. Afterwards, He goes down with His mother, and brethren, and disciples, to Capernaum, JOHN ii. 12, 13. but remains there only a few days as the Passover is at hand. From Capernaum He goes up to Jerusalem to attend this feast.

"And the third day there was a marriage" (verse 1). It is disputed from what point of time this third day is to be reckoned. Some would make it the third day after His arrival in Galilee;[3] others, as Alford, the third day from the calling of Nathanael, but one day intervening; and others, as Lange, identify it with the day last mentioned (verse 43). Blunt[4] supposes the Evangelist to have some event in his mind from which he dates, but which he does not mention. But most count from the day of the departure to Galilee (verse 43).[5]

The order of events may be thus given, John i. 19—ii. 1.

1st day. Visit of Deputation and John's testimony to them (verses 19-27).

---

[1] So author of " The Messiah," 73.

[2] For the former, Meyer, Alford ; for the latter, Tholuck, M. and M.

[3] So Friedlieb, Leben Jesu, 189; Trench, Mir., 83.

[4] Script. Coincidences, 261.

[5] So Robinson, Meyer, Lichtenstein, Ellicott, M. and M.

2d.   Jesus returns to John, who bears a second witness (verses 29-34).

3d.   The two disciples visit Jesus (verses 35-42).

4th.   He begins his journey to Cana (verse 43).

5th.   On the way.

6th.   On the way.   Reaches Cana.

7th.   At Cana.   The marriage (ii. 1).

We give the following variations:

Luthardt —

1st, 2d, and 3d days, same as before.

4th.   Simon brought to Him (verses 41–42).

5th.   Philip and Nathanael brought (verses 43-45).

6th.   Departs for Cana.

7th.   Arrives at Cana.

8th.   The marriage.

Thus the Lord's ministry begins as it ends, with seven days whose events are specifically mentioned.

Godet —

1st, 2d, and 3d days, as before.

4th.   Departs for Cana, meets Philip on the way (verse 43).

5th.   Meets Nathanael (verses 45-47).

6th.   Arrives at Cana.

7th.   The marriage.

Edersheim (i. 344) assumes that the marriage in Cana was of a maiden, not of a widow, and if so, that the marriage was on a Wednesday.   With this assumption, we have the following order of days:

1st, Thursday.   Visit of Deputation.

2d, Friday.   Jesus returns.

3d, Sabbath.   The two disciples meet **Him.**

4th, Sunday.   Departs for Cana.

5th, Monday.   On the way.

6th, Tuesday.   Reaches Cana.

7th, Wednesday.   The Marriage.

Caspari, (115,) counts " the third day," or day of the marriage, from the day when the two disciples visited Jesus (verse 35).   The next day He called Philip and Nathanael.   The third day He went to Cana, a distance, according to Caspari, of only twenty-two miles.   This supposes Bethabara to have been high up on the Jordan.

Whether the Lord passed through Nazareth on His way to Cana, depends upon the position of Cana; if at Kana el Jelil, He would reach Nazareth first.   Ewald supposes that the family of Joseph had at this time left Nazareth, and were already settled at Cana.[1]   But it seems conclusive against this that Philip should speak to Nathanael of Jesus as Jesus of Nazareth (John i. 45), and that Nathanael, who was of Cana, should know nothing of Him.   The mother of Jesus seems to have been intimate in the family where the wedding took place, from which it has been inferred that she was a relative of one of the parties.   One tradition makes Alpheus and Mary, the sister of the Lord's mother, to have resided at Cana, and the marriage to have been that of one of their sons.   According to Greswell, it was the marriage of Alpheus and Mary themselves.   Another tradition, current among the Mohammedans, and maintained by some in the Church, makes John the apostle to have been the bridegroom; another, that the bridegroom was Simon the Canaanite, the latter epithet being a designation of his residence, not of his party.   As no allusion is made to Joseph, the most obvious inference is that he was already dead.   From the fact that His disciples were invited with the Lord, it would appear that they were friends of the married pair, or that they were present as friends of Jesus.   It is not certain that all the disciples are here included; perhaps only Philip and Nathanael went with Him.[2] Some, however, find in the six water pots an allusion to the Lord and His five disciples.[3]

The marriage took place at "Cana of Galilee."   The name signifies, in Hebrew, a "place of reeds," and is used in the Old Testament as the name of a stream on the borders of Ephraim and Manasseh (Josh. xvi. 8), and of a city in Asher (Josh. xix. 28). With this city of Asher Greswell identifies the Cana of the Gospels. The addition "of Galilee" here seems designed to distinguish it from some other Cana.   There are now two Canas in Galilee; one, Kana el Jelil, north, and the other, Kefr Kenna, northeast of Nazareth, and it is disputed which is meant.   Robinson (ii. 347) shows that upon etymological grounds the former is to be' preferred, the present Arabic name Kana el Jelil being identical with Cana of Galilee, while Kefr Kenna "can only be twisted by force into a like shape."   He shows also that the former was by early tradition pointed out as the true site of the miracle, and that only since the sixteenth century, and for the convenience of monks and travellers, was the latter selected.   This view of Robinson has found much acceptance.[4]

---

[1] So Stanley, 359, note; Weiss.   [2] Trench, Mir., 84.   [3] See Luthardt, i. 77
[4] So Winer, Raumer, Ritter, Meyer, Porter, Van de Velde, Sepp. Socin.

De Saulcy, however (ii. 376), maintains the claims of Kefr Kenna, affirming that the present name of Kana el Jelil does not mean Cana of Galilee, but Cana the great, or illustrious. He also objects that this village is too far from Nazareth, and in the wrong direction, to answer to the narrative.[1] Stanley speaks of the claims of the two Canas as "being about equally balanced." Thomson speaks hesitatingly. Making inquiries, when in the neighborhood, of all he met, where the water was made wine, "with one consent they pointed to Kefr Kenna. Some of them knew of a ruin called Kanna on the north side of the great plain of Bŭttauf, but only one had ever heard of the word 'Jelil' as a part of the name, and from hesitancy with which this one admitted it, I was left in doubt whether he did not merely acquiesce in it at my suggestion. It is certain that very few, even of the Moslems, know the full name of Kana el Jelil; and yet I think Dr. Robinson has about settled the question in its favor." Osborne says that at Kefr Kenna he inquired its name of his guides and Arabs, who said it was also called Kenna el Jelil. Also one of the natives called it Jelil. He considered it, however, a new name, devised to preserve the character of the place as Cana of Galilee. It is said by Zeller (Qt. St., 1869, 71) that the name of Kana el Jelil is known only since Robinson's discovery; the Arabs know it only by the name of Khurbet Kana; and that the Christians of Palestine never doubted the identity of Kefr Kenna with the Cana of the Gospels. Some think "Galilee" was added by the Evangelist in order to lay stress upon the province. It was in Galilee, not in Judæa, where the miracle took place. (M. and M.)

Kana el Jelil lies 12 or 15 miles north of Nazareth, on the southern declivity of a hill that overlooks the plain El Bŭttauf. According to Robinson: "The situation is fine. It was once a considerable village of well-built houses, now deserted. Many of the dwellings are in ruins; we could discover no traces of antiquity." Thomson says that there is not now a habitable house in the village, though some of them may have been inhabited within the last fifty years. There are many ancient cisterns about it, and fragments of water-jars in abundance, not, however, of stone, but of baked earth. Not only is the village deserted, but the near neighborhood is so wild that it is the favorite hunting ground for the inhabitants of Kefr Kenna.

Kefr Kenna lies about 4 miles northeast of Nazareth, in a small valley upon the border of a plain. At the entrance of the village is a fountain made out of an ancient sarcophagus, which the inhabitants

---

[1] See Robinson's Reply, iii. 108, note. Ewald, Christus, 170, note, decides against De Saulcy

show as the fountain from which the water-pots were filled. A
Greek church is built upon the site of the miracle, but is a modern
structure. In this church are shown two enormous stone vases, as
two of the six water-pots. De Saulcy maintains that they are as old
as the period at which the miracle took place. There are some ruins
apparently ancient, and among them is shown the house of Simon the
Canaanite.

The village is thus described by a recent traveller (Prof. Stevens,
S. S. Times, Feb. 7, 1885): "From a broad ridge we descended into a
valley green with orchards and planted grain; and beyond it at the
foot of a long slope lies Kefr Kenna, where is a copious spring.
Groves of fruit trees fill in the foreground of the valley. Ruins that
bear the name Kenna are found a half mile or more to the northwest,
a still earlier site, it would seem, of the village."

The question has some importance from its bearing on the length
of the Lord's journey from Bethabara to Cana, and so on the position
of Bethabara. If the marriage was at Kana el Jelil, it would lengthen
the distance some eleven miles, or, according to Conder, some eight
miles, and make more time necessary than the narrative implies
(see Pict. Pal., 300). There is also no mention by the Evangelists of
the Lord's ever having been at Sepphoris, lying six miles south of Kana
el Jelil, through which He must often have passed had Cana been
there. The mention of Cana in Josephus (Life, 16; War, i. 17. 5),
points to Kefr Kenna, as Kana el Jelil would have been out of his way.
The question cannot be considered as finally settled, but the words of
Tristram have much force: "The modern name, Kana el Jelil, is
closer to the ancient; yet the proximity of Kefr Kenna to Nazareth,
and the fact of its being on the direct road between Nazareth and
Gennesareth, seem to me to far outweigh the claims of the northern and
more remote site." Many of the more recent explorers and writers
are disposed to accept Kefr Kenna as the Cana of the miracle. (So
Zeller, Tristram, Godet, Eders., Farrar, Dixon, see Qt. St. 1878, 67;
Qt. St. 1883, 43.)

The marriage festivities among the Jews usually continued
six or seven days, and it is not certain upon which of these
days the miracle was wrought, but probably toward the last.
At their expiration Jesus went with His mother and brethren
and disciples to Capernaum. The occasion of this journey is not
mentioned; probably, because He was invited by Peter and
Andrew, who seem now to have resided there. Wieseler (Syn.
169, note) thinks that the family had already left Nazareth, and

settled at Capernaum, or now did so. (So Tholuck, Ewald.) Friedlieb (191) suggests that, as the Passover was now not dis- tant, they might have desired to join a party of pilgrims going up to the feast from that city. Pressensé infers from Luke iv. 23, that He must have wrought some miracles there at this time, and Godet places at this time the miraculous draught of fishes, and the calling of the four disciples (Luke v. 1 ff.). But the fact that He did not remain there many days, is mentioned as indicating that His public ministry had not yet begun. There is no intimation that He taught, or made any public manifesta- tion of Himself while at Capernaum. Weiss (i. 386) says: "It is incomprehensible how, not only the beginning of Jesus' public ministry, but also the calling of the disciples, should be placed in these 'not many days.'" Almost all harmonists agree in this, that His public work in Galilee did not begin till a later period. Probably His time was spent in private intercourse with His disciples. Lightfoot (iii. 44), who makes four months to inter- vene between the temptation and the first Passover, supposes Him to have spent this interval in a " perambulation of Galilee." Of this there is no hint in the narrative. As the Passover drew nigh, He went up to Jerusalem. Whether the disciples accom- panied Him is not stated; but as they would naturally attend the feast, and as afterward they are found with Him (John ii. 22), we infer that they did so.

PART III.

THE JUDÆAN MINISTRY.

The cleansing of the Temple may be regarded as the first step in the Lord's Judæan work, the first public manifestation of Himself before the rulers and the people. All that He had done since His baptism to this time was in its nature preparatory; one miracle He had wrought at Cana, but it was in a small family circle, and there is no likelihood that it had been heard of at Jerusalem ; it was not for the people at large, but for His little body of believers.

It is ever to be kept in mind that the Lord was the Messiah, and it is this Messianic relation to the nation that determines the character of the first stage of His ministry. Had he come simply as a teacher or a prophet, He would not have waited for any national acceptance, but would, like the Baptist, have entered at once upon His work. But He came to do the work of the Messiah, not that of a simple teacher or prophet. The rulers were to recognize in Him the Son of David, the King, the Representative of God in His theocratic administration, whom all were to honor and obey (Matt. xxi. 37). Whether He knew, when He began His ministry, that the rulers would reject Him, we cannot say ; but even if this was known to Him, His first act must be to present Himself to them, that their feelings toward Him might be publicly expressed. Till this was done, and His rejection made morally certain, He could not begin His work of gathering disciples, and of separating them from the disbelieving with reference to the founding of His church. What was due at this stage, was to give sufficient proof by word and work that He was sent of God, their Messiah; then it was for the nation in its representatives to seek Him out, and be taught of Him how the purpose of God in Him was to be fulfilled.

That the rulers had the right, and, indeed, were in duty bound to demand proof of His Messianic claims, the Lord Himself declared (John v. 31). This proof was threefold. 1. The testimony of the Baptist (John v. 33). This was to the Deputation sent from Jerusalem to inquire as to his authority to institute such a rite, and what was the meaning of it ; and his answers to their questions could not leave them in doubt that he believed the Messiah to have already come.

2. The testimony of the Father from whom He received power to do His works (John v. 36). Thus Nicodemus said, "No man can do these miracles that thou doest, except God be with him."

3. The prophetic testimony given to Him in the Scriptures : "They are they which testify of me" (verse 39). To these may be added the truth of His words, the conformity of His teachings to all that God had revealed in the Law and the prophets.

The first public act of the Lord — the cleansing of the temple — was not so much in proof of His Messianic claims, as an assertion of them. It was an act that had a twofold bearing; on the one side it asserted His prerogative as the Son to preserve in purity the worship appointed of His Father, and on the other it was a severe rebuke to the priests and rulers. They had desecrated and defiled the holy House. He will reassert its sanctity and purify it. This act, done at the most solemn and generally attended of all the feasts, and before the assembled multitudes, did not leave any in ignorance that one had come with higher claims, at least, than belonged to a teacher, or even to a prophet.

The proof that He gave at this feast of His Divine mission was in the miracles which He wrought. "Many believed in His name when they saw the miracles which He did." (R. V., "signs.") It is not said of what nature were these signs, or how many; they were such as it pleased Him to give, and were sufficient to convince all willing to be convinced that He came from God, and to prepare them to hear His words of truth. But the faith begotten by the mere signs did not rest on that sense of spiritual need and perception of spiritual truth which alone give a solid and permanent basis of discipleship, and therefore He could not trust Himself to them (verses 23–25).

As none of the rulers or leaders acknowledge Him, or, perhaps, seek Him out, except the doubting Nicodemus, He leaves the city, and begins somewhere in the province the work of baptizing. This work He performed by the hands of His disciples. All this is in harmony with His position as one waiting for the recognition of the nation. In all that He does during this period, there is no act looking forward to the abrogation of the Mosaic institutions, and to the formation of a church on a new foundation. He does not, so far we know, go about preaching in the synagogues. He works no new miracles. Although assisted in His baptismal work by the few who early discerned in Him the Messiah, He seems to have organized no body of disciples, and to have done nothing that indicated a purpose to gather out a few from the nation at large. It was not for Him at this early stage to take any step that pointed to His rejection by the nation. It was the time of their trial, and their treatment of Him would indicate what His future acts should be. The whole Judæan ministry was an appeal to the people, and primarily to the rulers, to receive Him as the Messiah.

Passover, April 11–17, 780. A. D. 27.

At this feast Jesus with a scourge drives out of the temple the sellers of animals for sacrifice, and the money-changers. To the Jews, demanding His authority to do such things, He replies in a parable. During the feast He works miracles, which lead many to believe on Him. He is visited at night by Nicodemus, to whom he explains the nature of the new birth. Afterward He departs from Jerusalem into the land of Judæa, where He tarries with His disciples, and they baptize.

John ii. 14–22.

John ii. 23–25.
John iii. 1–21.
John iii. 22.

John iv. 2.

This Passover, according to Greswell and Lewin, was on the 9th April, to McClellan, the 10th. Friedlieb makes it to have been on the 11th. We follow the latter. If the Lord's baptism was, as we have supposed, early in January, between the baptism and the Passover was an interval of some three months.[1] The exact length of this interval depends, of course, upon the date of the baptism. With this Passover His public ministry may properly be said to begin.

This purification of the temple is plainly a different one to

---

[1] Paschale Chronicon, 76 days; Friedlieb, 87 days; Greswell, 64 days.

3

that mentioned by the Synoptists (Matt. xxi. 12–16; Mark xi. 15–19; Luke xix. 45–48). This occurred at the beginning, that at the end, of His ministry. The act, in all its essential outward features, must have been the same; but its significance varied with the time. The point of its repetition will be considered when the synoptical account comes before us. As now performed, it was a plain and open avowal of His Divine authority, and a public reproof of the wickedness of the priests and rulers who permitted His Father's house to be made a house of merchandise. Nothing could have brought Him more publicly before the ecclesiastical authorities and the multitudes who thronged to the feast, than this act, nor have shown more distinctly the nature and extent of His claims. Although He does not name Himself the Messiah, He could not be classed as a reformer of ecclesiastical abuses merely. He was the Son of God, jealous of His Father's honor, and to whom it especially belonged to see that His courts were not defiled. It is said by Edersheim (i. 38): " With this first bold purgation of the temple, a deadly feud between Jesus and the Jewish authorities had begun."

As the chief sacrifice, that of the Paschal Lamb, was offered on the first day of the feast, it is probable that this purification took place before that day. Although the act must have drawn to Him popular attention, and awakened general inquiry who He was, no hostile measures seem to have been taken at this time by the Jewish authorities. They asked for a sign (ii. 18) as a voucher for His Divine commission, which He declined to give, and answered them in an enigmatical manner. Still He wrought afterward during the feast miracles which caused many to believe in Him. Of the nature of these miracles nothing is said; probably they were miracles of healing. But their faith resting merely upon the exhibitions of power which they saw, not upon any perceptions of the moral character of His works, He did not commit Himself to them, or enter into any intimate relations with them, as with His disciples from Galilee. But in Nicodemus, whom Lightfoot calls "one of the judges of the great Sanhedrin," — ἄρχων — and Godet, "one of the lay members," He found one in whom were the germs of a true faith, and to whom He could reveal Himself not only through work but through word. The subject of His teaching was the nature of the kingdom of God, and how men were to enter into it. This conception of the kingdom, involving the gift of a new life from the Messiah as the second Adam, was one that the Lord could not then fully unfold, but which lies as the source of all His subsequent teachings. That Nicodemus should come secretly by night shows that there was, even now, among the priests and rulers with whom he had most intercourse, a feeling of dislike to Jesus, and that some degree of odium attached to all who were known to visit Him. Some infer from the plural, " We know," that Nicodemus came as the representative of others in the Sanhedrin. If John, the Evangelist, had a house in the city, as some think, the conversation may have been in his presence.

After the feast was over, Jesus leaving the city, went into some part of the territory adjacent, and began to baptize. Here several questions meet us: How early did His baptismal work begin? How long did it continue? Where was it carried on? What was its significance?

When did it begin? The only mark of time we have is in the words, "after these things,"— $\mu\epsilon\tau\grave{a}$ $\tau a\hat{v}\tau a$— after the events of the Passover (John iii. 22). This phrase, according to the Evangelist's usage, permits a considerable interval of time to have elapsed. "The sequence is not immediate;" (Alford, in loco, see v. 1; vi. 1; vii. 1.) If we suppose an interval of some weeks between the Passover and the beginning of His baptismal work, how and where was the time spent? According to Lichtenstein (157), He now returned to Galilee with His relatives and disciples, and lived there in retirement till the late autumn — from April to October, — the disciples going to their own homes. At this time He reassembled them, and going into Judæa, began to baptize. There is, perhaps, in this nothing intrinsically improbable, but there are no indications in the narrative of such a return to Galilee, and no convincing arguments for it. The impression made by the Evangelist's statement is that the Lord remained at Jerusalem or in its neighborhood for a time, longer or shorter, after the Passover, and then, going to some place He had selected in "the land of Judæa" — the country as distinguished

from the city — began there to baptize.   This was sometime
in the early summer of 780 ; more definitely, we cannot speak.

How long did His baptism continue ?   The only datum we
have is the word of the Lord after His baptismal work had
ceased, and while in Samaria on His way to Galilee: "There
are yet four months, and then cometh the harvest."   This saying,
which will be considered later, has been understood by some as
showing that the harvest was already ripe, and the time, therefore,
May; by others, that four months must pass before the harvest
began, and the time, therefore, December.   If we take the former date, His baptism, if begun immediately after the feast, continued only some four or five weeks; if the latter, it continued till
December, several months.   That it was brief, it is said, appears
from the manner in which one of John's disciples speaks (John iii.
26): " Behold the same baptizeth, and all come to Him," as if His
baptism had but recently begun.   But it is not the announcement
of the fact that He baptized as if it were a new thing, that is
emphatic, since what follows — " all come to Him,"— clearly implies some considerable period of activity.   The complaint is that
He, to whom John had borne witness, should also baptize.   "He
baptizeth," as if becoming John's rival.[1]

Where was this work carried on ?   All agree that it was
somewhere in the province of Judæa.   Some suppose Him to
have gone to the Jordan, or to some stream running into it.
(So Friedlieb, Thomson, Weiss.)   Others think that He was not
confined to one place, but went from place to place, baptizing
wherever He found water; and that He visited in southern
Judæa, Hebron, and the chief cities, going as far south as
Beersheba.   (So Sepp, Godet)   Others infer from the words
(John iv. 4), "And He must needs go through Samaria," that
He went at this time into the northern part of Judæa.   (So
Meyer.)   He may have been at Wady Farah, some six miles north-
east of Jerusalem, where is abundance of water.   (Baed., 322.
This wady will soon be spoken of again.)   It is more in harmony

---

[1] Opinions vary much as to the length of the Lord's work in baptizing: Norton, two or
three weeks; Greswell, less than a month; McClellan, Caspari, five weeks; Weiss, seven
months; Godet, eight months.   Greswell (ii. 215) thinks the statement that there was
much water there, " a proof that the rainy season had been some time over, and water was
beginning to be scarce," thus showing that it was near mid-summer.   Little reliance
can be placed on this.

with the general scope of His Judæan ministry that He should have continued in the neighborhood of the city, but the place where He baptized cannot be determined. While Jesus was baptizing, John was also carrying on his baptismal work. He had, however, left the Jordan — whether before or after the Passover we do not know — and had gone to Ænon. Let us inquire here where it is to be found.

Ænon — Αἰνών — is by some regarded as a Chaldaic plural, meaning "fountains" (T. G. Lex., *sub voce*), and by some as a compound, "dove-fountain" (so Meyer). It is doubtful whether it denotes here a district, or a village in which were springs (Lightfoot), or a fountain near a village. In any case its position is defined by saying that it was "near to Salim." But this helps us little, since the place of this Salim is also undetermined. Jerome speaks of a town called in his day Salem, eight Roman miles south of Scythopolis or Bethshean, where the ruins of a palace of Melchizedek were shown. He also speaks of a Salumias, which he apparently identifies with Salem, as lying in the plain or valley of the Jordan. Here he places Ænon, near to Salem and to the Jordan. (Raumer, 142; so Edersheim, i. 393; Caspari, 122; Ebrard, 313.) Here, at the base of a hill at the side of a beautiful spring, is a saint's tomb, to which the natives have given the name of Sheik Salim (Van der Velde, Mem., 345). But Robinson, who made special search for Salim in the Jordan valley, found no ruins, and no trace of the name. He considers this name as too frequent to be taken into account, and regards the search for Salim here as fruitless (iii. 298. See Drake, Qt. St. 1875, 32; 1874, 91). It is rightly objected by Stevens that an Ænon here is too near the Jordan (Jour. Bibl. Lit. and Ex. 1883, p. 130).

Another Salim is found a few miles east of Nablous, and some miles north from this Salim a ruined village called Ænon, which is believed by many to be the same place mentioned by the Evangelist, because of copious springs of water near it on the Wady Far'ah. All travellers agree in praising the beauty and fruitfulness of this valley, through which a permanent stream runs to the Jordan, and in which are many broad meadows, expansions well fitted for the accommodation of such as might come to be baptized. Robinson says: "Nowhere in Palestine had I seen such noble brooks of water" (iii. 305; see Stevens, 134).

It is here in this valley that many moderns find the place of John's baptism (Tristram, Conder, McGarvey, Stevens, Porter, Wilson, Schaff, Henderson). But to this there are two objections; one is the distance of the ruin Ænon from Salem some seven miles, and from Wady Far'ah some four miles. (Conder, H. B.) Of Ænon, Robinson says: "Here is precisely the name, but unfortunately there is no Salem near, nor a drop of water." Stevens (198), who defends this site, feels the force of this objection, and suggests a modern transfer from some earlier site. Another objection is, that it makes John to have been baptizing in Samaria. It is difficult to believe that John, the preacher of the Law, could have entered Samaritan territory for any such purpose, when, at a later period, the Lord forbade the Twelve to enter into any of its cities (Matt. x. 5; xv. 24). It was not to be expected that the Jews would follow John there, nor would the Samaritans accept baptism at his hands. It is said by Weiss, "It is perfectly impossible that John can have taken up his station in Samaria" (John iv. 9; Luke xvii. 18). Nor is there any trace in the conversation of the Samaritan woman or of her people with the Lord, that there had been any such ministry among them. On these grounds it is said by Meyer *in loco*: "Ænon must have been in Judæa, not in Samaria." (So Wieseler, Luthardt, Godet, Edersheim, McClellan. As to the relation of the Jews to the Samaritans, see Edersheim, 398; Hamburger, Talmud, 1068). The reasoning of Stevens on this point is not satisfactory. If the Baptist had no special mission to the Samaritans, as he most plainly had not, why go to Samaria where the Jews, to whom he had a special mission, would not follow him? That the Lord crossed Samaria on His way to and from Galilee to Jerusalem on one occasion, and spent two days there teaching, does not show that the work of the Baptist was among them.

If we cannot find Ænon in either of the two places already named, we must look for it in some other direction. Was it east of the Jordan, or somewhere in the interior of Judæa? That it was not east of the Jordan, appears from John iii. 26: "He that was with thee beyond Jordan," thus contrasting Ænon with his former place of baptism at Bethabara, and implying that John was now on the west side. That he was not in the valley of the Jordan, and near the river, appears from the description, "because there was much water"— many springs — which, in that case, would have been superfluous. Weiss, i. 34, supposes a contrast meant between the land of Judæa and Ænon, vs. 22–23 as if the latter were not in Judæa; but this is forcing the passage. The contrast is not local, but personal. Some would find Ænon in Southern Judæa. Wieseler (Syn. 248), refers to Joshua, xv. 32, where among the cities of Judah on the borders of Edom, mention is made of Shilhim, Ain, and Rimmon. (See

Riehm under Ain.) Ain and Rimmon being places near each other, were in time blended as one under the name En-Rimmon, now known by the name er Rumamim, about twelve miles north of Beersheba (Tristram, B. P. 26; Conder, H. B., so Godet, Pressensé). Lichtenstein finds Ænon in Wady el Khulil, a little northwest of Hebron; Sepp, in Beit Ænon a little north of Hebron; Ewald, in the southeast of Judæa; Luthardt, in south Judæa; Light-foot, "near the Essenes in the Judæan wilderness." To all these sites in Southern Judæa the general objection is made, that as John was not long after arrested by Herod, he must have been bap-tizing somewhere in the north, and in or near Galilee, and so brought under his jurisdiction, and that here Ænon must be sought.[1] Bar-clay finds it in Wady Farah, six miles northeast of Jerusalem, of which he speaks as having the most copious fountains to be found in the neighborhood of Jerusalem, one of them being capable of driving several mills as it gushes forth from the earth; but it is intermittent. Below, the stream is called the Kelt, emptying into the Jordan by Jericho. Baedeker mentions Wady Farah as "beautifully green, and containing excellent springs." But others find Barclay's account of the copiousness of the waters exaggerated. (So Stevens.) This site has not found much acceptance. Dixon (Qt. St. 1877) puts Ænon on a road from Jericho to Jerusalem. That John was within the territory of Herod when arrested, does not show that he was not at this earlier time engaged in baptizing somewhere in Judæa. If the Lord's work was now limited to Judæa, on grounds already stated, it was fitting that John should have carried on his work in His vicinity, and that is implied in the narrative. So M. and M.: "Ænon and Salem were in Judæa, so that Jesus and the Baptist were at this time in the same region of the country." Whether, when the Lord ceased to baptize and went into Galilee, John ceased his work in Judæa, and was in Galilee at the time of his arrest some months later, will be considered in its order.

Among so many discordant opinions, the true site of Ænon must be left undecided. Most agree in placing it on the west side of the Jordan, as it is contrasted (verse 26) with John's former place of bap-tism at Bethabara. We best meet the scope of the narrative if we suppose that Jesus and John were not very far distant from each other, and both in Judæa.

---

[1] So Lightfoot, Friedlieb, and Edersheim, but they are not agreed as to the place. Friedlieb (178) accepting the statement of Jerome, places Ænon in Peræa or Galilee; Edersheim (i. 393) thinks this most probable. But as some interval of time may have elapsed between the cessation of his baptism at Ænon and his arrest, the argument has little force.

We have still to ask what was the significance of the Lord's baptism ?

With the coming of Jesus to enter upon His work, it might have been supposed that the mission of the Baptist would cease, its end being accomplished. As we have seen, however, it did not wholly cease, for he had not brought the nation to repentance; but it changed its form. And it is probably from this point of view that we are to explain the departure of John from the Jordan to Ænon. And as the place of baptism was changed, so also in some degree the rite. His baptism could no more have a general and indefinite reference to one still to come. (See Acts xix. 4, "Saying unto the people that they should believe on Him which should come after him.") Having declared Jesus of Nazareth to be the Messiah, the undefined Messianic hopes of the nation were now to be concentrated upon Him. All the teachings and labors of the Baptist pointed to Him, and all tended to prepare the people to receive Him. Whether there was any change in the baptismal formula may be doubted, but the immediate and personal reference to Jesus as the Messiah was that which distinctively characterized the last stage of John's work, and explains why his baptism still continued.

To this form of John's ministry the ministry of Jesus, at its beginning, corresponded. The former had borne his witness to Him, and He must now confirm that witness; must show Himself to be the Messiah through His own words and acts. Before the priests and the people He asserted His Messianic claims by the purifying of the temple, and attested them by the miracles He subsequently wrought at the feast. But why should John continue to baptize ? It need not be said that if the rulers and people had responded to his preaching of repentance, and thus been prepared to receive the Lord, he would not have continued this work. But it was an indispensable condition to the reception of the Christ, the Holy One of God, that sin should be repented of and put away. Upon this John had insisted in his preaching, "Repent, for the kingdom of God is at hand." But this preaching and this baptism, both pointing to repentance, were no less important now that the Messiah had actually come. Without holiness of heart they could not receive Him, could not even discern Him as the Messiah. John had already baptized many into the hope of His coming, but others had equal need to be baptized into the reality of it.

We can now see why John should have continued baptizing after the Lord came, and why Jesus should Himself, through His disciples, also baptize. It was not enough that He had personally come.

Would the Jews receive Him ?   None could do so but the repentant. All those that, with hearts conscious of guilt, both personal and national, and truly penitent, were "waiting for the consolation of Israel," were willing to be baptized, confessing their sins; but the unrepentant, the unbelieving, the self-righteous, all who justified themselves, rejected the rite (Luke vii. 29, 30).   Hence it was a most decisive test of the spiritual state of the people.   And tried by this test, the nation, as such, was condemned.   Neither the baptism of John, nor that of the Lord, brought it to repentance.   True, great numbers went at first to John, and afterward many resorted to Jesus, and were baptized; but these were the common people, those without reputation or authority.   Those who ruled in all religious matters and gave direction to public opinion, the priests, the scribes the Pharisees, the Sadducees, and the rich and influential, held themselves almost wholly aloof.   Hence, as regarded the nation at large, John's baptismal work failed of its end.   The true and divinely appointed representatives of the people, the ecclesiastical authorities who sat in Moses' seat, were not brought to repentance, and, therefore, could not receive the Messiah.

Thus Jesus began His work as the Baptizer with water unto repentance.   It was this baptism that gave to His Judæan ministry its distinctive character.   It was an attempt to bring the nation, as headed up in its ecclesiastical rulers, to repentance.   Had these come to Him or to John confessing their sins, His way would have been prepared, and He could then have proceeded to teach them the true nature of the Messianic kingdom, and prepare them for the baptism of the Holy Ghost.   But as they had "frustrated the counsel of God within themselves, being not baptized of John" ("rejected for themselves the counsel of God," R. V.), so they continued to frustrate it by rejecting the work in which John and Jesus were jointly engaged.

In the act of baptizing Jesus personally took no part.   It was done by His disciples.   The names of these disciples are not mentioned, but they were doubtless the same whose names had been already mentioned (John, ch. i.), and who came with Him to the Passover from Galilee.   As the former disciples of John, and perhaps his assistants, this rite was not new to them.   Having, also, been for some time in company with Jesus, they were prepared by His teachings to understand the meaning of the service He required from them.   As yet, however, their relations

8*

to Him were much the same as their former relations to John, and very unlike what they afterward became.

These contemporaneous baptismal labors of the Lord and of John present many interesting questions, but most of them lie out of the pale of our inquiry. As the former did not Himself baptize, it is a question how His time was spent. Probably He taught the crowds that came to His baptism, but there is no hint that He healed the sick, or wrought any miracles. We can scarce doubt that He went up to Jerusalem to attend the two great feasts during this period, that of Pentecost and of Tabernacles, and here He must have come more or less into contact with the priests and Pharisees. It does not appear, however, that He went about from place to place to teach, or that He taught in any of the synagogues. Still it is not improbable that before He began to baptize, or at intervals during His labors, He may have visited many parts of Judæa, and have noted and tested the spiritual condition of the people. It may be, also, that at this time He formed those friendships of which we later find traces, as that with Joseph of Arimathea, and that with Mary and Martha.

DECEMBER, 780 — MARCH, 781. A. D. 27–28.

The Pharisees hearing that Jesus baptized more disciples than John, He gives up his work of baptizing and goes back to Galilee. The Baptist, in reply to the complaints of his disciples, bears a fresh testimony to Jesus as the Messiah. Jesus takes His way to Galilee, through Samaria, and abides there two days teaching, and many believe on Him. Upon reaching Galilee His disciples depart to their respective homes. He is received with honor by the Galilæans, because of the works which He did at Jerusalem at the feast. Coming to Cana, He heals the nobleman's son at Capernaum. He afterward lives in retirement till called to go up to Jerusalem at the following feast. — JOHN iii. 25, 26. JOHN iv. 1–3. JOHN iii. 27–36. JOHN iv. 4–42. JOHN iv. 43–45. JOHN iv. 46–54. JOHN v. 1.

The first point that meets us here is, why did the Lord cease to baptize? An answer very generally given is, that the Baptist was at the time cast into prison at the instigation of the Pharisees, and that He, fearing a like arrest, withdrew for safety from Judæa into Galilee. This point, as one of much importance in

determining the order of the events following, must be carefully considered.

It has been said by some that the Baptist was twice arrested.[1]
This rests upon the supposed force of the verb "was delivered up,"
παρεδόθη, (this is rendered, A. V. Matt. iv. 12, "was cast into prison,"
but in the margin "delivered up"; in Mark i. 14, "was put in
prison"; the rendering in the R. V. is in both cases "delivered up.")
This delivering up was, they say, not his imprisonment by Herod, but
a delivery of him by Herod to the Sanhedrin soon after the visit of
the Deputation. From this imprisonment, however, he was soon released, and later was imprisoned by Herod.

This theory of two arrests seems to have been devised to explain
the difficulty of the common interpretation, that Jesus going to Galilee immediately after John's arrest should then begin His work under
the very eye of Herod. But this view of two arrests of the Baptist has
no recent advocates.

The last notice we have of John as engaged in his baptismal
work, is that given by John iii. 23: while Jesus was baptizing somewhere in Judæa, John was baptizing at Ænon. When did his work at
Ænon cease, and why did it cease? It is held by many that it ceased
before Jesus left Judæa (John iv. 3), sometime in the summer or
autumn of 780, and ceased because he was then imprisoned by Herod.[2]
It is admitted that the Evangelist says nothing of John's imprisonment as the cause of the Lord's leaving Judæa; his language
rather gives the impression that John was still active.

The ground on which his imprisonment is here asserted, is a chronological rather than an exegetical one. As the Lord now went from
Judæa into Galilee, it is said that this departure into Galilee must be
the same as that in Matt. iv. 12, Mark i. 14, Luke iv. 14; and therefore we must put the Baptist's imprisonment at this time. Assuming
that this must be so, the inference is drawn from John iv. 1, that the
Lord's motive in leaving Judæa was fear of the Pharisees; He was
afraid of a like imprisonment. Thus Lightfoot says: "Herod had
imprisoned John the Baptist under pretense of his growing too popular. Our Saviour, understanding this, and that the Sanhedrin had
heard of the increase of His disciples, withdrew too from Judæa
into Galilee, that He might be more remote from that kind of thunder-
bolt John had been struck with." But here we meet some difficul-

---

[1] So Pound, ii. 137. Wies., Syn. 223, refers to the old harmonist, Lamy, as presenting the same view.

[2] So in general, with some differences as to the time, Rob., Fried., Gard., McClel.,
Eders., Ell., and others,

ties; if the Baptist had been arrested by Herod, he must have been in Herod's territory, in Peræa or Galilee, but we have no proof that Ænon was within it; and if it was not in Peræa or Galilee but in Judæa, John must have given up baptizing there before the Lord ceased His baptismal work, which is not implied in the narrative, and for which there is no authority. Some suppose that John, being in territory under Roman rule, was arrested by Pilate at Herod's request, and sent into Galilee; this is obviously a makeshift for there is no probability that Pilate, who did not love Herod, would make himself an instrument to gratify the king's personal enmity.

That the Pharisees at this time were becoming more determined in their hostility both to Jesus and John, we may well believe, but that they now, or later, instigated Herod to arrest the Baptist, is not shown. According to the Synoptists (Matt. xiv. 3, and parallels) it was the reproof of Herod for his adulterous marriage with his brother's wife, that led to John's arrest; Josephus ascribes it to political motives, but nowhere speaks as if the Pharisees instigated it. If their hostility had now reached this stage, and they had caused the Baptist's arrest through Herod, it is not likely that they would have permitted Jesus to carry on His work unmolested in Galilee for two years when they had such a convenient tool in Herod to carry out their purposes. That Jesus did not fear any arrest from Herod, is apparent from the fact that He now goes into his territory, and moreover takes up His abode in the near vicinity of his capital. It seems from the Synoptists, that it was not till the death of the Baptist that Herod heard of Jesus (Matt. xiv. 2,) a fact which clearly shows that up to this time the Pharisees had not sought to arouse his hostility to Him, and that he had not known of Him as an ally of John's.

Dismissing then as groundless the statement that Jesus left Judæa through fear of the Pharisees and of Herod, what was the ground of His action?

The words of the Evangelist are, "When the Lord knew how the Pharisees had heard that Jesus made and baptized ("was making and baptizing," R. V.), more disciples than John; He left Judæa and departed again into Galilee." We have here the facts, first, that Jesus baptized more disciples than John; second, that this was known to the Pharisees; third, that Jesus, knowing that this was known to them, left Judæa. The inference clearly is, though not expressed, that the greater success of Jesus was offensive to the Pharisees; but that it led them to any overt act is not implied, much less that they then procured the arrest of John, and that Jesus, through fear of them, went into Galilee. The Lord's motive seems to have been to avoid any hindrance which His own baptismal work might put in John's way through the misrepresentations of the Pharisees. Evidently the jealousy of John's disciples was awakened by the greater popularity of the Lord (John iii. 25), and this gave occasion to the enemies of both to stir up dissensions between their respective disciples. (So Licht., Luthardt.) It is to be noted also, that those who came to the Lord's baptism were not of the rulers and priests, or of the Pharisaic party (Luke vii. 30), so that it failed of its end to bring the nation in its chief representatives to repentance.

There is another interpretation of the Evangelist's statement which lays the stress on the knowledge which the Pharisees had of the Lord's baptismal success. The Lord knew that He had thus been brought sufficiently into prominence to make it plain that they refused to come to His baptism, and so rejected Him with full knowledge. Any further presentation of His baptismal work could, therefore, be of no profit.

But this is not inconsistent with the fact of the growing Pharisaic enmity. The increasing influence of Jesus, as shown by the numbers that came to His baptism, only brought out more strongly the envy and dislike of the Pharisees, and confirmed them in their hostility. To have continued His work could, therefore, have answered no good end, since it was not now the gathering of a body of disciples around Him at which He aimed, but the repentance of the priests and leaders of the people. As said by Weiss (ii. 30, note): "It is in no way indicated that Jesus here gathered a congregation around Him; that is contradicted by everything we hear as to His baptismal ministry in Judæa."

We conclude, then, that in John iv. 1, there is no intimation that the Baptist's work had ended, but rather a plain intimation that it was still in progress, for there is a comparison between them, and the result is, that Jesus is baptizing more than John. By M. and M. it is said: "We regard the ministry of John as still enduring at the period to which this verse relates"; and by Caspari, "John was still at liberty." (So Bengel, Wies., Licht., Luthardt.) Greswell (ii. 212), who admits that the words of the Evangelist imply that, when Jesus set out on His return to Galilee, John was not yet cast into prison, supposes that before he reached there he was imprisoned. This, however, contradicts the Synoptists, who imply that Jesus was in Judæa when He heard of John's imprisonment, and that this was the cause of His departure into Galilee; "Now when He heard that John was delivered up, He withdrew into Galilee" (Matt. iv. 12).

We give the following arrangements of events: 1st, of most harmonists. Soon after the Passover, Jesus and John entered upon their baptismal work in Judæa. After a time —longer or shorter— John is arrested and imprisoned; Jesus, through fear of a like arrest, leaves Judæa and goes to Galilee, and begins His public ministry there; some say in the early summer, others in the late autumn.

2d, of Lichtenstein. After the Passover Jesus returns to Nazareth; remains there in retirement till the late summer, perhaps till feast of Tabernacles in October; goes into Judæa and begins to baptize, John also baptizing at Ænon. John is imprisoned after a few weeks; Jesus then ceases His baptism, and returns to Galilee. Thence He goes up to the unnamed feast (John v. 1).

3d, of this book. Soon after the Passover—time undefined — Jesus and John begin to baptize in Judæa. Jesus ceases to baptize in the late autumn and goes to Galilee, John probably still continuing his work. Jesus remains in retirement three or four months, then goes up to the unnamed feast; and about this time John was imprisoned. After this feast Jesus goes to Galilee, and begins His ministry there.

How long after Jesus ceased baptizing and left Judæa John continued to baptize, we do not know, but the strong probability is that he continued to baptize till his imprisonment. Nor do we know whether he continued his work at Ænon or went to some other place. That at the time of his arrest he was within the jurisdiction of Herod Antipas, is scarcely to be doubted. But where he met with Herod, whether in Galilee or Peræa, and under what circumstances, we have no information. The grounds of his imprisonment will be later considered.

We conclude that John was not imprisoned when Jesus ceased to baptize and left Judæa. His imprisonment was some months later, and the Lord's Galilean ministry began soon after it.

The only datum we have by which to determine the time of the year when Jesus went into Galilee, is found in His words to His disciples when seated by the well in Sychar: " Say not ye, There are yet four months, and then cometh harvest ? behold, I say unto you," etc. (John iv. 35). Some, however, deny that this reference to the harvest as yet four months distant is of any chronological value, because the expression is a proverbial one, based upon the fact that there is an average interval of

four months between the sowing and harvesting.[1] But the form
of the expression seems to forbid that we regard it as a proverb,
"Say not ye, There are yet four months," etc.; here "yet," ἔτι,
obviously refers to the time when the words were spoken.
From this time, not from the time of sowing, are four months,
and then the harvest.[2] We are, then, to determine the time of
the harvest, and counting backward four months reach the
time when the words were spoken. Upon the 16th Nisan, a sheaf
of the first fruits of the barley harvest was to be waved before
the Lord in the Temple. Till this was done no one might lawfully gather his grain.[3] From this legal commencement of the
harvest about the first of April, we obtain the month of December as that in which the words were spoken.[4] Tholuck (*in loco*)
regards the expression as proverbial, yet reaches nearly the
same result. "As our Lord points them to the fields, it is
highly probable that it was just then seed-time, and we are thus
furnished with the date, to wit, that Jesus had remained in
Judæa from April, when the Passover occurred, till November."[5]

A very different result is reached by some who take the
Lord's words, "Lift up your eyes, and look on the fields; for
they are white already to harvest," as not figurative but literal,
and expressive of an actual fact. The harvest, they infer, was
not four months distant but just at hand. Upon this ground
Greswell (ii. 229) decides "that the time of the journey coincided
with the acme of wheat harvest, or was but a little before it,"
and puts it two or three weeks before Pentecost, or about the
middle of May.[6]

The direct route from Judæa to Nazareth led through Samaria by
Sichem, and was generally taken by the companies attending the
feast from Galilee, although the enmity of the Samaritans to the

---

[1] Norton, Krafft, Greswell, Alford, Westcott.

[2] Lightfoot, Baronius, Litchtenstein, Wieseler, Stier, Meyer, Robinson, Godet, Luthardt.

[3] Levit. xxiii. 10, etc.; Deut. xvi. 9, etc.; Josephus, Antiq. iii. 10. 5.

[4] Lightfoot, Lichtenstein, Meyer, Ellicott.

[5] A. Clarke and Stier, putting the harvest in May, make the departure to have been in
January; Stanley, in January or February.

[6] So Townsend, *in loco*, "The Messiah," 101; Caspari, Eders., Alford regards all chronological inferences built on this passage, as unwarranted. A writer in the *Dublin Review*,
April, 1890, finds the following meaning: Say ye not that the crop is already four months
old, and the harvest is coming ?

Jews seems especially to have manifested itself on such occasions. Josephus says[2] that it was necessary for those that would travel quickly to take that route, as by it Jerusalem could be reached in three days from Galilee. Sychar, the city of Samaria through which He passed, is regarded by many as a corruption of Sychem (Acts vii. 16), which stood upon the site of the present Neapolis or Nablous, and is often mentioned in biblical history.[3] For a time after the return from the captivity, Samaria (1 Kings xvi. 24) was the chief city, but Sichem soon gained the ascendency; and though Herod had recently rebuilt Samaria with much magnificence, yet Sichem retained its place as the leading city of the province. The change from Sichem to Sychar is supposed to mark the contempt of the Jews toward the Sichemites, the Sychar meaning the "toper city," or the "heathen city"; but it may have been made by those speaking Greek for easier pronunciation. Alexander calls it "a later Aramaic form." It is not to be supposed that this change was made by John in his narrative to express his own dislike, or that, as said by Stier, "it was an intentional intimation of the relation and position of things between Judæa and Samaria." Unless the name Sychar was in common use, we can scarce suppose him to have employed it; for in a simple historical statement the intentional use of any mock name or opprobrious epithet would be out of keeping.

Some make Sychar a village near Sichem, but distinct from it.[4] This was the early opinion. They were distinguished by Eusebius, and in the Jerusalem Itinerarium.[5] Raumer supposes that the city of Sichem was a long straggling one, and that the east end of it near Jacob's well was called Sychar. There is now a village near the well called El Askar, which some have supposed to be Sychar. Thomson (ii. 206) says: "This is so like John's Sychar that I feel inclined to adopt it."[6] The most recent investigation accepts this conclusion. (For a discussion of the matter, see Eders., ii. App., 767; Tristram, B. P., 192).

Jacob's well, where Jesus was resting Himself when He met the Samaritan woman, "is on the end of a low spur or swell running out from the northeastern base of Gerizim; and is still 15 or 20 feet above the level of the plain below."[7] It was formerly believed to have been dug out of the solid rock, but we now know that the upper

---

[1] Josephus, Antiq. xx. 6. 1.   [2] Life, 52.

[3] So Meyer, Wieseler, Raumer, Robinson, Ritter, Alford.

[4] Hug, Luthardt, Lichtenstein.   [5] See Raumer, 146, note.

[6] So Godet, Luthardt, M. and M., Westcott. See *contra* Robinson, iii. 133; see also Wieseler, 256, note.

[7] Robinson, iii. 132.

part is through a mixture of alluvium and limestone fragments, and the interior seem to have been lined throughout with rough masonry. The diameter is seven or eight feet. Anderson, in "*Twenty-one Years' Work*," (192) says: the well was doubtless sunk deep at first, but its original depth cannot now be ascertained, it having gradually filled up, but was probably near one hundred feet. Its present depth is about seventy-five. The quantity of water in it greatly varies; Maundrell found it five yards in depth. Sometimes it is nearly or wholly dry. Dr. Wilson in 1842 found so little water in it, that a servant, whom he let down to the bottom, was able by means of dry sticks thrown to him, to kindle a blaze which distinctly showed the whole of the well from the top to the bottom. Osborne says [1]: "There was no water at the time of our visit, near the close of December." "Formerly there was a square hole opening into a carefully built vaulted chamber, about 10 feet square, in the floor of which was the true mouth of the well. Now a portion of the vault has fallen in, and completely covered up the mouth, so that nothing can be seen but a shallow pit half filled with stones and rubbish." [2] A church was built near this spot, of which few traces remain. It is said that the Russians have bought the site, and are about to rebuild the church.

It has been much questioned why a well should have been dug here, since there are several springs within a little distance giving an abundance of water. Some suppose that earthquakes may have caused the springs to flow since the well was dug. More probable is the supposition that Jacob found the springs in the possession of others, who were unwilling to share the water with him, and therefore, as a matter of necessity, he must obtain it from a well (Tristram, B. P., 187). Why the woman should have come to this well to draw water, which was so much more easily attainable near by, cannot now be explained. It may be, as suggested by Caspari, that the village was much larger in the Lord's day, and stretched near to the well; or, if the city itself was at some distance, and the language seems to imply this (verses 8, 28–30), she may have lived in the suburbs, for it is not said that she resided in the city; but if she did so, she may have had special reasons for wishing the water of this well, because of its coolness or other qualities; or as especially valuable because of its association with Jacob. Porter (ii. 342) speaks of those at Damascus, who send to a particular fountain a mile or more distant from their homes, although water is everywhere very abundant.

It was about the sixth hour that Jesus sat on the well.

---

[1] Palestine, 335.   [2] Porter, ii. 340.

This, according to Jewish reckoning, would be 12 M. or noon; if reckoned according to Roman computation, 5 to 6 P. M., or as some say,[1] 5 to 6 A. M.   Ebrard (296), who contends that John always uses the Roman computation, prefers the evening here on the grounds that the noonday was an unfit time to travel, and that wells were usually visited for water at evening.   But if we remember that this was in December, travelling at midday will not appear strange.   Noon was not, indeed, the time for general resort to the well, but such resort must be determined in particular cases by individual need; and that the woman was alone, and held so long a private conversation uninterrupted, shows that it was an hour when the well was not generally visited. There seems, then, no reason to depart from the common opinion that it was about noon.[2]   At this hour the Jews were accustomed to take their principal meal.[3]

The reception which the Lord met with among the Samaritans was in striking contrast with His reception in Judæa; yet among them He seems to have wrought no miracles, and to have been received because the truth He taught was the convincing proof of His Messianic character.

Arriving in Galilee, Jesus was honorably received by the Galilæans, for they had been at the Passover, and had "seen all the things that He did at Jerusalem at the feast" (John iv. 43–45).   Of "the many that then believed on Him," a considerable part may have been Galilæan pilgrims.   But in face of this honorable reception, how are His words (verse 44) to be understood, "that a prophet hath no honor in his own country," which are apparently cited as explaining why He went into Galilee? There are several interpretations, the chief of which are : 1. Galilee is to be taken in opposition to Nazareth.   In this city, His own country, Jesus had no honor, but elsewhere in Galilee He was received as a prophet.[4]   2.   Galilee is to be taken in opposition to Judæa.   Judæa was His birthplace, and so His own country, and it was also the land of the prophets; but there

---

[1] Greswell, ii. 216; McKnight.

[2] For this, Luthardt, Meyer, Godet. For 6 P. M., M. and M., Westcott. The point how John computed time, has been already discussed (John i. 39).

[3] Winer, ii. 47.

[4] Lightfoot, Krafft, Lange with a slight modification.

He had found no reception, and had been compelled to discontinue His ministry. In Galilee, on the contrary, all were ready to honor Him.[1] 3. Galilee is His own country, where, according to the proverb, He would have had no honor unless He had first gone into Judæa and distinguished Himself there. It was His miracles and works abroad that gave Him fame and favor at home.[2]

The last interpretation appears best to suit the scope of the narrative. The connection between verses 43 and 44 is this. In verse 43, the fact is stated that He went into Galilee; and in verse 44, the reason is assigned why He went. As, according to the proverb, a prophet is without honor in his own country, by retiring into Galilee He could avoid all publicity and find retirement. "He went to Galilee because there in His own country He could expect no honor, . . and could hope not to be observed there, but to remain in rest and quiet." (Luthardt.) But in verse 45, the fact is stated that the Galilæans, notwithstanding the proverb, did receive Him, and the reason is also added. because they had been at Jerusalem and had seen what He did there. And in verses 46–53, a particular instance is given, showing how high was His reputation in Galilee, and what publicity attended His movements. His arrival at Cana was soon known at Capernaum, and a nobleman from the latter city, supposed by many to be Chuza, steward of Herod (Luke viii. 3), by others, Manaen (Acts xiii. 1), coming to Him, desired that He would return with him, and heal his son. Without leaving Cana, Jesus healed him. This was His second Galilæan miracle.

From the time of this miracle at Cana, we lose sight of the Lord till He reappears going up to a feast at Jerusalem (John v. 1). If, as we have supposed, He left Judæa in December, this miracle must have been wrought soon after His arrival in Galilee. "This second time, as at the first, He signalized His return to Galilee by a new miracle at Cana." (Godet.) As the first feast which He could attend was that of Purim, in March, an interval of some two or three months must have elapsed. If this feast was the Passover, or any of the later feasts, this interval was correspondingly prolonged. How was this time spent?

---

[1] Ebrard, Norton, Westcott, M. and M.   [2] Meyer, Alford, Godet, Luthardt.

Those who make the imprisonment of the Baptist to have taken place before He left Judæa, suppose that He now entered upon His Galilæan work. But, upon grounds already stated, we conclude that John was not yet imprisoned, and therefore, His Galilæan work could not now begin, as the two are closely connected by the Synoptists (Matt. iv. 12, Mark i. 14, Luke iii. 20 and iv. 14). Several additional considerations induce us to think that this period was not spent in any public labors. 1. When, after the imprisonment of John Jesus went into Galilee to teach and to preach His disciples were not with Him, and not till He had begun His labors at Capernaum did they rejoin Him (Matt. iv. 18, Mark i. 16, Luke v. 2–11). There was, then, an interval after He had ended His baptismal labors in Judæa, in which labors they were His helpers, and before the beginning of His ministry in Galilee, during which His disciples were separated from Him, and seem to have returned to their accustomed avocations. But if His Galilæan work began as soon as His Judæan work ended, there was no time for them to have thus returned to their homes, and, therefore, no opportunity to recall them to His service.

2. The Lord gave up baptizing, as we have seen, because of the hostility of the Pharisees, and their rejection of the rite; not because the Baptist was then imprisoned. So long as John was able, both in word and act, to bear witness to Him as the Messiah, He could Himself seek retirement, and wait the issue of John's ministry. He could not, till the Baptist was imprisoned and his voice thus silenced, leave Judæa and begin His work in Galilee. To Galilee He went, therefore, as a place of seclusion, not of publicity; of rest, not of activity. The proverb that a prophet has no honor in his own country, did not indeed prove true in His case. He was honorably received, and immediately besought to heal the sick. Still there is no record that He entered upon any public labors, that He preached or taught in the synagogues, or wrought any miracle beside that recorded of the nobleman's son. How or where His time was spent, can only be conjectured. From the fact that no mention is made of Nazareth, it has been inferred that He purposely avoided that city, and took another route to Cana. That

He is spoken of as being at Cana, gives a show of confirmation
to the supposition already alluded to, that Mary and her child
ren had now left Nazareth, and were dwelling at Cana.   But
we may as readily suppose that He was now visiting at the house
of the friends, or relatives, where He changed the water into
wine.

PASSOVER, MARCH 30 — APRIL 5, 781. A. D. 28.

From Galilee Jesus goes up to a feast, and at the pool of   JOHN v. 1.
Bethesda heals an impotent man. This act, done on the Sab- JOHN v. 2-9.
bath day, arouses the anger of the Jews, who conspire against JOHN v. 10-16.
His life. He defends His right to heal on the Sabbath upon   JOHN v. 17-47.
grounds that still more exasperate them. At this time He   MATT. iv. 12.
hears of the imprisonment of the Baptist, and retires to Gali- MARK i. 14.
lee, to begin His work there.   LUKE iv. 14.

"After this there was a feast of the Jews, and Jesus went up
to Jerusalem." Which feast was this? Opinions are divided
between Purim in March, Passover in April, Pentecost in May,
and Tabernacles in September; and some minor feasts have also
found advocates. Before considering the arguments urged in
favor of each, let us examine the statement of John: "After
this there was a feast of the Jews."

There has been much doubt as to the true reading, whether
a feast or the feast — ἑορτή or ἡ ἑορτή — but the weight of
authority is against the article. W. and H. omit it, Tischendorf inserts it.   In R. V. it is omitted: "There was a feast of
the Jews"; but in the margin it says "Many ancient authorities read, the feast." Accepting the reading, "a feast," does not
the absence of the article determine what kind of feast it was?
It is generally held that if the article was used, this would show
only that one of the three great feasts could be meant; not being
used, one of the minor feasts must be meant.   But are these certain inferences? Why might not the writer speak of one of the
greater feasts simply as a feast? He would unquestionably do
this if he saw any ground for it.   The mere absence of the article does not warrant us in saying that the Evangelist must have
meant a minor feast, nor does its presence define which of the
greater feasts is intended.   Tholuck says: "The Passover may
be meant, or other feasts"; and Abp. Thomson observes, that "all

its omission could prove, would be that the Evangelist did not think it needful to describe the feast more particularly." It is said by Robinson and others, that if the article was used, the feast must have been the Passover as the most ancient of all feasts. But Josephus speaks of the feast of Tabernacles as "a feast most holy and eminent" (Antiq., viii. 4. 1). If the article was used, this feast would have the preference. (So Browne, Westcott.)

But, if the article be wanting, it is said that the feast is still defined by the addition to it of the explanatory words "of the Jews," τῶν Ἰουδαίων.[1] It is given as a rule of Hebrew, and so transferred to Scripture Greek, that the "noun before a genitive is made definite by prefixing the article, not to the noun itself, but to the genitive."[2] Thus, the phrase before us should be rendered "the feast of the Jews," or "the Jews' festival," which must be understood of the Passover. But the rule is given with an important qualification by Winer:[3] "The article is frequently omitted, when a noun, denoting an object of which the individual referred to possesses but one, is clearly defined by means of a genitive following."[4] As there was but one feast of Tabernacles, the phrase ἑορτὴ τῶν σκηνῶν would be properly rendered "the feast of Tabernacles;" but as there were several feasts kept by the Jews, "feast of the Jews," may mean any feast.

From the form of the expression, then, nothing certain can be determined. We learn simply that Jesus went up to Jerusalem at one of the Jewish feasts. We not even learn whether it was one of the greater or lesser feasts. It seems to be mentioned only as giving the occasion why He went up to Jerusalem. He would not have gone except there had been a feast, but its name was unimportant to the Evangelist's purpose.[5] Let us then enquire what light is thrown upon it from the general scope of this Gospel.

---

[1] Hug, Int., 449. See John vii. 2, "Now the feast of the Jews, the feast of tabernacles, was at hand," R. V.

[2] Robinson, Har., 190. See in the Septuagint, Deut. xvi. 13; 2 Kings, xviii. 15; also Matt. xii. 24; Luke ii. 11; Acts viii. 5.

[3] Gram. Thayer's trans., page 125.

[4] See also Lücke *in loco*, who agrees that only where the governing noun exists singly in its kind, is it rendered definite by a noun following.

[5] See Luthardt *in loco*. It is said by Robinson, that John "uses the festivals as measures of time," but this is an over-statement of the chronological element.

It is apparent that John does not design, any more than the other Evangelists, to give us a complete chronological outline of the Lord's life. But we see that he mentions by name several feasts which the Lord attended which the Synoptists do not mention at all;[1] and these so mentioned were by no means all the feasts that occurred during His ministry. That of Pentecost is nowhere mentioned, nor does John say that those mentioned by him were all that Jesus attended. During the first year of His labors, or while baptizing in Judæa — supposing His baptism to have extended to December — there is good ground to believe that He was present at the three chief feasts, though the Passover only is mentioned. On the other hand, one Passover is mentioned which it is probable He did not attend (John vi. 4). Upon examination, we see that the feasts which are named stand in some close connection with the Lord's words or acts, so that it is necessary to specify them. Thus in ii. 13, the mention of the Passover explains the purification of the temple, or driving out of the sellers of oxen and sheep; in vi. 4, it explains how such a great company should have gathered to Him in so lonely a region across the sea; in vii. 2, His words take their significance from the special ceremonies connected with that feast; in x. 22, His presence in Solomon's porch is thus explained. In each of these cases the name of the feast is mentioned, not primarily as a datum of time, but as explanatory of something in the narrative; and as the mention of the other feasts was unimportant to his purpose, John passes them by in silence. But the feast before us he mentions, yet does not give its name. What shall we infer from this? Some, as has been said, infer that it must have been one of the minor feasts, for had it been one of the chief feasts it would have been named. But, as he specifies (x. 22) one of the minor feasts, there seems no sufficient reason why he should not specify this, had it been such. All that we can say is, that there was no such connection between this feast and what Jesus said or did while attending it, that it was necessary to specify it. The healing of the impotent man and the events that followed might have taken place at any feast.

The silence, then, of John determines nothing respecting

---

[1] See ii. 13; vi. 4; vii. 2; x. 22.

the nature of this feast.   We cannot infer with any assurance, because he has mentioned three Passovers beside, that this was a fourth; nor, on the other hand, that he would have so specified it had it been a Passover.

As this feast is not named, and the presence or absence of the article does not determine which it was, we must examine it from the chronological point of view, and learn its relations to the feasts before and after.   And the first element to be taken into account is the length of the Lord's baptismal work following His first Passover (John ii. 13).   Opinions are here divided, as we have already seen; some suppose Him to have ceased that work, and to have left Judæa in May, a few weeks after that Passover (John iv. 3; so Gres., Caspari, Eders., McClel.).   If this be so, in the remainder of this year, for we may believe that the feast of Pentecost was already past, would fall the greater feast of Tabernacles, preceded by the Day of Atonement, and the minor feasts of Wood-gathering in August ; of Trumpets in September; of Dedication in December.   Each of these, except the last, has its advocates; for Wood-gathering, Edersheim ; for Trumpets, Westcott.   Caspari defends the Day of Atonement.   But the first two have small claim for consideration.   The feast of Wood-offering (Nehemiah x. 34 ; Joseph., War, ii. 17. 6) whose object was to bring wood for the altar, was observed several times in the course of the year, of which the 15 Ab-(August), was the most important, and it is the feast at this time which is advocated by Edersheim (ii. App., see Reland, Antiq., 308).   As to the monthly feasts of Trumpets, Westcott selects that on the first of September.   It is a sufficient answer to the claims of these two feasts, that both were of subordinate importance, and little attended by the Jews.   As to the Day of Atonement, from the very nature of its services, it cannot be called a feast (Levit. xvi. 29 ff.).

But most put the Lord's departure from Judæa not in April or May, but much later, in November or December.   The feast of Dedication was observed about the middle of December, and it is generally agreed that this cannot be the feast intended by the Evangelist.   The next was that in March, the feast of Purim. That this feast is the one in question was first suggested by Kepler, and has since found many eminent supporters.   But before we consider the arguments in its favor, let us examine its origin and history.

Purim was not a Mosaic feast, or of divine appointment, but one established by the Jews while in captivity in commemoration of their deliverance from the murderous plans of Haman (Esther iii. 7; ix. 24). It is derived from "pur," the Persian word for lot. Haman sought to find an auspicious day for the execution of his design by casting lots. The lot fell on the 14th Adar. Failing in his purpose, this day was kept thereafter by the Jews as a festival. It seems to have been first observed by th Jews out of Palestine, and eighty-five elders made exceptions against it as an innovation against the Law.[1] It is mentioned in Maccabees (2 Mac. xv. 36) as Mordecai's day. It is also mentioned by Josephus,[2] who says "that even now all the Jews that are in the habitable earth keep these days festival." It is often alluded to in the Talmud.[3] Of the two days originally set, (Esther ix. 21,) the first was chiefly observed.

Such was the origin of the feast. It was commemorated by the reading of Esther in the synagogues, and by general festivity, with plays and masquerades. Maimonides says it was forbidden to fast or weep on this day. It was rather a national and political than religious solemnity;[4] and as no special services were appointed for its observance at the temple, there was no necessity of going up to Jerusalem; nor does it appear that this was their custom. In this respect it was unlike the feast of Dedication, which, as commemorating the purification of the temple, had a religious character. Each Jew observed it as a day of patriotic rejoicing and festivity, wherever he chanced to be.[5] Lightfoot (on Mark i. 38) remarks that if the feast did not come on a synagogue day, those living in a village where was no synagogue, need not go to some other village to read the book of Esther, but could wait till a synagogue day.[6]

From this brief survey of the history, and the manner of observance of this feast, it is highly improbable that it is the feast meant by John. It was not one of their divinely appointed feasts, nor was there any legal obligation to keep it. It was not a feast specifically religious, but patriotic; a day, making due allowance for difference

---

[1] Lightfoot, on John x. 22.　　　　　　[2] Antiq., xi. 6. 13.

[3] Winer, ii. 289; Wieseler, 206.　　　　[4] Ewald, iv. 261.

[5] Of the mode of its observance in this country at the present time, a recent New York journal gives the following account : "The day is devoted to mirth and merry-making. In the evening and morning the synagogues are lighted up, and the reader chants the book of Esther. It is a custom among the Jews on this occasion to visit each other's houses in masked attire and exchange joyful greetings."

[6] See generally, Hengstenberg, Christol., iii. 240; Hug, Int., 449; Wieseler, 222; Brown, Jew. Antiq., i. 574.

9

in customs and institutions, not unlike the day that commemorates our own national independence. There were no special rites that made it necessary to go up to Jerusalem, and even those residing in villages where was no synagogue were not obliged to go to a village where one was to be found. Why, then, should Jesus go up from Galilee to be present at this feast? It was not a time in which men's minds were prepared to hear spiritual instruction, nor could He sympathize with the rude and boisterous, not to say disorderly and drunken manner in which the day was kept. Stier (v. 75), who defends Purim, admits "the revengeful and extravagant spirit which animated it," and "the debauched manner in which these days of excess were spent." Yet he thinks motives of compassion disposed the Lord to visit once "this melancholy caricature of a holy festivity;" but it is well said by Edersheim: "I can scarcely conceive our Lord going to a feast observed with such boisterous merriment." We can see no sufficient motive for such a journey. The tenor of the narrative naturally leads us to think of one of the greater and generally attended festivals. If it be said of a Jew that he went up to Jerusalem to a feast, the obvious understanding would be that it was a feast that he was legally bound to attend, and which could be rightly kept only at Jerusalem.

The chief argument in favor of Purim, and, indeed, the only one of importance, is that this feast is brought by John into such close connection with the Passover (vi. 4), and that if it be not Purim, then a year and a half, at least, must have elapsed ere Jesus visited Jerusalem again, the next recorded visit being that to the feast of Tabernacles (John vii. 2). But this is not the only instance in which John narrates events widely separated in time, without noting the interval. Thus, ch. vi. relates what took place before a Passover, and ch. vii. what took place at the feast of Tabernacles, six months later. In like manner, in x. 22, is a sudden transition from this feast of Tabernacles to that of Dedication. Why the intervening events are not mentioned, finds explanation in the peculiar character of this gospel. That Jesus should have absented Himself for so long a time from the feasts, is explained by the hostility of the Jews, and their purpose to slay Him (John v. 16-18; vii. 1).

On the other hand, if this feast be Purim, and the Passover in vi. 4, be the first Passover after it, or the second of the Lord's ministry, then the interval between them, about three weeks, is not sufficient for all the events that must have taken place. And still less is the interval between December, when most of the advocates of Purim suppose the Lord's Galilæan work to have begun, and the following Passover (vi.

4) sufficient to include all that the Synoptists relate. The feeding of the five thousand, as is generally agreed, and as will be hereafter shown, marks the culmination of His work in Galilee; yet this took place according to this view in three or four months after His work began, for it was a little before the Passover (vi. 4). And into this short space are crowded two-thirds, at least, of all that He did in Galilee, so far as recorded. This would be very improbable, even if, as is supposed, His labors there extended only through a year. In the highest degree improbable is the view of Wieseler, followed by Ellicott, that for all this the little interval between Purim and Passover was sufficient.[1]

The order of events thus presented to us must be more fully examined. If this feast was Purim, and was followed a few days after by the Passover (vi. 4), the Evangelist mentions only three Passovers, ii. 13, vi. 4, xi. 55, and consequently, the Lord's ministry was only of two years and some months duration; and this conclusion is accepted by most who accept Purim. We have then this order: 1st, Passover, cleansing of Temple. 2d, Baptismal work in Judæa till December. 3d, Departure to Galilee and sojourn there till Purim in March, preaching and teaching. 4th, Returns after Purim to Galilee, and continues His work there till Autumn. 5th, He goes up to the Tabernacles in October (John vii. 1. ff.). 6th, He is in Jerusalem at the feast of Dedication in December (x. 22). 7th, He goes up to the last Passover in April. Thus we have a ministry of little more than two years.

The general objection to this shorter ministry is, that it crowds too many events into the Galilæan period. It is said to begin in December and to end in April of the second year following, leaving only the interval between December and the following October when He left Galilee — less than a year — for His work of gathering disciples there. Whoever reflects on the nature of the Lord's mission, how difficult it was for the Jews to understand the significance of His words and His works, and what misconceptions respecting Him prevailed, must see that time was a most essential element. He must give the people, even those best prepared to hear Him, some time for reflection. Their conceptions of the nature of the kingdom of God could not be changed in a moment; their discernment of the failure of the covenant people and of their unfitness for the Messiah, must be of gradual growth. It is true that in some very receptive minds faith in His person might be quickly formed, but a right knowledge

---

[1] See Lichtenstein, 174; Riggenbach, 406.

of His Messianic work was, of necessity, one that required much teaching.[1]

Upon these grounds we think the feast of Purim is to be rejected. It was a feast which it is not at all probable Jesus would go up to Jerusalem to attend, and whose introduction here brings chronological confusion into the gospel history.

The next feast in order of time is that of the Passover in April. In favor of this feast it may be said, that it was one which Jesus would naturally attend as having for Him a special significance. It was also the feast that had the most distinctly religious character, and it was very generally attended by the people, especially the most serious and devout. According to Hengstenberg, "it was the only one at which it was a universal custom to make a pilgrimage to Jerusalem."[2] We may thus infer that He would certainly go, unless prevented by the open hostility of the Jews. But no such hostility now appears. It was aroused into activity by the healing of the impotent man (John v. 16–18) but till this event, He was unmolested.

But the objection is taken that if this be a Passover, and another is mentioned (vi. 4) which apparently He did not attend, then He was not present at any feast till the feast of Tabernacles (vii. 2), a period of a year and a half.[3] This objection has been already alluded to. Whether the Lord did actually go up to any feast between that of v. 1 and that of vii. 2, cannot be determined.[4] We know, at least, that He would not, after the rulers at Jerusalem had sought to slay Him, needlessly expose His life to peril. To the laws of God respecting the feasts He would render all obedience, but with the liberty of a son, not with the servile scrupulosity of a Pharisee. As He was Lord of the Sabbath, so He was Lord of the feasts, and He attended them or did not attend them, as seemed best to Him. From John (vii. 21, 23), where He refers to a work which He had previously done at Jerusalem, and which we must identify with the healing of the impotent man (John v. 5), it appears obvious that He had not, during the interval, been publicly teaching there, and therefore had not attended any feast. Still the point is not certain, as He might

---

[1] If, indeed, we suppose, with Edersheim and Westcott, this unnamed feast to have been in the August or September following the first Passover in April, and to have been followed by that in John vi. 4, as the second, we gain more time, and so better meet the statements of the Evangelists; but, even here, events are too much crowded, as we shall see when we examine them in detail.

[2] See Luke ii. 41, where this feast is specially mentioned.

[3] Hug, Int., 448 ; Pressensé.

[4] Jarvis, Int., 570–576, makes Him to have attended them all, even that of Dedication. This is in the highest degree improbable.

have been present as a private worshipper, and without attracting public attention; yet this is improbable.[1]

Another objection to identifying this feast with the Passover, is that John relates nothing as having occurred between the feasts v. 1 and vi. 4, an interval of a year. This objection has already been sufficiently noticed.

Pentecost is the feast next in order, and occurred this year on the 19th of May. This feast is not mentioned by any of the Evangelists, nor do we know that the Lord was ever present at it. Though it has had some able advocates, as Calvin, Bengel, and lately, Townsend, and was adopted by many of the ancients, it has no special arguments in its favor. It was not so generally attended as Passover or Tabernacles, and no reason appears why Jesus should have omitted Passover and gone up to Pentecost.

The feast of Tabernacles followed upon the 23d of September. The chief argument in its favor is, that it brings the feast of v. 1 into closer connection with that of vii. 2, only a year intervening, and thus best explains his words vii. 21–23.[2] But some months more or less are not under the circumstances important, for the miracle with its results must have been fresh in their minds even after a much longer interval. If He had not in the interval between these feasts been at Jerusalem, as is most probable, His reappearance would naturally carry their minds back to the time when they last saw Him, and recall both His work and their own machinations against Him. Lichtenstein (175) defends this feast, but it is in connection with the view which we cannot adopt, that our Lord spent the summer of 780 in retirement.

The great objection to identifying the feast before us with that of Tabernacles, is, that it puts between the end of Chapter iv. and the beginning of Chapter v. a period of eight or nine months, which the Evangelists are said to pass over in silence.[3]

Comparing these various feasts together, that of the Passover seems to have most in its favor, and that of Purim least. Some incidental points bearing upon this question will be discussed as we proceed. We give the following order as the result of our inquiries: Jesus ceases baptizing and leaves Judæa in December, 780. His disciples depart to their homes, and He lives in retirement till March, 781, when He goes up to this feast, the Passover. At this time, on

---

[1] See Greswell, ii. 247, who maintains that the five instances recorded by John " embrace all the instances of our Saviour's attendance in Jerusalem at any of the feasts."

[2] So Riggenbach, 408.

[3] Ebrard avoids this objection, but falls into another as great, by supposing nothing recorded between the two feasts (John v. 1 and vii. 2), but the sending of the twelve and the feeding of the five thousand.

His way or after His arrival, He hears of the imprisonment of John, and returns to Galilee to begin His work there.

Recent writers are much divided in opinion.

For Purim: Tisch., Meyer, Stroud, Pressensé, Wieseler, Lange, Farrar, Godet, Dwight, M. and M., Bäumlein, Weiss.

Pentecost: Bengel, Browne, Lewin, Friedlieb, McClellan, Grenville.

Passover: Lightfoot, Grotius, Robinson, Sepp, Greswell, Gardiner, Wordsworth, Weitbrecht.

Tabernacles: Ewald, Ebrard, Licht.

Day of Atonement: Caspari.

Feast of Trumpets: Westcott.

Feast of Wood-gathering: Edersheim.

Undecided: Tholuck, Geikie, Neander, Alford, Luthardt.

For early opinions, see commentary of Maldonatus *in loco*, also Bengel, Meyer.

At this feast the Lord healed an impotent man at the pool of Bethesda. This was a place of resort for the sick, and its waters were supposed to have, naturally or supernaturally, healing virtue.[1] Let us inquire as to its position.

The first point is the right rendering : What is to follow the adjective, "sheep,"—$\pi\rho\sigma\beta\alpha\tau\iota\kappa\hat{\eta}$? In A. V., "There is by the sheep *market* a pool"; in R. V., "by the sheep *gate*"; others render it, "There is by the sheep pool *a pool*" (so DeSaulcy, M. and M.); others still, "There is by the sheep pool a "place" or "building"" (so Meyer, Weiss). The Evangelist's intention plainly is to define the position of the pool Bethesda by reference to another place, whether market, or gate, or pool. If "market" be inserted, there is the objection that no sheep market is mentioned in the Old Testament. There is mention of the "sheep gate" (Neh. iii. 32; xii. 39), but if the Evangelist meant this, why not mention it ? If we insert "pool," where it is said by some the sacrifices were washed, we have no account of any such "sheep pool," nor is there any proof that the sacrifices were washed before offering. For the washing of the entrails there was in the temple a washing room (Lightfoot, *in loco*), but that there was a pool where they were washed, is only conjecture. It seems, therefore, more probable that the pool obtained its name from the sheep gate in its vicinity; and this gate is placed by many at the east or northeast side of the temple, and, perhaps, is the same as the present St. Stephen's gate.

---

[1] It will be remembered that verse 4, "For an angel went down at a certain season into the pool, ff.," is of doubtful genuineness. It is omitted by Tisch., W. and H., and in the R. V. See Trench, Mir. 203. It is said by Pusey, *Baptism*, 277, that the fathers understood a "certain season" to mean yearly and that the annual cure was at Pentecost.

The name Bethesda gives us no certain information, the right reading being in dispute. Some ancient authorities having Bethsaida, others Bethzatha (the last is adopted by W. and H., Tisch., R. V. Margin. See Edersheim, i. 462; Qt. St., 1888, p. 124). If, as has been said, Bethzatha is the same as Bezetha, the hill north of the temple, the name may be local — the pool of Bezetha. If the name Bethesda be retained, it is generally rendered "the house of mercy," *domus benignitatis* — perhaps, as Meyer suggests, "a charitable foundation"; others, "house of offence." (See Herzog, Encyc., ii. 118, and commentators.)

We turn now to tradition. Eusebius, *Onomasticon* as translated by Jerome, speaks of Bethesda as a pool bearing the name *Probatike*, and yet as having two parts: *Bethesda, Piscina in Jerusalem quae vocabatur — haec quinque quondam porticus habuit ostendunturque gemini lacus.* Of these one is filled with rain-water, but the other with red water, as if reddened with the blood of the victims washed in it. Thus the name Bethesda seemed to have included two pools near each other. (So in *Itin. Hieros.* mention is made of twin pools — *—piscinae gemillares — quae appellantur Bethsadi.*)

Where were these twin pools? There has been a current belief for centuries that the deep excavation on the northeast corner of the temple area known as Birket Israel, is Bethesda. It is said by De Saulcy (ii. 285): "The two pools of St. John's gospel were close to, and in communication with, each other—*piscinae gemillares*— probably by the vaulted arches which are still to be seen at the extremity of Birket Israel. One of these pools was the Probatica, the other, Bethesda." But Robinson (i. 293) says: "There is not the slightest evidence that can identify them, and the tradition goes no further back than the thirteenth century." With Robinson almost all now agree. It is the general opinion that this excavation, 360 feet long, 130 broad, and 75 deep, was a part of the trench that once separated the temple enclosure from the adjoining hill, that it extended to the northwest corner of Antonia, and that it was afterward used as a reservoir. Fergusson, on the other hand, affirms that it was always meant for a reservoir.

Putting Birket Israel aside, two other pools have been suggested, both fed, as supposed, by intermittent springs: the fountain of the Virgin, which Robinson adopts; and the fountain on the west side of the temple area now called Hamman Esh-Shifa. (See Williams, Holy City, ii. 458.) But these are both single pools, and the last has no claim to be called intermittent. (Another view in Stewart, Tent and Khan, 277 ff., and another in Barclay, 326.) Some have thought that these pools may lie under the convent of the Sisters of Zion, a little

to the northwest of the temple. Thus Sir C. Wilson says: "These
accounts seem to indicate that Bethesda was identical with the twin
pools now known as the Souterrains of the convent. Here are two
pools in the rock, side by side, with a partition five feet wide between
them." (Qt. St., 1872, 147; Qt. St., 1888, 127.) Lightfoot thinks
Siloam, to whose waters he ascribes supernatural virtues, to be
Bethesda. In regard to the latter, he says: "The general silence
of the Jews about the wondrous virtue of this pool is something
strange, who, in the abundant praises, and particularly of Jerusalem,
yet speak not one word, that I have ever found, toward the story of
Bethesda."

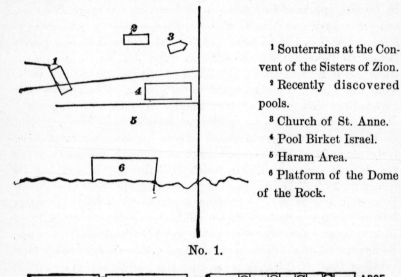

[1] Souterrains at the Convent of the Sisters of Zion.

[2] Recently discovered
pools.

[3] Church of St. Anne.

[4] Pool Birket Israel.

[5] Haram Area.

[6] Platform of the Dome
of the Rock.

No. 1.

No. 2. PLAN OF THE TWO POOLS.

But very recent explorations seem to leave little doubt that the
pool Bethesda is to be found a little northwest of the church of
St. Anne, and not far from the present St. Stephen's gate. In 1856,
the site of this church, perhaps built as early as the seventh century,
and rebuilt in the twelfth, was given by the Sultan to the French:
and, clearing up the ruins, they discovered a pool about 100 feet to
the northwest, lying under a small church, of which a part of the apse
remains. The pool is 55 feet in length, east and west, and 12 in
breadth; but perhaps these dimensions should be reversed, the

breadth being 55 feet, and the length north and south undetermined, since the north wall is wooden, and the pool may have been much longer than now appears.   It is cut in solid rock to the depth of thirty feet, and there are remaining the bases of five pillars cut out of the rock.   Upon the top of these pillars was formerly a stone roofing, and upon these were probably placed the five arches mentioned in the Gospel, and which were afterwards destroyed.   There are twenty-four steps originally cut in the rock, and thus it would be very difficult for the lame and feeble to get down to the water.

Sometime after this discovery a second pool was discovered, lying to the west of the first, but no full statement respecting it has yet been made.

It is admitted that these new pools lie in the very place where tradition placed them, and where they would now be looked for. Says Sir C. Wilson: "The pilgrims, in their accounts of Jerusalem, generally describe the pool with five arches as near the church of St. Anne."   Saewulf (1102 A. D., Early Trav., 41) speaks of the church of St. Anne, and near it the pool called in the Hebrew Bethsaida, having five porticoes of which the Gospel speaks.   (See Maundeville, Early Trav., 172: "In that church is a well, in manner of a cistern, which is called *Probatica Piscina*, which hath five entrances."   Rob., i. 331, Qt. St., 1888, 125.)   From these and other early testimonies, Williams (Holy City, ii. 483) inferred that in this place the pool would be found.   See Prof. Paine in The Independent, Aug. 16, 1888, who regards the "identification as complete."

There is good reason to believe that the lost pool has been found. This is, however, questioned by Conder, apparently upon the ground that there is no proof that the water of the pool recently found was intermittent.   The matter cannot be considered as absolutely determined; we must await further investigation.

As the healing of the impotent man took place on the Sabbath, it gave the Jews the desired opportunity of accusing Him of a breach of the law; and it seems, indeed, as if the Lord desired to judge their whole system of legal righteousness by an emphatic condemnation of the interpretation they gave to one of the most important of the commandments.   Lightfoot (*in loco*) observes: "It is worthy our observation that our Saviour did not think it enough merely to heal the impotent man on the Sabbath day, which was against their rules, but farther commanded him to take up his bed, which was much more against that rule."   A rigid observance of the Sabbath, even to the prohibition of the healing of the sick on that day (Luke xiii. 14), was a main element of Pharisaic righteousness, and therefore on this point He took issue with them.[1] It is said by Pressensé: "*Ultra sabbatarianism* was the very genius of the Pharisaic religion." According to the order we follow, it was the first time that He had healed on the Sabbath, and the question how such a work should be regarded, whether as lawful or unlawful, came before the ecclesiastical authorities at Jerusalem for their decision. That they decided it to be unlawful appears from the angry opposition which subsequent cases of healing on that day called forth.

The grounds of our Lord's defense (vs. 17–47) must be here considered. But first the question arises, Before whom was it spoken? There can be little doubt that He was now brought before the Sanhedrin. (So Licht., Meyer, Lange, Tholuck, Edersheim: "The masters in Israel"; Farrar: "summoned before the great Rabbis and chief priests.") That some interval of time elapsed between verses 17 and 19 is probable. That those before whom the Lord now stood, were the same who sent the Deputation from Jerusalem to the Baptist, appears from verse 33: "Ye sent unto John, and he bare witness unto the truth." Thus regarded as spoken before the ecclesiastical rulers and masters, and His final testimony to them before He entered upon a new stage of His work, His words demand our special attention.

The right of the Lord to heal on the Sabbath day He puts on the ground of His divine Sonship. As the Son, He did nothing of Himself, He did only what His Father did: "My Father worketh hitherto, and I work." This defense only angered them the more, because "He made Himself equal with God." This Sonship they could not comprehend; it was not an element that entered, at least distinctly, into their Messianic conceptions. There was much confusion in the Jewish mind as to the person of the Messiah and His prerogatives, most regarding Him as a mere man to be raised up of God for their deliverance; and as to the respective works to be wrought by Him and by Jehovah at the setting up of the Messianic kingdom. Would the Messiah raise the dead and sit in judgment, or would Jehovah? The Lord's words carried the Messianic claims far beyond the general belief; they seemed to affirm an equality with Jehovah in His actings which was blasphemous. They were also very mysterious. Not content with claiming to be the executor of His Father's will in all His works, even the highest — those of resurrection and judgment — He adds: "As the Father hath life in Himself, so hath He given to the Son to have life in Himself"; thus pointing to Himself as the second Adam, to become in resurrection the new and immortal Head of the race in the Messianic age.

---

[1] See Eders., ii. 56 ff., and Appendix 17.

Having stated His relation to His Father and His claim to equal honor, He proceeds to state the evidences of His divine mission. He accepts the truth that a man's own testimony is not sufficient. But there was other testimony: 1st, that of the Baptist, borne publicly, and of which they had official knowledge; 2d, that of His works wrought in the name and in the power of the Father, a sufficient proof that God had sent Him (see John iii. 2, "No man can do these miracles that Thou doest except God be with Him"); 3d, that given by the Holy Scriptures. Many refer, verse 37, "the Father Himself which hath sent me hath borne witness of me," to the voice heard at His baptism and the descent of the Spirit upon Him. But if evidence to the Jews, they must have heard the voice and seen the dove (Matt. iii. 17, which apparently they did not.) Why then, did they not receive Him? Because they had not the love of God in them. They had the Scriptures and searched them but did not understand them, because "His word did not abide in them." A Messiah not honored by men, though honored by God, they could not receive. Coming in the name of His Father they rejected Him, but another coming in his own name they would receive. It was Moses who accused them of unbelief, for he wrote of Him, and disbelieving Moses they disbelieved Him.

The Lord's justification of Himself before the Sanhedrin based upon His divine Sonship and His equality with God, only the more inflamed the anger of His enemies. He had broken the law of the Sabbath by healing the impotent man on that day, and now He puts forth in defense blasphemous claims to be greater than the Messiah, even to be equal with God. With such a law-breaker and blasphemer there could be no peace. It was a duty to reject Him, nay more, to put Him to death.

Thus, His presentation of Himself to the nation in its chiefs had been unavailing. It only brought out their enmity into fuller manifestation, and showed how unprepared were all — priests, scribes, and elders — to receive Him. The suspicion with which they had regarded Him from the first, arising from His peculiar relations to the Baptist, whom they disliked and whose baptism they refused, had continually strengthened; and this His defense brought their hostility to a head. Whether any official action was now taken, does not appear; but it is not improbable, since the Evangelist a little later explains the fact of His ministry in Galilee by saying that He could not walk in Judæa "because the Jews sought to kill Him." From this we may infer that it was then determined upon to seize Him and put Him to death if found in Judæa. (Compare verses 25–32.) From this province He was thus, by the act of the ecclesiastical rulers, excluded.

It is well said by Ellicott (141): "This is the turning point in the Gospel history. Up to this time the preaching of our Lord at Jerusalem and in Judæa had met with a certain degree of toleration, and in many cases even of acceptance; but after this all becomes changed. Henceforth the city of David is no meet or safe abode for the Son of David; the earthly house of His Heavenly Father is no longer a secure hall of audience for the preaching of the Eternal Son."

It will be well at this point to consider the Lord's rejection by the Jews at Jerusalem, both as to its grounds, and its effects upon His subsequent ministry. The warrant for this rejection was found in the direction given in Deuteronomy xiii. 1–5, by which to test the claims of one pretending to a divine mission. The sign or wonder which he might give, was not to be of itself sufficient proof; his words and teaching must also be taken into account. If he spake anything contrary to the law, the wonder or sign did not compel the people to give him credence: rather they must reject him, and if he taught idolatry, must put him to death. (See Cohen, *Les Deicides*, Paris, 1864.)

Let us admit that this divine direction was to the Jews of the Lord's day the rule of their action. Jesus appeared before them as one sent of God; He was to be tested by a two-fold standard, His words and His works. His words were of the first importance, His works were subordinate. A man might be a prophet and prophesy and teach, and yet work no miracle, as was the case with most of the Old Testament prophets. It was their words that proved their divine mission. If Jesus had claimed to be simply a prophet, one sent from God with a message, He need not work any miracle; His message would prove itself by its conformity to the law, and by its spirit. It would appeal to the spiritual discernment of the people (John x. 4 ff.). Conformity to the old revelation, and a true development of it, was the test of the new; and it was in this way that the Baptist attested his mission.

But if He claimed to be the Messiah, He must give the appointed signs, for the Messiah's work was a great step forward; His coming brought in a new epoch. The proof that sufficed for a prophet, would not suffice for the Messiah. There must be both the word of truth and the sign or wonder; and more, He must set up the Messianic kingdom.

What, then, might the Jews rightly demand of Jesus as the Messiah, as to His teaching, and as to His work? 1st, that personally He would keep the law, and would enforce its universal observance; 2d, that He would fulfill the words of the prophets as to the Messianic kingdom.   These were in themselves just demands, but they implied two things: first, that they themselves knew the meaning of the law, and kept it without adding to it or taking from it; second, that their Messianic beliefs were in conformity to the prophets.   But in both these respects they failed.   They had added to the law many traditions, and made it in some points void, and in many others burdensome. Therefore, when they came to judge His teachings and acts by it, they made Him a transgressor when He was not; He kept the law in letter and in spirit, but they condemned Him for not keeping it. Their expectations, also, of the Messianic kingdom were not according to the prophets.   They did not understand that the people must be keeping all God's ordinances, must be obedient, righteous, holy, or they were not ready for the Messiah.   The prophets always spoke of their captivity and subjection to the nations around them as a punishment of their sins, and demanded repentance and humble confession as a preliminary to their restoration.   The Jews in this day were in sore bondage under the Roman yoke, but there was no consciousness of guilt on their part, no true sense of God's anger with them, no humiliation, no confession.   Therefore, the first step on God's part was to call them to repentance; without this His promises of restoration could not be fulfilled.   But they did not hear the Baptist calling them to repentance.   They believed that the Messiah would take them in their then condition, organize them, overthrow the Romans, and make them a great nation.   It was these beliefs and expectations by which they tested the Lord, and He did not fulfill them.   On the contrary, He began by trying to awake in them a sense of sin.   He did not accept their traditions, but showed them plainly what God demanded of them; He did not even assume the title of the Messiah, lest He should be understood as confirming their unfounded hopes.

Thus we see that, however right the rule of their action in demanding conformity to the law and the prophets in the teachings and works of one claiming a divine mission, the Jews were in no position to apply it to the Lord; they did not know the law, they did not understand the prophets, and thus had no right criterion, no standard by which to judge His teachings or His works.

But the Lord was more than the Messiah, He was the Incarnate Son of God.   He did not, indeed, now present Himself as such to the Jews, but He could not separate His Person from His office.   (See John iii. 13.)   He who was the God-Man, was both Prophet and Messiah.   The

Jews understood Him to assert a certain filial relation to God as lying
at the basis of His Messiahship, a kind of equality with the Father.
(Whether His words here imply partaking of the divine essence, or an
equality in action and honor, is a matter for theological interpretation.) What ground should the Jews take in regard to claims like
these? They could reject them as absolutely incredible, so palpably
false as to be self-condemned; or they could compare them with
what their Scriptures taught them of the Person of the Messiah.
They took the first. His words were blasphemous, and on this ground
He was put to death (Matt. xxvi. 63 ff.).

But it is to be noted that the Lord did not, first of all, reveal the
mystery of His Person. This revelation could be made only when those
who had received Him as the Messiah had learned through His teaching what was involved in the title Son of God. It was as more than a
prophet that He presented Himself to the people, for in Him all the predictions of the prophets were to be fulfilled. If they, seeing His works
and hearing His words, received Him as the Messiah, then He could
lead them on to a fuller knowledge of His Person, and reveal to them
what had been the purpose of God from the first—that the Word should
be made flesh and dwell among men. But to those who could not
rise above the current worldly conceptions of the Messiah, every intimation which He gave of His divine Sonship was both unintelligible
and offensive.

We have also to ask, What was the effect of this rejection by the
rulers upon the Lord's subsequent ministry? That the Galilæans were
ignorant of their hostility toward Him, as shown by their attitude
from the first, and especially after the healing of the impotent man,
is not probable. He went down into Galilee to begin His ministry
there as a proscribed man, one under the ban; whoever accepted Him
as the Messiah, or even as a prophet, did it knowing that he exposed
himself to the ill-will and rebukes of his spiritual leaders. Whether
the ecclesiastical jurisdiction of the Sanhedrin extended to all parts
of the land, so that the power "to put out of the Synagogue" (John
ix. 22) was in force in Galilee, we do not certainly know, but probably it did. (See Schürer, ii. 1. 185.) Thus it demanded a high
measure of faith and much self-sacrifice to confess Him as the Messiah. In a real sense every one who followed Him must take up His
cross. The call to leave all and follow Him, even if attended by no
civil punishments, could be heard only by those over whom truth was
all powerful, and who could say with St. Peter, "Thou hast the
words of eternal life." We may find in the records of the Galilæan
ministry, how much it cost to be known as one of His adherents,

although at the first there was a strong popular feeling in His favor.

With this miracle, the healing of the impotent man, the Lord's Judæan work, or the first stage of His ministry, came to an end. As Jesus now left Judæa, and only returned to it after a considerable interval, and then only for very brief periods at the feasts, His enemies in that province had little opportunity to arrest Him. We know, however, that in point of fact they attempted to do so at the very first feast He attended (John vii. 32). So long as He was in Galilee, all they could do to Him was to watch His proceedings there, and seize upon every occasion that presented itself to destroy His reputation, and hinder His work. How zealously they labored to this end will appear as our history proceeds.

PART IV.

The Lord's Ministry in Galilee to the Death of the Baptist.

Of the general character of the Lord's work in Galilee, as
distinguished from His work in Judæa, we have already spoken,
when considering the divisions of His ministry. It is in the light
of this distinction that certain remarkable, and to some readers
perplexing, features of the synoptical Gospels find their explanation. As is patent upon their narratives, they relate nothing that
the Lord did prior to John the Baptist's imprisonment. Only
from the Evangelist John do we learn that His field of labor, till
the Baptist was imprisoned, was Judæa. Here His time was
spent from the Passover of 780 till the December following, and
if He resided in Galilee a few weeks till the feast (John v. 1),
as He seems to have done, this was in consequence of the enmity
of the Jews, and the time was apparently spent in seclusion.
So far as the narratives of Matthew, Mark, and Luke go, the
beginning of His public labors is to be dated from the time
when, the Baptist being cast into prison, He went from Judæa
into Galilee. They all assume that He was in Judæa up to this
time, this being the province to which His early labors were
confined. The reasons why they pass over in silence this first
year of His ministry, and why they bring His work in Galilee
into such close connection with the Baptist, we now proceed to
consider.

The silence of the Synoptists respecting the Judæan work of
the Lord will not appear strange, if we recall the purpose and
result of that work. As we have seen, John, after the baptism of Jesus, was visited by a Deputation of priests and Levites
from Jerusalem, to whom he bore formal witness that the Messiah

had come (John i. 19–28).   Perhaps, also, he pointed out Jesus
to them in person.   It was now a question distinctly before the
ecclesiastical rulers, Would they receive Jesus thus pointed out
to them as the Christ, or reject Him ?   As they took no steps to
seek Him, thus showing their disregard of the Baptist's testimony, at the first feast after this testimony He appeared in the
temple, and there assumed authority to purge it.   He also
worked miracles, and taught, and many believed in Him as
one sent from God.   Still the ecclesiastical rulers did not receive
Him.   He therefore begins to baptize ; but they do not come
to His baptism ; the gathering to Him of the people only aug-
ments their hostility; and they seek to cast impediments in His
way by sowing dissensions between His disciples and those of
John.   As they will not come to receive baptism, or be taught by
Him, no further step can now be taken in the regular development of His Messianic work.   He, therefore, ceases to baptize, and
retires from Judæa.   Still the time is not yet come for Him to
begin His work in Galilee, for the Baptist is at liberty, and
through his witness and labors the rulers may yet be brought to
repentance, and the nation be saved.   He will wait till His forerunner has finished his work ere He commences His new work in
Galilee.   Once more He presents Himself in Jerusalem at a feast,
and works a miracle, but is called a blasphemer, and His life is
endangered ; and John's ministry also comes to a sudden and
untimely end.   The Baptist is shut up in prison, and can
bear no further witness.   There is now no place for the Lord
in Judæa.   All the labors of the Baptist and His own labors
had been unavailing to turn the hearts of those in authority, and
to insure His reception as the Messiah.   By their own unbelief,
those who sat in Moses' seat, the priests and Levites, had made it
impossible that He could use them in His service, and continuing to reject Him they themselves must be rejected.   The
Mosaic institutions must be set aside, and their priesthood cease ;
the defiled temple be destroyed, and the Christian Church be
founded.

It is here that we find the essential distinction between the
Lord's work in Judæa and that in Galilee.   The former had reference to the Jewish people in their corporate capacity, a nation

in covenant with God; He addressed Himself to the nation as represented in its ecclesiastical rulers, and aimed to produce in them that sense of sin, and that true repentance, which were indispensable to His reception. The latter was based upon the fact that the ecclesiastical rulers of the Jews did not receive Him, and had sought to kill Him ; and that, therefore, if they persisted in their wickedness, God was about to cast them out of their peculiar relations to Him, and establish a church, of which the elect of all nations should be members (Matt. viii. 11, 12). Going into Galilee, the Lord will gather there a body of disciples, who shall bear witness to Him before the nation; but who, if this testimony is unavailing, will serve as the foundations of the new institutions resting upon the New Covenant.

Thus the departure from Judæa into Galilee does not imply that the Lord regarded this rejection of Himself by the Jews as final, and that nothing remained but to lay new foundations and choose a new priesthood. He will leave Judæa, but after a time He will return. He will to the last make every effort to save them (Matt. xxiii. 37). His work in Galilee still has reference to national salvation through the faith of those who should believe on Him there; and to this end, as we shall see, He sent out the seventy at the close of the Galilean ministry. If, however, the nation will not hear them, then from among them He will select those who shall take the place of the priests of the Aaronic line, and be builders and rulers under Him — the Stone which the builders had refused, but now become the Head of the corner.

Thus it will not appear strange that the Synoptists, writing after all these events had developed themselves, and when the Jews had lost their high place by disobedience, and the new Covenant had been established, should pass over in silence the Lord's Judæan work. It was, indeed, a matter of highest interest to the Jews, but regarded in its relations to the Christian Church, its mention was comparatively unimportant; and the Synoptists could well commence their narratives with that work in Galilee, which, looking forward to the future, was already developing itself so widely and powerfully. It was comparatively of little moment that their Gentile readers should know, in detail, that the Lord first began His labors in Judæa, and that, after a few months.

He was compelled to abandon them through the enmity of the rulers; since all Christians knew in general that He was finally rejected by them, and suffered death at their hands. But the Galilæan work was of the highest moment, as it marked where the dividing line began between the old and the new, between Moses and Christ. And this may also explain their silence in respect to the feasts which the Lord attended while in Galilee, and are mentioned by John. Any transient work at Jerusalem, addressing itself especially to the hierarchy, had had no important bearing upon the great result, as time had shown, and need not therefore be mentioned by them.

Thus the silence of the Synoptists respecting the early work of Jesus in Judæa is satisfactorily explained; and we also see why the imprisonment of the Baptist is made so prominent in their narratives. It marks the time when He left Judæa for Galilee, and is thus the great turning point in His ministry. So long as John was free to prosecute his work of calling the nation to repentance, He could take no steps looking forward to the establishment of new institutions. He could not begin to preach or teach in Galilee. But John in prison could no more prepare His way, could no more testify of Him to the nation, or administer the baptism of repentance. The voice of the forerunner thus silenced, Jesus, departing to Galilee, can there begin Himself to preach, and to gather disciples, and to prepare them for their future work.

As the primary object of the ministry in Galilee was to gather disciples, the Lord directs His teachings and works to that end. Hence, His visits to all parts of the land, His use of the synagogues for preaching, His teachings in the streets, in the fields, upon the sea-shore, wherever the people gather to Him. He speaks to all, that whoever has ears to hear may hear. Hence, also, His readiness to heal all who may come unto Him, that the faith which the word could not draw forth, might be drawn forth by the work. Thus by degrees He gathered around Him the most spiritually-minded and receptive of the Galilæans, and of the inhabitants of the adjacent regions. From these in due time He chose a small body of men whom He kept near Himself, and to whom He explained what was obscure in His public discourses, as they were able to hear; and these, after He had instructed them, He sent forth to be witnesses to the people at large.

This work of Jesus in Galilee, gathering and educating His disciples, continued from the Passover of 781 till the Feast of Tabernacles in 782, or a period of about one year and six months. The death of the Baptist, which we place in the spring of 782, had an important bearing upon His labors, and divides this Galilean ministry into two parts, which are easily distinguishable from each other. The grounds of this distinction will be noted hereafter. Our present period ends with the Baptist's death. The important events that mark its progress will be noticed as we proceed.

THE PROVINCE OF GALILEE.

This departure of the Lord into Galilee to make this the field of His labors, offers us a fit opportunity to describe it in its general features.[1] Palestine proper, west of Jordan, according to the latest explorations, has about 6,000 square miles, and Galilee something less than a third of this. In the Lord's day it was very populous. Josephus (War, iii. 3. 2) says, "the towns were numerous, and the multitude of villages so crowded with men, owing to the fecundity of the soil, that the smallest of them contained about 15,000 inhabitants"; and in his Life (xlv. 4), incidentally mentions that "there were 204 cities and villages," thus giving it a population of more than 3,000,000. Almost all writers agree that this is an exaggeration, but Merrill thinks the number not incredible. Making all allowance for this, Galilee must have been very full of people. (See Raumer, 81, who cites Dion Cassius as stating that in the war under Hadrian, 985 villages of the Jews were laid waste.) Nor were these towns and villages inert and sluggish, but full of life and energy. The richness of the soil abundantly repaid the labors of the cultivators, and it was a thoroughfare through which passed great quantities of merchandise from Damascus and the East to the Mediterranean, and from the coast to the interior. The lake of Galilee was covered with ships engaged in fishing and traffic, and its shores were dotted with cities and villages. Taricheæ, at its lower end, contained about 40,000 inhabitants (Josephus, War, iii. 10. 10), and there were other cities probably not less populous. In a region so

---

[1] See "Galilee at the time of Christ," by Rev. S. Merrill, LL.D.; Conder, Hand-Book; Stanley, Sinai and Palestine; Schürer, I. ii., and Bible Dictionaries.

fertile by nature, and inhabited by an industrious people, there could not be wanting many rich families ; and to this the Gospels bear witness, as also the ruins of buildings, palaces, and tombs. It was a common saying, quoted by Edersheim: "If a person wishes to be rich, let him go north; if he wants to be wise, let him come south."

Although patriotic and courageous, there was for a long time little of political disturbance, Galilee standing in this respect in striking contrast with Judæa under the Roman governors. After Herod the Great's death, Galilee and Peræa were allotted by the emperor to his son Herod Antipas, who ruled there during the Lord's whole life. This shows that his general administration, whatever his personal character, was not cruel or unjust. But the spirit of nationalism was stronger in Galilee than in Judæa, and any tidings of a coming Messiah were more gladly received.

It is generally said that Galilee, being surrounded on the east and south and west by alien peoples, had in it a large foreign and heathen element, and that its inhabitants were much less strict in the observance of the law than those in Judæa, and were therefore looked down upon by the latter, and treated with disdain ("out of Galilee ariseth no prophet," John vii. 52). Their language was not so pure (Matt. xxvi. 73), nor were they learned in the law. But Merrill thinks these charges of ignorance and of irreligion unfounded, and denies that there was so large a heathen element as is asserted, and their language so corrupt. Conder (Hand-Book, 313) agrees with him, and affirms that although "the Talmudic writers speak with contempt of the Galilæans, they do not say anything which would lead to the supposition that the Galilæans were less orthodox than the inhabitants of Judæa." But we may infer from the statements of Josephus that, while the bulk of the Galilæans were Jews, there were many Phœnicians, Arabians, Syrians, and some Greeks among them; and if so, it was natural, perhaps inevitable, that there should be a less strict observance of the law than in Judæa, more freedom from traditional bonds, more openness to hear new things (see Eders. i. 223 ff.).

It was to this province that the Lord went when driven from Judæa by the ecclesiastical rulers. He must enter upon His new work of gathering disciples, and here He would find freedom of movement. The Sanhedrin had no civil jurisdiction in Galilee, and the king was not likely to interfere. Indeed, we know that for a considerable time he took no notice at all of the Lord and His work, and if he heard of Him, looked upon Him as one of the Rabbis who was gathering disciples around Him, and His work without political significance. Not till the Baptist's death did he desire to see Him;

and thus the Lord, unmolested by the authorities, — for the alliance of the Pharisees and Herodians, or partisans of Herod (Mark iii. 6), was apparently without the knowledge of the king, — could visit all parts of the province, and teach openly in all places.

That the Pharisees and Scribes of Galilee stood to the Lord from the first, in an attitude of suspicion and dislike, which gradually became one of positive hostility, appears from the Synoptists, and will be noticed more particularly as we examine them. The nationalists, or those opposed to all foreign domination, affirming that God alone was their king, and who are called by Josephus the Zealots, do not seem at this time to have been politically organized, but their principles were spreading among the people, and from them the Lord took one of His apostles.

April, 781.   A. D. 28.

The Baptist being now imprisoned, the Lord leaves Judæa Matt. iv. 12. and goes into Galilee to begin His ministry there. In His Mark i. 14, 15. progress He comes to Nazareth and teaches in its synagogue. Luke iv. 14, 15. His words enraging the people, and His life being in danger, Luke iv. 16–31. He leaves Nazareth, and going to Capernaum there takes up Matt. iv. 12–17. His abode.

The manner in which John relates what the Lord did in Galilee up to the time of the feast (v. 1) shows that he regarded Judæa as the proper field of His labors during this period, and His works in Galilee as only exceptional. Only two miracles were wrought in Galilee during this period, and both when He was at Cana (John ii. 1; iv. 46). Of the first, the Evangelist says: "This beginning of miracles did Jesus in Cana of Galilee, and manifested forth His glory;" of the second: "This is again the second miracle that Jesus did, when He was come out of Judæa into Galilee." Both these miracles were wrought under peculiar circumstances, and for special ends, not in the ordinary course of His ministry. Those wrought by Him in Jerusalem at the first Passover (John ii. 23, compare iii. 2) are merely alluded to, although they seem to have been of a striking character; but these are specified as wrought by Jesus coming out of Judæa, the proper place of His ministry, into Galilee where His ministry had not yet begun, John not being imprisoned.

It is to be remembered that Galilee had been spoken of several centuries before the Saviour's birth by the prophet

Isaiah (ix. 1, 2) as that part of the Holy Land to be especially blessed by His labors. It had been the part least esteemed, not only because in the division of the kingdom it was joined to Israel in opposition to Judah, but also as especially exposed to foreign invasion, and had in fact been repeatedly conquered. Here was the greatest admixture of foreign elements, the natural result of these conquests, and hence the name, "Galilee of the Gentiles." The prophet mentions the two tribes of Zebulon and Napthali as peculiarly depised; and within the bounds of the first was Nazareth, and within the bounds of the second was Capernaum. How wonderfully this prophecy, so dark in its literal interpretation, was fulfilled, the history of the Lord's ministry shows. His own in Judæa and Jerusalem would not walk in His light, and thus it was that, in "Galilee of the Gentiles, the people which sat in darkness saw great light."

To the prediction of Isaiah, the Evangelist Matthew, according to his custom, calls the attention of his readers, and affirms that in Galilee thus prophetically marked out the preaching of the Lord actually began (iv. 17). "From that time," that is, from the imprisonment of John, and the departure into Galilee that immediately followed it, "Jesus began to preach," etc. "His earlier appearance in Judæa, though full of striking incidents and proofs of His divine legation, was preliminary to His ministry or preaching, properly so called, which now began."[1] Luke connects His teaching in the synagogue with His return into Galilee (iv. 14–15). That His enemies at Jerusalem regarded His labors as first taking positive form and character in Galilee, appears from their accusation (Luke xxiii. 5), "He stirreth up the people, teaching throughout all Jewry, beginning from Galilee to this place." (See also the words of Peter, Acts x. 37, "That word which was published throughout all Judæa, and began from Galilee.") And as God had ordered that Galilee should be the chief theatre of His teaching, so He providentially overruled the political arrangements of the time that He could labor without hindrance, since the tetrarch Herod Antipas did not trouble himself concerning any ecclesiastical movements that did not disturb the public peace. And

---

[1] Alexander, *in loco*; so Greswell, ii. 274; Stier, on Luke iv. 18.

here, also, the people were less under the influence of the hierarchy, and more open to His words.

If we are right in putting the imprisonment of the Baptist just before the unnamed feast, it is the return to Galilee after this feast that is meant by the Synoptists (Matt. iv. 12; Mark i. 14, 15; Luke iv. 14, 15.) Comparing their account of what followed this return, with that given by John (iv. 43–54), we find full proof that they refer to different periods. According to the latter, Jesus went to Galilee, not to begin public labors but to find retirement. The prophet, as a rule, having no honor in his own country, He might well hope to pass the time there in seclusion, without attracting public attention, till the issue of John's ministry was determined. He did not indeed find the privacy which He sought, because the Galileans had been eye witnesses of what He had done at Jerusalem, and were favorably inclined toward Him. Very soon after His return a nobleman from Capernaum sought His aid; but aside from this, there is no indication that He performed any miracles or engaged in any teaching. No disciples are spoken of as with Him, nor any crowds of people. Nor when He goes up to the feast (v. 1) does He appear to have been attended by any disciples. On the other hand, according to the Synoptists, so soon as He heard of John's imprisonment He began His labors in Galilee, very early gathering again His disciples, and working miracles, and teaching in all the synagogues. His fame spread immediately through the whole region, and wherever He went great crowds followed Him.

Some find difficulty in reconciling the Synoptists with John ii. 12; iv. 46, because the former say that Jesus went to Capernaum to begin His ministry after the imprisonment of the Baptist. But these earlier visits they might well pass over in silence, as not at all affecting the general fact that the field of labor during the first part of His ministry was Judæa, and not Galilee. The first of these visits to Galilee was before the first Passover, and of short duration; the second was after the work in Judæa had been interrupted, and was also brief, and neither of them was marked by public labors. He began to preach in Galilee only when He had ended for the time His work in Judæa, and this was after the imprisonment of the Baptist and the attempt of the Jews on His own life (John v. 18).

10

From Matthew's words (iv. 13): "Leaving Nazareth, He came and dwelt in Capernaum," we may infer that up to this time Nazareth was his fixed place of residence, although the two miracles — the change of water into wine and the healing of the nobleman's son — were wrought by Him being at Cana. If the words are taken in their strict sense, we may say that leaving Jerusalem after the unnamed feast He went first to Nazareth, where He taught in the synagogue, and thence to Capernaum. Mark says only in general terms that "He came into Galilee." Luke (iv. 16, 31) speaks as if He went from Nazareth to Capernaum. Are we to assume that he is narrating chronologically, and that the Lord's Galilæan ministry, His first teaching in a synagogue, began at Nazareth? This may be doubted. We find in this Evangelist (iv. 15, 16) a brief but comprehensive statement of His work in Galilee, that His fame went abroad, and that "He taught in their synagogues, being glorified of all." Is the mention of His teaching at Nazareth which immediately follows, an instance illustrating the general character of His ministry, and without regard to the time when it occurred? (So Keil, and many.)

Before we answer this question, we must ask whether the Lord twice visited and preached in Nazareth? As Matthew (xiii. 53–58) and Mark (vi. 1–6) both speak of a visit of Jesus to Nazareth, but apparently at a later period, it is a question whether this visit can be identified with that mentioned by Luke (iv. 16–30), or whether they are to be regarded as distinct.[1] There are several points of likeness, but not more than would naturally exist in two visits made under such peculiar circumstances. In both, His words excite the astonishment, not unmixed with envy, of His fellow-townsmen; and recalling to mind His origin and His education amongst themselves, and His family, whose members they knew, they are offended at His prophetic claims. In both, He repeats the proverb, so strikingly applicable, that "a prophet is not without honor save in his own country;" but with this difference, that at the second visit He

---

[1] Opinions of recent inquirers are about equally divided. In favor of their identity are Lange, Alford, Bucher, Friedlieb, Lichtenstein, Farrar, Bleek, Weiss; against it, Meyer, Stier, Robinson, Tischendorf, Wieseler, Krafft, Townsend, Ellicott, Keil on Matt. xiii. 54 ff., Godet; and, hesitatingly, Edersheim.

adds, with apparent reference to His brothers and sisters, "and among his own kin and in his own house." On the other hand, the points of difference are more numerous, and more plainly marked. In the former visit, He is alone, in the latter, He is accompanied by His disciples (Mark vi. 1). In the former, He is attacked by the enraged populace, and escapes through supernatural aid the threatened death; in the latter, though He marvelled at their unbelief, He continued there for a time, and healed a few sick folk. In the former, " passing through the midst of them He went His way and came to Capernaum, a city of Galilee"; in the latter, He " went round about the villages teaching." The mention of the healing of the sick by Mark clearly shows the visits to have been distinct, for it could not have taken place before His first teaching in the synagogue on the Sabbath, and immediately afterward He was obliged to flee from their rage.

But if we find two distinct visits to Nazareth, this does not show that this in Luke was before He went to Capernaum, and the first instance of His teaching in a synagogue. This will depend upon the meaning of Luke's words (iv. 16), " And as His custom was, He went into the synagogue on the Sabbath day, and stood up for to read." Was it His custom, while yet living at Nazareth and before His ministry began, not only to attend the service but to take part in it ? There were two parts of the service in which He may have assisted — the offering of the prayers; the reading of the Scriptures, first the Law, then the Prophets; and the exposition or sermon following, if any was made. But those who took part were asked to do so by the president or superintendent of the service, and none did so but those thus asked. (As to the mode of conducting the service, see Eders., i. 439 ff.) Whether the Lord may not, as a private man, have offered the prayers and read the Scriptures, we cannot say, but that He had never preached, may be fairly inferred from verse 22 : " They wondered at the gracious words which proceeded out of His mouth." It certainly had not been His custom to expound the Scriptures or preach at Nazareth ; and that He was now called up to read and expound, was doubtless owing to the reputation He had already acquired as a teacher (John iii. 2 ; Eders., i. 445).

It seems, therefore, better to confine "as His custom was" either to His attendance on the synagogue service, or to interpret it by the general statement in the verse preceding: "And He taught in their synagogues," *i. e.*, He did at Nazareth only what He was accustomed to do elsewhere. (So Bleek *in loco.*)

If we accept this visit at Nazareth as before His settlement at Capernaum, how are the words, verse 23, to be understood "Whatsoever we have heard done in Capernaum, do here also in thy country"? This implies that He had already wrought miracles in Capernaum. Some (as Ebrard and Edersheim) explain this by saying that this may refer to the healing of the nobleman's son, which took place at Capernaum, though Jesus Himself was at Cana; others (as Godet), that He wrought some miracles when earlier at Capernaum (John ii. 12) though they are not mentioned; and others still, that He may have gone to Nazareth at this time by way of Capernaum, and wrought some miracles on the way. It must be admitted that these explanations are not wholly satisfactory; and the natural inference is, that this visit at Nazareth was, if distinct from and earlier than that in Matthew and Mark, still after the beginning of His labors in Capernaum.

A chronological datum has been found by Bengel in the fact that the passage of Isaiah read by the Lord (Luke iv. 18, 19) was that appointed to be read on the morning of the great day of Atonement.[1] But it is by no means certain that such was the order at this time; nor does it appear whether Jesus read the passage appointed for the day, or that to which He opened intentionally or under divine direction. Some of the fathers, from verse 19, where mention is made of "the acceptable year of the Lord," inferred that His ministry continued but a single year.[2] That no definite period of time is meant, sufficiently appears, however, from the context (Is. lxi. 2).

The city of Nazareth, being built upon the side of a steep hill, presents several precipices down which a person might be

---

[1] See also McKnight, Har. *in loco.* Edersheim, i. 444, objects that the modern Lectionary readings from the prophets are not the same as in the time of Christ; and that in the modern lectionary this part of Isaiah is not read at all.

[2] See Wieseler, Syn., 272, who makes an interval of a year from this Sabbath to His death.

cast. It is said that the ancient city stood higher on the slope
than the modern. That which has for many years been pointed
out as the place where the attempt was made on the Lord's life,
and called the Mount of Precipitation, lies some two miles from
the village. It is a conspicuous object from the plain of Esdraelon,
which it overlooks. Its distance from the village is a sufficient
proof that it cannot have been the real scene of the event. The
cliff which travellers have generally fixed upon as best answering to the narrative, lies just back of the Maronite church, and
is some thirty or forty feet in height.[1]

The wrath of the people, so unprovoked, and their effort to
kill Him, seem sufficiently to justify the opinion of Nathanael in
regard to Nazareth. From this incident it is plain that they
were fierce and cruel, and ready from mere envy to imbrue their
hands in the blood of one who had lived among them, a neighbor
and a friend, all His life. It is not improbable, however, that
they may long have been conscious that, though dwelling among
them, He was not of them, and thus a secret feeling of dislike
and ill-will may have been slumbering in their hearts. This is
the only instance recorded of the Lord's reading in a synagogue.
Elsewhere it is said that He preached in the synagogues, permission being everywhere given Him, apparently in virtue of
His prophetic claims. (Compare Acts xiii. 15.)

Thus rejected at Nazareth, Jesus departs to Capernaum.
The natural interest which all feel in a place which was so long
the Lord's residence and the central point of His labors, leads us
to inquire with some minuteness as to its site. As Bethsaida
and Chorazin were adjacent cities, joined with Capernaum in the
same high privileges, and falling under the same condemnation
(Matt. xi. 21; Luke x. 13), and their sites are subjects of dispute, we shall embrace them in this topographical inquiry; and
we begin with some account of the Sea of Galilee upon whose
shores they stood.

The sea of Galilee is formed by the waters of the Jordan, which

---

[1] Robinson, ii. 285; Ritter, Theil, xvi. 744. Van der Velde, Journey, ii. 385, thinks
that this cannot be the place, and supposes that the precipice where the Saviour's life
was threatened, has crumbled away from the effect of earthquakes and other causes.
Conder, Tent Life, i. 140, suggests that the brow of the hill may now be hidden under
one of the houses.

enter at the northern end and flow out at the southern. Its shape is that of an irregular oval, or pear-shaped, somewhat broader at the upper part, it is twelve and a quarter miles in length, its greatest breadth six and three-quarters; its lowest depth 106 feet. The water is clear and sweet, and is used for drinking by the inhabitants along its shore, many of whom ascribe to it medicinal qualities. It is 650 feet lower than the Mediterranean, and was once thought to fill the crater of an extinct volcano, and there are now hot springs on its western shore; but Col. Wilson (B. E., iii. 170) says that there does not appear to be anything volcanic in its origin. The west shore of the lake is more precipitous, except at one or two points, than that of the east. Lying so low and surrounded with hills, those on the east nearly 2,000 feet above the level of the sea, and seamed with deep ravines down which the winds sweep with great violence, it is very much exposed to sudden furious storms. (Stanley, 361; Rob., ii. 426.) McGregor (Rob Roy. 508) says: "On the sea of Galilee the wind has a singular force and suddenness, and this is no doubt because the sea is so deep in the world that the sun rarefies the air in it enormously, and the wind speeding swift along a level plateau, till suddenly it meets the huge gap in the way, and tumbles down here irresistible." The sea swarms with fish, and its waters in the Lord's day were covered with boats. At that time its shores were densely peopled, nine cities being mentioned and many villages; now are found only the city of Tiberias and a collection of hovels at Magdala.

Nearly midway on the west side of the lake is "the land of Gennesaret" (Matt. xiv. 34; Mark vi. 53; Jos., War, iii. 10. 8). It is made by a recession of the hills from the shore, and forms a segment of a circle, a crescent shape, being, according to Col. Wilson (Recov. Jer., 264), two and a half miles long, and one mile broad. It begins on the south just above the village Mejdel or Magdala, and extends northward to the point where the promontory of Khan Minyeh comes down to the water. "The plain is almost a paralellogram, shut in on the north and south sides by steep cliffs nearly a thousand feet high. On the west the hills recede not quite so precipitously. The shore line is gently embayed, and the beach is pearly white, one mass of triturated fresh water shells, and edged by a fringe of the exquisitely lovely oleander." (Tristram, B. P., 273.) It is well watered, two fountains arising in it large and copious, and several permanent streams flow from the hills west and north, whose waters were carried right and left by aqueducts to irrigate the plain. (Rob., ii. 402; Baedeker, 370.)

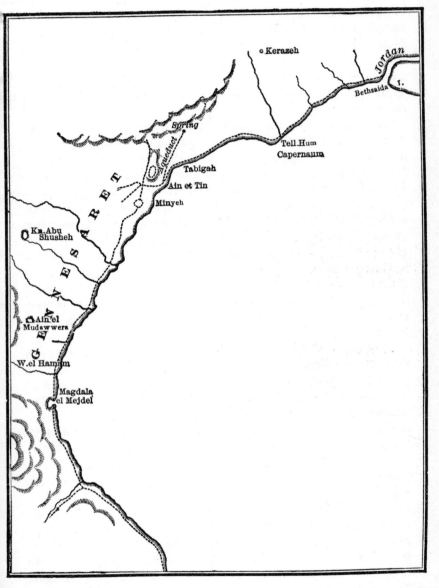

NORTHWESTERN COAST OF THE SEA OF GALILEE, WITH THE PLAIN OF GENNESARET
AND THE TOWNS LYING IN IT AND NEAR IT.

In or near the land of Gennesaret was the city of Capernaum. Its site has been long the subject of dispute. Neither the statements of the Evangelists, nor of Josephus, nor of the early fathers and travellers, are so definite that we can determine from them the exact spot; and even now moder ntravellers and Palestinian explorers who have carefully examined all possible sites along the lake, are by no means agreed in their conclusions. All, therefore, that we can now do, is to give a summary of the question as it stands in the light of the most recent investigations.

It is known from the gospels (Matt. iv. 13; ix. 1; xiii. 1; Mark ii. 13; John vi. 17) that Capernaum was built on the sea shore, and it appears from a comparison of John vi. 17 with Matt. xiv. 34 and Mark vi. 53 that it was either in or near "the land of Gennesaret." As to its position we have more distinct information incidentally given us by Josephus, who, speaking of the plain of Gennesaret, says: "It is irrigated by a highly fertile spring called Capharnaum by the people of the country." (War, iii. 10. 8.) Elsewhere (Life, 72) he speaks of a village on the lake called Cepharnome to which he, having been wounded in a skirmish, was taken. We can scarcely doubt that the fountain he speaks of as called Capharnaum, took its name from the city, and that the two were not far from each other. Can this spring be identified with either of those now watering the plain?

Josephus mentions as a peculiarity of the spring of Capernaum that "it was thought by some to be a vein of the Nile from its producing a fish similar to the coracin of the lake of Alexandria." Are such fish now found in any fountain of Gennesaret? The southernmost fountain lying near the western range of hills, is the Round Fountain — Ain Mudawarah — which is described by Robinson as forming "an oval reservoir more than 50 feet in diameter; the water is perhaps two feet deep, beautifully limpid and sweet, bubbling up and flowing out rapidly in a large stream to water the plain below." Here Tristram (Land of Israel, 46), found the coracin or cat-fish, and was therefore inclined to regard it as the fountain of Capernaum, but he afterwards found the same fish in the lake. Fishermen of the coast told McGregor (Rob Roy, 359) that this fish is found in summer time in other fountains, and is always to be found in the lake; and afterward he saw one in the hot spring of Tabigah. The presence of the coracin, therefore, in a fountain ceases to be any certain proof that it is the fountain mentioned by Josephus.

Assuming that the fountain was near the city, we must further inquire as to the existence of any ruins in its neighborhood. Robinson, who searched for them at the Round Fountain, says : "There was nothing that would indicate that any town or village had ever occupied the spot." And Col. Wilson says (B. E., iii. 281): "No ruins of any consequence have been discovered in this neighborhood"; and with them Dr. Thomson agrees. But, on the other hand, the claims of the Round Fountain to be the fountain of Capernaum are strenuously defended by DeSaulcy (ii. 423), who asserts that he found distinct traces of the ruins of a city upon the adjacent hills. McGregor says, that "various ruins are found not far from the fountain, though not distinct." The absence of ruins, though admitted by Caspari, proves to his mind nothing against the former existence of a city there, as it might have been destroyed by an earthquake. (Matt. xi. 23.)

Dismissing, then, the claim of the Round Fountain, because of the absence of any ruins in its neighborhood, and because to-day it has very few advocates, we proceed to the next fountain in the plain, which some regard as the fountain of Capernaum. This is called Ain et-Tin — the fountain of the fig-tree — and rises near Khan Minyeh at the northwestern extremity of the plain, where the western hills approach the lake shore. Robinson (ii. 403) thus describes it: "Between the Khan and the shore a large fountain gushes out from beneath the rocks, and forms a brook flowing into the lake a few rods distant. Near by are several other springs. Our guide said these springs were brackish. . . . Along the lake is a tract of luxuriant herbage occasioned by the spring." McGregor (Rob Roy, 355) speaks of it as a perennial fountain, pouring out from the rock about eight feet higher than the lake. The water descends into a long marshy lagoon, into which he paddled his canoe from the lake, and searched for some trace of a building, but found none. The water is strongly brackish, and is not used by the inmates of the Khan near by.

That this fountain cannot be that mentioned by Josephus is plain from the fact that it could not irrigate the plain. "Most of the land of Gennesaret," says McGregor, "is above the level of the fountain head." Robinson says: "The lake, when full, sets up nearly or quite to the fountain"; and Thomson, that "it comes out close to the lake and on a level with its surface." It is impossible, therefore, that it could ever have had any value for purposes of irrigation. Nor are there any ruins of importance yet discovered near this fountain such as would naturally mark the site of a city like Capernaum. They are thus spoken of by Robinson when he first saw them: "A few rods south of the Khan and fountain is a low mound or swell, with ruins occupying a considerable circumference. The few remains seem to be mostly dwellings of no very remote date, but there was not enough to make out anything with certainty." Upon his second journey the ruins appeared to him more extensive. "The remains are strewed around in shapeless heaps, but are much more considerable and extensive than my former impressions had led me to suppose. Indeed, there are here remains enough, not only to warrant, but to require the hypothesis of a large ancient place" (ii. 345). Thomson (i. 545), on the contrary, speaks of the ruins as "not adequate to answer the demands of history. No one would think of them, if he had not a theory to maintain which required them to represent Capernaum." Bonar also affirms, "that no large town surely stood here, else it would have left some traces of itself." The later explorers speak in the same way. Col. Wilson (Recov. Jer., 273) says of the ruins described by Robinson: "They form a series of mounds covering an extent of ground small in comparison with either those of Tell Hum or Korazeh," nor do they contain the ruins of any important building. As no fragments of columns, capitals, or carved stones were found, he concludes that the ruins are of modern date. And the ruins on the hill above Khan Minyeh where some place Capernaum, he regards as unimportant.

These differing, and somewhat conflicting, statements show, at least, that whatever may have been the cause, whether by the transportation of the hewn stones to Tiberias or elsewhere, as said by Robinson, or as the more direct result of a divine judgment through some physical catastrophe, almost all traces of Capernaum, if it stood here, have disappeared.

If, then, neither the Round Fountain, nor Ain et-Tin, answers to that described by Josephus, and if they are the only fountains lying in the plain, we must seek this fountain without the plain, and yet so near it that it might be irrigated by it; and such a one may be found at et-Tabigah, some three-quarters of a mile or a mile north of Khan Minyeh. Here are several hot springs, issuing from a limestone rock some thirty or forty feet above the plain; one is much larger than the rest, and is said by Col. Wilson to be by far the largest spring in Galilee. It rises in an octagonal reservoir of stone, originally some twenty feet high, but now the wall is broken, and the water is only about ten feet in depth. For what purpose was this reservoir? Not apparently to gain power to turn mills, but to supply water to irrigate the plain of Gennesaret; and this could be done only through an aqueduct. Are there now any traces of one? In going northward along the shore from Khan Minyeh toward

the bay of et-Tabigah, says Robinson (iii. 345), " we struck upon the
rocky and precipitous point of the hill above the fountain, toward
the northeast.   There is no passage along its base, which is washed
by waters of the lake.   A path has been cut in ancient times along
the rock some twenty feet above the water, and we found no difficulty
in passing.   One feature of the excavation surprised us, namely, that
for most the way there is a channel cut in the rock, about three feet
deep and as many wide, which seemed evidently to have been an
aqueduct once conveying water for irrigating the northern part of
the plain El-Ghuweir (Gennesaret).   There was no mistaking the nature and object of this channel; and yet no waters were near which
could be thus conveyed except from the fountains of et-Tabigah.
Tha fountains issue from under the hill, just back of the village.
We went thither, and found built up solidly around the main
fountain an octagonal Roman reservoir, now in ruins.   Like those at
Ras el-Ain, near Tyre, it was obviously built in order to raise the water
to a certain height for an aqueduct.   The head of water was sufficient
to carry it to the channel around the point of the opposite hill into the
plain El-Ghuweir; but whether this was done by a canal around the
sides of the valley, or whether even it was done at all, there are now no
further traces from which to form a judgment.   The water has a
saltish taste, but is not unpalatable."   Porter (ii. 429) gives substantially the same description.

Almost all later travellers and explorers have spoken in a like
way.   Col. Wilson (Recov. Jer., 272) says: " Connected with this
fountain are the remains of some remarkable works, which at one
time raised its waters to a higher level, and conveyed them bodily
into the plain of Gennesaret for the purposes of irrigation.   After
leaving the reservoir, the aqueduct can be traced at intervals, following the contour of the ground, to the point where it crossed the beds
of two water courses on arches, the piers of which may still be seen;
it then turns down towards the lake, and runs along the hillside on
the top of a massive retaining wall, of which fifty or sixty yards remain; and lastly passes round the Khan Minyeh cliff by a remarkable
excavation in the solid rock, which has been noticed by all travellers.
The elevation of the aqueduct at this point is sufficient to have enabled the water brought by it to irrigate the whole plain of Gennesaret."   McGregor (Rob Roy, 360) confirms Col. Wilson.   " We
easily trace the ancient remains of the ancient aqueduct all the way
to the rocky cliff. . . .   Then we ride up the cliff and find the
level waterway has come there too. . . .   The channel is cut
round the rocky slope, and we go inside the old dry aqueduct, long

used as a riding path, but now plainly seen to be a way for water by its section like an inverted horseshoe; the very least convenient form for a road and the very best for a channel." (Of this rocky cut a photograph may be found in Dr. Thomson's Central Palestine.)

To the general assent of travellers that this cut was for a water-way, Captain Conder takes exception. He says (Qt. St., 1882, 222): "The total length of the rock-cut passage is 150 yards, the width from four to six feet, but generally not more than from three to six feet on the lower side. Between this spring and the passage there are no traces of any aqueduct, nor any indication of any wall on piers. The level of the passage appears to be higher than the top of the reservoir." His conclusion is, that "the spring and rock-cut channel have no connection with one another. It seems far more probable that the passage was intended for a road in order to avoid the necessity of climbing over the promontory."

If future examinations shall sustain the positions of Conder, the spring at et-Tabigah cannot be that mentioned by Josephus as watering the plain of Gennesaret. But at present we must accept the general statement of travellers, that the channel in the rock was for an aqueduct, and was connected with the spring at et-Tabigah. We have then a spring, not itself in the plain, and yet capable of irrigating it, and apparently once used for that purpose; and so far answering to the description of Josephus.

But two other questions here arise: First, Has this spring in it the coracin or cat-fish of which Josephus speaks? This fish, it is admitted, is found in the lake, and may easily ascend to the neighboring fountains, and, according to McGregor, is found not only in the Round Fountain, and at Ain et-Tin, but here also at et-Tabigah. Second, If this be the fountain at Capernaum, where was the city? Are there any ruins near? It is admitted that in its immediate vicinity are no ruins of importance; apparently no city stood near it. The nearest places, which, by their ruins, show that they were large villages or cities, are Khan Minyeh on the south, a mile distant, and Tell Hum on the northwest, two or two and a half miles distant. Between these we must choose. The argument in favor of Khan Minyeh is, that it is nearer the fountain, and directly connected with the aqueduct already mentioned. In favor of Tell Hum are the greater extent of the ruins, indicating a larger city, and their greater antiquity. These are found on "a little low promontory running out into the lake," about two and a half miles from where the Jordan enters it. Here, says Robinson (ii. 246), are the remains of a place of considerable extent, covering a tract of at least half a mile along the shore, and about half that breadth inland. They consist chiefly of the fallen walls of dwellings and other buildings, all of unhewn stone, except two ruins. Thomson speaks of them as "much more extensive and striking than those of any other ancient city on this part of the lake." But the recent explorations of the Palestinian Fund Society have given us more definite information. Col. Wilson (Recov. Jer., 269) says: "The whole area, half a mile in length and a quarter in breadth, was thickly covered with the ruined walls of private houses." The foundations of a large building were found, which is supposed to have been a Jewish synagogue, and of which he says: "Built entirely of white limestone, it must once have been a conspicuous object standing out from the dark basaltic background." There are also the remains of a later building, probably those of a church, perhaps that built about 600 A. D., and enclosing the supposed house of St. Peter. Two remarkable tombs were also found.

Between these two claimants to be Capernaum, the position of the fountain at et-Tabigah, admitting it to be the fountain of Capernaum, does not enable us to decide. If the fountain and the city were near each other, Khan Minyeh has the preference. But some affirm that the fountain might have been quite remote from the city. It is, doubtless, generally true that among the brookless hills the site of a fountain determines the site of a village, as at Nazareth; but the same necessity would not exist in the case of villages built along the lake, and thus amply supplied with water for domestic uses. Here, the position of a village would naturally be governed by other considerations. We are not, then, to think it necessary that a city on the lake should be close to a fountain, as said by Dr. Robinson (*contra* Dr. Thomson, Van der Velde). If the latter were in its territory, and used by its citizens for irrigation, or for mills, or other purposes, both would naturally be called by the same name. The existence of Tell Hum itself away from any fountain is its own proof.

As we have seen, the quantity of water at et-Tabigah is very abundant, but it is slightly brackish and is not drunk, so that its distance from the city was in this respect of no importance. Its chief value was to drive mills, one of which is still in use. Thomson thinks et-Tabigah may have been "the great manufacturing suburb of Capernaum," where were clustered together the mills, potteries, and tanneries, and other operations of this sort, the traces of which are still to be seen. "I even derive this name Tabiga from this business of tanning." If Tabigah were thus a suburb of Capernaum, we should naturally expect to find remains of former habitations scattered along between them. Thomson states that "traces of old buildings extend all the way along the shore from Tabiga to Tell Hum," thus connecting them together as city and suburb. Robinson, on the other hand, speaks of "other fountains and a town" as lying between. In this we have Thomson's personal assurance that he is in error. So far, then, as regards "the fertilizing spring" of Josephus, we must place it at et-Tabigah, and the probabilities are that it was in the territory of Tell Hum, not in that of Khan Minyeh.

Let us now examine the second topographical datum given by Josephus. He tells us (Life, 72), that being bruised by a fall from his horse in a skirmish near the mouth of the Jordan, he was carried to a village called Cepharnome. Here he remained during the day, but was removed that night by medical direction to Taricheæ, at the south side of the lake. From this it is inferred that Capernaum was the first town of any importance along the shore from the mouth of the Jordan southward, since the soldiers would not have carried a wounded man any further than was necessary. Hence, Tell Hum, as several miles nearer the place of the skirmish, is more likely to have been Capernaum than Khan Minyeh. (Stanley, 376, note; Wilson, B. E., ii. 139.) This is very probable, but as we know not whether special reasons may not have led Josephus to prefer Capernaum to any other city on that shore, irrespective of distance, the argument is not at all decisive.

We have now to consider the statements of the Gospels, which seem to place Capernaum in the plain of Gennesaret, and, if so, would exclude Tell Hum (Rob. iii. 349 and 353); and since these demand some previous examination as to the site of Bethsaida, we must inquire here as to this place, and our knowledge of it.

Let us first sum up all that we know from other sources respecting Bethsaida. In Josephus [1] we find mention made of a village of this name. "Philip the Tetrarch also advanced the village Bethsaida, situate at the lake of Gennesaret, unto the dignity of a city, both by the number of inhabitants it contained, and its other grandeur, and called it by the name of Julias, the same name with Cæsar's daughter." Elsewhere he states that it was "in the lower Gaulanitis" [2] and in describing the course of the Jordan, he says [3] that it "divided the marshes and fens of the lake Semechonitis; when it hath run another hundred and twenty furlongs, it first passes by the city Julias, and then passes through the middle of the lake Gennesaret." Thus Josephus places Bethsaida at or near the entrance of the Jordan into the sea of Galilee. It is placed, also, by Pliny, upon the east side of the Jordan, and by St. Jerome upon the shore of Gennesaret. There is not in Josephus, nor in any of the early fathers, any mention of another Bethsaida.

---

[1] Antiq., xviii. 2. 1.   [2] War, ii. 9. 1.   [3] War, iii. 10. 7.

If, then, there was in the Lord's day a well-known Bethsaida on the northeast side of the lake, not far from the entrance of the Jordan, can its site now be found? Robinson places it on a hill — et-Tell — two or three miles above the entrance of the Jordan on the east side, but some distance from its banks (ii. 413). " The ruins cover a large portion of it, and are quite extensive, but, so far as we could observe, consist entirely of unhewn volcanic stones, without any distinct trace of ancient architecture."

It is said by Wilson: " Et-Tell has been identified with Bethsaida Julias . . . but there is no trace of that magnificence with which, according to Josephus, Julias was built." Socin (Baedeker) says: " The ruins consist only of a few ancient fragments." Thus it appears that, if Bethsaida was at et-Tell, almost all traces of it have disappeared. But there are some who do not put it at et-Tell. Thomson, with whom Wilson and others agree, objects that the hill is too far from the mouth of the Jordan, and that as Bethsaida — "house of fish " — derived its name from its fisheries, it must have been located on the shore. Thomson is therefore inclined to put it at the mouth, and suggests that the town would naturally extend to both sides of the river, here some seventy feet wide. As the stream is so narrow, it is almost certain that, even if the main part of the city was on one bank, the other bank would also be built upon. Philip, in enlarging and ornamenting it, doubtless confined himself to the eastern side, the part which lay in his own territory; and this would then become, if it were not at the first, distinctively the city to which the western side would stand as the suburb. This is the view long since defended by Hess (*Lehre u. Thaten unsers Herrn*, 1806), and upon his map Bethsaida is placed on the west side of the Jordan near its mouth, and Bethsaida Julias opposite to it on the east. It is said by Rohr (Palestine, 154), " Bethsaida Julias lay on the northeast shore of the lake near the influx of the Jordan, and probably on both sides of the river." (So Calmet and others. Wilson, B. E., iii. 170.) In this way the objection is met that Bethsaida is called " Bethsaida of Galilee " (John xii. 21), for if the town was built on both banks of the river, a part was in Gaulanitis, as said by Josephus, and a part in Galilee.

But are there any ruins on either bank? Thomson finds on the west side some remains of ancient buildings, and Col. Wilson speaks of a "few small mounds and heaps of stone." (Recov. Jer., 269.) On the eastern side not far from the bank, are traces of an ancient village, foundations of old walls, which Dr. Thomson identifies, and with great probability, with Bethsaida Julias."

Schumacher, the latest explorer of that region (The Jaulan, Qt. St., April, 1888), places Bethsaida Julias at El Mesadiyeh, a little way from the Jordan's mouth, on the east shore, quite near the lake. He says that while et-Tell has the more commanding position, no more ornaments or inscriptions have been found there than at El Mesadiyeh. He suggests that the residence of Philip may have been on the hill et-Tell, and the fishing village at El Araj near the mouth of the Jordan, where are ruins, and that "both were closely united by the beautiful road still visible."

Was this Bethsaida on the east side of the Jordan, of which we have been speaking, the Bethsaida of the Evangelists, in which the Lord wrought His miracles, and on which He pronounced judgment? Let us examine the several places where it is mentioned. John (i. 44) speaks of a "city" — πόλις — of this name: "Philip was of Bethsaida, the city of Andrew and Peter." And again (xii. 21): "Philip was of Bethsaida of Galilee." In Matthew (xi. 21) it is classed with Capernaum and Chorazin as a city that had seen the great works of the Lord, and yet had not repented. (See also Luke x. 13.) In its vicinity was the healing of the blind man (Mark viii. 22): "He cometh to Bethsaida, and they bring a blind man unto Him . . . and He took him by the hand and led him out of the town and healed him." And not far from it was the feeding of the five thousand (Luke ix. 10): "He took the disciples, and went aside privately into a desert place belonging to the city called Bethsaida." (According to the R. V.: "He took them and withdrew apart to a city called Bethsaida." But that Luke puts this miracle at some distance from the city itself, appears from verse 12: "for we are here in a desert place.") Of this "desert place" apart, both Matthew and Mark speak, but do not mention it as at or near Bethsaida. (The place where the 5,000 were fed will be more fully examined in its order.)

That this desert place was on the east side of the lake, appears from the statements of all the Evangelists. The Lord and His disciples went to it by a ship or boat, and after the feeding of the multitude, they returned in the same way. But being on the east side, how could the Lord (Mark vi. 45) "constrain the disciples to get into the ship, and to go to the other side before unto Bethsaida" (in R. V. "to go before Him unto the other side to Bethsaida")? Does not this imply that there was, also, a Bethsaida on the west side? This seems to be confirmed by John's statement, vi. 17, that "the disciples went over the sea toward Capernaum." Matthew and Mark say only that when they were gone over they came to Gennesaret. From all this the inference is drawn that there was a Bethsaida on the west side of

the lake, and near or in the plain of Gennesaret. After the feeding
of the multitude near the eastern Bethsaida, the disciples returned
across the sea to the western Bethsaida. Thus there were two
Bethsaidas, the eastern in Gaulanitis, in Philip's territory; the western in Galilee, and under Herod. It is also said that John speaks
of "Bethsaida of Galilee," as if to distinguish it from another of the
same name, not of Galilee.

But apparently to the time of Reland (1714 A. D.) only one Bethsaida had been thought of, although the difficulties of the matter as
just stated had been felt and various solutions proposed. (Raumer,
109, note; Rob., ii. 413, note 6.)

Reland (653) conjectured that there were two Bethsaidas, one on
the east of Jordan in Gaulanitis, and one on the west side of the
lake in Galilee, and this conjecture has been almost universally
received as the true solution. But he himself was aware of the
improbability that two towns of the same name should lie upon
the same lake only a few miles apart, and adopted this solution
only because he had no other to give. *Atque ita, quamvis non sim
proclivis ad statuendas duas pluresve urbes ejusdem nominis (quod ple-
rumque ad solvendam aliquam difficultatem ultimum est refugium), hic
tamen puto id necessario fieri oportere.* He does not, however, allow
that there is any mention by the Lord of the Bethsaida east of Jordan. *Christus de Bethsaida loquens non potuit nisi de sola Galilaica
intelligi.*

But do the accounts of the feeding of the five thousand, and the
subsequent crossing of the lake, make imperative the theory of two
Bethsaidas? Most agree that somewhere in the territory of the Bethsaida east of the lake, the multitude was fed. But the exact site of
the city we do not know, nor where was "the desert place" of the feeding. Thomson thinks that he finds this place at "the point where
the hills on the east side of the plain Butaiha come to the edge of
the lake." This plain is said by Col. Wilson to be two and a half
miles long, and one and a half wide, but some make it much larger.
The place of feeding must have been some two or three miles southeasterly of the Jordan, Tell Hum lying a little northwest across the
end of the lake, and the land of Gennesaret lying to the south of
Tell Hum. "At the southeastern end of this plain, Butaiha, the
hills which bound it approach within a half mile of the lake shore,
where they form an angle with those which extend due south along
the eastern side of the lake." At the foot of the high hill at this
angle is located the feeding of the five thousand. McGarvey (328)
says: "Here is a smooth grassy plain, the lake near at hand, and not

far away the mountain where the Lord went up to pray when He had sent away the multitude."

Accepting this as the "desert place," a place uninhabited, belonging to Bethsaida, and the city Bethsaida as near the Jordan, let us put in order the events of the afternoon and night. Jesus leaving the west side, probably at Capernaum, with His disciples seeks some place on the eastern shore where He may be alone with them. There is no reason to think that He would go further than to attain this end, and such a retreat He would find at the place we have mentioned. The people at Capernaum see Him go, and they and the people of the adjacent villages follow Him by land. After the feeding of the multitude, He constrains His disciples to depart in the boat while He remains to dismiss the people. He directs them to go before Him to Bethsaida, for this was not far distant, and there He will rejoin them and go with them to Capernaum. But the wind arising, they are driven down to the middle of the lake where it is some six miles broad, and opposite to Gennesaret. Here, early in the morning, the Lord meets them, walking upon the sea, and the wind ceasing, "immediately the ship was at the land," and they go thence to Capernaum.

That the disciples expected Jesus to rejoin them and go with them to Capernaum appears from John (vi. 17): "They were going over the sea to Capernaum, and it was now dark, and Jesus had not yet come to them." Godet remarks: "It is more simple to suppose that, inasmuch as the direction from Bethsaida Julias is nearly parallel with the northern shore, Jesus had appointed for them a meeting place at some point on that side, at the mouth of the Jordan, for example, where He counted upon joining them again." "Probably they were intending to coast along the shore between Bethsaida Julias and Capernaum; in this they were, no doubt, following their Master's directions. The words that follow show clearly that they expected Him to rejoin them at some point on the coast." (M. and M. *in loco*. Rob. iii. 378. See Gardiner, Har. 101, note.)

Let us examine the reasoning of those who affirm a western Bethsaida near Capernaum. When Jesus directed His disciples to enter the ship, and go before Him to the western side of the lake (R. V. "to go before Him unto the other side to Bethsaida"), He mentions, according to Mark (vi. 45), Bethsaida as their point of destination; according to John (vi. 17), Capernaum (R. V., "they were going over the sea unto Capernaum"). The inference, therefore, is that the two cities were situated near each other on the shore of the lake. That they were in the land of Gennesaret, or near it, it is said, appears from the statement of John (vi. 21), that after Jesus joined them in the ship, "it was immediately at the land whither they went," *i. e.*, at Capernaum. But Matthew says: "When they were gone over, they came into the land of Gennesaret." R. V., "They came to the land, unto Gennesaret." (So Mark vi. 53.) The inference, therefore, is that Capernaum was in or near Gennesaret, and Bethsaida adjacent to it. This conclusion, Robinson, who puts Capernaum at Khan Minyeh and Bethsaida at et-Tabigah, holds "to be incontrovertible."

But let us briefly consider it. The first proposition is, that as both Capernaum and Bethsaida are mentioned as the point to which the disciples should sail, they must have been near each other. According to Mark, the Lord directed them to go to Bethsaida; what is said in John is simply narrative: "They were going over the sea to Capernaum." This is rendered by Alford: "They were making for the other side of the sea, in the direction of Capernaum"; this city being, as the Lord's residence, the point of ultimate destination.

But, if we put Bethsaida at the mouth of the Jordan, and Capernaum at Tell Hum, the two cities were, in point of fact, near to each other, the distance between them being only about two or two and a half miles. The relative positions of the two places, according to Col. Wilson, are such, that to reach Tell Hum from the point on the eastern shore where the Lord then was, a boat would naturally go in a northwesterly direction, and so pass near Bethsaida at the mouth of the Jordan; and here the disciples expected Him to rejoin them. McGregor (Rob Roy, 364 ff.) argues from the usual force and direction of the winds, that to put Bethsaida at Ain Tabigah best meets the natural conditions. But his experience was too brief for a conclusive judgment.

The second proposition is, that as the disciples were going to Capernaum, and landed at some point in Gennesaret, Capernaum must have been at or near that point. But it is clear from Mark vi. 53) that He did not land at Capernaum, and was at some distance from it; and went thither slowly, healing the sick by the way. It is said by Robinson (iii. 350, note): "During the early part of the day Jesus healed many, apparently before reaching Capernaum."

We do not, then, feel compelled to put another Bethsaida on the west side of the lake, in or near Gennesaret. If at the mouth of the Jordan, it would answer to the statements of the Evangelists, and would be, in fact, a little distance from Tell Hum.

The various opinions respecting Bethsaida may be thus summed **up:**

I. 1.   That there was but one Bethsaida, and this on the west side of the lake.   This was the early and general belief.   But as to the exact site there was no agreement.   (a.) Some said that it was near Tiberias, and here was put the feeding of the five thousand in the "desert place." To reach it, the Lord crossed from one side of a bay to the other side in a ship, but did not cross the lake.   (b.) That its territory extended along the northern shore of the lake to the east side where was the desert place.   (c.) That it was a suburb of Capernaum.

2.   That it was on the southeast side of the lake, and nearer the exit than the entrance of the Jordan.

II.   That there was one Bethsaida, at the entrance of the Jordan, and lying on both sides of the river.

Thomson, DeSaulcy, Col. Wilson, Conder, Riddle, and Gardiner doubtful.

III.   That there were two Bethsaidas, one on the east, and one on the west side.

The advocates of the last view are the most numerous.

For two Bethsaidas, one at B. Julias on east side, and one somewhere on the western shore: Ritter, Robinson, Caspari, Godet, Ellicott, Wieseler, Edersheim, Geikie, Socin, Farrar, Weiss, Tristram, Henderson, Van der Velde.   But these are not agreed where the western Bethsaida is to be placed.

For Khan Minyeh: Ritter, Van der Velde, Caspari, Weiss.

Ain Tabigah: Robinson, Tristram, McGregor.

A suburb of Capernaum: Caspari, Edersheim.

On southeast side of the lake: Lightfoot.

Returning now to the site of Capernaum; in favor of Tell Hum is its name.   Caphernaum is generally derived from Kefr Nahum — "the village of Nahum," or as others, "the village of consolation."   (See T. G. Lex.)   Of this name the Talmudists give several variations, but all agree in retaining the syllable *houm*, which favors its identification with Tell Hum.   (Neubauer, 221; Hamburger, ii. 636.) Thomson explains the substitution of Tell-(hill) for Kefr-(village,) by the fact that the Arabs apply to a heap of ruins the term Tell.   Thus Kefr Nahum becoming ruinous was changed into Tell Nahum, and then abbreviated into Tell Hum.

The extent and antiquity of its ruins are also in its favor; and its position, as near the border line of the territories of Herod and Philip, thus making it a fit place for the receipt of customs (Matt. ix. 9).   Had Capernaum been at Khan Minyeh, it would have been too far from the border, the tolls being paid to Herod not to the Romans (see Schürer, in Riehm, Art. Zoll).   These remarks will also apply to it as a garrison town.

There is, however, one objection to be noticed — the absence of any harbor at Tell Hum, natural or artificial. Fishing boats could not lie there safely, but would go south toward Tabigah, where there is a little bay of which Tristram says: "The white beach gently shelves, and is admirably adapted for fishing boats. . . . The sand has just the gentle slope fitted for the fishermen running up their boats and beaching them." (See McGregor, Rob Roy, 342.) But in this respect Tell Hum and Khan Minyeh seem to have been in the same position, the latter having to find its harborage south of it on the shore of Gennesaret.

In favor of Tell Hum, Thomson appeals to tradition: "So far as I can discover, after spending many weeks in this neighborhood off and on for a quarter of a century, the invariable tradition of the Arabs and Jews fixes Capernaum at Tell Hum, and I believe correctly." (See also Col. Wilson, Recov. Jer., 298.)

Some notice must be taken here of the argument in favor of Khan Minyeh derived from its name. It is said that Minyeh in its original form Mini, meant, according to the Rabbis, heretics, or Jews who had become Christians. Kefr Minyeh was "the village of the heretics." It was in this opprobious way that they named Capernaum, it having been the place where Jesus lived. We are therefore to regard Khan Minyeh as Capernaum. (So Conder, H. B. 326, Sepp. ii. 2 Theil, 243. See Art. Capernaum in Riehm.)

But on the other side, it is said by Edersheim, i. 365, that "certain vile insinuations of the Rabbis connecting it with heresy, point to Kepher Nachum — Capernaum — as the home of Jesus." It is evident that little reliance can be placed upon Jewish tradition in the matter.

We have still to inquire respecting the site of Chorazin. Two or three miles northwest from Tell Hum are some ruins called Khirbet Kerazeh. They were visited by Robinson, who describes them as "a few foundations of black stones, the remains evidently of a poor and inconsiderable village," and regards them as "too trivial ever to have belonged to a place of any importance. Chorazin too, according to Jerome, lay upon the shore of the lake, but the site is an hour distant, shut in among the hills, without any view of the lake, and remote from any public road, ancient or modern." While Robinson thus rejects Kerazeh as the site of Chorazin, Thomson is equally decided in its favor. "I have scarcely a doubt about the correctness of the identification, though Dr. Robinson rejects it almost with contempt. But the name Korazy is nearly the Arabic for Chorazin; the situation, two miles north of Tell Hum, is just where we might expect to find it; the ruins are quite adequate to answer the demands

of history, and there is no rival site." With Thomson Keith agrees:[1]
"There seems no reason for questioning that Korazy is the Chorazin
of Scripture, in which it is not said to stand on the *shore* of the lake
of Tiberias, as Capernaum and Bethsaida are. We reached it in
fifty-five minutes from the chief ruin of Tell Hum, from three to four
miles distant. It lies almost directly to the west of the point where
the Jordan flows into the lake. It retains the name and is known by
it still among the inhabitants of the country round, and, as we
repeatedly inquired, especially at Safet, by no other. Of these ruins
Col. Wilson (Recov. Jer., 270) says: "They cover an area as large,
if not larger, than the ruins of Capernaum." He finds the distance
from Tell Hum north to be two and one-half miles. The identification of these ruins with Chorazin is now generally accepted.

This topographical discussion, extended as it is, by no means ex-
hausts the subject. Certainty as regards these sites is at present
unattainable; but as the question now stands, it is most probable that
Capernaum was at Tell Hum, that Chorazin was a little to the north
of it; and that there was but one Bethsaida, and this near the
entrance of the Jordan into the lake, and lying on both banks. All
these places seem to have been of considerable size and importance,
and nea to one another. It is a strong objection to a western
Bethsaida that the only "mighty works" that are recorded as done
by the Lord in any Bethsaida, are the feeding of the five thousand
(Luke ix. 10), and the healing of a blind man (Mark viii. 22). That
these were both at Bethsaida Julias is generally admitted. It would
be strange, therefore, if the woes pronounced by Him (Matt. xi. 21)
were not on the city where these miracles were done, but on another,
in which, as far as recorded, He wrought none.

We have therefore left unnoticed the position taken by some that
"the land of Gennesaret" is to be identified with the plain El Batihah at the mouth of the Jordan.[2] The arguments by which it is
supported are briefly these, that the political divisions, which assigned
the Jordan as the eastern limit of Galilee, had no existence prior to
the will of Herod partitioning his dominions among his sons; that
there was but one Bethsaida, and that Bethsaida Julias at the mouth
of the Jordan; that the Scriptures show that Capernaum and Bethsaida were but a step apart, and therefore Capernaum was in the
plain El Batihah; and that this site best corresponds to the language
of Josephus. Admitting that there is some force in these considera-

---

[1] So Norton, Notes, 115; Winer, i. 238; Van der Velde, Memoir, 304.
[2] See article by Tregelles, in Journal of Classical and Sacred Philology, vol. iii. p.
145. See also article, vol. ii. p. 220, by Thrupp, who regards Gennesaret as El Batihah,
but identifies Capernaum with Tell Hum, and finds no trace or tradition of a Bethsaida
on the western side of the lake.

tions, still they are by no means so weighty as to lead us to change the position of the land of Gennesaret from the west to the north of the lake.[1]

We know not whether private and personal reasons had any influence in the selection of this city as the central point of His labors in Galilee. Some, as Lightfoot and Ewald, have supposed that Joseph had possessions there, and that the family, the Lord's mother and brethren, were now residing there (John ii. 12). More probably, in the selection of Capernaum He was determined chiefly by local position and relations. Lying upon the sea of Galilee, and the great roads from Egypt to Syria running through it, and in the direct line from Jerusalem to Damascus,[2] it gave Him such facilities of intercourse with men as He could not have had in more secluded Nazareth. Not only could He readily visit all parts of Galilee, but by means of the lake He had ready access also to the region upon the other side, and to the towns both north and south in the valley of the Jordan. From it he could easily make circuits into Galilee on the west, into Trachonitis on the north, and into Decapolis and Peræa on the east and south. Besides this local fitness for His work, it was also the residence of Simon and Andrew, and but a little way from Bethsaida, the city of Philip.

It does not appear from the Gospels whether the Lord had a house of His own at Capernaum, or dwelt with some relative or disciple. His own words (Matt. viii. 20), "the Son of Man hath not where to lay His head," seem decisive that He did not own any dwelling, but was dependent upon others even for a place where to sleep. He is spoken of as entering the house of Peter (Matt. viii. 14), and the form of expression (Mark ii. 1), "it was noised abroad that He was at home," (R. V. margin, compare iii. 19) implies that He had a fixed place of abode. Norton, in common with many, supposes that He resided in the house of Peter; Alexander (on Mark i. 29) suggests that Peter may "have opened a house for the convenience of his Lord and master in the intervals of His itinerant labors." If, however, His mother was now living at Capernaum, which is by no means certain,

---

[1] See Ewald, Jahrbuch, 1856, p. 144, who also places Gennesaret on the north of the sea.

[2] Robinson, ii. 405; Ritter, Theil, xv. 271.

He would naturally take up His abode with her. "The change of abode," says Alford, "seems to have included the whole family, except the sisters, who may have been married at Nazareth." Greswell asserts that the incident respecting the tribute money (Matt. xvii. 24) proves indisputably that He was a legal inhabitant of Capernaum.

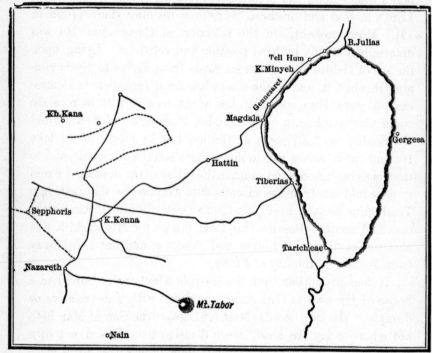

SEA OF GALILEE, AND THE PART OF EASTERN GALILEE ADJACENT.

The arrival of the Lord at Capernaum, there to take up His abode, offers us a fitting place in which to speak of His Galilæan work in its general practical features, and to give a brief out-line of it.

In many points it was very unlike His earlier work in Judæa. So far as we can learn, He did not then go from place to place baptizing, nor does He seem to have made any use of the synagogues for the purpose of teaching. Like the Baptist, He did not seek the people in their cities and villages, but made the people seek Him (Matt. iii. 5; xi. 7). In Galilee the Lord began immediately to visit the people in all their cities and villages, making Capernaum the central point of His labors, and this He did in a systematic manner; "He went round about the villages teaching " (Mark vi. 6).   "In a circle," says Alexander, "or circuit, that is, not merely round about, but on a regular concerted plan of periodical visitation."   We have not sufficient data to determine the local order of these visitations ; but it is natural to suppose that He would first visit the places near Capernaum, and then those more remote (Mark i. 38).   From this city as a centre He would go forth to preach in the adjoining towns, and by degrees extend His labors to those more distant.   And His course would be directed rather to the west than to the east, both because Galilee lay to the westward, and because of the semi-heathenish character of the people who lived beyond the lake.   It was, in fact, a considerable time, as we we shall see, ere He visited the regions of Cæsarea Philippi and of Decapolis.

During these circuits we find the Lord journeying from place to place, remaining for the most part only a little while in a village.   In these journeys He was attended by His disciples; at first by those who had before been with Him in Judæa, and whom He recalled ; and then by others; and afterward by the body of the Apostles, who became His constant attendants.   At a later period of His ministry, His mother and other women accompanied Him in some of His circuits (Luke viii. 2); and He was followed by crowds who were drawn to Him by various motives.   His common mode of procedure was apparently this: on entering a city where was a synagogue, He availed Himself of the privilege which His reputation as a rabbi and prophet gave Him, to teach the people from the Scriptures.   This He did upon the Sabbaths and synagogue days.   These synagogue days were Mondays and Thursdays, being the ordinary market days when the country people came into the town, and for this reason the services on these days were of a more elaborate character (Eders., i. 432).   At other times He preached in the streets or fields, or sitting in a boat upon the sea; in every convenient place where the people were willing to hear Him.   His fame as a healer of the sick caused many to be brought to Him, and He appears in general to have healed all (Mark vi. 56; Matt. ix. 35).

11

His sojourn in any single village was necessarily brief, and therefore those who had been really impressed by His works or words, and desired to see or hear Him more, followed Him to the adjoining towns, or sought Him at Capernaum. The disciples do not appear to have taken any public part as teachers, but may privately have aided Him in various ways to disseminate truth among the people. The expenses of these journeys were probably borne by the contributions of the disciples, and by the voluntary offerings of the grateful who had been healed, and of their friends. After the Twelve had been chosen, one of their number seem to have acted as treasurer, taking charge of the moneys designed for the common use (see John xii. 6).

A specimen of the daily activity of the Lord may be found in the narrative of His early work in Capernaum. He enters upon the Sabbath into the synagogue and teaches, filling all His hearers with astonishment at His words. He there heals a demoniac, probably immediately after the discourse. Leaving the synagogue, He enters Peter's house and heals a sick woman, and crowds coming to Him at evening, He heals many others. The next morning, after a time of meditation and prayer, He departs to another city. Similar, doubtless, in their main features to this, were His labors upon subsequent Sabbaths. In mentioning these circuits, none of the Evangelists gives them in regular order, or relates the events in chronological succession. Each has his own principle of selection and of arrangement, with which we are not now concerned; but it is obvious when we remember how great was the Lord's activity, how many His works and words, that within the limits of their narratives only very brief outlines can be given.

The stages of progress in the Lord's labors in Galilee will be noticed as we meet them. Yet it should be noted as characteristic of the beginning of His ministry, that we do not find any open avowal of His Messianic claims. He wished the people to infer who He was from His words and works rather than to learn it from any express declarations of His own. He preached the kingdom of heaven as at hand, and illustrated it by His miracles. (Of the nature and number of these we shall speak later.) If the people had sufficient spiritual discernment to see

the true import of what He said and did, this was all the proof
that was needed that He was the Messiah.

We give at this point, for the sake of convenient reference,
an outline of the Lord's Galilæan work to the death of the Baptist, divided into periods of sojourn in Capernaum, and of circuits in the adjacent territories. The grounds for the order will
be stated as the particular periods come under consideration.

First Sojourn in Capernaum.

Rejected at Nazareth, He comes to Capernaum. In its
neighborhood He calls the four disciples while fishing upon the
lake, and works the miracle of the draught of fishes. On the
following Sabbath He preaches in the synagogue, and heals the
demoniac, and afterward heals the mother of Peter's wife. In
the afternoon, after the sun had set, He heals many others.
Early the next morning He rises to pray, and then departs to
preach and heal in the adjacent cities and villages.

FIRST CIRCUIT.

He visits the "next towns," probably those lying nearest
Capernaum, as Chorazin and Bethsaida. No particulars of this
circuit are given, except that He heals a leper "in one of the
cities." This being noised abroad, He is for a time unable to
enter any city, and retires to secluded places where the people
gather to Him. After an absence, it may be of some weeks,
He returns to Capernaum.

Second Sojourn in Capernaum.

Crowds begin to gather to Him so soon as it is known that
He is at home. A paralytic is brought to Him, whom He heals,
forgiving his sins. This awakens the anger of the Scribes, who
regard it as an assumption of the Divine prerogative. He
goes forth again by the seaside, and teaches. Walking along
the shore, He calls Levi. He goes upon a Sabbath through a
field in the neighborhood of Capernaum with His disciples, and
on the way plucks and eats the ears of corn. This is noted by
the Pharisees of the city who are watching Him. He enters
the second time into the synagogue, and heals the man with a
withered hand. The Pharisees and the Herodians now conspire
against Him. He departs to the seaside, and is followed by
crowds.

Leaving Capernaum, the Lord goes to a mountain in the neighborhood, and after a night spent in prayer, calls His disciples, and from them chooses the twelve apostles. Great multitudes now gathering to Him. He delivers the Sermon on the Mount, and returns, apparently the same day, to Capernaum, still followed by the multitudes. He heals, immediately upon His return, the Centurion's servant. The people so throng Him, and His labors are so incessant, that He has not time even to eat, and His friends fear for His sanity.

SECOND CIRCUIT.

Soon after, He goes to Nain, and raises from death the widow's son. He continues His ministry in the adjacent region. John Baptist sends a message to Him from his prison ; to which He replies, and addresses the people respecting John. He dines with Simon, a Pharisee, and is anointed by a woman who is a sinner. He returns again to Capernaum.

Third Sojourn in Capernaum.

He heals a blind and dumb possessed man, whereupon the Pharisees blaspheme, saying that He is aided by Beelzebub. His mother and brethren come to Him, but He rejects their claims. He goes to the sea-shore and teaches in parables.

THIRD CIRCUIT.

The same day at even He crosses the sea with His disciples, and stills the tempest. He heals the Gergesene demoniacs; and the devils, entering into a herd of swine, destroy them. The people of the country entreat Him to depart, and He returns to Capernaum.

Fourth Sojourn in Capernaum.

Here Levi makes Him a feast. He raises from death the the daughter of Jairus, and heals the woman with an issue of blood, the two blind men, and a dumb possessed man.

FOURTH CIRCUIT.

He goes to Nazareth, and is a second time rejected. He teaches in the villages of that part of Galilee, and sends out the twelve apostles on their mission. About this time Herod puts the Baptist to death, and now hearing of Jesus and His miracles wishes to see Him.   Jesus returns to Capernaum, and the apostles gather to Him there.

APRIL–MAY, 781.   A. D. 28.

Arriving at Capernaum, the Lord begins to gather about	MATT. iv. 18–22.
Him His former disciples, that they may accompany and	MARK i. 16–34.
assist Him in His work. The miracle of the draught of fishes.	LUKE v. 1–11.
He enters the synagogue on the Sabbath, and there heals a	LUKE iv. 31–41.
demoniac. Thence He goes the same day to the house of	
Peter, and heals his wife's mother of a fever, and in the	MATT. viii. 14–17.
evening He heals many sick persons who are brought to Him.	

The first notice we have of the Lord after leaving Nazareth (Matt. iv. 18; Mark i. 16; Luke v. 1), brings Him before us standing on the shore of the lake, and surrounded by people that pressed upon Him to hear the word of God.   How long an interval had elapsed since He left Nazareth we have no data to decide, but this gathering of the people to Him presupposes a period, longer or shorter, during which He had been teaching. Not improbably He may have been several days upon the journey, and His growing reputation as a prophet, joined to rumors of what had taken place at Nazareth, would procure Him audience in whatever village He entered.   Especially as He came near the lake, the numerous cities and villages would furnish crowds of listeners to hear one who spake as never man spake.

It was as He thus approached Capernaum that He met upon the lake His former disciples, Simon, Andrew, James (this is the first time James is mentioned, but it is generally accepted that he was with his brother John at Bethabara), and John, and called them again into His service.   We have already seen that on leaving Judæa, His baptismal work ceasing, His disciples left Him and returned to their homes and usual pursuits.   To the feast (John v. 1) He seems to have gone unattended, nor apparently were any disciples with Him at Nazareth.   But now that John's imprisonment had determined the character of His future ministry, He proceeds to gather around Him those who had already been workers with Him, that they might enter upon this new sphere of labor.   Heretofore their relations to Him had been similar to their previous relations to John the Baptist, involving only a temporary absence from their families and business. "These disciples, hitherto," says Lightfoot, "were only as private men following Christ." It is well said by Bruce (*"The Training of the Twelve,"* Edin. 1887) that there were three stages in the fellowship of the Apostles with Christ: 1st, as simple believers in Him as the Christ, and His occasional companions; 2d, the abandonment of secular occupations, and a constant attendance on His person; 3d, when called especially to be Apostles. Now the Lord sought to engage them in a work which should be life-long, and which was incompatible with other pursuits. They should now be His constant attendants, going with Him wherever He went, and thus be necessarily separated from their families and friends. This call at the sea of Galilee to follow Him was not, indeed, as Alford, Caspari, and others suppose, a call to the apostleship, but to a preliminary service; and those thus called had as yet little understanding what labors, dangers, or dignities it involved.

To one who considers the essentially different character of Christ's work in Judæa and in Galilee, it will not appear surprising that, when beginning the latter, He should give to these disciples a new and distinct call. Only neglect to note this difference permits anyone to speak of a want of harmony between John and the Synoptists upon this ground.

From the narrative of Mark (i. 16–21; see also Matt. iv. 18–23), we should infer that the call of Peter and Andrew, James and John, was the Lord's first act after He came to the sea, and perhaps before He went to Capernaum. Luke, however (iv. 31–42), places the preaching in the synagogue, the healing of the demoniac and of Peter's wife's mother and others, and His first circuit, before this call (v. 1–11), and connects it with the wonderful draught of fishes. But we shall find abundant proof that Luke does not follow the chronological order, and that nothing decisive can be inferred from the fact that he places the call after the miracles and teaching. Still, as his accounts of this call differ somewhat from those of Mark and Matthew, many have been led to regard them as distinct, and as happening at different times.[1] The peculiarity of the call in Luke, according

---

[1] So early, Augustine, and recently, Krafft, Stier, Greswell, Alford, Rig., Lex., Keil. See Trench, 106, Ellicott, 164, note.

to this view, is that it was later than that in Matthew and Mark, and that now "the disciples forsook all, and followed Him." Now they became fishers of men (Luke v. 10), in fulfillment of His previous promise (Matt. iv. 19). This involved the entire relinquishment of their secular callings, and to convince them of His ability to take care of them and supply every temporal need, not excluding other and higher symbolical meanings, the Lord worked the miracle of the draught of fishes. But the words of both Matthew (iv. 20) and Mark (i. 18) are express that "they straightway forsook their nets and followed Him." How, then, should they be found several days after engaged in their usual occupations? That, whenever the Lord was at Capernaum, these disciples were wont to follow their calling as fishermen, as said by Alford, is plainly inconsistent with their relations to Him, and with the service He sought from them. Certainly they could have had little time for such labors amidst the pressure of the crowds which seem to have ever gathered around Him when He came to Capernaum.[1]

The circumstances attending the call of the disciples, as related by the several Evangelists, may be thus arranged: As Jesus approaches the plain of Gennesaret from Nazareth, teaching by the way, many flock round Him to hear His wonderful words. Passing along the level and sandy shore, where the fishermen's boats were drawn up, (which Tristram thinks to have been the beach at et-Tabigah) He sees among them the boats of Simon and Andrew, and of James and John, who, having been fishing, are now washing their nets. As the people press upon Him, He requests Simon to push off his boat from the shore a little way, that from it He may teach the multitude as they stand before Him. After His discourse is ended, He directs Simon and Andrew, and perhaps also others with them, to push out into the deep waters and let down the net. This, after a little hesitation arising from the ill-success of their labors the previous night, Simon does, and they take so great a number of fish that the net begins to break. He now beckons to those in the other boat, James and John and their companions, who had doubtless been watching the whole proceeding, and

---

[1] See Ebrard, 307.

who now come to their help, and both boats are so filled as to be in danger of sinking. This unexpected success, and all the attendant circumstances, make such a powerful impression upon Simon's mind, that, acting with his usual impetuosity, he casts himself at the Lord's feet, saying, "Depart from me for I am a sinful man, O Lord." All are astonished, and see a Divine hand in what had happened. Soon after this, probably so soon as they reach the shore, He calls Simon and Andrew, in whose ship He still is, to follow Him, for He will make them fishers of men. During this time James and John have gone a little distance from them, and are engaged in repairing the net that had been broken. Walking upon the shore, He goes to them and calls them also to follow Him, and they, leaving their father and servants, follow Him.

In this way may we find a natural and easy solution of the apparent discrepancies between Matthew and Mark, on the one hand, and Luke, on the other Luke alone relates that Jesus spake to the people from Simon's boat, and afterward directed him to fish, and shows in what relation this fishing stood to the subsequent call of the fishermen. Matthew and Mark omit all but the fact that they were engaged in their usual work of fishing when thus called. There is then no such opposition in the accounts as to make it necessary to refer them to different events.[1]

On the first Sabbath following the call of the four disciples, he entered the synagogue and taught. His teaching excited general astonishment, but not the envy that manifested itself at Nazareth. Present in the synagogue was a man possessed with a devil, whom He healed, and through this miracle thus publicly performed, His fame spread rapidly through all Galilee (Mark i. 28). It is to be noted that He did not here, or subsequently, permit evil spirits to bear witness to His Divine character or Messianic claims. (Mark i. 34; Luke iv. 41). The ground of this imposition of silence may have been, that the intent with which such witness was offered was evil ; and that it would also have tended to evil by awaking premature and unfounded expec-

---

[1] In this general result agree Lightfoot, Newcome, Townsend, Robinson, Wieseler, Tischendorf, Lichtenstein, Ebrard, Edersheim, Gardiner, Godet, Fuller. For an answer to objections, see Blunt, Scriptural Coincidences, 256, note.

tations as to His future work. It will be noted that no objection was now made by any one that these healings were on the Sabbath.

From the synagogue the Lord proceeded to the house of Simon and Andrew, where He healed Simon's wife's mother. As mention is made by John (i. 44) of Bethsaida, as the city of Andrew and Peter, it has been conjectured that the house at Capernaum was that of the parents of Simon's wife ; but against this is the expression "house of Simon and Andrew," which implies the joint ownership of the two brothers. It is therefore more probable that they had now left Bethsaida and taken up their residence at Capernaum.[1] The healing of Peter's wife's mother seems to have been at the close of the synagogue service, and before evening, for at evening all that were diseased and possessed were brought to Him. The synagogue service closed at or before noon, and it may be inferred from the fact that she "ministered unto them," that she served them at the table at the midday meal. According to Josephus, the hour of this meal was, on the Sabbath, the sixth, or twelve o'clock. That the sick should wait till the sun was gone down (Mark i. 32), may be referred to the great scrupulosity of the Jews in regard to the Sabbath.

MAY, 781. A. D. 28.

The next morning, rising up early, Jesus goes out into a solitary place to pray. Simon and others go out to seek Him because the multitude waits for Him. He replies, that He must also preach in the neighboring towns. He goes preaching in the synagogues and working miracles.	MARK i. 35–37. LUKE iv. 42. MATT. iv. 23. MARK i. 38–39. LUKE iv. 43–44.

This quick departure from Capernaum may perhaps be explained from the Lord's desire that a period of reflection should follow the surprise and wonder which His words and works had excited in the minds of the people. Their astonishment at the supernatural power He manifested, and their readiness to come to Him as a healer of the sick, did not prove the possession of true faith. He, therefore, will leave them to meditate on what they have seen and heard, and depart to visit the other cities

---

[1] This may be a slight confirmation of the supposition that there was but one Bethsaida, and that east of the Jordan.

11*

and villages of Galilee,[1] probably, as has been suggested, follow
ing some fixed order of visitation.

That this, the Lord's first circuit with His disciples, must
have continued some time, appears from the statements of the
Evangelists (Mark i. 39–ii. 1; Luke iv. 44; Matt. iv. 23), though
their language may, perhaps, describe His general activity
rather than any particular period of it. The expression in
Mark ii. 1, δὶ ἡμερῶν, "after some days," is indefinite, and its
length must be otherwise determined. The attempt of Greswell to show, from the number of places He would visit, and
the length of the stay He would make in each, that the duration of a circuit would never be less than three months, and
probably never less than four, rests upon no sound basis. Ellicott
(168), going to the other extreme, makes this circuit to have
lasted only four or five days. It is intrinsically improbable
that, as Greswell supposes, Jesus should have journeyed now
wholly around Galilee, keeping on its boundary lines. What
particular parts of the province He at this time visited, we have
no data to decide; but it is certain that early in His ministry
He visited the cities of Bethsaida and Chorazin, adjacent to
Capernaum, and labored much in them, though of these labors
there is little or no mention (Matt. xi. 21). His fame rapidly
spread, and soon the people from the regions adjacent to Galilee
began to gather to Him.

Of His works of healing during the first circuit, no instance
is given, unless the healing of the leper (Matt. viii. 2; Luke v.
12; Mark i. 40) took place at this time. Matthew places it
immediately after the Sermon on the Mount. Luke introduces
it with no mark of time: "And it came to pass when He was
in a certain city," etc. Mark connects it with the first circuit in
Galilee, but with no mention of place. That this healing is not
chronologically placed by Matthew, appears from the whole

---

[1] It is said by Schürer, ii. 1. 154, that the New Testament and Josephus uniformly
distinguish between the two notions, city or town — πόλις — and village — κώμη. Once
the term κωμοπόλεις is used, Mark i. 38, meaning towns which only enjoyed the rank of
a village. The village was in some way subordinate to the town, and the smaller towns
to the larger. See Weiss, ii. 510. The several Evangelists in one or two instances, apply
these different terms to the same place. Thus, Bethsaida is called by Mark viii. 22, 23, a
κώμη; Luke ix. 10, a πόλις. See Matt. xi. 20. Bethany, Bethlehem, Bethphage, Emmaus, are villages; Capernaum, Nain, Chorazin, Ephraim, are cities.

arrangement of chapters viii. and ix.   The first verse of chapter
viii. more properly belongs to the conclusion of the history of
the Sermon on the Mount; verse second begins the narrative of
healings and other miracles, of which ten particular examples
are successively recorded, but without regard to the exact order
of time in which they occurred.   After healing the leper, Jesus
commands him to go and show himself to the priests, and to
say nothing to any one else of the miracle (Matt. viii 4).   This
command of silence plainly implies that the miracle had been
done privately, and not in the presence of the multitude; and
could not have been, therefore, as He came from the Mount, for
great crowds then followed Him.   Nor in the presence of the
people could a leper have approached Him.[1]   This command to
keep silence the leper disobeys, and everywhere publishes abroad
what Jesus had done.   This wonderful cure, for leprosy was
deemed incurable, made the people throng to Him in such
crowds, that He could no more enter into any city.[2]   It is said
by some that He was made unclean by touching the leper, and
therefore was forbidden to enter the city by the local magistrates;
this is not probable.   He was obliged to retire to desert, or
uninhabited places, to avoid them ; but even then they gathered to Him from every quarter.   (For the order in Matthew,
Bengel, Quandt, Godet; for an earlier period, Rob., Gardiner,
Caspari, Ellicott.)

If, then, the healing of the leper be placed during this circuit, it was probably during the latter part of it.   As He proceeded from place to place He healed such sick persons as were
brought to Him, and the reports of these cures spreading in
every direction, all in every city would be brought so soon as
His presence was known.   The leprosy may have been one of
the last forms of disease He healed, partly because of want of
faith on the part of the lepers, and partly because it was difficult
for them, amidst such crowds, to get access to Him.   But why
in this case should silence be enjoined ?   And why, after He
had wrought so many other cures, should this have aroused so

---

[1] Greswell, ii. 296, note, infers that Jesus was in some house apart when the leper
applied to Him, and that his cure took place in private.   *Contra*, Godet: " A leper would
hardly have been able to make his way into a house."   See Eders. i. 496, note.

[2] Or into *the* city, *i. e.* Capernaum.   So Norton.   R. V. " a city."

much attention as to make it necessary for Him to avoid the cities, and go into uninhabited places? The most probable answer is, that the public proclamation of this miracle gave the people such conceptions of His mighty power to heal, that all thronged to Him to be healed, and thus His teachings, the moral side of His work, were thrust into the shade. It was the word which He wished to make prominent, and the work was but subsidiary. He would not that the people should merely wonder after Him as a miracle-worker, but should learn through His words the true nature of the redemption He came to proclaim, and so be able to understand His works as redemptive.

EARLY SUMMER, 781. A. D. 28.

After some time, the Lord returns to Capernaum. So soon as it is known that He is returned, the multitudes begin to gather, bringing their sick, whom He heals. The Pharisees and doctors of the law from all parts of the land come to Capernaum to see and hear the new prophet. A paralytic is brought to His house upon a bed, whom He heals, forgiving his sins. This awakens the indignation of the Pharisees, who regard him as a blasphemer. Leaving the city, He goes to the seaside and there teaches. Afterward walking on the shore, He sees Levi, the publican, sitting at the receipt of custom, whom He calls to follow Him.

MARK ii. 1–12.

LUKE v. 17–26.

MATT. ix. 2–6.

MARK ii. 13, 14.
MATT. ix. 9.

LUKE v. 27, 28.

The order of Mark, who places the healing of the paralytic after the return to Capernaum, is plainly the right one.[1] Matthew in his grouping of the miracles in chapters viii. and ix., does not follow the order of time. Luke narrates it after the healing of the leper, but without specifying time or place. He mentions, however, the fact, that there were "Pharisees and doctors of the law sitting by, which were come out of every town of Galilee, and Judæa, and Jerusalem; and the power of the Lord was present to heal them." (W. and H., Tisch., for ἀυτούς have ἀυτόν. In R. V., "The power of the Lord was with Him to heal"). It is not wholly clear who these persons were, or why they were now present. Greswell (ii. 298) cites Josephus to show that they were "a sort of village school masters, or a class of inferior municipal magistrates, who might conse-

---

[1] So Robinson, Tischendorf, Alford, Greswell. As to the details of this healing see Eders. i. 502.

quently be met with everywhere." So Edersheim (i. 87) speaks of the scribes as having civil administration in villages and town-ships. (As to the scribes as teachers, see i. 93 ff.). Schürer (ii. 1. 333) describes them as men who made acquaintance with the law a profession, and who, rather than the priests, were at this time its zealous guardians, and the real teachers of the peo-ple. Whether these are to be distinguished from the scribes who came down from Jerusalem at a later period to watch Him (Mark iii. 22), is in dispute. Most suppose them to have been present with evil intent, but it is possible that they came to be healed, or to see and hear Him whose fame had gone so widely abroad. There is no distinction taken by the Evangelist between those from Galilee and those from Judæa and Jerusa-lem, as if the latter were present from any special cause. At this period of the Lord's career, the nature of His work was very imperfectly understood, and many in every part of the land and of every class, looking for the Messiah, would be naturally attracted to one who showed such wonderful power in word and deed. But in a little time as His teachings became more dis-tinctly known, His disregard of merely legal righteousness, His neglect of their traditions, His high claims, awakened great and general hostility. We see here how these scribes, who came, perhaps hoping to find in Him their Messiah, perhaps to judge by personal observation how far the popular reports respecting Him were true, were turned into enemies and accusers when He said to the paralytic, "Thy sins be forgiven thee," which was to speak blasphemy, because He assumed a prerogative which belonged to God only.

There are several allusions to the Lord's teaching by the seaside. Whether He now stood upon the shore, or entered a boat, does not appear. It was not, however, till afterward (Mark iii. 9) that He commanded that a small ship should wait on Him. Thomson (i. 548) speaks of the small creeks or inlets near Tell Hum, "where the ship could ride in safety only a few feet from the shore, and where the multitude, seated on both sides, and before the boat, could listen without distraction or fatigue. As if on purpose to furnish seats, the shore on both sides of those narrow inlets is piled up with smooth boulders of basalt." Others find a more convenient place along the shelving beach further to the south.

The road from Damascus to the cities along the coast passed by "Jacob's bridge" over the Jordan, and thence along the northern shore of the lake. It is probable that the place of toll, where Levi sat, was upon the road, near its entrance into the city.[1] The manner of this call, like the call of Simon and Andrew, and James and John from their work as fishermen, presupposes a prior acquaintance of Jesus with Levi. The tax-gatherer, from his occupation and local position, must have been aware of all that was taking place in the neighborhood, and could not easily have been ignorant of the Lord's person and work. Not improbably also, he was already a disciple in the wider sense of the term, this not involving the giving up of his usual calling. It would appear that the call was given on the same day in which Jesus taught the people, and soon after His discourse was ended.[2]

By some this call to Levi is placed after his election to the Apostleship. Having been already chosen one of the Twelve, he returned to his ordinary labors ; and now, they say, was called to enter upon his apostolic duties, to leave all and follow Christ. But this in itself is exceedingly improbable, and we shall soon see that the election to the apostleship is later.

The call of Levi to stand in such intimate relations to the Lord, must have been a stumbling-block to all the Pharisaic party, and to all those in whose hearts national pride and hatred of foreign rule were ardent. The occupation of the publican was odious, if not in itself disgraceful, as a sign and proof of their national degradation ; and the selection of a disciple from this class to be His constant attendant, by one who claimed to be the Messiah, must have strongly prejudiced many against Him and His work.[3]

Such selection implies, also, that already the Lord was turn-

---

[1] See Lichtenstein, 230; Herz., Encyc., xv. 161.

[2] Bleek, Synoptische Erklarung, i. 384. As to the identity of Matthew and Levi, see Winer, ii. 61; Godet, on Luke v. 27; Eders., i. 574.

[3] "The Talmud," says Lightfoot, iii. 61, hath this canon: "' A Pharisee that turns publican, they turn him out of his order.' " See Eders., i. 515 ff.: "Levi was not only a publican, but of the worst kind, a douanier a custom-house official," and as such most obnoxious.

ing away from the legally righteous, the Pharisees, because His words had so little entrance into their hearts; and was turning to those who, though despised as publicans and sinners, were nevertheless ready to receive the truth.   Unable to draw the priests into His service, He calls fishermen ; and what He cannot accomplish because of the unbelief of Pharisees, He will do through the faith of publicans.

Many bring the feast which Levi made for the Lord (Luke v. 29 ; see also, Matt. ix. 10 ; Mark ii. 15) into immediate connection with his call.[1]   Still there is nothing in the language of the Evangelists that implies sequence, and as Capernaum doubtless continued to be Levi's residence, to which he frequently returned from his journeyings with the Lord, the feast may with equal likelihood have taken place at a later time, and be here related, in order to bring together all that concerned him personally.[2]

This point, and the chronological connection between this feast and the healing of the daughter of Jairus (Matt. ix. 18–25), will be examined when we reach this miracle.

Greswell (ii. 397) attempts to show that the feast of Matthew (Matt. ix. 10) was different from that mentioned by Mark and Luke; that the first was later, and not in the house of Levi ; and that at this feast, only the disciples of John were present. This view removes some difficulties, but the arguments in its favor are more ingenious than convincing.

Early Summer, 781.   A. D. 28.

During this sojourn in Capernaum, the Lord with His disciples walks through the fields upon a Sabbath, and plucks and eats the ears of corn. This is observed by some of the Pharisees who are watching Him, and who complain of it to Him as a violation of the Sabbath. He answers them by referring to what David did, and asserts His power as Son of man over the Sabbath. Upon another Sabbath He heals a man with a withered hand, which leads the Pharisees to conspire with the Herodians to destroy Him.

Matt. xii. 1–8.
Mark ii. 23–28.
Luke vi. 1–5.

Luke vi. 6–11.
Matt. xii. 9–14.
Mark iii. 1–6.

---

[1] Lichtenstein, Tischendorf, Stier, Godet, Caspari.

[2] So Lightfoot, Newcome, Townsend, Robinson. Newcome (259) refers to the Harmony of Chemnitius, "where it appears that Levi's call and feast were separated in the most ancient harmonies from Tatian, A. D. 170 to Gerson, A. D. 1400."

Both the time and place of this event — the plucking of the ears of corn — have been much disputed; and both are therefore to be considered. It is mentioned by all the Synoptists, by Matthew in one connection, by Mark and Luke in another, but by none in such a way as to determine its place, or its chronological position. Its importance in this respect makes it necessary that we give it a careful examination.

All agree that it took place on a Sabbath, and Luke (vi. 1) defines this Sabbath as "the second Sabbath after the first," or "second-first — ἐν σαββάτῳ δευτεροπρώτῳ. But what was this second-first Sabbath? The first point is as to the true reading. Many, on various grounds, omit the adjective. (So Meyer, W. and H., Bleek; Weiss regards the text as corrupted; Riddle, that a marginal note has found its way into the text. Retained by Tisch., Winer, Wies., Ellicott, Keil, McClel., Eders.)

If rejected as not genuine, the text will read: "And it came to pass on a Sabbath that He was going through the cornfields." (So R. V.) In this case the only clew to the time of the year is the fact, that "the disciples plucked the ears of corn and did eat." The grain, therefore, was ripe, and from this we may infer that it could not have been earlier than the time set for the reaping of the barley harvest, for it is generally accepted that the sheaf of first-fruits offered at the Passover (Levit. xxiii. 10), and before which no grain was reaped, was of barley; but whether the barley is here meant is in question. It is said by Lightfoot (on Matthew xii. 1): "Barley was sown at the coming in of winter, and when the Passover came in, became ripe, so that from that time barley-harvest took its beginning." The wheat harvest was later, and not gathered till May or June. Robinson speaks of seeing wheat ripe upon the 9th of May, and he also speaks of the people near Tiberias as engaged in gathering the wheat harvest upon the 19th of June. The uncertainty as to the kind of grain gathered by the disciples, whether wheat or barley; and also as to the place, whether in Judæa or Galilee, on the highlands or lowlands, permits us to put this event either in April, or May, or June. The field was not yet reaped, but it was not unusual to let the grain remain in the field some time after ripening. Thomson says that the Syrian harvest extends through several months, and "the wheat is suffered to become dead ripe, and as dry as tinder before it is cut." Even if, in the case before us, the harvest generally was reaped, this particular field may still have been ungathered; or possibly this grain had been left for gleaners.

But if we accept the reading, "second-first," what was the Sabbath so distinguished? As no other writer uses this designation, shall we say that it was invented by Luke? This is not likely; we may rather suppose that it was a technical term, the meaning of which he supposed his readers to be acquainted with. But its meaning is not plain. There are two suppositions: "second" may be understood as defining "first;" there being two or more first Sabbaths, of which one is marked out as the second. ("The second of two firsts" Meyer.) Or "second" may be understood as marking some well-defined Sabbath, from which second Sabbath others are counted; the first after the second, the second after the second, the third after the second, etc. (So Campbell and Norton in their translations; Rob., Gres.)

If we adopt the first supposition, there must be a class of two or more first-Sabbaths which can be numerically distinguished; and we must ask after the several classes of first-Sabbaths which have been proposed.

I. 1. That which takes a cycle of seven years from the end of one Sabbatic year to another, the year commencing at Nisan or April; of these seven yearly first-Sabbaths the first Sabbath of the second year is the second-first. But if, as is generally agreed, the Sabbatic year began in October not in April, this would bring the second-first Sabbath into the Autumn. (See Winer, ii. 348; Wies., Syn., 204.)

2. That which, dividing the year into two parts, the ecclesiastical and the civil, the one beginning with Nisan (April) the other with Tizri (October) finds two yearly first-Sabbaths, the first-first in Tizri, the second-first in Nisan; or this order may be reversed if we begin the year with Nisan.

3. That which, dividing the year into twelve months, finds twelve first-Sabbaths, or the first Sabbath of each month. The second-first is the first Sabbath of the second month. If Nisan (April) be the first month, Ijar (May) is the second month.

4. That which finds a class of first-Sabbaths marked out by the three great feasts, Passover, Pentecost, and Tabernacles. Of these that of Pentecost would be the second-first.

5. That which takes a cycle of seven weeks from the second day of the Passover, which was a Sabbatic day, to Pentecost; the Sabbaths of these seven weeks making a class of first Sabbaths, the second of which is the second-first.

II. If we take the second view of the meaning of the phrase, "second-first," that it is the first after a second, we have two chief explanations:

1. The second day of the Passover (Levit. xxiii. 10) is selected as the starting-point from which the Sabbaths are counted to Pente-

cost; the first Sabbath after this second day being the second-first, and in like order.

2. The fifteenth and twenty-first days of Nisan being feast Sabbaths, if a week Sabbath came between them, it was called the second-first.

Still another solution has been proposed. The first day of a new month being determined by the appearance of the new moon, when this could not be ascertained, the day was counted as the 30th of the old month, and the next day as the commencement of the new. In this case both days were sanctified, and the first called the first Sabbath, and the second the second-first.

With the uncertainty as to the right reading, and the multiplicity of interpretations, it is obvious that the designation of this Sabbath as the second-first gives no certain chronological datum.

It is a valid objection to some of them that they bring the plucking of the corn too early, before the offering of the wave sheaf, and so before the legal time. To others it may be objected that they are merely ingenious conjectures, sustained by no proof. That which has the larger number of names in its favor is that which is said to have been originally propounded by Scaliger, and maintained by Lightfoot (*in loco*, also on Matt. xii. 1). "It was the first Sabbath after the second day of the Passover." If the Passover this year began on March 30, the plucking of the corn was early in April. Others prefer the view which regards the second-first Sabbath as the first after the second of the three great feasts, that after the Passover being the first-first, and that after Pentecost, the second-first. In like manner we have in common use the designations, the first Sunday after Epiphany, first after Easter, and the like. Brown (657) remarks: "Of all the explanations known to me, this seems the best, indeed, the only likely one." Clinton calls it "equally probable" as the first mentioned. But eminent names can be cited for other interpretations. (For a brief statement of opinions, see Winer, ii. 348; Greswell, ii. 300; Meyer and Godet, *in loco*.)

The bearing of this incident on the point of the length of the Lord's public ministry, is to be noted. It is held by those who affirm that there were but three Passovers, and consequently that it continued but little more than two years, that the plucking of the corn must have been just, after the Passover mentioned in John vi. 4, the second one. If so, it must have been just at the close of the Galilæan ministry. It is said by Edersheim (ii. 54) that it was just before the feeding of the four thousand; and if so, the whole Judæan and Galilæan ministries must be compressed within a period of little more than a year, leaving nearly a year for His last journey from Galilee to Jerusalem. This statement is its own condemnation.

In this chaos of interpretations, the mention of this Sabbath as the second-first gives us no certain chronological aid. The circumstance, however, that the disciples plucked the ears of corn and did eat, defines the season of the year as that when the corn was ripe. The kind of grain is not mentioned, whether barley which is earliest, or wheat which was later. Many have assumed, with Lightfoot, that this corn was barley, but this is not easily rubbed in the hands, and it was the food of the very poor, and of horses. Though the disciples may have eaten it in their hunger, yet wheat is the more probable grain. But if it were barley, the Passover of the year beginning on the 30th March, the barley harvest would begin about the 1st April, and continue till May or later. If the corn was wheat, the harvest would begin some weeks later, and many fields may have remained unreaped as late as June, much depending on the position of the field as to latitude and elevation.

Thus no definite chronological datum can be obtained in this way. We have only the general result that the plucking of the corn may have been in April or May or June. If we regard this second-first Sabbath as the first after Pentecost, which was on this year the 19th May, we must put the event about the end of this month. If this be correct, the ministry of the Lord in Galilee had now continued about two months.

Where did this event take place? It is narrated by all the Synoptists as occurring just before the healing of the man with the withered hand, and this healing was probably in the synagogue at Capernaum. "And He entered again into the synagogue" (Mark iii. 1), that is, the synagogue already mentioned.[1] The article is omitted by Tisch., W. and H., and others, yet if rendered "into a synagogue," the reference would not necessarily be to i. 39, "And He preached in their synagogues throughout all Galilee," but rather to i. 21, where the synagogue at Capernaum is mentioned. This appears also from the mention of His withdrawal to the sea after the healing (Mark iii. 7 ; see also Luke vi. 6). That the field where the ears were plucked was not far distant from Capernaum, appears from Matthew xii. 9, for the Pharisees who had blamed the disciples for that act,

---

[1] Alexander, Meyer.

are spoken of as members of that synagogue. "He went into their synagogue." [1]   They were, therefore, the Pharisees of Capernaum, and the field of corn was in the neighborhood of that city, and within the limits of a Sabbath day's journey.

We may, then, give the following order of events as one intrinsically probable. The Lord, after His return from His first circuit, remained some days or weeks at Capernaum, and upon a Sabbath walked out with His disciples through the fields in the vicinity of the city. As He had already, in the opinion of the Pharisees, broken the sanctity of the Sabbath by healing upon it (Mark i. 23 and 30), they followed Him to watch Him, perhaps to note whether His walk upon that day was longer than the law permitted (Acts i. 12). Seeing His disciples plucking and rubbing the ears of corn in their hands, they saw in the act a violation of the law. It has sometimes been said that the Pharisees did not think it sinful to pull and eat the grain, but it was so to rub it in their hands, all preparation of food being forbidden. This is doubtful. Lightfoot says : "The plucking of ears of corn on the Sabbath was forbidden by their canons, *verbatim :* 'He that reapeth corn on the Sabbath, to the quantity of a fig, is guilty. And plucking corn is as reaping.'" [2]   It is said by Edersheim (ii. 56) that the act involved two sins, — first, that of plucking the ears; second, that of rubbing them. If done presumptuously, or without necessity, the punishment was death by stoning, and hence the Lord's defense of the disciples. His answer to their complaints could only have angered them still more, and when, therefore, He entered the following Sabbath into the synagogue (Luke vi. 6), it was to be expected that they would carefully watch all that He did to find some sufficient ground of accusation against Him. His renewed violation of the Sabbath by healing the man with a withered hand, added to their indignation, and they now began to plot how they might destroy Him.

Luke (vi. 6) defines the time of this work of healing as "on another Sabbath." That this was the Sabbath immediately fol-

---

[1] Meyer, Norton. But others do not accept this; see Keil. DeWette: "the people of the place where He then was."

[2] See also Meyer on Matt. xii. 1; and Eders., ii. 56 ff., and as to Rabbinical Sabbath law, App., xvii.

lowing that on which He walked through the corn-field, is not said, though it may have been.[1] The alliance of the Herodians with the Pharisees does not prove that Herod himself had at this time any knowledge of Jesus, or took any steps against Him. The Herodians were those among the people who, though hating the Roman rule, favored the pretensions of Herod's family to kingly power (Lindsay, on Mark iii. 6). In case of national independence, this family should reign rather than the house of the Maccabees, or any other claimant. They were never numerous, for the great body of the nation looked upon that family as foreigners and usurpers. " Why the Pharisees and Herodians," says Alford, "should *now* combine, is not apparent." The Herodians would, however, be naturally jealous and watchful of any one whom they supposed to put forth any Messianic pretensions; and the Pharisees being angry at Jesus on religious grounds, yet unable to take any measures against Him without the assent of Herod, a union of the two for His destruction was very easily made. Indeed, the Herodians may have been themselves of the Pharisaic party. We need not suppose that this conspiracy against Him as yet included others than the Pharisees and Herodians of Capernaum and its immediate vicinity (see Matt. xii. 14 ; Mark iii. 6), and seems to have been the beginning of the organized hostility to Him in Galilee. Doubtless, very soon after this, His enemies here took counsel with His enemies at Jerusalem, and the conspiracy against Him became general.

It appears from these narratives that, almost from the very beginning of His Galilæan work, the Lord encountered the active hostility of the Pharisees of that province. The grounds of offense may be stated in general terms: 1st, that He disregarded their traditions in not a few points, as in fasting, in purifications ; 2d, He associated with publicans and sinners ; 3d, He broke the Sabbath ; 4th, He assumed the right to forgive sins. Of these, the breaking of the Sabbath and forgiveness of sins were the most offensive. At the feast (John v. 1), He had aroused the anger

---

[1] Wieseler (237) conjectures that it was a feast Sabbath, and the day following that mentioned in verse 1st. This seems to have little or no ground for it. Meyer's assertion, that Matthew (xii. 9) puts the two events on the same Sabbath in opposition to Luke, has no sufficient basis. See Keil, *in loco.*

of the Pharisees at Jerusalem by healing the impotent man on
the Sabbath (verses 16 and 18) ; and at Capernaum He continued again and again to heal upon that day, and in the syna-
gague itself.[1] Their fanatical zeal could not allow such violations of the law to pass unnoticed, and as Jesus defended them on
the ground of His divine right to work, even on the Sabbath,
He seemed to them not only a Sabbath-breaker, but also a
blasphemer. At first they plotted secretly against Him, the people at large being friendly to Him. While in the full flush of
His popularity, they dared take no steps openly against Him, but
waited till some imprudence, or error, or folly on His part,
or the fickleness of the multitude, might put Him in their
power. There was early an active and constant correspondence
between the scribes and Pharisees in Galilee and those in
Jerusalem ; and at intervals deputations from the latter came
down to consult with the former, and to devise means to hinder
Him in His work, and to bring Him to punishment. As
yet the fact that He had broken the Sabbath by healing upon it,
does not seem to have turned the popular feeling at all against
Him, nor even the assertion of His power to forgive sins. This
was doubtless due to His many miracles of healing, which for a
time repressed all open attempts against Him.

It is at this point that we may properly consider a most important feature of the Galilæan ministry, — the many miracles
of the Lord. On this first Sabbath in Capernaum He healed in
the synagogue a man possessed of a devil, then the mother in-
law of Peter, and, after the sun was set, all in the city who came
to be healed (Matt. viii. 16). The same is said by Mark (i. 32 ff.),
and by Luke (iv. 40): "Now when the sun was setting, all they
that had any sick with divers diseases brought them unto Him ;
and He laid His hands on every one of them, and healed them; and
devils also came out of many." And this universality of healing
was not confined to the beginning of His ministry, or to any one
place. It is said by Matthew (iv. 23) that "Jesus went about
all Galilee, . . . healing all manner of sickness and all
manner of disease among the people." And this is often re-

---

[1] There are seven recorded cases of healing on the Sabbath, and a general intimation of many more. (Mark i. 34. See Trench, Mir., 250.)

peated (ix. 35; xii. 15; xiv. 14; xv. 30; xix. 2; xxi. 14; Mark iii. 10; Luke v. 15; vi. 17 ff.; vii. 21).

Not only did the Lord heal all who came to Him, but He gave also like power to heal to His disciples when He sent them forth as His witnesses. Thus it is said by Matthew (x. 1): "When He had called unto Him His twelve disciples, He gave them power against unclean spirits, to cast them out, and to heal all manner of sickness and all manner of disease." (See Mark iii. 15; Luke ix. 1.) And when the Seventy were sent forth, they were empowered to heal the sick in every city that received them. (Luke x. 9.)

Let us inquire as to the significance of this plenitude of miracles during the Galilæan ministry.

A miracle may be wrought by any one sent of God with a message or to do a work, as a credential — a means to beget faith ; or in answer to a special request springing from faith; or as a necessary element in the work to be done. Thus in the case of Moses (Ex. iv. 1–9), certain signs were wrought by him before the people as his credentials, proofs that God had sent him. Afterward he did many miracles, at the Red Sea and in the wilderness, not as credentials, but in the prosecution of His work of delivering the people from their bondage.

In the case of the Lord, the signs wrought by Him at Jerusalem before the rulers and people (John ii. 23) did not beget faith. He, therefore, went into Galilee "preaching the gospel of the kingdom of God." And it is in the connection of this preaching of the kingdom with the healing of all the sick, that we find the key to this wonderful miraculous activity. His miracles in Galilee were not wrought as credentials, though they were such, nor were they, for the most part, in answer to prayers of faith ; they were proofs, outward and visible to all, of the presence of the kingdom of God. He was the Redeemer, and His whole work was redemptive — a prefiguration of what should be when redemption was completed. He did not simply proclaim a coming kingdom, but showed it to be now present, in that devils were cast out and the sick healed. He said on one occasion to the Pharisees : "If I by the Spirit of God cast out devils, then the Kingdom of God is come unto you" (Matt. xii.

28, Luke xi. 20). This supremacy over evil, manifested, as was necessarily the case, in external forms, was to all, who knew the relation of sin to death, of moral to physical disorder, the sure proof that He was the healer of the soul as well as the body; that He came to destroy the works of the devil, and to teach the truth, and to show forth the righteousness of God.

That this readiness to heal all who came to Him should have gathered great multitudes around Him, was to be expected. He did not demand of them individual faith as a condition of healing, and we know from the result that in most cases faith in Him did not follow. But His work, while it testified that He was the King, and that the kingdom was present in His Person, answered another purpose. It enabled Him to find those among the multitudes who felt the burden of sin and longed for spiritual deliverance, and came to Him that they might have life; and from these were His true disciples gathered.

But the question may be asked, Why did not the Lord begin His ministry in Judæa with such general healing? Would it not have been to all the strongest confirmatory evidence that He was the Messiah? A little reflection will show us that such a putting forth of healing power would have been quite inconsistent with His purpose in the first stage of His ministry. Had He then done this, the holy city would have been crowded by multitudes from every part of the land, and from all Syria; and the tumult and excitement consequent would have been destructive of that calm self-examination and searching of heart, and study of the Scriptures, which He sought to effect in the rulers. For this the quiet of His baptismal work, a work calling for repentance and confession of sin, was best fitted. It was not the mere number of His miracles that was to decide whether He was sent of God; and to multiply them as proofs before those who had no real discernment of their nature and purpose, and might ascribe them to demons, could only have afforded new occasions for dispute and strife. To those who sat in Moses' seat He must first show that Moses wrote of Him.

MIDSUMMER, 781. A. D. 28.

After healing the man with a withered hand, Jesus withdraws to the seashore. Here great multitudes from all parts of the land resort to Him, and He heals many. As they press upon Him to touch Him, He directs that a small ship be prepared to wait upon Him. Leaving the seaside, He goes up into a neighboring mountain and spends the night in prayer. In the morning He calls the disciples to Him, and from them chooses the twelve Apostles. The multitudes now gathering to Him, He proceeds to deliver the discourse called the Sermon on the Mount.	MATT. xii. 15–21. MARK iii. 7–12. MATT. iv. 25. LUKE vi. 12–16. MARK iii. 13–19. MATT. v., vi., vii. LUKE vi. 17–49.

From Matthew (xii. 15) it would appear that Jesus was aware of the purpose of the Pharisees, and therefore avoided them. He would not, except so far as was necessary, come into collision with them, or expose His work to injury through their opposition. It was for this reason that, having healed all the sick among the multitudes that followed Him, He charged them that they should not make Him known (verse 16). He was now seeking for the humble and repentant, all in whom He could discern any sense of sin or germs of faith, and He would not for their sakes suffer Himself to be forced into a hostile attitude to the spiritual leaders of the people. This was the rule of His conduct, as it had been prophetically laid down by the prophet Isaiah (xlii. 2): "He shall not cry, nor lift up, nor cause His voice to be heard in the street."

The withdrawal from the city to the seashore (Mark iii. 7), while it thus had for one end, to avoid His enemies, seems also to have been to find a more convenient place for teaching and healing. In the city, He was exposed to constant interruption through the eagerness of the sick and their friends, who pressed upon Him to touch Him; and when at the seaside, to secure personal freedom He was compelled to order a boat to attend upon Him, that He might, when necessary, use it as a pulpit to address the multitude standing before Him on the shore, and perhaps also withdraw Himself wholly from them by crossing the lake.

The fame of Jesus seems at this time to have reached every part of the land. Crowds came, not only from Galilee and Judæa, but also from Idumæa and from beyond Jordan, and from the territories about Tyre and Sidon. That so great num-

12

bers, and from such remote regions, should gather at Capernaum, shows that He remained at that city for some time after His return from His first circuit. It was, doubtless, not his teachings but His miracles of healing, that awakened such general attention, and drew such multitudes after Him. Most came attracted by His reputation as a healer of the sick. After making all allowance for the degraded condition of the present inhabitants of Palestine, the following remarks of Thomson (ii. 84) would not be inapplicable to the Jews of the Lord's day : "Should a prophet now arise with a tithe of the celebrity of Jesus of Nazareth, there would quickly be immense assemblies about him from Galilee, and from Decapolis, and from Jerusalem, and from Judæa, and from beyond Jordan. Bad and stupid and ignorant and worldly as the people are, their attention would be instantly arrested by the name of a prophet, and they would flock from all parts to see, hear, and be healed. There is an irresistible bias in Orientals of all religions to run after the mere shadow of a prophet, or a miracle worker."

That the choice of the Twelve took place at this time, appears from the mention in Mark and Luke of the various parts of the country from which the multitudes came. According to Luke (vi. 17), they that heard the discourse upon the mount were from Judæa and Jerusalem, and from the sea-coast of Tyre and Sidon. Mark (iii. 7, 8) mentions Galilee, Judæa, Jerusalem, Idumæa, beyond Jordan, and about Tyre and Sidon. Matthew (iv. 25), who does not mention the choice of the Apostles, but gives the sermon on the Mount, speaks of the great multitudes that followed Him from Galilee, Decapolis, Jerusalem, Judæa, and beyond Jordan. It was at this point, when He had special need of their services, that He selected twelve out of the body of His disciples whom He named Apostles. The importance of this act demands our consideration.

As has been already said, the choice of the Twelve had a twofold aspect; it looked both to the present, and to the future. They were chosen, as said by Mark (iii. 14), "that they should be with Him, and that He might send them forth to preach." They were to be His present helpers in proclaiming the kingdom of God, thus calling the attention of their countrymen to Jesus as the Messiah. But their work had its chief significance, as the result showed, not in their present witness but in their relation to the new election, the Church, of which they were to be the foundation. Their choice at this time did not, however, show that the Lord had cast off the Jews, but rather that He would, if it were possible, save them; and to this end the Apostles were to go forth among the people at large, and give the utmost publicity to His mission. But to do this they must first themselves be instructed as to His Person and mission; and therefore must be with Him in daily intercourse, not only to behold His works and hear His words in public, but also to be taught of Him in private.

On what grounds the Lord made this choice just at this time, we are not told. It may be that not till now did He find among the disciples those whom He judged to be fit for this work; or that the concourse of the people from all quarters was now so great that their assistance was needed; or that He saw that the efforts of His enemies would soon bring His labors in Galilee to an end.

Without entering into disputed points as to the names and relationships of the several apostles, we may here note some particulars respecting their previous acquaintance with the Lord, and subsequent intercourse with Him. He first met, as we have seen, Andrew, Simon, and John at Bethabara. Whether James was there then, we do not know. Farrar supposes that he was following his calling as a fisherman in Galilee; but most infer from the language (John i. 41), "Andrew findeth first his own brother Simon," that John found later his own brother James. To these four Philip and Nathanael were added, so that we may believe that these six accompanied the Lord to Cana, and were present at the marriage there, and subsequently went with Him to Capernaum (John ii. 12). Whether they went up with Him to the Passover when He cleansed the temple, we do not know. (It is affirmed by Godet, and denied by Caspari. The words, verse 17, "His disciples remembered," etc., are not decisive to show that they were with Him when spoken.) But the fact that soon after this Passover "He came with His disciples into the land of Judæa," where they baptized, seems to show that some or all of these six were at this time with Him. Since, "of the many who believed on His name" at the feast (John ii. 23), it is said, "He did not trust Himself unto them," it is not probable that He chose any of them to be His special helpers.

It seems, therefore, not improbable that some of His earliest disciples were with the Lord during His Judæan ministry; and that they returned with Him when He left Judæa for Galilee. If from that time — December, 781 — to the unnamed feast in March, 782, the Lord lived in retirement, these disciples would return to their homes and their several occupations. When He began His Galilæan work, He called James and John and Andrew and Peter to follow and aid Him, but no mention is made of Philip and Nathanael. The only one of the Twelve of whom special mention is made as afterward called to follow the Lord, is Levi or Matthew.

Thus we have previous knowledge of seven of the Twelve, but of the earlier relation of the others to the Lord,— Thomas, Simon the Canaanite, James the son of Alphæus, Thaddæus, and Judas Iscariot, we know nothing. They may have been among the believers in Jerusalem at the first Passover, or later at His baptism in Judæa; they may perhaps have become such after He began His work in Galilee.[1] Whether they had had any intimation of His purpose to choose them as His apostles, we are not told; most suppose that He had previously made known to them what He proposed to do. (See the note of Lindsay on Mark iii. 14.) It is most improbable that He gave them at that time any intimation of their future relations to the Christian Church.

We may ask whether this choice of the Twelve was known to the Pharisees; and if so, how did they regard it? It is said by some that at the delivery of the Sermon on the Mount which soon followed, the Apostles stood next the Lord, then the disciples in general, and then the multitudes, thus forming three groups. If such distinction of place was made, it must have been seen, and the subsequent attendance of the Twelve upon the Lord also noticed, so that His enemies would not be ignorant that some step had been taken in the way of organizing His disciples, and they would be aroused to watch all His movements still more closely.

Whether some particular mountain is designated by the use of the article by the Synoptists, τὸ ὄρος, "the mountain," R. V., or generally, the ridges of hills on the sides of the Lake of Galilee as distinguished from the low shores, we cannot easily decide. (See Tholuck, *Die Bergrede Christi*, Gotha, 1872.) The Jews distinguished the face of the country into mountains, plains, and valleys; and according to Middleton,[2] by the mountain is here signified "the mountain district as distinguished from the other two."[3] It is most natural to refer it to some specific and well-known locality; but it is plain that the mountain here is not the same mentioned in Matt. xiv. 23, Mark vi. 46, John vi. 3, where the five thousand were fed, or

---

[1] Acts i. 21–2. One qualification of an apostle was that he should have been with the Lord, "beginning from the baptism of John, unto the day that He was received up." It is not plain from what point in John's baptismal work we are to reckon; not from its beginning, or from the Lord's baptism, perhaps from his imprisonment.

[2] Greek Article, 103.   [3] See Ebrard, 349; Meyer on Matt. v. 1.

that in Matt. xv. 29, where the four thousand were fed. We may then rather infer that in each of these cases the mountain is defined by the article because supposed to be already well known as the site of the event. Where this mountain was, is now only a matter of conjecture. (Eders., i. 524. "One of those mountain ranges which stretch to the north of Capernaum." So Keil.) Tradition has chosen the hill known as the Horns of Hattin from its peculiar shape, and called by the Latins the Mount of Beatitudes. It is on the road from Tiberias to Nazareth — a ridge about a quarter of a mile in length, running east and west. At each end rises a small cone or horn. Its peculiar shape attracts the attention of the traveller, and is probably the cause of its selection. Robinson contends that there are a dozen other mountains in the vicinity of the lake which would answer the purpose just as well; and that the tradition which has selected this as the site, goes no further back than the 13th century, and is confined to the Latin Church. As the same tradition places here also the feeding of the five thousand, which is certainly an error, we cannot attach much importance to it.[1] Stanley, however (360), says: "The situation so strikingly coincides with the intimations of the Gospel narrative as almost to force the inference, that in this instance the eye of those who selected the spot was for once rightly guided." With Stanley, Farrar agrees. On the other hand, Edersheim says, that "it is for many reasons unsuitable."

We may arrange the events preparatory to the delivery of the Sermon on the Mount in the following order. The Lord leaving Capernaum in the evening, went to the mount, which cannot have been at any great distance, and spent the night alone. Very early in the morning, His disciples, probably according to His direction, came to Him, and from them He selected the Twelve. By this time the multitudes who had lodged in Capernaum or in its neighborhood, learning whither He had gone, followed Him, and then He addressed them.

As Matthew (chs. v., vi., vii.) and Luke (vi. 17–49) introduce their reports of the Sermon on the Mount by the mention of differing circumstances, and as their reports differ in many points, it has been questioned whether both can refer to the same discourse. The various opinions may be thus classified : 1st. That they are reports of discourses wholly distinct, and spoken at different times, and perhaps, also, at different places.[2]

---

[1] Raumer, 32, note.   [2] Patritius, Krafft, Greswell.

2d.   That they are reports of distinct discourses, but spoken successively: the one, before the choice of the Apostles, the other,
after it; the one, to the disciples, the other, to the multitude;
the one, sitting upon the mountain, the other, standing upon the
plain.[1]   3d.   That they are two reports of one and the same
discourse, neither of the Evangelists giving it exactly as it was
spoken.[2]   4th.   That Matthew has brought together the Lord's
words spoken at different times and places — a kind of summary
of His teachings — while Luke gives a particular discourse as it
was delivered.   5th.   That Matthew's report is a full and accurate one of what the Lord said, and that Luke gives a condensed
account of it, adapting it to his readers.

To determine which of these views is correct, or how the respective discourses of Matthew and Luke stand related to each other, we
must examine in detail the several points of likeness and unlikeness.

1st.   Difference of place.   Matthew (v. 1) says: "And seeing
the multitudes, He went up into a mountain; and when He was set,
His disciples came unto Him, and He opened His mouth, and taught
them."   Luke (vi. 17–20) says, that after the choice of the Twelve,
"He came down with them, and stood in the plain ($\epsilon\pi\iota\ \tau\delta\pi o\upsilon\ \pi\epsilon\delta\iota\nu o\hat{\upsilon}$,
R. V. "on a level place"), and the company of His disciples, and a
great multitude of people   .   .   .   which came to hear Him, and to
be healed of their diseases; and they that were vexed with unclean
spirits: and they were healed.   And the whole multitude sought to
touch Him, for there went virtue out of Him and healed them all.
And He lifted up His eyes on His disciples, and said," etc.   Thus,
according to Matthew, the discourse was delivered by the Lord sitting upon the side or top of a mountain; according to Luke, after
He had chosen the Twelve He descended to the plain, and having
healed the sick, addressed those present.   But the latter does not say
that the discourse was spoken on the plain, although He does not
mention any re-ascent.   Such a re-ascent is however very probable,
for it is said "that the whole multitude sought to touch Him"; and
as, when similarly pressed upon the sea-shore (Mark iii. 9), He entered
a boat and taught from it, so now He would naturally ascend to a
point where they could not reach Him, and from which He could
easily be seen and heard by all.[3]   Some would understand the
"plain" of Luke of a level spot on the side of the mountain, or at its

---

[1] Augustine, Lange.
[2] Robinson, Tischendorf, Stier.
[3] So Robinson, Har., 193.

foot, where the multitude could sit or stand, this plain itself being, in reference to the sea-shore from whence they came, a part of the mountain.   Thus Stanley, speaking of the hill of Hattin, says: " The plain on which it stands is easily accessible from the lake, and from that plain to the summit is but a few minutes' walk.   The platform at the top is evidently suitable for the collection of a multitude, and corresponds precisely to the 'level place,' mistranslated 'plain,' to which He would ' come down,' as from one of its higher horns, to address the people." [1]   In this way, all seeming discrepancy between Matthew and Luke as to the place disappears.   The choice of the Twelve was made upon the mountain before the multitude gathered, which choice Matthew does not mention.   As the Lord beholds the people gathering to Him, He goes down with His disciples to meet them upon some level place; and after healing the sick, He seats Himself in a position, probably higher up upon the hill, where He can be seen and heard by the great crowds, and proceeds to address them. [2]

2d.   Difference of time.   Following his report of the sermon, Matthew relates (viii. 2–4) the healing of the leper, as immediately taking place.   Luke (vii. 2–10) relates the healing of the centurion's servant as immediately following.   As these events were separated by a considerable interval of time, so, it is said by Krafft and others, must have been the discourses which they respectively followed.   But we have already seen that Matthew is not narrating events in chronological order, and that the healing of the leper took place before the Sermon on the mount.   We are not, therefore, obliged to suppose the discourses distinct upon this ground.

3d.   Difference of audience.   Matthew (iv. 25) describes the multitudes present as from Galilee, Decapolis, Jerusalem, Judæa, and from beyond Jordan; Luke (vi. 17), as from all Judæa, Jerusalem, and the sea-coast of Tyre and Sidon.   From this partial difference of names Krafft (83) infers that those who heard the discourse reported by Matthew were mostly Jews, with perhaps a few Syrians; but that those who heard the discourse reported by Luke were mostly from the eastern side of Galilee, and the coasts of Tyre and Sidon.   But this inference is not warranted.   In this enumeration neither of the Evangelists designs to discriminate between Jewish and heathen lands.   This appears from Mark (iii. 7, 8), who mentions Galilee, Judæa, Jerusalem, Idumæa, beyond Jordan, and about Tyre and

---

[1] So Tholuck, Sermon on the Mount, 53, " a level place, not a plain." Weisäcker: ein ebenes Feld. *Contra*, McClel., 446.

[2] See Ebrard, 350; Stier, i. 327; Lichtenstein, 247. Alford, after Meyer, finds the two Evangelists in contradiction.

Sidon. If heathen were present, according to Luke, from Tyre and Sidon, so might they be also, according to Matthew, from Decapolis. The Evangelists plainly all intend to say, that the crowds who were present came from every part of the land, and any difference in the enumeration of the regions whence they came is unimportant. On the other hand, the very particularity of the mention of so many provinces by each, sufficiently shows that all point to one and the same period. As has been said, some affirm that the discourse in Matthew was spoken to the disciples, that in Luke to the multitude; and they understand Matthew's statement, "Seeing the multitudes He went up into a mountain," to mean, that He ascended up that He might avoid them, and address the disciples alone. But that He addressed the multitudes, is plain from the statement (vii. 28) that "the multitudes were astonished at His teaching."

The supposition that the Lord first addressed the apostles and disciples, which address Matthew gives, and then the multitudes, which address Luke gives, was advocated by Augustine, and has been the ruling one in the Latin Church. (See Maldonatus, *in loco*.) It has been also adopted by most of the Lutheran harmonists, though Calvin calls this view light and frivolous. That there is something esoteric in the former and exoteric in the latter, may be admitted; but this is owing, not to the different audiences to whom the discourses were spoken, but to the different classes of readers for which the two Gospels were designed.

4th. Difference of contents. "Of 107 verses in Matthew, Luke contains only 30; his four beatitudes are balanced by as many woes; and in his text parts of the sermon are introduced by sayings which do not precede them in Matthew, but which naturally connect with them."[1] But these differences are few when compared with the resemblances. The beginning and ending of both are the same; there is a general similarity in the order, and often identity in the expressions. Often in the Evangelists, when their reports are in substance the same, there are many variations.[2] That the two discourses should have so much in common if they were distinct, spoken at different times and to different audiences, is most improbable. That many of the shorter proverbial expressions might be used at various times is natural, but not that such similarity should prevail throughout.[3]

---

[1] Alford on Matt. v. 1. See also Greswell, ii. 429; Krafft, 83.

[2] Compare the Lord's Prayer as given Matt. vi. 9–13 and Luke xi. 2–4; and His discourse concerning the Pharisees, Matt. xxiii. and Luke xx. 46.

[3] Neander's explanation, 224, that the original document of Matthew being of Hebrew origin, "passed through the hands of the Greek editor, who has inserted other expressions of Christ allied to those in the organic connection of the discourse, but spoken on other occasions," is an arbitrary assumption.

Without entering into the vexed question of inspiration, its nature and degrees, we may say that each Evangelist, writing under the direction of the Holy Spirit, made such selection of the Lord's words, as well as of the events in His history, and so arranged them, as best to meet the wants of those for whom he wrote. That Luke should omit those portions of the discourse having special reference to the Jewish sects and to the Mosaic laws, was in accordance with the general scope of his Gospel as designed for Gentile Christians; while Matthew, on the other hand, writing for Jewish Christians, would retain them. (Wordsworth, on Luke vi. 17.)   To this Alford and others object that in some cases Luke is fuller than Matthew (compare Matt. vii. 1, 2, and Luke vi. 37, 38).   But, as has been said, Matthew may not give the words of the Lord in all their fullness; and it is not at all inconsistent with the fact of an epitome that certain thoughts should be more fully expanded than in the original, when this original is itself but an epitome.

There is still another argument against the identity of these two discourses, based upon the fact that Matthew does not relate his own call (ix. 9) till he had recorded the sermon.   But it is so abundantly established that Matthew does not follow chronological order, that this is of no importance.

We conclude, then, that Matthew gives this discourse substantially, if not literally, as it was spoken; and that Luke gives the same, but modified to meet the wants of that class of readers for whom he especially wrote.[1]

It is not in our province to interpret this discourse, but it gives some historical data which should be noted.   1st. His denial that He came to destroy the law and the prophets (Matt. v. 17). Charges of this kind were, undoubtedly, often made against Him. 2d.   His intimation that all who should receive Him, must suffer reproach and persecution (v. 11), "Blessed are ye when men shall reproach you, and persecute you. and say all manner of evil against you falsely, for my sake."   3d.   The authority with which He speaks, as shown in the frequent recurrence of the words, "But I say unto you"; and in His declaration (vii. 22),

---

[1] In this view of the matter, most agree; Rob., Tholuck, Alex., Fried., Ellicott, Eders.

12*

"Many will say to me in that day, Lord, Lord, . . . and then will I profess unto them, I never knew you, depart from me, ye that work iniquity." His language throughout is not that of a rabbi, or a prophet, but of a Law-giver and a King.

MIDSUMMER, 781. A. D. 28.

After the sermon is ended Jesus returns to Capernaum, still followed by the multitudes. Immediately after His return, He heals the centurion's servant. The crowds continuing to follow Him so that He has no time even to eat, His friends become alarmed at His incessant labors, and thinking Him beside Himself, attempt to restrain Him.

MATT. viii. 5–13.
LUKE vii. 1–10.
MARK iii. 20, 21.

It is said by Luke (vii. 1), "Now when He had ended all His sayings in the audience of the people, He entered into Capernaum." (R. V., "After He had ended.") Mark, after mentioning the choice of the Twelve, adds : "And they went into a house," or more literally, "went home" — εἰς οἶκον — that is, to His house in Capernaum. (See ii. 1.) It is probable that the healing of the centurion's servant was on the day of His return (Matt. viii. 5). The mention of this centurion seems to be the ground of the general belief that a Roman garrison was stationed here, but it is more probable that the centurion was under Herod.[1]

The difference between Matthew and Luke, that according to the former, the centurion came unto the Lord in person, but according to the latter, he made his request by the elders, is unimportant. That the synagogue here spoken of as built by the centurion, is the same as that the ruins of which are now to be seen at Tell Hum, is not improbable. It is said by Tristram (B. P. 279) : "If this be Capernaum, then this must, beyond doubt, be the synagogue built by the Roman centurion." (So Eders., i. 546, and Col. Wilson; but it is objected by others that its architecture shows it to be of later date.) That the elders should come to make the request is wholly in accordance with oriental usage (Thomson, i. 313), and that they were willing to make it shows that at this time no general hostility had yet developed itself against the Lord in Capernaum.

---

[1] So Keil, Meyer, Godet. As to Roman garrisons in Jewish cities, see Schürer, I. ii.

Returning to Capernaum, the Lord found no rest.   So earnest were the people to see and hear Him, and to bring to Him their sick, that He found no time even to eat (Mark iii. 20).   This intense activity alarmed His friends for His sanity (verse 21, " He is beside Himself ") and " they went out to lay hold on Him."   Mark mentions a little later (verse 31) a visit of His mother and brethren, apparently to restrain Him from such excessive labors.   Are these two events the same ? Are " His friends " in verse 21, the same as " His mother and His brethren " in verse 31 ?   This point we will briefly consider.

We must first ask how the expression, οἱ παρ' αὐτοῦ, literally " those from Him," is to be understood?   It is said that the only allowable translation is that of " relatives " or " kinsmen," and that, therefore, these here mentioned must have been His mother and brethren.[1]   But in the R. V., the translation " His friends " of the A. V. is retained. The question is, whether kinship is meant, or some relation of discipleship or friendship.   It is said by Lichtenstein that they were disciples in the larger sense, not of the Twelve; by Ebrard, that they were the people of the house where He was; by Keil, that they were not distinctively His disciples, but some in Capernaum friendly to Him, who, knowing how great the pressure upon Him, came out of their houses to interfere.

If we distinguish His friends from His relatives — His mother and brethren — we find two events, and we must enquire as to the order of their occurrence.   Mark alone makes mention of His friends, but all the Synoptists mention the visit of His relatives.   In Matthew, this stands in immediate relation to the request of the Pharisees for a sign (xii. 38–46), and after He had been accused by them of being in alliance with Beelzebub (verse 24).   Mark (iii. 31) also brings it into immediate connection with this accusation (verse 22).   Luke (viii. 19) puts it after the teaching in parables, but without any special indication as to the time.   It seems, therefore, most probable that the visit of His relatives must be put somewhat later than the visit of His friends, and when the enmity of the Pharisees was more developed. As to the chronological place of the first interference, we are to note that Mark does not say that it was immediately after the descent from the mount.   In the R. V. (verse 19) it reads, " And He cometh into a house," or in the margin, " cometh home," beginning here a new paragraph.   This was the original division when the Bible was

---

[1] So T. G. Lex. *sub voce,* παρά, Meyer, Alex., Stier, Alford, Norton: in the Vulgate it is rendered, *et cum audissent sui ;* by De Wette and Weisäcker, die Seinigen.

divided into verses, and is retained by many modern editors and translators; it is also the division in the Vulgate. It is, therefore, possible,
that this attempt of His friends was some days or even weeks after
the Sermon on the Mount. But it may very well have been immediately after this, and the expression, "The multitude cometh together
again," seems to indicate that after a temporary dispersion, such as
was natural in coming from the mount, they had reassembled in the
city, and doubtless before His own dwelling.[1]

How are we to understand the words of His friends, "He is beside Himself?" Did they really question His sanity? The expression,
ἐξέστη, does not necessarily mean this. (See Mark ii. 12; T. G. Lex.,
Eders. i. 543.) It is most probable that they thought Him over-
excited, and attempting labors beyond His strength, and therefore
needing to be restrained. But if it were their belief that He was
really insane, it would simply show how incapable they were of
understanding what zeal for God possessed Him, and what strength
He received from His Father for His work.

If, however, on the other hand, we identify, as many or perhaps
most do, His friends with His mother and brethren, and find one
event only, this is not, as we have seen, necessarily to be put immediately after the Sermon on the Mount. Some put it after the healing of the demoniac (Matt. xii. 22 ; so Light., Fried., Gardiner,
Eders.), when the charge of the Pharisees that He cast out devils by
the aid of Beelzebub, must have greatly agitated His relatives.

While, then, we cannot positively assert that the two events are
not to be identified, yet the probability is, that they are distinct. If
distinct, the first is to be put at or soon after the descent from the
mount; and the second, after the healing of the dumb and blind demoniacs. If identified, the latter date is the more probable.[2] The place
from which His relatives came will be later considered.

MIDSUMMER, 781.   A. D. 28.

Soon after the healing of the centurion's servant He   LUKE vii. 11–17.
goes to Nain, accompanied by the disciples and many
people. He there restores to life the son of a widow as
they were bearing him to the grave. While continuing   MATT. xi. 1–19.
His ministry in that part of Galilee, John the Baptist,   LUKE vii. 18–35.
who hears of His works, sends from his prison a message
to Him by two of his disciples. Jesus answers their
question, and addresses the multitude respecting John.

---

[1] In Tisch., the article is omitted before multitude, in W. and H. it is bracketed.
If we omit it, it reads " a multitude," not identifying it with that from the mount.

[2] The two are distinguished by Bengel, Rob., Farrar, Lex., Fuller, Keil, Eders.;
and identified by Light., Ellicott, Gardiner, Quandt, Meyer.

The order of events here will depend upon the reading,
Luke vii. 11, whether ἐν τῇ ἐξῆς, or ἐν τῷ ἐξῆς, "the day after,"
or "afterward."[1]   (In R. V. "It came to pass afterwards," but
see margin. We accept the R. V.) But how long He now remained at Capernaum we are not told. Some interval must
have elapsed before His relatives came from Nazareth — if this
was their residence — to Capernaum. His departure to Nain
was the beginning of His second circuit.

The Lord gave Himself no rest, but entered immediately
upon new labors. From this time the Twelve were constantly
with Him till sent forth upon their mission. Beside them many
of the other disciples now accompanied Him, as well as much
people.

Nain lies on the northwest declivity of the hill of Little
Hermon, commanding an extensive view over the plain of
Esdraelon and the northern hills. It is now an insignificant
village, with no remains of any importance. "No convent, no
tradition marks the spot. But under these circumstances, the
name is sufficient to guarantee its authenticity."[2]   Tristram
(B. P., 241) says of it : "Nain must have been a city ; the
ruined heaps and traces of walls prove that it was of considerable extent, and a walled town, and therefore with gates, according to the Gospel narrative."

As the Jews usually buried the dead upon the same day they
died and before sundown,[3] it has been questioned how the Lord
could have reached Nain from Capernaum so early in the day as
to meet the funeral procession. But it is uncertain whether He
left Capernaum that morning. He may have been at some point
much nearer to Nain, and if not, as the distance is only about
twenty-five miles, and probably less, it might be walked in seven
or eight hours. As the orientals walk rapidly, and commence
their journeys early in the morning, He might have reached
Nain by noon, or a little after.[4]

The restoration to life of the widow's son was the first work of
this kind the Lord had wrought, and naturally produced a most

---

[1] For the first, Tischendorf, Robinson, Wieseler, Alford, Keil ; *contra*, Meyer,
Stier, W. and H.

[2] Stanley, 349.   [3] Winer, ii. 16, note 1.

[4] For details of this miracle, see Edersheim, i. 553.

powerful impression on all who heard of it. All saw in it
the mighty hand of God, who alone could bring the dead to life.
The Evangelist mentions (Luke vii. 16) that "there came a fear
on all, and they glorified God, saying, that a great prophet is
risen up among us ; and that God hath visited His people."
Keil understands this as expressing the popular feeling that
Jesus was not the Messiah, but His forerunner. No such miracle
had been wrought since the days of Elisha; the fame of it
"went forth through all Judæa, and throughout all the region
round about," and thus coming to the ears of some of John's
disciples, was told by them to their master. Luke says (vii.
18), "And the disciples of John showed him of all these things."
This may mean that they told him of all that Jesus had recently
done, His works of healing, the choice of the Twelve, the Sermon on the Mount, as well as of this work at Nain ; and also
of His great popularity, and of the crowds that continually followed Him. If we assume that the place of John's imprisonment was Machaerus,[1] a fortress in the southern part of Peræa,
just on the confines of Arabia, some days at least must have
elapsed between this miracle and the coming of John's messengers.[2] Perhaps our Lord continued during this interval at Nain,
teaching all who had been so impressed by His mighty work
that they had ears to hear ; or He may have visited the adjacent
cities and villages ; or He may, after a brief circuit, have returned to Capernaum, and hither, as the place of His residence,
John's disciples have come.

Some place this miracle after the raising of the daughter of
Jairus, chiefly because the former is a greater exhibition of the
power of Christ. Thus Trench[3] says of the three miracles of
raising the dead, that "they are not exactly the same miracle
repeated three times over, but may be contemplated as an ever-
ascending scale of difficulty, each a greater outcoming of the
power of Christ than the preceding." But this is more plausible
than sound. If there be such "an ever-ascending scale of difficulty," we should find the Lord's first works of healing less
mighty than the later ; but this is not the case. If we compare

---

[1] Josephus, War, vii. 6. 1–3.   [2] See Greswell, ii. 327.
[3] Mir., 152.

the two miracles of feeding the multitude, the first is the more stupendous.   The impression which the raising of the widow's son made on all, seems plainly to show that it was the first of its kind (Luke vii. 16, 17).

Perhaps the message of the Baptist may stand in close connection with the great miracle at Nain.   It is not within our scope to ask what motives may have controlled him, but such a miracle must have convinced him, had he before had any doubts, that Jesus was divinely sent, and that the mighty power of God was indeed with Him.   The question then, "Art thou He that should come, or look we for another?" may be an intimation that Jesus should now put forth in direct act that power of which He had just shown Himself to be possessed; a question of impatience rather than of doubt.

The answer of the Lord to the messengers meets this state of mind.   He refers to His daily works as being truly Messianic, and such as befitted Him to perform.   Not acts of judgment but of mercy belong to His office.   His work is now to heal the sick, to preach the Gospel to the poor, to raise the dead. He adds, as a caution to John, "Blessed is he whosoever shall not be offended in me."   "Blessed is he who shall understand the work I now do, and not stumble at it."

This question of John, which some, as Jones, suppose to have arisen from no doubt on John's part, but to have been suggested by the Holy Spirit for the confirmation of the faith of others, gives Jesus an opportunity to bear His direct witness to him as a prophet, and more, as the herald of the Messiah (Matt. xi. 9, 10).   He declares also to the people, that if they will receive him, he is the Elias that was for to come; and reproaches them that they would not receive John or Himself in either of their different modes of working or teaching (Matt. xi. 16–19; Luke vii. 31–35).   His testimony to John was well received by the people and the publicans, all those who had been baptized by him; but not by the Pharisees and lawyers, who had rejected his baptism (Luke vii. 29, 30).

This testimony of Jesus to John as the herald of the Messiah, was a plain assertion, though an indirect one, of His own Messianic character.   But John was now in prison.   How was

this compatible with his being Elias ? How could he prepare
the Lord's way ? Did not this very fact of his imprisonment
conclusively disprove all his claims to be the forerunner of the
Messiah ? This tacit objection Jesus meets by showing that it
depended on them, whether or no John was the Elias. If they
received him, if they hearkened to his words, and permitted him
to do his work, then he would be to them that prophet, and fulfill
all that was said of Elias. But they had not so received him ;
they had said of him that he had a devil ; and now he was shut
up in prison ; and thus the Jews were made clearly to understand the connection between John's ministry and that of Jesus,
and how the rejection of the former involved that of the latter.

Immediately upon these words concerning John, follows in
Matthew (xi. 20–24) an apostrophe to the cities of Bethsaida, Chorazin, and Capernaum. It is given by Luke later, and in connection with the mission of the seventy disciples (Luke x. 13–16).
The point is of some importance as bearing on the question,
how long the Lord's work in Galilee had now continued.

It is said by Matthew : "Then began He to upbraid the cities
wherein most of His mighty works were done, because they repented not." This would indicate that a considerable time had
elapsed since His ministry began in Galilee, and that it was now
drawing to a close. In Matthew's arrangement it is put after
the Twelve were sent out, and John's messengers had come to
Him (xi. 1–2). Is "then" — τότε — here a mark of time ?
There seems no good reason why it is not to be so taken here,
for the woes on the cities that follow are in keeping with His
words respecting John and Himself (xi. 18, 19). But the position of these woes in Luke at the time of sending out the
Seventy, and at the end of His Galilæan ministry, is rather to be
preferred. And some think that the Lord repeated them. It
is suggested by Alexander that a part spoken to the Seventy is
given by Matthew "on account of its affinity with what precedes." As he does not mention the sending of the Seventy,
there seems to be no valid objection to this view of a repetition.[1]

---

[1] Opinions are much divided. Of those who think them spoken once, and follow-
ing Matthew, are Caspari, Keil ; following Luke, Bleek, Godet, Friedlieb, Gardiner, Krafft,
Edersheim, and many. Of those who think them spoken twice, Lightfoot, Robinson,
Meyer, Stroud; Farrar, not twice spoken, but placed too early by Matthew.

Whether the journey (Luke viii. 1–3) made in company with "the Twelve and certain women," was a continuation of the circuit from Nain, is not certain, though most probable. Edersheim (i. 573) supposes Him to have returned to Capernaum after the miracle at Nain, and on this return journey to have healed the two blind men and the demonized dumb mentioned by Matthew (ix. 27–31). If, however, the anointing was at Capernaum, this may refer to a new circuit. The remark of Ellicott (184) that "this circuit could not have lasted much above a day or two after the miracle at Nain," is plainly at variance with the Evangelist's language (viii. 1), that "He went throughout every city and village preaching," which upon its face implies a circuit of considerable duration.[1] This circuit is distinguished from His former ones by the attendance of the women, whose names are mentioned : Mary Magdalene, Joanna, wife of Chuza, Herod's steward, and Susanna, and many others. Nothing is historically known of any of these persons more than is here related. Their attendance on the Lord may perhaps be regarded as marking an onward step in His ministry. Whether from this time they generally accompanied Him in His journeys is not stated, but is not improbable. (See Luke xxiii. 55; compare Matt. xx. 17, 20.)

Autumn, 781.   A. D. 28.

Jesus dines with a Pharisee named Simon, and while at   Luke vii. 36–50.
the table is anointed by a woman who is a sinner. In reply to Simon's complaint He relates the parable of the two
debtors. He continues His circuit in Galilee with the   Luke viii. 1–3.
Twelve, and also accompanied by certain women.

It is much disputed whether one, two, or three anointings of the Lord are mentioned by the Evangelists, and whether these were by one or two women, and when, and where they took place. A brief discussion of these points is therefore necessary.

We first ask how many times was the Lord anointed ? (Matt. xxv. 6; Mark xiv. 3; Luke vii. 36; John xii. 2.) A few of the early fathers said three times; Matthew and Mark relating one instance,

---

[1] It is impossible, without great violence to language, to compress so much of the Lord's work into the brief interval between Purim and the Passover following, as Ellicott is compelled to do by assuming that the feast (John v. 1) is Purim.

John another, and Luke a third. But more said, He was twice anointed, Matthew and Mark and John relating one instance, and Luke a second. On the other hand, some said, He was anointed only once, all the Evangelists relating the same. (For the early opinions, see Maldonatus, *in locis*; Nebe, Leidensgeschichte, 120.) And down to the present time each of these opinions has its advocates.

Assuming here, what is generally admitted but which will be examined when the events of Passion week are considered, that Matthew and Mark and John all refer to the same anointing, we shall now consider only the point whether this is the one mentioned by Luke.

The ground upon which one anointing only has been affirmed is in general the similarity of the narratives as seen in three particulars: first, the identity of the names of the givers of the feasts, being both Simon; second, the very unusual character of the act, and the consequent improbability that it would be repeated; third, the offense taken in both cases by persons present.

As to the first, the identity of names, this has little force. The name Simon was one of the most common among the Jews, and in the New Testament some eight persons of this name are mentioned. Besides, the two Simons are here distinguished; in Luke "Simon the Pharisee," in Matthew and Mark "Simon the leper." We cannot then, on this ground, affirm that they are one and the same person.

As to the second, that such an act with its attendant circumstances could scarcely have been repeated, we know that the anointing of the head was common, and not uncommon the anointing of the feet. (Hamburg., i. 887.) The wiping of His feet with the hairs of the head was most remarkable, but the same feeling of humility, reverence, and love that called it forth from one person, might also from another. Luthardt suggests that Mary of Bethany (John xii. 3) may have heard what the woman, "a sinner," did to the Lord (Luke vii. 38), and she would not do less.

As to the third, that some of those present should on both occasions take offense, it is quite what we might expect from the peculiar character of the act. But the persons are not the same, nor the ground of the offense. Some of the disciples, represented by Judas Iscariot, blamed Mary for her waste; Simon the Pharisee found fault that the Lord, if a prophet, should have received such an anointing from a woman, a sinner.

If we now note the dissimilarities, we find them to be many and important. As against the identity of the two Simons, besides their differing designations, "Pharisee" and "leper," we must take into

account the differences of time and place.   Luke puts this anointing in
the midst of the Lord's Galilæan ministry, and somewhere in Galilee;
the other Evangelists, some days only before His death, and at Bethany
near Jerusalem.   It may be said, as by Grotius, that Luke often dis-
regards time and place, but it is scarcely credible that he should take
this event so wholly out of its actual connections.   Nor can the language
of Simon the Pharisee be put into the mouth of Simon the leper; nor
can the words of the Lord to the two women have been spoken to one
and the same person.   To the sinner He said, " Thy sins are forgiven";
of Mary, "She did it for my burial" . . . ("to prepare me for
my burial," R. V.).   And it is most unlikely that after the Pharisees
had resolved to put the Lord to death, a Pharisee would have
received Him into his house, and honored Him with a feast.[1]

But the more general belief has been from the first that there were
two anointings.[2] If we accept two anointings, one in Galilee and
one in Bethany, were there two women anointing, or one? If one,
since Mary of Bethany is expressly named (John xii. 3), the "the
sinner" of Luke, must be identified with her.   This identification
was held by some, perhaps most, of the Latin fathers.   Thus
Augustine says: *eandem Mariam bis hoc fecisse.*   On the other side,
many held that there were two women, Mary of B. and "the sinner"
being distinct persons.[3]

Before we examine the grounds on which the belief rests that
there was but one woman, and she Mary of B., let us examine the
statement in Luke (vii. 37).   And first, the right reading.   In the
received text it reads γυνὴ ἐν τῇ πόλει ἥτις ἦν ἁμαρτωλός, and is translated
" a woman in the city, which was a sinner "; in W. and H., γυνὴ
ἥτις ἦν ἐν τῇ πόλει ἁμαρτωλός, translated in the R. V., "a woman which
was in the city, a sinner."   Accepting the last as the true reading, the
natural construction is, that she was a woman residing in the city
where Jesus then was; and her character is marked by the word
"sinner," which, we can scarce doubt, indicates here a woman of unchaste life.   This has been the very general belief from earliest times.
It is said by Maldonatus : " *Constans omnium veterum auctorum opinio
est fuisse meretricem* "; and this is generally accepted by recent commentators.

If, then, the Lord was anointed twice by the same woman, the
sinner of Luke must have been Mary the sister of Martha and

---

[1] Among those in recent times who have maintained only one anointing are Lightfoot, Grotius, Ewald, Bleek, Hengstenberg.

[2] So of the fathers, Augustine, Chrysostom. Of the moderns, Meyer, Rob., Elli
cott, Caspari, Ebrard, Godet, Edersheim, Friedlieb, Farrar, Gardiner.

[3] So Origen, Jerome, Chrysostom, and others. See Friedlieb, 438.

Lazarus. (John xi. 2; xii. 3.) And this is the belief of the Latin church, at least since Gregory (604 A. D.), and is affirmed by most of its commentators and harmonists. (So Maldonatus and a Lapide, but *contra*, Friedlieb.)

But on what grounds are we to identify the two? There is nothing in the narrative that points to it. If there were two anointings, one in Bethany and one in Galilee, how do we explain the presence of Mary of B. at both? If leading an impure life in Galilee, when and why did she transfer her residence to Bethany? The explanation usually given supposes that there was but one Simon, a leper whom the Lord had healed, that he lived at Bethany, that Martha, Mary, and Lazarus lived at Magdala in Galilee, that Simon married Martha, that Mary was unchaste, but lived with her sister, that she first met the Lord at Bethany at the house of her brother-in-law, and there anointed Him, and afterward anointed Him again before His passion. (So in substance the Latins; Hengstenberg gives a somewhat different version.) For all this there is no historical basis. All depends upon a supposed relationship of Simon to the family of Martha and Mary, either of marriage or of blood. The variations of this tradition, as that this Simon lived first in Galilee, that there Mary his relative had free entrance to his house, and there anointed the Lord, that he afterwards settled in Bethany, and that she repeated the anointing there, are all equally unsupported.

To the identification of Mary of Bethany with the sinful woman, it may be replied, (*a*) that the woman mentioned by Luke is not called Mary, and therefore the woman mentioned by John is sufficiently distinguished from her by the name, while the fact of the anointing is used by him to distinguish this Mary from others of the same name; and (*b*) that the objection is of weight only in case the anointing mentioned by Luke as occurring in Galilee is the same with the one mentioned by John as occurring in Jerusalem, an identification on other grounds improbable.

We do not, then, find any ground to identify the sinful woman of Galilee with Mary of Bethany. Of the former we know absolutely nothing, neither her name, nor her family or friends, nor even her city. But Mary never appears anywhere else but in Bethany, her relatives are always mentioned; and our Christian feeling is wounded when we are asked to believe that one, so highly commended by the Lord, had led a notoriously wicked life. It is true, she is said by the advocates of this identity to have repented, *tunc peccatrix fuerat, nunc sancta;* but the shame of her earlier life must have remained in the memories of all.

We conclude, then, that the woman a sinner and **Mary of B. were** distinct persons; the former anointed the Lord in Galilee during His ministry there, the latter in Bethany when His ministry had come to its close.

But another question meets us: Can the sinful woman of Galilee be identified with Mary Magdalene? It has been the general opinion of the Latin Church, at least since Gregory I., that Mary of B. and the sinful woman and Mary M. are all one and the same; we must, there-fore, also ask what we know of Mary M. It is generally accepted that she was so called from Magdala, a town on the sea of Galilee.[1] She is mentioned by Luke (viii. 2) as one of the women whom the Lord had "healed of evil spirits and infirmities; Mary called Magda-lene, out of whom went seven devils." Only once again is she spoken of in this way (Mark xvi. 9); in all other cases, fourteen in number, she is called Mary Magdalene, or simply Mary, and all later mention of her is in connection with the crucifixion and resurrection.

This is all we can be said to know of Mary M., but from the fact that she "ministered to the Lord of her substance," the inference has been drawn that she had some wealth; and from the position of her name before those of Joanna and Susanna (Luke viii. 3), and also before those who were with her at the cross (Matt. xxvii. 56, and elsewhere), we may infer that she was a woman of rank. (See Lard-ner, x. 238.) But whether these inferences be or be not correct, she was certainly very prominent among the disciples. That she was ever an immoral woman, is not said, nor is it implied in the fact that she had been under the power of evil spirits. (See Trench, Miracles, 131.) A life of unchastity is precluded by the place she held in the ranks of those faithful and honorable women who followed the Lord.

It is hard to see why Mary M., of all the women mentioned as believers, should have been selected to stand as the unknown sinner. How strong and general this belief had become, is seen in the heading of the chapter (Luke vii.) in the A. V. of the English Bible: "Our Lord showeth by occasion of Mary M. how He is a friend to sinners;" and it is now a case of inseparable association. But the early church was by no means unanimous in this identity; it was not for some centuries that it was generally accepted, and there have been many dissentients. The Greek Church never identified the three. In the *Apostolic Constitutions* (iii. 6), Mary of B. is distin-guished from Mary M.: "There were with us Mary Magdalene, and Mary and Martha, the sisters of Lazarus," and the two have different days of commemoration. In the Roman Church, the feast of Mary

---

[1] Lightfoot attempts to identify Magdala with Bethany, but on no sufficient ground. See Reland, 883.

M. is on the 22d of July, and she is identified with Mary of B. and with the sinful woman. The Church of England dropped this commemoration in 1552. (For a full account of the honors paid Mary M., see Binterim, Denk, v. 395; in favor of the identity of Mary Magdalene with this sinner, see Sepp, iii. 243; Oosterzee *in loco; contra*, Meyer, Winer. For a general discussion of the point, see Herzog's Encyc., vol. ix. 102.)

As there is much confusion arising from the great diversity of opinions respecting the number of the women, and the number of the anointings, and their place and time, a brief summary may be useful.

I. Number of women anointing. *First.* Three women: 1. The unknown sinner; 2. Mary of B.; 3. Mary M.; *Second.* Two women: 1. Mary of B.; 2. Mary M. One of these must be the same as the unknown sinner; (*a*) Mary of B. and the sinner the same; (*b*) Mary M. and the sinner the same. *Third.* One woman only; the sinful woman, Mary of B., and Mary M., all one and the same person.

II. Number of anointings. *First.* Three anointings, one in Luke, one in Matthew and Mark, and one in John. *Second.* Two anointings, one in Luke; one in Matthew, Mark, and John. *Third.* One anointing. All the Evangelists describe the same.

III. Place and time: if three anointings, one in Galilee during the second year, two in Bethany six days and two days respectively before the crucifixion; if two anointings, either (*a*) one in Galilee during the second year, the other in Bethany during Passion Week, or (*b*) both in Bethany, one six days, the other two days before the crucifixion; if one anointing, this in Bethany during Passion Week.

AUTUMN, 781. A. D. 28.

Returning to Capernaum, the Lord heals one possessed with a devil, blind and dumb. The Pharisees hereupon charge Him with casting out devils by the help of Beelzebub, and some, tempting Him, ask a sign from Heaven. He replies to their charge, and while speaking it is announced to Him that His mother and brethren stand without, desiring to see Him. He points to His disciples, and says, Behold my mother and my brethren.

MATT. xii. 22–45.
MARK iii. 22–30.

MATT. xii. 46–50.
LUKE viii. 19–21.
MARK iii. 31–35.

There is not a little difficulty in the arrangement of these events. There are two cases of healing of dumb possessed persons related by Matthew, first in ix. 32, second in xii. 22. They have much in common, and at both did the Pharisees make the charge that Jesus cast out devils through the prince of the devils. There is, however, this important difference, that in the former the possessed was dumb only, in the latter, both dumb and blind.

It has been said by some, as DeWette, that these are the same; but almost all make them distinct. (See Meyer on Matt. xii. 22.) Does Matthew relate them in the order of their occurrence? This is not certain. He collects in chapters viii. and ix. a number of miracles, but their chronological relations he does not define, and to know when they occurred we must examine the attendant circumstances. The healing of this dumb man is put as following immediately after the healing of the blind men (ix. 27), and this immediately after the raising to life of the daughter of Jairus (verse 23 ff.). But in the latter case the connecting links are too vague to demand an immediate sequence, and perhaps also in the first. (See Trench, Mir., 160.) The healing of the blind and dumb possessed man is mentioned without any clear indication of the time.

In both these cases the charge was made that the Lord cast out devils by the aid of Beelzebub. To this charge in ix. 34, He made no reply, so far as is reported; but in xii. 25 He replied, showing both its folly and its wickedness.

In Luke xi. 14 we find an instance of the healing of a dumb possessed man followed by a like charge, and the Lord's reply. Is it to be identified with either of those mentioned by Matthew? That he is spoken of only as dumb and not also blind, would seem to identify him with the man in Matthew ix. 32; but the Lord's reply in Luke is so like that in Matt. xii. 25 that we seem almost compelled to identify them. We have also in Mark iii. 22 the same charge, and a reply much briefer, but in substantially the same words.

The arrangement of harmonists as to number of healings and times of occurrence is various.

I. Those who find three cases of healing:

Lightfoot — 1st, Matt. xii.; 2d, Matt. ix.; 3d, Luke xi.

Bengel, Greswell — 1st, Matt. ix.; 2d, Matt. xii.; 3d, Luke xi.

II. Those who find two cases:

Robinson, Gardiner, Friedlieb — 1st, Matt. xii., Luke xi.; 2d, Matt. ix.

Edersheim — 1st, Matthew ix. ; 2d, Matthew xii. ; Luke xi.[1]

It is very difficult to choose among these several arrangements. It is remarked by Greswell that cases of dispossession were among the earliest and commonest of the Saviour's miracles; it is not, therefore, to be thought strange that His replies upon these different occasions should be substantially the same. And we are also to remember that the Evangelist having once given His reply, would not repeat it unless some new elements were woven into it. It is then not at all improbable that Matthew, who simply mentions the charge in ix. 34, should, in xii. 25, have brought together after his manner, the substance of all the Lord had said in His replies. The same may be true of the report in Luke. In both, the demand of His enemies for a sign is mentioned in immediate connection with their charge of demoniac help, and this points strongly to their identity. But while there is much to be said in favor of this, yet the probability is that Matthew and Luke refer to different cases of healing and give different discourses, that in Luke being during the last journey to Jerusalem. (See Greswell, ii. 581 ff.)

Two points still remain. Is the discourse in Mark iii. 23 ff. the same as in Matthew xii. 25 ? This is most probable, Mark omitting the miracle which occasioned the charge against the Lord. Of the healings in Matthew, which is to be put first in time ? As we have seen, the harmonists are divided, but there seem to be less difficulties in putting the healing of the blind and dumb possessed (Matthew xii. 22) before that of the dumb possessed (Matt. ix. 32).[2]

The order of events is of importance only as showing how early in His ministry the Pharisees charged the Lord with being aided by Beelzebub. It is easily credible that they brought the charge early, but at first in a reserved way, and afterward more openly.

---

[1] Krafft (85) attempts to show that the discourse (Matt. xii. 25-45) was not all spoken at once, nor has reference to the same miracle, but all from verse 38 on has reference to the miracle in Matt. ix. But this division is arbitrary.

[2] It has been questioned whether the words (ix. 34): "But the Pharisees said, He casteth out devils through the prince of the devils," are not to be regarded as an interpolation. They are put by W. and H. in brackets, but are kept by Tisch., and in R. V. and generally. See Eders., i. 516.

That the healing of the dumb and blind possessed man took place at Capernaum, may be inferred from the mention of "the scribes which came down from Jerusalem" (Mark iii. 22), and who would naturally seek Him in the place of His residence. Their presence at this time may be ascribed to the powerful impression which the raising of the widow's son at Nain had made upon all who heard of it, and the consequent necessity on the part of His enemies of taking some steps to counteract it. The cure of the possessed, it is said, amazed the people, and led them to ask, "Is not this the Son of David?" So far as we know, this was the first time that this specially Messianic title had been given Him; nor does it clearly appear what there was in this miracle that should lead them thus to speak. It would, however, naturally arouse the jealousy of the Pharisees, and make them the more eager to oppose Him. As the fact of the healing was beyond dispute, they could only assert that it was done through the aid of the prince of the devils. This ascription of His miracles to Satanic agency marks a decided progress in Pharisaic hostility. Heretofore they had said of Him that He was a Sabbath breaker and a blasphemer; now they say that He is in league with evil spirits. And this charge reached much farther than to this particular miracle. It was virtually ascribing all that He said and did to a diabolical origin, and made the Spirit of God that rested upon Him to be the spirit of Beelzebub; and hence the severity of His language in reply (Matt. xii. 34). To understand this charge of the Pharisees, we must remember the common belief of the day, that miracles could be wrought by the help of evil spirits; and that therefore the possession of miraculous power did not prove that a man was sent from God. It was necessary for the Lord's enemies to explain His many mighty works; for if He did them by the help of God, there was no alternative but to receive Him and His teachings. The only way of escape was to ascribe His miracles to the powers of darkness. Aside from the folly of supposing that Satan would cast out Satan, there was the blasphemy against the Holy Ghost in ascribing works wrought by His help, and manifestly good, to the prince of the demons.[1]

---

[1] Those who wish to see how a modern Jew defends the action of the Pharisees and Scribes, will find a defense of them in Cohen, Les Déicides, 39 ff. The writer leaves

13

It appears from Mark (iii. 22), that those who made this charge were the scribes which came down from Jerusalem. Luke (xi. 15) uses the indefinite expression, "some of them said." Matthew (xii. 24) refers it to the Pharisees. (In Mark ii. 16 R. V. "The scribes of the Pharisees" are spoken of; in Luke v. 30, "The Pharisees and their scribes." While the scribes were generally of the Pharisaic party, there were some of the Sadducees. Schürer, ii. 1. 313.) These scribes were doubtless themselves Pharisees, possibly also priests or Levites. Alexander remarks: "It is a serious error to suppose that these descriptive titles are exclusive of each other, and denote so many independent classes, whereas they only denote different characters or relations, which might all meet in one and the same person, as being at the same time a priest and Levite by descent and sacred office, a scribe by profession, and a Pharisee in sentiment and party connection." But although originally the priests were scribes, as Ezra (Neh. viii. 9), yet at this period the scribes made a distinct class. It is not improbable that they came as a formal deputation to watch His proceedings, and to organize His enemies against Him throughout Galilee. Doubtless their calumny, that He was aided by Beelzebub, was caught up and reiterated by the Pharisees of Capernaum.

The visit of His mother and brethren is mentioned by all the Synoptists; and that it occurred during, or immediately after, the reply to the Pharisees, appears from Matt. xii. 46. Luke (viii. 19) has it in another connection, but without any note of time. We distinguish it from the visit of His friends (Mark iii. 21), which took place soon after the choice of Apostles, and of which we have already spoken. We cannot tell where His mother and brethren were at this time residing; some say at Cana, others at Nazareth, others at Capernaum. The Roman Catholic writers in general attempt to separate His mother from His brethren, as not acting with them. (See Maldonatus on Mark iii. 31.) It is evident that Mary and His brethren were presuming too much on their near relationship to Him; and that He wished to teach them that, when engaged in His Father's work, merely

it uncertain whether the Lord really wrought miracles, or only pretended so to do; nor does he mention the fact that the Jews believed them to be real, but attributed them to evil spirits. As to Jewish belief respecting miracles, see Eders., i. 574.

human bonds must give place to higher obligations. Mary here showed the same spirit that twice before He had gently rebuked (Luke ii. 49 ; John ii. 4).

AUTUMN, 781. A. D. 28.

The same day He leaves His house and sits by the sea-side, and as the multitudes gather to Him, He enters a ship, and teaches them in parables. At the close of the day, He gives commandment to depart to the other side. As they are preparing to go, He holds a conversation with a scribe, and with one of His disciples about following Him. He enters the ship with the disciples, and crosses the sea. Upon the way a violent tempest arises, Jesus rebukes the wind and waves, and there is a great calm.	MATT. xiii. 1–52. MARK iv. 1–34. LUKE viii. 4–18. MATT. viii. 18–27. LUKE ix. 57–60. MARK iv. 35–41. LUKE viii. 22–25.

There is no reason why the language of Matthew "in the same day " — ἐν τῇ ἡμέρᾳ ἐκείνῃ — should not here be taken strictly, although sometimes used indefinitely (Acts viii. 1). It was the same day as that on which His mother and brethren visited Him, and on which He healed the blind and dumb possessed. Mark (iv. 1) has the same order. Luke (viii. 4–19) narrates the teaching in parables before His mother's visit. Whether the narration of the two who would follow Him (Matt. viii. 19–22), is the same as that mentioned by Luke (ix. 57–60), who speaks of three ; and whether we are to follow the order of Matthew or Luke, will be considered when the Lord's last journey is examined.

It is a question whether all the parables given by Matthew (xiii.) were spoken at once, and if not, when and where ? Mark, although he gives only those of the sower and the mustard seed, implies that there were others (iv. 2): "And He taught them many things by parables," language almost the same as that of Matthew (xiii. 3): "And He spake many things unto them in parables." After He had spoken the parable of the sower, it is said (Matt. xiii. 10) that His disciples came to ask Him why He spake in parables. Mark (iv. 10) says: "When He was alone, they that were about Him with the Twelve asked of Him the parable." Whether He was yet in the ship, or had gone to the shore. does not appear. Greswell attempts to show that the disciples did not ask any explanation of the parable of the sower at this time, but only why He spake in parables at all. Afterward, when He had gone into the house (Matt. xiii. 36), they asked Him the meaning of this particular parable, and also of that of the tares. This involves more difficulties than it removes. Krafft makes the teaching in parables to have occupied at least two days. (See Luke viii. 22, who makes a distinction between the day of the visit of His mother and brethren, and that when He spake the parable of the sower.) In this case, Mark (iv. 35) refers not to the day when He went down to the seaside, but to the day following. Stier supposes the seven parables of Matthew to have been spoken on one day: the first four to the people on the shore, the last three to the disciples in the house. (So Keil.) Trench remarks: "The first four were spoken to the multitude while He taught them out of the ship; the three last on the same day in the narrow circle of His disciples at His own house." After several parables had been spoken, there was a pause (Mark iv. 10; Matt. xiii. 10), and then the questions following were asked.

It must remain doubtful whether this teaching in parables did not occupy more than one day. If, however, we limit it to one, we may give the following order of events as a probable one. After Jesus had spoken the parable of the sower, He paused for a while, perhaps to give His hearers time to reflect upon it. During this interval, the Twelve and other disciples asked Him, first, why He taught in parables; and second, what this parable was? Where these questions were asked, is uncertain. Two circumstances only define it: that "He was alone" (Mark iv. 10), or separated from the multitude; and that "the disciples came to Him" (Matt. xiii. 10). All this may have taken place while He was still in the boat, in which with Him were doubtless the Twelve, and others may have joined them. By withdrawing a little way from the shore, they would be strictly alone. Greswell (ii. 440) objects that the multitude could not be called "those that are without" (Mark iv. 11), unless Jesus and the disciples were somewhere within, that is, in a house; but the distinction is not one of locality, but of moral preparedness. After His explanations to the disciples, Jesus again teaches the people, and adds the parables of the tares and wheat, the mustard seed, and the leaven.   At this point, dismissing the multitude, He returns to His house, and His disciples coming to Him, He expounds to them the tares and wheat, and adds the parables of the hid treasure, the pearl, and the net.   Going again at even to the shore, and the multitudes gathering around Him, He gives order to pass to the other side.   The disciples, therefore, send away the people, and take Him as He is in the ship.[1]

This teaching in parables plainly marks an onward step in the Lord's ministry.   He had now testified of Himself both in word and deed, had manifested Himself as the Messiah ; and it was becoming apparent to Him that the great body of the people had no discernment of His divine character and mission, and would not receive Him, however they might for a time be personally attracted to Him, and marvel at His words and works. The Pharisees, the spiritual leaders, both at Jerusalem and in Galilee, had not only taken decided steps against Him, but had accused Him of being helped in His work by Beelzebub.   This utter spiritual incapacity to see the true nature of His teachings and acts, and the determined hostility which it manifested, showed Him that the time had come when He must change the form of His speech, and not expose the holy things of God to reproach.   Though with the common people His popularity seemed now at its height, He discerned that there was no root of faith, and that most followed Him through motives of wonder or idle curiosity.   He could, therefore, well speak of them (Matt. xiii. 13–15) as hearing His words, and yet not understanding them; as seeing His works, and not perceiving their significance.   To them He could not explain the mysteries of the kingdom.   He must use the form of the parable which, hiding its meaning from the careless and foolish, opened it to the diligent and wise seeker after truth.   As is well said by Thiersch (Parables): "These parables are of the nature of warnings to the disciples, and contain also great promises and mysteries of the kingdom of heaven.   The Lord declared these warnings and prophecies purposely in obscure language, in order to hide their meaning from blasphemers and skeptics, whose anger He was

---

[1] See Newcome, Har., 256.

unwilling to excite; and yet so as to confirm the faith of His disciples, to whom He explained all things." To the same effect Abp. Thomson styles a parable, "a mode for keeping the seed safe till the time should arrive for the quickening spirit to come down and give it growth."

The motive of the Lord in crossing the lake is not stated, but apparently it was to escape the crowds, never satisfied with hearing Him, and to find rest (Matt. viii. 18). His disciples 'took Him as He was in the ship," or without any preparation for the journey; which implies that it was not premeditated, but suddenly determined on (Mark iv. 36). It was "even," probably near sundown, when they left the shore, and wearied by the labors of the day the Lord soon fell asleep. While thus sleeping a fierce storm burst upon them. How exposed is the Sea of Galilee, from its peculiar position, to these storms, all travellers have remarked; but few have had any personal experience of their fury. Thomson (ii. 32), however, was for several days upon its shores during one of them, the character of which he thus describes : "To understand the causes of these sudden and violent tempests we must remember that the lake lies low, six hundred feet lower than the ocean ; that the vast and naked plateaus of the Jaulan rise to a great height, spreading backwards to the wilds of the Hauran, and upward to snowy Hermon; that the water courses have cut out profound ravines, and wild gorges converging to the head of the lake, and that these act like gigantic funnels to draw down the cold winds from the mountains. And, moreover, these winds are not only violent, but they come down suddenly, and often when the sky is perfectly clear. I once went in to swim near the hot baths, and before I was aware, a wind came rushing over the cliffs with such force that it was with great difficulty I could regain the shore." Of another storm, when on the eastern shore, he says: "The sun had scarcely set when the wind began to rush down toward the lake, and it continued all night long with constantly increasing violence, so that when we reached the shore next morning, the face of the lake was like a huge boiling caldron." "We had to double-pin all the tent ropes, and frequently were obliged to hang with our whole weight upon them to keep the quivering tabernacle from being carried off bodily into the **air."** (See Wilson, Bib. Ed., iii. 284.)

The attempts to determine at what season of **the year the** parables were spoken through the natural analogies **upon which** they are based, as Norton inferred that it was **seed-time, or** about November, because of the reference to the sowing **of** seed, lead to no substantial result. So also the storm **does not,** as said by him, define the time as winter; or as **an equinoctial** quarter of the year, as said by Greswell. That it **was during the** late autumn or early winter, is upon other grounds **probable.**

AUTUMN, 781. A. D. 28.

After the stilling of the tempest, He comes to the country of the Gergesenes. As He lands, He is met by two men possessed by demons, whose dwelling is in the tombs near by. Beholding Jesus, they run to meet Him, and He, casting out the demons, permits them to enter a herd of swine that is feeding near. The swine, so possessed, run down the hill-side into the sea and perish, and the inhabitants, coming to Him, desire Him to depart from their coasts. After directing the healed demoniacs to proclaim through Decapolis what had been done for them, He returns to Capernaum.

MATT. viii. 28–34.
MARK v. 1–18.
LUKE viii. 26–39.

MARK v. 19, 20.
MATT. ix. 1.

Several questions meet us here. First, as to the time when the Lord reached Gergesa. He left Capernaum, as we are told in Mark, "when the even was come "; that He reached the opposite shore while it was broad daylight, is shown by the fact that the demoniacs "saw Jesus afar off." Was this on the evening of the day, or the next morning? It is said by Edersheim (i. 606) that He landed on the east shore late in the evening: "All the circumstances lead us to regard the healing of the demonized at Gerasa as a night scene." If we take " the even," as it is sometimes to be taken. as the latter part of the afternoon, or from three to six o'clock, the Lord may have reached Gergesa. notwithstanding the storm, before sundown. But it may have been that the departure was later, during the second evening — six to nine — and that, delayed by the storm, the landing on the east shore was not till the next morning. This is the more general view, and seems to find confirmation in the fact that the Lord was asleep. Greswell (ii. 204), thinks that the Lord did not sail till after sunset; that He spent the night on the lake, and landed on the east side in the early morning. (See also ii. 338.)

Another question concerns the place where the Lord met the demoniacs. As this has been much discussed, a brief statement of the points in dispute must be made.

The first point is to determine the reading. Three places, or districts, are mentioned: the country — χώρα — of the Gadarenes, of the Gergesenes, and of the Gerasenes. In the *Textus receptus*, Matthew (viii. 28) has "of the Gergesenes;" but Tisch., W. and H., and R. V., "of the Gadarenes"; Mark (v. 1) has "of the Gadarenes"; but Tisch., W. and H., and R. V., "of the Gerasenes"; Luke (viii. 26) has "of the Gadarenes"; but W. and H. and R. V., "of the Gerasenes"; Tisch., Keil, and Riddle, "of the Gergesenes". We have thus three places before us: Gadara, Gerasa, and Gergesa, and we must ask what knowledge we have of their positions. Gadara is mentioned by Josephus (War, iv. 7. 3) as the capital of Peræa, and as destroyed by Vespasian; it is counted as one of the cities of the Decapolis (Casp., 97; Schürer, ii. 1. 100). It is generally admitted that it stood upon the site now known as Um Keis, lying some six or eight miles southeast of the sea of Galilee, and three south of the Yarmuk or ancient Hieromax (Thomson, ii. 35). It is plain that Gadara, if the city be meant, is too remote to answer to the conditions of the narrative, for this plainly implies that the place of meeting the demoniacs was upon or near the shore. Mark (v. 2) says: "And when He was come out of the ship, immediately there met Him out of the tombs," ff. This statement cannot well be understood, as observed by Alexander, otherwise than that He was met "as He landed, not merely after he had done so, which would admit of an indefinite interval; whereas the landing and the meeting were simultaneous, or immediately successive." The narrative, however, does not say that the event took place in the immediate vicinity of the city — πόλις — but implies the contrary (Matt. viii. 33).

Gerasa is mentioned by Josephus (War, iii. 3. 3; iv. 9. 1) as lying upon the eastern border of Peræa; and is now known as Jerash. It was one of the chief cities of the Decapolis, and its ruins are among the most beautiful and best preserved in all Palestine. (See Baedeker, 391, for full description and plans.) It is some twenty miles east of the Jordan, and far distant from the sea of Galilee, and cannot be meant as the place where the demoniacs were met.

"Gergesenes" is the rendering of the received text (Matthew viii.

28), but is now generally rejected on critical grounds as an emend-
ation of Origen, and "Gadarenes" preferred. That there was a
city called Gergesa is affirmed by Origen, but his testimony has been
generally rejected as unsupported (Godet on Luke viii. 26; see Re-

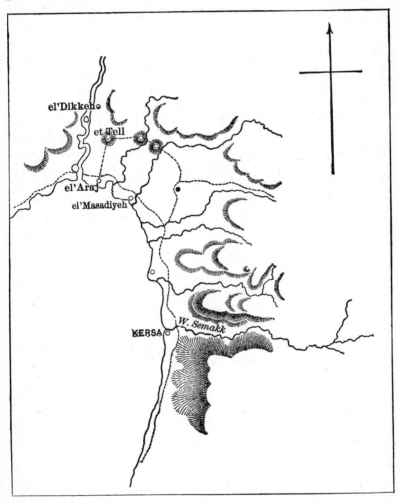

NORTHEASTERN PART OF THE SEA OF GALILEE SHOWING THE ENTRANCE OF
THE JORDAN, AND THE SITE OF KERSA OR GERGESA.

land, 806). He places it upon the Lake of Tiberias, and near the
shore; and adds that the precipice is still pointed out where the
swine rushed into the sea. Alford (on Matt. viii. 28) doubts the
existence of such a city; but still questions whether "Gergesenes"
could, as a mere conjecture of Origen's, have found its way into so

13*

many ancient versions, and adopts it as the true reading. (So Farrar, 254, note; McClellan, 650.) Bleek thinks that Origen's words
show that there was such a place in his day, the traditional site of
the miracle, and one answering to its conditions (see T. G. Lex., *sub
voce*). This seems to be a fair statement of the matter, and it is confirmed by Eusebius, who says that in his day a village was shown
upon the mountain near Lake Tiberias, where the swine ran down
(see also Jerome; McClellan, 649; Raumer, 218 note, and 331).
We may, then, accept as credible the statement of Origen, that there
was in his day a town by the name of Gergesa near the lake, which
tradition made the scene of the miracle; and the absence of all later
mention of it by name would show only that it had fallen into decay.
But, within a few years, its site has been re-discovered under the various names, Kersa, Chersa, or Gersa. Dr. Thomson, (Land and Book,
ii. 25), to whom this discovery is owing, found Gersa near the point
where Wady Semak enters the lake, nearly opposite the plain of
Gennesaret. "In this Gersa, we have a position which fulfills every
requirement of the narrative, and with a name so near that in Matthew,
as to be in itself a strong corroboration of the truth of this identification. It is within a few rods of the shore, and an immense mountain
rises directly above it, in which are ancient tombs, out of some of
which the two men possessed of the devils may have issued to meet
Jesus. The lake is so near the base of the mountain that the swine,
rushing madly down it could not stop, but would be hurried on into
the water and drowned. The place is one which our Lord would be
likely to visit, having Capernaum in full view to the north, and Galilee 'over against it,' as Luke says it was (viii. 26). The name, however, pronounced by Bedawin Arabs, is so similar to Gergesa, that, to
all my inquiries for this place, they invariably said it was at Chersa,
and they insisted that they were identical, and I agree with them in
this opinion." Here Dr. T. found some ruins. "It was a small
place, but the walls can be traced all around, and there seems to
have been considerable suburbs." Col. Wilson (Recovery of Jer.,
286) says: "On the left bank of Wady Semak, and at the point where
the hills end and the plain stretches out toward the lake, are the
ruins of Khersa — Gergesa. The site is enclosed by a wall three feet
thick. The remains are not of much importance. . . . On the
shore of the lake are a few ruined buildings, to which the same name
was given by the Bedawin. About a mile south of this, the hills,
which everywhere else on the eastern side are recessed from half to
three-quarters of a mile from the water's edge, approach within forty
feet of it; they do not terminate abruptly, but there is a steep even

slope, which we would identify with the 'steep place' down which
the herd of swine ran violently into the sea, and so were choked."
Schumacher (The Jaulan, Qt. St. 1888, 179) says: "The remains date
from two periods, a more ancient one, from which only scattered
building stones and foundations are still extant; and a more recent
one, probably Roman. . . . . The ruins are extended, and it is
thought that traces of aqueducts can be distinguished." Merrill
places Kersa six miles south from the entrance of the Jordan into the
lake.

Thus one chief condition of the miracle is fully satisfied. There
is a short strip of the coast, and only one on the east side, where the
mountain is so near the water, that the herd rushing down would
plunge into the lake. That there should be herds of swine in this
region is explained by the fact that the population was in great part
heathen and not Jewish. Schürer, speaking of Gadara, says: "There
is abundant evidence that it was already in pre-Christian times, a
flourishing Hellenistic town" (Joseph., Antiq., vii. 11. 4). The Jews,
living in such a community, might breed them for sale, if they
did not themselves eat them. It is said by Pressensé, that "they
carried on without scruple a forbidden traffic, keeping herds of
swine on their hills." And here good feeding ground was found.
Of the hill-sides at Gergesa, McGregor says: "A verdant sward is
here with many bulbous fruits, which swine might feed upon; and
here I saw a very large herd of oxen, horses, camels, sheep, asses,
and goats, all feeding together."

Other conditions are also met. There are natural cavities in the
rocks which might serve well for tombs. Schumacher (179) says:
"The lime rocks of the neighborhood have several large natural
cavities, especially on the lower ruin over the slope." Although Sir
C. Wilson did not see any rock-hewn tombs near Kersa, yet he thinks
that the demoniacs may have lived in the tombs built above ground,
such as are still seen at Tell Hum, and of which he saw some traces
not far from the shore. But Thomson says that "an immense
mountain lies directly above Kersa, in which are ancient tombs."

There is also the steep descent or slope, not a cliff or precipice,
which the word — κρημνός — does not mean. It is possible that
it may refer to the peculiar formation of the beach for half a
mile in length, which is thus described by McGregor (411): "It is
flat until close to the edge. There a hedge of oleanders fringes the
end of the plain, and immediately below these is a gravel beach, inclined so steep that, when my boat was at the shore, I could not see
over the top even by standing up; while the water along-side is so

deep that it covered my paddle (seven feet long) when dipped in
vertically a few feet from the shore."

Thus the miracle finds abundant confirmation in all its local
details.   Just at the point where all other conditions of the narrative
are met, we find the ruins of a town known to the Bedawin as Kersa,
and this is now generally accepted as the place of the miracle.   The
real difficulty, as long since said by Wieseler, is to reconcile the variations of the text.   But into this we are not called to enter.
Whether Kersa can be derived from Gergesa (*contra*, Riehm, i. 454)
or must represent Gerasa (Edersheim, i. 607), or whether the place was
anciently called Gergesa, and afterwards Gerasa (McClellan), we must
leave to the philologist.

We may picture the scene in Thomson's words: "Take your
stand a little south of this Chersa.   A great herd of swine, we will
suppose, is feeding on this mountain that towers above it.   They are
seized with a sudden panic, rush madly down the almost perpendicular
declivity, those behind tumbling over and thrusting forward those before, and, as there is neither time nor space to recover on the narrow
shelf between the base and the lake, they are crowded headlong into
the water, and perish.   All is perfectly natural just at this point,
and here, I suppose, it did actually occur."

This discovery of the site of Gergesa removes all topographical difficulties from the sacred narratives.   It is therefore unnecessary to mention in detail the other solutions that have been
proposed, as that of Ebrard (324), who, in answer to DeWette,
attempts to show that Gadara was but an hour distant from the
sea; and that of Stanley (372) who places the scene of these
events in Wady Feik, nearly opposite Tiberias.

We may then thus picture this incident to ourselves.   The
Lord, leaving Capernaum at even to avoid the ever-thronging
multitude, directs his course southeasterly toward Gergesa.
The storm bursting suddenly upon them during the evening,
He by His word calms the sea.   Very early in the morning He
lands upon the coast of Gergesa, a little way south from the city.
Here He is met, as He lands, by the demoniacs.   Upon the
steep slopes of the adjacent mountain the swine are feeding,
and to Him upon the shore come out the inhabitants of the city,
beseeching Him to depart from their coasts.

Matthew mentions two demoniacs; Mark and Luke but one.
How shall this discrepancy be explained ?   Lightfoot (on Mark

v. 1), who supposes that Gergesa was the name of a district embracing within it Gadara, which was a heathen city, makes one
of the two to have been a Gadarene, and the other a Gergesene.
Matthew, he says, mentions both, but Mark and Luke mention only
him from Gadara as a heathen demoniac, "that so they might make
the story more famous." Some, as Ebrard, make Matthew to have
blended this case with that of the possessed healed at Capernaum (Mark i. 23). Da Costa supposes that Matthew knew that
there was in fact but one, but that he might have seen a man
attacked by the demoniac, and so gives the impression upon his
mind as if there were two !

The common and most probable explanation is, that there
were indeed two, but that one was much more prominent than
the other, either as the fiercer of the two, or as of a higher rank
and better known, and therefore alone mentioned by Mark and
Luke.[1] That their silence respecting one of the demoniacs does
not exclude him, Robinson thus illustrates:[2] "In the year 1824
Lafayette visited the United States, and was everywhere welcomed with honors and pageants. Historians will describe these
as a noble incident in his life. Other writers will relate the
same visit as made, and the same honors as enjoyed, by two persons, viz., Lafayette and his son. Will there be any contradiction between these two classes of writers? Will not both record the truth?" Greswell (i. 210) thinks that one of those
thus healed became a disciple, and that the other did not. The
former being thus better known, and his case invested with a
personal interest, Mark and Luke speak of him only, and in
much detail; while Matthew, who desires only to illustrate the
power of Christ over evil spirits, mentions the healing of both,
but says nothing of their subsequent history. He prefers, however, the conjecture based on Luke viii. 27, that this one
demoniac was an inhabitant, and probably a native of Gergesa,
but not the other.

Meyer, on the other hand, rejects all attempts to explain
away the discrepancy; and Alford, who supposes that there was
but one demoniac, thinks that perhaps his words, " My name is

---

[1] So early, Augustine; and recently, Alexander, Krafft, Stier, Greswell, Ellicott
McClel., Godet.

[2] Har., 195.

Legion, for we are many " (Mark v. 9), may have given rise
to the report of two demoniacs in Matthew.

The request of the Gergesenes that Jesus would depart from
their coasts, shows how material interests ruled in their minds,
and how unprepared were they to understand the real significance of His work. The healing of the demoniacs, so mighty a
miracle, and their restoration to sound mind and to their
families and friends, were of less value than the loss of their
swine.

The direction to the healed to go to their homes (Mark v. 19)
and proclaim what the Lord had done for them, so contrary to His
general custom, shows that it was His desire to call attention to
Himself in this section of the land, and, by making this miracle
widely known, prepare the way for subsequent labors. Perhaps,
also, something in the moral condition of the healed made this
desirable for them.

AUTUMN, 781. A. D. 28.

Immediately upon His return to Capernaum He is | LUKE viii. 40–56.
surrounded by the multitude, which has been waiting for | MARK v. 21–43.
Him. Being invited by Matthew to a feast at his house, | MARK ii. 15–22.
He there holds conversation with some Pharisees, and | LUKE v. 29–39.
afterward with some of John's disciples. While yet | MATT. ix. 10–17.
speaking with them, comes Jairus, a ruler of the syna- | MATT. ix. 18–26.
gogue, praying for the healing of his daughter. As Jesus
is on His way to the house of Jairus, He heals a woman with an issue of blood. A messenger meeting Him
announces the death of the girl, but He proceeds, and,
entering the house, restores her to life.

We may put His arrival at Capernaum about midday. The
crowds that for several days had been following Him, were
awaiting eagerly His return, and now gladly received Him.
According to Matthew (ix. 2), after this return He healed the
paralytic, but according to Mark (ii. 3 ff.), this was earlier, and
after the Lord's return from His first circuit. We have followed
the order in Mark.[1] All the Synoptists mention the call of Levi as
immediately following the healing of the paralytic. The question

[1] So Rob., Alex., Licht., Ellicott, Fried., McClel., Stroud, Fuller; following Matthew, Bengel, Farrar, Keil.

that here meets us, and upon the answer to which the order of
subsequent events depends, is, Did the feast given by Levi
follow immediately upon his call, or was it after the Lord
returned from Gergesa? In the order we follow, the two are
separated. The question cannot be answered upon any ground of
intrinsic fitness. It is said by Plumptre (in Ellicott's Com.) that
this feast was a "farewell feast to his friends and neighbors before he entered upon his new calling." But such a feast would
not have been in harmony with his new calling. It is more
probable that he made it to give the Lord and the disciples an
opportunity to meet the guests in this social way, with reference
to a better knowledge of Him. But we may believe that this
"great feast," for which special preparation was needed, was
after some days or weeks, rather than that it was on the day of
the call.[1] That the feast was a few days later than the call
appears from the relations in which it is placed to the Lord's
words addressed to the Pharisees in regard to eating with publicans and sinners, and to those addressed to John's disciples in
regard to fasting. It seems from Matthew's words (ix. 10 ff.),
that this feast gave occasion to their questions and His replies,
for we are told that "many publicans and sinners came and sat
down with Him and His disciples." And from the offense
taken by John's disciples and the Pharisees in regard to fasting,
we may infer that the supper was upon a day in which they
fasted. (That this was a fasting day, one of the two — Monday
and Thursday — which were observed by the more scrupulous,
(Luke xviii. 12,) is probable, if we accept the rendering in Mark
ii. 18, R. V.: "And John's disciples and the Pharisees were
fasting, and they came.") We cannot well separate these replies
of the Lord from the feast of Levi, which would naturally give
occasion to the questions addressed to Him and to His disciples; and in this most are agreed. But we have still to ask how
these replies stand in order of time to the raising of the daughter of Jairus. Matthew alone of the Synoptists, brings the two
into immediate connection, verse 18: "While He spake these
things unto them" — to John's disciples — "behold there came

---

[1] Opinions are much divided; for uniting the two, Gardiner, Caspari, Friedlieb.
Ellicott, Stroud, Fuller; for separating them by some interval, Robinson, McClel., Far
rar, Riggenbach.

a certain ruler, . . . and Jesus arose and followed him."
Some say (so Meyer) that Jairus came to the house of Levi during the feast, and that the Lord arose from the table, and went
with him. It is said by McClellan: "He passed from Levi's
house of feasting to Jairus' house of mourning." But that the
Pharisees were any of them present at the feast, whether
as spectators or spies, as held by Alexander, cannot be
affirmed, though oriental freedom on such occasions would
have permitted it, and the words of Matthew point to it; on
the other hand, it is almost certain that their scruples in regard to ceremonial defilement would have prevented them.
Probably the same scruples would have made John's disciples to
stand aloof. But, if not present, the fact of the Lord's presence
at such a feast must very soon have become generally known.
It is said by Alford that "the remonstrance addressed to the
disciples, 'Why eateth your Master with publicans and sinners?'
cannot have taken place at the feast, but denotes an occasion
when the Lord and the disciples were present, and not intermixed with the great crowd of publicans."

There are some who separate the Lord's answer to the Pharisees from that to John's disciples, and put some interval
between them. But, they cannot well be separated, the
internal connection showing that both were spoken on the same
occasion. Gardiner, who follows Mark's order, supposes that
the discourse concerning fasting may have been repeated.
Greswell (ii. 398) thinks that as Matthew puts the feast just
after the return from Gergesa, and Mark and Luke put it
immediately after his call, we must accept two feasts, one
in Levi's own house, the other in the house of Simon and
Andrew, where the Lord had His abode. There seems little
ground for this. As it is clear from Mark (v. 22, 23) and Luke
(viii. 40, 41) that the raising of the daughter of Jairus was
after the return from Gergesa, we put the feast of Levi or
Matthew after this return. Still it is admitted that the coming of Jairus may have been some time subsequent to the feast,
for it is not certain that the reply to the Pharisees took place at
the feast; or, if it did so, that the reply to John's disciples was
at the same time; but the probabilities are, that all took place
on the same evening in which He went with Jairus.

As there is much difference of opinion among harmonists, where this feast is to be placed, we give some of the proposed arrangements, which connect as immediately successive the call of Levi and his feast.

1. Lichtenstein: The Lord teaches in parables; crosses the sea, and heals the demoniacs at Gergesa; returns to Capernaum; heals the paralytic ; calls Matthew ; attends Matthew's feast; raises up the daughter of Jairus; chooses Apostles; and delivers Sermon on the Mount. This is open to the insuperable objection that the teaching in parables precedes the choice of Apostles and the Sermon on the Mount.

2. Stier: The Lord chooses Apostles; teaches in parables; crosses the sea, and heals the demoniacs; returns to Capernaum; heals the paralytic; calls Matthew; attends his feast; raises up the daughter of Jairus. It is a sufficient objection to this order, that the choice of Matthew as an Apostle precedes his call.

3. Ebrard: The Lord teaches in parables ; crosses the sea, and heals the demoniacs ; returns to Capernaum ; answers the questions of John's disciples respecting fasting; raises the daughter of Jairus; heals the blind, and the dumb possessed, and the paralytic; calls Levi, and attends his feast; chooses the Apostles; and delivers the Sermon on the Mount. This arrangement is open to the same objection as the first, that it puts the teaching in parables before the choice of the Apostles and the Sermon on the Mount.

In the above arrangements, the call of Levi and the feast are both put after the teaching in parables and the healing of the Gergasene demoniacs, but others put them much earlier. Thus, Friedlieb and Fuller put them before the unnamed feast (John v. 1); and so generally those who suppose the Lord to have begun His Galilæan ministry in the summer or autumn of the first year of His public work. But if this ministry began after this unnamed feast, and the call of Levi was before the choice of Apostles, we must bring the narratives into accord by separating the call from the feast.

The mention of John's disciples at Capernaum is to be noted as showing that there were some there who did not follow Jesus, and their affinity with the Pharisees in ceremonial observances.

(Luke v. 30, does not mention these disciples, but the Pharisees only.)

The selection of Peter, James, and John, to go with Him to the house of Jairus, is the first instance recorded of special preference of these three above the other nine Apostles. It is hardly to be questioned that this selection was determined by the personal peculiarities of these three, which made them more ready than the others to understand the real meaning of Christ's words and works, and to sympathize with Him in His trials and griefs. But why they should have been selected to be present at this particular miracle, is not apparent. It was not, according to the order which we follow, the first case of raising the dead; and therefore they were not present, as Trench supposes, on this ground. But, unlike the raising of the widow's son at Nain, which was in public before all the funeral procession, the Lord will here have no witnesses but His three Apostles and the father and mother of the maiden. Nor will He allow the wonderful work to be proclaimed abroad: "He charged them strictly that no man should know it." The grounds of these differences in the Lord's actings are probably beyond our knowledge, and cannot be explained. That He now enjoined silence because He had ceased to work publicly in Capernaum, is disproved by His later miracles. The healing of the woman with an issue of blood presents nothing for our notice here.

AUTUMN, 781.   A. D. 28.

Returning homeward from the house of Jairus, He is followed by two blind men, saying, "Son of David, have mercy on us." They enter His house and are healed, and He charges them not to speak of what He had done; but they, going forth, everywhere proclaim it. As they depart, a dumb possessed is brought to Him, whom He heals, to the astonishment of the multitude. This gives the Pharisees new occasion to say that He casts out devils through Satan.   MATT. ix. 27-31.

MATT. ix. 32-34.

These cases of healing are mentioned only by Matthew, and by him in immediate connection with the raising to life of the daughter of Jairus. We assume that he here narrates in chron-

ological order.[1] Some[2] identify Matt. ix. 32–34 with Luke xi.
14, 15; and as the healing of the possessed was immediately
after that of the blind, place all these miracles at a much later
period, and after the sending of the Seventy.

By these blind men was Jesus for the first time addressed as
"the Son of David." This shows that His descent from that
royal house was known and recognized. Already the people
had asked of Him (Matt. xii. 23), "Is not this the Son of
David?" (The American Committee read: "Can this be the Son
of David?") and the use of the title by the blind men shows
their disposition to honor Him whose help they sought.[3]

The impression which the miracle of healing the dumb possessed made upon the multitude, was very great, and explains
why the Pharisees should repeat the charge that He cast out
devils through the prince of devils.

WINTER, 781–782. A.D. 29.

Leaving Capernaum, Jesus goes, accompanied by His disciples, into lower Galilee, and again visits Nazareth. Rejected here the second time, He goes about through the cities and villages in that region. During this circuit He commissions and sends out the Twelve. In their absence He continues His work. About this time John is beheaded in prison, and the news of his death is brought to Jesus by some of John's disciples. Herod now hears of Christ, and expresses a desire to see Him. Jesus returns to Capernaum, and the Twelve gather to Him there.	MATT. xiii. 53–58 MARK vi. 1–6. MATT. ix. 35–38. MARK vi. 7–13. MATT. x. 1–42. LUKE ix. 1–9. MATT. xiv. 1–12. MARK vi. 14–30.

In the order of events we follow Mark : " And He went out
from thence, and came into His own country; and His disciples
follow Him." The place of departure was the house of Jairus
(Meyer, Keil), or Capernaum and its neighborhood (Alexander).

---

1 Robinson, Greswell, Lichtenstein, Lange, Ebrard, Gardiner. Alford, however,
observes that παράγοντι ἐκεῖθεν is too vague to be taken as a fixed note of sequence;
for ἐκεῖθεν, 'thence,' may mean the house of Jairus, or the town itself, or even that part
of the country, as verse 26 has generalized the locality, and implied some pause of time."
Edersheim puts them at or near Capernaum on His return from Nain, and the healing of
the blind and dumb possessed (Matt. xii. 22), at a later period. The point has already
been considered.

2 Krafft, Tischendorf.

3 Compare (Matt. xx. 30) the healing of the two blind men at Jericho, when the
same title was used; as also by the woman of Canaan (xv. 22).

Matthew (xiii. 53–58) narrates this visit to Nazareth immediately
after his account of the teaching in parables: "And it came to
pass when Jesus had finished these parables He departed thence.
And when He was come into His own country," etc.   Here it is
not said that this coming to Nazareth was immediately subsequent to the departure after the parables were spoken.   That
departure was not to Nazareth, but across the sea to Gergesa
(Mark iv. 35).   We must then place between verses 53 and 54
the healing of the demoniacs, of Jairus's daughter, of the woman with issue of blood, of the two blind men, and of the dumb
possessed.   All these may have taken place on the day of the
return from Gergesa; and thus, between the teaching in parables
and the departure to Nazareth, only an interval of two days
may have elapsed; but in all probability the period was much
longer.

The grounds upon which this visit at Nazareth is to be distinguished from the earlier one mentioned by Luke (iv. 16),
have been already stated.   The circumstances under which He
now returns to His early home are very unlike those of that former visit.   Then, He had but newly begun His public labors,
and was comparatively little known ; and great surprise was felt
that one, who only a few months before had been an undistin-
guished resident among them, should make so high pretensions.
How could He, whom they had known from childhood up, be a
prophet, and possess such powers?   Now, His fame was spread
throughout the whole land, and His character as a prophet was
established.   Crowds followed Him from all parts of the land.
His miracles were familiar to all.   He had, in the immediate
neighborhood of Nazareth, raised a dead man to life.   But His
now enlarged and confirmed reputation did not weaken the feeling
of surprise.   All His life was familiar to them, and they could not
believe that He was in aught greater than themselves.   Jesus,
therefore, could now well, and even with greater emphasis, repeat the proverb, "A prophet is not without honor but in his
own country"; adding, with reference to the continued unbelief
of His brethren, "and among his own kin, and in his own
house."   (See John vii. 5.)   The Nazarenes did not now take any
violent measures against Him, though "offended at Him "; and

after teaching in the synagogue and healing a few sick folk, He
made a circuit through the adjacent villages (Mark vi. 6).   It is
probable that Matthew (ix. 35–38) has reference to this circuit.

That the sending of the Twelve upon their mission was during this journey, appears from the order in which it stands in
all the Synoptists.   Matthew (ix. 35, ff.) connects it with the
journey following the healing of the blind men and the dumb
possessed; and Mark (vi. 7), with that following the departure
from Nazareth.   Luke does not mention this visit at Nazareth,
but narrates the sending of the Twelve (ix. 1–6) directly after
the healing of Jairus's daughter.   How long the circuit continued, or at what point in it the Twelve were sent out, we have
no data to determine.   That it was extensive and occupied a
considerable period may be fairly inferred from Matthew's language (ix. 35), that "He went about *all* the cities and villages."
Nor can we tell from what place they were sent.   Greswell (ii.
342) supposes it to have been Capernaum, and that therefore
the sending was just at the close of the circuit.   "It is certain
that after their mission they rejoined our Lord at Capernaum;
and it is not probable that they would be sent from one quarter
and be expected to rejoin Him at another."   On the other hand,
Alford observes that no fixed locality can be assigned to their
commission.   "It was not delivered at Capernaum, but on a
journey."   The view of Krafft (99), that they were sent from
Jerusalem when Jesus was at the feast of Tabernacles (John v.
1), is in every point of view unsatisfactory, and is refuted by the
fact that the theatre of His activity was now Galilee, and not
Judæa.

Where did the Twelve labor?   Luke (ix. 6) says, "they departed and went through the towns."   It has been supposed
that this expression "towns," κώμας, may be used here in opposition to cities, implying that the Twelve visited only the
smaller places.   But the same expression is used of the Lord
Himself (Mark vi. 6).   Probably their labors were confined to
Galilee.   They were forbidden to enter Samaria; and it is not
likely that they would enter Judæa from which the Lord was
excluded.   As they journeyed two by two, this would enable
them to visit many towns in a few days.   How long they were

2 days
1 day
2 weeks

absent upon their mission does not appear. Wieseler. followed by Tischendorf, would limit it to a single day; Ellicott, to two days; Edersheim, to two weeks; Krafft extends it to several months; Greswell makes them to have been sent upon their ministry in February, and to have returned in March, an interval of near two months. That they were engaged in their labors several weeks at least, is plainly implied in the terms of their commission; and is confirmed by the brief statements of their actual labors. It is said in Luke ix. 6: "They went throughout the villages." (See Godet, *in loco:* "They went through the country in general, staying in every little town.") Their mission must have been of some considerable duration.

The same question meets us in regard to the commission given to the Twelve as recorded by Matthew, that meet us in his record of the Sermon on the Mount. Is it a summary of all the instructions the Lord gave them respecting their work, instructions given on different occasions? (So Ellicott, 194.) Or since we find some parts of it in Mark and Luke in different relations, did He repeat them as He judged fitting? Perhaps both may be true. It is wholly credible, that, in preparing them for their future work, He should often have spoken of the way in which it should be conducted, and of the opposition and perils which they would meet. But it is apparent upon its face that their commission had a far larger scope than of their first temporary work under it.[1] It had prospective reference to their larger work after the Lord's ascension, and also in some measure to all the missionary work of the Church till His return. Some directions in it are plainly temporary, as those not to visit the heathen or Samaritans, and to make no provision of money or clothing. The prediction of persecutions and scourgings, on the other hand, had at this time no fulfillment. It is on this ground that some make a division of its contents, applying verses 5 to 15 to this first mission (compare Mark vi. 8–12, Luke ix. 1–6), and the remainder to their future labors. It is said by Alexander, that "the charge relating to the first mission ends with verse 15, and with verse 16 begins a more general and prospective charge relating to their subsequent Apostolic labors."

---

[1] So Jones, Notes on Scripture, 100; Stier, ii. 2; Eders., i. 640.

With the correctness of this or other divisions we are not here concerned; what is of importance to us is the light which this commission casts upon the relations of the people to the Lord. If it was all spoken at this time, it was a plain declaration to the Twelve that they, going out in His name, would meet not merely a temporary outburst of hostility, but the persistent and bitter enmity of those to whom they should go : " Ye shall be hated of all men for my name's sake." Yet they would find some who would receive them, some " sons of peace." That they did not understand the large significance of the Lord's words is clear, for their conception of the future was very confused, and the thought of a permanent separation from Him had not yet entered their minds. His declarations respecting their persecutions must have been in striking contrast to the opinions the Apostles were yet cherishing respecting the reign of the Messiah, and His general reception by the people. By speaking of their sufferings and persecutions, He announced, by implication, His own sufferings and rejection.

There are two aspects in which this mission of the Twelve may be regarded: First, as that of heralds proclaiming wherever they went that the Kingdom of God is at hand. It has been questioned whether the Lord's purpose in sending them was to draw attention to Himself, proclaiming by them that the Messiah had come and was among them, or to announce the approach of the Messianic kingdom, to call to repentance, and to confirm their message by their miracles. But we can scarce doubt that their commission was rather that of heralds than of preachers. They could not themselves at this time have understood sufficiently the nature of the kingdom they proclaimed to be able to teach others. Plumptre *in loco*, holds that they were to go as heralds: " The two envoys of the kingdom were to enter into a town or village, and there standing in the gate, to announce that the kingdom had come near, and when this had drawn crowds to listen, to call men to repentance, without which they could not enter it." But, as said by Pressensé, it is most probable that their mission did not " go beyond a general announcement that the Messiah had appeared." It was not that they should be teachers of the people, but that they should bring them to their Lord that He might teach them.

Secondly, as that of men endowed with miraculous powers, whose works were not less important than their message (Matt. x. 7, 8). Their endowment with such powers was a thing unknown in Jewish history, and this in two respects — (a) that no limitation was put on their exercise, (b) that they were conferred by a Man upon them that, as one body, they might bear witness to Him. As in the case of the Lord, the healings wrought by the Twelve were not of certain individuals alone who had faith, but were general. As it is said of Him, that He went "round about the villages teaching," "entering into all the synagogues, and healing every sickness and every disease among the people," so their commission was "to cast out unclean spirits, and to heal all manner of sickness, and all manner of disease." The end of both was the same — to show that the kingdom of God is present in the person of the King. It was bringing that kingdom through these works of deliverance into sharpest contrast with the bondage of soul and body under the rule of evil spirits. Thus their works, even more impressively than their words, testified that the day of redemption and the Redeemer were at hand.

The fact that they possessed such powers as the heralds of Jesus must have led many to ask, Is not He who sent them forth, and who not only Himself heals all, but is able to give like power to others, the Messiah? No prophet in the past had ever been able to do this, not even Moses. Is not He who does this a King, and even more than a King?

These miraculous endowments were doubtless confined to this mission. Up to this time there is no mention that the Twelve had wrought any miracles, nor is it recorded that they did so after they rejoined the Lord. (See however Matt. xxi. 19, 20, as showing that the power to work miracles was not absolutely withdrawn, but was dependent on their faith.)

That Jesus continued His own personal labors during the absence of the Twelve, appears from Matthew (xi. 1), that "when He had made an end of commanding His Twelve disciples, He departed thence to teach and preach in their cities." In these journeyings He was probably accompanied by other disciples, doubtless by some of those who were afterward chosen among the seventy (Luke x. 1), and perhaps also by the women who had before been with Him.   If, as is probable, He had given direction to the Twelve to rejoin Him at Capernaum at some fixed time, He would now so direct His own course as to meet them there.

It was during the mission of the Twelve that the death of John the Baptist occurred.   The news of it seems to have been communicated to Jesus by John's disciples (Matt. xiv. 12), but this must have been some days at least after the event.   The date of his death has been already discussed (Chronological Essay, 46 ff.), and the conclusion reached that it was in the latter part of March or the beginning of April, 782.

From Mark vi. 13, 14, and Luke ix. 6, 7, it appears that it was not till after the death of John that Herod heard of Jesus. But how could he have been so long active in one of Herod's provinces, followed by great multitudes, performing daily the most wonderful works, and His residence only a very few miles from Sepphoris, where the king kept his court, and yet His fame never reach the royal ears?   Tiberias was built about 779, but whether Herod's palace was completed and he resided there at this time, we do not know.   The most ready explanation would be, that during His ministry Herod had been absent from Galilee on a visit at Rome, whither he went about this time; or had been engaged in hostilities with Aretas, and thus remained in good measure ignorant of what was taking place.[1]   There is much probability in this supposition of Herod's absence, but decisive proof is wanting.   If, however, he was in Galilee during this period, his ignorance of Jesus finds a sufficient explanation in his own personal character.   We know from Josephus that he was a lover of ease and pleasure, and a man who occupied himself more in erecting fine buildings than in public affairs. Like all the Herodian family, he treated the Jewish religion with respect as a matter of policy, but did not interfere with ecclesiastical matters, except he saw movements dangerous to the public peace.   The disputes of contending sects, or the theological discussions of the Rabbins, had no attractions for him ; and, provided the Jews were orderly and peaceful, he cared not to

---

[1] Greswell, iii. 428; Edersheim, i. 654, says that he was during the Galilæan ministry in his dominions east of the Jordan, at Julias or Machaerus

14

interfere in their religious quarrels. John's ministry continued a considerable period without any interruption on his part; and when he at last imprisoned him, it was on personal, not on political or religious, grounds. Hence, we can understand how Jesus might prosecute His work in Galilee in the vicinity of Herod, without the latter learning anything definite respecting it, or having his attention specially directed to His character or designs. As a new religious teacher, the founder of a new sect, an opponent of the Pharisees and scribes, the matter was unimportant, and beneath the royal notice. Unless the public tranquility was actually disturbed or seriously threatened, Herod, like Gallio, cared for none of these things.

During the imprisonment of the Baptist, Herod seems to have had several interviews with him, and learned to appreciate his bold and fearless honesty (Mark vi. 20). He did many things that John recommended, and heard him gladly. Hence, when, in his drunken revelry, he had given up the Baptist to the malice of Herodias, he was troubled in conscience; and his ears were open to any tidings that had connection with the departed prophet. It was a short time before this that Jesus had sent out the Twelve, a step which would naturally turn public attention to Him, and which might easily be misinterpreted. It would arouse His watchful enemies to action, for it apparently indicated a purpose to disseminate His doctrine more widely, and to make disciples in larger numbers. It might thus easily, through them, reach the ears of Herod, who would be led to inquire more particularly into the character and works of the new Rabbi. But his informants gave him different answers (Mark vi. 14, 15; Luke ix. 7, 8). Some said that He was Elias; others, that He was a prophet, or as one of the prophets; and others still, ignorant of His earlier work, said that He was John the Baptist risen from the dead. This last account, to the uneasy and superstitious mind of Herod, was most credible, and explained how He wrought such mighty works as were ascribed to Him. Returned to life, he could do what could be done by no one in mortal flesh (Matt. xiv. 2; Mark vi. 14). All this awakened in Herod a lively desire to see Jesus, but no intimation is given us that he designed to arrest Him or to hinder Him in His work.

Thus far the Messianic claims of the Lord had been so presented, that there was nothing in His teachings or actions to awaken Herod's jealousy of Him as a claimant of the throne. At no period does the king seem to have looked upon Him with any dislike or fear as a political leader. The threatenings of the Pharisees at a later period, that Herod would kill Him (Luke xiii. 31), seem to have been a device of their own to frighten Him from His labors.

According to Josephus,[1] John was put to death at Machaerus, a fortress at the southern extremity of Peræa on the borders of Arabia.[2] It has been questioned whether Herod would have made a birthday feast at the southern extremity of his dominions, where it would be difficult for the courtiers and noblemen of his court to attend. Still, if we remember that the Jews generally were in the habit of going up from the most remote parts of the land to Jerusalem once or more every year to the feasts, the journey of a few courtiers to Machaerus will not seem strange. Besides, if Herod was detained there through a war, or other cause, the feast must follow his pleasure; and if Machaerus was not convenient to his guests from Galilee, it was more convenient to those from Peræa.

Some, however, have supposed that the feast did not take place at Machaerus, although John was beheaded there, but at Tiberias, or at Julias. (For Machaerus: Meyer, Lewin, Gams, Alford, and most; for Tiberias: Grotius, Lightfoot; for Livias or Julias: Wieseler, Lange.) But although it is possible that the head of the Baptist should have been taken from Machaerus to Tiberias before the feast ended, yet the obvious interpretation of the narrative is, that he was beheaded the same night in which the daughter of Herodias danced before the king, or at least, that no long interval elapsed. If the feast was not at Machaerus, where most place it, it was most probably at Julias,[3] which was at no great distance, and where Herod had a summer palace.

---

[1] Antiq., xviii. 5. 2.

[2] The question respecting the possession of this fortress at this time, whether it was held by Herod or by Aretas, was considered in the inquiry as to the time of the Baptist's imprisonment. That he was beheaded there is generally accepted.

[3] The modern Beit-Haran. See Tristram, B. P., 348.

PART V.

FROM THE DEATH OF THE BAPTIST TO THE FINAL DEPARTURE FROM GALILEE, OR FROM APRIL TO NOVEMBER, 782. A. D. 29.

The Lord's Ministry in Galilee from the Death of the Baptist till its Close.

The connection between the imprisonment of the Baptist and the commencement of the Lord's ministry in Galilee has been already considered. The same moral causes that determined this connection, make the death of the Baptist important in its influence upon the subsequent character of that ministry. It appears from the notices of the Evangelists that when this event occurred, the popularity of Jesus, if we may use this word, was at its height in Galilee. Great multitudes followed Him wherever He went, and so thronged Him that He had no leisure even to eat. From every part of the land they came to listen to His teachings and to be healed. Nor may we ascribe this concourse merely to curiosity and selfishness. These doubtless ruled in many; but that there was also at this period a large measure of faith in Him as one sent from God, appears from the fact that " whithersoever He entered, into villages, or cities, or country, they laid the sick in the streets, and besought Him that they might touch if it were but the border of His garment; and as many as touched it were made whole." As His healing power seems now to have been manifested in its greatest activity, so now He performed one of the most stupendous of His miracles, the feeding of the five thousand. At no period of His ministry did He stand in such high reputation with the people at large as a Teacher and Prophet; and to the human eye, His labors seemed about to be crowned with great results.

It was at this stage of His ministry that He heard of the Baptist's death. To His clear-seeing eye the fate of His forerunner was prophetic of His own. As the Jews " had done unto the Baptist whatsoever they listed, as it was written of Him," so He knew that He also "must suffer many things and be set at naught" (Mark ix. 12, 13). However well disposed toward Him individuals among the people might be, there was no longer hope that the nation, as such, would receive Him. The more clearly He revealed His Messianic character in its higher features, the more all the worldly minded, the unspiritual, turned away from Him. His popularity rested upon no solid or permanent basis, as there was no recognition of His true mission, and He was deemed merely the equal of John or Elijah. He was in a position in which He must either fulfill their Messianic expectations, and begin the struggle for political freedom, or meet the reaction which His refusal would inevitably bring. From this time, therefore, He begins to act as in view of His approaching death. More and more He withdraws Himself from the crowds that follow Him, and devotes Himself to the instruction of His disciples. It is not now so much His purpose to gather new adherents, as to teach those already believing on Him the great mysteries of His Person and work. As yet the knowledge even of the Twelve was very imperfect; and He could not be personally separated from them till He had taught them of His divine origin; and as subsequent to this, of His death, resurrection, ascension, and of His coming again in glory.

As the Lord seemed thus to shun public observation, it was natural that the popular favor which had followed Him should suffer at least a temporary diminution; and that this should have been the signal for increased activity on the part of His enemies. As He made no distinct assertion of His Messianic claims before the people at large, and so far from assuming royal dignity, seemed rather to take the position of a mere Rabbi, the fickle multitude was the more easily affected by the accusations and invectives of His foes. His teachings also seem to have gradually assumed a more mysterious and even repellent character. He speaks of Himself as "the bread of life"; of the necessity of "eating His flesh and drinking His blood"; language so incomprehensible and so offensive, that many, even of His disciples, forsook Him. To the Scribes and Pharisees He addresses reproaches of unwonted severity. Up to this time He had been engaged in gathering disciples, and for their sake He would not willingly array against Himself those whom all the people had been taught to honor as their ecclesiastical rulers and teachers. Such open hostility on their part, and a corresponding severity of rebuke on His, would have been a stumbling-block to the tender conscience and half-enlightened mind. But the time is come that the line of separation must be clearly drawn, and the truth respecting Himself and His enemies be openly spoken; and His disciples learn that to follow Him involves the fierce and persistent enmity of their spiritual rulers and guides — an enmity which should follow them even after His own death.

That which specially characterizes the second part of the Lord's ministry in Galilee, or that from the death of the Baptist onward, we thus find to be a gradual withdrawal of Himself from the multitude and from public labors, and the devotion of Himself to the instruction of His disciples. When by these instructions He has prepared them to understand His Divine Sonship, and what should befall Him at Jerusalem, His Galilæan ministry comes to its end.

Outline of the second part of the Galilæan ministry :

Fifth Sojourn in Capernaum.

Hearing of the death of the Baptist, the Lord returns to Capernaum. No event is narrated as having occurred during this sojourn. Probably it was very brief — a mere passage through the city.

FIFTH CIRCUIT.

He crosses the sea with the Twelve to seek retirement, but the multitude immediately follow Him. He feeds the 5,000, and sending away the apostles by ship He rejoins them the next morning, walking on the sea. Landing on the plain of Gennesaret, He heals the sick, and they return to Capernaum.

Sixth Sojourn in Capernaum.

He discourses in the synagogue on the bread of life. His discourse causes many of His disciples to forsake Him. He addresses the Pharisees, and heals the sick.

SIXTH CIRCUIT.

He goes to the coasts of Tyre and Sidon to find retirement. Here He heals the daughter of the Syro-Phœnician woman. Crossing the northern part of the Jordan, He goes to Decapolis He heals a deaf man, and feeds the 4,000, and returns by Dalmanutha to Capernaum.

Seventh Sojourn in Capernaum.

He is tempted by the Pharisees, who seek a sign.

SEVENTH CIRCUIT.

He goes to Bethsaida, and there heals a blind man. He returns to Capernaum, and there meets His brethren, who wish Him to go up to the Feast of Tabernacles, and show Himself openly at Jerusalem.

Eighth Sojourn at Capernaum.

He remains at Capernaum till the feast had begun, and then goes up privately to Jerusalem, and teaches. A woman taken in adultery is then brought before Him; He heals a blind man; and after a time returns to Capernaum.

EIGHTH CIRCUIT.

He leaves Capernaum and goes to Cæsarea Philippi. The confession of Peter, and the Transfiguration. He heals the lunatic child, and returns to Capernaum.

Ninth Sojourn at Capernaum.

He pays the tribute money.

Final Departure from Capernaum and Galilee.

APRIL, 782. A. D. 29.

After the return of the Twelve to Him at Capernaum, Jesus prepares to go with them across the sea to find seclusion and rest. They desire to go privately, but the multitudes seeing them departing by ship, follow them on foot along the shore, and come to the place where He had gone. He heals their sick, and the same evening feeds 5,000 men, beside women and children. Immediately

MARK vi. 31-44.
LUKE ix. 10-17.
JOHN vi. 1-4.
MATT. xiv. 13-14.

MATT. xiv. 15-21.

after, He compels the disciples to return in the ship to   JOHN vi. 5–14.
Capernaum, and remains to dismiss the people. He spends   MARK vi. 45–53.
the night alone, and early in the morning walks upon the   JOHN vi. 15–21.
sea to rejoin the disciples who have been driven from their
course by the wind, and are unable to make the land.
Having rescued Peter, who attempts to walk upon the   MATT. xiv. 22–34.
water to meet Him, they both enter the boat, and immediately come to the shore in the land of Gennesaret.

It is not said where Jesus was when the disciples of John
came to Him to announce their master's death (Matt. xiv. 12),
but it was natural that they should seek Him at Capernaum.
About the same time the Twelve, who had been absent on their
mission, rejoined Him. Perhaps their return at this juncture
may have been determined by the tidings of the death of the
Baptist, which must very soon have become widely and generally known. As usual whenever Jesus after one of His circuits
returned to Capernaum, the people of the surrounding cities and
villages flocked to see Him, bringing with them their sick.
"Many were coming and going, and they had no leisure so
much as to eat " (Mark vi. 31). Jesus therefore determined to
cross the sea, and find repose in the uninhabited hills upon the
eastern shore. Some attribute this departure to fear of Herod's
hostility, and this has some countenance in the language of
Matt. xiv. 13. Caspari says: "The Lord, to avoid the tyrant,
repaired to the eastern part of the lake." But a more careful
examination shows us that this could not have been His motive. Luke (ix. 9) mentions that Herod "desired to see Him,"
but this seems to have been rather from curiosity than from any
purpose to arrest Him. Mark gives the Lord's own words to
the Apostles, "Come ye yourselves apart into a desert place, and
rest awhile "; adding the explanatory remark that "they had no
leisure so much as to eat." He desired to separate the Apostles
from the multitude; and to give them after their labors a little
period of repose, such as was not possible for them to obtain at
Capernaum. Perhaps, also, He Himself desired a few hours for
solitary communion with God for the refreshment of His own
spirit, agitated by the death of John, whom He mourned as a
faithful friend; and in whose untimely and violent end He saw
the sign and foreshadowing of His own approaching death.

That the departure across the sea was not through fear of
14*

personal violence of Herod, appears also from the fact that Jesus
the next day returned, landing publicly upon the shore of
Gennesaret; and thence attended by crowds went to Capernaum, where He taught openly in the synagogue (Mark vi. 53–
55; John vi. 22–59). And after this, as before, He continued
to make Capernaum His abode, and was not molested by Herod.
Norton suggests that the death of John had produced a sudden
excitement among the people; and that public attention began
to be turned to Jesus as one who might avenge his murder, and
become Himself their king; and that it was to escape the people
rather than Herod, that He crossed the sea. But the desire to
make Him king (John vi. 15), seems to have been rather the
effect of the miracle He wrought than of any popular indignation because of John's death.

The place to which the Lord directed His course across the sea,
was "a desert place belonging to the city called Bethsaida" (Luke
ix. 10). The position of this city has been already discussed.
According to the conclusion then reached, it was situated just at the
entrance of the Jordan into the sea, and upon both banks of the
stream. Upon the east side lies the rich level plain of Butaiha
(Batihah), a plain a little larger than Gennesaret, forming a triangle,
of which the eastern mountains make one side, and the river bank
and the lake shore the two other. This plain, with its bordering hills,
probably belonged to Bethsaida. It was at the southeastern angle
of this plain, where the hills come down close to the shore, that
Thomson (ii. 29) places the site of the feeding of the five thousand.

"From the four narratives of this stupendous miracle, we gather, 1st,
that the place belonged to Bethsaida; 2d, that it was a desert place;
3d, that it was near the shore of the lake, for they came to it by
boats; 4th, that there was a mountain close at hand; 5th, that it was
a smooth, grassy spot, capable of seating many thousand people.
Now all these requisites are found in this exact locality, and nowhere
else, so far as I can discover. This Butaiha belonged to Bethsaida.
At this extreme southeast corner of it, the mountain shuts down
upon the lake, bleak and barren. It was, doubtless, desert then as
now, for it is not capable of cultivation. In this little cove the ships
(boats) were anchored. On this beautiful sward, at the base of the
rocky hill, the people were seated."

We see no reason to doubt that Thomson has rightly fixed upon
the site of the miracle. A generally received tradition placed it

upon the west side of the lake, and near to Tiberias; but there was no agreement as to the exact spot. The earliest tradition, going back to the fourth century, placed it, according to Robinson (ii. 372), "on the broad ridge about an hour southeast of the Mount of the Beatitudes," where are four or five blocks of black stone called by the Arabs "stones of the Christians," and by the Latins, *mensa Christi,* "table of Christ." A later tradition — not older, according to Robinson, than the twelfth century — put it on the mountain where the Lord's Sermon was delivered. As early as 700 A. D. Arculf was shown here "a grassy and level plain which had never been ploughed since that event." Col. Wilson (Bib. Ed., iii. 186) thinks it may have been near Ain Baridah, which is between Tiberias and Magdala.[1]

There is some question as to the right reading. In the A. V., Luke ix. 10, it reads: "And He took them, and went aside privately into a desert place belonging to the city called Bethsaida;" in R. V., "And He took them, and withdrew apart to a city called Bethsaida." (So Tisch., W. and H., Meyer; others, as Godet: "into a desert place called Bethsaida"; others, accepting the Sinaitic reading: "into a desert place." Matthew says (xiv. 13, R. V.), "He withdrew in a boat to a desert place apart." Luke does not mention any crossing of the lake, probably because the mention of Bethsaida sufficiently indicated that it was upon the east side. In John (vi. 23) there has been found an intimation that the place of this miracle was near Tiberias: "Howbeit there came other boats from Tiberias nigh unto the place where they did eat bread " — (Vul., *a Tiberiade juxta locum ubi manducaverant panem.*) This has been understood as meaning that Tiberias was nigh unto the place. It is said by a Lapide: *Hinc patet locum. . . . fuisse juxta Tiberiadem.* In his note on Matt. xiv. 13, he repeats this, and puts the place between Tiberias and Bethsaida, and of course, on the west side.

It is to be kept in mind that the Lord sought "a desert " or " un-inhabited " place, and this place stood in some local relation to the city Bethsaida, probably as a part of its territory, or at least under its jurisdiction. Now, if we put the place of the feeding on the western side of the lake, somewhere between Tiberias and Tell Hum, we must put Bethsaida not far from it; but if, as the narratives show, the feeding of the people was on the east side, we must put it in the territory of Bethsaida Julias. The statement of John (vi. 23) is to the effect that boats from Tiberias on the west side came to some point on the east side near the place of the miracle.

---

[1] That it was on the west side is defended by Thrupp, Journal of Class. and Sac. Philology, ii. 290. So DeSaulcy.

There is a slight seeming discrepancy in the statements of Matthew and Mark respecting the meeting of Jesus with the multitude that followed Him. Matthew relates that "Jesus went forth and saw a great multitude, and was moved with compassion," etc., implying that He had already reached the place He sought ere the crowds came. Mark relates that the crowds "outwent them, and came together unto Him. And Jesus, when He came out," i. e., from the ship, "saw much people, and was moved with compassion toward them," etc. Whether any discrepancy exists depends upon the meaning of "went forth," ἐξελθών, in Matthew. Meyer refers it to His coming forth from His place of retirement.[1] In his note on Mark (vi. 34), Alford remarks: "There is nothing in Matthew to imply that He had reached His place of solitude before the multitudes came up." There seems to be no good reason why the "went forth" in Matthew, should be differently understood from the "came out" of Mark; the word in both cases being the same, and in both may refer to His coming out of the ship. Lichtenstein reconciles the discrepancy by supposing that a few came before Jesus reached the shore, but unwilling to intrude upon Him waited till the others came, so that He had a little interval of retirement ere He went forth to heal the sick and teach.

Some have supposed that John (vi. 4) mentions the fact that "the Passover was nigh," to explain why so great a company should have gathered to Him of men, women, and children. They were composed, at least in part, of those that were journeying toward Jerusalem to keep the feast.[2] Alexander, on the other hand, objects that, from the fact that they had nothing to eat, they could scarcely be a caravan of pilgrims, but were probably just come from their own homes. This is confirmed by the statement in verse second, giving the reason why they followed Him, because of the healing of the sick. It would seem that the people were mostly from Capernaum, Bethsaida, and the towns adjacent. (See Mark vi. 33.)

It was, as has already been shown, the Lord's desire to go privately with the Apostles across the sea, and thus escape the

---

[1] So Norton, Bengel, Trench.
[2] So Trench, Mir., 214; Bengel, Meyer, Edersheim, Westcott. Alford doubts.

multitudes; but as His preparations to depart were necessarily made in public, and the departure itself was in sight of all, He could not prevent them from following Him. It strikingly marks the strong hold He now had upon the people at large, that so great a number should follow Him so far. That they should be able to keep pace with those in the boat, will not appear strange if we remember the relative positions of Caper-naum and Bethsaida, as already defined. From the former city, which we identify with Tell Hum, to the entrance of the Jordan, where we place Bethsaida, according to Robinson, is one hour and five minutes, or about two and a half geographical miles. The distance from the entrance of the Jordan along the eastern shore to the point where the mountains approach the lake, is also about an hour. The whole distance, then, which the people from Capernaum had to travel, was not more than six or eight miles; and from the conformation of the coast, could be almost as rapidly passed by those on the shore as by those in the boat. If the place where they were fed was two or three miles up the river on the east bank, the distance would be a little less. Edersheim puts it some three or four miles; Tris-tram, some two miles. In this case, it was a considerable distance from the lake shore. Greswell,[1] who puts this Bethsaida at the southeastern angle of the lake, supposes that Jesus set out from Capernaum in the evening, and landed at Bethsaida in the morning; and that the people, who ran before on foot, travelled all night, a distance of about sixteen Roman miles. This needs no refutation.

The presence of this multitude that had followed Him so far, awakened the Lord's compassion ; and receiving them, He "spake unto them of the kingdom of God, and healed them that had need of healing" (Luke ix. 11). From John's lan-guage (vi. 5), it would seem that the Lord first addressed Philip with the inquiry, "Whence shall we buy bread that these may eat ?" According to the Synoptists, it was the disciples who proposed to Him that He should send them away that they might buy themselves victuals. But none of the Evangelists narrate all the conversation that passed between Jesus and the

---

[1] ii. 344, note.

disciples. Probably the disciples first proposed to send the people away to get food, and He replies, "Give ye them to eat" (Mark vi. 35–37). This leads to a general conversation in which He specially addresses Philip, and asks where bread could be bought. He then directs them to make inquiry how many loaves they had. After making inquiry, Andrew reports that there were five barley loaves and two small fishes, and hereupon He proceeds to feed the multitude. As residents of Bethsaida, Philip and Andrew would naturally know better than the other Apostles how food could be procured in that region.

The effect of this miracle upon the minds of those present was very great. So mighty and wonderful an exhibition of power, reminding them, perhaps, of the feeding of their fathers in the wilderness by Moses, led them to say, "This is of a truth that prophet that should come into the world." We can scarce doubt from the context that they meant the Messiah, for so great was their enthusiasm that they proposed among themselves to take Him by force and make Him king (John vi. 14, 15). It is said by Pressensé: "The multitudes are ravished, enthusiastic; now, indeed, they believe that they have found the Messiah after their own heart." Thus, the effect of the miracle was to confirm them in their false Messianic hopes, for they interpreted it as a sign and pledge of the highest temporal prosperity under His rule, who could not only heal the sick of all their diseases, but feed five thousand men with five loaves of barley bread. Hence, He must immediately dismiss them. It appears from Matthew and Mark that He sent away the disciples first, perhaps that the excitement of the multitude might not seize upon them. That they were unwilling to leave Him, and that He was obliged to "constrain" them to depart, is not strange, if we remember that they knew no way by which He could rejoin them but by a long walk along the shore; and this in the solitude and darkness of the night, for it was evening when they left the place. (Compare Matt. xiv. 15, 23, where both evenings, the early and late, are distinguished.) Aside from their reluctance to leave Him alone at such an hour, there may also have been fear upon their own part of crossing the lake in the night, remembering their great peril from which He had a little while before delivered them (Matt. viii. 24) and perhaps also, seeing signs of an approaching storm.

After His disciples had departed, the Lord proceeded to dismiss the multitude, perhaps now more willing to leave Him that they saw His special attendants had gone. So soon as all had left Him, He went up into the mountain alone to pray — the *Note* second instance mentioned of a night so spent; the first being the night prior to the choice of Apostles (Luke vi. 12, 13), and both marking important points in His life.

The details of the voyage of the disciples in their topographical bearings, have been already considered (p. 233), and need not be re-stated here.   We assume that the place where the people were fed was the southern angle of the plain of Butaiha, where the mountains meet the lake.   From this point the Apostles, to reach Capernaum, would pass near Bethsaida at the mouth of the Jordan; and as Jesus proceeding along the shore must necessarily pass through it, we find no difficulty in supposing that they directed their course toward it with the design of stopping there, and taking Him with them into the boat when He should arrive.   This is plainly intimated by Mark vi. 45,[1] and is wholly consistent with John vi. 17.   This latter passage is thus translated by Alford: "They were making for the other side of the sea in the direction of Capernaum."   He adds: "It would appear as if the disciples were lingering along shore, with the expectation of taking in Jesus; but night had fallen and He had not yet come to them, and the sea began to be stormy."   "The great wind that blew" and the tossing waves made all their efforts to reach Bethsaida useless.   Nor could they even make Capernaum.   In spite of all their endeavors, they were driven out into the middle of the lake and southerly, down opposite the plain of Gennesaret.

Thomson (ii. 32), referring to this night voyage of the disciples, says: "My experience in this region enables me to sympathize with the disciples in their long night's contest with the

---

[1] See Wieseler, 274, note 1; Newcome, 263. "They were to make Bethsaida in their passage, at which place it was understood that Jesus was to meet them by land, there to embark with them." So Eders., i. 690; Rob., iii. 358: "The apparent discrepancy between Mark and John disappears at once, if Bethsaida lay near to Capernaum, and if the disciples intended first to touch at the former place before landing at the latter."

wind. I spent a night in that Wady Shukaiyif, some three miles up it, to the left of us. The sun had scarcely set, when the wind began to rush down toward the lake, and it continued all night long with constantly increasing violence, so that when we reached the shore next morning, the face of the lake was like a huge boiling caldron. The wind howled down every wady, from the northeast and east, with such fury that no efforts of rowers could have brought a boat to shore at any point along that coast. In a wind like that, the disciples must have been driven quite across to Gennesaret, as we know they were. We subsequently pitched our tents at the shore, and remained for three days and nights exposed to this tremendous wind. No wonder the disciples toiled and rowed hard all that night, and how natural their amazement and terror at the sight of Jesus walking on the waves. The whole lake, as we had it, was lashed into fury; the waves repeatedly rolled up to our tent door, tumbling on the ropes with such violence as to carry away the tent pins." The width of the sea opposite the plain of Gennesaret is about six miles, and the disciples, who "had rowed about five and twenty or thirty furlongs" when Jesus met them, were thus something more than half the way over. As this was "about the fourth watch of the night" (Mark vi. 48), or from 3–6 A. M., the disciples must have been struggling against the wind and waves some eight or ten hours.

The incident respecting Peter's attempt to walk on the water to meet Jesus is mentioned only by Matthew. That after he had been rescued they entered the ship, is expressly said: "And when they were come into the ship, the wind ceased" (Matt. xiv. 32). In like manner Mark (vi. 51): "And He went up unto them into the ship; and the wind ceased." But with this John's narrative has been thought by some to be in contradiction (vi. 21): "Then they willingly received Him into the ship, ἤθελον οὖν λαβεῖν αὐτὸν εἰς τὸ πλοῖον; and immediately the ship was at the land whither they went" (R. V., "They were willing therefore to receive Him into the boat"). It is said that the disciples willed or desired to take Him into the ship with them, but did not, because the ship immediately came to the shore.[1]

---

[1] So Meyer, *in loco*; Bleek, Beiträge, 28.

Tholuck, however, defends the translation of Beza, "they received Him with willingness," which is the same as our English version.[1] "John mentions the will only, assuming that every reader would understand that the will was carried into effect" (M. and M).   Some deny that the ship came to the shore by miracle, but suppose that it came rapidly in comparison with the earlier part of the voyage, the wind having subsided and the sea become smooth.[2] On the other hand, Luthardt and most rightly regard it as supernatural.

APRIL, 782.   A. D.   29.

The people of Gennesaret, so soon as they know that Jesus has landed upon their coasts, bring unto Him their sick, who are healed by only touching the hem of His garment.   Those whom He had fed, and who had spent the night upon the eastern shore, now returning seek Him at Capernaum, whither He goes.   In answer to their question how He came over the sea, He discourses to them concerning the bread of life.   His words are so offensive to many of His disciples that they henceforth forsake Him.   The Twelve continue with Him, but He declares that one of them is a devil.

MATT. xiv. 34-36.

MARK vi. 53-56.
JOHN vi. 22-59.

JOHN vi. 60-66.
JOHN vi. 67-71.

The language of Matthew and of Mark is so express in connecting these miracles of healing with the return after the feeding of the five thousand, that there is no room for doubt that they then took place.   It is not, however, necessary to regard their statements as descriptive of an activity confined to that one day, but rather as embracing the whole period after His return till He again departed.   All the accounts of this period indicate that He had now come to the culminating point of His labors. Never was His popularity so great, and never His mighty power so marvellously displayed.   He could go nowhere, into country, or village, or city, that they did not bring the sick into the streets, that they might at least touch the hem of His garment; "and as many as touched were made perfectly whole." The fact that the men of Gennesaret "sent out into all that country round about and brought unto Him all that were diseased" (Matt. xiv. 35), indicates their great confidence in His

---

[1] Alford; see Winer, Gram., 363; Trench, Mir., 228, note; Eders., i. 692; Godet, *in loco*.   [2] Alford, Tholuck.

ability and willingness to heal all that should be brought to
Him; and perhaps also their expectation that, according to His
custom, He would soon depart to other fields of labor.

Of those who had been present among the five thousand,
some, and probably many, remained in the villages and towns
on the eastern and northern shores during the night.   The
statement of John (vi. 22–25), though not without grammatical
difficulties, is clear as to its general meaning. The multitude
saw that the disciples had gone in the boat in which they came,
and that the Lord was not with them, and naturally inferred
that He was still somewhere in the neighborhood, and that the
disciples would return the next morning to rejoin Him; but
when in the morning they saw boats come over from Tiberias,
and that the disciples were not in them, and that Jesus was not
to be found, they took the same boats, and went to Capernaum
to find Him.   These boats may have been sent over by the
boatmen from Tiberias for passengers, the gathering of the
crowd on the eastern shore being now known.   As He had
landed very early upon the plain of Gennesaret, for it was about
the fourth watch when He met the disciples, He had probably,
ere their arrival, reached the city. The discourse concerning
the bread of life was spoken in the synagogue at Capernaum
(John vi. 59), and most probably upon the Sabbath.   Still, no
certain inference can be drawn from this mention of the
synagogue, as it was used for teaching upon other days than the
Sabbath.[1]   According to Lightfoot, it may have been on a
Monday or Thursday. Edersheim (ii. 4), assuming that this
was a Sabbath and reckoning backward, gives the following
order of events: Jesus left Capernaum to go across the lake on
a Thursday, and on that evening was the feeding of the five
thousand, and other events; on Friday those remaining on the
east side returned; and on Saturday He met them in the synagogue, where He made a discourse.   Wieseler (Syn., 276) makes
the feeding of the five thousand to have been on the 14th Nisan
or 16th April, at the same time when the paschal lamb was
eaten at Jerusalem; and this day, therefore, was the 15th of
Nisan, or the first feast Sabbath.[2]   But this is inconsistent with

---

[1] Winer, ii. 549.   [2] So Tischendorf.

the notice of John (vi. 4), that the Passover was nigh, which implies that an interval of a day at least, if not of days, intervened.

It is in question whether this discourse was spoken all at once on this day and in the synagogue, or on successive days. Some think that all from verses 26 to 41 was spoken to the multitudes, and before the Passover; and all from verses 41 to 58 was spoken later, and after the Passover. The data are not sufficient to warrant this inference. (As to the divisions of the discourse, see Eders., ii. 26; Westcott, and Luthardt, *in loco*.)

It has been often said that the Lord went up to Jerusalem to this Passover. (So Lightfoot.) Luthardt thinks that the people here gathered went up also with Him. But for this there is no good ground, and, when viewed in the light of their desire to make Him king, it is most improbable. The suggestion of Godet that the Lord regarded this feeding of the multitude as His passover, and in contrast with the paschal feast in Jerusalem, is fanciful; nor is there any reason to attach a sacramental character to it, as many have done.

This discourse of the Lord so offended many of His disciples that from this time they walked no more with Him. Up to this time His works of healing had been so many and marvellous, that notwithstanding the open hostility of the scribes and Pharisees, the people continued to gather to Him in crowds. And the last miracle, the feeding of the five thousand, was such an exhibition of power that it affected the popular imagination far more than many cases of individual healing, or even than the two instances of the raising of the dead. The time had now come when the true believers among the miscellaneous multitude must be separated. The Lord would find those who had ears to hear the higher truths respecting His Person and the purpose of the Father in Him, which He wished them to know before He was taken from them. This separation could be effected in no external way; but according to the measure of spiritual discernment. He would find those who would follow Him because of the truth of His words, not as dazzled by the splendor of His works. His teaching respecting Himself as the Bread of

Life which came down out of heaven, was a crucial test. It was doubtless "a hard saying" even to the most discerning of the Apostles; and to many of the disciples, perhaps to a majority, they were so repellent that they now turned away from Him. The answer of Peter to the question addressed to the Twelve, " Will ye also go away?" marks a crisis in their relations to Him. Now, for the first time, so far as we know, there was a defection among His disciples. His teachings were too high for them, even when confirmed by such great miracles. But it was His words, not His works, that held the Twelve faithful. "Thou hast the words of eternal life," said Peter. The right reading of the confession of Peter immediately following this is, according to Tischendorf : [1] "And we believe and are sure that thou art the Holy One of God ; " (R. V.: " And we have believed and know that thou art the Holy One of God.") This confession is to be distinguished from that made later (see Matt. xvi. 16), which displays a higher knowledge of the mystery of the Lord's Person.

SUMMER, 782. A. D. 29.

While still at Capernaum, some of the scribes and Pharisees who have come from Jerusalem, see His disciples eating with unwashed hands, and find fault. This leads to a discussion of Pharisaic traditions and sharp reproofs of their hypocrisy. Leaving Capernaum, He goes with the Twelve into the coasts of Tyre and Sidon, avoiding all publicity. But He can not be hid, and a woman of that region coming to Him with urgent request, He heals her daughter. From thence He departs to the egion of Decapolis, where He heals many, and one with an impediment in his speech, and afterward feeds a multitude of 4,000 persons. Recrossing the sea He returns to Capernaum.

MATT. xv. 1–20.
MARK vii. 1–23.

MATT. xv. 21–28.
MARK vii. 24–30.

MATT. xv. 29–39.
MARK vii. 31–37.
MARK viii. 1–10.

How long after the feeding of the five thousand the Lord continued at Capernaum, we cannot tell ; but it is plain that He was found there by the Pharisees and scribes which came down from Jerusalem. Edersheim (ii. 7) puts the eating with unwashed hands on the day of the Lord's return from Bethsaida, and on the way to Capernaum, and before the discourse in the synagogue there ; McClellan, some two months after the dis-

---

[1] So W. and H., Meyer; Ellicott, undecided.

course; out most follow the order of Matthew. That this was as Wieseler maintains,[1] upon the 15th Nisan, the day when he supposes the discourse in the synagogue to have been delivered, is highly improbable. It is not likely that His enemies would leave Jerusalem till the Passover was fully over.[2] Much earlier in the Lord's ministry, as we have seen, a deputation of scribes had been sent from Jerusalem to watch and oppose Him. The presence of this new deputation may be ascribed to the reports that had been borne to that city by the pilgrims going to the feast, of the feeding of the five thousand, and of the wish of the people to make Him king. So great a miracle, and its effect on the popular mind, could not be overlooked, and they hastened to counteract, if possible, His growing influence. Arriving at Capernaum, and watchful to seize every possible ground of accusation against Him, they noticed that some of His disciples did not wash their hands in the prescribed manner before eating; a sign that they were already in some degree becoming indifferent to Pharisaic traditions.[3] The words of the Lord in reply to the Pharisees are full of severity, and show that He knew that they were, and would continue to be, His enemies. Now for the first time He addresses them openly as hypocrites, and reproaches them, that they set aside by their traditions the commandments of God. He proceeds to address the people upon the distinction between internal and external defilement; and afterward, when He was alone with the disciples, He explains to them more clearly what He had said. Afterward He goes with the Twelve into the region of Tyre and Sidon.

Many ascribe the departure of the Lord into Phœnician territory to the fear of Herod. (So Keim.) But there is no evidence of this. If Herod had really wished to arrest Him, it would have been easy for him to do so when the Lord returned, as He did later, to Capernaum. And when the Lord was in Peræa after He had left Galilee, He was still within Herod's jurisdiction, and yet was unmolested. (The message of the Pharisees, Luke xiii. 31, will be later examined.) If the king had felt any apprehension of political disturbance from His Messianic claims, he must have known that, aside from the oppo-

---

[1] Syn., 311, note 1.

[2] Tischendorf, Greswell.

[3] As to these traditions, see Lightfoot, Har., *in loco ;* Edersheim, ii. 8, who suggests that the real offense was, that the five thousand ate with unwashed hands.

sition to Him of the Pharisees, His position was so much an enigma
to the people that they were falling away from Him. (So Weiss,
iii. 42.) Others make Him to have left Galilee through fear of the
Pharisees. (So Greswell, ii. 354, who thinks His object was concealment.) But these had no power to arrest Him, or to interfere with
His labors, except by seeking to entrap Him upon points of the law,
and otherwise to annoy Him, and to turn away the people from Him
by threats of excommunication. The obvious ground of His retirement was not to escape personal danger but for the instruction of His
disciples.

It has been questioned whether the Lord went merely to the
borders of Tyre and Sidon, or actually crossed them (Matt. xv.
21; Mark vii. 24).[1] Some light may be cast on this point if we
consider His motive in the journey. That it was not to teach
publicly seems plain from Mark's words (vii. 24), "He would
have no man know it." He desired that His arrival should be
kept secret. As He had directed the Twelve when upon their
mission, not to "go into the way of the Gentiles" to preach, it
is not probable that He would now do so. Nor is there any
mention of teaching and healing, except in the case of the woman and her daughter. His motive in this journey obviously
was to find the seclusion and rest which He had sought but in
vain, to find on the east side of the lake, and could not find in
Capernaum. He hoped on the remote frontiers of Galilee to
escape for a time popular attention, and to be hid from the
crowds that followed Him. It was for the Twelve that He
sought a temporary retirement, and to them did He address
His teachings.

It would not then be inconsistent with His purpose that He
should enter the heathen provinces of Tyre and Sidon. Some
have objected that He would not have entered heathen territory,
since He would thus become ceremonially defiled. But the fear
of this could scarcely have affected His action. In this
region He may obtain a little interval of repose. But He cannot
be hid, and after healing the daughter of the Syrophœnican woman in answer to her importunity, He is compelled to leave

---

[1] In favor of the latter, Alford, Alexander, Bleek, DeWette, Greswell; of the former, Stier and Meyer, who refer to Matt. xv. 22, as showing that the Syrophœnician
woman came out of the coasts of Tyre and Sidon to meet Jesus, so that He was not within
them. Keil thinks it cannot be decided.

that region.   The route He followed is uncertain.   It is said by
Mark (vii. 31): "And again departing from the coasts of Tyre
and Sidon, He came unto the Sea of Galilee through the midst of
the coasts of Decapolis."   (R. V., "He went out from the borders
of Tyre, and came through Sidon unto the Sea of Galilee").
"As most of the cities of the Decapolis were situated southeast
of the Sea of Tiberias, it is not improbable that our Lord, having gone to the east of Phœnicia through Upper Galilee, returned
thence, by way of Lower Galilee through the plain of Esdraelon,
to Bethshean (Scythopolis), the only city of Decapolis which is
to the west of Jordan.   Here He would cross the river, perhaps
at the bridge now called Jisr Majumah, then possibly make a
circuit about the district of Pella and Philadelphia to the south,
about Gerasa to the east, and Gadara, Dios, and Hippo to the
north.   Thus He would 'come unto the Sea of Galilee through the
midst of the coasts of Decapolis.'"[1]   But according to the reading
of Tischendorf:[2] "Departing from the coasts of Tyre He came
through Sidon— διὰ Σιδῶνος — to the Sea of Galilee."   He went
therefore northward from Tyre, and passing through Sidon, not
the city but the territory (*contra*, Keil), probably proceeded along
the Phœnician border line to the Jordan, near Dan[3] (Laish), and
journeying along its eastern bank came to the Decapolis.   He may
thus have visited the province of Herod Philip and Cæsarea
Philippi, although no special mention is made of it.   "He went
first northward (perhaps for the same reason of privacy as before) through Sidon, then crossed the Jordan, and so approached
the lake on its east side."[4]   How long the Lord continued in
Gentile territory we do not know.   Weiss says several months;
there is no ground for this.   It may have been as many weeks.

What part of the Decapolis the Lord visited is not mentioned
by any of the Evangelists.   Under this title were included ten
cities, eight or nine of which were on the east side of the Jordan, and east or southeast of the Sea of Galilee.   It is spoken of
by Josephus as a well-known territorial designation, embracing
towns and villages.   After Syria had been conquered by the

---

[1] G. Williams, in "The Messiah," 268, note.
[2] So W. and H., Meyer, and Alford.
[3] Josephus, War, iii. 3. 1.
[4] Alford; see Lichtenstein, 284; Lindsay, *in loco*; Weiss, iii. 41.

Romans, ten cities seem, on some grounds not well known, to have been placed under certain peculiar municipal arrangements, and brought directly under Roman rule. It is probable that their population was chiefly heathen. The names of the ten cities are differently given. To the original ten cities others were probably added, though at no time do they seem to have constituted a distinct province.[1]

It is impossible to tell where the healing of the deaf man with an impediment in his speech took place (Mark vii. 32). It may have been one of the cures mentioned by Matthew (xv. 29–31), and it was near the sea, and in the region of the Decapolis; but why Jesus enjoined silence upon the deaf man and his friends, when He directed the demoniacs at Gergesa to make their healing known, we cannot tell. The injunction of silence was not heeded: "The more He charged them, so much the more a great deal they published it." The effect of this was, as related by Matthew, a great gathering to Him of "the lame, blind, dumb, maimed, and many others," whom He healed. Both Matthew and Mark speak of the wonder and astonishment of the multitude as they saw these healings. It is to be remembered that Jesus had not visited this region at all, except for the few hours when He healed the demoniacs of Gergesa, and afterward when He fed the five thousand; and the great body of the people now saw Him for the first time. The expression (Matt. xv. 31), "they glorified the God of Israel," may indicate that part of the multitude were heathen, and now glorified Jehovah in contrast with their own deities; or it may have reference to the Jews as dwelling among the heathen, who saw in these miracles new proofs of the power of their God, before whom all others were but idols.

Three days this great concourse of people to the number of four thousand, continued with the Lord, beholding His works, and listening to His words; and at their close He fed them with the seven loaves and a few fishes. The place where they were assembled was, beyond question, on the east side of the lake, and some suppose at the same place where He had fed the five thousand.[2] Matthew (xv. 29) relates that "He came nigh unto

---

[1] See Winer, i. 263; Smith's Dict. of Bible, i. 419; Schürer, ii. 118.
[2] So Trench, Mir., 285; Greswell, ii. 357.

the Sea of Galilee, and went up into a mountain and sat down there." The use of the article, τὸ ὄρος, "the mountain," does not determine the spot, as it may be used to denote the high land in distinction from the lake shore. It seems, however, more probable that it was at some point near the south end of the lake, as several cities of the Decapolis were in that vicinity. Caspari thinks it was south of the place of the feeding of the five thousand; Edersheim, in the Decapolis near the eastern shore. Ellicott [1] suggests that its site may have been "the high ground" in the neighborhood of the ravine nearly opposite to Magdala, which is now called "Wady Semak." While there are several points of resemblance between this miracle and that of the feeding of the five thousand, there are many of difference: as to the number of persons fed, the quantity of food, the quantity of fragments gathered up, the time the multitude had been with Jesus, and the events both preceding and following the miracle. (See Mark viii. 19 ff., where the Lord distinguishes the two.) It is probable that many of the four thousand were heathen, or those who had come from the east side of the sea; while most of the five thousand seem to have followed Him from the western shore. [2]

After sending away the multitudes, He took ship, perhaps the ship kept specially for His use, and crossed the sea. He came, according to Matthew (xv. 39), "into the coasts of Magdala" (R. V. "into the borders of Magadan"); according to Mark (viii. 10), "into the parts of Dalmanutha." Magdala — the Greek form of Migdol — watch-tower — is generally identified with El Mejdel, a miserable village on the south side of the plain of Gennesaret, near the lake. [3] It is only a collection of filthy hovels with ruins of an old watch-tower, but was formerly a place of some importance. It is about three miles north of Tiberias, and probably at one time the two places may have been closely connected, as the remains of buildings are found all along the way between them.

But it is not certain that this Magdala — el Mejdel — was the place to which the Lord went after the feeding of the four thousand (Matthew xv. 39). The reading Magadan is adopted

---

[1] 221, note 1.   [2] Trench, Mir., 286.

[3] Rob., ii. 397; Porter, ii. 431; See, *contra*, Norton, notes, 153.

by Tisch., W. and H., and Alford.   Are Magdala and Magadan
variations of the one name, or were there two distinct towns bearing these names ?   (In favor of the former, Gratz, Riehm, Herzog;
of the latter, Robinson, Caspari, Edersheim.)   If we accept Magadan as the right reading, and a place distinct from Magdala,
where was it ?   Caspari says: "The region of Magadan is the
western domain of Scythopolis, or the region of the Ten Cities
on this side Jordan."   Edersheim (ii. 67) would put Magadan
south of the lake, and near the border of Galilee, but within
the Decapolis; he does not, however, assign it any definite position.   Ewald would identify it with Megiddo near Mt. Carmel.

For the Magadan of Matthew, Mark (viii. 10) has Dalmanutha.   Are we to identify Magadan and Dalmanutha?   This is
said by Edersheim (ii. 67): "The borders of Magadan must
evidently refer to the same district as the parts of Dalmanutha."   If not different names for the same place, we may infer
that they were so near each other that the adjacent territory
might be called from either.   It is said by Lightfoot (Choro.
Decad., 225) that Dalmanutha is the name of a town or village
not far from Magadan, or lying within its territories; and
both are put in his map south of the lake and east of the Jordan.
Some later writers are inclined to put Dalmanutha on the
south or southeast of the lake.   Edersheim (ii. 67), on etymological grounds, thinks it may have been Tarichæa at the exit of
the Jordan.   Thomson (Cen. Pal., 335) speaks of the ruins of a
considerable town on the east bank of the Jordan five miles south
of the lake, called Dalhuminyeh.   (In Fischer & Guthe's Map,
Ed-Delhemije.)   This is apparently the same place meant by
Caspari (106), and accepted by him as Dalmanutha.

But most, identifying Magadan and Magdala, put Dalmanutha near it on the west shore.   Porter and Tristram find it at
Ain el Barideh, lying a little south of Magdala.   Keim (ii. 528)
thinks Gadara is meant.   The matter is unimportant, except as to
its bearing on the place of the feeding of the four thousand.
Did the Lord after this event return to the west shore, or did
He keep within the limits of the Decapolitan territory to avoid
the Pharisees?   The latter view is not in itself improbable; it
may be that He did not return to Capernaum at this time, but

being disturbed by the Pharisees who sought Him at Dalmanutha, He crossed the lake to escape them (Mark viii. 13).   Yet,
upon grounds to be mentioned, it seems more probable that
Dalmanutha was near Magdala, and that He returned to Capernaum after feeding the four thousand.   (See Weiss, iii. 12.)

SUMMER, 782.   A. D. 29.

So soon as Jesus returns to Capernaum, the Pharisees and Sadducees begin to tempt Him by asking a sign from Heaven. He reproves their hypocrisy, and declares that no sign shall be given them but the sign of the prophet Jonas.	MATT. xvi. 1–4. MARK. viii. 11, 12.
Leaving them, He enters a ship, and again departs across the lake toward Bethsaida. Upon the way He discourses to the disciples respecting the leaven of	MATT. xvi. 5–13. MARK viii. 13–21.
the Pharisees. Arriving at Bethsaida, He heals a blind man and sends him privately home.	MARK viii. 22–26.

It is not expressly said that Jesus went from Magdala, or
Dalmanutha, to Capernaum, and it is possible that He may have
met Pharisees and Sadducees at either of the former places; yet
as the latter city was His home, to which He returned after all
His circuits, and was but few miles from Magdala, we have no
reason to doubt that He went thither as usual.   But some, as
Farrar, hold that He was at Dalmanutha or Magdala, and that
His enemies went there to find Him.   All depends on the posi
tion of Dalmanutha; if it was in Decapolitan territory, we may
infer that the Lord went there to avoid the Pharisees of Galilee,
and that they sought Him out in His retreat.   But if Dalmanutha
was near Magdala on the west shore, there seems no good reason
why He should not have gone to Capernaum, and the Pharisees
and Sadducees have found Him there; for this meeting does not
seem to have been accidental but premeditated on their part.
It is the first time the latter are named in conjunction with the
former, as acting unitedly in opposition to Him.   Apparently as
a party, the Sadducees had up to this time looked upon Him with
indifference, if not contempt.   But as His teachings began to
expose their errors, and His reputation was too wide-spread to be
overlooked, their hostility was aroused; and from this time they
seem to have acted in unison with the Pharisees against Him.
The peculiarity of the sign which His enemies now sought from

Him, was that it should be from heaven, or something visible in the heavens; perhaps some change in the sun or moon, or a meteor, or fire, or thunder and lightning. Denouncing them as hypocrites, who could discern the face of the sky but could not discern the signs of the times, He refuses to give them any other sign than one too late to profit them — His own resurrection.

The departure from Capernaum, or, as some think, from Dalmanutha, across the sea, seems to have followed close upon this temptation of the Pharisees and Sadducees. That the Lord was greatly grieved at this new instance of their unbelief, appears from Mark viii. 12, where it is said: "He sighed deeply in His spirit." Alexander also observes that the expression, verse 13, "'He left them,' suggests the idea of abandonment, letting them alone, leaving them to themselves, giving them up to hopeless unbelief." According to Matthew, He admonished His disciples to beware of the leaven of the Pharisees and Sadducees; according to Mark, of the leaven of the Pharisees and of Herod. This slight discrepancy is generally explained by saying that Herod was a Sadducee. This is in itself probable, for none of the Herodian princes seem to have imbibed the true Jewish spirit; and though fearing the Pharisees, because of their great influence over the people, yet they favored the Sadducees, and gave office so far as possible to men of that party. But it may be that the Lord speaks of hypocrisy in general as leaven, and so the same in whatsoever person or party it appeared.

If Bethsaida were, as we suppose, at the mouth of the Jordan, its position would correspond with all the conditions of the present narrative. Although we know from the Lord's own words (Matt. xi. 21) that He had wrought many mighty works in Bethsaida, yet the healing of the blind man is the only one recorded, except the feeding of the five thousand, which took place upon its territory. For some reason not stated (Mark viii. 23), the blind man was healed without the city. There are many points of resemblance between this miracle and that of the healing of the deaf man with an impediment in his speech (Mark vii. 32–37). In both the Lord is besought to touch them; He takes them aside from the people; He uses spittle; He enjoins silence.

11th–18th October, 782. A.D. 29.

Jesus goes up secretly to Feast of Tabernacles. During the first days of the feast there is much inquiry among the people concerning Him, and His probable appearance at the feast, but no one speaks openly through fear of the Jews. After His arrival at Jerusalem He goes into the temple and teaches. His enemies wish to arrest Him but do not, and many people believe on Him. Upon a subsequent day of the feast the Pharisees make an attempt to arrest Him, but it fails, and the officers they had sent return, declaring, "Never man spake like this man." Nicodemus makes an useless effort to induce them to act with equity.

John vii. 2–10.
John vii. 11–13.

John vii. 14–31

John vii. 32–53.

It is at this period that we put the Lord's journey to Jerusalem to the Feast of Tabernacles recorded by John (vii. 2–10). By many this journey and that mentioned by Luke (ix. 51–53) are regarded as identical. But a careful comparison shows so many points of difference that it is very difficult to believe them the same. These will be hereafter examined. For the present it will be assumed that the journeys are distinct, and that the one mentioned by Luke was later. But if there were two journeys, is that to Tabernacles to be inserted here? Did not the journey to Cæsarea Philippi follow immediately upon the miracle at Bethsaida? (Mark viii. 22–27; see Matt. xvi. 12–13.) This is said by many. But we leave this point also for future discussion ; and here assume that the Lord after this miracle went to Jerusalem to the feast, and returning to Galilee, went to Cæsarea Philippi.

In what place Jesus met His brethren (John vii. 3), and whence He departed to the feast, is not certain, but most probably it was Capernaum.[1] His brethren appear not as wholly unbelievers, but as those who, recognizing His works as wonderful, do not understand His course of conduct. Sharing the common opinions respecting the Messiah, they felt that if His Messianic claims were well founded, there could be no general recognition of them so long as He confined His labors to Galilee (see verses 41 and 52). In advising Him to go and show Himself in Judæa, their motives were friendly rather than evil. They knew that Jerusalem was the ecclesiastical centre, and that if He desired to

---

[1] Greswell, ii. 482; Caspari, 168.

be received by the nation at large, He must first find reception there. His works in Galilee, however great they might be, could avail little so long as the priests and scribes did not give Him their countenance and aid. The disciples He had already made were men of no reputation. Their adhesion gave Him no strength, for they were but Galilæan fishermen and publicans, and, with few exceptions, poor and obscure people. He must then stay no longer in that remote province, but go up to Jerusalem, and there in the temple, and before the priests and rulers, do His works.[1] If once recognized there, He would be everywhere received. Had Jesus been such a Messiah as they supposed was to come, their advice was good. It is plain that they did not in any true sense believe on Him, but in a spirit of purely worldly wisdom attempted to guide Him in His conduct. Their advice was in its nature a temptation like that of the devil (Matthew iv. 5); a temptation to reveal Himself before the time, and in a presumptuous way.

To the counsel of His brethren Jesus replies in substance, that His time is not come; that they are always sure of a friendly reception from the world, but Him it must hate, because He testifies against it. "Go ye up to the feast. I do not go up to it, for my time is not yet come." Some think to find a contradiction here, since, saying, "I go not up to this feast," He afterward went.[2] One solution makes Him to have had no intention at this time to go, but that afterward He changed His purpose in obedience to divine direction, and went. Another lays weight upon the use of the present tense, "I go not," which means "I go not now, or yet"; or, as given by Alford, "I am not at present going up." Another lays some weight upon "this feast," counting it to begin on the 10th, the day of Atonement (so Caspari), which it is said He did not in fact attend, except in its last days. Still another thus defines His words: "I go not up with you, or in public with the company of pilgrims," or, "I go not up in such way as you think or advise." The matter to one who considers the scope of Christ's reply to His brethren, presents no real dif-

---

[1] This advice seems to show that the Lord had not been in Jerusalem since the beginning of His Galilæan ministry.

[2] For the reading in the received text, "I go not up yet," οὔπω ἀναβαίνω, which is retained in W. and H., and R. V., Tischendorf has "I go not up," οὐκ ἀναβαίνω. So Alford, Meyer, Godet.

ficulty.   They had said: "Go up to this feast and manifest thyself.   Show thyself to the world, and work thy miracles in
Judæa."   He replied: "My time to manifest myself is not yet
come; I go not up to this feast with such intent.   At some subsequent feast I shall manifest myself."   (See Godet, *in loco*.)
As He had said, so He acted, going up to Jerusalem in a secret
way, avoiding all publicity, nor arriving there till the feast was
partially past.   At the following Passover He acted in substance
as ___ brethren had advised, showing Himself to the world,
and entering the holy city as a King, amid the shouts of the
multitude.

The Feast of Tabernacles was preceded by the Fast of Atonement, upon the 10th Tisri, or the 6th of October of this year,
the feast itself beginning on the 15th Tisri, or 11th of October.
The Lord probably reached Jerusalem on the 13th or 14th of
October.   That He had reached the city earlier, and only now
first showed Himself in the temple, is not implied in the narrative.[1]   We know not whether the apostles waited for Him, or
went up at the usual time, but the latter is more probable.   He
went "as it were in secret," which may imply not only that He
went unattended, but went by some unusual and obscure route.
That there was anything supernatural in His journey, or in His
appearance in the temple, as some have supposed, does not appear
in the narrative.

Here, as elsewhere in the Gospel of John, a distinction is to
be noticed, although not always preserved, between the "Jews"
and the "people."   By the former he means the nation as headed
up in its rulers, and represented by them, and ever hostile to the
Lord.   Thus he says (verse 11): "The Jews sought Him at the
feast, and said, 'Where is He?'"   Again (verse 13): "No man
spake openly of Him, for fear of the Jews."   By the people
he means the "crowd," "multitude," $\delta\chi\lambda o\varsigma$, regarded as an
assemblage of individuals; among whom there were many differences of opinion, some favorable and some unfavorable to
Jesus.   (See verse 12.)   A large portion of the crowd on this occasion was composed of pilgrims to the feast, and these are dis-

---

[1] So Edersheim; He went up later than His brethren, but still before the feast
began; and at that time visited Mary at Bethany, but did not enter the temple till two or
three days had passed.

tinguished from the citizens of Jerusalem (verse 25).   But there was no public expression of opinion in His favor, all His friends being afraid of the hierarchy.   His sudden appearance in the temple at so late a period of the feast surprised all; and the power of His speech, not the truths that He uttered, made His enemies to marvel.   It will serve to the understanding of the present narrative to keep in mind that at the time of the healing of the impotent man the Jewish rulers determined, perhaps formally in full Sanhedrin, to put Him to death (John v. 16–18); that this determination was known to some at least of the citizens of Jerusalem; and that Jesus had not, from that time to the present, entered Judæa.   He could now, therefore, refer back to that miracle, and to the purpose to kill Him, as to things well known to the rulers and to Jerusalemites, although most of the multitude, doubtless the feast pilgrims (verse 20), were ignorant of this purpose.   Thus we readily see why the citizens were surprised that He should be allowed to speak at all in the temple.

It is not plain when the Pharisees and chief priests (verse 32) sent officers to take Him.   (The seeking to take Him — verse 30 — seems to have been earlier, and not an official act.   See verse 44.)   It was perhaps, as said by Stier, upon the day following His appearance in the temple, and before the last day of the feast. Greswell supposes that for prudential reasons they deferred the attempt till the last day.   It was plainly an act not of individuals, but whether that of the Sanhedrin, now assembled specially for the purpose, is in question.   This is commonly said (so Meyer, Godet), but it is denied by Edersheim (ii. 155): "Here was neither meeting, nor decree of the Sanhedrin, nor, indeeed, could be."   He supposes a conference between the heads of the priesthood and the chief Temple officials, and that the officers were of the Temple-guard.   They were induced to take this step by the great impression His teachings had made upon the people.   But, if the officers were sent before the last day, they seem to have waited for a more favorable hour, perhaps fearing to attempt an arrest, and to have contented themselves with watching Him till the conclusion of the feast.   Upon the last day some of the multitude (v. 44) would have taken Him, but the officers, who had been greatly moved by His words, made no effort to do so; much to the vexation of those who had sent them, and to whom they now made their report.

The haughtiness of the priests and Pharisees, and their contempt for all not of themselves, are strikingly displayed in their remarks upon the return of the officers; and their rejection of the manifestly just and legal proposition of Nicodemus shows that they were bound by no considerations of equity. It is possible that others agreed with Nicodemus, and that there were internal dissensions in the council.

It is disputed whether "the last, the great day of the feast" (verse 37) was the seventh or eighth. Most maintain the latter.[1] According to the law (Numb. xxix. 35), upon the eighth day a solemn assembly should be held and special sacrifices offered. This day seems to have become in popular estimation the great day of the feast. Lightfoot (*in loco*), after stating the Jewish opinions as to the meaning of the several sacrifices, adds: "On the other seven days they thought supplications and sacrifices were offered, not so much for themselves as for the nations of the world; but the solemnities of the eighth day were wholly in their own behalf. They did not reckon the eighth day as included within the feast, but a festival day, separately and by itself."[2] It is questioned whether the drawing of water, to which the Lord is supposed to allude (verses 37, 38), and which took place upon each of the seven days, took place also upon the eighth.[3] But if it did not, as Alford rightly remarks, it would not exclude a reference to what had been done on the preceding days. Many, however, maintain that water was also poured out on the eighth day, and that Christ's words were spoken as the priest who bore it entered the court.

OCTOBER, 781. A. D. 29.

[The Lord spends the night following at the Mount of   [JOHN viii. 1–11.]
Olives, and returning early next morning to the temple,
teaches the people. An adulteress is brought before Him,
whom He directs to go and sin no more.] He answers the

---

[1] So Meyer, Alford, Tholuck, Lichtenstein, Godet, Westcott, M. and M.; *contra*, Greswell, Edersheim (ii. 176), who mentions six points which mark the octave as a separate feast.

[2] See Josephus, Antiq., iii. 10. 4.

[3] See Winer, ii. 8, note 2; Alford *in loco*.

15*

Pharisees from the treasury, and continues to speak to the people. Many believe on Him, but others are angry, and take up stones to cast at Him. As He goes, He meets and heals a blind man, who had been blind from birth, and it is the Sabbath. So soon as this miracle is reported to the Pharisees, they call him and his parents, and examine him and cast him out. He afterward meets Jesus, and believes and worships Him. Some Pharisees who are present ask Him a question, to which He replies in the parable of the Good Shepherd. There is great division of sentiment among the Jews in regard to Him.

JOHN viii. 12–59.

JOHN ix. 1–12.

JOHN ix. 13–34.

JOHN ix. 35–38.
JOHN ix. 39– x. 18.
JOHN x. 19–21.

The exact order of the events given above is not certain. The best authorities reject as not genuine the account of the adulterous woman.[1] If this be rejected, commencing vii. 53, and extending to viii. 12, it will read: "Search and look, for out of Galilee ariseth no prophet. Then spake Jesus again unto them" (R. V., "Again, therefore, Jesus spake unto them"), and in this case, His words from viii. 12–20 were spoken in the treasury upon the last day of the feast, and perhaps also the subsequent words to verse 59. We give the probable order. The feast began on the 15th Tisri, and ended on the 21st. The eighth day was the 22d, which was observed as a Sabbath. We cannot tell whether Jesus appeared in the temple and taught (vii. 14) on the 17th, 18th, or 19th day. According to Wieseler (309), it was the 18th, which he makes to have been a Sabbath; according to Greswell (ii. 491) it was the 19th. It may, with equal probability, have been the 17th. Assuming that the last great day of the feast was the 22d, an interval of three or more days must have elapsed after His appearance in the temple. Upon the first of these days occurred what is narrated in vii. 14–31, or, as some prefer, in 14–27. The next event mentioned (verse 32), the sending of officers, was probably on the next day, and they were directed to watch Him, and arrest Him when they found a good occasion. When the words in verses 33–36 were spoken is not said, but probably after the officers began to watch Him. There are then two or three days of the feast during which Jesus was present, of which nothing is related. Upon the last day He speaks of Himself as giving living water (vii. 37–38). Whether His words in viii. 12–20 and 21–59, omitting

---

[1] So Tischendorf, W. and H., Meyer, Alford, Tholuck, Trench.

here the account of the adulterous woman as not genuine, were
all spoken afterward upon the same day, or upon successive days,
it is difficult to decide. Some infer from the mention of the
"treasury" in verse 20, and the use of "again" in verse 21 (see
verse 12), that these words were spoken after the eighth day, and
upon different days.[1]   Some, on the other hand, making the
healing of the blind man (ix. 1–7) to have taken place on the
last day of the feast, which was a Sabbath, refer all His words
(ch. viii.) to this day. The former is most probable, and from
viii. 21–59 we find but the events of a single day. Was the
blind man healed on this day? So say many, bringing the
attempt to stone Him and the miracle into immediate connection.[2]
But it is more probable that some interval elapsed.[3] It is not
likely that Jesus, when "He hid Himself and went out of the
temple," was accompanied by His disciples; yet they were with
Him when He saw the blind man (ix. 2). Nor would they in
such a moment be likely to ask speculative questions respecting
the cause of the man's blindness. We conclude, then, that the
Sabbath upon which the blind man was healed (ix. 14) was not
the eighth day of the feast, but the first week-Sabbath following.

The view of Westcott should be mentioned here. He sup·
poses that the Lord's acts and words from ix. 1 to x. 20 were not
at this Feast of Tabernacles, but at the later Feast of Dedication.
This is based upon the reading ἐγένετο τότε τὰ ἐνκαίνια — "Then
was the Feast of Dedication." But Tisch. and the revisers retain
the *textus receptus;* in R.V.: "And it was the Feast of the Dedication. It was winter."

The effect of Christ's words (viii. 21–29) was such that
"many believed on Him." It is questioned whether these believers are meant in verse 33, and whether to them, in common
with others, are addressed the subsequent words (34–38). "The
Lord mingles them indiscriminately in the general mass of the
people, in spite of the transient and indistinct impulse of faith."[4]
But it seems more probable that He speaks to the Jews gener-
erally, and does not include them, for those could not in any
sense be said to believe on Him to whom He immediately ad·

---

[1] So Meyer.

[2] Meyer, Luthardt, Trench.

[3] See Alford, *in loco.*

[4] Stier; so Alford.

dresses the reproach: "Ye seek to kill me because my word hath no place in you."[1]

The attempt to stone Him (verse 59) was the fruit of sudden rage. It is denied by many, as Meyer and Alford, that the Lord's escape from their violence involved anything supernatural. The language may be construed either way; but, as said by Winer,[2] the supernatural interpretation is to be preferred as more correspondent with the character of this Evangelist. Tholuck does not find the intimation of a miracle in the strict sense of the word, but of a special providence.

The position of the pool of Siloam, where the blind man was sent to wash, had been much disputed, but all modern writers agree that it lies at the mouth of the valley of the Tyropœon, near the base of Ophel.[3] The waters of this pool come from the fountain of the Virgin, which lies on the west side of the valley of Jehosaphat, through a subterranean passage cut in the rock. It is a current belief that the water of the fountain comes from a living spring beneath the temple. Barclay (523), however, asserts that the subterranean canal derived its former supply of water, not from Moriah but from Zion.[4] It is still in dispute whether any of the water of Siloam comes from the temple.[5]

The effect of this miracle was to make a division among the Pharisees. Some said that it was a violation of the law, being done on the Sabbath; others, that no sinner could do such miracles. At first there was a general disposition to doubt the reality of the miracle, perhaps, as said by Weiss, to regard it as a concerted deception. As this, however, was established by the testimony of his parents, they reviled the man and cast him out. This may refer to his being thrust from the room where they

---

[1] In the Greek text, Tisch., W. and H., 59 ends with ἱεροῦ. R. V. "went out of the temple." Edersheim thinks He hid Himself for a moment in one of the many chambers of the temple, and then passed out.

[2] Gram., 264; see Bengel, *in loco*.

[3] Robinson, i. 333; Raumer, 296; Lewis, 119.

[4] See Robinson, i. 343; Porter, i. 138.

[5] For the latest examination of this pool, see Qt. St., January, 1891, 13, and the references there to earlier statements. It will be noted that the healing of the impotent man was at the pool of Bethesda.

were assembled,[1] or to the sentence of excommunication.[2] Some
suppose that He was now before the great Sanhedrin; others,
that He was before the lesser; others still, that he was not before
any judicial tribunal, but before some of the chief Pharisees in-
formally assembled. From the manner of the examination and
their action at its close, it is most probable that they were clothed
with some ecclesiastical authority.

How soon after the blind man was cast out the Lord met
him, is not stated. Not improbably, He may have met Him the
same day toward evening. It is in question what is the right
reading of the Lord's words in verse 35: "Dost thou believe on
the Son of God"? Tisch., W. and H., read, "Son of Man."
(In R. V., "Son of God" is retained; so Edersheim, who relies
on "the internal evidence.") The words in verse 39 seem to
have been addressed to the disciples, and probably after His
meeting with the blind man, and the words to the Pharisees
immediately followed. The effect of these words was again to
work a division of opinion respecting Him, some saying that
He had a devil, others, that neither His words nor works
were those of a man who had a devil.

From Jerusalem, as we here assume, the Lord returns to
Galilee. Of His return the Evangelist gives us no information.
Many suppose that He did not return to Galilee at this time,
but spent the interval between the feasts of Tabernacles and of
Dedication at Jerusalem or in its vicinity.[3] It will be shown
that this journey to the feast of Tabernacles is not identical
with that in Luke ix. 51, and that the latter was subsequent.
A full discussion of all these points is reserved to the part following.

If we compare the discourse of the Lord when at the unnamed
feast (John v. 1) with those at this later feast of Tabernacles, and
their attendant circumstances, we find many important differences,
showing that a considerable interval of time had elapsed. In the first,
though there is mention of a multitude as present (verse 13), yet they
apparently take no part in the proceedings against Him, and are

---

[1] Meyer, Lichtenstein.

[2] Alford. Trench embraces both. As to the effect of excommunication, see
Eders., ii. 183.

[3] So Meyer, Alford, Tholuck, Robinson, Tischendorf.

either ignorant or uninterested. There is evidently no popular excitement about Him, and nothing is said of any Messianic claims. All this corresponds to the fact that up to this time He had been laboring in Judæa, and with special reference to the rulers at Jerusalem, and to them His discourse was addressed. The public at large knew little of Him. But at the last feast the multitude is plainly much excited in regard to Him. The question is earnestly asked whether He will come to the feast, and they dispute as to His character and work and His Messianic claims. All this shows that He had at this time become well known throughout the land, for these multitudes were doubtless the feast-pilgrims coming from all parts of it; and that there was a very deep interest in His personal movements.

Comparing the conduct of the Jews toward the Lord at the two feasts, we see that their hostility had greatly increased. At the first, the charge brought against Him was that He had broken the Sabbath by the healing of the impotent man; now, the charge against Him, one made by the Pharisees in Galilee, and become current among the multitudes, is that He has a devil. His enemies had taken the position that all His words and works were those of a man possessed. This permitted no compromise, no middle ground was possible. He was not, they said, sent of God, a teacher, a prophet, much less the Christ, but sent of the devil; and hence the greater severity of the Lord's words, and the clear, and strong, and oft-repeated affirmations of His divine mission and of His relations to the Father.

It is important to note what knowledge the people at large had of His Messianic character, at this late stage of His ministry, and the division of sentiment respecting Him which His words at this feast made. That which had kept them so long in doubt, was His refusal to take any such step to assert His royal claims as they expected the Messiah would do when He came. His miracles made a deep impression, and they asked: "When the Christ shall come, will He do more signs than those which this man hath done?" But this inactivity led them to believe that He Himself was not the Messiah, but His forerunner. In this state of uncertainty it was natural that His words should have caused frequent and rapid transition of feeling. Now many believed on Him, now they argued against Him, now they took up stones to stone Him. The Pharisees, seeing these alternations of popular feeling, were alarmed, and asked anxiously: "Have any of the rulers or of the Pharisees believed on Him?" Even among these was at last a division (x. 20–1); for while many said (R. V.): "He hath a devil, and is mad; why hear ye Him?" others said, "These are not the sayings of one possessed with a devil. Can a devil open the eyes of the blind?"

It was apparent to the Lord that the hatred of the rulers at Jerusalem had only intensified with time.   All that was remained was to return to Galilee and prepare His disciples for that hour which was rapidly approaching, when His words would be fulfilled: "Yet a little while I am with you, and I go unto Him that sent me."

AUTUMN, OCTOBER TO NOVEMBER, 782. A.D. 29.

Returning to Galilee, Jesus goes with His disciples to the region of Cæsarea Philippi.   While upon the way, He asked them, "Whom do men say that I am?"   He then asks them their opinion of Him, and Peter replies that He is the Christ, the Son of the living God.   This truth He commands them to tell to no one; and now begins to teach them respecting His approaching rejection by the Jews, His death, and resurrection after three days. Peter would rebuke Him for these words, but is himself rebuked.   Jesus afterward addresses the disciples and people, and teaches them what is involved in following Him, and speaks of the rewards He will give to all when He shall come again in the glory of His Father. He adds, that some standing before Him should see Him come in the glory of His kingdom.   Six days after He goes to a high mountain, taking with Him Peter, James, and John, and is transfigured before them.

MARK viii. 27–33.
MATT. xvi. 13–23.
LUKE ix. 18–22.

MARK viii. 34–38.
MATT. xvi. 24–28.
LUKE ix. 23–27.

MARK ix. 1–10.
MATT. xvii. 1–9.
LUKE ix. 28–36.

To what place in Galilee the Lord returned after the feast in Jerusalem we do not know, but probably He went to Capernaum, and from thence to Cæsarea Philippi.   (The point of departure, whether from Capernaum or Bethsaida, will be later considered.)

It is said by Mark (viii. 27): "Jesus went out and His disciples into the towns — κώμας — of Cæsarea Philippi."   As His chief purpose in this journey was that He might instruct His disciples, it is not probable that He taught in these towns, but passed quietly through them, avoiding publicity as far as possible. Still in this circuit, as in that through Tyre and Sidon, "He could not be hid."   It is said by Alexander that "the multitude was never far off, even when the Lord was most retired."   It is therefore not in contradiction to this that the Lord is said by Mark (viii. 34), at a little later period during this circuit, "to have called the people unto Him, with His disciples also," His teaching respecting the self-denial needed in a disciple, having an equal application to both.   That "He called the people unto Him " marks this as a special act (see vii. 14); and it does not follow from this, as Ellicott says, that His object in His journey was public preaching and teaching.

We do not know where the Lord was when He asked the disciples, " Whom do men say that I am ? "   Matthew says (xvi. 13): " When Jesus came unto the coasts — parts — of Cæsarea Philippi, He asked," etc.   Mark (viii. 27): " And by the way, He asked," etc.   Luke (ix. 18), who makes no mention of this circuit, and gives no indication of the place, says: " And it came to pass, as He was alone praying, His disciples were with Him, and He asked them." [1]   Whether the Lord actually entered the city of Cæsarea Philippi, we cannot tell, but the probability is that He did not.

The apostles, in their answer to the Lord's question, " Whom do men say that I am ? " give the opinions then most current among the people generally in Galilee.   It is not certain whether He was through ignorance confounded with John the Baptist, as if the latter were still living, or was thought to be the Baptist raised from the dead.   The latter is most probable, and perhaps reference may be made to the opinion of Herod and his party.   It will be remembered that the Lord did not begin His Galilæan ministry till the Baptist was imprisoned, and so removed from public observation.   We do not know that he carried on any baptismal work in Galilee, and it is not strange, therefore, that there should have been some confusion in the popular mind respecting him.   Those who knew that Jesus and John had carried on contemporaneous labors in Judæa, could not possibly have identified them as one; but many in Galilee were doubtless ignorant of this.   How intimate was the connection in the Jewish mind between the resurrection and the kingdom of heaven and the advent of Christ, is shown by Lightfoot (on John i. 25): " The Jews believed that at the coming of the Messiah the prophets were to rise again.   The nearer still the ' kingdom of heaven ' came, by so much the more did they dream of the resurrection of the prophets."

It is to be noted that no important part of the people seem to

---

[1] This mention of His being alone (see Mark iv. 10) shows that none but the disciples were with Him.

have regarded Jesus as the Christ, or else it would have been
mentioned by the apostles.   It is apparent that He was regarded
rather as a forerunner of the Messiah than as the Messiah Himself, though public sentiment may have changed from time to
time in regard to His Messianic claims.[1]   On the one hand, He
had been pointed out as the Messiah by John, and His mighty
works manifestly proved His divine commission; yet, on the
other hand, He did not openly avow Himself to be the Messiah,
and His whole course of conduct was in striking contrast to their
Messianic expectations.   While a few here and there said, "He
is the Christ," the general voice began to be that He was but a
forerunner.   Weiss (ii. 52) thinks that the answer shows only
that the people no longer considered Him as the Messiah, not
that many had not formerly done so.   After the feeding of
the five thousand, there was a desire to make Him king; it
was the natural effect of so stupendous a miracle upon the restless Jewish mind, eager to cast off the Roman and Idumæan yoke;
but the next day many of His disciples, and perhaps those most
zealous to make Him a king, repelled by His words, "went
back and walked no more with Him."   It is said by Lindsay:
"The people had fancied that He was the Messiah; they did so
no longer."   This confession of Peter, which was that of all the
apostles, was therefore a great turning point in their history.
To others He was only the Baptist, or Elias, or one of the prophets; to them "He was the Christ, the Son of the living God."

We are not concerned in these discussions to enter upon
points of interpretation, except so far as they bear directly upon
our historical understanding of the Gospels.   That there was
during the Lord's ministry a development in the minds of His
disciples, and especially of the Twelve, of their conceptions as to
His Person, is undoubted; and we may briefly outline the
progress of this development as it is made known in their
successive confessions.

The first confession made was that of Andrew at Bethabara
(John i. 41) to his brother Peter : "We have found the Messiah."   The second was that of Philip (verse 45) : "We have
found Him of whom Moses in the law and the prophets did

[1] Lange, on Matt. xvi. 14.

write, Jesus of Nazareth, the Son of Joseph." The third was that of Nathanael (verse 49): "Rabbi, thou art the Son of God; thou art the King of Israel." The comparison of these several confessions shows that in their minds the terms "Messiah" and "Son of God" were interchangeable, and that both were compatible with the fact that He so designated should be born of a human father, and at Nazareth in Galilee. A later confession was that of those in the ship when the Lord walked upon the water (Matt. xiv. 33): "Of a truth thou art the Son of God." After the discourse in Capernaum (John vi. 69) Peter made the confession: "We believe, and are sure that thou art that Christ, the Son of the living God." (The best authorities substitute for this reading that of the R. V., "that thou art the Holy One of God."[1])

The last of these confessions — that now before us, made in answer to the Lord's question — is briefest in Mark: "Thou art the Christ"; in Luke: "The Christ of God"; in Matthew more full: "Thou art the Christ, the Son of the living God."

As we must believe that the imperfect conceptions of the disciples in regard to the Lord's Person were much enlarged through His teachings, we ask as to the new elements now made known. They were two: first, that of His pre-existence; and as involved in this, His coming down from heaven. To Nicodemus He said: "No man hath ascended up to heaven, but He that came down from heaven, even the Son of man which is in heaven." So to the disciples at Capernaum He said (John vi. 38): "For I came down from heaven, not to do mine own will but the will of Him that sent me." Again (viii. 42), "I proceeded forth and came from God." And even more distinctly (John viii. 58): "Before Abraham was, I am." (See also vi. 33, 51, 62.) If pre-existence had already entered as an element into the Jewish conception of the Messiah, it was now confirmed; but probably it had never been held unless in a very vague way.

The second element was that of Sonship as involving unity of essence. The Son's relation to the Father was not that of a man sent and endowed by the Father to do His work, His servant; but of one equal to the Father, yet as Son subordinate to Him. Of this Sonship He had spoken to the Jews (John v

---

[1] So Tisch., W. and H., Meyer, Gardiner, Riddle, and many; *contra*, McClellan.

17 ff.), and they had understood Him as "making Himself equal with God." His words spoken at the Feast of Dedication (x. 30): "I and my Father are One," were understood in the same sense: "Thou, being a man, makest thyself God."

These declarations of the Lord respecting His Person publicly made, must not only have been known, but also believed by His disciples, even if He had not Himself taught them in private more fully and plainly. We must, therefore, believe that in this confession of Peter was embraced the fact of the Incarnation, though doubtless in a very undefined way, for it could not have been rightly understood till after His death and resurrection and ascension. The mystery of His Person — "the Word made flesh" — was something not to be known through the senses, or through any exercise of the understanding. Nor could it be proved by any miracles, even the most stupendous. If known, it must be through the revelation of God.

This truth, so far surpassing all the common Jewish conceptions of the Messiah, of the united Divinity and humanity of the Lord, being known and confessed by the Twelve, Jesus could begin to open to them other truths till this time concealed. Now He could teach them that His first work was to suffer; that He must be rejected by the Jews and be put to death; that He must rise from the dead; and would afterward establish His kingdom. These truths, so new and strange to the disciples, so foreign to all their modes of thinking, they could not for a long time comprehend. The very fact of the Divinity of Jesus, even as now imperfectly understood by them, made it still more incomprehensible how He could suffer and die; nor could the plainest words of the Lord make it intelligible. How repugnant to their feelings was the announcement of His sufferings is graphically shown in the language of the impetuous Peter: "Be it far from thee, Lord; this shall not be unto thee"—language which brought upon him the severest rebuke.

From this time the teaching of Jesus to His disciples, and also to the people at large (see Mark viii. 34; Luke ix. 23) assumed a new character. Gradually, as the Twelve were able to bear it, He showed them how the great purpose of God in the Messiah must be effected through His death, and how

His sufferings had been foretold by the prophets So far from
now establishing any earthly kingdom in which they should
have distinguished places, He must be put to a most ignominious
death, and all who received Him as the Messiah would do it at
the peril of their lives.   Yet, as a counterpoise to the gloomy
picture, He speaks of an hour when He would come again, and
then every disciple should have His reward.   (What the disciples
understood by His coming again, whether He was to be hidden
from them for a time and then reappear as King; or that He
would suddenly manifest Himself as King, will be later considered.)   Thus He confirmed to them the great fact that He was
to establish a kingdom in power and glory.   To prevent the
disciples from seizing upon this fact, and indulging in dreams of
a reign corresponding to that of earthly kings, the Lord was
pleased to show certain of the apostles, by a momentary transfiguration of His body, the supernatural character of His kingdom, and into what new and higher conditions of being both
He and they must be brought ere it could come.   The promise
that some then standing before Him should not taste death till
they had seen "the Son of man coming in His kingdom" (Matt.
xvi. 28), or had seen "the kingdom of God come with power"
Mark ix. 1), was fulfilled when, after six days, He took Peter,
James, and John into a high mountain apart, and was transfigured before them.   Trench (Studies in the Gospels, 188) remarks that "nearly all the early expositors, the fathers and
the mediæval interpreters find in the glory of the Transfiguration the fulfillment of the promise."   These apostles now saw
Him as He should appear when, risen from the dead and
glorified, He should come again from heaven to take His great
power and to reign.   They saw in the ineffable glory of His
Person and in the brightness around them, a foreshadowing of the
kingdom of God as it should come with power, and were for a
moment "eye-witnesses of His majesty" (2 Peter i. 16).   Many
errors still remained to be removed from their minds, especially
respecting the time of its establishment (Acts i. 6), but the great
fact of its supernatural character they could not mistake.
Henceforth the phrase "kingdom of God" had to these apostles
a significance which it probably had not had to any of the prophets,
and certainly had not to any of the Rabbis or priests.

The three apostles were commanded to tell no one of the vision till Jesus had risen from the dead. It therefore remained for a considerable period unknown to the other apostles and disciples. It was natural that they should question one with another, as they descended the mount, what the rising from the dead should mean (Mark ix. 10). They had just seen the Lord transfigured. He had not died, yet had His body been invested with heavenly glory. It was not then necessary to die and to rise again in order to be glorified. What, then, should the death and resurrection of which He had spoken mean ? Not a literal death and resurrection, but a spiritual death — some act of suffering or self-sacrifice, upon which supernatural glory would follow. And thus the resurrection from the dead, as a preliminary to the kingdom, became still more incomprehensible.

The statements of the Evangelists do not enable us to decide where the Transfiguration took place. Matthew and Mark speak of it as " a high mountain "; Luke, as "the mountain," τὸ ὄρος. A tradition, dating back to the fourth century, gives Tabor in Galilee as the site. · This is a very conspicuous mount rising out of the plain of Esdraelon, cone-shaped, about 1,400 above the plain or 1,900 above the sea, its slopes wooded, and only a few miles from Nazareth. All travellers speak of it as in itself a beautiful object, and presenting a wide view from the summit. So generally received for many centuries was this tradition, that Lightfoot (Mark ix. 2) says: " I know it will be laughed at if I should doubt whether Christ was transfigured on Mount Tabor, for who ever doubted of this thing? " [1] According to Robinson (ii. 358) the first notice of Tabor as the place of the Transfiguration is as a passing remark by Cyril of Jerusalem, and afterward by Jerome. Before the close of the sixth century three churches were builded there, and afterward a monastery was founded. Arculf, A. D. 700,[2] says : " At the top is a pleasant and extensive meadow surrounded by a thick wood, and in the middle of the meadow a great monastery with numerous cells of monks. There are also three handsome churches, according to the number of tabernacles described by Peter."

---

[1] The feast of the Transfiguration is called by the Greeks the " Tabor feast " — τὸ Θαβώριον.

[2] Early Travels, 9.

Robinson and Stanley think it conclusive against this tradition,
that at the time of the Transfiguration " the summit of Tabor was
occupied by a fortified city." Thomson, however (ii. 139), does
not regard this as presenting any difficulty. " There are many secluded or densely-wooded terraces on the north and northeast sides,
admirably adapted to the scenes of the Transfiguration. After
all that the critics have advanced against the current tradition,
I am not fully convinced." Admitting that much may be said in
favor of Mount Tabor as " the high mountain " of the Evangelists,
still their narratives lead us to place this event in the neighborhood
of Cæsarea Philippi rather than on the west of the lake. " The
Evangelists," says Lightfoot, " intimate no change from place to
place." The expression of Mark (ix. 30), that " departing thence
He passed through Galilee," would imply that He was not
then in Galilee. We are therefore made to look for some
mountain in the vicinity of Cæsarea, and Mount Hermon at once
rises before us.[1] "Standing amid the ruins of Cæsarea we do
not need to ask what that ' high mountain ' is. The lofty ridge
of Hermon rises over us, and probably on one or other of those
wooded peaks above us that wondrous event took place."[2]

The difference in the computation of Matthew and Mark on
one side, who say, " After six days He taketh Peter, James, and
John into a high mountain apart," and Luke, who says, " About
an eight days after these sayings, He took," etc., is easily reconciled if we suppose that the latter included, while the former
excluded, both the day on which the words were spoken and
the day of the Transfiguration. Some, as Meyer, prefer to take
Luke's phrase "about an eight days" as indefinite, but this is
contrary to the use of ὡσεὶ, with numerals by this Evangelist.
The six days, according to Lange, are probably to be counted
from the day of Peter's confession. Others, as Lightfoot,
count from the day the words of Matt. xvi. 28 were spoken.
Not improbably the days were identical. It is not certain
at what period of the day the Transfiguration took place,
but most probably during the night, or at the early dawn.
(Greswell, ii. 368.) Darkness was not indeed, as some have sup

---

[1] Lightfoot, Reland.
[2] Porter, ii. 447; so Stanley, Lichtenstein, Ritter, Eders. Godet; Keil and Weiss
uncertain.

posed, necessary that the glory of the Lord's Person might be plainly visible, for when He appeared to Paul (Acts xxvi. 13) it was midday, yet the light that shone around Him was brighter than the sun. Nor does the fact that the apostles slept, show that it was night, for their sleep seems to have been not so much natural sleep, the result of fatigue, as stupefaction caused by the marvellous apparition (Rev. i. 17). Nor does the fact that He was at that time engaged in prayer (Luke ix. 29) determine it. But as He did not descend from the mount till the day follow ing, it is not probable that He ascended upon one day, was transfigured, remained after this during the night, and the next day returned to the disciples. It is most reasonable to suppose that the Lord went upon the mount at even, that He was transfigured at the early dawn, and soon after descended.

The feast of the Transfiguration was not one of the very early feasts, though observed in the East as early as the 6th century; its general observance in the West was due to a bull of Pope Calixtus in 1457. It was held on the 6th August. This time was selected, not as the date of the event, but for symbolical reasons. The Transfiguration showing forth the new life, the Eucharist on that day, it was said, ought to be celebrated with new wine, and hence the feast was put as early as the grapes were ripe. So early a period is inconsistent with the arrangements of most harmonists. (See Binterim, Denk., v. 1, 414 ff.)

AUTUMN, 782. A. D. 29.

Descending from the mount, Jesus explains, in answer to a question from the Apostles, how Elias must be the forerunner of the Messiah. At the foot of the mountain, they meet the other Apostles surrounded by a multitude, among whom are scribes questioning with them. The Lord heals a lunatic child, whom the Apostles have not been able to heal.	MATT. xvii. 10–13. MARK ix. 11–13. MATT. xvii. 14–21. MARK ix. 14–29. LUKE ix. 37–42.

That Elijah must personally precede the Messiah, was one of the firmest and most undoubted convictions of the Jews; and the fact that the Baptist denied himself to be Elijah, was a circumstance that went far to discredit his mission. If he was not Elijah, then Jesus could not be the Christ. If he was a prophet, and so all the people regarded him, it by no means followed that the Messiah must immediately follow him, for there might be

many prophets who could act as forerunners, and yet Elijah
alone should prepare His way. As we have seen, most of the
people seem to have regarded Jesus Himself only as one of the
prophetic forerunners of the Messiah. Educated in the current
belief respecting the office of Elijah, the three apostles could
not reconcile it with his appearance upon the mount. The Lord
clears up this great difficulty by explaining to them the truth, so
strange, that there should be two comings of the Messiah, and so
two forerunners. Thus, the mystery of two Elijahs was cleared
up so soon as the mystery of the two comings was known. It is
remarked by Alford: " The double allusion is only the assertion
that the Elias (in spirit and power) who foreran our Lord's first
coming, was a partial fulfillment of the great prophecy, which
announces the real Elias (the words of Malachi iv. 5, 6, will
hardly bear any other than a personal meaning), who is to fore-
run His greater and second coming."

The other apostles and disciples had remained at the foot of
the mount, probably in some town or village, during the absence
of the Lord. In the morning, before He descended, a crowd
had gathered around them, doubtless seeking Him ; and in the
crowd was a man who had brought his lunatic son to be healed.
In the absence of Jesus he presented him to the disciples, who
could not heal him. Among those present were certain scribes,
who, apparently taking occasion from their ill success, began to
question with them, and plainly with an evil intent. While
they were disputing with the disciples, Jesus appeared, and was
gladly received by the multitude. In answer to the father's
prayer He healed the child, after a severe rebuke of the general
unbelief. The question afterward addressed to Him by the disciples when alone: " Why could not we cast him out ? " shows
that they supposed the power to work miracles, which had
been given the Twelve when they were sent forth upon their
mission, was still continued to them.

Autumn, 782. A. D. 29.

Departing from the place where He healed the lunatic   Mark ix. 30–32.
child, He passes through Galilee, avoiding, as far as
possible, public attention, and giving Himself to the   Matt. xvii. 22, 23.
instruction of His disciples. He repeats the announce-
ment respecting His death and resurrection, but they   Luke ix. 43–45.

do not understand Him, and are afraid to ask. After
some time thus spent they come to Capernaum. Peter,
having declared to the tax-gatherer that his master is MARK ix. 33–50.
liable to pay tribute, goes by Christ's direction to the MATT. xvii. 24–27.
sea, and finds the tribute-money in the mouth of a fish.
At Capernaum He discourses to them of their equality as MATT. xviii. 1–35.
brethren, and teaches them who shall be regarded as the LUKE ix. 46–50.
greatest in the kingdom of Heaven.

If the healing of the lunatic child was, as we have supposed,
in the neighborhood of Cæsarea Philippi, the Lord, crossing the
Jordan near its sources, would enter the northern parts of Galilee, and thus journey toward Capernaum. That this circuit
was not for the purpose of public teaching, is expressly said by
Mark (ix. 30): "And they departed thence, and passed through
Galilee; and He would not that any man should know." And
the reason is added why He would not be known, "for He
taught His disciples." To instruct them more fully in the truths
He had just opened to them of His approaching death and resurrection, now occupied Him, and the presence of large crowds
would have hindered Him in His purpose. How long this circuit continued we do not know, nor what particular parts of
Galilee He visited. The order of events is as follows: healing
of the lunatic child; teaching as to the power of prayer; repetition of the prediction of His death and resurrection; dispute
of the disciples by the way which should be the greatest; payment of the tribute-money; teaching upon rank in the kingdom
of heaven. Matthew's language (xvii. 22): "And while they
abode in Galilee," or more literally, "while they were going
about in Galilee," implies that some time was spent there.[1]
The continued inability of the disciples to understand the Lord's
words respecting His death and resurrection will surprise no
one acquainted with the Messianic expectations of the Jews.
They found it impossible to give a literal interpretation to His
words, but they were afraid to ask Him what He meant.

During these journeyings, and probably just before their
arrival at Capernaum, a dispute had arisen among the disciples,

---

[1] But Tisch., W. and H., have συστρεφομένων for ἀναστρεφομένων, meaning "uniting or assembling themselves." See T. G. Lex, and R. V. margin; compare Acts
xix. 40; xxiii. 12, and xxviii. 3. This seems to point to a gathering together for a departure from Galilee.

who should be the greatest in the kingdom.   That He was about
to reveal Himself as the Messiah and set up His kingdom, was a
belief still firmly rooted in their minds, and which His mysterious words about His death and resurrection seemed only to confirm.   They knew that some great event was approaching; what
should it be but this long-hoped-for manifestation of the kingdom, when David's son should sit on David's throne?   It, therefore, naturally became now a question of deep personal interest
to those most ambitious among them, who should fill the highest
places under the new government.   Perhaps the preference shown
by Jesus to the three whom He took with Him upon the mount,
and whom He had before specially honored, may have provoked
envy and occasioned this dispute.   It was not till after His arrival at Capernaum that Jesus took notice of it.   From Matthew
(xviii. 1) it seems that the incident of the tribute-money had
some connection with the strife, as some of the disciples coming
to Him immediately after asked Him directly, "Who is the
greatest in the kingdom of heaven?"[1]   In the most expressive
way, by means of a little child, He teaches them that only those
like little children, trustful, humble, unambitious, could even
enter the heavenly kingdom.

The tax demanded of Jesus was the temple tax, which all
Jews were obliged to pay yearly (Ex. xxx. 13).[2]   Some, as Wieseler (Syn., 265; Beiträge, 108), have understood a civil tax payable
to the Romans; but against this is the use of "didrachma" for
the tribute, a sum equal to the half shekel, the legal due.   It is
said by Schürer (II. i. 250): "The actual payment of the temple
tax in the time of Christ is beyond doubt. . . .   After the
destruction of the temple it was converted into a Roman tax."
Besides this, the scope of the Lord's reply shows that the temple
tax is meant.   As the Son of God, He was exempt from the
payment to which others were bound for the support of ecclesiastical services.   Had it been a civil tax, this reply would not
have been so directly to the purpose.[3]

---

[1] Greswell (ii. 462) attempts to show that the question in Matthew to Jesus was subsequent to His question to the Apostles in Mark (ix. 33) and in Luke (ix. 46). Some
suppose, as Keil, that the others were displeased with the prominence given to
Peter at his confession, at the Transfiguration, and in the matter of the tribute money.

[2] Josephus, Antiq., xviii. 9.

[3] Meyer; Winer, ii. 588, note 3; Trench, Mir., 399; Alford; Ellicott, 229; Keil.

According to the Rabbins this temple tax was due between the 15th and 25th Adar.[1] This would be about the time of the Passover. Greswell, however, maintains, upon rabbinic author ity, that it was paid at each of the three great feasts. We cannot then determine at what period of the year this demand of the tax-gatherer was made. If payment was legally due at the Passover, still it may not have actually been demanded till a later period. It may be that, being regarded as a prophet, up to this time no tax at all had been demanded of Jesus; and that now, at the instigation of His enemies, and for the first time, the demand was made.[2] Some suppose that the Rabbins were exempt from taxation; and that the question of the tax-gatherer shows that he had not previously collected it of the Lord; but others draw the exactly opposite conclusion, that He had been accustomed to pay it. That he should ask the question of Peter, may be explained from his prominent position as a disci- ple, or because as a resident in the city he was well known. The inference of Bengel, from the fact that the Lord paid the tax for Himself and Peter but for none other of the apostles, that the others were too young to be taxed, is wholly improbable and unnecessary.

---

[1] See Winer, i. 4. Caspari puts the payment at this time, but thinks the time of the collection of the temple tribute uncertain; Godet, that the form of the Collector's question supposes a payment which was at once voluntary and in arrears.

[2] See Lightfoot, *in loco*.

PART VI.

The Lord's Last Journey from Galilee.

If the views that have already been presented in regard to
the divisions of the Lord's ministry are correct, we are in a position to judge rightly the statements of the Evangelists respecting the period that intervened between the departure from Galilee and the commencement of Passion Week, a period of about
five months. In Galilee the Lord had accomplished His work.
He had gathered about Him a considerable body of disciples (1
Cor. xv. 6) who saw in Him, with more or less clearness of vision, the Christ of the prophets and Son of the living God; and
there was also a much larger number, who, unable to see in Him
the Messiah of their hopes, still believed that He was a prophet
sent from God, and heard His words with reverence. Besides,
there must have been very many in all parts of the land, who
had seen His works, and been more or less impressed by them,
and yet had not felt the power of the truths He taught, and
were waiting to see what His future course would be. His
labors had by no means been in vain, although, as set forth in
His own parable, but little of the seed He had so diligently
sown fell into good ground.

There are two circumstances that seemed to have marked,
if they did not determine, the conclusion of the Galilean ministry: first, that the Apostles, not to speak of other disciples, had
learned, if imperfectly, the mystery of the Lord's Person as the
Son of God; second, that the machinations of His enemies at
Jerusalem were arousing great hostility against Him in Galilee,

(365)

and making the further prosecution of His labors there full of difficulty and danger.   Both of these points demand attention.

It needs no argument to show that the Lord's ministry must primarily aim at the recognition, on the part of His disciples, of the great fact that in His Person "God was manifest in flesh." Until they were able to rise above the ordinary Jewish concep‑ tions of the Messiah, and to see in Him the Son of God, He could open to them but little of the divine purpose.   He could say nothing to them in distinct terms of His death, resurrection, and ascension.   He must continue with them in person till, through their communion with Him, they should learn who He was, and what were His relations to the Father.   And, as we have seen, when Peter, in the name of all the Apostles, made the confession that He was " the Christ, the Son of the living God," He for the first time announced to them His approaching death (Matt. xvi. 21).   This announcement it was still very hard for them to understand, and perhaps the more that they now knew Him to be the Son of God; for how could men have power over Him, and what had death to do with Him?   But, however imperfectly held, the germ of this great truth of His divinity was in their hearts, and they were now in a state to receive those teachings of Jesus which had reference to a heavenly kingdom, one corresponding to the Person of the King.   Thus the foundation was laid of that high knowledge of God's pur‑ pose in Him, which they needed in their subsequent work, and for which they were further prepared, first by the teachings of the Lord Himself after His resurrection, and then by the descent of the Spirit at Pentecost.

The recognition on the part of His disciples of His divine Sonship, and the consequent announcement to them of His ap‑ proaching death, mark, therefore, the end of His Galilean min‑ istry.   Yet a little time must elapse that these truths might get more firmly rooted in their faith ere the terrible hour of His suf‑ ferings should come.

That, as His disciples grew in knowledge and faith, the dark‑ ness and bitterness of His enemies should increase, was but what Jesus Himself had foretold.   All who loved the light gathered around Him, the true light.   His words were the test by which the thoughts of all hearts were revealed; and as His ministry was prolonged, and the truths He taught were more distinctly apprehended, the line of separation between His friends and His enemies became more and more marked.   His popularity among the people seems to have been at its height about the time of the Baptist's death, when, after the feeding of the five thousand, many wished to take Him by force and make Him a king.   But the nature of His teachings soon repelled not a few who had been counted among His disciples (John vi. 66), and the Pharisees at Capernaum and elsewhere in Galilee became daily more open and virulent in their opposition.   Gradually the great crowds that at first thronged around Him diminished; the novelty of His first appearance passed away; His calls to repentance were by most disregarded; His miracles, wonderful as they were, were not of a kind to satisfy the populace that He was the expected Messiah; His enemies were active and unscrupulous in representing Him as a blasphemer ; His nearest and most trusted disciples were uninfluential and obscure men, publicans, fishermen, and the like.   It is not, therefore, in itself at all strange that there was not in Galilee at the end of His ministry any general belief in His Messianic character.   Against those cities which He had often visited, and where He had wrought many works, He pronounced a fearful judgment.   Thus, in Galilee, as in Judæa, Jesus was despised and rejected of men.

But the Lord did not yet forsake His people.   He would make one more, and a final appeal.   Up to this time He had not openly and expressly declared Himself to be the Messiah, either in Judæa or in Galilee.   He had left the Jews to judge for themselves from His teachings and His works, who He was. But they did not for the most part discern Him.   Their preconceived opinions of the Messiah and of His work prevented them from recognizing Him in the obscure, humble, peaceful Galilean, mighty as were His miracles and sublime as were His teachings.   If the Messiah, why did He not establish His kingdom?   Yet, while thus not answering to the popular apprehensions of the Messiah, He seemed in His discourses to claim higher rank and power than even the Messiah could claim, a mysterious relationship to God which was blasphemous.   Thus, on the one side, His silence respecting His Messiahship and His inactivity caused many, who were astonished at His works and words, to look upon Him only as a prophet; and on the other, His repeated allusions to His divine Sonship drew upon Him the enmity of many as a blasphemer.

But while it was the will of God that His people should be left at first to recognize His Son by His words and works, and thus to test them, yet He willed also that there should be borne clear and full testimony to His Messianic character, that all might be without excuse. Such testimony John the Baptist had borne; and to this was now added that of all His disciples, who in the very fact of their discipleship proclaimed Him to be the Messiah. He had not indeed permitted the Apostles to proclaim Him by name (Matt. xvi. 20), because He then for their sake avoided publicity. Had they done so, such an announcement made authoritatively by those nearest Him, would at once have rallied around Him all those cherishing the current Messianic hopes, and have cast the Apostles back into that lower region of thought and feeling, from which He was endeavoring to lift them. But the time had now come when His Messianic character must be publicly asserted, that the whole nation might know that He was the Christ, the Son of David, the King of Israel; and if rejected, He must be rejected as such. The people should not be left in doubt whether He asserted Himself to be more than a simple prophet, or, like the Baptist, a forerunner of the Messiah. He will go up to Jerusalem; for if it cannot be that a prophet perish out of Jerusalem, how much more is this true of the Son of God? and He will go with every circumstance of publicity, to be received or finally rejected by those whom God had set to be the heads of the people. It must be a national act, and must not be done in ignorance. In Judæa, He had testified of Himself as the Son of God, but in vain. Now He will return thither, and His disciples shall bear witness to Him, if, perchance, the nation will hear them. To this end His messengers shall go before Him into every place where He designed to go, and announce the kingdom of God at hand in the Person of the King.

Here, then, we find the grand peculiarity of the Lord's last

journey to Jerusalem. As He knew, and had declared to His
Apostles, He went up to die; but to the Jewish people the issue of
His journey was not known, and the secret purpose of God did
not hinder this last appeal to them to repent and receive their
Lord.

Before entering upon the details of this last journey, it will be
well to consider its general features. To reconcile the various statements of the Evangelists respecting it, is one of the most difficult
tasks that meet the harmonist. That we may see clearly the points
of difference, it will be well to examine the statements of each
Evangelist separately.

1. *The time of the final departure.* As John gives the most dis
tinct notices of time, we begin with his narrative.

About the middle of October 782 (A. D. 29) the Lord goes up
to the Feast of Tabernacles (John vii. 10). As to the time of this
feast and the manner of its observance, and the Lord's words and
work during it, we have already spoken. He went up, "not openly,
but as it were in secret," and continued in Jerusalem to the end of
the feast. Whether He then left the city, is not said, and we find
Him there some two months later at the Feast of Dedication in
December. After this feast, His enemies seeking to arrest Him, "He
escaped out of their hand, and went away again beyond Jordan unto
the place where John at first baptized, and there He abode" (x. 40).
How long He abode here is not said, but after an interval, longer or
shorter, He was called to go up to Bethany to see Lazarus about to
die (xi. 1). After the resurrection of Lazarus He did not return at
once beyond Jordan; and His enemies becoming more hostile, "He
walked no more openly among the Jews, but went thence unto a
country near to the wilderness, into a city called Ephraim, and there
continued with His disciples" (xi. 54). From Ephraim a little before
the Passover of April 783 (30 A. D.), He went up to that feast by way
of Bethany (xi. 55; xii. 1).

We have thus in John a chronological outline of the chief events
of the last six months of the Lord's life and ministry. He was in
Galilee, and went thence to Jerusalem, and was in that city in October and again in December. Afterward He was beyond Jordan,
where John at first baptized, and from there went to Bethany close
by Jerusalem. From Bethany He went to Ephraim, and from
Ephraim went up a little later to the Passover. He was thus
present at three consecutive feasts, and the time of these feasts is
known — Tabernacles in October, Dedication in December, 782, and
Passover in April, 783; but where He was in the interval from

16*

Tabernacles to Dedication — October to December; or how long was
the interval between His journey beyond Jordan and His going up to
raise Lazarus; and how long his sojourn at Ephraim, we are not
told.   Had we John's narrative only, we should infer that He did not
return to Galilee at all after He went up to the Feast of Tabernacles.
His journey to this feast "not openly, but as it were in secret," six
months before His death, was the final departure from Galilee.

But we have still to examine the accounts of the Synoptists.
Matthew (xix. 1) mentions a departure from Galilee: "When Jesus
had finished these sayings, He departed from Galilee, and came into
the coasts of Judæa beyond Jordan."   Mark says (x. 1): "And
He arose from thence, and cometh into the coasts of Judæa by the
farther side of Jordan."   Without entering now into a particular
examination of these statements, we find mention here of a departure
from Galilee, and the only one mentioned by them; but there is nothing to indicate the time of the departure, and the events mentioned
as taking place after it and before His arrival at Jericho are very few.
(Matt. xix. 2. — xx. 28; Mark x. 1–45.)   Turning to Luke we find no
mention in so many words of a departure from Galilee, but a statement equivalent to it (ix. 51): "And it came to pass when the time
was come that He should be received up, He steadfastly set His face
to go to Jerusalem."   That the starting point of this journey was in
Galilee cannot be doubted; and the words clearly imply that, knowing
the time of His death and ascension to be at hand, He left Galilee and
went up to Jerusalem to suffer and die.   That this was not intention
only, is shown by the context: "He sent messengers before His face,
and they went," etc.   This, therefore, seems to have been the final
departure from Galilee, and the same as the departure spoken of by
Matthew and Mark.   But is it to be identified with that to the Feast
of Tabernacles (John vii. 10)?   Although the identification is accepted
by many, the arguments for it are insufficient.   They are in substance
these; that the Lord did not, so far as is said in John, return to
Galilee after the Feast of Tabernacles, and if He had done so, John
would have mentioned it; that the Lord went up "as in secret" by
avoiding the pilgrim caravans, and taking the route through Samaria;
and that much that Luke relates after ix. 51 took place earlier in
Galilee, showing that he does not speak of a continuous journey.

But, on the other hand, there are very strong objections to this identification; we mention some of the most important.   (a.) The Lord
refused to go up with His brethren (John vii. 6): "My time is not
yet come.   .   .   .   Go ye up unto this feast; I go not up yet unto
this feast; for my time is not yet full come.")   This solemn assur-

ance: "My time is not yet full come, but your time is always ready," must mean more than that they would go up two or three days before Him. The reference is clearly to the time of His suffering, and to the Messianic manifestation that should precede it. He would show Himself openly to the world in Judæa as His brethren desired, but not till the time appointed of God had come; till then He must avoid publicity. And this time was when, the Passover drawing near when He must suffer, He steadfastly set His face to go to Jerusalem.

(b.) The manner of the two journeys is wholly unlike. According to Luke, He goes with great publicity, accompanied by the apostles and probably other disciples, so that it is necessary to send messengers before Him "to make ready for Him"; according to John, "not publicly, but as it were in secret." That He went by way of Samaria is no indication that He sought privacy by avoiding the train of Galilæan pilgrims, for Josephus expressly says (Antiq., xx. 6. 1) that it was the custom of Galilæan feast-pilgrims to take their journeys through the country of the Samaritans. (But see Edersheim, ii. 131.) In this last journey He was preceded by the Seventy (Luke x. 1), whose words announcing the kingdom of God as at hand, must have called general attention to Him; and in fact He was followed by crowds of people. "Great multitudes followed Him" (Matt. xix. 2).

(c.) According to John, He went from Galilee to Jerusalem very rapidly, since, leaving after His brethren had gone, He appeared there about the middle of the feast. There is nothing in Luke to imply such rapidity, rather that He went slowly, following the Seventy, making wide circuits, and passing through many villages, teaching and working miracles.

On these grounds we must refuse to identify the journey of Luke (ix. 51) with that of John (vii. 10), and must accept the judgment of Neander (303, note) that "the two accounts are utterly in conflict."[1]

Whether a return to Galilee after Tabernacles. — If, then, we conclude that the departure in Luke (ix. 51) is not the same with the journey to the Feast of Tabernacles, it must have been later, and the Lord must, therefore, have returned to Galilee after that feast. When did He return ? On examining John's narrative, we find that He might have returned: 1st, after Tabernacles,

---

[1] So Bengel, DeWette, Greswell, Ebrard, Alford, Licht., Godet, Meyer, Baumgarten, Riggenbach, Lewin, Farrar, McClellan, Pressensé.

For their identity: Lightfoot, Robinson, Wieseler, Abp. Thomson, Friedlieb, M. and M., Caspari, Ellicott, Oosterzee, Gardiner, Edersheim, Fuller. It does not follow that all who identify the two look upon this journey to Tabernacles as the final departure from Galilee. Not a few hold that he did, after the feast, return there. So Lightfoot, Caspari, Abp. Thomson, Oosterzee.

either immediately or sometime in the interval between this feast and Dedication (John x. 22); 2d, after Dedication (John x. 39); 3d, after the sojourn in Ephraim (John xi. 54). Each of these times has its advocates. Which of these is to be preferred will be later considered.

It will help to give clearer conceptions of the points before us, if we examine several differing arrangements of the events from the Feast of Tabernacles to the arrival at Bethany six days before the last Passover. We have here a period of six months, which may be divided into two: from Tabernacles to Dedication, two months; from Dedication to last Passover, four months.

I. Arrangements which make no return to Galilee after the Feast of Tabernacles in October, His Galilæan ministry being completed.

Robinson: 1. The Lord goes up from Galilee to Tabernacles (Luke ix. 51, John vii. 10). On the way heals ten lepers (Luke xvii. 11). 2. After the feast, remains in Judæa; visits the house of Martha (Luke x. 38); the Seventy, sent out before He left Galilee, now return to Him at Jerusalem; heals the blind man there, and teaches. 3. In Jerusalem at Dedication. 4. Goes thence beyond Jordan where John baptized (John x. 40). 5. Goes up to Bethany to raise Lazarus. 6. Retires to Ephraim. 7. Leaves Ephraim to go to last Passover by way of Peræa and Jericho. It is this journey from Ephraim which is spoken of by Matt. xix. 1, Mark x. 1; and during it most of the events (Luke xiii. 10 to xviii. 35) took place.

Wieseler: 1. Goes up to Tabernacles (Luke ix. 51, John vii. 10), on the way sends the Seventy, and visits the house of Martha. 2. After the feast, remains till Dedication in Judæa. 3. Goes to Jerusalem to Dedication. 4. Goes to Peræa where John baptized. 5. Goes to Bethany to raise Lazarus (Luke xiii. 22 to xvii. 10). 6. Retires to Ephraim. 7. Leaves Ephraim for last Passover, and on the way heals the ten lepers. This is the same journey as Matt. xix. 1, and Mark x. 1, and Luke xvii. 11.

Gardiner: 1. Goes up to Tabernacles (Matt. xix. 1, Mark x. 1, Luke ix. 51, John vii. 10); unable to pass through Samaria, He enters Peræa, and on the way sends the Seventy; heals the ten lepers; visits Martha. 2. After the feast, returns to Peræa and teaches (Luke x. 17 to xiii. 17). 3. Goes up to Dedication. 4. After Dedication, retires beyond Jordan (Luke xiii. 22 to xvii. 10). 5. Goes up to Bethany to raise Lazarus. 6. Retires to Ephraim. 7. Goes up to Jerusalem to last Passover by Jericho (Luke xvii. 20 to xviii. 34).

II. Arrangements which make one return to Galilee after the Feast of Tabernacles.

(*a*) After Tabernacles and before Dedication.

Ebrard: 1. The Lord returns to Galilee. 2. Journeys to Tyre and Sidon; comes to Decapolis; feeds the four thousand. 3. Goes to Cæsarea Philippi; the Transfiguration; returns to Capernaum. 4. Goes up to Dedication (Luke ix. 51, John x. 22). 5. Retires beyond Jordan (Matt. xix. 1, Mark x. 1, John x. 40). 6. Goes up to raise Lazarus. 7. Returns to Ephraim. 8. Journeys to Jerusalem by Jericho.

Lichtenstein: 1. The Lord returns to Galilee. 2. Goes to Cæsarea Philippi, is transfigured, returns to Capernaum. 3. Leaves Galilee and goes by way of Samaria (Luke ix. 51); heals the ten lepers on the border of Samaria and Galilee; crosses the Jordan into Peræa; ministers there, and sends the Seventy. 4. Goes up to Dedication. 5. Returns to Peræa. 6. Goes to raise Lazarus. 7. Sojourns in Ephraim; and goes from there by Jericho to last Passover.

It will be noted that these two arrangements differ in this: that the first puts both the journey to Tyre and Sidon and that to Cæsarea Philippi after the Lord's return to Galilee; the last, only that to Cæsarea Philippi.

(*b*)   After Dedication.

Bengel: 1. The Lord goes to Galilee by way of Peræa, visits Cæsarea Philippi, is transfigured, returns to Capernaum. 2. Leaves Capernaum and goes by way of Samaria, crosses the Jordan into Peræa, from Peræa sends the Seventy, remains there preaching and teaching (Luke x. 25 to xviii. 14). 3. Goes up to raise Lazarus. 4. Retires to Ephraim. 5. Goes up by Jericho to last Passover.

McClellan: 1. The Lord returns to Capernaum, goes to Cæsarea Philippi, is transfigured, returns to Capernaum. 2. Goes through lower Galilee and along the confines of Samaria and Galilee to Peræa, and there teaches. 3. Goes up to raise Lazarus. 4. Retires to Ephraim. 5. From Ephraim returns to east side of the Jordan, and goes to last Passover by Jericho.

(*c*)   After the sojourn in Ephraim.

Pound: 1. Goes from Ephraim through Samaria into Galilee (Luke xvii. 11). 2. Goes into Peræa (Matt. xix. 13 to xx. 28). 3. Goes up to Jerusalem by Jericho.

III.   Arrangements which make two returns to Galilee after Tabernacles. One return after Tabernacles, and another after Dedication.

Caspari: 1. The Lord returns to Capernaum after Tabernacles, from there sends the Seventy. 2. Goes up to Dedication, visits Martha. 3. After Dedication, goes into Peræa (Matt. xix. 1, Mark x. 1). 4. Goes up to raise Lazarus. 5. Retires to Ephraim. 6. Journeys through the confines of Samaria to Galilee, heals the ten lepers, and goes to Jerusalem by way of Jericho.

Greswell: 1. The Lord returns to Capernaum after Tabernacles (of what He did at this time we have no account). 2. Goes up to Dedication. 3. Goes into Peræa. 4. Goes up to raise Lazarus. 5. Retires to Ephraim. 6. Goes into Galilee by way of Samaria, sends out the Seventy, goes to Capernaum where the Seventy rejoin Him. 7. Leaves Capernaum (Luke ix. 51), and goes up by Jericho to last Passover.

Edersheim, who puts no return to Galilee after Tabernacles, makes the Lord, after leaving Ephraim, to have passed on the border line of Galilee and Samaria, and to have healed the ten lepers.

In choosing among these several arrangements there is much difficulty; it must be a matter of probabilities, and it will be necessary to examine them somewhat in detail.

Arrangement which denies any return to Galilee after the Feast of Tabernacles.—(The fact that the Lord, after He left Ephraim, may have passed over the border into Galilee, is not important if He did not go there for any act of ministry.) If, then, His Galilæan work was completed when He went up to Tabernacles in October, there remained a period of two months to Dedication, and one of four months after it. How was this time from Tabernacles to Dedication spent? According to McClellan, in seclusion; according to Robinson, He taught in Judæa and Jerusalem; according to Gardiner, He went to Peræa and taught; according to Pound, He taught both in South Judæa and in Peræa.

Against the supposition that He spent this interval in Jerusalem or in Judæa, is the statement (John vii. 1) that "He would not walk in Jewry because the Jews sought to kill Him." The hatred of the Jews did not permit Him to remain in Judæa to teach; and on this ground He appears to have passed by several of the feasts. It is highly improbable, then, that after the reception He had met at the Feast of Tabernacles, when a formal attempt was made to arrest Him, and the populace had taken up stones to stone Him, He should have remained in Judæa till the next feast, exposed to their machinations.[1]

If the Lord remained after the feast to carry on a work in Judæa, of what nature was it? Was it a repetition of His earlier work of witness to the rulers? There is no hint of this, and they had long since arrayed themselves against Him. Was it a repetition of His work in Galilee, having for its end the gathering of disciples? There is no hint of this. It is not said that He went about teaching and preaching in the synagogues; all His public activity, so far as re-

---

[1] Luthardt. ii. 74; Lichtenstein. 299.

corded, both at this feast and at Dedication, was in the temple. At this time the Twelve were doubtless with Him, for at such a critical period He would not be separated from them; and their presence would have aroused in still greater degree the anger of the rulers, and prompted them to His immediate arrest while still in their power. If, then, for these reasons we cannot believe that the Lord carried on a Galilæan ministry in Jerusalem and Judæa, and if He could not have remained so long in seclusion unmolested, we must either hold that He began at this time His ministry in Peræa, or returned to Galilee. That He did not go to Peræa from Jerusalem, appears from the statement of Matthew xix. 1, that He went from Galilee to the region beyond Jordan. We conclude then, that the Lord had not finished His work in Galilee when He went up to the Feast of Tabernacles, and that He returned soon after it to Galilee.

Return after Tabernacles. — Accepting this return, we ask, What was the Lord's work in Galilee after His return ? Here there is not agreement among harmonists. The question is, where to find in the Synoptists a place to insert this journey to Tabernacles, and where to find in John a place to insert a return to Galilee. Of the two possible arrangements, one puts the journey to Tabernacles just before the circuit through Tyre and Sidon (in Matt. xv. after verse 20, in Mark vii. after verse 23). We thus obtain the following order: 1. The Lord returns from Tabernacles to Galilee. 2. Makes a circuit through Tyre and Sidon to the Decapolis. 3. Heals the man with an impediment in his speech; feeds the four thousand. 4. Goes to Dalmanutha; goes to Bethsaida, heals a blind man. 5. Goes to Cæsarea Philippi; Transfiguration. 6. Returns to Capernaum; pays temple tax. 7. Final departure from Galilee.

If we grant that there is nothing, so far as the language of Matthew and Mark is concerned, that forbids us to insert this journey to Tabernacles before the journey to Tyre and Sidon, yet there is a very strong objection from the fact that so little is recorded of the Lord's ministry during the period — some six months — from the Passover (John vi. 4) to the Feast of Tabernacles following in October. Matthew (xv. 1, ff.) and Mark (vii. 2, ff.) give the Lord's discourse to the Pharisees about eating with unwashen hands, which was soon after the feeding of the five thousand; and then speak of the circuit in Tyre and Sidon. We must, therefore, conclude, either that this circuit was before Tabernacles, or that several months passed of which the Synoptists say nothing; and the former is far the more probable.

If, then, we cannot put the journey to Tabernacles before the circuit in Tyre and Sidon, can we put it later? Such later period we find just before the circuit through Cæsarea Philippi, and inserting it in Matthew xvi. after verse 12, and in Mark viii. after verse 26; we obtain the following order: 1. The Lord returns from Tabernacles to Galilee. 2. Goes up to Cæsarea Philippi; the Transfiguration. 3. Returns to Capernaum, pays the temple tax. 4. Final departure from Galilee.

That this journey to Tabernacles may be inserted in Matthew at the place mentioned, is plain, there being nothing in the narrative to intimate strict chronological sequence. But in Mark such sequence is affirmed by many. His words are: "And Jesus went out and His disciples into the towns of Cæsarea Philippi." The phrase "went out"— ἐξῆλθεν — it is said, refers to His departure from the place just before mentioned — Bethsaida (verse 22); and as this was on the east of the Jordan, the inference is that He now went immediately up on the east side to Cæsarea Philippi. But it is observed by Alexander, *in loco :* "Neither Evangelist assigns the date of this transaction, even by connecting it expressly with the previous context as immediately successive. Into the towns dependent upon this important city, Jesus came with His disciples, when or whence is not recorded. 'Went out' throws no light upon this point, as it may refer to any going forth for any purpose, even from a private house, or from Capernaum, as the center of His operations, on a new official circuit."

We may, then, without violence, insert after the miracle at Bethsaida the journey to Tabernacles. The Lord returns from Bethsaida to Capernaum — an hour's walk — where He probably meets His brethren (John vii. 3), and from thence goes up to Jerusalem.

In all these questions Luke gives us no help, since he says nothing of the circuit in Tyre and Sidon, of the feeding of the four thousand, of the journey to Cæsarea; but passes at once from the feeding of the five thousand to the confession of Peter and the Transfiguration, and without any mention of the region where these occurred (Luke ix. 18).

But the point remains; Where in John's narrative can we insert this return to Galilee? It must be in ch. x. between verses 21 and 22. There seems to be no valid objection to this, as there is an interval of two months which this Evangelist passes over in silence (see Godet, *in loco*).

(In former editions of this book, the order was followed which makes the Lord to have returned to Galilee after Tabernacles, but only to send the Seventy, His ministry there having been completed. A more careful consideration leads to the conclusion that He went to

Tabernacles before His Galilæan ministry was ended, and that He returned to complete it.)

Return after Dedication.— But many affirm that the Lord did not go to Galilee after Tabernacles, but later, after Dedication. This order must therefore be examined. In this case we meet, first, the improbability that He remained all the interval from Tabernacles to Dedication in Jerusalem or Judæa. This has been already spoken of.

A second objection is found in the difficulty of inserting a journey to Galilee after Dedication in the narrative of John. The only place for it is in ch. x. after verse 39: "They sought again to take Him, but He escaped out of their hand, and went away again beyond Jordan." (In the R. V.: "He went forth out of their hand." Verse 40 begins a new paragraph. So in Greek text of Tisch., W. and H., and in several translations.) It is certainly possible to put here after His escape from Jerusalem a journey to Galilee, a ministry there of some duration, and a return to the Jordan; but the scope of the narrative is against it.

Those who hold this order are not agreed as to the Lord's work after He returned to Galilee; but most, as Stier, say that the circuit to Cæsarea Philippi then took place, the return to Capernaum, and the final departure to the last Passover. But so late a departure increases the difficulty of explaining the circuitous route, the Lord's visit to Martha at Bethany, and His presence later in "the midst of Samaria and Galilee."

Return after sojourn in Ephraim.—Again, as we have seen, some hold that the Lord returned to Galilee at a much later period — after the sojourn in Ephraim (John xi. 54) — to complete His ministry. The chief representative of this order is Greswell, who says (ii. 529), that "all the notices in Luke from ix. 51 to xvii. 11 belong to the course and continuance of one and the same journey, begun at Ephraim and terminated at Jerusalem, but visiting in the interim Galilee and Peræa also." This is the final departure from Galilee, and is that mentioned in Matt. xix. 1; Mark x. 1; Luke xvii. 11; and it is on this journey that He was accompanied by the women (Luke xxiii. 49). Edersheim agrees with Greswell in putting a return to Galilee after the sojourn in Ephraim; but it was not to resume His ministry there, only to meet His disciples and go up with them to the Passover.

But against this late return to Galilee there are strong objections. The retirement of the Lord to Ephraim was to escape the notice of His enemies, who had determined to put Him to death. It was clearly chosen as a hiding place, because they "had given a commandment,[1] that if any knew where He were, they should show it that they might take Him"; and we are told that "He continued there with His disciples." We cannot, therefore, suppose that He would engage in any public labors which would draw to Him the attention of His enemies; rather He would devote Himself to the instruction of those with Him — perhaps the Apostles only. As we do not know how soon after the Feast of Dedication the Lord went to Bethany to raise Lazarus, nor how soon after that resurrection He went to Ephraim, so we do not know how long was His sojourn there. The impression made by the narrative is that He left Ephraim only a short time before the Passover (verse 55): "Now the feast of the Passover was nigh at hand." This may mean that the feast was nigh at hand when Jesus went to Ephraim, or that He left Ephraim when it was nigh; but in either case it allows no time for a journey to Galilee, and for all the events which preceded His final departure from that province.

We thus seem to have sufficient grounds to reject the order advocated by Greswell, Sepp, and Caspari. The first of these puts the resurrection of Lazarus in December, very soon after the Feast of Dedication, the flight to Ephraim the last of December, the sojourn there a month, or to the end of January, and then a departure to Galilee. (So in substance Sepp and Caspari.) But if the Lord went to Galilee at the end of January, and was for some weeks active there, and sent the Seventy from Capernaum; how could those who went up from Galilee to the Passover have been ignorant of His work there, and of the sending of the Seventy, and that He was already following them on His way to Jerusalem — to say nothing of the ignorance of the chief priests and Pharisees? (John xi. 55–57.)

There is still another objection to this order. If the words of Luke (ix. 51): "He steadfastly set His face to go to Jerusalem," are applied, as by Greswell, to His departure from Ephraim, and Ephraim was in Judæa on its northern border, the first stage of His journey was not southward to Jerusalem, but northward to Galilee. But if going from Jerusalem and not to it, why did the Samaritans refuse to receive Him? Greswell gives the very insufficient answer, that they knew, indeed, that He was journeying toward Galilee, but knew also that He was "to commence a public tour from there" back to Jerusalem. But the statement is perfectly plain that they refused to receive Him because He was going up to Jerusalem. And how did they know what His intentions were as to His return?

---

[1] Tisch., W. and H. read ἐντολάς, "commandments," perhaps orders sent to different parts of the land. See M. and M., in loco.

We must reject, then, the arrangement which denies any return to Galilee after Tabernacles; and of those which affirm such a return either after Tabernacles and before Dedication, or after Dedication, or after the sojourn in Ephraim, we accept the first as most probable, and put the final departure from Galilee a few days before the Feast of Dedication.

THE LAST JOURNEY.

Let us now note the general features of this last journey — its starting point and goal, its continuity, by whom the Lord was attended, the mission of the Seventy, the crowds that gathered to Him, the opposition of His enemies, and the character of his teachings.

Its starting point and goal. — It is generally admitted that the starting point was Capernaum; the goal was Jerusalem. Two ways were open to Him: through Samaria, or along the Jordan valley; and He took the former. To reach Samaria from Capernaum, He must pass through lower Galilee on its eastern side. The Samaritan village which refused to receive His messengers was probably one on the frontier; the ground of rejection being that His face was as though He would go to Jerusalem. Whither did He then turn? We are told simply that "they went to another village." Was this village in Samaria or Galilee?[1] Assuming that it was in Galilee, what was the Lord's further course? Certainly He did not turn back to Galilee, but kept on His course, either southward into Samaria, or eastward along the border line of the two provinces, so crossing the Jordan into Peræa; from whence when the time came, He might go up to Jerusalem.

Its continuity. — Was this last journey continuous? By this is not meant that He went forward every day nearer and nearer to Jerusalem; but that, having ended His work in Galilee, and Jerusalem being the goal of His journey, all His steps were determined by this chief end. It is true that in Luke we find few data as to times or places. The first local notice is that of "a certain village" (x. 38), where He visits Martha; then we read of His being in "a certain place" where He gave the disciples a form of prayer (xi. 1). Still later we have the general statement that "He went through the cities and villages, teaching, and journeying towards Jerusalem" (xiii. 22); and the more particular one, "and it came to pass as He came to Jerusalem that He passed through the midst of Samaria and Galilee" (xvii. 11). A little before His arrival at Jericho "He took unto Him

---

[1] Most commentators say in Galilee: Meyer, Godet, Edersheim; *contra*, Bleek; undecided, Keil; this point will be further spoken of when considering the mission of the Seventy.

the twelve, and said unto them: 'Behold we go up to Jerusalem'" (xviii. 31). Another note of place is given in the words of the Phari-sees: "Get thee out, and depart hence" (xiii. 31), showing that He must have been at that time in Herod's dominions, in Galilee or Peræa. But although we have so few data of time or place, yet all these statements agree in this, that the Lord, enlightened by the Father, and knowing that His decease should be accomplished at Jerusalem, and during the Passover, so directed His steps that He might fulfill His Father's will.

We must, then, regard this last journey as a continuous one, with a definite purpose and a progressive movement beginning in Galilee and ending in Jerusalem. Thus it is said by Meyer: "It is to be con-ceived of as a slow circuit whose final goal is Jerusalem."

The Lord's attendants.—By whom was the Lord attended on this journey? Certainly by the Apostles, and perhaps by the other dis-ciples. It is said by Godet that "Jesus carried with Him to Judæa all the following of devoted believers which He had found in Gali-lee"; but this is too broad. Was He also attended by the women spoken of by Matthew (xxvii. 51), "which followed Him from Galilee, ministering unto Him"? This is questioned by Edersheim (ii. 327), who affirms, that "any lengthened journeying, and for an indefinite purpose, would have been quite contrary to Jewish man-ners"; and he suggests that their accompanying Him was not till He left Ephraim, and went to Galilee to meet the festal bands going up to the Paschal Feast. But the words of Luke (viii. 2, 3), and of Mark (xv. 41), speaking of the women, who, when He was in Galilee, followed Him and ministered unto Him, serve to show that they were with Him at other times than in journeys to the feasts. And some of the women were doubtless the wives or mothers of the apostles or disciples (1 Cor. ix. 5). It is not, then, improbable that His mother and other female relatives, and female relatives of the disciples, and probably some of those whom He had healed, as Mary Magdalene, went with Him when He finally left Galilee.

The sending of the Seventy.—But the sending of the Seventy before Him is, as has been said, the most marked feature of this last journey. "After these things the Lord appointed other Seventy also, and sent them two and two before His face into every city and place whither He Himself would come" (Luke x. 1). What was His pur-pose in sending them before Him? When and from what place did He send them? Where did they fulfill their mission? And when and where did they return to Him?

Their commission.—The end for which they were sent forth was, as expressed in their commission (verse 9), to proclaim "The king-

dom of God is come nigh unto you"; and as an evidence of this, to
heal the sick in such cities as should receive them.   What was the
significance of this proclamation?   Was it merely the repetition of
what had been preached by the Baptist, by the Lord, and by the
apostles: "The kingdom of heaven is at hand"?   Did it not, rather,
derive a peculiar character from the relation in which the mission of
the Seventy stood to His last journey?   The apostles had earlier been
sent "to the lost sheep of the house of Israel" without distinction
(Matthew x. 6); but these were directed to go only to those "cities
and places whither He Himself would come."   The Seventy were to
go before Him as His heralds or forerunners; and it seems clear that
they did not merely announce in general terms that the kingdom of
God was at hand, but made a specific mention of Jesus who was to
follow them as the King.   They were to give notice that the Messiah was coming, and that in those places only which He had chosen.
What determined the Lord's choice of those cities and places we are
not told, but we may believe that He went only to those where His
heralds found reception.   "The Twelve apostles were sent to declare
the coming of the kingdom, these the coming of the King."   (Lightfoot, *in loco*.)   Jesus was soon to follow them on His way to the Holy
City; and thus the eyes of all who heard them were turned to Him,
not as a great Rabbi or Teacher, or as a Prophet, but as the long-
promised Son of David and Redeemer of Israel.

Time and place of their sending.— Such being the purpose of the
mission, when and from what place were the Seventy sent?   The time
of their sending depends upon the time of the final departure from
Galilee, for all agree that it was a little before or after that departure
that the Lord sent them.   The place from which they were sent,
whether from Galilee, or from some point on the way to Jerusalem,
or from the city itself, is clearly connected with the time.   We may
give the following classification of opinions: 1. From Capernaum,
and before going up to the Feast of Tabernacles.   Robinson, Newcome, Pound.   2. After the departure from Galilee, and on the way
to Tabernacles.   Lightfoot, Wieseler, Friedlieb, Gardiner, Edersheim.   3. In the interval between Tabernacles and Dedication.   (a.)
From Jerusalem, Krafft; (b.) from Judæa, Ellicott; (c.) from Galilee,
Caspari, Farrar, Neander, Pressensé; (d.) from Peræa, Bengel.   4.
After sojourn at Ephraim, and from Capernaum, Greswell.[1]

Whither sent.— Whither were the Seventy sent?   It may be said
that they were to precede Him all the way to Jerusalem, and there-

---

[1] McClellan (453 ff.), who puts the sending of the Seventy soon after the sending of
the Twelve (Luke ix. 1), and brings it into no relation with the last journey, thinks the
field of their mission to have been Galilee; so, apparently, Calvin.

fore would fulfill their mission in each province through which He
passed till He reached the city. We may accept this, and yet ask
after the more special field of their activity. Was it Galilee?[1] It
is, indeed, not unlikely, if we suppose the Lord to have sent them
from Capernaum, that they preceded Him through lower Galilee, and
announced His coming; but there is no mention of any Galilæan
town as now visited by Him. It is most probable that the woes on
the Galilæan cities with which their commission ends, were spoken
when He was about to leave Galilee; but the Lord may have added
them as an example of like judgment to come upon the cities that
rejected His messengers. It seems, therefore, very doubtful whether
the Seventy were sent out till the Lord was leaving, or had finally left
Galilee.

Did the Lord send them into Samaria? This is said by some.
(So Wieseler, Lange, Cook.) Godet says: "He intended to do a
work in the north of Samaria like that which had succeeded so
admirably in the south." It is true that in their commission they
were not forbidden, as were the apostles, to enter Samaria; but nevertheless the nature of their message makes it most improbable that
they would proclaim it in the Samaritan cities. (So Robinson and
most.) They were to announce that the kingdom in the person of
the King was at hand. Such announcement could be made to those
only who were already familiar with the Jewish conceptions of the
Messiah, and friendly to them. But the Messianic expectations of the
Samaritans were not those of the Jews, for, as they accepted the law
only as Divinely inspired, not the prophets, they knew nothing of
the promises made to the Son of David.[2] Nor did the welcome they
gave to the Lord in the first stage of His ministry (John iv. 39)
prove their willingness now to receive Him as the Jewish Messiah.[3]
Besides this ignorance of the true nature of His Messiahship, He had
been already rejected in Samaria by the rejection of His messengers,
and for the reason that His face was turned to Jerusalem. Meyer
quotes Weiss with approval: "Of any appointment of the Seventy
for Samaria, or for the heathen world at all, there is not a single
word said."

Were the Seventy sent to Judæa? The commentators, Maldonatus

---

[1] Sepp thinks that they were sent before the Lord as He journeyed into the regions
of Tyre and Sidon, and of the Decapolis (Matthew xv. 21). But we must remember that
the Lord's work in Galilee was at this time finished, and He was about to leave it, and
that the Seventy were not sent to the heathen.

[2] Hamburger, ii. 1,063; Lightfoot, on John iv. 25.

[3] The reading of the A. V.: "We know that this is indeed the Christ, the Saviour
of the world," in the R. V. is, "We know that this is indeed the Saviour of the
world." John iv. 42. (So Tisch., W. and H.)

and a Lapide, make Judæa the place of their labors, as Galilee had been that of the Apostles. (With them agree Ellicott, Oosterzee, and others.) Considered as a testimony to the Messianic claims of Jesus, their mission would have found in Judæa — the seat of the hierarchy — its most fitting field; but the Lord had been compelled to leave that province long before because the ecclesiastical rulers sought to kill Him (John vii. 1), and their hostility was shown anew at the Feasts of Tabernacles and Dedication. It is not likely, therefore, that He sent them to cities where He could not follow them without endangering His life, not to speak of the improbability that they would have been allowed to deliver their message. And it is not intimated that He visited any part of Judæa during this last journey except when going to Bethany (Luke x. 38; John xi. 1), or that the Seventy went there; but if their mission was of necessity executed elsewhere, it was doubtless well known in Judæa and the Holy City, and served its purpose as a witness.

Were they sent to Peræa? As all are agreed that this was the chief region of our Lord's labors in this last stage of His ministry, the strong presumption is that they would go before Him there. And this is made certain by the statements of Matthew and Mark, which will be examined later.

We conclude, then, that the mission of the Seventy was chiefly fulfilled in Peræa, though we cannot tell what parts of it they visited. If the Lord, after His rejection in Samaria, passed along its north border eastward, and crossed the Jordan near Bethshean, they may have preceded Him into north Peræa. How far to the northeast or south they went is mere conjecture; there were many large towns east of the Dead Sea, some of which they may have visited.

Their return.—We have still to ask, When and to what place did the Seventy return? In Luke (x. 17) their return is mentioned in immediate connection with their sending forth, but some considerable interval must have elapsed; how long was this interval depends upon the manner of their mission. Were they all sent at once, and from one place, or two by two, at different times, and from different places? In the former case, did the Lord wait in the place from which they were sent till all returned to Him, and then begin His circuit after them, or did He follow those first sent, and then the rest, in the order of their return? The last seems most probable. Meyer says, "Some must have returned very soon, others later." We can scarce doubt that the Lord made known to them the names of the cities and places He would visit (A. V.: "whither He Himself would come"; R. V.: "was about to come"), and these in some definite order; and it is probable that He would visit the nearest first, and the more remote later, but always advancing towards Jerusalem. But this order might be broken in two ways: first, by the refusal of a city to receive the messengers; second, by the hostility of the Pharisees preventing Him from following them. That ultimately all the Seventy rejoined Him, we learn, but when and where we are not told. It may have been after Dedication, and at that place beyond Jordan where He abode (John x. 40). After all had returned to him, he spake to them the words in Luke x. 17-24.

Effect of their mission.—Such a mission must, in the nature of the case, have excited a very wide and deep interest throughout the whole country, for He was now everywhere well known, and all knew the goal of His journey. That such interest was awakened is shown by the crowds that gathered to Him and accompanied Him. Matthew says (xix. 2): "Great multitudes followed Him." Mark says (x. 1): "The people"—ὄχλοι—"multitudes"—"resort unto Him again." Luke says (xi. 29): "When the people were gathered thick together." Again (xii. 1): "When there were gathered together an innumerable multitude of people, insomuch that they trode one upon another." ("The many thousands of the multitude," R. V.) Again (xiv. 25): "And there went great multitudes with Him." This language, perhaps, warrants us in saying, that at no previous period of His ministry had such crowds gathered to hear Him, or such intense excitement prevailed.

It is obvious that through such concourse of the people His enemies would be even more inflamed against Him, and aroused to take more active measures to destroy Him. Their emissaries would follow Him from place to place, and watch carefully all His acts and words, to find some new grounds of accusation against Him as breaking the law, or to turn His teachings into ridicule, and so discredit them. How often during this journey He came into hostile contact with the Pharisees and their allies, will be seen in our examination of the narratives.

Character of His teaching.—If the object of the Lord in sending the Seventy was to bring before the people His Messianic claims, His teachings would naturally take upon themselves a corresponding character. And this was the case, as we shall by and by see. That there was a very strong and general belief among the people that the Lord would avow Himself the Messiah when He reached Jerusalem, and there proclaim the Messianic kingdom, there can be no doubt (Luke xix. 11). A large part of His teachings related, directly or indirectly, to this kingdom. But the public mind was not assured. While He distinctly claimed to be the Messiah, His acts did not at all correspond to the popular expectation. He did not

ınflame men's hearts against the Roman yoke, or take any stcps look
ıng to its overthrow.   He made no overtures to the Pharisees, and
what could He do without their help?   His words were often very
mysterious, and we cannot wonder that at the Feast of Dedication
the Jews should say to Him: "How long dost Thou make us to
doubt?   If Thou be the Christ, tell us plainly."   Still those who saw
in Him a possible Messiah, though they understood Him not — probably a large number — must have had their hopes quickened and
strengthened during this last journey.   And even His apostles,
though plainly told of His approaching death, were so far affected
by the popular excitement and under the power of the current
Messianic beliefs, that they could not understand His words about
His rejection and sufferings, but believed that as a reward for their
fidelity high places would soon be given them in His kingdom
(Matt. xix. 27; xx. 20).

NOVEMBER — DECEMBER, 782.   A. D. 29.

The time when He should be received up approaching,
the Lord sets His face to go to Jerusalem.   He sends mes-   LUKE ix. 51–56.
sengers before Him, who, entering into a Samaritan village,
are rejected by the inhabitants.   He reproves His angry
disciples, James and John, and departs to another village.
He replies to one who proposes to follow Him.   He now   LUKE ix. 61, 62.
sends out seventy of His disciples, to go two and two into   LUKE x. 1–24.
every city and place where He Himself would come.   They   MATT. xi. 20–30.
depart, and return from time to time as they fulfill their   MATT. xix. 1.
commission.   He follows in their steps, journeying through   MARK x. 1.
Peræa toward Jerusalem.

Having already discussed the statements of the Evangelists
respecting the Lord's last journey, in their general features, we
have here to deal only with details.

Some have thought to find a chronological datum in His
words: "When the time was come that He should be received
up" — ἐν τῷ συμπληροῦσθαι τὰς ἡμέρας.   If it be read as mean·
ing, "when the days were entirely completed," the Passover at
which He suffered must have been close at hand.   But the
words are generally understood as meaning that the time of His
passion was approaching, but not giving any definite indication
how near.[1]   We cannot, therefore, find in this, a specific chron·

---

[1] So Norton: "When the time was near for His being received into heaven."   In
the R. V.: "When the days were well-nigh come": in margin: "were being fulfilled."
In Bleek, der Zeit war nahe, stand bevor, kam heran.   See Gardiner, 129, note ; and
Godet, *in loco*.

ological datum.   The view of Wieseler (Syn., 324), that "the being received up"— τῆς ἀναλήμψεως — refers to His favorable reception by the Galilæans, and that the meaning is, "When He no longer found Himself received in Galilee, He left that province and went up to Jerusalem to labor there," is very arbitrary and finds little support.[1]   The messengers sent before Him to the Samaritan village are said by some early writers to have been the two Apostles, James and John, but without authority, traditional or otherwise.   The village where He was rejected is thought by many to be the present Ginnea or Jenin, situated upon the north border of Samaria, and overlooking the plain of Esdraelon.   It is mentioned by Josephus (Antiq., xx. 6. 1) as the place where some pilgrims at a later period, going up to the feast, were attacked and killed.   It is probable that the road from Nazareth to Jerusalem always passed this way (Baed., 343), and as a frontier town it might have been the first reached by the Lord.[2]

It is not certain that the Lord passed out of Galilee into Samaria at all.   Very probably He waited on the border till the return of His messengers.   The "other village" to which they went was not in Samaria.   (So Meyer.)

The intentions to follow the Lord expressed by the three men (Luke ix. 57–62), suit very well this beginning of the last journey, but Matthew mentions the like intentions of two men just before the journey to Gergesa (viii. 19–22).   As it is improbable that the Lord would have repeated the same words on two such occasions, many say that Luke inserts verses 57–60 out of the chronological order.[3]   Matthew certainly gives the incidents a more definite setting, but it is probable that the man mentioned in verses 61, 62, met the Lord on this last journey. That the three here spoken of were Judas Iscariot, and Thomas, and Matthew (Lange), or that one of them was Philip (Godet), are merely traditional conjectures.

---

[1] See his Beiträge, 130; *contra*, Meyer and Bleek, *in loco*, and Edersheim, vol. ii. 128.

[2] So Licht., Farrar, and many others.   Maldonatus thinks the village to have been Samaria, the capital, but this is too far from the border, and was a city while this is called a village.

[3] So Meyer, Bleek, Lange, Licht., Rob.; *contra*, Tisch., Neander, Gardiner, Fuller, and, in substance, Godet.   In favor of Luke's order it may be said that the Lord's words : "The Son of man has not where to lay His head," better apply to this journey than to His residence in Galilee.

That the number of the Seventy was not an arbitrary one but had some significance, is apparent. Some think it to correspond to the "seventy elders" (Numbers xi. 16); and others find an allusion to the later Sanhedrin; Godet supposes that the Lord may have constituted an anti-Sanhedrin, as in the twelve apostles he finds new spiritual patriarchs set over against the twelve sons of Jacob. This is fanciful. Others find in the number a reference to the belief that there were seventy heathen nations (Gen. x. 32), and see in the mission now set forth a foreshadowing of the preaching of the Gospel to all nations.[1] That there is some prophetic reference in the mission of the Seventy to a preaching of the gospel of the kingdom before the Lord's return in glory, is probable; but analogy leads us to refer it to those in covenant, rather than to the heathen. (Winer, i. 569; Licht., 327.)

We have already referred to the various opinions respecting the time when, and the place whence, the Seventy were sent. If we accept Luke as here following the order of events, this sending was after the rejection in Samaria. If He then journeyed along the border eastward, He may have chosen and sent them before He reached the Jordan valley, or soon after He entered Peræa. We know, at least, that the chief region of their mission was beyond Jordan, and it will be in place here briefly to describe this region.

PROVINCE OF PERÆA.

Peræa is mentioned in the gospels (Matt. iv. 25) under the term "beyond Jordan"—πέραν τοῦ Ἰορδάνου; in Mark x. 1, translated "The farther side of Jordan." But there is here question as to the text. Mark (x. 1) says: "He arose from thence, and cometh into the coasts of Judæa by the further side of Jordan." In R. V.: He cometh into the borders of Judæa and beyond Jordan. (So Tisch., W. and H.) Is "beyond Jordan" to be taken as the name of Peræa, as in iii. 8 ? In this case the Lord would have gone from Galilee to Judæa, and thence over the Jordan. But it may be understood, He cometh to Judæa by way of beyond Jordan, or by Peræa (so Meyer, Keil, and most). But there is another interpretation of the words.

---

[1] So Bleek, Wieseler, and many; *contra*, Meyer, who denies any reference to the Gentile nations. As to the Jewish offering of the seventy bullocks at the Feast of Tabernacles, according to the number of the nations, see Lightfoot on John vii. 37.

It is said by Caspari (89) that the district mentioned in Joshua xix.
34, "Judah at Jordan", is to be identified with the ancient Gaulanitis or modern Jolan, and was north of the Sea of Galilee. (For earlier
discussion see Reland, 33; later, see Riehm, 789.) Thomson (ii. 391)
finds a place on the easternmost branch of the Jordan, now called Seid
Yehudah, which he thinks to have been in Judæa beyond Jordan.
It is to this district, not to Peræa, that Caspari supposes Matthew
and Mark to refer.

The west border of Peræa was the Jordan; on the east its border
was undefined;[1] on the north it extended to the Jarmuk; on the
south, to the Arnon, a length of some sixty miles. Its capital,
according to Josephus, was Gadara (War, iv. 7. 3). It is distinguished by Matthew (iv. 25) from the Decapolis. It was a part
of the territory of Herod Antipas, and Machærus, where John was
imprisoned, was in the southern part of it. Josephus speaks of it
as larger than Galilee, but not so fertile. Modern travellers, however,
speak of the great richness of the soil, especially in the central part
known as Gilead. Tristram (B. P. 335) says: "None can fairly judge
of Israel's heritage who has not seen the luxuriance of Gilead. To
compare Judæa with it is to contrast nakedness and luxuriance."[2]
That it was filled in the Lord's day with cities and villages is certain,
though none are mentioned by name in the Gospels, and many ruined
places are still to be seen on the east bank of the Jordan. The population was not purely Jewish, but rather a mixed one; not so largely
heathen as in the Decapolis, and not likely to be so easily stirred up
against the Lord as the inhabitants of Judæa, or even of Galilee.[3]
It, therefore, presented, in some respects, a better field for His present activity, though we can hardly agree with Pressensé, that "it
offered to Him the quiet retreat which He could no longer find in
Galilee." As the population was in some degree a mixed one, the
Lord would find less of bigoted opposition than in Judæa or even
than in Galilee, while it was so near these provinces that information
of all His movements would soon be known in them. We may infer
that the spirit of the people in general was friendly, since many came
to hear Him, remembering John's words respecting Him; "And
many believed on Him there."

The central point of the Lord's activity after the Feast of Dedi-

---

[1] According to Josephus, War, iii. 3. 3, it reached to Arabia, Gerasa, and Philadelphia.

[2] See also Oliphant's " Land of Gilead."

[3] See Neubauer, page 241, who quotes the Rabbins that Judæa was the wheat, Gal
ilee, chaff, Peræa, tares; and adds that there were many long discussions whether the
trans-Jordanic region enjoyed all the religious privileges belonging to Judæa and Galilee.

cation was at "the place where John at first baptized." It is said
"that there He abode — ἔμεινεν — and many resorted unto Him"
(John x. 40, 41). This did not hinder Him from going from place
to place following the Seventy, but we may infer that the zeal of His
enemies hampered in some degree the freedom of His movements.
So far as we know, the place where John at first baptized was Bethabara, the site of which has already been discussed. If we place it a
little northeast of Jericho, it would have given a central and convenient point from which to visit the various towns in the province. If
He came hither from Galilee, crossing the Jordan at Bethshean, or
some ford higher up, and descended the river, there were many
places He might have visited in northern Peræa, following the
Seventy, before He reached Bethabara. But it is idle to attempt to
mark out their route, and to inquire to what cities they may have
gone.

November — December, 782.   A. D.   29.

During the journey through Peræa, the Lord is attended   MATT. xix. 2.
by great multitudes, whom He teaches and heals. Upon   MARK x. 1.
the way He is tempted by a lawyer, who asks Him how   LUKE x. 25–37.
he shall inherit eternal life. In reply, He relates the
parable of the Good Samaritan. One of His disciples asks   LUKE xi. 1–13.
for a form of prayer. He gives Him the form, and adds
some remarks on the right method of prayer.

The Lord was now entering upon a field of labor almost new,
and yet prophetically foretold — πέραν τοῦ Ἰορδάνου, "beyond
Jordan" (Isaiah ix. 1, 2). Four districts are spoken of by the
prophet: 1. Zebulon, Lower Galilee; 2. Naphtali, Upper Galilee
(these are more particularly designated by the words following
— "way of the sea," or "seawards"); 3. Beyond Jordan, Peræa;
4. Galilee of the Gentiles, the northern border of Galilee
adjacent to the Gentile provinces. (See Meyer and Keil, in loco.)
Comparatively few in Peræa, we may believe, had seen or heard
Him; and the announcement of the Seventy that He was about
to follow them, would naturally call general attention to His
movements, and gather great crowds around Him. It is apparent, also, that the peculiar character of this journey gave
new impulse to the prevalent Messianic expectations. It is
mentioned by Matthew (xix. 2) in general terms, that He healed,
but no specific cases are given. Mark speaks only of teaching.

We have no data to determine when the inquiry of the

lawyer was made. It may have been early in the journey, while the Lord was yet on the border of Samaria; and His reply derives a special significance from the fact that He Himself had just been rejected by the Samaritans; or it may have been a little later, when He was on His way to the Feast of Dedication, and was near Jericho. Still, the bitter hostility of the Jews to the Samaritans would have given point to the parable, wherever He may have been.

Luke (xi. 1) introduces the request for a form of prayer, with the remark, that "as He was praying in a certain place, when He ceased, one of His disciples said unto Him," etc. From this it has been inferred by some (as Oosterzee and Godet) that the incident stands here in its historical connection, and is inserted by Matthew out of its place in the Sermon on the Mount (vi. 9–13); and they find in its brevity proof that it was spoken as given by Luke. It certainly appears more probable that it should be given in answer to a disciple than spoken to the multitude; and if it had been spoken on that occasion, it might have simply been referred to here. Still, many make it to have been original in Matthew, and repeated here; and others, as Alford, that it stands in close connection with what goes before in both Evangelists. Tholuck takes the distinction, that in the first instance it was generally given, but in the latter as a specific form. The difference of expression in the two cases is explained by the fact that Luke gives here, as often, a less complete report of Christ's words. (See Keil, *in loco.*)

NOVEMBER — DECEMBER, 782.   A. D. 29.

The Lord heals a dumb possessed man. The Pharisees accuse Him of casting out the devils through Beelzebub.	LUKE xi. 14–28
He replies to them, and while He is speaking a woman in the crowd blesses Him. He continues to discourse to the	LUKE xi. 27–36.
multitude on the desire for signs. He dines with a Pharisee, and sharply rebukes Pharisaical hypocrisy. The Pharisees	LUKE xi. 37–54.
sees are greatly enraged, a great crowd gathers, and He	LUKE xii. 1–12.
proceeds to address the disciples, admonishing them to beware of the leaven of the Pharisees, and to fear God only.	LUKE xii. 13–22.
One of those present desires of Him that He will make his brother divide the inheritance with him. He denies his request, and speaks the parable of the rich fool. He ad-	LUKE xii. 22–53.

monishes the disciples to watch for the coming of the Son
of Man, and, after answering a question of Peter, proceeds   LUKE xii. 54–59.
to address the people respecting their inability to discern
the signs of the times.

The relation of this miracle of the dumb possessed and of
the discourse following it, to the healing mentioned by Matthew
(xii. 22), and the discourse there given, has been already discussed (p. 287).   Most agree that Luke has placed them here
out of their historical connections.[1]   Tischendorf identifies this
healing with the miracle in Matt. ix. 32–34, but regards it
rightly placed here.   Greswell strongly insists that this account
is wholly distinct from those in Matthew and Mark.   It being
impossible to come to any certain result, and as it is at least possible that Matthew relates another case of healing and another
discourse, we will follow Luke's order.   (See Godet and Keil,
in loco.)   In regard to the rebukes of the Pharisees by the Lord,
spoken at the house of a Pharisee (verses 37–52), we cite the
just observation of Alford, that He " spoke at this meal parts of
that discourse with which He afterward solemnly closed His
public ministry."

That Jesus should have been invited by a Pharisee to dine
with him, or rather to breakfast with him, when the sect in
general was so hostile to Him, may have been owing to the
desire to have one so famous for a guest, or perhaps to a true
impulse of hospitality; but more probably with evil intention,
hoping to entrap Him.   This better agrees with the seeming
abruptness and sharpness of the Lord's words.   (See, however,
contra, Edersheim, ii. 205, and his observations upon the Jewish
rules of etiquette at table.)   The severity of His language seems
directed rather against Pharisaism than against the individuals
then present, except so far as their consciences should compel a
self-application.   The sins are rebuked which were characteristic
of that party.   The lawyer (xi. 45) makes a distinction between
his class and the Pharisees in general, as if the former were a
kind of higher order, a learned aristocracy.   That the Lord
touched his hearers to the quick is apparent from their vehement attempts to entangle Him by their questions.

---

[1] So Robinson, Alford, Lichtenstein.

It is said by Godet that verses 53, 54 describe "a scene of violence probably unique in the life of Jesus." If we suppose the Pharisee to have resided in some city which had been visited by two of the Seventy, and in which were many Pharisees and scribes, who had been excited by their message, and perhaps had gathered their adherents from the neighboring towns, we may better understand the narrative. The "innumerable multitude" (R. V.: "The many thousands of the multitude"), composed in part of the citizens, and in part of the crowds that were following Him, so many that in their eagerness "they trode one upon another," seems to have been much like a modern mob. That the feeling in general was hostile to the Lord may be inferred from His words addressed to His friends (xii. 4): "Be not afraid of them that kill the body."

In regard to the discourses found in this chapter (Luke xii.), it is impossible to say whether they have their right place here or in Matthew, or whether the Lord may not have repeated them. A considerable part is found in the Sermon on the Mount as given by Matthew (vi. 25 ff.); and another part in the last discourse on the Mount of Olives (xxiv. 42 ff.); and still another in the commission given to the Twelve (x. 34 ff.); and smaller portions elsewhere. As Matthew brings together in his report of the discourse much that was beyond doubt spoken at other times, we are inclined to believe that Luke here in the main follows the order of events. (See Oosterzee, *in loco*; also Alford.)

We may ask here in what way the disciples understood the Lord's instructions to watch for His return (verses 35–40). He had spoken to them after His transfiguration of His death and resurrection, and of His coming in glory (Matt. xvi. 21–27). And at Jerusalem (John vii. 33, 34) He had spoken of a going away: "I go unto Him that sent me; ye shall seek me, and not find me." But neither the disciples nor the Jews understood what this departure was (Luke xviii. 34; John viii. 22), nor did they connect His return with the resurrection. Probably the Jewish belief, though very vaguely held, that the Messiah would come, and then be hidden for a time, and then reappear as King, may have helped to explain His words; and perhaps also His appearance on the Mount of Transfiguration, showing that a

change was to pass upon Him before He entered upon His kingdom, may have been understood by the three apostles present
as pointing to a departure and return.   But evidently if the
disciples looked forward to any separation from Him, it was
only for the briefest period.   It is not probable that His words
now spoken, in which His personal absence from them was
assumed as a fundamental condition of their future trials, and to
wait for His return made a continual duty, were understood by
them.   It was not till after His resurrection and ascension
that they could know what His coming, and the waiting for it,
meant.

The request of one of the company that the Lord should
speak to his brother to divide the inheritance with him, and the
following parable of the rich fool, are mentioned only by Luke.
The request shows how much the attention of men was now
turned to Jesus as the Messiah, and this fact doubtless greatly
inflamed the hostility of the Pharisees.

NOVEMBER — DECEMBER, 782.   A. D. 29.

Being told of the murder of the Galilæans by Pilate, **LUKE xiii. 1–9.**
he replies, and adds a parable respecting the fig tree.
While teaching in the synagogue upon the Sabbath, He **LUKE xiii. 10–17.**
heals a woman who has been sick eighteen years.   He is **LUKE xiii. 18–21.**
rebuked for this by the master of the synagogue, but puts
him to shame.   He continues His journey toward Jerusa-
lem, and replies to the question of one who asked Him, **LUKE xiii. 22–35.**
" Are there few that be saved ? "   The same day He is
warned by certain Pharisees against Herod.

Of these Galilæans so murdered by Pilate we have no other
mention, and cannot tell when the event occurred.   There can
be little doubt that it was at Jerusalem, and during a feast.[1]
The relations of Pilate to the Jews were such as to make this
act of cruelty highly probable.   He was no respecter of places,
and did not hesitate upon occasion to violate the sanctity of the
temple.   Some suppose these Galilæans to have been the followers of Judas of Galilee (Acts v. 37), but without any good
grounds.   Probably there was some sudden outbreak at one of
the feasts; and they, perhaps taking part in it, perhaps only

---

[1] See analogous cases in Josephus, Antiq., xvii. 9, 10; xviii. 3. 2.

17*

mere spectators, were slain by the Roman soldiers in the outer
court. Some see in this the cause, or an effect, of the enmity
between Pilate and Herod (Luke xxiii. 12). That the event was
recent, and that it excited great indignation, are apparent from
the narrative. The attempt of Greswell (iii. 26) to connect it
with the sedition of Barabbas (Luke xxiii. 19), and to place it at
the beginning of the last Passover, and thus to find in it a note
of time, is more subtle than forcible. Hengstenberg,[1] supposing that the parable of the fig tree was spoken a year before the
Lord's death, makes the murder of these Galilæans to have been
at the last Passover but one, or that mentioned in John vi. 4,
which the Lord did not attend. Edersheim, with more ground,
infers that it had just occurred, as else they would not have
spoken of it. Of the tower that fell in Siloam we have no
knowledge, but as Josephus (War, v. 4. 3) speaks of the towers
on the city walls, it has been conjectured that it was one of
them. It is said by some, as Pressensé, that it occurred during
the building of his aqueduct by Pilate.

The parable of the fig tree has been regarded by many as
giving a datum to determine the length of the Lord's ministry [2]
But it is doubtful whether it has any chronological value,[3] and
the point has been already discussed in the chronological essay.
Some refer the three years to the whole period before Christ,
during which God was waiting for the Jews;[4] some to the three
polities, those of the judges, kings, and high priests.

The healing of the sick woman is mentioned by Luke, without any mark of time or place, except generally, that it was in
a synagogue and upon the Sabbath. The decided manner in
which the ruler of the synagogue expressed himself against the
lawfulness of healing on this day, indicates that the Pharisaic
party had determined to treat such works of healing as a violation of its sanctity. There is no expression of sympathy with
the woman, of sorrow at her sickness, or joy at her recovery.
That in this condemnation of the Lord's act he was supported
by others, appears from verse 17. Such a literal adherence to
the law and violation of its spirit awakened Christ's just indigna

---

[1] Christol., iii. 249.   [2] Bengel, Krafft, Wieseler, Stier.
[3] So Meyer, Lichtenstein, Trench.   [4] Grotius.

tion, and He denounced him as a hypocrite. Perhaps, the parables of the mustard seed and leaven may have been originally
spoken here, or at least repeated here.[1]

The account of the Lord's progress (verse 22) that "He
went through the cities and villages — κατὰ πόλεις καὶ κώμας,—
teaching and journeying toward Jerusalem," is too indefinite to
determine what stage of His journey He had now reached, but
it indicates that He visited many places on the way.   This language is over-pressed by Godet, who speaks of " His stopping at
every city, and even at every village."   Some would refer it to
His work after Dedication; others, to His going up from Peræa
to Bethany at the resurrection of Lazarus (John xi. 1–17).[2]
Some support is thought to be found for the last in the Lord's
words (verses 32, 33): "Behold, I cast out devils, and I do
cures to-day and to-morrow, and the third I shall be perfected.
Nevertheless I must walk to-day, and to-morrow, and the
day following."   The three days are said to refer to the time
necessary to go up from Peræa to Bethany, and so are to be literally taken.   The meaning of His words then is, " In three days
I perfect this part of my work, and not till then do I leave
Herod's dominions."   But even if the language is capable of
this interpretation, it is certain that verse 22, which speaks of a
journey to Jerusalem, would not be applied to a journey to
Bethany, which was rather a turning aside from His fixed route
in answer to a special request.

The time when the Pharisees came to Him to warn Him to
depart or Herod would kill Him, is designated as the same day
when the question was asked Him, " Are there few that be
saved? " (Tisch., and W. and H., have ὥρᾳ.   R. V.: " In that
very hour.")   This was one of the days during which He was
teaching and journeying toward Jerusalem (verse 22).   That
Herod should be spoken of, shows that Jesus was now either in
Galilee or Peræa, and so under his jurisdiction and exposed to
his anger.   Meyer supposes Him to be still in Galilee, and that
His reply to the Pharisees (verse 32) is to be understood: " I
have yet three days in which to labor in Galilee, and to complete
my work of casting out devils and of healing, and then I must

---

[1] McKnight, Meyer, Alford, Godet.
[2] Wieseler, Oosterzee.

go up to Jerusalem." On the third day He comes to the border, as related in xvii. 11. Wieseler (Syn., 322) makes Him to have journeyed three days to reach Bethany. But are the Lord's words to be understood of three literal days?[1] This literal interpretation is not to be pressed. The number three seems here, as in the three years (verse 7), to denote a period of time as complete in itself, with a beginning, middle, and end, and does not give us any chronological help. There is no good reason why the language may not be understood as a general statement, that His labors must be continued till He should perfect them at His death in Jerusalem.[2]

The motive of these Pharisees in thus warning the Lord to depart, is not clear. It is possible that they were His friends, and that their message was based upon some information which they possessed of the purposes of Herod, who may have been in Peræa, at Livias or Machaerus. Had he been, the great publicity with which the Lord journeyed could scarcely have failed to draw the king's attention to Him, and to awaken some suspicion of His designs. If not His friends, some suppose them to have been sent by Herod in order to frighten Him from his territories.[3] This supposition finds some support in His reply, " Go ye, and tell that fox." Less probable is the supposition that they feigned themselves to be Herod's messengers, in order to drive Him into Judæa where He could be more readily arrested by the priests and rulers. Perhaps the simpler explanation is that, without being sent by Herod, or having any special knowledge of his plans, they gratify their malice by uttering the threat that he will kill Him if He does not depart.

The apostrophe to Jerusalem (verses 34, 35) is found also in Matt. xxiii. 37–39, where it was spoken after the Lord left the temple for the last time. From its nature, and from the connection in which it stands in both Evangelists, it is probable that it was twice spoken.[4] Those who think it to have been spoken but once, find its most fitting place in Matthew.[5]

---

[1] So Meyer, Alford, Ellicott. This, however, makes it necessary to render τελειοῦμαι, " I perfect my works," or, " I close my ministry," not as in our version, " I shall be perfected." R. V.: " I am perfected."

[2] So Lichtenstein Stier, Owen, Godet.   [3] McKnight, Meyer, Alford, Weiss.

[4] So Stier, Alford, Ellicott   [5] Meyer, Lange, DeWette.

It has been questioned how the words, "Ye shall not see me, until the time come when ye shall say, Blessed is He that cometh in the name of the Lord," are to be understood. The most obvious meaning is, that they are to be taken in the large prophetic sense, and refer to His departure into heaven, and to His joyful reception by the nation when He should come again in His kingdom. And this also best fits the connection of the thought. No prophet could perish out of Jerusalem. There He must die, and afterward ascend to God, to be seen no more till the hearts of the people should be made ready for Him. Till then, their house was left unto them desolate.[1] Here is brought out the truth that He would return when His people should desire it, and welcome His heralds. The supposition that He foretold His purpose to go up to the coming Passover, and that it then found its entire fulfilment,[2] is erroneous. That some of the people did then say (Luke xix. 38), "Blessed be the King that cometh in the name of the Lord," was no general, much less national, acceptance of Him, and no real fulfillment of His words. Still, some allusion to the shouts of the multitude at His is triumphal entry need not be denied.[3]

DECEMBER 20–27, 782. A. D. 29.

From Peræa He goes up to Jerusalem to be present at the Feast of Dedication. Upon the way He passes through the village of Bethany, and visits Mary and Martha. Reaching Jerusalem, the Jews demand that He declare plainly whether He is or is not the Messiah. He answers them by referring to His past words and works. The Jews, thinking His answer blasphemous, take up stones to stone Him. He continues His discourse to them, but as they seek to arrest Him He escapes from them, and goes beyond Jordan to Bethany (Bethabara), and abides there. Many resort to Him, and believe on Him.

JOHN x. 22–24.

LUKE x. 38–42.

JOHN x. 25–42.

It is at this point, after Luke xiii., that we would insert the narrative of John (x. 22–42), embracing the visit to the Feast of Dedication, and the return to Peræa. These events are omitted by the Synoptists as not falling into the scope of their

---

[1] Tisch. and W. and H. omit " desolate " — ἔρημος. Tisch. retains it, Matt. xxiii. 38, but W. and H. mark it as a secondary reading.

[2] Wieseler, 321.   [3] Meyer, *in loco*.

narratives, which leads them to mention no visit to Jerusalem but the last.

That the visit at Bethany to Martha and Mary, mentioned by Luke only, took place at this time, cannot be positively affirmed, but it cannot well be put earlier. It may be placed by the Evangelist in its present position in the narrative upon other than chronological grounds, but there are no very strong chronological objections to the place here given it.

The journey, as it has been traced, brings Him into the neighborhood of Jerusalem. His presence at the Feast of Dedication, which was celebrated for eight days, from the 20th to the 27th of December, is often ascribed to the fact of His proximity to the city, rather than to any design on leaving Galilee to be present.[1] It is not indeed probable that He would go up simply because of the feast, which He might have observed elsewhere. The three great feasts, says Lightfoot, "might not be celebrated in any other place, but the Encenia was kept everywhere throughout the whole land." As one of the minor feasts, His presence implies some special motive. May we not find this in the character of the Lord's last journey? For a considerable period He had avoided Jerusalem; at the Feast of Tabernacles He went up secretly. Now He seeks publicity. Wherever the Seventy go they proclaim Him, and all understand that He appears as the Messiah. Perhaps, as has been already intimated, He may have designed to send His messengers into Judæa, and if they found a favorable reception, to follow them. The great desire of His heart is to save Jerusalem from its impending destruction (Matt. xxiii. 37). He will present Himself again before the priests and scribes and rulers that they may show forth what is in their hearts, show whether they can yet recognize in Him the Messiah. And the Feast of Dedication had special significance as the time of such a visit. It was appointed in commemoration of the national deliverance by the Maccabees from the oppression of the Syrians (B. C. 164), and of the cleansing of the temple and restoration of the appointed worship.[2] It should not only have reminded the Jews of the sins that brought them under the tyranny of Antiochus, and of

---

[1] Lichtenstein.   [2] 1 Maccabees iv. 52-59.

the goodness of God in their deliverance; but have taught them the true cause of their present bondage, and awakened in them hopes of a more glorious deliverance through the Son of David. Had the Lord found them conscious of sin, and humbling themselves under the punishments of God, the way would have been opened for a new cleansing of the temple, and the bringing in of a new and nobler worship. But, as the event showed, the feast served only to feed their pride, to foster their hate of Roman rule, and to turn their hearts away from the true Deliverer. A Judas Maccabæus they would have welcomed; but Jesus, whose first work must be to deliver them from sin, found no favor in their eyes.

It is possible that some of the Seventy may have preceded Jesus to Jerusalem, announcing His coming; but if not, His movements must have been well known there. The manner in which the Jews gather around Him, and the character of their question: "How long dost Thou make us to doubt? (R. V.: 'How long dost Thou hold us in suspense?') If Thou be the Christ, tell us plainly," clearly indicate that in some way their attention had been especially drawn to Him as something more than a prophet, as indeed the Christ. If we compare this language with that uttered but two months earlier, it appears evident that His Messianic claims had now become more prominent. That the Jews asked the question with the intent to make an affirmative answer the basis of accusation,[1] is not improbable; but it may also have been an honest expression of doubt. It is to be noticed that no mention is made of any preliminary teaching or healing, nothing to call forth the question. He is silent till it is addressed Him by the people, and this was as soon as He appeared in the temple. The place of His teaching was Solomon's porch,[2] probably selected because of the cold.

The Lord's reply: "I told you, and ye believed not," must refer to the general sentiment and scope of His teachings; for we nowhere have on record any express avowal to the Jews that He was the Messiah. Such an avowal He seems purposely to have avoided. His own words were: "If I bear witness of

---

[1] So Meyer after Luther, M. and M., Eders.
[2] See Caspari, 298, and Edersheim, ii. 229, who differ as to its locality.

myself, my witness is not true. There is another that beareth
witness of me" (John v. 31, 32). In conformity to this general
rule, He here refers the Jews to His works. "The works that
I do in my Father's name, they bear witness of me"; and that
this evidence was not sufficient, He ascribes to their unbelief.
This was not what they wanted, and they must have thought it
very remarkable that if He were the Christ, He did not explicitly
and openly affirm it. They did not consider that "with the
heart man believeth unto righteousness"; and that the evidence
that was convincing to a Nathanael, was wholly unsatisfactory
to a Caiaphas. That in their question they had no other than
the current conceptions of the Messiah, appears from the effect
of His reply upon them. So soon as He began to speak of His
relations to God as His Father, and said, "I and My Father are
one," they sought to stone Him. This was open blasphemy, and
the blasphemer must be stoned.

His reference to the figure of the sheep (verse 26), as it had
been used by Him at the Feast of Tabernacles (x. 1–18), is not
strange, for probably most of those now present, priests, scribes,
and Pharisees, were residents in Jerusalem, and had heard His
words at that time. The interval was but two months, not so
long that they could have forgotten what He then said,
especially if they had not heard Him since. At all His former
visits to the Holy City He wrought a miracle or miracles, but
none are recorded of Him at this time.

This attempt to take His life, compared with that at the Feast
of Tabernacles (viii. 59), may perhaps show less of hasty passion,
but indicates a fixed purpose to destroy Him.[1] The attempt to
take Him (verse 39) may have been with design to keep Him
in custody till He could be formally tried; or to remove Him
from the temple that they might immediately stone Him.
That His escape was miraculous is not said, though so regarded
by many.[2] If He had designed to send His messengers into
Judæa, this new manifestation of hostility may have prevented
it; for if His life was in danger at Jerusalem, He could not have
journeyed safely into other parts of the province. No other
place of refuge was open to Him than Peræa. Thus the

---

[1] Luthardt, ii. 190.   [2] So Luthardt; *contra*, Meyer.

Seventy may but partially have completed their intended circuit, Judæa being shut against them; and this will explain why their labors are so briefly noticed by the Evangelist.

The Lord, now leaving Judæa, goes beyond Jordan, "into the place where John at first baptized." There is no doubt that this was Bethabara or Bethany (John i. 28). Its position has already been considered, though no positive result was reached. The strong probability is that John began his baptism near Jericho, and this place would seem to be meant here, even if he later went higher up the river to other baptismal places. The matter will meet us again in connection with the death of Lazarus. The motives that led to its selection are wholly conjectural. That He sought it merely as a place of safety from the Jews, is possible; but here, on the other hand, He was exposed to the anger of Herod (Luke xiii. 31, 32). Aside from considerations of His personal safety, there is much significance in this return to the place of His baptism. He might expect to find there, as He did, many whose hearts had been prepared by the teachings and baptism of John for the reception of His own words. It is said that "there He abode." [1] This, as has been said, would not forbid that He should make short circuits through the surrounding towns. It was while in this place, whether town or district, that many resorted unto Him, and here Mary and Martha sent to Him during the sickness of Lazarus. How long He sojourned here ere He went up to Bethany near Jerusalem, to raise Lazarus, does not clearly appear. It is inferred by some, from the language of His disciples after He had proposed to return to Judæa (xi. 7, 8): "The Jews of late sought to stone Thee" — νῦν ἐζήτουν — (R. V.: "Were but now seeking to stone Thee,") that He had but just come from Jerusalem. [2] Much stress, however, cannot be laid on this. (See Acts vii. 52.) From the Feast of Dedication to the Passover was about four months, and it is not improbable that half of this, or more, was spent "beyond Jordan," in the neighborhood of Bethany. Many would place during this time much that Luke relates. Upon grounds already stated, we shall assign to this period all from chap. xiv. to xvii. 10.

---

[1] As to the use of "abode," μένειν, see John iv. 40; vii. 9; xi. 6.   [2] Meyer.

January, 783.   A. D. 30.

The Lord is invited to feast with one of the chief Pharisees on the Sabbath day, and there heals a man who had the dropsy, and defends the lawfulness of the act. He addresses the guests, reproving them for choosing the highest seats, and reminds His host of his duty to the poor, and speaks the parable of the great supper. As He journeys on, great multitudes go with Him, and He addresses them upon the self-denial required in disciples. Publicans and sinners coming in large numbers to hear Him, the scribes and Pharisees murmur that He should receive them, and eat with them. He, therefore, utters several parables, those of the lost sheep, of the lost piece of silver, and of the prodigal son; and to His disciples that of the wasteful steward, adding admonitions against covetousness. The Pharisees deriding Him, He rebukes them, and utters the parable of the rich man and Lazarus. He addresses the disciples upon offenses, and forgiveness, and faith.	LUKE xiv. 1–6. LUKE xiv. 7–14. LUKE xiv. 15–24. LUKE xiv. 25–35. LUKE xv. 1–32. LUKE xvi. 1–13. LUKE xvi. 14–31. LUKE xvii. 1–10.

The Pharisee by whom the Lord was invited to eat bread is described as "one of the chief Pharisees."   This may denote that he was of high social position, but probably includes some official distinction, as that he was chief of a synagogue, or member of the local Sanhedrin.   His motive in thus seeking the Lord's society does not clearly appear; and it is possible that, unlike most of his sect, he wished to show him some mark of respect, perhaps as a prophet, perhaps as the Messiah.   Still the Lord's words (verse 12) imply that He made the feast in a self-seeking, ostentatious spirit, and under the pretence of hospitality he may have hidden an evil design.   (So Trench, Godet.)   It appears that there were many invited, and that they were of the rich and better class.   It was customary for the Jews to entertain their friends upon the Sabbath, although they cooked no food.   "The Jews' tables were generally better spread on that day than on any other." [1]

The appearance of the dropsical man at such a feast, it is not easy to explain.   He could hardly, if severely ill, have been invited as a guest; and it is said that after the Lord had "healed him, He let him go," as if he were only accidentally present.   Nor is it probable that he came merely as a spectator, although

---

[1] Lightfoot; see Trench, Mir., 263.

eastern customs permit strangers to enter houses at all hours with great freedom, and they are often present at feasts merely to look on. Some have therefore supposed that he was intentionally brought in by the Pharisees, to see if the Lord would heal him on that day,[1] he assenting to it. But had he been a mere tool in the hands of the Pharisees, it may well be doubted if the Lord would have healed him. It is more probable that he came in faith to be healed, and unable, perhaps, to approach the Lord before He entered into the house, now forced himself into the room where He was.

McKnight supposes the parable of the great supper to be the same as that mentioned by Matthew xxii. 2–14, and to have been spoken a second time in the temple. But the parables are wholly distinct, as a comparison of the details plainly shows. (So Trench, Meyer, Godet, Keil.)

As the end of His ministry drew nigh, and the hostility of His enemies became more open, the Lord's words became more and more plain in showing how much of self-denial was involved in becoming one of His disciples. The same remarks in substance He had before made (Matt. x. 37); but He here adds new illustrations. He compares Himself to a man who wishes to build a tower, His Church; and to a king who goes to make war with another king, with the prince of this world; and they who would aid Him in this building, or in this warfare, must be ready to sacrifice all.

The great concourse of publicans and sinners to Him cannot be explained from anything in His language (xiv. 25–35) as especially applicable to them, nor as springing from their exclusion from the feast. It rather marks the fact that, now that His words had become more sharp against the Pharisees, and the breach between them and Him more apparent, this class rallied around Him and thronged to hear Him. Much to the disgust of the Pharisees, He did not disdain even to eat with them. Such an act they deemed in the highest degree unbecoming in one who claimed to be the Messiah; and it was also a keen reproof to themselves, who so scrupulously excluded all publicans and sinners from their society.

---

[1] McKnight, Oosterzee, Stier, Keil.

It is disputed whether the parable of the lost sheep, as here given by Luke, is the same as that given by Matt. xviii. 12, 13. From the relation in which it stands to the other parables which Luke has recorded, we cannot well doubt that it was spoken at the same time. But such an illustration, so natural and apt, may have been used more than once, and been spoken earlier in Galilee, as Matthew relates. Perhaps, both in form and in meaning, some distinction may be drawn between them.

The parables of the lost sheep, of the lost piece of silver, and of the prodigal son, seem to have been all uttered at once to the Pharisees and scribes, who murmured at His reception of publicans and sinners. That which immediately follows, of the unjust steward, was spoken to the disciples; but whether immediately or after a little interval, we have no data to decide.

It is not easy to see how the words addressed to the Pharisees in verse 18, respecting divorce and adultery, are to be connected with the verses immediately preceding; perhaps they may be an abstract of some discourse not otherwise mentioned; but the parable that follows, of the rich man and Lazarus, has plain reference to that sect. Whether the words to the disciples (xvii. 1–10) followed at once upon the parable, we cannot determine.

JANUARY—FEBRUARY, 783. A. D. 30.

Lazarus, the brother of Mary and Martha, being sick, they send a messenger to the Lord in Peræa to inform Him of his sickness. After receiving the message, He abides still two days in the place where He is. Taking the disciples with them, He then goes to Bethany and raises Lazarus from the dead. Many of the Jews present believe on Him, but others departing to Jerusalem tell what has occurred to the Pharisees. A council is summoned, and Caiaphas the high priest advises that He be put to death. Jesus, learning this, goes with His disciples to a city, called Ephraim, and His enemies give a commandment, that, if any man know where He is, he shall show it, that they may take Him.　　JOHN xi. 1–46.

JOHN xi. 47–54.

At this point in Luke's narrative (xvii. 11) we insert the account given by John of the journey of Jesus from Peræa to Bethany to raise Lazarus, and of His subsequent departure to Ephraim and sojourn there. The exact order of events connected with the death and resurrection of Lazarus, is not clear. The Lord waits two days after receiving the message of the sisters ere He departs for Bethany. It is not certain how long after the death of Lazarus He arrived there. It is said (verse 17) that "when He came He found that he had lain in the grave four days already." We may then count as the first day that on which the message was sent and received; the two follow· ing days of waiting; and on the fourth He departs from Peræa and arrives at Bethany. If we thus suppose Lazarus to have died on the same day that the message was sent, and to have been buried the same day, as was customary, (see Acts v. 6 and 10) the day of the Lord's arrival was the fourth after the interment. Reckoning a part of a day as a whole, we have thus the four days. Lardner [1] supposes that his burial was the day following his death. "If he died on the first day of the week, he was buried on the second, and raised on the fifth. He had been dead four days complete, and buried four days incomplete."

Tholuck (in loco) thinks it improbable that Jesus could have made the journey (perhaps 23–29 miles) in one day, and yet arrive in Bethany in season to do all that is recorded of Him. He must have spent parts of two days upon the road. He supposes, therefore, that Lazarus died the night following the arrival of the messenger and was buried the next day, and that Jesus reached Bethany the fifth day. The first day was that of the burial; the second and third were spent in waiting; the fourth in journeying; on the fifth He reaches Bethany and raises Lazarus.

Some place the death of Lazarus on the last of the two days of waiting, referring in proof to Christ's words (verses 11 and 14).[2] He had waited till the death should take place, and, so soon as it did, He announced it to the disciples, saying, "Lazarus is dead." Thus He is made to reach Bethany on the sixth day.[3]

Edersheim (ii. 315), supposing the journey to Bethany to have occupied a day, thinks that the messenger left Bethany on

---

[1] Works, x. 26, note.   [2] Bengel, Krafft.
[3] See Greswell, ii. 513; Ebrard, 456; Stud. u. Krit., 1862, p. 65.

a Sunday and reached Jesus on Monday. He continued where
He was two days — Tuesday, Wednesday — and reached Beth-
any on Thursday, and raised Lazarus the same day, and on
Friday the chief priests and Pharisees gathered a council.

That the Lord, after He commenced this journey, went directly to
Bethany, lies upon the face of the narrative.[1] Yet some suppose that much related by the Synoptists finds here its proper
place. Krafft (117) identifies the beginning of the journey with
Mark x. 17: "And when He was gone forth into the way," etc.; and
Mark x. 32, Matt. xx. 17, and Luke xviii. 31, with its progress. An
enumeration of the events which he here brings together will show
the great improbability of his arrangement: the discourse upon the
danger of riches, the reward of the apostles, the third announcement
of His approaching death, the strife of the apostles for supremacy,
the entrance into Jericho attended by crowds, healing of the blind
men, interview with Zacchæus, parable of the pounds; all this on the
way to Bethany. Ebrard does not follow Krafft, yet supposes that,
as He was two or more days on the way, He may have made several
circuits. All suppositions of this kind are wholly untenable. The
Lord went to Bethany for a special purpose, attended only by His
followers, and without publicity.[2]

Bethany lies on the eastern slope of the Mount of Olives, some
fifteen furlongs (nearly two miles) southeast from Jerusalem. The
etymology of the name is uncertain. According to some it means
" a low place," *locus depressionis*, as lying in a little valley; according
to others, a "house of dates," or " place of palms," *locus dactylorum.*[3]
It is not mentioned in the Old Testament. Its chief interest to us is
in its connection with Lazarus and his two sisters; and with the Lord's
Ascension. Its proximity to Jerusalem and its retired position made
it a convenient and pleasant resting place for the Lord upon His journeys to and from the feasts, although there is mention made but once
of His presence there (Luke x. 38–42) prior to the resurrection of
Lazarus. It is now a small village of some twenty houses, occupied
by Bedouin Arabs. "A wild mountain hamlet, screened by an intervening ridge from the view of the top of Olivet, perched on its broken
plateau of rock, the last collection of human habitations before the

---

[1] So Meyer, Tischendorf, Lichtenstein, Robinson.

[2] The arrangement of McKnight is extraordinary. Placing Bethany, where He
was sojourning, on the Jordan in northern Peræa, he supposes Jesus to have gone
through Samaria and Galilee, and on the way to have healed the ten lepers (Luke xvii.
11), and thence to Jerusalem, and from Jerusalem to Bethany of Judæa.

[3] Lightfoot, x. 85; Winer, i. 67.

desert hills which reach to Jericho — this is the modern village of El-Azariyeh."[1] Little that is ancient is now to be found. A tradition that dates back to an early period, points out the sites of the houses of Simon and of Lazarus, and the sepulchre of the latter. "This," says Porter,[2] "is a deep vault, partly excavated in the rock, and partly lined with masonry. The entrance is low, and opens on a long, winding, half-ruinous staircase, leading down to a small chamber, and from this a few steps more lead down to another smaller vault, in which the body of Lazarus is supposed to have lain. This situation of the tomb in the centre of the village scarcely agrees with the Gospel narrative, and the masonry of the interior has no appearance of antiquity. But the real tomb could not have been far distant." Thomson says (ii. 599): "By the dim light of a taper we descended very cautiously by twenty-five slippery steps to the reputed sepulchre of Lazarus, or El-Azariyeh, as both tomb and village are now called. But I have no description of it to give, and no questions about it to ask. It is a wretched concern, every way unsatisfactory, and almost disgusting." Robinson denies that the sepulchre now shown could have been that of Lazarus. In this, Tristram agrees (B. P. 130): "It is in the middle of the village, and most unlike the character and situation of Jewish sepulchres." Edersheim supposes him to have been buried "in his own private tomb in a cave, and probably in a garden."

The impression which the miracle of the resurrection of Lazarus made upon the people at large, was very great. It was in all its circumstances so public and so well authenticated that it was impossible for the most skeptical to deny it, even if it did not lead them to faith in Jesus. It is said (vs. 45, 46) "Then many of the Jews which came to Mary . . . . believed on Him. But some of them went their ways to the Pharisees and told them what things Jesus had done." Two classes are here spoken of: the first, which included those who came to Mary and saw the things which Jesus did — all these believed; the second, other Jews who had not seen, and these are they who went to the Pharisees. (So M. and M., Godet.) From the grammatical construction, Meyer infers that those who went to the Pharisees were of those who believed, and that they went that they might testify to them of the miracle.[3] As all did not believe on Him, it is more probable that some of these unbelievers went to the

---

[1] Stanley, 186; Baed., 258.   [2] Hand-Book, i. 188.

[3] See, *contra*, Luthardt and Alford, *in loco*.

Pharisees, and that their motive was evil. The ecclesiastical
rulers felt that it was now high time that something should be
done, and they proceed at once to call a council to determine
what steps should be taken. Their deliberations ended with the
resolve that He should be put to death. This may be regarded
as the decisive and final rejection of Jesus by the Jewish authorities. Much earlier the Jews at Jerusalem had sought to slay
Him as a Sabbath-breaker and blasphemer (John v. 16–18); the
Pharisees and Herodians in Galilee had taken counsel how they
might destroy Him (Mark iii. 6); the Sanhedrin had agreed to
excommunicate any one who should confess that He was Christ
(John ix. 22); on one occasion officers had been sent to arrest
Him (John vii. 32); tumultuous attempts had been made to stone
Him; and there was a general belief that His enemies would not
rest till He was removed out of the way (John vii. 25). But it
does not appear that to this time there had been a determination
of the Sanhedrin in formal session, that He should die. It is
questioned whether this was a formal session. It certainly was
not a judicial one in fact, for the Lord was not before them for
trial, but judicial in effect, since His death was then determined
on. The miracle at Bethany, and its great popular effect, brought
the matter to a crisis. The nation, in its highest council,
presided over by the high priest, decided in the most solemn
manner that the public safety demanded His death. All that
now remained to be done was to determine how His death could
be best effected, and formally to condemn Him.

It is to be noticed how, in the deliberations of the Sanhedrin, truth and justice were made wholly subservient to selfish
policy. That Jesus had wrought a great and wonderful miracle
at Bethany, was not denied. Indeed it was admitted, and made
the basis of their action against Him: "If we let Him thus
alone, all will believe on Him." Still they did not believe that
He wrought His miracles by the power of God, but ascribed them
all to a satanic origin, and as wrought to deceive the people. But
on what ground rested their fear that "the Romans would come
and take away both their place and nation"? It seems plain
that they did not look upon Jesus as one who, under any circumstances, could fulfill their Messianic hopes, and establish a
victorious kingdom. Even if all were to believe on Him, and

He should set up Himself as King, He could not resist the
Romans.   This strikingly shows how little the impression made
by the character of Jesus, His works and teachings, corresponded
to the prevalent conceptions of the Messiah.   It was to the
Pharisees impossible, that He, the teacher, the prophet, should
become the leader of armies, the asserter of their national rights,
the warrior like David.   They felt that in Him their hopes
never could be fulfilled.   His growing popularity with the people, if it led to insurrection, could only bring upon them severer
oppression.   In this point of view, it was better that He should
die, whatever might be His miraculous powers, than that all
through Him should perish.

If, as the narrative plainly implies, the Sanhedrin held its
session as soon as possible after the knowledge of the resurrection of Lazarus reached it, the Lord's departure to Ephraim
could not have been long delayed.   He could not remain in
Bethany without each hour putting His life in peril.   According
to Edersheim (ii. 326), He remained in Bethany Friday and Saturday, and the next day went to Ephraim.   That He went secretly
to Ephraim, appears from the commandment given by the chief
priests and Pharisees that "if any man knew where He were,
he should show it, that they might take Him."   Yet the Twelve
seem to have accompanied Him, or, which is more probable, to
have gathered to Him there, and possibly Lazarus was with
them.   It is not improbable that others, also, may have resorted
to Him.   The mention of Salome (Matt. xx. 20) does not show
that the women with the Lord went to Ephraim.

Of the city Ephraim, in which He took refuge, little is known, and
different sites have been assigned it.   In Joshua xviii. 23, mention is
made of an Ophrah as one of the cities of Benjamin, and in 2 Chronicles xiii. 19, of an Ephron, or Ephrain, in connection with Bethel
and Jeshanah.   Josephus [1] speaks of an Ephraim in connection with
Bethela, or Bethel.   It was a small town lying in the mountainous
district of Judah, and was captured by Vespasian.   Eusebius mentions
an Ephron as lying eight Roman miles north of Jerusalem, but Jerome, [2]
who mentions the same place, puts it at twenty miles.   Lightfoot
identifies the Ephraim of Chronicles, of Josephus, and of the text. [3]

---

[1] War, iv. 9. 9.   [2] Raumer, 171.
[3] So Tischendorf, Wieseler.
18.

That the Ephron of Eusebius and Jerome is the same place can scarcely be questioned, and their conflicting statements as to its distance from Jerusalem may be explained, as Robinson does, by the supposition that the latter corrects the former. Wieseler maintains that Eusebius is right. Proceeding upon these data, Robinson thinks that he finds the site of Ephraim in the modern Taiyibeh, which is situated about twenty Roman miles northeast of Jerusalem, and some five or six miles northeast of Bethel, upon a lofty hill, overlooking all the valleys of the Jordan, and said by Tristram to be "peculiarly isolated and secluded, truly 'the lonely Ephraim.'" This identification is accepted by many.[1] Ebrard, however, denies that the Ephraim of Josephus can be identified with that of the Evangelist, and places the latter southeast from Jerusalem, because Jesus on His way from it to Jerusalem passed through Jericho. Sepp places it in the land of Gilead; Luthardt regards its position as doubtful; Edersheim, starting from the statement that it was "near the wilderness," and finding this wilderness in the north of Peræa (see Luke viii. 29), places it east of the Jordan and close to Galilee. This position has this in its favor that it would have given a safer retreat.

FEBRUARY — MARCH, 783. A. D. 30.

In Ephraim the Lord abides with the disciples till the approach of the Passover. A little before the feast, many go up out of the country to Jerusalem to perform the necessary purifications, and there is much discussion as to the probability of His presence. He leaves Ephraim, and begins His journey toward Jerusalem, passing along the border line of Samaria and Galilee. Upon the way He meets and heals ten lepers. Being asked by the Pharisees when the kingdom of God shall come, He replies, and adds the parable of the unjust judge. To certain self-righteous persons He speaks the parable of the Pharisee and the publican. He replies to the question of the Pharisees respecting divorce. Little children are brought to Him, whom He blesses. As He is journeying, a young man follows Him to know how he may inherit eternal life. Jesus bids him sell all that he has and follow Him, and proceeds to address the disciples upon the dangers incident to riches. In answer to Peter, He speaks of the rewards that shall be given to the Twelve, and to all faithful disciples. He adds the parable of the laborers in the vineyard.

JOHN xi. 54–57.

LUKE xvii. 11–19.
LUKE xvii. 20–37.

LUKE xviii. 1–14.
MATT. xix. 3–12.
MARK x. 2–12.
MATT. xix. 13–15.
MARK x. 13–16.
LUKE xviii. 15–30.
MATT. xix. 16–30.
MARK x. 17–31.

MATT. xx. 1–16.

---

[1] So, Ritter, Porter, Lange, Lichtenstein, Smith's Dict. of Bible, Ellicott, Conder Tristram.

Supposing the Lord to have gone to Bethany — Bethabara—beyond Jordan, immediately after the Feast of Dedication, or in the latter part of December, and that He remained there several weeks before He heard that Lazarus was sick, we may put His departure to Ephraim in the latter part of February or early in March. Here He continued till the Passover, which fell this year on the seventh of April. He was thus at Ephraim several weeks. How was this time spent? It is said by some,[1] that He may have made excursions to the neighboring villages, or even to the Jordan valley. But, as His object in seeking this secluded spot on the edge of the wilderness was to avoid the observation of His enemies till the appointed hour had come, how could He go about the country teaching and preaching? The place of His retreat must thus have come very speedily to the knowledge of the Pharisees. How little the people at large knew where He was, appears from the fact that those who went up early to the feast out of the country,[2] sought Him at Jerusalem. Besides, the position of Ephraim, though well fitted for seclusion, was not so for teaching. We conclude, then, as the narrative plainly implies, that He was spending the few days that remained to Him, not amidst crowds, nor renewing in some scattered villages the labors of His early ministry, but in the society of His disciples, teaching them such truths as they could receive, and preparing them for their labors after He should Himself be taken from them. Doubtless, also, this period gave Him many desired opportunities of solitary communion with His Father.

The fact that He had been present at the last two feasts in Jerusalem led the people to expect that Jesus would also be present at the Passover. But, on the other hand, as He had withdrawn from public observation, and as the Jews had endeavored to learn the place of His concealment in order to arrest Him, they thought it doubtful whether He would dare to come and brave their enmity. That many should assemble some days before the feast, was made neceesary by the laws respecting purification.[3]

---

[1] So Robinson. Har., 201.

[2] Some suppose "the country" to be the region about Ephraim, so Bäumlein; others. the country in general as contrasted with Jerusalem; so Meyer.

[3] See Numbers ix. 10, and Ainsworth's note; 2 Chron. xxx. 17.

We meet here the very difficult point, the route by which Jesus went from Ephraim to Bethany. Upon this neither Matthew, Mark, nor John give any light. Does the statement of Luke (xvii. 11) find its right place here: "And it came to pass as He went to Jerusalem, that He passed through the midst of Samaria and Galilee"? (For διὰ μέσου, Tisch., W. and Hort. have διὰ μέσον ; in R. V. margin, "between Samaria and Galilee"; Vulgate, *transibat per mediam*.) Some think that He passed through Samaria and Galilee. But this cannot be the meaning, as the goal was Jerusalem in the south, and to go through Samaria, and then Galilee, was to go north. Most, therefore, understand the words, that He went eastwards between the two provinces, having Samaria on His right hand and Galilee on His left. (So Meyer, Godet, Keil, Eders. ; Lightfoot thinks that Peræa may be meant here under the term Galilee, and refers to Luke iii. 1, where Galilee includes Peræa.) But how did He reach the border line from Ephraim? If we identify Ephraim with the modern Taiyibeh, the distance to the border was not great. If He left the former in the morning, He would reach the frontier in the afternoon. But what was His motive in thus going northward ? It is said by some that it was to meet a pilgrim caravan, which having assembled in Galilee, would proceed along its southern border down to the Jordan, and go thence to Jerusalem by way of Jericho. This is not improbable. If His Galilæan disciples and friends formed such a caravan, it was easy for Him to join them with His apostles.[1]

That He was accompanied by others than the Twelve appears from the statement (Matt. xx. 17) that " He took them apart in the way "; and from the mention of Salome (verse 20). As the time for concealment was now past, and it was His purpose to enter Jerusalem with all publicity, it is probable that He directed His course from Ephraim northward with a view to meet the pilgrims from Galilee. So soon as He came into the valley of the Jordan, He would meet the larger processions that came from the neighborhood of the Sea of Galilee by the road down the west bank of the river; and in the neighborhood of Jericho would meet those that crossed the ford from the eastern side. What multitudes attended the feasts, especially this feast, appears from Josephus.[2] From actual count, it was shown that at a given Passover 256,500 paschal lambs were slain ; and allowing ten persons to each lamb, which was the smallest allowable number, the participants amounted to 2,565,000 persons. Admitting that this number is greatly

---

[1] It does not seem necessary, with McKnight, Edersheim, and others to put Ephraim in northern Peræa, and near Galilee; but such a position would afford an easier explanation of His presence on the frontier.

[2] War, vi. 9. 3.

exaggerated, there is no question that immense multitudes were always present; and all the roads leading to Jerusalem, for several days before and after the feasts, were thronged with passengers.

As to the name or position of the village where the ten lepers met Him, we know nothing more than that it was on the border of Samaria. It would seem, from the gathering together of so many lepers in one place apparently to meet Him, that the Lord's journey was widely known. The title by which they address Him, "Jesus, Master," indicates faith in Him as a prophet rather than as Messiah.

When or where the question of the Pharisees (Luke xvii. 20) respecting the coming of the kingdom of God, was addressed to Him, we have no data to determine. It is probable that He was now in Peræa, and these may have been in fact the same Pharisees whom He had rebuked before. The point of the question concerns the time: When wilt Thou, now announcing Thyself as the Messiah, visibly set up Thy kingdom? Probably it was asked in mockery, or to tempt Him; but, if honestly meant, it could not be answered as a matter of mere chronology. The words, "The kingdom is within you" (in the R. V. margin, "in the midst of you"), is best understood with Meyer: "It was in the midst of them so far as He the Messiah was and worked among them; for where He was and worked, there was the Messianic kingdom." (See Godet, who says, "almost all modern interpreters explain, 'in the midst of you,'" though he opposes it.) The words that follow to the disciples (verses 22–37) contain many expressions almost identical with those afterward employed by Him in His discourses respecting the destruction of Jerusalem (Matt. xxiv), giving some reason to believe that they are here recorded out of their order. (See, however, Meyer, *in loco;* Eders., ii. 328, thinks them in the right place here.)

The parable of the unjust judge stands in obvious connection with the discourse immediately preceding; but that of the publican and the Pharisee may have been spoken later.

The question concerning divorce is found both in Matthew and Mark, and is the first event related by them in their account of the last journey from Galilee to Judæa. Whether it belongs here, or took place earlier, we have no data to determine; but it stands in obvious connection with what is reported in Luke xvi. 18. Being mentioned, however, by them both just

before the incident of the blessing of the children, which Luke
also mentions, this seems the most fitting place.   Perhaps this
question may refer to the disputes of the Jewish schools, one of
which permitted divorces for many causes, even very slight
ones; the other only for adultery.[1]

All the Synoptists mention the blessing of the children.   It
is plain that their parents were those who honored the Lord and
valued His blessing; and it shows that the enmity of the Pharisees was by no means general among the people.   Perhaps it
may point to His near departure from this scene of labor.[2]   The
demand of Jesus upon the young ruler to sell all that he had
and give to the poor, was something unexpected.   Such a demand was totally at variance with the popular conceptions of the
Messianic kingdom, in which all Jews confidently believed that
every form of temporal blessing would abound.   The question
of Peter indicates how much his thoughts were engrossed with
the rewards and honors of that kingdom, which all now thought
to be near at hand.   The prophets had spoken of a new heaven
and earth, and probably the apostles connected them in some
indistinct way with "the regeneration," and the Messianic reign.

MARCH, 783.   A. D. 30.

Upon the way to Jerusalem the disciples are amazed
and filled with fear, beholding Jesus going before them.
He announces to the Twelve privately His approaching
death and resurrection, but His words are not understood.   Afterward James and John, with their mother
Salome, come to Him, asking for the seats of honor in
His kingdom.   He denies their request.   The jealousy
of the other apostles.

MARK x. 32–34.
MATT. xx. 17–19.
LUKE xviii. 31–34.

MATT. xx. 20–28.
MARK x. 35–45.

Upon the way, and probably soon after reaching the valley
of the Jordan, or at least before arriving at Jericho, He took
the Twelve apart, and announced to them, for the third time,
His approaching death, but with greater particularity than before.   He now speaks of the mode of His death: that it must
be by crucifixion; that He should be delivered unto chief priests
and scribes, and be by them condemned to death, and delivered

---

[1] Lightfoot, on Matt. v. 31 and xix. 3; Eders., ii. 382.
[2] See Oosterzee, on Luke xviii. 15.

unto the Gentiles, who should mock, and scourge, and kill Him.
That this announcement was made early in the journey, appears
from the use of the present tense: "Behold, we go up to Jerusalem."[1]   Mark adds, "And Jesus went before them; and they
were amazed; and as they followed they were afraid."[2]
(R. V., "and they that followed were afraid.")   As this
amazement and fear were previous to His informing them
what was about to befall Him, it indicates that there was
something unusual in His manner, something that awed and
appalled them.   Luke informs us that, notwithstanding the
Lord's words were so plain and express, "they understood none
of these things, and this saying was hid from them, neither
knew they the things which were spoken."   An undefined sense
that some great and awful event was impending, seems for a
little while to have had possession of their minds; but, even now,
of its real nature they had no just conceptions.   They knew
why He had sought refuge in Ephraim, and that to go to
Jerusalem was to expose Himself to the deadly malice of the
Pharisees (John xi. 8 and 16), and momentary doubts of the
result troubled and depressed them.   Yet, on the other hand,
they had seen so many proofs of His mighty power in Galilee,
and the resurrection of Lazarus was so fresh in their memories,
that they could not believe that His life could be taken by
violence, or against His will.   That He should voluntarily yield
Himself up as a victim, was wholly inconceivable; and His
plainest words could not change their long preconceived and
deeply-rooted opinions as to the nature of the Messianic kingdom.   All His predictions respecting His sufferings and death,
though explicit in the letter, they so interpreted as to harmonize
with a victory over all His enemies, and a triumphant reign.   As
said by Alexander: "The correct understanding does not depend upon the plainness of the language, but upon the principle
of interpretation."

A striking commentary upon Luke's statement, that the dis-

---

[1] See Lichtenstein, 370.

[2] Meyer, following a different reading, makes two parties: some who remained
behind in their amazement, and others who followed Him, but with fear. See R. V.
margin.   Keil distinguishes the two parties: the first, the Twelve; the second, His
disciples among the crowd following Him.

ciples understood none of the Lord's words, is found in the
request of Salome that her two sons, James and John, might
fill the highest places in His kingdom.   It has already been
noted, that the sending out of the Seventy, and the peculiar
character of this journey to Jerusalem, had awakened strong
expectations that the day was very near when He would
openly and successfully assert His claims to the throne of His
father David.   Perhaps Salome and her sons may have had in
mind His promise, spoken earlier (Matt. xix. 28), that the
twelve apostles should sit in the regeneration on twelve thrones,
judging the twelve tribes of Israel, and believed that the time
for its fulfillment was near.   The request was made by her in
person, but her sons were also present, and the Lord's reply was
addressed to them.   Probably it was made some few hours after
He had spoken to the Twelve of His sufferings and death; perhaps when they were drawing near to Jericho, and had already
been joined by troops of the pilgrims on their way to the feast.
The excitement of the occasion, the tumult of the multitude,
and the joy and honor with which the Lord was greeted, would
naturally drive from their minds the sombre impression of the
earlier part of the journey.   What the expectations of most of
those who accompanied Him were, clearly appears from Luke's
words (xix. 11): "They thought that the kingdom of God
should immediately appear."   Under these circumstances, it
was not strange that Salome and her sons should present their
request.

MARCH, 783.   A. D. 30.

As in company with the crowd of pilgrims He approaches Jericho, two blind men, sitting by the way-
side begging, address Him as the Son of David, beseeching Him to restore their sight. He heals them,
and they follow Him. Entering Jericho, He meets
Zacchæus, and goes to his house, where He remains
during the night. In the morning, when about to depart, He speaks to the people the parable of the pounds.
He leaves Jericho, and the same day reaches Bethany,
near Jerusalem.

LUKE xviii. 35-43.
MATT. xx. 29-34.
MARK x. 46-52.

LUKE xix. 1-10.

LUKE xix. 11-28.

The account of the healing of the blind men is differently related by the Synoptists, both as to the place and the number of

persons.   Matthew and Mark make it to have taken place as
Jesus was leaving Jericho; Luke, as He was entering it.
Matthew mentions two blind men; Mark and Luke mention
but one.   Of these discrepancies there are several solutions :

1st. — That three blind men were healed: the one mentioned
by Luke, as He approached the city; the two mentioned by
Matthew, as He was leaving the city.[1]   Some, as Osiander and
Pound, make four to have been healed.

2d.— That one was healed on His entry into the city, the other,
on His departure.[2]   According to this solution, Matthew combines the two in one, and, deeming the exact time and place unimportant, represents them as both occurring at the departure of
the Lord from the city.

3d. — That two were healed, and both at His entry; but
one being better known than the other, he only is mentioned by
Mark and Luke.[3]

4th. — That one of the blind men sought to be healed as the
Lord approached the city, but was not; that the next morning,
joining himself to another, they waited for Him by the gate as
He was leaving the city, and were both healed together.   Luke,
in order to preserve the unity of his narrative, relates the healing of the former as if it had taken place on the afternoon of
the entry.[4]

5th.— That only one was healed, and he when the Lord left
the city; and that Matthew, according to his custom, uses the
plural where the other Evangelists use the singular.[5]

6th.— That Luke's variance with Matthew and Mark, in regard to place, may be removed by interpreting (xviii. 35) "as
He was come nigh to Jericho," in the general sense of being
near to Jericho, but without defining whether He was approaching to it or departing from it.   Its meaning here is determined
by Matthew and Mark: He was leaving the city, but still near
to it.   Keil's solution is that Luke puts the healing of the blind
man before the entrance into the city in order that he may give

---

[1] Kitto, Augustine, Morrison.

[2] Lightfoot, Ebrard, Krafft, Tischendorf, Wieseler, Bucher, Lex, Neander.

[3] Doddridge, Newcome, Lichtenstein, Friedlieb.

[4] Bengel, Stier, Trench, Ellicott.   See a modification of this view in McKnight,
and another in Lange on Matt. xx. 30.

[5] Oosterzee on Luke; Da Costa.

18*

the account of Zacchæus and the parable following without interruption.[1]

Other solutions of the discrepancy in regard to place have
been given; as by Newcome,[2] that Jesus spent several days at
Jericho, that He went out of the city as mentioned by Matthew
and Mark, for a temporary purpose, and that on His return He
healed the blind men; by McKnight,[3] preferred by Farrar, that
there were two Jerichos, old and new, and the blind men, sitting
on the road between them, were healed as the Lord was departing from one and entering the other; by Paulus (iii. 44), that
there was a multitude of pilgrims with Jesus, and that the front
ranks of the procession were leaving the city as He was entering
it.   Riddle refers Luke xviii. 35 to the first approach to the city,
and xix. 1, to the final departure from it.

Olshausen and Riggenbach decline to attempt to harmonize
the accounts, regarding the differences as unimportant.   Meyer
and DeWette suppose the Evangelists to have followed different
traditions, and find the discrepancies invincible.   With them
Alford agrees in substance: "The only fair account of such differences is, that they existed in the sources from which each Evangelist took his narrative."   The supposition that two were healed
separately, or that there were two distinct miracles combined by
Matthew in one, he characterizes as "perfectly monstrous, and
would at once destroy the credit of Matthew as a truthful re-
lator."   Norton (ii. 302) observes: "The difference in the accounts of the Evangelists is entirely unimportant except as serving to show that they are independent historians; and it is idle
to try to make them agree by the forced suppositions to which
some commentators have resorted."   It is most probable that
two were healed, though one only is mentioned by Mark and
Luke.

Jericho — This city in the Lord's day was one of much importance,
probably among the Judæan cities second only to Jerusalem.   It was
of great antiquity because of its position, being on the west side of
the large plain of the Jordan, which, well watered by the large fountain and by streams from the western hills, was very productive.   The

---

[1] Grotius on Matt. xx. 30; Clericus, Diss. ii., Canon vi.; Pilkington, cited in Town
send, Robinson, Jarvis, Owen.

[2] Har., 275.   [3] Har., ii. 93.

position of the city was several times changed: its original site was probably near Elisha's fountain (2 Kings ii. 19–22) —'Ain es-Sultân— the Jericho of the Roman period more to the south; the modern Jericho — Es-Riha — is about two miles southeast. "Back of the fountain," says Robinson, "rises up the tall and perpendicular face of the mountain Quarantana." Another fountain — 'Ain Dûk — which is said to be as large or larger than the first, lies some two or three miles northwest of it. Destroyed by Joshua, Jericho was subsequently rebuilt, and here in Elisha's day were the schools of the prophets (2 Kings ii. 5). It was a favorite city of Herod the Great; here he built a hippodrome and here he died (Joseph., Antiq., xxii. 10); here his son Archelaus built or rebuilt a palace. The region being rich in palms, the city was sometimes called "the city of palms." Most tropical fruits flourished there, and especially balsams from which large revenues were derived. This Jericho had considerable commercial importance, and lying on the caravan route from Damascus, was a place of toll. Being near the mountain passes leading up to Jerusalem and Bethel, and commanding the lower fords of the Jordan, it was of much consequence in a military point of view, and here the Romans in the Lord's day had a garrison. It was also the last station through which the pilgrims passed who came from Galilee by way of the Jordan valley and then from Peræa.

It is to be noted that Jericho was one of the cities where many priests resided at this time; about one-half of the whole number is said to have dwelt permanently in Jerusalem, and a large part of the residue in Jericho.[1] Probably the same feeling of dislike to the Lord that prevailed among the priests at Jerusalem, prevailed here. There is no mention of any ministry by the Lord there except at this time.

The present Jericho is composed of hovels inhabited by some sixty families. Robinson (ii. 554) speaks of it as "the most miserable and filthy that he saw in Palestine." Very recently the Russians have begun some building here.

None of the Evangelists state at what time of the day Jesus reached Jericho, but it was probably in the afternoon. The distance to Jerusalem, about seventeen miles, and the nature of the country through which the road passed, may have made it difficult or impossible to go on to Bethany that night, and there was no intervening village where they could encamp. That Jesus did spend the night at Jericho appears from His words to Zacchæus (Luke xix. 5): "To-day I must abide at thy house,"

---

[1] Lightfoot, Temple Service, 49; Eders., The Temple, 59.

and from the murmurings of the people (verse 7): "That He was gone to be a guest (καταλῦσαι) with a man that is a sinner."[1] This visit of the Lord to the house of a publican, although a chief among his class and rich, did not escape strong animadversion. It was regarded by the people at large, and perhaps also by some of His own disciples, as an act unworthy of His high claims. In popular estimation, publicans, whose calling so odiously reminded them of Roman domination, were no fit hosts for Him whom they fondly believed to be now on His way to Jerusalem to proclaim Himself the King. The conversation between the Lord and Zacchæus (verses 8–10) apparently took place in the court of his house, or near the entrance, where the crowd had followed. Olshausen supposes it to have been on the morning of His departure, but there is no good ground for this. It is not certain where the parable of the nobleman (verses 11–27) was spoken, but it would seem from the connection that He was still standing by the door of Zacchæus' house.[2] Some, who suppose that He merely passed a few hours with Zacchæus, and then journeyed on toward Bethany the same day, make all from verse 8 to 27 to have been spoken at His departure.[3] We need not, however, understand verse 28 as meaning that immediately after He had uttered the parable, He went up to Jerusalem.

Of Zacchæus little more is known than is here related. He was not, as some have said, a heathen, but, as appears both from his name and from verse 9, of Jewish descent.[4] He was a chief publican or head collector of the taxes, having the other publicans of that region under him. Jericho was rich in balsams, and therefore much toll was collected here. According to tradition, Zacchæus became bishop of Cæsarea. A tower, standing in the modern village of Riha, is still shown as the "house of Zacchæus."

---

[1] For the usage of καταλῦσαι, see Luke ix. 12; so Meyer, Alford, Greswell, Lichtenstein, T. G. Lex.

[2] So Meyer, Lichtenstein.   [3] Oosterzee, *in loco;* Stier, iv. 318.

[4] So Meyer, Alford.

PART VII.

FROM THE ARRIVAL AT BETHANY TO THE RESURRECTION; OR,
FROM MARCH 31st [8TH NISAN] TO APRIL 9TH [17TH NISAN], 783.
A. D. 30.

This period, from the arrival at Bethany to the resurrection,
nay be divided into two parts; the first embracing the close of
the Lord's active ministry; the second, the paschal supper, His
arrest, and the events following till He left the sepulchre.   His
work in Jerusalem was in substance of the same nature as in
Peræa — a witness to Himself as the Messiah.   But He was now
in a new position.   He stood face to face with His declared enemies, who had already condemned Him to death, and were waiting only for a fitting opportunity to carry their determination into
effect.   He would that Caiaphas and all the rulers should know
that "the one man who should die for the people" (John xi. 50),
was their King.   He therefore enters the city as the King, the
Son of David.   He goes into the temple, and for the second
time cleanses it; He asserts His prerogative as the Judge in
the symbolical withering of the fig tree.   In His parables, He
teaches the rulers that they had been false to their trust as the
husbandmen of God's vineyard; and that as their fathers had
killed His prophets and messengers, so they were about to kill
His Son, the Heir; that they would not come to the marriage supper of the King's Son, though all things were ready, but were
despising the call and would slay His servants.   Thus He made
plain the enormity of the crime they were about to commit, one
far greater than any which their fathers had committed in killing
the prophets; and foretold that their punishment would be as their
crime.   God would destroy these husbandmen, and give the vineyard to others; His holy city would be burnt up, and His servants sent into the highways to bring in the believing Gentiles.

Thus the Lord showed to His enemies that He knew that His
death was at hand, and warned them of the terrible conse-

(421)

quences to themselves and to the nation of their act. His murder, which they meant to be for their salvation, would become
their destruction. At last, in the audience of all the people and
in the temple, He pronounced upon them the seven-fold woe,
whose burden remains to this day.

But while thus severe to His unrelenting enemies, denouncing their iniquity in the majesty of His righteousness, He yet
shows Himself to be the Saviour by healing the lame and blind
who come to Him in the temple. He teaches them that the
scanty offerings of the very poorest, as seen in the widow's mite,
are acceptable to God. Notwithstanding the great influence
which His enemies had over the popular mind, it is plain that for
some days He had in a large degree the sympathy and approval
of the people. It is said by Luke that "all the people were
very attentive to hear Him"; and by Mark, that "they sought
to lay hold on Him, but feared the people"; and by John, that
"among the chief rulers also many believed on Him," but were
afraid to confess Him. Apparently, it needed but a word from
Him to have set the nation ablaze. But He knew that the
hour of the kingdom had not yet come; and now, as in the
wilderness, He would not take His throne till given Him by His
Father's hand. To His disciples He gave but little direct teaching, though His answers to the questions of the scribes and Sad-
duces, and His parables, must have been full of instruction for
them. But the discourses especially addressed to them, the prophetic opening of the future of Jerusalem and of the people;
the promise of His return, the tribulation that should precede it,
and the parables descriptive of several phases of the judgment;
and also, the promise of the Comforter to abide during His personal absence, were probably very imperfectly understood at the
time, nor could they have apprehended with any clearness the
meaning of His great prayer of intercession.

FRIDAY, 31ST MARCH, 8TH NISAN — SATURDAY, 1ST APRIL, 9TH NISAN.

Arriving at Bethany, He abides there for the night. JOHN xii. 1-9.
The next day He sups with Simon, the leper — Lazarus, MATT. xxvi. 6-13
Martha, and Mary being present. Here He is anointed MARK xiv. 3-9.
by Mary, while Judas and others are angry at so great

waste. At even, many come out of Jerusalem to see
Him and Lazarus. The rulers in the city hearing this,   JOHN xii. 10, 11.
consult how they may put Lazarus also to death.

The date of the arrival at Bethany is to be determined from
the statement of John (xii. 1), that He came "six days before
the Passover." But how shall these six days be reckoned?
Shall both extremes, the day of His arrival and the first day of
the Passover, be included, or both excluded? or one included
and one excluded? The latter mode of computation is more
generally received. Adopting this mode, we reckon from the
Passover exclusive to the day of arrival inclusive. But here a
new question meets us: What day shall be reckoned as the first
of the Passover, the 14th or 15th Nisan? The language of
Moses is (Levit xxiii. 5), "In the fourteenth day of the first
month at even is the Lord's Passover." Counting backward
from the fourteenth and excluding it, the sixth day, or the day
of the arrival at Bethany, was the 8th Nisan. What day of the
week was this? If the fourteenth fell on Thursday, the eighth
was on Friday preceding; if on Friday, the eighth was on
Saturday, or the Jewish Sabbath.[1]

Most.	Robin- son.	The 14th on Thursday.	Modern Time.	Jewish Time.	The 14th on Friday.	Strong.	Gres- well.
6	..	Friday	March 31	Nisan 8	Saturday	..	6
5	6	Saturday	April 1	" 9	Sunday	6	5
4	5	Sunday	" 2	" 10	Monday	5	4
3	4	Monday	" 3	" 11	Tuesday	4	3
2	3	Tuesday	" 4	" 12	Wedn'sd'y	3	2
1	2	Wedn'sd'y	" 5	" 13	Thursday	2	1
..	1	Thursday	" 6	" 14	Friday	1	..
..	..	Friday	" 7	" 15	....	..	..

Owing to these differences in the modes of computation, very
different results are reached by harmonists. Robinson, including both extremes, and counting from the fourteenth, or Thursday, makes Him to have arrived on Saturday, the ninth.
Strong, computing the same way, but making the fourteenth to
fall on Friday, makes the arrival on Sunday, the ninth. Gres

---

[1] So Meyer, Alford,

well, including one extreme, and placing the Passover on Friday, the fourteenth, makes it to have been on Saturday. Most,
however, making the fourteenth Thursday, place it on Friday
the eighth.[1] And this seems, on other grounds, the most likely.
That Jesus would, without necessity, travel on the Sabbath,
we cannot suppose; much less that He would go on that day
from Jericho to Bethany, a distance of fourteen or fifteen miles.[2]
Caspari thinks that He remained with Zacchæus at Jericho over
the Sabbath, and on Sunday went to Bethany. Some, as Robinson, suppose that He went on Saturday only a Sabbath day's
journey; but that He should have come on Friday so near to
Bethany and then have encamped, to finish the journey after
sunset of the Sabbath, is not probable. The supposition of
Greswell that He spent the night at the house of Zacchæus, who
lived between Jericho and Bethany, and went on to Bethany the
next day, is wholly without proof, and besides, does not meet
the difficulty. We infer that He did journey directly from
Jericho to Bethany; first, from the fact that the whole intervening country is a wilderness, without city or village, where no
one would, without necessity, spend the night; second, that He
was with the crowd of pilgrims, whose course was direct to
Jerusalem, and who would naturally so arrange their movements
as to reach it before the Sabbath. From Matthew (xxi. 1) and
Mark (xi. 1) it might be inferred that the Lord went on at once
to Jerusalem, without stopping at Bethany, as said by John.
But the silence of the Synoptists is not a contradiction; it does
not exclude such a stop. All that took place from the departure
from Jericho to the arrival at the Mount of Olives is passed over.
There is nothing to forbid us to insert a stop at Bethany for a
night and day, and longer, if we have other sources of information.

We can easily understand why the Lord should desire to
stop at Bethany rather than go on to the city. Here He found
repose and peace in a household whose members were bound
to Him by the strongest ties; and here, in seclusion and quiet,
He could prepare Himself for the trials and anguish of the

---

[1] Friedlieb, Bucher, Wieseler, Lichtenstein, Tholuck, Keil.
[2] Wieseler, 378.

coming week; and this continued to be His home till His
arrest.

The distance from Jericho to Jerusalem is, according to
Josephus, a hundred and fifty furlongs; and from the Jordan to Jericho, sixty.   From Jericho to Bethany is about fifteen
miles; and all travellers agree in describing the way as most
difficult and dreary.

It is much disputed when the supper was made for the
Lord.   John merely says, xii. 1: "Then Jesus, six days before the
Passover, came to Bethany . . . there they made Him a supper."
This does not determine whether the supper was upon the day
of His arrival, or the next, or even later; still the more obvious
interpretation is, that it was that day, or the next.   He also gives
us another note of time, in verse 12: "On the next day much
people . . . . took branches of palm trees."

But to what is this "next day" related? to the events immediately preceding (verses 9, 10) — the visit of many of the Jews
to Bethany and the consultation of the chief priests — or to the
day of His arrival at Bethany; or to the supper? If to the consultation of the priests, as by Friedlieb, the day is undetermined;
if to the day of His arrival, as by Meyer, the supper must have
been on the evening of that day; if to the feast, as by M. and M.,
we are still uncertain.   Those who put His arrival at Bethany
on Saturday or on Sunday, put the supper on the evening of the
same day; but most of those who put the arrival on Friday, put
the supper on the evening of the next day, or Sabbath evening.
And this seems most probable if we understand the words,
"There they made Him a supper," to mean that it was a supper
given specially in His honor, and not an ordinary repast.
It is so understood by Westcott: "They, the people of the village"; and by Godet, who connects the "therefore" — οὖν — of
verse second with the mention of the resurrection of Lazarus in
the first verse.   In this case, some time would be needed for
preparation, and this was gained if the feast was on the day following His arrival.   We can also thus easily explain the presence of the Jews from Jerusalem, the sojourn of the Lord at
Bethany over the Sabbath giving opportunity for all who wished
to visit Him.

But the more common opinion is, that the supper was given either by the family of Lazarus, or by Simon the leper. That it was at the house of Simon is said by Mark (xiv. 3), and the more natural understanding is, that it was made by him. It is in favor of this that Lazarus is mentioned as "one that sat at meat with Jesus," apparently one of the invited guests; for if the supper had been given by himself or by his sisters, his presence would have been taken as a matter of course. But this is by no means convincing; even if at his own table the peculiar position in which he stood as one raised from the dead, would cause special mention of him. That "Martha served," does not show that she was in her own house; her feeling of gratitude would impel her to render her service in the house of a friend or neighbor. There is nothing that enables us to decide positively where the supper was given; Meyer, who supposes it to have been made by Martha on the evening of the day of His arrival, describes it as only "the usual domestic entertainment a little more richly set forth." Of this Simon nothing is known but what is implied in the name "leper." He is generally supposed to have been healed by the Lord. One tradition makes him to have been the father of Lazarus; another, the husband of Martha (Winer, ii. 464).

We meet here the question whether the supper mentioned by Matthew (xxvi. 6–13) and Mark (xiv. 3–9) is identical with that of John (xii. 2–8.) They have all in common an anointing of the Lord, but differ as to the time; John putting this supper six days before Passover, the Synoptists two days. Lightfoot makes them on this ground to be distinct: one given by Lazarus on the evening of the Sabbath, the 9th Nisan; the other, given by Simon on Tuesday evening, the 12th Nisan.[1] Most identify the two, but do not agree as to the time, some affirming that John puts it in its right order, and that the Synoptists mention it later only for the purpose of explanation; others, that John anticipates it, and that the Synoptists have the right order.[2] A close examination of Matthew and Mark shows us that their account of the supper

---

[1] Clericus, A. Clarke, McKnight, Whitby, make them distinct. See *contra* Michaelis, in Townsend, part v. note 37.

[2] For John's order the great majority of harmonists; for that of Matthew and Mark: Bynaeus, Newcome, Da Costa, Wichelaus, Röpe, McClellan; some put it on Wednesday evening, so Rob.; but see Riddle, Har., 237.

is brought in parenthetically.[1] Two days before the feast of the
Passover, the chief priests and elders hold a council at the
palace of Caiaphas the high priest, and consult how they may
kill Jesus. They dare not arrest Him openly and with violence,
but will do it by subtlety; yet, even this they fear to do during
the feast. The result of their consultation thus is, that the
arrest be postponed till the feast is past, or, as some say, that
it be made before the feast. But the Lord had declared, that
after two days was the Passover, and then He should be betrayed
to be crucified. Matthew and Mark, therefore, proceed to show
how the Lord's words were fulfilled through the treachery of
Judas, and the priests and elders made to change their resolution.
This apostate, coming to the priests, offers to betray Him into
their hands, and will do it so soon as an opportunity presents.
Thus the matter is left between Judas and them, and they await
his action.

Turning now to the account of the supper, we ask why it is
thus interposed between the consultation of the priests and the
action of Judas? Plainly, that it may explain his action. He
was offended that so much money should be wasted at the
anointing of the Lord, and in his covetousness, as here revealed,
we find the explanation of his subsequent treachery. But it is
said that neither Matthew nor Mark makes any special mention
of Judas at the supper, and, therefore, give no explanation of
his treachery. They say only that certain of the disciples were
displeased. It must be admitted that, had we not the narrative
of John, it would not be obvious why they should mention this
supper in this connection. There may be some reason unknown
to us why they omit the name of Judas as the one chiefly
offended. Yet, even with this omission, an impartial reader
could hardly fail to infer that to the supper at Bethany we should
trace the immediate origin of the treachery they relate. Some,
however, think the supper to be mentioned here upon other
grounds,[2] perhaps because of the anointing, of which McClellan
speaks " as a memorable act of faith in the coming Passion."
There is nothing in the language of Matthew or Mark which

---

[1] Wieseler, Stier, Greswell, Lewin, Ellicott, and many.

[2] Ebrard, 474; Strong, Har., note 51.

necessarily implies that this supper took place two days before
the Passover, for the statement of the former (verse 14), " Then
Judas . . . went unto the chief priests," does not connect
the time of his visit with the supper, but with their council
(verses 3-5). (So Keil.) All between verses 6-13 comes in
parenthetically as an explanatory statement. But against this it
is objected,[1] that Judas would not have cherished a purpose of
treachery four days in his heart without executing it. But the
betrayal of his Lord was not a hasty, passionate act, done in a
moment of excitement. It was done coolly, deliberately, and it
is this which gave it its atrocious character. Greswell remarks
(iii. 129) that " this history is divisible into three stages, each of
which has been accurately defined: the first cause and conception of his purpose; the overt step toward its execution; and
lastly, its consummation. The consummation took place in the
garden of Gethsemane; the overt step was the compact with the
Sanhedrin; the first cause and conception of the purpose, if they
are to be traced up to anything on record, must be referred to
what happened at Bethany."

We give the following as the probable order of events:
Jesus, leaving Jericho on the morning of Friday, reaches Bethany in the afternoon, perhaps about sunset. He leaves the pilgrims with whom He has journeyed, and who go on to Jerusalem, and with His apostles stops till the Sabbath should be
past; they being probably received by some of His friends, and
He Himself doubtless finding a home in the dwelling of Lazarus and his sisters. The next day, being the Sabbath, is spent at
Bethany; and in the afternoon Simon the leper makes Him a
supper, at which His disciples and Lazarus and his sisters were
present. During the afternoon much people of the Jews, —
"the common people of the Jews," (John xii. 9) R. V., — who had
heard through the pilgrims of His arrival, go out to see Him
and Lazarus; from this desire to see Lazarus we may infer either
that he had been with Jesus at Ephraim, or that those who went
to see him were pilgrims; and many of them believe on Him.
This, coming to the ears of the chief priests, leads to a consulta
tion how Lazarus may be put to death with Jesus.

---

[1] Robinson, Har., 210.

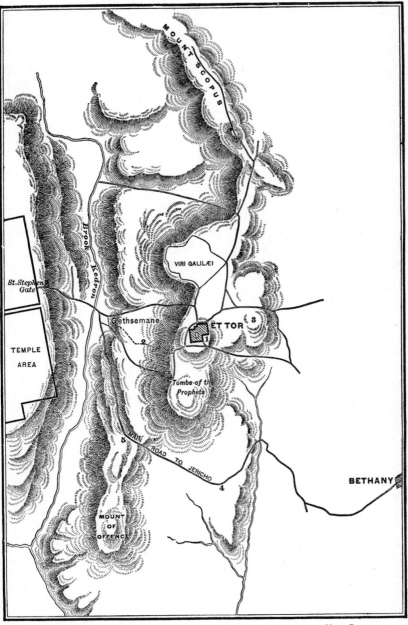

SUNDAY, 2D APRIL, 10TH NISAN, 783. A. D. 30.

Leaving Bethany, He sends to an unnamed village for an ass upon which to ride, and sitting upon it He enters Jerusalem amidst the shouts of His disciples and of the populace. As He looks upon the city from the Mount of Olives, He weeps over it. All the city is greatly moved, and the Pharisees desire Him to rebuke His disciples. He visits the temple; but, after looking around Him, leaves it and goes out with the Twelve to Bethany, where He passes the night.

MATT. xxi. 1–11.
MARK xi. 1–10.
LUKE xix. 29–44.
JOHN xii. 12–19.

MARK xi. 11.

The day following the supper at Bethany, the Lord sent two of His disciples to a village which is described as lying "over against them;" where they would find an ass and her colt, and these they were to bring to Him. Some suppose that the owners, if not His disciples, were at least friendly, and learning for whose use the animals were desired, at once consented; others, without sufficient ground, suppose them to have been strangers, and infer a supernatural knowledge on the Lord's part of the ownership of the animals.

As this village is generally supposed to be Bethphage, and Bethphage lay upon the Mount of Olives, some notice of this mount is necessary.

MOUNT OF OLIVES AND BETHPHAGE.

Under the general term, Mount of Olives, is included the long ridge of chalky limestone east of Jerusalem, running north and south, and separated from the city by the valley of the Kidron. This ridge has three peaks or eminences: that to the north known as Mt. Scopus; that in the middle, the Mount of Olives distinctively so called; that to the south, the Mount of Offence (Rob., i. 274). We are here concerned only with the middle one, which lies directly east of the temple. This is also divided into three points or tops: the northern, bearing the traditional name of Viri Galilæi (Acts i. 12); the middle one, where is the Moslem village et Tôr of some dozen houses, and the Church of the Ascension; and the southern, enclosed and in possession of the Roman Catholics, who have here two churches and a convent. With the northern one we are interested as the place where the Twelve are said to have stood when the Lord ascended, but it will be examined when the Ascension comes before us. The central eminence has two points, of which the eastern is the highest, some 2,664 feet above the Mediterranean, and about 200 feet above the temple. This point is owned by the Russians, who have here rebuilt an old church and some small convents, planted trees, "and above all erected a very high, square-shaped belfry, standing alone, with very many bells of various sizes, amongst which is one very large" (Qt. St., Oct., 1889). Another church after the Muscovite style has been built lower down on the west slope.

The road from Jericho to Jerusalem through Bethany runs between the Mount of Offence and the Mount of Olives, but there is another more direct running over the central summit.

Bethphage. — There are two chief opinions respecting the position of Bethphage: 1. That it was a village distinct from Bethany, but adjacent to it, and the same mentioned by Matthew (xxi. 2), by Mark (xi. 2,) and by Luke (xix. 30); 2. That it was an ecclesiastical suburb of Jerusalem, rather a district than a village.

1. It may be inferred from Mark (xi. 1): "And when they came nigh to Jerusalem, unto Bethphage and Bethany at the Mount of Olives, He sendeth forth two of His disciples," and from the like expression in Luke (xix. 29), that they were two distinct yet adjacent villages, and both upon the Mount of Olives. In Matthew (xxi. 1) Bethphage only is mentioned: "And when they drew nigh unto Jerusalem, and were come unto Bethphage, unto the Mount of Olives, then sent, ff." In John (xii. 1) mention is made of Bethany, but not of Bethphage. As the journey from Jericho to Jerusalem was from northeast to southwest, it is supposed that Bethphage was first reached, and therefore was east or northeast of Bethany, and more remote from the city. (So Winer, Rob., Meyer, Tristram.) Others, however, maintain that the Evangelists in their narratives take Jerusalem as the centre, and mention Bethphage first because first reached by one going eastward to Jericho, and so nearer the city than Bethany. (So Licht., Ellicott, Farrar, Lange.) Another reason for this order is given by Greswell (iii. 75): "Bethphage lay upon the direct line of this route, but Bethany did not, so that one travelling from Jericho would come to Bethphage first, and would have to turn off from the road to go to Bethany."

But before we can define the relative positions of the two places, we must examine their supposed sites; several have been suggested.

Barclay (65) finds a site which he thinks answers all demands of the narrative, a little south of the road from Jericho to Jerusalem. It is upon "a spur of Olivet distant rather more than a mile from the city, situated between two deep valleys, on which are tanks, foundations, and other indubitable evidences of the former existence of a village." Porter (Hand-Book) refers to a site upon the projecting point of a ridge, "and marked by scarped rocks, cisterns, and old stones." In the twelfth century Bethphage was placed by tradition between Bethany and the Mount of Olives, and no other traditional site was known. Modern explorations give us little knowledge. In 1879 the ruins of a mediæval church were discovered on the ridge joining the Mount of Olives to the hill above Bethany, in which was found a slab of stone having on it paintings and inscriptions (See Pict. Pal., 83; Twenty-one Years' Work, 177.) This is ascribed to the twelfth century, but gives no help as to the true site of Bethphage; it shows only the tradition of that time.

2. That Bethphage was counted as an ecclesiastical suburb of Jerusalem, and was on the western slope of the Mount. This is often said by the Talmudists, some of whom speak as if it were locally within the city walls; but their meaning seems to be, that lying outside the walls but contiguous to them, it was reckoned as holy as the city itself. The reason of this is found in the fact that at the great feasts too many were present to be able to find lodging in the city, and hence it was necessary to enlarge it by sanctifying some space without the walls. The western slope of the Mount of Olives, and perhaps also its summit, were so sanctified and regarded as holy. Lightfoot (Vol. X., Chronograph. Cent., 76) quotes several writers to show that a sentence of the Sanhedrin pronounced at Bethphage was valid; that the Passover might be eaten there, and the shewbread be baked there. He thinks that Bethphage was "a tract without the walls, but regarded as holy as if in the city itself"; and that the outermost street of the city but within the walls, was called by the same name. Edersheim (ii. 364) observes that Bethphage is sometimes spoken of as distinct from Jerusalem, while at others it is described as, for ecclesiastical purposes, part of the city itself. Neubauer (147) to reconcile the Talmudists, supposes it to have been near to Jerusalem, but not in it. Thus, when many were present at the feasts, and the city was not able to hold them, Bethphage was included in the holy limits, and the offerings of those in it were accepted (Hamburger, ii. 109; Sepp, v. 421).

But how far from city walls eastward did this suburb extend? Lightfoot says, 2,000 cubits, or a Sabbath day's journey; and that certain marks were set that its bounds might be known. The point on the Mount of Olives where Bethany and Bethphage touched on each other, was at this distance; and the place where the ass was tied may have been where one of these marks was set up (Luke xix. 29–30). To the same effect Conder says (H. B., 326): "It appears clear from a number of passages in the Talmud that Bethphage marked the Sabbatical line east of Jerusalem. The limit called 'the wall of

Bethphage' is about two thousand feet east of the east wall of
Jerusalem" (Caspari, 190). Assuming these statements to be well
founded, Bethphage was the name given to a district extending a
Sabbath day's journey east of the city up the slopes of Olivet, and
regarded as holy.

We must now further ask, Was there also a village called Bethphage? This is denied by Lightfoot: "There was no town at all
named Bethphage." (III. Har., 131; so Godet, Caspari.) Others
hold that there was a village, but that it later fell into decay, and its
site is unknown. But most commentators take Bethpage to be the
village mentioned by the Lord (Matt. xxi. 2): "Go into the village over
against you, and ye shall find an ass tied." (Meyer, Ellicott, Keil;
Weiss thinks that the village was Bethany; Ebrard, neither Bethany
nor Bethphage, but a third and unknown village. Schick, Qt. St.,
Oct., 1889, thinks this village to be that where the Bethphage stone
was found. See Jerusalem Survey, p. 331 ff.)

On the other hand, Caspari, who makes Bethphage a district embracing the whole of the Mount of Olives, and denies any village
of the name, thinks Bethany to be the particular spot within
Bethphage to which Jesus came. It is said by Godet: "He came to
Bethphage, the sacred district; and to Bethany, the hamlet where this
district began." But we may rather say, with Lightfoot, that they
were two distinct districts or townships; and that when it is said
(Acts i. 12) that "the Lord led His disciples out to Bethany, a Sabbath day's journey," this "brought them to the tract of Olivet where
the name of Bethphage ceased and that of Bethany began; and here
He ascended." The language of Luke: "When He was come nigh
to Bethphage and Bethany," implies that He was on the border line
of the two. (Thus in substance Williams, Holy City, ii. 443.) This
does not forbid the existence of two villages or hamlets, one, Bethphage, giving its name to the western, the other, Bethany, to the
eastern slope of the mount. (See McClellan, 589; Winer, i. 174.)

We may, then, believe that the Lord had reached the point where
the two districts, Bethany and Bethphage, joined, when He sent the
two disciples for the colt. Whether the village to which He sent
them was called Bethphage, and, if so, where this village stood, are
questions which our present knowledge does not enable us to answer.

Without, then, attempting to define the exact position of Bethphage, we may thus arrange the circumstances connected with the
Lord's departure from Bethany: Leaving this village on foot, attended
by His disciples and others, He comes to the place where a neighboring village, probably Bethphage, is in view over against them, perhaps separated from them by a valley. At this point He arrests His

march, and sends two of His disciples to find and bring to Him an
ass tied and her colt with her. When her owners demanded of them
why they took the ass, they had only to say that the Lord had need
of it, and the sight of Jesus with the attendant crowds would at once
explain why He needed it. It is not, therefore, necessary to suppose
that the owners were His disciples, much less that any previous
arrangement had been made with them. The animals being
brought to Him, He is seated upon the colt, and amidst the acclamations of the multitude, ascends to the top of the Mount.

As both the ass and her colt were brought, it has been questioned
upon which the Lord rode. But Mark and Luke are express that it
was the colt.[1] The multitude that accompanied the Lord was composed, in part, of those going up to the city from the neighborhood,
and of the pilgrims from Galilee and Peræa on their way thither; and
in part, of those who, hearing of His coming, had gone out from the
city to meet Him (John xii. 12, 13). It is probable that most of the
latter were pilgrims, not inhabitants of the city, and are spoken of
by John as "people that were come to the feast." The priests and
scribes and Pharisees stood as angry or contemptuous spectators, and
not only refused to join in the rejoicings and hosannas, but bade Him
rebuke His disciples, and command them to be silent (Luke xix. 39).

The road by which the Lord passed over Olivet was probably the
southern or main road which passes between the summit which contains the Tombs of the Prophets, and that called the Mount of
Offence. This was the usual road for horsemen and caravans; a steep
footpath leads over the central peak, and a winding road over the
northern shoulder, neither of which could He have taken. Stanley
(187) thus describes the procession: "Two vast streams of people
met on that day. The one poured out from the city, and, as they
came through the gardens whose clusters of palm rose on the southeastern corner of Olivet, they cut down the long branches, as was
their wont at the Feast of Tabernacles, and moved upward toward
Bethany with loud shouts of welcome. From Bethany streamed forth
the crowds who had assembled there the previous night. The road soon
loses sight of Bethany. . . . The two streams met midway.
Half of the vast mass turning round, preceded, the other half followed.
Gradually the long procession swept up over the ridge where first
begins ' the descent of the Mount of Olives ' toward Jerusalem. At
this point the first view is caught of the southeastern corner of the
city. The temple and the more northern portions are hid by the
slope of Olivet on the right; what is seen is only Mount Zion. . .

---

[1] Ebrard, 480; Meyer, *in loco.*

It was at this precise point, 'as He drew near at the descent of the Mount of Olives,' (may it not have been from the sight thus opening upon them?) that the shout of triumph burst forth from the multitude: 'Hosanna to the Son of David! Blessed is He that cometh in the name of the Lord!' Again the procession advanced. The road descends a slight declivity and the glimpse of the city is again withdrawn behind the intervening ridge of Olivet. A few moments, and the path mounts again; it climbs a rugged ascent; it reaches a ledge of smooth rock, and in an instant the whole city bursts into view. It is hardly possible to doubt that this rise and turn of the road, this rocky ledge, was the exact point where the multitude paused again; and 'He, when He beheld the city,' wept over it." [1]

Tradition makes the Lord to have crossed the summit of the Mount of Olives, and puts the spot where He wept over the city about half-way down on its western slope. [2]

Placing the Lord's arrival at Bethany on Friday, the supper and anointing on Saturday, His solemn entry into the city took place on Sunday. [3] As to the hour of the entry nothing is said, but from Mark xi. 11 it appears that it was late in the afternoon when He entered the temple; and, as no events intermediate are mentioned, the entry into the temple seems to have been soon after the entry into the city. It was, then, probably near the middle of the day when He left Bethany. Luthardt, who puts the supper on Sunday, makes the entry to have been still later upon the same day; but this would have brought it to the verge of evening. Greswell puts His departure from Bethany about the ninth hour, or 3 P. M.; His arrival in the temple before the eleventh; His departure before sunset.

This entry of Jesus into Jerusalem, "the city of the great king," was a formal assertion of His Messianic claims. It was the last appeal to the Jews to discern and recognize His royal character. He came as a king, and permitted His disciples and the multitudes to pay Him kingly honors. He received, as rightly belonging to Him, the acclamations, "Hosanna to the Son of David! Blessed is He that cometh in the name of the Lord;" "Blessed be the kingdom of our father David, that cometh in the name of the Lord;" "Blessed be the King that cometh in the name of the Lord: peace in heaven, and glory in the highest;" "Hosanna! Blessed is the King of Israel, that cometh in the name of the Lord." He was the Son of David, the King of Israel, coming in the name of the Lord. But,

---

[1] This point is about 100 feet higher than the valley of the Kidron near St. Stephen's gate.

[2] See Van der Velde's Map of Jerusalem ; Ellicott, 288, note 1.

[3] So Lichtenstein, Robinson, Wieseler, Gardiner, Friedlieb, Wichelhaus, Meyer.

although this triumphal entry excited general attention — "all the city was moved" (Matthew xxi. 10), — yet it is plain from the question put by the citizens, "Who is this?" that, as a body, they had taken little part in the matter. "And the multitude said, This is Jesus, the prophet of Nazareth of Galilee" (verse 11). This multitude, thus distinguished from the citizens, consisted doubtless of those who had escorted Him from Bethany, and who were mostly Galilæans; and their answer, as remarked by Meyer, seems to show a kind of local pride in Him as from Galilee, their own prophet. But this very answer was peculiarly adapted to set the people of Judæa against Him. (See John vii. 52.)

The visit to the temple, for this was the goal to which the procession directed its march,[1] and its purification, are put by Matthew (xxi. 12) as if immediately following the entry; but Mark states that He merely entered the temple, and, looking around Him, went out because the even had come, and returned to Bethany with the Twelve. Luke (xix. 45) gives us no mark of time. The statement of Mark is so precise, that we cannot hesitate to give it the preference.[2] Some suppose the Lord to have twice purified the temple; on the day of His entry, and again the next day.[3] Others, that He began it on one day and finished it on the next, cleansing first the inner and then the outer court. Patritius makes Him to have healed the blind and lame, to have answered the priests and scribes (Matt. xxi. 14–16), and to have heard the request of the Greeks (John xii. 20–22), on this first entry. Alford's supposition,[4] that Mark relates the triumphal entry a day too soon, that Jesus, in fact, first entered the city privately, noticed the abuses in the temple, and returning to Bethany, the next day made His triumphal entry, has no good basis. A private entry before the public one conflicts with the whole tenor of the narrative.

After looking about the temple ("round about upon all things," Mark), as if He would observe whether all was done according to His Father's will, He goes out, and returns to Bethany. Greswell (iii. 100) remarks: "It is probable that the traders, with their droves of cattle and their other effects, had already removed them for the day." But if so, He saw by plain marks that His Father's house was still made a house of merchandise. There can be little doubt that He

---

[1] See Mark xi. 11; R. V.: "He entered into Jerusalem, into the temple."

[2] Wieseler, Lange, Alexander, Robinson, Tischendorf, Gardiner, Meyer, Ellicott, McClel., Eders. For the order of Matthew, Farrar, Weitbrecht.

[3] Lightfoot, Townsend; Greswell, iii. 99. Found, once on Friday and again on Sunday; so apparently Neander.

[4] Note on Matt. xxi. 1.

spent the nights during Passion week in Bethany, and probably in the house of Lazarus.   Matthew says (xxi. 17): "He went out of the city into Bethany, and He lodged there."   Luke, speaking in general terms, says (xxi. 37): "And in the day-time He was teaching in the temple, and at night He went out and abode (lodged) in the mount that is called the Mount of Olives."   Probably Bethany is here meant as a district embracing a part of the mount, for He could not well, at this season of the year, without a tent, lodge in the open air. Alexander supposes that Luke would suggest that "a part of these nights was employed in prayer amidst the solitudes of Olivet." Some would put the request of the Greeks to see Jesus, and His answer to them (John xii. 20–36) upon this day; but it may better be referred to Tuesday, upon grounds to be there given.

Many would bring this visit of Jesus to the temple on the 10th Nisan into connection with the divine command to choose this day a lamb for the paschal sacrifice and supper (Ex. xii. 3–6), and thus find in it a mystical significance.   He was the true Paschal Lamb, and was now set apart for the sacrifice.[1]

MONDAY, 3D APRIL, 11TH NISAN, 783.   A. D. 30.

Jesus, leaving Bethany early with His disciples, is hungry, and beholding a fig tree by the way which has no fruit, He pronounces a curse against it.   Proceeding to the city, He enters the temple and purifies it. He heals there the blind and lame, and the children cry, "Hosanna to the Son of David."   His reproofs enrage the priests and scribes, who seek how to destroy Him.   In the evening He departs, and returns to Bethany.

MATT. xxi. 18, 19.
MARK xi. 12–14.

MATT. xxi. 12–17.
MARK xi. 15–19.
LUKE xix. 45–48.

Both Matthew and Mark relate that the Lord was hungry as He returned into the city; but upon what ground He had abstained from food that morning does not appear.   It could not well have been from the early hour of His departure from Bethany, but was probably a self-imposed fast.   It has been inferred from this circumstance that He could not have spent the night with His friends.   It may have been spent in solitude and prayer.

Into an examination of the supposed moral difficulties connected with the cursing of the fig tree, we cannot here enter.[2]   It is plain that this miracle was wrought because of its symbolic teachings.   The fig tree was the type of the Jewish people (Luke xiii. 6–9).   They

[1] Whitby, Greswell, Alford, Wieseler.
[2] See Trench, Miracles, p. 346.

had the law, the temple, all rites of worship, the externals of righteousness; but bore none of its true fruits.   Christ found nothing but leaves.   Some think the tree to have been unhealthy, and therefore a better symbol of the nation.   It is said by Neander: "A sound tree, suddenly destroyed, would certainly be no fitting type of the Jewish people."

Matthew relates the withering of the fig tree as if it took place, not only on the same day on which it was cursed, but within a few moments (verses 19, 20).   Mark, on the other hand, speaks as if the withering was not seen by the disciples till the next day (xi. 20).   Greswell, who supposes that the malediction instantly took effect, and that the tree began at once to wither, would make Matthew and Mark refer to two distinct conversations between the Lord and the disciples, — one that day, and the other upon the next.   More probably, Matthew brings together all that occurred upon both days, in order to complete his narrative.[1]

That this purification of the temple is distinct from that at the beginning of His ministry (John ii. 13–17) has been already shown. That the latter was passed over by the Synoptists, is explained from the fact that they begin their account of Jesus' ministry with His departure to Galilee after John the Baptist's imprisonment.   That John should omit the last, is wholly in keeping with the character of his Gospel.[2]   The first cleansing and rebuke had wrought no permanent results, and the old abuses were restored in full vigor.

After cleansing the temple, or that part of the court of the Gentiles called "the shops," where every day was sold wine, salt, oil, as also oxen and sheep,[3] He permits the blind and lame, probably those who asked alms at the gates, to come to Him, and He healed them.   These are the only cases of healing recorded as wrought by the Lord in the temple.   These healings, and the expressions of wonder and gratitude which they called forth, joined to the remembrance of the acclamations that had greeted Him the day before, led the children in the temple, who may have been members of the choir of singers employed in the temple service,[4] to cry, "Hosanna to the Son of David," greatly to the displeasure of the priests and scribes.   It is remarkable that children only are mentioned, and may indicate that already the multitude, overawed by the firm and hostile bearing of His enemies, had begun to waver, and dared no more openly express their good-will.   (See, however, Mark xi. 18.)

---

[1] So Alford, Trench, Krafft, Wieseler.

[2] See Edersheim, ii. 389, note.

[3] See Lightfoot, on Matt. xxi. 12.

[4] Lightfoot, The Temple Service, p. 56; Sepp, v. 439.

Some, from the fact that the children are here mentioned as cry-
ing Hosanna, and that in the temple, make it to have been on the day of
the Lord's entry.[1] But there is no difficulty in believing that the
children might now re-echo what they had heard the day before.[2]

Tuesday, 4th April, 12th Nisan, 783.   A. D. 30.

Returning into the city in the morning with His dis-ciples, they see the fig tree dried up from the roots, and this leads Jesus to speak to them respecting faith. As He enters the temple, the Pharisees ask Him by what authority He acts. He replies by a question respecting the baptism of John, and adds the parables of the two sons and of the wicked husbandmen. The Pharisees wish to arrest Him, but are afraid of the people. He speaks the parable of the king's son. The Pharisees and Herodians propose to Him the question concern-ing the lawfulness of tribute to Cæsar. The Sadducees question Him respecting the resurrection of the dead; and a lawyer, Which is the chief commandment in the law? He asks the Pharisees a question respecting the Messiah, and puts them to silence, and addressing the disciples and people denounces their hypocrisy.	Mark xi. 20-26. Matt. xxi. 20-22. Matt. xxi. 23-46. Mark xi. 27-33. Luke xx. 1-19. Mark xii. 1-12. Matt. xxii. 1-14. Matt. xxii. 15-46. Mark xii. 13-40. Luke xx. 20-47. Matt. xxiii.
After this He watches the people casting in their gifts, and praises the poor widow who casts in two mites. Some Greeks desiring to see Him, He prophe-sies of His death. A voice is heard from heaven. He speaks a few words to the people and leaves the tem-ple. As He goes out, the disciples point out to Him the size and splendor of the buildings, to whom He replies that all shall be thrown down. Ascending the Mount of Olives He seats Himself, and explains to Peter, James, John, and Andrew, the course of events till His return. He adds, that after two days was the Passover, when He should be betrayed. He goes to Bethany, and the same evening His enemies hold a council and agree with Judas respecting His betrayal.	Mark xii. 41-44. Luke xxi. 1-4. John xii. 20-50. Mark xiii. Luke xxi. 5-36. Matt. xxiv., xxv. Matt. xxvi. 1-5. Mark xiv. 1, 2. Matt. xxvi. 14-16. Mark xiv. 10, 11. Luke xxii. 1-6.

The withering of the fig tree seems to have begun as soon as
the Lord had spoken the curse against it. Matthew says,
"presently the fig tree withered away." Mark says, "it was
dried up from the roots." In twenty-four hours it was completely dead. That the disciples did not, at evening upon their
return to Bethany, see that it had withered, may be owing to
the late hour of their return, or that they did not pass by it.

---

[1] Alford, Newcome, Robinson.
[2] Krafft, Wieseler, Lichtenstein, Ellicott.

The people assembling at an early hour in the temple, Jesus
went thither immediately upon His arrival in the city, and began
to teach.   Very soon the chief priests and elders of the people,
and the scribes, came to Him, demanding by what authority He
acted.   It seems a question formally put to Him, and probably
by a deputation from the Sanhedrin.[1]   It differs essentially from
the question put to Him after the first purification (John ii. 18):
" What sign shewest thou unto us, seeing thou doest these
things ? "   Now it is : " By what authority doest thou these
things ?   And who gave thee this authority ? "   Then, they desired that He should work miracles as signs or proofs of His
divine mission.   But His miracles had not been sufficient to
convince them.   Now, he must give other vouchers.   He must
show himself to be authorized by those who, sitting in Moses'
seat, could alone confer authority.   But they had not authorized Him, and He was therefore acting in an arbitrary and illegal manner.   To this question He replies by another respecting
the baptism of John.   The Baptist had borne his testimony to
Him when, three years before, they had sent a deputation
to him (John i. 26).   If John was a prophet, and divinely commissioned, why had they not received his testimony?   This was
a dilemma they could not escape.   They could not condemn
themselves; they dared not offend the people; they must remain
silent.

Although thus repulsed, His enemies did not leave the temple, and He began to speak to them in parables (Mark xii. 1);
" the second beginning," says Stier, " as before in Galilee, so
now in Jerusalem."   It is to be noted that now, for the first
time, the Lord uttered plainly the truth in the hearing of the
Pharisees, that they would kill Him, and that in consequence the
kingdom would be taken from them.[2]   The point of these
parables was not missed by the Pharisees, but they dared not
arrest Him.

The parable of the marriage of the king's son is related by
Matthew only, for that in Luke (xiv. 16–24) was spoken much

---

[1] So Alexander, Meyer, Keil; Edersheim (ii. 381) thinks there could not have been
any formal meeting of the Sanhedrin, but only an informal gathering of the authorities.

[2] See Matt. viii. 11, 12.   These words seem to have been spoken to the disciples.

earlier.[1] It set forth more distinctly than the parables preceding, the rejection of the Jews, — those bidden of old; the
bidding of others in their place; and the destruction of their city.

Stung by these parables, so full of sharp rebuke, the Pharisees now consulted together how "they might entangle Him in His
talk," and they sent out to Him certain of their number, and of
the Herodians.   There is by no means agreement as to the position
of these Herodians, or why they are now acting with the Pharisees.
They are generally regarded as partizans of the Herods (Josephus,
Antiq., xv. 15. 9).   Edersheim (ii. 384) thinks them a party which
"honestly accepted the house of Herod as occupants of the Jewish throne"; Greswell (iii. 111), as "holding covertly the principles of Judas of Galilee," or, in other words, as secret nationalists.
Lutteroth, *in loco*, thinks them so called simply because subjects
of one of the Herods, and thus to distinguish them from the
Jews under Roman rule.   Never were Pharisaic craft and in-
veterate hostility more strikingly shown than in these attempts
to draw something from His own mouth which might serve as
the basis of accusation against Him.   The first question would
have been full of peril to one less wise than Himself, for
it appealed to the most lively political susceptibilities of the people.   No zealous Jew could admit that tribute was rightly due
to Cæsar, and much less could one who claimed to be the Messiah
admit this; for it was to confess that He was the vassal of the
Romans, a confession utterly incompatible with Messianic claims.
Yet if He denied this, the Herodians were at hand to accuse
him of treason, an accusation which the Romans were always
quick to hear.   But He avoided the artfully contrived snare
by referring the question to their own discernment.   God had
chosen them for His people, and He alone should be their king,
and therefore it was not right for them to be under heathen
domination.   Yet, because of their sins, God had given them
into the hands of their enemies, and they were now under
Roman rule.   This fact they must recognize, and in view of this
they must fulfil all duties, those to Cæsar as well as those to
God.

The question of the Sadducees was in keeping with the

---

[1] Meyer, Alford, Robinson, Tischendorf, Lichtenstein, Trench.

skeptical, scoffing character of that sect. Apparently, it was not so much designed to awake popular hatred against Him as to cast ridicule upon Him, and also upon their rivals, the Pharisees, by showing the absurd consequences of one of the most cherished pharisaic dogmas, the resurrection of the dead. Perhaps, also, they were curious to see how He would meet an argument to which their rivals had been able to give no satisfactory answer.[1]

The question of the lawyer seems to have been without any malicious motive on his part.[2] It referred to a disputed point among the schools of the Rabbis, one which he, admiring the wisdom of Jesus, wished to hear solved. Some, however, suppose (see Matt. xxii. 34) that the lawyer was sent by the Pharisees who had gathered together to devise a new attack.[3] But these two views are not really inconsistent. The lawyer, a man of ability and reputation, and on these grounds chosen to be their representative and spokesman, may have had a sincere respect for the wisdom that had marked Christ's previous answers; and proposed this question respecting the comparative value of the commandments rather to test His knowledge in the law than to array the people against him. Had the answer been erroneous, doubtless advantage would have been taken of it to His injury, although it is not obvious to us in what way; but it so commended itself to the intelligence of the lawyer, that he honestly and frankly expressed his approbation. (See Mark xii. 32–34.)

All his adversaries being silenced, the Lord proceeds in His turn to ask a question that should test their own knowledge, and inquires how the Messiah could be the Son of David, and yet David call Him Lord? Their inability to answer Him shows us how little the truth that the Messiah should be a divine being, the Son of God as well as Son of Man, was yet apprehended by them; and how all Christ's efforts to reveal His true nature had failed through their wickedness and unbelief.

It is questioned whether the Lord's words spoken of the scribes (Mark xii. 38–40; Luke xx. 45–47) are to be distinguished from those recorded by Matthew xxiii. Greswell (iii. 121) gives

---

[1] See Meyer, *in loco*. [2] Greswell, Alford.
[3] Meyer, Ebrard.

ten reasons for distinguishing between them, which, however, have no great weight. Most regard them as identical.[1] Wieseler (395) and Godet suppose Matthew to have included the address to the Pharisees recorded by Luke (xi. 39–52). We can scarce doubt that the Lord's address (Matt. xxiii.) was spoken as given by that Evangelist. Some parts of it are found in Luke, but, as said by Meyer, "The entire discourse has so much the character of a living whole, that although much that was spoken on other occasions may, perhaps, be mixed up with it, it is scarcely possible to disjoin such passages from those that are essentially original." (Verse 14 is put in R. V. in the margin.) The attempts of the Pharisees to entrap Him, their malice and wickedness veiled under the show of righteousness, awakened the Lord's deepest indignation, and explain the terrible severity of His language. They had proved that "they were the children of them which killed the prophets," and as the old messengers of God had been rejected and slain, so would they reject and slay those whom He was about to send. Thus should all the righteous blood shed upon the earth come upon them.

It is not certain who was the "Zacharias, son of Barachias," to whom the Lord refers as slain between the temple and the altar. Many identify him with the Zechariah son of Jehoiada, who was "stoned with stones at the commandment of the king in the court of the house of the Lord" (2 Chron. xxiv. 20, 21). In this case Barachias may have been another name of Jehoiada, as the Jews had often two names; or Barachias may have been the father and Jehoiada the grandfather; or, as it is omitted by Luke xi. 51, some, as Meyer, infer that it was not mentioned by Christ, but was added from tradition, and erroneously given, perhaps confounding him with the Zechariah son of Berechiah (Zech. i. 1). But if this Zacharias was meant, why is he called the last of the martyrs, since there were others later? The explanation given by Lightfoot is at least probable, that it was the last example in the Old Testament as the canon is arranged in the Hebrew, the books of Chronicles being at the end; and therefore the Lord cites the first, that of Abel, and this as the last. Both have also another circumstance in common — a call of the

---

[1] Ebrard, Meyer, Alford, Robinson, Krafft.

murdered for vengeance.   Thus Lightfoot says: "The requiring
of vengeance is mentioned only concerning Abel and Zacharias.
'Behold, the voice of thy brother's blood crieth unto me' (Gen.
iv. 10).   'Let the Lord look upon it, and require it'" (2 Chron.
xxii. 22).[1]   Lutteroth, *in loco*, thinks Zacharias to have been one
of "the many priests" mentioned by Josephus (War, i. 7. 5), who
were slain by Pompey's soldiers while carrying on services at
the altar, and whose name was known to the Jews.   Others
make this Zacharias to be prophetically spoken of, and identify him with the Zacharias, son of Baruch, mentioned by
Josephus,[2] who was slain by the Zealots in the midst of the
temple, and the body cast into the valley of the Kidron.   But
the Lord does not speak of blood to be yet shed, but of that
which had been shed ; and as the death of Abel was a well-
known historical event, so also was that of Zacharias.   Others refer to a tradition that Zacharias, father of John the
Baptist, was murdered by the Jews.[3]

Many make this discourse to the Pharisees to have been
spoken just before He left the temple, and His last words
there.   "It is morally certain," says Greswell, "that our Lord
immediately left the temple and never returned to it again."
But most follow the order of Mark (xii. 41–44), who places the
visit of Jesus to the treasury after this discourse.[4]   Seating Himself by the treasury or treasure chests in the court of the women
in which offerings were placed, He watches those who come to
bring their gifts ; and commendeth the gift of the poor widow.

The visit of the Greeks to Him, who are generally regarded as
proselytes of the gate, who had come to Jerusalem to worship,
is mentioned only by John (xii. 20–36).   From whence they
came, we do not know.   Some suppose them to have lived in
one of the cities of the Decapolis, and find here the reason why
they should have presented their request through Philip of Bethsaida.   (Sepp, v. 447, thinks them deputies of Abgarus king of
Edessa; see Westcott, *in loco*).   The occasion of their desire to

---

[1] So Meyer, Alford, Eders., Lange ; see Winer, ii. 711.   [2] War, iv. 5. 4.

[3] Thilo, Codex Apoc., i. 267; Hofmann, Leben Jesu, 134; Jones on the Canon of
the New Testament, ii. 134.   According to the latter, this tradition was very generally
credited in early times, as by Tertullian, Origen, Epiphanius.   See also Baronius, who
defends it.

[4] Krafft, Friedlieb, Robinson, Wieseler. Ellicott, Tischendorf.

see the Lord some have found in the words which they had
heard, that the kingdom of God should be taken from the Jews
and given to others. The time of their visit is not clear.
Some place it upon the evening of the triumphal entry.[1] But
the Lord's language fits better to the final departure from the
temple than to the time of the entry. Beside, if He was now
in the court of the women, it explains the request of the Greeks
to see Him, for if He had been in the outer court, all could
have seen Him, but into the inner court they could not come.
Upon these and other grounds it is placed here by many.[2] It is
not certain whether these Greeks did actually meet the Lord.
His words (verses 23–27) were not addressed directly to them,
but they may have been within hearing. Their coming is a
sign that His end is nigh, and that the great work for which
He came into the world is about to be fulfilled. Stier sets this
visit of the Greeks from the west in contrast to the visit of the
Magi from the east; the one at the end, the other at the beginning
of His life.

In reply to the Lord's prayer — " Glorify Thy name " (verse
28) — there " came a voice from heaven, I have both glorified it
and will glorify it again." These words, according to most
interpreters, were spoken in an audible voice. It is said by
Alford: " This voice can no otherwise be understood than as a
plain articulate sound, miraculously spoken, heard by all and
variously interpreted." This would imply that all present heard
the words plainly articulated. But this is not said. They heard
a voice, yet some said, " It thundered," and others, " An angel
spake to Him," which could not have been the case if the words
had been distinctly spoken. Probably, the capacity to understand the voice was dependent upon each man's spiritual condition and receptivity. To Jesus, and perhaps to the apostles
and disciples, it was an articulate voice ; to others, it was
indistinct, yet they recognized it as a voice, perhaps of an angel;
to others still, it was mere sound as if it thundered.[3] Townsend
would make it an answer to the Greeks who desired to see
Jesus, or, at least, spoken in their hearing. We find, however,

---

[1] Greswell, Krafft, Ebrard, Townsend, Stier.
[2] Robinson, Lichtenstein, Tischendorf, Wieseler, Ellicott, Gardiner.
[3] See Luthardt, *in loco.*

its true significance if we compare it with those other testimonies
of the Father to Him at His baptism and at His transfiguration
(Matt. iii. 17; xvii. 5).

After Jesus had finished His words in the temple, He " departed, and did hide Himself from them " (verse 36).   This was,
according to our order, on Tuesday evening, but others, as Godet,
put it on Wednesday evening.   His departing and hiding are
not to be understood of a night's sojourn in Bethany, but of His
final departure from the temple, and His sojourn in retirement
till His arrest.   His public work is over.   He appears no more
in His Father's house as a preacher of righteousness.   Henceforth all His words of wisdom are addressed to His own disciples.   The statements in verses 37–43 are those of the Evangelist.   But when were the Lord's words (verses 44–50) spoken?
Most regard them as a citation by the Evangelist from earlier
discourses, and introduced here as confirming his own remarks.[1]
" The words were spoken by Jesus; the selection is made by
John " (M. and M.); but according to others, they were spoken
by the Lord at this time.

The allusion of the disciples to the size and splendor of the
temple buildings seems to have been occasioned by His words
to the Pharisees foretelling its desolation (Matt. xxiii. 38).   That
so substantial and massive a structure could become desolate
was incredible to them, for they had as yet no distinct conception
that God was about to cast off His own covenant people, and
bring the worship He had appointed to an end.   This manifestation of incredulity led Him to say with great emphasis, that
the buildings should be utterly destroyed, not one stone being
left upon another.   This was literally fulfilled in the destruction
of the temple, though some of the foundation walls were not
wholly cast down.

It was probably at the close of the day, whether before or
after sunset we cannot tell, that He sat down on the Mount of
Olives over against the temple.   The city lay in full view before
Him.   Mark (xiii. 3) speaks of only four of the apostles —
Peter and James and John and Andrew, who asked Him

---

[1] So Lichtenstein, Meyer, Alford, Tholuck, Tischendorf, Godet; Luthardt and
Wieseler make them to have been spoken to the disciples.

privately when these things should be. Matthew (xxiv. 3) states that "the disciples came unto Him privately"; Luke (xxi. 7), that "they asked Him." There can be little doubt that Mark gives the more accurate account, and that these four only were present.[1] The remainder of the Twelve may have preceded Him on the way to Bethany. Alexander supposes that all were present, and that "the four are only mentioned as particularly earnest in making this inquiry, although speaking with and for the rest;" Ellicott takes the same view.

If His words were spoken to these four only, it implies that the predictions He uttered could not at that time be fittingly spoken to the body of the apostles; if to the apostles only, it shows that He would not have His predictions made public, as they would greatly have angered the Jews and their publicity have answered no good purpose.

The announcement to the disciples (Matt. xxvi. 1, 2) that "after two days was the Passover, when the Son of Man should be betrayed to be crucified," was probably made soon after His discourse upon the Mount of Olives, and so upon the evening of Tuesday. Perhaps He wished distinctly to remind them that His coming in glory must be preceded by His death and resurrection. Whether it was made to all the disciples or to the four, is not certain, but probably to all. Alford thinks that "it gives no certainty as to the time when the words were said; we do not know whether the current day was included or otherwise." If, however, Thursday was the 14th Nisan, which was popularly regarded as the first day of the Passover, according to the rule already adopted excluding one of the extremes and including the other, the announcement was made on Tuesday.[2] The meeting of the chief priests and the scribes and elders at the palace of Caiaphas for consultation, was upon the same evening. This may be inferred, at least, from Matthew's words (xxvi. 3), "Then assembled together," etc., the assembly being on the same day when the words were spoken (verse 2).[3] From the fact that the council met at the palace of Caiaphas, and also that its session was in the evening, we may infer that it was

---

[1] Lichtenstein, Alford, Lange, Greswell, McClellan.

[2] Meyer, Lichtenstein, DeWette.

[3] Meyer; Ellicott places it on Wednesday.

an extraordinary meeting, held for secret consultation.[1] (See Luke xxii. 4, where mention is made of "the captains"; as to the regular place of session, the hall Gazith, see Lightfoot, *in loco;* Schürer, ii. 1. 190.)   It may readily be supposed that the severe language of the Lord had greatly enraged His enemies, and that they felt the necessity of taking immediate steps against Him.   But they dared not arrest Him during the feast because of the people, and determined to postpone it till the feast was past.   Thus, it may be, at the same hour when Jesus was foretelling that He should suffer at the Passover, His enemies were resolving that they would not arrest Him during the feast.[2]   But the divine prediction was accomplished in a way they had not anticipated.   Judas, one of the Twelve, coming to them, offered for money to betray Him into their hands. They at once made a covenant with him, and he watched for an opportunity.   Still it does not appear that he designed to betray Him during the feast, and his action on the evening following the Paschal supper was, as we shall see, forced upon him by the Lord.   Whether Judas presented himself to the council at their session, is not said ; but it is not improbable that, hearing the Lord's rebukes of their hypocrisy, and seeing how great was their exasperation against Him, he had watched their movements, and learned of their assembly at the high priest's palace. This gave him the wished-for opportunity to enter into an agreement with them.

Assuming without further discussion the correctness of the order of events already given — that the Lord reached Bethany on Friday the 8th Nisan, that a supper was given Him that evening or the next, that He made His entry into the city on Sunday the 10th, that He cleansed the temple on Monday the 11th, that He taught in the temple on Tuesday the 12th, and that He spent Wednesday the 13th in retirement, there are still some minor points to be examined ; and here, as in our examination of other points during this week, we

---

[1] Tradition makes the bargain with Judas to have been entered into at the country house of Caiaphas, the ruins of which are still shown upon the summit of the Hill of Evil Counsel. The tradition is not ancient, but it is mentioned as a singular fact, that the monument of Annas, who may have had a country seat near his son-in-law, is found in this neighborhood. Williams, H. C., ii. 496.

[2] Some understand that they proposed to arrest Him before the feast. So Neander. Ewald; see contra, Meyer, *in loco.*

are to keep clearly in mind that the Jews computed the days from sunset to sunset.

(*a*) The time of the supper at Bethany, whether at the beginning or end of the Sabbath ? If the Lord reached Bethany before sunset on Friday, He might have partaken of the opening Sabbath meal, when the Sabbath lamp was lighted, and which was as good and bountiful as the family could afford. In this case we must, however, suppose that it was known to the givers of the supper that He was coming, and so all necessary preparations were made before His and the guest's arrival. But Lightfoot and others think it to have been at "the going out of the Sabbath." This best corresponds to the circumstances, and is more generally received.

(*b*) The time when the Lord spake the discourse in Matthew xxiv., xxv., and parallels. No one of the Evangelists gives us a distinct note of time, but from the fact that He was sitting on the Mount of Olives apparently on His way to Bethany, the natural inference is, that it was at the close of Tuesday, and the probability is that it was before or soon after sunset.

(*c*) The time of the coming of the Greeks. This we have put on Tuesday, after the Lord's words about the widow's mite. If so, His words spoken in answer to their request may be regarded as the last He ever spake in the temple, and thus as having a special significance. It is said (John xii. 36): "These things spake Jesus and departed, and did hide himself from them." The words in verses 44 to 50 are not to be understood as a later address, but as said by Godet, "a summary of all the testimonies of Jesus which the Jews ought to have believed, but which they rejected." (So, in substance, Meyer and most.)

(*d*) The visit of Judas to the chief priests. Was this on the same evening as the supper at Bethany, and after it, or four days later, either on Tuesday evening or on Wednesday ? Assuming, as we do, that the supper was on the evening following the Sabbath, and that Judas was then meditating his treachery, why should he delay so long to seek out the chief priests? It may be that he had formed the purpose to betray Him, but was made to waver in it by seeing how many friends the Lord had among the people, and the evident powerlessness of the rulers to arrest Him. It may have been the Lord's words addressed to the disciples, which he heard: "Ye know that after two days is the Passover, and the Son of Man is betrayed to be crucified," and which showed to him the impolicy and danger of any longer delay, so that he hastened that same evening to make his bargain with them. The note of time (Matt. xxvi. 14), "then — τότε

— Judas went unto the chief priests," refers back to the events in verses 1 to 5, and not 'to the supper. It cannot be decided with any certainty whether the consultation at the palace of Caiaphas was held on Tuesday or Wednesday, but from the words of Matthew, "From that time he sought opportunity to betray Him," the earlier period is preferable.

It is to be noted that, although the Lord spake early in His ministry (Matt. viii. 12) of the casting out of "the children of the kingdom," and the admission of the Gentiles, yet it was not till this time that He foretold the destruction of the holy city. On the day of His entry when He came in view of it, "He wept over it" as not knowing the time of its visitation, and therefore to be given into the hands of its enemies. (See also Matt. xxii. 7.) He did not, however, speak specifically of the temple and its destruction till His final departure from it (Matt. xxiv. 1), unless we regard His words in Luke (xxi. 20 ff.) as spoken earlier in the day.

It is in question whether the Lord's discourse in Matthew xxiv. and xxv. is to be identified with that in Luke xxi. 5 ff. They are said by some to be distinct discourses, and spoken at different places and times: one during the day and in the temple, the other at evening and on the Mount of Olives. It is said by Meyer: "There is no trace in Luke that this discourse was spoken on the Mount of Olives, but belongs to the transactions in the temple." The same conclusion is reached by some on internal grounds. (See Marquis in the Lutheran Qt. Rev., Jan., 1887.) It is a point which cannot be discussed here; but it may be remarked that Matthew's words seem to embrace some events subsequent in time to those foretold in Luke. It may be that some of the predictions given by the former which do not find any obvious applications to the destruction of Jerusalem by Titus, may look forward to events yet to come, since it is plain that God's purpose in the Jews is not yet accomplished. His declaration, "Heaven and earth shall pass away, but my words shall not pass away," implies that His predictions run far into the future, and cannot be fully comprehended till the consummation is reached.

We have still to ask how the disciples understood the Lord's prediction of the overthrow of the temple in its relation to the Messianic kingdom. It must at this time have been plain to them that the rulers would not receive Him as the Messiah, and that if He was to reign in Jerusalem, He must cast them out. It may have been this establishment of His authority which they understood by His "coming" — παρουσία — regarding it, on the one side, as the end of the present age — ὁ αἰὼν οὗτος — and on the other, as the beginning of the new

— ὁ αἰὼν ὁ μέλλων — "the world to come." Clear and oft-repeated as His declarations had been respecting His death, they were not understood; and therefore, they had no conception of a resurrection and return to earth as His coming; nor did they think of any personal departure, unless they held what Edersheim (ii. 436) affirms to have been the general opinion, that "the Messiah would appear, carry on His work, then disappear, probably for forty-five days, then reappear, and destroy the hostile powers of the world." That a period of great trouble would precede the setting up of the Messianic kingdom, was generally believed, and the wars of that time were designated as the "travail pangs" or "birth throes." (See Matt. xxiv. 8, in R. V.: "All these things are the beginning of travail." Hamburger, ii. 735.) The disciples would naturally understand that during this time the temple would be destroyed, and that the Lord would rebuild it at His coming or assumption of the kingdom.

WEDNESDAY, 5TH APRIL, 13TH NISAN, 783. A. D. 30.

During this day the Lord remained in seclusion at Bethany.

The Lord left the temple for the last time on Tuesday afternoon. His public labors were ended. There remained, however, a few hours before the Passover. How was this period spent? We can well believe that some part of it was spent alone that He might enjoy that free communion with God which He had so earnestly sought in the midst of His active labors, and which was now doubly dear to Him in view of His speedy death. Some part of it also was doubtless devoted to His disciples, giving them such counsel and encouragement as was demanded by the very peculiar and trying circumstances in which they were placed. That Wednesday was spent in retirement is generally admitted,[1] but is questioned by Stroud, who affirms that Jesus returned to Jerusalem on the morning of that day, and places at this time all in John xii. 20 ff.

THURSDAY, 6TH APRIL, 14TH NISAN, 783. A. D. 30.

From Bethany the Lord sends Peter and John into the city to prepare the Passover. He describes a man whom they would meet, and who would show them a room furnished, where they should make ready for the supper.

MATT. xxvi. 17-19
MARK xiv. 12-16.
LUKE xxii. 7-13.

---

[1] Wieseler, Robinson, Ellicott.

He remains at Bethany till toward evening, when He   MATT. xxvi. 20.
enters the city, and goes to the room where the supper   MARK xiv. 17.
is to be eaten.   LUKE xxii. 14.

At this feast the Jews divided themselves into companies or
households, of not less than ten nor more than twenty persons;
and these together consumed the paschal lamb.[1] One of the
number, acting as the representative of all, presented the lamb
in the court of the temple, and aided the Levites in its sacrifice.
The victim was then carried away by the offerer to the house
where it was to be eaten, and there wholly consumed. On this
occasion Peter and John acted as the representatives of the Lord
and of His apostles at the temple, and provided the bread, wine,
bitter herbs, and all that was necessary for the proper celebration of the feast; and it is probable, therefore, that they went
early in the day, though the cleansing of the house from leaven
was the work of the owner. It appears that, up to this time, the
disciples did not know where the Lord would eat the Passover,
and, as the hour drew nigh, inquired of Him (Matt. xxvi. 17).
The ground of His silence is supposed to have been the desire
to keep Judas in ignorance of the place, lest he should attempt
to arrest the Lord there. According to Mark and Luke, the two
apostles were to go to the city, and a man should meet them bearing a pitcher of water, whom they should follow into whatsoever
house he entered. There they should find a guest-chamber,
furnished and prepared, which the master of the house should
place at their disposal. Matthew says nothing of their meeting
the man with the pitcher, but makes the two to have gone
directly to the house. Meyer supposes that Matthew follows the
early tradition, which represents the master of the house as a
disciple of Jesus, who had, earlier in the week, arranged with
Him for the use of the guest-chamber; and that Mark and Luke
follow a later tradition, which represents the Lord as ignorant
of the man, but giving directions to the two through prophetic
foresight. There is no need of thus supposing two traditions.
Matthew passes over in silence the incident of the man with the
pitcher, upon what grounds we cannot state, but this silence is
no way inconsistent with the statements of the other Evangelists.

---

[1] Exod. xii. 3, 4; Josephus, War, vi. 9. 3.

From Mark and Luke it is apparent that no agreement had been made by the Lord for the room; else He would not have given such directions to the two apostles, but have sent them directly to the house.[1] Whether the master of the house was an entire stranger to Jesus, or a concealed disciple, like Joseph or Nicodemus, or an open follower, perhaps the father of the Evangelist Mark, is not certain.[2] The Lord's message to Him, "My time is at hand, I will keep the Passover at thy house, with my disciples," seems, however, to presuppose some previous acquaintance; as also the phrase, "the Master saith." This, however, is not necessary, if, as said by Alexander, "the whole proceeding be regarded as extraordinary, and the result secured by a special superhuman influence."

It is at this point that we meet the difficult questions connected with the last Passover, but before we enter upon them, it is necessary to have clearly before us the origin and nature of this feast, and the peculiarities of its observance.

THE PASSOVER.

1. Its origin and design. It was instituted in commemoration of the deliverance of the Jews in Egypt from the destroying angel when all the first-born of the Egyptians were slain (Ex. xii. 14 ff.). This remarkable deliverance was ever after to be commemorated by a feast of seven days, the feast of unleavened bread — τὰ ἄζυμα. But distinct from this feast and introductory to it, was the paschal supper, or "the Lord's passover," — τὸ πάσχα. The people being divided into households or families of not less than ten or more than twenty persons, a lamb was slain for each family, and afterwards eaten with unleavened bread and bitter herbs. Now followed a feast of seven days's continuance in which the bread eaten was unleavened.

2. The paschal supper. Distinguishing the paschal supper from the feast following, we ask the manner of its celebration. A lamb or goat was to be selected on the 10th Nisan, a male without blemish, and slain on the 14th "between the evenings" (Ex. xii. 6; Levit. xxiii. 5; Num. ix. 3). The expression, "between the evenings," was generally understood by the Jews of the period from the decline of the sun to its setting, or from 3–6 P. M. This was without doubt the

---

[1] Alford, Alexander.

[2] See Bynaeus, i. 480, who gives an account of early opinions. In proof of His discipleship, Edersheim refers to the fact that the Lord asked for a common apartment, but was assigned "the upper chamber," the largest and best room.

ruling mode of computation in the Lord's day (Josephus, War, vi. 9. 3; Antiq. v. 4. 3; Lightfoot, Temple Service, ix. 139; Eders., ii. 490). The Karaites and Samaritans, however, referred it to the period between sunset and dark, or from 6–7 P. M. (Winer, ii. 198). Wieseler refers it to a period a little before and a little after the going down of the sun, say from 5–7 P. M., citing Deut. xvi. 6 in proof. Ewald makes it to include three hours before and three hours after sunset.

The paschal lamb was originally slain by the head of each family in his own house, but afterward in the court of the temple where stood the brazen altar (Deut. xvi. 2–6). (As to the changes between the early and later usages, see Eders., "Temple," 180 ff.). After it was slain came the supper set out in some place prepared. This was upon the evening following the 14th Nisan; or, since the Jews counted the day to begin at sunset, on the beginning of the 15th. The lamb was to be wholly consumed before morning either by eating or by fire.

3. Feast of unleavened bread. The feast of unleavened bread, though to be distinguished from the paschal supper, yet began at the same time, inasmuch as all leaven was removed from the house by noon of the 14th, and no leavened bread eaten after this. But while the paschal supper was with unleavened bread, as was the rest of the feast, it had two elements peculiar to itself, the lamb and the bitter herbs. In one sense it was the beginning of the feast, but in another, it was regarded as distinct from it. As the paschal lamb was wholly consumed at the paschal supper, and as unleavened bread would but poorly furnish a festal table, other food must be provided, and was done in the Chagigah. These embraced the sacrifices of sheep and bullocks voluntarily made. Concerning them Maimonides (quoted by Ainsworth on Deut. xvi. 2) says: "When they offer the passover in the first month, they offer it with peace-offerings on the 14th day, of the flock and of the herd; and this is called the Chagigah, a feast offering of the 14th day. And of this it is said that "thou shalt sacrifice the passover to the Lord thy God of the flock and the herd."

To understand the relation of the Chagigah to the Passover in general, we must remember that this festival was the commemoration of a great national deliverance, and, as such, to be kept with thanksgiving and joy. The paschal supper, strictly speaking, seems to have had much less of the joyous element in it than the rest of the feast. As said by Lightfoot: "The eating of the lamb was the very least part of the joy; a thing rubbing up the remembrance of affliction, rather than denoting gladness and making merry." The lamb, which constituted the chief part of the supper, reminded them of that fearful

night when all the first-born of Egypt died; the bitter herbs with
which it was eaten, reminded them of the bitterness of their Egyptian
bondage; and all the attendant circumstances would tend to beget
seriousness and reflection. The festival character of the season appeared much more upon the succeeding day when the peace-offerings
voluntarily presented to God in token of thankfulness were eaten.

It was the word of the Lord: "None shall appear before me
empty" (Ex. xxiii. 15), and this was understood of the burnt-offerings
and peace-offerings in addition to the paschal lamb. It is said by
Maimonides (quoted by Ainsworth, *in loco*): "The rejoicing spoken
of at the feasts is that he offers peace-offerings . . . . and these
are called peace-offerings of the rejoicing of the feast" (Deut. xxvii. 7).
The day when they were offered is called "the first great day of the
feast"; at the passover, on the 15th Nisan. But were they also eaten
at the paschal supper? That they sometimes were, is admitted; but,
according to Lightfoot (on John xviii. 28), only when the lamb was
not sufficient for the company. It is said by Edersheim ("Temple,"
186): "The Chagigah might be twofold. The first Chagigah was
offered on the 14th Nisan, the day of the paschal sacrifice, and
formed afterwards part of the paschal supper. The second Chagigah
was offered on the 15th Nisan, on the first day of the feast of unleavened bread." But the first was only offered when the lamb was
not sufficient for a meal. The usual time for the Chagigah was on
the 15th after the morning sacrifice, and with them the rejoicing was
more directly connected.

4. The wave sheaf. The ceremonies of the second day of the
feast — the 16th Nisan — were peculiar, and are important to be
noted. Upon this day the first fruits of the barley harvest were
brought to the temple, and waved before the Lord to consecrate the
harvest, and not till this was done might any one begin his reaping
(Levit. xxiii. 10–12; Josephus, Antiq., iii. 10. 5). (As to the connection of this rite with the general scope of the passover, see Winer,
ii. 201; Bähr, ii. 638.)

Thus we find in the paschal festival three distinct solemnities:
First. The killing of the paschal lamb on the afternoon of the 14th
Nisan, and the eating of it the evening following, or on the beginning of the 15th. Second. The feast of unleavened bread exclusive
of the paschal supper, and continuing to the close of the 21st day
of Nisan. Third. The offering of the first fruits of the barley harvest
on the 16th Nisan, or second day of the feast. To the latter no distinct allusion is made by the Evangelists.

The removal of the leaven from their houses, the preparations for
the paschal supper, and the sacrifice of the lamb, all taking place on

the 14th Nisan, this day was popularly called the first day of the feast, thus extending it to eight days.[1] The Evangelists follow this popular usage (Matt. xxvi. 17; Mark xiv. 12; Luke xxii. 7). Upon each of the seven days of the feast was offered a sacrifice for the whole people (Num. xxviii. 19–24). The first and last days of the feast, or the 15th and 21st, were holy days, or sabbaths (Lev. xxiii. 7, 8). But these feast sabbaths do not seem ever to have been regarded as equal in sacredness to the week-Sabbaths; and it is important that the distinction between them should be clearly seen, as it has an important bearing upon several points to be hereafter discussed.

5. Feast Sabbaths. Besides the weekly Sabbath, there were seven days of the year that had a sabbatical character: the first and seventh of the feast of unleavened bread; the day of Pentecost; the first and the tenth of the seventh month; and the first and eighth of the feast of Tabernacles. Of these, one, the tenth of the seventh month, the day of Atonement, was put on the same footing as the weekly Sabbath in respect to labor. No work at all could be done upon it; but on the other six feast sabbaths they could do no servile work (Lev. xxiii. 3–39). These were called by the Talmudists "good days." It is not wholly clear what kind of work was not servile, but the preparation of food was expressly permitted (Exod. xii. 16). Maimonides (quoted by Ainsworth) says: "All work needful about meat is lawful, as killing of beasts, and baking of bread, and kneading of dough, and the like. But such work as may be done in the evening of a feast day they do not on a feast day, as they may not reap, nor thrash, nor winnow, nor grind the corn, nor the like. Bathing and anointing are contained under the general head of meat and drink, and may be done on the feast day." The penalty for doing servile work on these days was, according to Maimonides, to be beaten; but the penalty for working on the Sabbath was death (Num. xv. 32–35).

To these feast sabbaths we find few allusions in Jewish history, either in the Old Testament or in Josephus. All the violations of the Sabbath with which the Lord was charged were those of the weekly Sabbath.

6. Use of terms. With these preliminary observations upon the question of time, we pass to the consideration of the terms applied to the passover, first in the Old Testament and then in the New. The Hebrew *pesach*, or Aramaic *pascah*, refers commonly to the paschal lamb. "Draw out and take you a lamb, and kill the passover" (Ex. xii. 21). To kill the passover, and to eat the passover, is to kill and eat the paschal lamb (see Exod. xii. 11; Num. ix. 2–6; 2

---

[1] Josephus, Antiq., ii. 15. 1.

Chron. xxx. 15).   But as with the flesh of the lamb unleavened bread
was eaten, the phrase "to eat the passover" naturally came to embrace the whole feast, including the peace offerings (Deut. xvi. 2; 2
Chron. xxx. 1); and on the other hand, "the feast of unleavened
bread" embraced the paschal lamb, as well as all the sacrifices that
followed it (Deut. xvi. 16; 2 Chron. xxx. 21).   In the days of Josiah,
he and his princes gave small cattle and oxen for passovers—*pesachim*
(2 Chron. xxxv. 7–9).   But some distinguish these, the lamb and
kid only—the small cattle—being killed for the paschal supper, the
oxen for the peace-offerings.   (So Schürer, 12.) [1]   Thus, as the initial
act and giving character to all that followed, the word *pesach* became
a designation of the feast in general.   "To keep the passover,"
was to observe all the solemnities of the feast without distinction
of special acts, unless through the force of the context the meaning
must be limited to the paschal supper.   It is thus used in 2 Kings
xxiii. 21; 2 Chron. xxx. 1; 2 Chron. xxxv. 1; Ezek. xlv. 21.

From this examination of the terms in the Old Testament, we
find that there is no exact discrimination in their use.   Sometimes
the passover and the feast of unleavened bread are expressly distinguished, and the former limited to the paschal supper (Lev. xxiii. 5,
6; Num. xxviii. 16, 17).   At other times they are used interchange-
ably.   The precise meaning in each case must be determined by the
connection in which it stands.

We proceed to consider the usage of these terms in the New
Testament.   And first their usage by the Synoptists.   Here also the
term passover, τὸ πάσχα, is used in its narrowest sense, of the paschal
lamb.   Thus in Mark xiv. 12, "when they killed the passover"; in
Luke xxii. 7, "when the passover must be killed."   It is used in the
large sense, including both the sacrifice of the lamb and the supper,
Matt. xxvi. 17; Mark xiv. 14; Luke xxii. 11.   It is used as a
designation of the feast in its whole extent, Matt. xxvi. 2; Luke
xxii. 1.   (See also Mark xiv. 1.)   That the phrase, "feast of unleavened bread," τὰ ἄζυμα, embraced the paschal supper, appears from
Matt. xxvi. 17; Mark xiv. 12; Luke xxii. 7.

Turning from the Synoptists to John, it is at once apparent that
he generally uses the term passover, τὸ πάσχα, in its largest sense, as embracing the whole feast.   So ii. 13 and 23; vi. 4; xi. 55; xii. 1; in
xiii. 1, it is "the feast of the passover."   So also in the references to
it as the feast, ἑορτή, iv. 45; xi. 56; xii. 12 and 20; xiii. 29.   In

---

[1] So Bleek, Beiträge, 111.   See other constructions in Cudworth, ii. 522.   Schürer,
Akademische Festschrift über, φαγεῖν τὸ πάσχα, 1883, 13, affirms that at that time both
of the flock and herd might be eaten at the paschal supper.   As against Schürer, see
Eders., ii. 566, note; also Bissell, *Pentateuch*, 108.

xiii. 29, in xviii. 28 and 39, and in xix. 14, its meaning is in dispute.

Our way being now prepared, we enter upon the discussion of the disputed points connected with the Lord's last paschal supper. For the sake of clearness we may divide them into two classes: I. Those relating to His legal observance of the supper, as both to the time, and the manner. II. Those relating to the accounts which the Evangelists give of the observance, whether in any, or in what, particulars discrepant.

I. 1. *The time.* Did the Lord observe the legal prescription as to the time, and did He eat the supper at the same time as the Jews? It is said by some that there were two legal days, one of which He observed; while the Jews observed the other. The ground of this is found in the two ways of determining the first day of the month, and consequently the right day of the feast, one by astronomical calculation, and the other by ocular observation; and thus the paschal lamb might be slain on the 14th Nisan of real, or the 14th of apparent, time. One of these modes, it is said, was followed by the Sadducees, and the other by the Pharisees; Jesus, with the Sadducees, kept the true day, the Pharisees and most of the Jews the apparent day. If, however, such a difference in the mode of computation did actually exist between the Rabbinites and Karaites after the destruction of Jerusalem, there is no proof that it did before.[1] The only way of determining the beginning of the month practised by the Jews before the capture of the city by Titus, A. D. 70, was the appearance of the new moon. Thus there could not have been, during the Lord's ministry, two legal days for the observance of the passover; and the supposition that He, with one part of the Jews, rightly observed Thursday as astronomically correct, and that another part rightly observed Friday as determined by the appearance of the new moon, is without any foundation.

A modification of this view has lately been presented by Serno.[2] He supposes that, as the moon in some sections of the country might be seen at its first appearance, and in others be hidden by the clouds, and thus a difference in computation arise, the first day of the feast was doubled, and the paschal supper was lawfully eaten on either. But this was true only of the Jews living without Palestine, and not of those within it. When the authorities at Jerusalem had determined the first of the month, all succeeding days were reckoned from it; and

---

[1] Winer, ii. 150; Paulus, iii. 486.
[2] Der Tag des letzten Passahmahles. Berlin, 1859, 35 ff.

20

if a Jew from any distant part of the land had mistaken the day of the month through ignorance of the appearing of the moon, he must make the later feast days conform to those fixed upon by the Sanhedrin. Even if the latter had erred, their decision was final.   Nor was an exception made, as affirmed by Serno, in favor of the Galilæans, so that the Lord following their usage could keep the feast a day earlier than the citizens of Judæa.   (See Langen, 87.)

A little different position is taken by Cudworth (*True Notion of the Lord's Supper*, ii. 528), who says, that the Jews having erred this year in the day, placing it too late, the Lord corrected the error, and directed the supper to be prepared at the legal time, on Thursday evening.   He affirms, also, that it was "a custom among the Jews in such doubtful cases as these, which oftentimes fell out, to permit the feasts to be solemnized, or passover killed on two serial days together."   He quotes Scaliger to the same effect.   But all this is without good basis.   There is not any sufficient evidence that the paschal supper ever was, or could have been, observed upon two successive days.

Some have affirmed that a second day of sacrifice was made necessary through the multitude of the paschal lambs to be slain, and therefore permitted by the authorities.   But Josephus, who (as already quoted) mentions the great number of the sacrifices, says nothing of this difficulty, nor do contemporaneous writers refer to it.   (See Sepp, vi. 41.)

We find, then, no good grounds for believing that the Jews recognized two distinct days as equally legal for the paschal solemnities; or that, through error of computation, they observed the wrong day, and the Lord the right one.

2.   It is said that the Lord kept the passover on Thursday, at the appointed time, but that the Jews delayed it till the next evening. The ground of this delay is found in the statement, that when the 15th Nisan, the first day of the feast, and so a sabbath (Lev. xxiii. 7, 8), fell upon Friday, and thus two sabbaths, the feast sabbath and week sabbath, would immediately follow each other, the Jews united them in one, and the sacrifice of the paschal lamb on the 14th was postponed to the 15th.   Thus the Lord, according to the law, ate the paschal supper on Thursday evening, but the Jews on Friday evening.[1]   But this explanation has no sufficient basis, as there is no room for doubt that such changes of the feasts, and particularly

---

[1] So Calvin, on Matt. xxvi. 17, who remarks that the Jews affirm that this was done by them after their return from Babylon, and by God's express direction.   See Maldonatus, *in loco*, who takes the same view.

the rule forbidding that the passover should fall on Friday, were posterior to the destruction of Jerusalem, probably about 400 A. D.[1]

Another ground of delay applying only to this time, was given early by Eusebius and others, that the Jews were so busy with their accusations against Christ that they postponed the feast till His trial and crucifixion should be over. This is so intrinsically improbable that it now finds no defenders. A modification of this is still supported by some: that those most active against Him, and who are specially alluded to (John xviii. 28) as not willing to enter the judgment hall, did delay their paschal supper on this account.[2] This view will be hereafter noticed.

We do not thus find any proof that the Jews delayed the passover after the legal time.

3.   That the Lord anticipated the true day upon typical grounds. That He anticipated the day, was very early affirmed by some of the fathers, supposing, that as the true Paschal Lamb — the Antitype — He must have suffered at the hour when the typical lamb was slain, and so upon the 14th Nisan. The supper He observed must, therefore, have been on the evening following the 13th. This point had in the first days of the church a special importance, because of the controversy with some of the Christian Jews in regard to the binding force of the Mosaic laws. It was asserted by them, that as Jesus kept the legal passover, the paschal sacrifice and supper, these were still binding, and to be kept in the Church. In reply, it was asserted by many of the Christians that He did not eat the paschal supper, but, as the true Paschal Lamb, was slain at the hour appointed for the sacrifice of the passover. In the Greek Church this become by degrees the ruling opinion, and is generally defended by her writers.[3] In the Latin Church, on the other hand, it was generally denied; but in neither is it made an article of faith. The question as to the use of leavened or unleavened bread in the Eucharist may have had some influence upon the matter; the Greeks, using the former, were led to say that the Lord used it at the institution of the rite, and that, therefore, it was not the true paschal supper, at which only unleavened bread was used; while the Latins, using unleavened bread, maintained that the Eucharist was instituted at the true paschal supper.

This view, that the Lord of His own authority anticipated the paschal supper, because of its antiquity, has found much favor; and is

---

[1] Wichelhaus, 203; Paulus, iii. 487, note; Cudworth, ii. 524; Roth, 15 ff.

[2] Fairbairn, Her. Man., 382; Wordsworth, *in loco*.

[3] See Maldonatus, Matt. xxvi. 1: *Ut veritas figurae responderet, et verus agnus eodem die, quo typicus, occideretur.*   Wichelhaus, 190; Greswell, ii. 162 ff.

now supported by many.[1] The particular passages urged in its support will be later considered.

But, beside other objections drawn from the accounts of the Synoptists, it was intrinsically impossible that He could have anticipated it. The paschal lamb must have been slain in the temple by the priests, and they would not have aided in its sacrifice upon a day which they did not recognize as the legal one. Still less would they have done this for the Lord and His disciples. To avoid this difficulty, Greswell quotes Philo (iii. 146) to show that each man was at this time his own priest, and could slay the lamb, if he pleased, in his own dwelling, and that this was now done. But the weight of authority is all against him. The lamb must be slain, not in any private house, but in the temple, and its blood sprinkled upon the altar. Had the Lord not done this, it doubtless would have been known, and have strengthened the feeling against Him.

We thus find it difficult to believe that the Lord anticipated the paschal supper, observing all the legal prescriptions, except that as to time. He who came to fulfill, not to destroy, the law, would not in so important a matter have set it aside. We may rather say, in the words of another: "There seem insuperable objections to the idea, either that the Lord did not keep the true passover, or that He could have kept it according to the law, unless on the day recognized by the Jews and their rulers. . . . . Moreover, there is something very significant in the Lord observing the legal type before He fulfilled it anti-typically. Dying on the 15th, He rose again on the 17th of the month, as the passover had been slain on the 14th at even, and the first fruit omer or sheaf had been waved on the 16th, the like interval of one day occurring in both in the type and the antitype." It will be seen that the real question is, whether the Lord, being the Antitype, should first have observed the type. We cannot doubt that He who came to fulfill the law, would do this, and therefore that He kept the passover at the legal time. It is not essential to the typical relation, that as the lamb was killed on the afternoon of the 14th Nisan, He should be crucified at the same hour.

4. *The manner.* Did the Lord observe the legal prescriptions as to the manner of the supper? It is said by some (*a*) that it was a memorial supper. Such a memorial supper, it is said by some, the Jews who could not be present at the feast, were permitted to observe in their own homes when all the forms of the passover were kept,

---

[1] So Krafft, 129; Greswell, iii. 133; Ellicott, 322; J. Müller, in Herzog's Real Encyc., i. 22; Clinton, ii. 240; The Author of "The Messiah," Lindsay, Sepp, Norris, Westcott, Farrar, Aldrich.

except the eating of the lamb.[1] But such a supper could be only eaten out of Jerusalem, and upon the legal day, not in the city, and upon the day previous. Nor is there any evidence that this memorial passover was ever observed till after the destruction of Jerusalem, when it became impossible that the lamb could be slain in the temple, and the supper was necessarily limited to unleavened bread and bitter herbs.

(b) That it was a farewell supper, and not in any true sense a paschal supper, although the usual elements of such supper were on the table. It is said that the Mosaic type was fulfilled in the institution of the Lord's Supper; what took place at the meal before this institution, was unimportant. But against this is the fact that the Lord used in the institution of His supper not merely some of the materials, bread and wine; but the forms, which, as well as the directions given by Him respecting its preparation, show that He did keep the true paschal supper.

We find, then, no sufficient grounds for the belief that the Lord did not observe the legal prescriptions respecting the paschal supper, both as to the time, and the manner of its observance.

II.   Are there in the accounts of the Evangelists discrepancies as to the time or manner of the paschal supper ?

1.   As to time:

It is admitted on all sides, and therefore, need not be here considered, that Jesus died on Friday in the afternoon.[2] The eating of the supper on the evening previous was, therefore, on Thursday evening; His resurrection was on the Sunday following. The point in question is not respecting the day of the week, but the day of the month. Was Friday the 14th or 15th Nisan? It is said that John asserts the former, the Synoptists the latter. We give the discrepancy in tabular form:

St. John.	Synoptists.
Supper eaten, evening of Thursday, 13th Nisan.	Evening of Thursday, 14th Nisan.
Jesus crucified, Friday, 14th Nisan.	Friday, 15th Nisan.
Was in the grave, Saturday, 15th Nisan.	Saturday, 16th Nisan.
Resurrection, Sunday, 16th Nisan.	Sunday, 17th Nisan.

The supper of the Synoptists. We may best begin our enquiry by asking: Do the Synoptists put the supper on the evening following the 14th Nisan? Their language on its face clearly affirms this: " Now

---

[1] So Grotius, on Matt. xxvi. 11.
[2] See, however, Westcott, Introduction, 317 ff.

the first day of the feast of unleavened bread — τῇ δὲ πρώτῃ τῶν ἀζύμων — the disciples came to Jesus, saying, Where wilt Thou that we prepare for Thee to eat the passover?" . . . (Matt. xxvi. 17.) "And the first day of unleavened bread — καὶ τῇ πρώτῃ ἡμέρᾳ τῶν ἀζύμων — when they killed the passover, His disciples said unto Him" (Mark xiv. 12). "Then came the day of unleavened bread when the passover must be killed," — ἡ ἡμέρα τῶν ἀζύμων — (Luke xxii. 7. Compare this with verse 1: "Now the feast of unleavened bread drew nigh "). That this was the 14th Nisan seems beyond reasonable doubt, for on the afternoon of this day the paschal lamb was slain, and all preparations made for the feast that began at evening with the paschal supper. All the Evangelists say: "They made ready the passover — the paschal supper " — and this must have embraced the lamb. As has been already remarked, this was not, strictly speaking, the first day of the feast, for this began at sunset with the 15th, but, it was in popular language so called; and the circumstance that the lamb was yet to be slain sufficiently determines what day was meant. (Compare Exod. xii. 18.)

The attempts so to interpret these statements as to make them refer to an anticipatory supper on the evening following the 13th Nisan, are very forced and unsatisfactory, since neither according to the law nor to usage was the paschal lamb slain on that day.

It is said by Godet (on John xix. 41, 42), that as "the first day of unleavened bread," as used by the Synoptists, means the 14th Nisan, and as the day began at sunset, we are either obliged to hold that the commission given to the two apostles to prepare for the supper was at its beginning, i. e. after the sunset following the 13th (so Westcott), or that it was earlier and on the 13th itself, probably some hours before sunset. The two disciples indeed thought that they were to make ready for the evening of the next day, the 14th Nisan, but the Lord told them that His time was that very evening. Of course, as Godet admits, there was no sacrifice of the lamb in the temple, and without such a sacrifice the supper was only a private meal. But aside from this, we cannot, without great violence to the language of the Synoptists, make it to refer to an anticipatory sacrifice on the evening of the 13th Nisan. Its whole tenor makes the very strong impression upon us that the disciples prepared, and that the Lord ate the paschal lamb at the same time when it was prepared and eaten by the people in general. The indications, which a few think they find in certain expressions, are very slight and unimportant. Thus it is said that from the Lord's words (Matt. xxvi. 18): "My time is at hand, I will keep the passover at thy house," it is a valid inference

that this supper was " out of course," and before the usual time.
(Godet.)   But clearly by " my time " there is no reference to the hour
of the meal, but to the time of his suffering.   In like way, His words
(Luke xxii. 15): " With desire I have desired to eat this passover
with you before I suffer," have been understood as meaning that this
passover was peculiar in that it was before the usual time, or as one
at which there was no paschal lamb.   (Caspari.)   But the obvious
meaning is, that it had special significance because it was the last.
The truth is well expressed by Robinson: [1]   " Their language is full,
explicit, and decisive, to the effect that our Lord's last meal with His
disciples was the regular and ordinary paschal supper of the Jews,
introducing the festival of unleavened bread on the evening after
the 14th day of Nisan."

Taking then as established, that the Synoptists make the supper
eaten by the Lord to have been the true paschal supper, let us consider in detail the statements of John that bear upon the point.
The first of these we find in xiii. 1, ff., where mention is made of a
supper where Jesus washed the disciples' feet.   Was this the paschal
supper ? If so, when was it eaten ?

The supper of John.   Was this the paschal supper?   This is denied by not a few, who think it to have been a supper before the
paschal supper, and one not mentioned at all by the Synoptists.   The
grounds of this conclusion are : 1st, that it is not described by John
as a paschal meal; 2d, that the act of feet washing was incongruous
with such a meal; 3d, that comparing John xiii. 27 with Luke xxii.
3, where it is said that " Satan entered into Judas," both refer to the
same thing, and this supper must therefore have been before the paschal supper; 4th, that the interpretations of the Lord's words to
Judas (verse 29) show that this supper was still future; 5th, that His
words at the close of the supper (xiv. 31) " Arise, let us go hence,"
refer to His going with the disciples from the place of the supper to
Jerusalem, there to keep the paschal feast.   If not a paschal supper
eaten at the appointed time, when was it eaten?   Some say on Tuesday
evening, some on Wednesday evening.   The first is advocated by
Lightfoot, and for the purpose of comparison we give his order:

Saturday — Sabbath,— 9th Nisan, He sups with Lazarus at Bethany; Tuesday, 12th Nisan, He sups with Simon at Bethany.   It is
this supper which is mentioned by John when the feet were washed,
and the subsequent events and the Lord's discourse at this time are
contained in chapter xiii.   He continued in Bethany till Thursday,
14th Nisan, and His words, chapter xiv. were spoken at Bethany

---

[1] Har., 246.   See to same effect, Bleek, Beiträge, 134; Edersheim, ii. 481.

just before He went into the city to the paschal supper. Chapters
xv., xvi., and xvii. were spoken at the end of the paschal supper on
Thursday evening. Thus Lightfoot makes three suppers, of which
John mentions two (xii. 2 and xiii. 2); the paschal supper he does
not speak of, and there is consequently no discrepancy with the
Synoptists as to its time.

Among those who put this supper on Wednesday,[1] we take the
order of Wichelhaus (168).

On Tuesday, the 12th Nisan, was the supper at Bethany in the
house of Simon. On Wednesday morning, Judas made his bargain
with the priests, and in the evening was the supper of the feet washing
in Bethany or its neighborhood. On the next afternoon, Thursday,
the 14th Nisan, was the paschal supper. All recorded in John after
this supper (xiii. 12 to xiv. 31) was before He went to Jerusalem, a
part on Wednesday evening and a part on the Thursday forenoon following. If not the paschal supper, but one on the Tuesday or
Wednesday evening preceding, the accounts of the Synoptists and of
John cannot conflict.

Upon the other hand, it is said that this supper was the paschal
supper, and so to be identified with that of the Synoptists, upon the
following grounds: First, Through the designation of Judas by the
Lord as he that should betray Him. (Compare John xiii. 21–30 with
Matt. xxvi. 21–25, Mark xiv. 18–21, Luke xxii. 21–23.) Second,
Through the prophecy that Peter should thrice deny Him, and of the
crowing of the cock. (Compare John xiii. 38 with Matt. xxvi. 34,
Luke xxii. 34.) Third, Through the connection between the Lord's
words recorded in John, chapters xiv., xv., xvi., showing that they
were all spoken at once. Fourth, Through the statement (Luke
xxii. 24) that at the paschal supper there was a strife among them
who should be accounted greatest, which serves to explain His
conduct in washing His disciples' feet. (Compare John xiii. 13–17.)
It is impossible in our limited space to examine these points in
detail; some of them will meet us later. But most modern harmonists
and commentators find the points of similarity more marked than
those of difference, and so identify the supper of John with that of
the Synoptists.[2] But a few of them affirm that a discrepancy exists
as to the time, and that one of the accounts must be in error. This
point therefore demands our attention.

Time of the supper in John. Assuming that John and the Synopt-

---

[1] So Bengel, Krafft, Wichelhaus, Röpe. See Bynaeus, *De Morte Jesu Christi*,
l. 586, for an elaborate defense of this view.

[2] Tholuck, Greswell, Alford, Meyer, Tischendorf, Robinson, Friedlieb, Luthardt,
Edersheim, Gardiner, and others.

ists refer to the same supper, and having already seen that the latter put it on the evening following the 14th Nisan, we ask what note of time does John give us ? He says only that it was "before the feast of the passover." But to what does this mark of time refer ? Our answer must depend upon the relation in which verse 1 stands to the verses following. That it forms a sentence complete in itself, and grammatically independent upon what follows, is generally admitted.[1] If so, the words, "before the feast of the passover," must qualify either the main or one of the subordinate propositions. The main proposition is that "Jesus loved his own to the end, to the end of His life "; or, as some render it, "perfectly," or to "the uttermost." But clearly the Evangelist did not mean to say merely that Jesus before the feast of the passover loved His own to the end of His life, or that He then loved them perfectly. Although the sentence may be grammatically complete, yet all feel that the statement is incomplete. Love being a permanent feeling in His heart, we need not be told that He loved His disciples to the end; much less can we connect it with the note of time, "before the passover." Interpreters, therefore, understand love here not of the feeling in itself, but as manifested in some act or event of which a definite time may be predicated; and that this act was in the mind of the Evangelist. Accordingly, Meyer speaks of the manifestation of this love: "He loved, and gave to His own the closing proof of love." In like manner Godet: "He perfectly testified to them all His love." But there is in this first verse no mention of any such act; in the following verse there is mention of a supper, and of His act in the washing of the apostles' feet.

Let us, however, admit that this is the meaning of the Evangelist, and read: "Before the feast of the passover, Jesus gave the last proof of His love," or "perfectly testified His love," "by washing the disciples' feet at a supper." It is said that this supper, thus described as being before the feast of the passover, cannot have been the paschal supper, but must have been at least one day earlier.

But there are others who take the same view of the relation of the note of time, and yet reach an opposite conclusion. They take "before the feast of the passover" as an indefinite expression which may denote a longer or shorter interval, the Greek preposition — πρό — being in this respect like the preposition "before." As we use this of events which may immediately follow, in current expressions like these — before dinner, before sunset — when a very few moments may intervene; so "before the passover" may mean that the act spoken of took

---

[1] Meyer, Lange, Robinson, Alford, Tischendorf, W. and H., R. V.; but *contra*, Bleek, Beiträge, 126, DeWette, in his Translation, Ebrard.

place at a very brief interval before the paschal supper. (See Luke xi. 37; Bäumlein, *in loco*.) In this way it is understood by Luthardt, who contrasts (xii. 1) "Six days before the passover"—a definite interval—with the present, "now before the feast"—an indefinite interval—and explains the last as meaning, "now that the feast had come," or was about to begin. (So Stier: "was immediately before.") In this view of the matter the supper of the feet-washing was the paschal supper, the washing of the feet being introductory.

But to this there is the objection that the feet-washing was "during supper"—the meal being actually in progress,—and therefore cannot be fairly said to have been before the feast (Wies., Beiträge, 233).

To avoid this objection, it may be said that John, in speaking of the Feast of the Passover, followed the usual Jewish usage in counting the first day of the feast, or the 15th Nisan, not from the sunset of the 14th, but from the following morning (Levit. xxiii. 56). The feast beginning with the early daybreak of the 15th, the supper of the feet-washing on the evening before was in fact before the feast, and so might have been the paschal supper. (See Langen, 109; McClel., 482.)

To this it may be replied that it implies a distinction between sacred and secular time in the computation of the days, of which there is no sufficient proof.

We have assumed hitherto that the words "before the passover" qualify the main proposition, "Jesus loved His own to the end"; but they may qualify one of the two subordinate propositions or participial clauses—"Knowing that His hour was come that He should depart out of this world unto the Father," and "Having loved His own which were in the world." If they qualify the first, the rendering is, "Jesus, knowing before the feast of the passover that His hour was come," etc. ; if the second, the rendering is, "Jesus having loved His own before the feast of the passover" etc. Of these two qualifications the first is clearly to be preferred, the connection being closer and more obvious. The meaning of the verse is thus given by Norton in his translation: "But Jesus, before the feast of the passover, knew that the hour had come for him to pass from the world to the Father, and having loved His own who were to remain in this world, He loved them to the last." In a note he says: "It is a very forced interpretation to regard the words, 'before the feast of the passover,' as intended to fix the date of what follows."

That either of the participial clauses should be qualified by the note of time is said by Westcott to be "impossible." But the grounds of this impossibility are not apparent. Supposing the Evangelist to

have had in his mind the paschal supper, now near at hand, his statement is clear and consistent; and we find a sufficient reason for the
note of time.   The Lord's knowledge of the future determined His
action.   Knowing before the feast that He should die at the feast, He
would, before He left the world, show forth His love to His own;
and the paschal supper gave Him the last opportunity to do this, for
immediately after this they were all scattered.   It is as if a man,
knowing that a session of a court where he is to be tried for his
life is near, should assemble his friends and make an address to
them.   The exact hour when the Lord came to this knowledge is
unimportant, but the foreknowledge is an essential condition of His
action.   This interpretation is in perfect harmony with the whole
narrative.   Before Jesus left Galilee He announced His departure as
at hand (Matt. xvii. 22), and again after He left Ephraim (xx. 17).
Two days before the feast He repeated that at the Passover He should
be betrayed (Matt. xxvi. 2).   And now the feast had come, and with
it "His hour."   He, knowing all this, gives at this introductory
supper of the feast a new and last proof of the love with which He
had loved them.   With the full knowledge that the hour of His
arrest and death is come, and that He no more should thus meet
His disciples, He shows them in the most expressive way how great
and unchangeable His affection for them.   In this way the abrupt
and incidental mention of the supper (verse 2) is readily explained;
and that it was the paschal supper follows from the whole connection
of the thought.

If, however, we connect the clause, "before the feast of the passover," with "having loved," the meaning is, Jesus, that having loved
His own down to this time, or to the passover which is now come,
and knowing that the hour of His death is at hand, continues to
love them, even to the end, and now gives a fresh proof of it at the
paschal supper.   Here, as before, it is implied that this supper at
the beginning of the feast is the last opportunity He would have
of manifesting His love.   In this construction the antithesis between "before the feast" and "to the end," is most clearly
brought out.   The love which He had felt to His own before the
feast continued ardent to the end, and was shown in the act of washing their feet.   Still, the other participial connection is to be preferred.[1]

We conclude, then, that from the note of time "before the feast
f the passover," nothing definite in regard to the time of the supper can be determined.   Supposing all between verses 1 and 4 to be

---

[1] See Wieseler, Syn., 379; Beiträge, 231; Tholuck, *in loco;* Rob., Har., 249.

striken out, and the statement to read: "Now before the feast of the passover . . . . He riseth from supper, and laid aside His garments," it would still remain probable that the paschal supper is meant. The presumption is very strong that this meal, thus incidentally mentioned, must have been that so prominently and inseparably associated with the feast.

An additional proof that this was not the paschal supper, but one a day earlier, is found by many [1] in the fact mentioned (John xiii. 29), that none of the disciples knew what the Lord had said to Judas at the table, but some of them supposed He had told him to buy what was necessary for the feast, or to give something to the poor. It is said, if the disciples were now eating the feast no one could have thought that Judas went out for this purpose. Hence it follows that this supper was previous to the beginning of the feast, and that all the preparations were yet to be made. But this inference is not well grounded; it depends upon the determination of the time in verse first. The feast, for the needs of which Judas was to buy, is not to be limited to the paschal supper, for it continued seven days, and embraced various sacrifices and offerings other than the paschal lamb. It is not at all improbable that a master of a family, speaking at this first meal, should thus refer to the provision to be made for the further keeping of the feast. Judas, as the treasurer of the body of apostles, was in this case the person to make such provision. And the fact, that he went out immediately after the Lord had spoken to him, would naturally suggest to others that something necessary to the feast was to be at once procured; if it were to begin twenty-four hours later, there would be no need of haste. (The objection that nothing could be bought on a feast day, will be later examined.)

A careful examination of this passage seems rather to prove that this was the paschal supper than to disprove it. The disciples heard the Lord say to Judas, "That thou doest do quickly." He immediately arises and goes out, and "it was night." Supposing this to have been a supper on the night of the 13th Nisan, and a full day before the paschal supper, would they connect his departure with any preparations for the feast? The next day would give him abundant time to buy all that was necessary. Why hasten out at that hour of the night? But if we suppose that this was the paschal supper, and that the next day, the 15th, was the first day of the feast, we can readily explain their conjectures as to the cause of Judas's sudden departure. What he was to do must be done without delay. (So Stier, Luthardt, and others.)

---

[1] Meyer, Bleek, Alford, Godet, who does not, however, attach much importance to it.

The next passage in John, and that most relied on to prove that the Lord could not have eaten the paschal supper at the legal time, is found in xviii. 28: "Then led they Jesus from Caiaphas unto the hall of judgment, and it was early; and they themselves went not into the judgment hall lest they should be defiled, but that they might eat the passover." This, it is said, plainly proves that the Jews had not yet eaten the passover, and that the supper which Jesus had eaten on the previous evening could not have been the paschal supper as the Synoptists seem to state.[1]

Two solutions of this difficulty are given: First, that those who would not go into the judgment hall, were those Scribes and Pharisees who had been engaged during the night, while the other Jews were keeping the feast, in directing the proceedings against Jesus, and thus had had no time to partake of the paschal supper. Second, that John uses the expression, "eat the passover," in its larger meaning, not referring to the paschal lamb, but to the offerings eaten on the second day of the feast. The former of these solutions has never found many defenders, though not in itself impossible. So great was the hate against Jesus, and so little scrupulous were His enemies, that we cannot doubt, that to compass His death they would have postponed for a time the paschal supper, or even have neglected it altogether. There are, however, other obvious difficulties, which this explanation does not fully meet. (This view is best stated by Fairbairn, "Hermeneutical Manual," 382 ff.)

We must consider the second of these solutions. It is admitted, that as the Synoptists use the phrase "to eat the passover" — φαγεῖν τὸ πάσχα, — it always means to eat the paschal supper (Matt. xxvi. 17; Mark xiv. 12 and 14; Luke xxii. 11 and 15). If John uses it in the same sense, then the paschal supper was eaten by the Jews on the evening of the day when Jesus was crucified, and He must have anticipated it. But the usage of the Synoptists does not decide the usage of John. We must determine its meaning from the way in which he uses the phrase elsewhere, and from the general character of his writings. It has already been shown, that out of the nine times in which he uses the word πάσχα, — passover — in six it is applied to the feast generally, and not to the paschal supper only. The meaning in the other three passages is in dispute. Only in the passage before us does the phrase "eat the passover" occur. The simple point is, does John here use it in its wider or narrower meaning?

Some considerations, drawn from the character of John's Gospel, as influenced by the period of time at which he wrote, will serve to

---

[1] Meyer, Bleek, Browne, Alford, Godet, Schürer.

show how this marked distinction in the use of terms between him and the Synoptists may be explained.   John wrote toward the close of the century [1] and after the destruction of Jerusalem.   To him the Jews were no more the holy people of God.   Rejecting Jesus, and afterwards His apostles, they had themselves been rejected.   Everywhere he speaks of them distinctly as "the Jews," formerly the Church of God, but now cut off, and as a body standing in a hostile attitude to Christ and to that new, universal Church, composed both of Jews and Gentiles, of which He was the Head.[2]   Jewish institutions had in his eyes been emptied of their significance and value, since Christ, in whom all the law was fulfilled, had come.   Hence, he speaks of them commonly as the institutions of a people between whom and himself was a broad line of distinction.   Their purification is spoken of as that "of the Jews"; the passover, as "a feast of the Jews"; the preparation, as "preparation of the Jews"; Nicodemus, as "a ruler of the Jews."   The Synoptists, on the other hand, writing before the total rejection of Judaism, and while it still stood side by side with Christianity as of divine authority and sanctity, show by their mode of allusion that no such line of distinction then existed.   To them the Jews are not as aliens, but still the chosen people of God.

Placing ourselves in the position of John, and remembering the position of those for whom he wrote, how few of them had any real knowledge of Jewish laws and traditions; we shall readily understand why he speaks in such general and indefinite terms of Jewish rites as of things now superseded.   Since Jesus, the true Paschal Lamb, had been slain, the true paschal supper was kept only in the Christian Church.   To Christians, he could say with Paul (1 Cor. v. 7, 8), " Christ, our Passover, is sacrificed for us, therefore let us keep the feast."   The Jews in their passover had only the shell or shadow; the Church had the kernel or substance.   Hence, it is not to be expected that he would refer to any rites of the Jews at this feast with the care that marks the Synoptists.   He does not distinguish, as do they, its several component parts, but speaks of it only in general terms as one of the Jewish feasts.   There is not, in the other places in which he mentions the passover, any clear proof that he means to distinguish the paschal supper from the solemnities of the following days.   Why, then, in the passage before us, are we forced to believe that the passover which the Jews were about to eat on the day of the crucifixion, was the paschal supper, and that only?   Why may he not

---

[1] Meyer, about 80 A. D.

[2] See Meyer on John i. 19; Bleek, 247.

mean the subsequent sacrifices? Standing to the Jews in a position so unlike that of the Synoptists, it seems most arbitrary to assert that he must use language with precisely the same strictness, and that "to eat the passover" must mean to eat the paschal lamb.

As has been said, upon the first day of the feast or the 15th of Nisan thank offerings of the flock and herd were slain and eaten. There is certainly no intrinsic reason why John may not have meant these. But it is said in reply,[1] that if the phrase "to eat the passover" may be used of the other offerings inclusive of the paschal lamb, it cannot be exclusive of it. But this is by no means obvious. Passover, with John, is a term denoting the whole festival; and why, if the paschal supper was past, might he not employ it to designate the remaining feasts? To affirm that he could not is mere affirmation. Norton,[2] referring to the oft-repeated remark that the term passover is never used "absolutely" to denote the thank offerings considered apart from the paschal supper, observes: "This remark has been repeatedly praised for its acuteness by Kuinoel and Strauss. But, in fact, it only implies a forgetfulness of a very common metonymy by which the name of a whole is given to a part. If, when the paschal festival were half over, it had been said that certain Jews desired to avoid pollution that they might keep the passover, every one perceives that the expression would be unobjectionable, though no one would think of applying the name passover 'absolutely' to the last three or four days of the festival." Edersheim (ii. 568, note 1) observes: "No competent Jewish archæologist would care to deny that 'Pesach' [πάσχα] may refer to the Chagigah."

The exact nature of the defilement to which the Jews would have been exposed by entering the judgment hall, does not appear; but that they were at this time very strict in regard to entering the dwellings of the uncircumcised and eating with them, is plain from the accounts of Peter (Acts x. 28 and xi. 3. See Lightfoot on Matt. xxiii. 17). In the law, defilements are mentioned which were only for a day and which could be cleansed by ablution (Lev. xv. 5 -11 and xxii. 5–7). It is supposed by some that contact with the heathen was of this class, and that, therefore, if the day of the crucifixion had been the 14th Nisan, the Jews could still have cleansed themselves by evening and been ready to eat the paschal supper.

But it is said by Schürer, *Festschrift*, 24, that this defilement continued for seven days, and that it was therefore impossible for the Jews thus defiled to have eaten the paschal supper. On the other

---

[1] Meyer and others, after Mosheim, Delitzsch in Riehm, 1143; Schürer.

[2] Notes, ii. 466.

hand it is affirmed by Bynaeus, Edersheim, and many, that entering a
heathen house made one ceremonially unclean only for the day, or
till the evening.   In this case, if the paschal supper had not been
eaten by the Jews, but was still to be eaten, they would not have
been prevented from eating it, since, although the lamb was killed
in the afternoon, the supper was not served till after the sunset, or in
the beginning of the next day.   The Sanhedrists could not, therefore,
on this ground have refused to enter the judgment hall on the morning of the 14th.   But if it was the morning of the 15th, during which
day the thank offerings were sacrificed and eaten, they could not have
partaken of them.   Hence, it is inferred that the thank offerings,
rather than the paschal supper, were meant, and that this day was the
15th rather than the 14th.[1]   Much stress, however, in the present
state of our knowledge of Jewish customs, cannot be laid upon this
argument.[2]

This passage, then, affords no sufficient data for the final determination of the question as to the time of the paschal supper.   If any
think that John could not have used the phrase "to eat the passover" in any other sense than the Synoptists used it, they must
admit a chronological difference between him and them which we
find no satisfactory way to reconcile.   But if, on the other hand, we
find it not only possible, but also probable, that he should thus speak
of the festival apart from the supper, the supposed difference disappears.

The next important passage we find in xix. 14: "And it was the
preparation of the passover, and about the sixth hour; and he saith
unto the Jews, Behold your King."   A different punctuation of this
passage has been proposed, making it to read thus: "And it was the
preparation.   The hour of the passover was about the sixth."[3]
Though some plausible reasons may be given for this change, yet it
involves considerable difficulties.   We shall follow the generally
received punctuation.

Our first inquiry relates to the meaning of the term "preparation"
— παρασκευή.   It occurs in the Gospel five times besides the text:
Matt. xxvii. 62; Mark xv. 42; Luke xxiii. 54; John xix. 31; John
xix. 42.   In all these cases there is little doubt as to its meaning.   It
was, as Mark explains it, "the day before the Sabbath" — προσάββατον — or the day in which preparation was made for the Sabbath.
Such preparation, though not expressly prescribed in the law, was

---

[1] So Bynaeus, iii. 13; Eders., ii. 567; Langen, Keil, and many.
[2] See Friedlieb, Arch., 102; Bleek, 113; Nebe, i. 397 ff.
[3] So Hofmann, followed by Lichtenstein, 359.   See *contra*, Luthardt *in loco*.

yet made necessary by the strictness of the commands respecting the Sabbath, which forbade all labor even to prepare food on that day. (Compare Exod. xvi. 5.)   Hence, it became the habit of the Jews to observe the afternoon before from three o'clock, as a time of getting ready for the Sabbath which began at sunset.[1]   As they came more and more under bondage to that legal spirit which so characterized the Pharisees, and the rigor of the original Sabbath laws was augmented by burdensome additions, of which many examples are to be found in the Evangelists and in Josephus, this period of preparation became more and more important.   Thus, by degrees, Friday, or the προσάββατον, became known as the παρασκευή, or Preparation; as Saturday, the day of rest, was known as the Sabbath, all other days being distinguished only as the first, second, third, etc.   As the preparation was made in the afternoon preceding, or during that part of it which was known as "the evening," this term was generally applied to it in Hebrew and Chaldee: as by the Germans the day before the Sunday is called Sonnabend or Sun-evening.   Thus the sixth day of the week received its current name from its peculiar relations to the Sabbath; and παρασκευή became equivalent to Friday. As remarked by Westcott: " Being the preparation for the weekly Sabbath, it was natural that it should become at last the proper name of the day."

From this origin of the term, and from the fact that it was generally used to designate the sixth day of the week, and that it is so used both by the Synoptists and by John, we infer that, in the passage before us it means the preparation day before the Sabbath, or Friday.   As the feast of unleavened bread continued seven days, there would be in it one Sabbath, and so one preparation day, and to speak of the *paraskeue* of the passover week would sufficiently define it.

In its larger meaning of "preparation," the term might be used in connection with any of the feasts; and this leads us to ask as to preparation days other than that for the week-Sabbath.   That some preparation was necessary for the proper observance of every feast, even of those observed only for a day — as the new moon and pentecost — may be admitted, and probably some hours on the afternoon before may have been given to it; and especially before the feast Sabbaths, such as the first and last days of passover and of tabernacles.   But there seems no good reason why in these cases the day preceding should be known as the day of preparation.   The manner of celebrating the passover, indeed, made it necessary that the day before it began should

---

[1] Josephus, Antiq., xvi. 6. 2.

be spent in part in removing the leaven, and in killing the lamb; and in this sense the 14th Nisan was the preparation day for the 15th, and might be called the preparation day of the passover. But we find no proof that there were any such days of preparation for the feasts as for the weekly Sabbaths. The chief reason why such preparation was needed for the latter, was that on that day no food could be prepared; every kind of labor ceased as a mark of its greater dignity and sanctity. But preparation of food, and labor other than "servile," were permitted on the feast Sabbaths. Some have laid stress on the expression "passover eve," as showing that there was on the afternoon of the 14th Nisan a period thus designated and set apart; but it is said by Robinson (Har.) that the expression did not arise "till after the destruction of the temple and the consequent cessation of the regular and legal paschal meal, when, of course, the seven days of unleavened bread became the main festival." To such a passover eve the term "preparation day of the passover" could not apply; and as this feast came but once a year, there was no need that any special name should be given to the day preceding it.

Thus we seem to reach the result that the term παρασκευή — preparation — must mean the day before the Sabbath, or προσάββατον, unless the context forbids it. It is so used by the Synoptists in all the places where it occurs. Matt. xxvii. 62: "The next day, that followed the day of the preparation"; (R. V., "On the morrow which is the day after the preparation"); Mark xv. 42: "Because it was the preparation, that is, the day before the Sabbath"; Luke xxiii. 54: "And that day was the preparation, and the Sabbath drew on" (R. V.: "the day of the preparation"). In all these cases the obvious meaning is, that the preparation was that for the Sabbath, and the day on which it was made was Friday. In the three cases in which it occurs in John, of two — xix. 31 and 42 — the same may be said; but it is claimed that in the third, the passage before us, the day of the preparation is expressly defined by the addition "of the passover," and cannot, therefore, be the day of preparation for the weekly Sabbath, but must denote a day of preparation for the feast, and this day must have been the 14th Nisan, as the first day of the feast was the 15th. (So Meyer, Alford, Winer, Bleek.) It is said by Godet: "Every Greek reader would necessarily think of the 14th Nisan as the day on which the passover supper was prepared." But if it had become a technical term, a designation of Friday, and is so used by the Synoptists, and affirmed by them to have been the day of the crucifixion, it is very questionable whether John would here have used it in a different sense. It is remarked by Norton: "It would be very extraordinary if, in speaking of the same day, Friday, he had happened to use the proper name of that day in a sense different from its common one, and from that in which it is used by the other Evangelists, and especially in a sense of which no other example has been adduced."

Some light may be gained by asking what was the object of the Evangelist in mentioning that it was "the preparation of the passover" when Jesus was brought before Pilate. Was it chronological simply? This is possible, but he seems to have had a higher purpose. It was the time when the Jews should have been engaged in making themselves ready for the holiest services of God in His temple; but their preparation consisted in putting His Son to the shameful death of the cross. The incongruity of their labors with the character of the day is thus brought into the clearest contrast.[1]

The phrase "preparation of the passover," as used by John, does not then, we conclude, compel us to regard the day of the crucifixion as the day before the passover. It may be as Norton translates, "the preparation day of the paschal week"—the day before the Sabbath.

In still another passage (John xix. 31) we read "The Jews, therefore, because it was the preparation, that the bodies should not remain upon the cross on the Sabbath day (for that Sabbath day was a high day — μεγάλη), besought Pilate," etc. The ground upon which this Sabbath is designated as a high day, is supposed by many to be that the first day of the feast, or 15th Nisan, which was a feast Sabbath (Exod. xii. 16), fell upon the weekly Sabbath, and thus it was a double Sabbath, and "a high day." This, in itself considered, would be a sufficient and satisfactory explanation. But no weight can be attached to it as showing that this was actually the case. If the weekly Sabbath fell upon the 16th Nisan or the second day of the feast, a day distinguished from the other days as the time for the waving of the sheaf of first fruits, it would, with equal propriety, be called a high day.[2] As said by Robinson, " It was a high day, first, because it was the Sabbath; second, it was the day when all the people presented themselves in the temple; third, it was the day when the sheaf of first fruits was offered." There are no data for a positive decision of the question. In point of fact, this question is always decided according as the day of the crucifixion, for other reasons, is placed upon the 14th or 15th Nisan. Cudworth's assertion, that

---

[1] An attempt has been made to show (Journal Sac. Lit., July, 1850) that παρασκευή means properly " preparation time," and comprises the interval between mid-day or the sixth hour and sunset or the twelfth. Translated according to this view the passage before us would read: " For about the sixth hour the preparation time on passover day commenced." This is hardly satisfactory, and has not found favor.

[2] So Wies., Rob., Licht., and many.

"great day," in the Greek of the Hellenists, is used for the first or the last day of every feast, in which there was a holy convocation to the Lord, is not sustained by the passage to which he refers (Isa. i. 13). Every week Sabbath as well as every feast Sabbath, there was a holy convocation (Lev. xxiii. 3).

A new solution is proposed by Roth.[1] In place of reading "The day of that Sabbath was a high day," he would read "That day of the week was the great day" (of the passover). This rests on the fact that "Sabbath" has two meanings: first, that of the rest-day of the week, the last or seventh; second, that of the week itself, as in Luke xviii. 12: "I fast twice in the week" — δὶς τοῦ σαββάτου. That day, "the preparation" day, or Friday, was a high day because on it the Lord was crucified. This rendering, he thinks, would bring the passage into perfect harmony with the Synoptists. But there are here two questions, one, as to the meaning, the other, as to the differing uses of "Sabbath" in the same verse, which must be answered; and there is also the enquiry as to the bearing of the parenthesis, "the day of that Sabbath was a high day," on the taking down of the bodies from the cross. On this point, Roth's explanation does not help us.

Having now examined the passages in John usually cited to show that he puts the crucifixion on the 14th Nisan, and not on the 15th, let us notice some objections to the latter date. They all depend upon one thing — the legal sacredness of a feast Sabbath and the supposed strictness with which the Jews in the Lord's day observed it. Something has already been said upon these points, but we must enter into more detail.

1st. It is said that the Lord's trial and execution could not have taken place on the 15th Nisan. According to Rabbinical precepts, the Sanhedrin could not have held a session, they could not have sent armed men to arrest Jesus; in fine, no judicial proceedings were lawful on that day. But several elements are here to be taken into account. We must ask how far the part which the Romans took in these transactions — the employment of the Roman soldiers to make the arrest and guard the prisoner, the trial before Pilate, the sentence of crucifixion, a Roman not a Jewish punishment, and its execution by the centurion — may have seemed to the rulers and people to make their participation in it subordinate, and to relieve them from responsibility. And we must ask, also, whether these later Rabbinical precepts represent truly those then current and, if so, whether the Jews themselves strictly observed them. Bleek (Beiträge, 140) admits that

---

[1] "Die Zeit des letzen Abendmahles." Freiburg, 1874.

criminals were often arrested on the Sabbath, and of course, if necessary, by men bearing arms.   (See Winer, ii. 537.)   That the Sanhedrin did sometimes hold its sessions on feast days and Sabbaths is proved from the Gemara, and also that on those days sentence of death could be passed and executed.[1]   That the execution of criminals was purposely reserved till the feasts, in order to produce a greater impression upon the people, appears from Maimonides, quoted by Ainsworth, on Deut. xvii. 13: "They put him not to death in the judgment hall, that is, in his city, but carry him up to the high Synedrion in Jerusalem, and keep him until the feast, and strangle him at the feast, as it is said, ' all the people shall hear and fear.' " It seems, also, to have been the custom of Pilate and of other governors who always went up to Jerusalem at the feasts, then to try and punish criminals; and thus it was that the two malefactors were crucified at the same time with Jesus.   The crucifixion itself was performed, not by the Jews, but by Pilate and his soldiers.   The following observations of Tholuck seem well founded: " We consider it, therefore, as certain, that judicial proceedings were also held on the feast days, perhaps under certain legal provisos, and that this very period, when large assemblages of the people came together, was, for the reason mentioned in Deut. xvii. 13, selected for the execution of notorious criminals."

The assertion that the Synoptists could not have put the Lord's arrest, trial, and crucifixion on the first feast day because they must have known such acts to be unlawful, assumes the point to be proved. They say that certain things were done on a certain day; the objector replies, that the day was too sacred to be so desecrated, and, therefore, we must understand their words in some other way.   If, indeed, we knew from other sources that no such things could have been done on this feast day, then we might say that the Synoptists, who cannot have been ignorant of Jewish customs, must be interpreted accordingly. But our knowledge of the actual observance of the day is in large part derived from the Evangelists themselves.   The very fact, then, that these Evangelists do place the arrest, trial, and execution of Jesus upon a feast Sabbath, together with the judicial sessions of the Sanhedrin, and the subsequent purchase of spices and preparations for His embalming, gives the strongest presumptive proof that these were not incompatible with the character of the day.   As against their statements, any Rabbinical precepts of a later age cannot be considered as decisive.

---

[1] See the citations in Lightfoot; Tholuck on John xiii. 1: Wieseler, Syn., 361 ff.; Keim, iii. 473.

But even if we admit that, as a rule, the Jews did not arrest and try and execute criminals during the feasts, still the cases of those whose offenses were of a sacreligious character, as blasphemy and the like, may have been an exception. How great was the hate of the Pharisees and chief priests and elders to Jesus, as making Himself equal with God, we have already had abundant opportunities to observe. They stuck at nothing if they could but accomplish His death. Here, if ever, the end would in their eyes have justified the means, and when the long-desired opportunity of getting their dreaded enemy into their power came, they were not likely to be prevented from using it by any conscientious scruples respecting the sanctity of the day. That even the sanctity of the weekly Sabbath was no barrier against popular passion, appears from Luke iv. 16–30, where the inhabitants of Nazareth attempted to put Jesus to death on that day. So also the Jews at Jerusalem, at the Feast of Dedication, attempted first to stone Him, and afterward to arrest Him (John x. 22–39). Upon the last day of the Feast of Tabernacles, "the great day of the feast," the Sanhedrin was in session, and officers were engaged in the attempt to take Him (John vii. 32–52). Upon the weekly Sabbath the chief priests and Pharisees did not hesitate to go to Pilate to take measures for sealing the sepulchre (Matt. xxvii. 62–66).

2d. It is said that no one after the paschal supper could leave the city till the next morning, and that, therefore, Jesus, upon this evening, could not have gone to the garden of Gethsemane. But this was based upon the direction at its first appointment that "no one should go out of his house till the morning." (See Exod. xii. 22.) It seems evident, however, that this direction was not designed to be permanently observed any more than the command (verse 11) to eat it standing, with loins girded, shoes on the feet, and staff in the hand. We know, in point of fact, that the Jews in the Lord's time did not observe these and other directions, regarding them as peculiar to its first institution, and in the nature of the case not to be repeated. Besides we have seen reason to believe that all the western slope of the Mount of Olives was regarded as a part of the holy city.

3d. It is said that the preparation of spices and ointments for the Lord's embalming upon the afternoon of the day of the crucifixion (Luke xxiii. 56, John xix. 38–40), implies that it was not a feast Sabbath. Here, also, all depends upon the strictness with which the Jews observed the feast Sabbaths. As we have seen, Maimonides mentions bathing and anointing as things that might be done on the feast days ; and, in the very nature of the case, every thing necessary to prepare the dead for burial would then be permitted. But in cases of less urgency the same was true.   That purchases could be made even on the Sabbath, is shown by Tholuck (on John xiii. 1), if the price was not agreed upon and no money paid.   But with whatsoever strictness the feast Sabbath was usually observed, we cannot question that both Joseph and Nicodemus would have regarded themselves as fully warranted to perform, during its hours, the last offices of love to one who had taught in express words, and shown by His example, that He was Lord of the Sabbath.   That Judas was supposed to have gone out from the supper (John xiii. 29) to make purchases or to give something to the poor, does not show that this was not on the evening after the 14th, but rather that it was.   The evening was not a time when he could ordinarily have found the poor except in their own dwellings, and it is most improbable that he would this night have sought them there.   But if we remember that the poor gathered around the temple on the first day of the feast as early as the temple gates were opened for the offering of the peace and thank offering — the Chagigah — the eating of which on the first day was a chief element of the feast, there was nothing strange in the supposition that the Lord sent him there to help the poor to buy something for their festive meal.[1]

4th.   It is said that the account given of Simon of Cyrene (Mark xv. 21, Luke xxiii. 26), who, coming out of the country at the time when Jesus was on His way to the place of crucifixion, was compelled to bear His cross, is additional evidence that this was not a feast Sabbath, he having probably been at work.   But if this were so, we have still to inquire respecting the nature of the work.   Lightfoot supposes him to have come from the field bearing wood, which was lawful on a feast day.   But it is not said that he had been out in the fields at work, nor that he had travelled any distance; and to come from the country into the city upon a feast Sabbath was no violation of any law.   For aught that we know, he was a resident of Jerusalem who was casually without the wall, and was entering the gate when he met Jesus; or he may have been a pilgrim who had come up to the feast and was encamped without the city walls.

5th.   It is said that the Synoptists in their mention of the day of crucifixion, give no hint that it had a Sabbatical character.   It is true that they do not do this in express terms, but it is involved in their statement that the Lord ate the passover at the legal time; the day, therefore, of His death was the 15th, or the first feast Sabbath.   That they designate it as the preparation day without making prominent its Sabbatical character, simply shows what great im-

---

[1] Joseph., Antiq., xviii. 2. 2 ; Edersheim, ii. 508.

portance they attached to the fact that the Lord died and was buried before the weekly Sabbath began. This was of far more moment to them as illustrating the relation of the Jewish Sabbath to the Christian, than to make prominent the Sabbath character of the first day of the feast.

In summing up our inquiries, we may distinguish the two points: 1, the time of the paschal supper, 2, the time of the crucifixion.

1. (a) We accept as proved that the statements of the Synoptists show the Lord to have kept the paschal supper at the time when the Jews in general kept it, i. e. on the evening following the 14th Nisan, and in the same manner. All attempts to show that these statements are inconsistent with themselves, we must regard as inconclusive.

(b) We find no clear evidence that John, writing much later, and, as we must believe, with knowledge of what the Synoptists had written, intended in his account to correct them, and to put the supper on another and earlier day. If he did so intend, he would have represented the supper of the feet-washing as not a paschal supper, but as held before the legal time, and also as identical with theirs. It is claimed that he does represent it as not a paschal supper by the mention of the time, and by the absence in his account of all that indicates a paschal supper. But, admitting that it was not, does he identify his supper with that of the Synoptists? If not identical, he does not correct the Synoptists as they refer to a different event.

Let us assume that the supper in John was not the paschal supper, and that it was identical with that of the Synoptists; it must have been either an anticipatory supper or an ordinary meal. We find no good ground to believe that the Lord would have observed an anticipatory supper, whether eaten with a lamb or without, not only because of its illegality both as to time and manner, but also because of an element of unreality — a seeming observance — wholly foreign to Him who came to keep the law, and to fulfill all righteousness. We may rather believe that He observed no quasi-paschal supper, but met the apostles at an ordinary meal. In this case, however, why go to Jerusalem at all since this meal might have been at Bethany? And why do the Synoptists affirm so clearly that his messengers were sent to prepare, and did prepare the passover? And as it is admitted that the Lord instituted His supper in connection with a supper preceding it, if this was an ordinary meal, he must have instituted His supper in the absence of all those typical elements that gave to the paschal supper its significance; a view in itself incredible, and directly contradicted by the Synoptical accounts.

2. (a) We find no clear evidence that John intended to correct the

Synoptists as to the day of the crucifixion.   The argument derived from the fear of defilement on the part of the Jews, and from their desire to eat the passover (John xviii. 28), depends upon the meaning of a word which confessedly is used with large latitude, and its significance here is very uncertain.   The point is one that must be determined rather on historical than on grammatical grounds, and we seem to find it used in the large and indefinite sense which would naturally follow from John's Christian position, and the later date of his gospel.   The argument from the phrase, "preparation of the passover" (John xix. 14), is of a similar kind.

(b) We find no sufficient proof that the first feast day, the 15th Nisan, was held so sacred by the Jews that they would not have arrested and tried the Lord on that day, and the more readily that the chief responsibility and entire execution vested in the Roman governor.

(c) But if generally strictly keeping it, we can easily believe that the rulers would not have counted it a work unworthy of a holy day, to arrest and condemn one who blasphemously asserted Himself to be their Messiah, and more, to be the Son of God; and whose acceptance by the people would be the overthrow of the city and temple, and the destruction of the nation.   To destroy such a man, and to avoid so great danger, would justify a transgression of the feast laws.

Among the more important recent discussions of the questions connected with this last passover, are those of Wieseler, *Beiträge*, 230 ff.; Langen, *Die letzten Lebenstage Jesu*, 50 ff.; Farrar, *Life of Christ*, excursus X; Edersheim, *Temple Service*, appendix; Keim, *Geschichte Jesu*, iii. 460 ff.; McClellan, *Harmony*, 473 ff.; the monographs of Schürer, Roth, Röpe, and others; the articles in the Bible Dictionaries, of which may be mentioned that of Ginsberg in Alexander's Kitto Cyclopedia, and that of Delitzsch in Riehm's Handwörterbuch.

EVENING FOLLOWING THURSDAY, 14TH NISAN, BEGINNING OF 15TH NISAN, 7TH APRIL.

As the disciples are about to take their places at the table, Jesus observes a strife among them for precedency and seats of honor. To rebuke them, He arises and girds Himself, and proceeds to wash their feet. Afterward, while they are eating, He declares that one of them will betray Him. The declaration creates great excitement among the apostles, and they begin to ask anxiously, Is it I? The Lord describes the traitor as one that is eating with Him, but without designating him further. Peter makes a sign to John to ask Him who it is, which he does,	LUKE xxii. 24–30. JOHN xiii. 1–20. LUKE xxii. 15–18. MATT. xxvi. 21–24. MARK xiv. 18–21. LUKE xxii. 21–23. JOHN xiii. 21, 22. JOHN xiii. 23–35.

and Jesus gives him privately a sign ; and dipping the
sop, gives it to Judas, who asks, is it I ?   Jesus answers   MATT. xxvi. 25.
him affirmatively, and he immediately goes out, to the sur-   MATT. xxvi. 26–29.
prise of those apostles who do not understand the cause.   MARK xiv. 22–25.
After the departure of Judas, the Lord proceeds to the   LUKE xxii. 19, 20.
institution of the eucharistic supper.

Assuming, upon grounds already stated, that John and the
Synoptists both refer to the same supper, and that the paschal
supper, we may now attempt to arrange its events in a chronological order.   This is very difficult, as no one of the Evangelists
has so given them.   There are four points that especially demand our attention: The strife for precedency ; the washing of
the apostles' feet ; the announcement of Judas' treachery and
his departure; and the institution of the Lord's supper.   Let us
take the order of Luke (xxii. 14 ff.) as the fullest in its details.

1.   The Lord and the Twelve sit down to the paschal supper.   2.   The cup is divided among them, and the supper
follows, presumably in the accustomed order.   3.   Institution of
the Lord's supper.   4. Announcement of Judas' treachery.   5.
Strife for precedence.   John alone mentions two events additional, the feet washing and the departure of Judas, but he
omits the institution of the Lord's supper which the Synoptists
have.   All have in common the announcement of Judas' treachery, but Luke alone the strife for precedence.

The feet washing.   We may best examine the matter of order, if we
begin with the feet washing (John xiii. 2 ff.); at what period of the
supper is it to be placed? and the first inquiry must be as to the text.
In the Textus R. it is δείπνου γενομένου, translated "supper being
ended "; accepting this, the feet washing was after the supper.
(Others translate it, "during supper," Norton; "while they were at
supper," Campbell; "supper being prepared," or "going on," Alford.)
But Tisch. and W. and H. read δείπνου γινομένου, in R. V.: "during
supper;" in Meyer, "while it is becoming supper time," *i. e.*, they
had reclined at the table, but the supper had not yet begun.   (So
Luthardt: "They were on the point of beginning the meal.")

The feet washing may then be put at the beginning of the supper.
Was this an act customary on grounds of cleanliness?   It seems
not to have been uncommon at feasts, but was not always practiced (Luke vii. 44).   The references to the Old Testament show only
that it was customary to wash the feet after a journey, and not

always before a meal. But when this was done, it was by the ministry of slaves or servants. It is said by Thomson (i. 183), on the ground of oriental usage, that it was at the close of the meal, it being customary to wash the hands and mouth after eating. "The pitcher and ewer are always brought, and the servant with a napkin over his shoulder, pours water on your hands. If there is no servant, they perform this office for one another." But in this case the Lord must have washed both hands and feet; it is, however, plain from Peter's words (verse 9) that He washed their feet only. Some, assuming that it was customary, think that the Lord acted as the servant because no one of the apostles was willing to render this service to the rest, no servant being present to do it. (So Bengel, Ebrard, Nebe, Lindsay.) But we may rather regard it as unusual, and having now a special cause. All do not, however, put it at the beginning of the meal; some, as Langen, put it at the end of the paschal supper and before the institution of the Lord's supper; and others still later.

It does not appear with which of the apostles the Lord began the feet washing. According to Chrysostom, it was Judas; to Augustine, Peter; and with him agree the Roman Catholic commentators and many Protestants. "If He did observe any order," says Lightfoot, "He began with Peter who sat in the next place immediately to Himself." This commentator supposes that He washed only the feet of Peter, James, and John, thus avoiding the washing of Judas. Bengel infers from verse 6: "So He cometh to Simon Peter," that Peter was not the first. (So Luthardt.) It seems evident from verses 5 and 6, that He did not go first to Peter, and from verses 10 and 11 that the feet of Judas were washed, for had the Lord not done this, the neglect would at once have called attention to him. According to Greswell, He began with Peter and ended with Judas.

Strife for precedence. We may thus place the feet washing at the beginning of the supper, and find the special occasion for it in the strife of the apostles for precedence mentioned by Luke (xxii. 24): "And there was also a strife among them, which of them should be accounted the greatest." This strife would come most naturally at the beginning of the supper, and find its cause in the desire to be as near to the Lord as possible, the present degree of nearness to the King being an index of rank in the future Messianic kingdom. It is scarce possible that at a later period, after the discovery of the treason of Judas, and with the solemn impression which the Lord's words respecting his guilt and punishment must have made upon them, and after they had eaten His sacred supper, any such strife could have occurred.

If then we combine the two accounts of Luke and John, we find a consistent narrative. The Lord noting this strife as they were about to begin the meal, first rebukes the apostles in words, and then proceeds to teach them in a symbolic manner that their real greatness was in their humility, by girding Himself and proceeding to wash their feet — the duty of a servant. Both events are thus internally connected together, and both are to be placed at the beginning of the supper.

Announcement of Judas's treachery. The third point is the announcement by the Lord of the treachery of Judas, and the departure of the traitor. But before considering this, it is necessary to recall to mind the order of the paschal supper,[1] and to have before us the probable positions of Peter, John, and Judas at the table.

(*a*) The supper opens with a glass of wine mingled with water, preceded by a blessing, and followed by washing of the hands. 2. Giving of thanks and eating of the bitter herbs. 3. Bringing in of the unleavened bread, the sauce, the lamb, and the flesh of the chagigah, and thank offerings. 4. Benediction. The bitter herbs dipped in the sauce are eaten. 5. The second cup is mixed, and the father explains to his children the origin of the feast. 6. The first part of the Hallel (Psalms cxiii. and cxiv.) is sung, prayer offered, and the second cup drunk. 7. The father washes his hands, takes two loaves of bread, breaks one and blesses it, takes a piece and wrapping it in the bitter herbs, dips it in the sauce and eats it with thanksgiving. Giving thanks, he then eats of the chagigah, and again giving thanks, eats of the lamb. 8. The meal continues, each eating what he pleases, but eating last of the lamb. After this is consumed, no more is eaten. 9. He washes his hands and takes the third cup after giving thanks. 10. The second part of the Hallel (Psalms cxv.–cxviii.) is sung. 11. The fourth cup is taken, and sometimes a fifth. 12. The supper concludes with singing the great Hallel (Psalms cxx.–cxxvii.)

Upon several of these points there is dispute among the Jewish writers, but the order as here given is substantially according to the paschal ritual of the Talmudists. Whether this order was generally followed in our Saviour's time is very doubtful; nor if so, is it certain that He strictly followed it.

(*b*) The data to determine the positions of the apostles at the table are very scanty. As the Lord had often eaten with the Twelve, we may presume that there had been some order which they followed in

---

[1] For this, see Lightfoot and Meyer on Matt. xxvi. 26 ; Friedlieb, Arch., 54; Langen, 148; Weichel., 247; Eders., The Temple and its Services, ch. vi.

taking their places; whether hitherto Peter had had the place of honor
nearest the Lord and John next to him, we cannot tell. This is
said by Langen, who affirms that no one would think of disputing
Peter's place as the first in rank. It is said by Nebe that the Lord at
this time gave John the highest place, and that this occasioned the
strife; but this is not warranted by anything in the narrative. We
know only that John was nearest the Lord (xiii. 23). As to the position of Judas we have only the datum in Matt. xxvi. 23: "He that
dippeth his hand with me in the dish, the same shall betray me"; and
the giving of the sop to him (John xiii. 26), indicating that he was
not far from the Lord. It is said by Edersheim (ii. 493) that "he
claimed and obtained the chief seat at the table next the Lord." (So
Keil.) As this view of the positions of the chief actors is peculiar
we give his diagram.

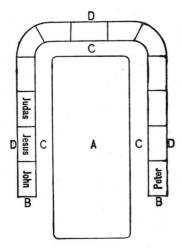

A. The table. B B. The heads of the divans on which the guests
reclined. The chief place, that occupied by the Lord. The next
place in honor, that occupied by Judas on the left of the Lord; the
lowest of all, that occupied by Peter. The lowest place was voluntarily taken by Peter, who felt keenly the Lord's rebuke of this strife
for precedence.

We give also a diagram of a Roman *triclinium* from Orelli's Hor-
ace, excursus to Sat. II. 8, furnished by Dr. Hart, who also suggests
the places occupied by the Lord and John and Judas.

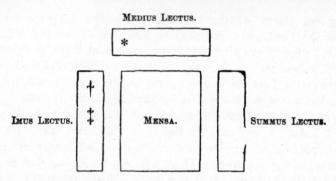

* Locus consularis, for the chief guest.   † Host's seat; here the
the Lord sat, St. John at ‡, Judas at *.[1]

We may now return to the announcement by the Lord of the
treachery of Judas, and enquire at what point in the meal it is to be
put.

Judas pointed out as the traitor.   The first allusion to him was
while washing the feet of Peter (John xiii.): " Ye are clean, but not
all."   Again, after the washing the Lord said: "I speak not of you
all. . . .   He that eateth bread with me hath lift up his heel
against me " (see Ps. xli. 9).   This prophecy was now finding its fulfillment in one sitting and eating at the same table with Him.   But
these intimations were too obscure to make any special impression upon
their minds, and He therefore, soon after declares in plain words that
one of them should betray Him.   (All the Evangelists mention this;
Luke with a little difference of phraseology, and John with the additional circumstance that " He was troubled in spirit and testified.")
This distinct utterance at once attracts their deep attention, and they
all begin to ask Him, " Lord, is it I? "   In reply He says (Matt. and
Mark), it is one of the Twelve who dippeth his hand with me in the
dish. . . .   (The R. V. reads in Matt. xxvi. 23: "he that dipped
his hand.")   In this designation of the traitor He does not seem to
refer to any present act of eating, but to the fact that he was sitting
and partaking with Him at the same table.   From these words, therefore, the apostles could not tell who of them was meant.   The same
indefiniteness of expression is found in Luke: " Behold, the hand of

[1] Pieritz: The Gospels from the Rabbinical Point of View, London, 1873 (15),
denies that there is reason to believe that the Jews at this time followed the Roman mode
of reclining at table.   He supposes that the Lord and the apostles sat in a circle around
a table on which was only one dish, into which all dipped.   But against this the language
of the Evangelists is decisive: Mark xiv. 18, Matt. xxvi. 20, in both cases, ἀνάκειμαι
Luke xxii. 14, John xiii. 12, ἀναπίπτω.   See T. G. Lex., *sub vocibus;* Light. on Matt. xxvi.
20.   Sepp (vi. 65) thinks Peter to have been on the right of Jesus, and John on his left.
He also gives the positions of all the rest, which is, of course, only conjecture.

him that betrayeth me is with me on the table." Some, however, find in the language of Mark xiv. 20, " One of the Twelve that dippeth with me in the dish," a specific designation of Judas. " The expression seems to describe the traitor as particularly near to Christ at table, and in some peculiar sense partaking with Him." [1] This is not likely unless there was more than one dish into which they dipped their morsels. It is possible that Judas may have been sitting near to Jesus, and both have been dipping at the time in the same dish; but, if so, it is plain that the others did not yet know who was meant.

At this point, when all doubtless had suspended eating, and their anxiety was at its height, and all were looking upon one another doubting of whom He spake, and asking, Is it I? Peter beckons to John to ask Him who it was (John xiii. 24). [2] To John's question, " Lord, who is it?" which, probably, from his position as lying on Jesus' breast, was unheard by the others, He replied, " He it is to whom I shall give a sop when I have dipped it." [3] It is not probable that this reply was heard by any one but John. Taking a piece of the bread and dipping it in the broth, He gives it to Judas, and thus he is revealed as the traitor to John, but to none of the others. It may be that, on receiving the sop, Judas saw that his treachery was known not only to Jesus but also to John; and, knowing that all longer concealment is useless, he now asks as the rest had done, but mockingly, " Lord, is it I?" (Matt. xxvi. 25). To his question the Lord replies, " Thou hast said," or in other words, " Thou art the man."

There is some difficulty in determining when Judas asked this question and the Lord replied, from the fact that John does not mention the question of Judas, " Lord, is it I?" and that when the former went out, none of the apostles seem to have known the cause of his departure (John xiii. 28, 29). Grotius supposes it to have been asked before Peter beckoned to John, the Lord's reply not being heard by him; and Friedlieb puts it before the sign of the sop given to John. In the general agitation and confusion the Lord's reply was unnoticed. According to Ebrard (518), the Lord answered John's question, " Who is it?" openly, so that all knew who was meant, and then Judas asked, " Is it I?" According to some, as Stier, all heard

---

[1] Alexander, *in loco ;* Meyer.

[2] The text, as given by Tischendorf, W. and H., makes the question to have been addressed by Peter to John. R. V.: " Simon Peter therefore beckoneth to him and saith to him, Tell us who it ⌐ ⌐ whom He speaketh." Peter first beckons to John to gain his attention, and then asks him, supposing that he may know, but he, being ignorant, asks Jesus.

[3] Tischendorf and W. and H. read βάψω. R. V.: " He it is, for whom I shall dip the sop, and give it him."

the question of Judas, but none specially marked it, as all had asked the same, and no suspicion seems to have attached to him in particular. The difficulty, however, is not with the question of Judas, which might easily have passed unnoticed, but with the Lord's reply, which, if heard, was too direct to have been misunderstood. If Judas had been thus openly designated as a traitor, how could the other apostles suppose that he was sent out to execute some official commission? Some, therefore, suppose that both question and reply were in a whisper or very low tone of voice, and inaudible to the others.[1] This is possible if Judas was very near the Lord, perhaps upon one side as John was upon the other, as some have inferred from Mark xiv. 18. In this case what was said might easily have escaped the ears of the other apostles ; and it seems that Judas must have been near Him when he received the sop. According to some, both question and reply were not by words, but by signs. Others still suppose that both were heard and understood by all present, but that the apostles, looking forward to the betrayal as not imminent, did not imagine that His words, spoken immediately after, "That thou doest, do quickly" (John xiii. 27–29), had any reference to the execution of his treacherous project. This is not impossible but improbable.

At what point during the supper Judas went out is uncertain, and we can best determine it when we have inquired as to the time when the Lord instituted His supper.

Institution of the Lord's supper. It is most likely that the Lord observed the usual paschal ritual to the end, and then took of the remaining bread and wine for His institution; and this is the more general opinion. But those who deny that this was the true paschal supper and regard it as anticipatory or commemorative, think that He did not follow this ritual, but blended the two, putting some interval of time between the blessing of the sacramental bread and of the cup; the former being during the feast and the latter after it. (So Greswell; Godet says that " He transformed, as He went along, the Jewish supper in such a way as to convert it into the sacred supper.") But assuming that this was the true paschal supper, let us examine the Synoptical accounts.

Order of the supper. The order may be most clearly seen in its relation to the evangelical narratives, if we consider it in connection with the several cups of wine. " Four cups of wine," says Lightfoot, " were to be drank up by every one." The first was introductory, with

---

[1] So Langen, Stroud, Eders.; Farrar thinks that Peter and John heard; Godet that the act of giving the sop to Judas was the reply to his question, and that Matthew has translated the act into words.

thanksgiving. This was followed by the bringing in of the bitter herbs
and partial eating of them; the bringing in of the bread, the sauce, the
lamb, and the chagigah; the explanation of the meaning of the feast,
and the first part of the Hallel. The second cup which was followed
by the eating of the unleavened bread, of the chagigah, and of the lamb.
The third cup, commonly called the cup of blessing, and after it, the
second part of the Hallel was sung. The fourth cup was drunk.
If the great Hallel was sung, there was a fifth cup. All that took
place between the first and second cups was introductory to the meal.
The feast proper began with the second cup and ended with the
third. Except the partial eating of the bitter herbs, nothing was
eaten before the second, and nothing at all was eaten after the third.
The singing of the second part of the Hallel, and the fourth cup,
generally closed the feast.

If we now turn to the Evangelists, we find that Luke only (xxii.
17, 20) mentions two cups of wine. To which of the four customary cups of the paschal supper shall these be referred? Many identify the first of Luke with the first of the supper.[1] But against this
an argument is found in the Lord's words (verses 16 and 18), that He
would no more eat or drink of the passover till the kingdom of God
should come, which seem to imply that He had already eaten and
drunken, and that the paschal supper was over. The words, however, may mean no more than that He would partake of no passover
after the present.

Some, however, make the first cup of Luke to have been the third
of the paschal supper.[2] The supper was then, so far as eating the
passover was concerned, fully over; and His words, "With desire
have I desired to eat this passover with you before I suffer," refer to
His own supper which He was about to establish. Bucher (742)
refers these words in Luke (verses 15–18) to the paschal supper just
ended; but Matt. xxvi. 29 and Mark xiv. 25, to the eucharistic supper.

The second cup of Luke (verse 20) was that "after supper" (see
also 1 Cor. xi. 25), and is the same as that mentioned by Matt. xxvi. 27
and Mark xiv. 23. To which of the four cups of the supper does this
correspond? Many refer it to the third.[3] Of this cup, Brown remarks:
"It was emphatically called 'the cup of blessing,' because, while it
stood before them, the president did what we commonly do at the
end of a feast — he returned thanks to the Father of all for every
temporal and spiritual blessing, but especially that of the passover."
To this some suppose St. Paul to refer (1 Cor. x. 16): "The cup of
blessing which we bless, is it not the communion of the blood of

---

[1] So Robinson, Stier, Alford, Godet.   [2] Brown, Antiq., 465.
[3] Lightfoot, Lange, Rob., Licht.

Christ?" It is observed by Lightfoot (Matt. xxvi. 27): "Here it is that Luke and Paul say that He took the cup after supper, that is, that cup which closed up the supper."

If the third cup or "cup of blessing" was the Lord's sacramental cup, as is most probable, the blessing of the sacramental bread must have preceded it. We may say, either that after the lamb had been eaten and before the drinking of the third cup, He took of the bread and blessed it and gave them tc eat; or that He partook of the third cup as the last part of the paschal supper and then proceeded to the institution of His supper by blessing the bread and giving the cup.

Some, however, make the second cup of Luke to have been the fourth cup.[1] The chief argument for this is, that if it was the third cup, the fourth cup must have been wholly omitted, which is not probable. Of this fourth cup, Brown remarks: "We are not particularly informed whether it immediately succeeded the third, or that a certain interval was between them. But we know that it was called the cup of the Hallel because the president finished over it the Hallel which he had begun over the second cup." Still, as this observance respecting the four cups of wine was not commanded in the law, Jesus might not have regarded it, and have sung the hymn after the third. It is said by Lightfoot: "Whether He made use of this cup also, we do not dispute, it is certain He used the hymn." If, however, a cup was taken after the sacramental cup, which is not probable, it is not mentioned.

Confining ourselves to those arrangements that assume the Lord to have kept the paschal supper according to the Jewish ritual, we may thus classify them:

1. That the paschal supper was wholly finished, the fourth cup having been drunk and the lesser Hallel sung, when the Lord instituted His supper. (Langen and many.)

2. That the paschal supper as to its essential part was ended, the lamb having been eaten. At this point the Lord blessed the bread, and made the third cup His sacramental cup. (Light., Eders., Tisch., and most.) Others, that the fourth cup was the sacramental cup. (Meyer, Brown; Bynaeus hesitates between the third and fourth. The arrangements of these who hold that the supper was anticipatory and without the lamb, are various and need not be stated here.)

We conclude that the second of the above arrangements has most in its favor. The Lord partook with the others of the paschal lamb, and when the law had been thus fulfilled and the supper ended, before proceeding to take the cup after supper, the cup of blessing, took bread, probably the unleavened bread upon the table, and gave

[1] Meyer, Brown.

thanks, and declaring it to be His body, gave them to eat. It had
been a rule that the paschal lamb should be the last thing eaten; but
He now set this aside and gave them the flesh of "the Lamb slain
from the foundation of the world." He now took the cup, and giving thanks, gave it to them that all might drink. By thus placing
the taking of the eucharistic bread immediately after, and in connection with, the eating of the paschal lamb, we best meet the statements of Matthew and Mark, that "as they were eating — ἐσθιόντων
αὐτῶν — He took bread," etc. (See Eders., ii. 511: "He connected
with the breaking of the unleavened cake at the close of the paschal
meal, the breaking of the bread and the eucharist.")

After this discussion as to the time of the institution of the sacramental supper, we return to the question whether Judas departed
before or after the institution.

Departure of Judas. Matthew (xxvi. 25), who alone relates the
question of Judas, "Master, is it I?" and the Lord's reply, "Thou
hast said," says nothing of his departure, but mentions the eucharistic supper as taking place after the question and reply. John
(xiii. 26–30), who mentions his departure immediately after receiving
the sop, says nothing of the eucharistic supper. The Evangelists
Mark and Luke do not speak of Judas by name. Where then, in
Matthew's narrative, shall we insert his departure? Probably between
verses 25 and 26. (So Ellicott, Meyer.) From the expression (verse
26): "And as they were eating, Jesus took bread," etc., some infer
the presence of Judas, the paschal supper not being yet ended.[1]
But the expression may mean no more than that, while yet at the
table Jesus took bread; or if the eating was that of the lamb of
which all were bound to partake, the peculiar position of Judas
would justify his exclusion. The argument from the Lord's words
(verse 27), "Drink ye all of it," as implying that Judas was to drink
with the others, is thus stated by Alford: "It is on all accounts
probable, and this account confirms the probability that Judas was
present and partook of both parts of this first communion. The expressions are such throughout as to lead us to suppose that the same
persons, the Twelve, were present." But Matthew uses the same expression: "All ye shall be offended in me this night" (verse 31, so
verses 33 and 35), when only eleven were present. Perhaps the right
explanation of the words "Drink ye all of it," may be that given by
Buxtorf,[2] who says, that it is the law among the Jews, that all who
were present at the paschal supper should drink of the four cups,

---

[1] Bengel; *ergo Judas aderat.* See his footnote.
[2] Cited by Bynaeus, i. 624.

whether men or women, adults or children; and especially of the
fourth or last cup.

If we turn to the narrative of John, we read that, after Jesus gave
Judas the sop, Satan entered into him, and "he went immediately
out." Some have attempted to determine from the mention of the
"sop" to what period of the meal this event is to be referred. But
it is uncertain whether this sop — $\psi\omega\mu\iota\sigma\nu$ — literally bit or morsel, was
of flesh or bread.[1] If of bread, as is most probable, it may have been
given immediately after the second cup when each of the company,
wrapping a piece of unleavened bread in bitter herbs, dipped it in the
sauce and ate it. This was before the paschal lamb was eaten. But,
as both the bread and the sauce continued on the table to the end of
the meal, the Lord may have given him the sop at a later period, and
no definite inference can be drawn from this circumstance. Edersheim
affirms that it was compounded of flesh of the lamb, unleavened
bread, and bitter herbs. The Lord dipped this and gave it to Judas,
after this the supper continued.

If Judas went out immediately after receiving the sop, and yet
was present at the Lord's supper, this supper must have been prior to
the dipping of the sop and the events immediately before it. But
where in John's narrative can it be placed? According to Stier, it
may find place between verses 22 and 23. But there is the greatest
intrinsic improbability, that after Jesus had solemnly announced to
them, "Verily, verily, I say unto you, that one of you shall betray
me," and "all were looking on one another doubting of whom He
spake," He should have proceeded at once to the institution of this
holy rite. It is to be noted, also, that in announcing the treachery
of Judas (verse 21), "He was troubled in spirit," but that after the
departure of Judas (verse 31), He said, "Now is the Son of Man glorified, and God is glorified in Him." There seems to be in John's
narrative no possible place for inserting the institution of the eucharist prior to the departure of Judas. Where, after that, it is to be
placed is disputed. Some place it between verses 30 and 31 (Ellicott,
Luthardt, Ebrard, Langen, McClel.); some between verses 32 and 33;
some after verse 33; some after verse 38; and others find no place
wholly satisfactory.

Some would make a distinction between the two parts of the
Lord's supper, an interval elapsing between the consecration of the
bread and that of the wine.[2] Hence, it is said that Judas partook of

---

[1] The opinion of Origen and others that this was the bread consecrated to be the
Lord's body, and now given to Judas, is refuted by Augustine. See Tholuck, *in loco.*

[2] Greswell, iii. 181. "The bread was ordained during the supper, the use of the
cup was prescribed after it." So Westcott, Godet. a Lapide on John xiii. 2, distinguishes

the bread but went out before the distribution of the cup.   There is no sound basis for this distinction.

Upon these grounds, we conclude that Judas left the paschal supper before the Lord instituted the eucharist.   This point has been connected with questions respecting the spiritual efficacy of the sacrament into which it would be foreign to our purpose to enter.   The weight of authority down to recent times is in favor of the view that he was present and partook with the other apostles of the bread and wine.[1]

Some minor questions remain.   Did the Lord partake of the paschal supper?   Meyer insists that the words (Luke xxii. 17, 18) "Take this and divide it among yourselves, for I say unto you, I will not drink of the fruit of the vine until the kingdom of God shall come," show conclusively that He did not Himself drink of the cup, which abstinence, if this were the first cup, is most improbable; and he therefore infers that those words which, according to Matthew (xxvi. 29), were later spoken, are erroneously inserted here.   But it is by no means certain that the words, "Take this and divide it among yourselves," do exclude His own participation in the first cup.   As Luke alone reports His words: "With desire I have desired to eat this passover with you," it is almost certain that He had Himself partaken of the cup ere He gave it to the disciples.[2]

Many identify Matt. xxvi. 29 and Mark xiv. 25 with Luke xxii. 18, but this is doubtful ; the similarity may best be explained by supposing that the latter was spoken in reference to the paschal supper and before it began, the former in reference to the eucharistic supper.   He kept the passover with His disciples according to the law, and thus fulfilled it; and He would no more partake of it till it should be observed in its new and higher form in the kingdom of God.   He established the eucharistic supper, and henceforth would no more partake of it till He partook of it new in the kingdom of His Father.   It

---

three suppers: *Cæremonialis*, the eating of the paschal lamb; *Communis*, the eating of other viands; *Cœna Eucharistiæ*. It was before this third and last that He washed their feet—not an ordinary rite, but a *lotio sacramentalis*, to prepare them for His supper. The Lord twice pointed out Judas as His betrayer, once before His supper, and once after; he was thus present at it. See Maldonatus on Matt. xxvi. 20.

[1] Wichelhaus (257) enumerates as its defenders, Cyprian, Jerome, Augustine, Chrysostom, the two Cyrils, Theodoret; and later, Bellarmine, Baronius, Maldonatus, Gerhard, Beza, Bucer, Lightfoot, Bengel. Calvin is undecided; *Probabile tamen esse non nego Judam affuisse.* It is affirmed by the Lutherans but denied by the Reformed. Of the later commentators affirming it are McKnight, Krafft, Patritius, Stier, Alford, Stroud, Caspari; denying it, Meyer, Tischendorf, Robinson, Lichtenstein, Friedlieb, Bucher, Ebrard, Lange, Wieseler, Riggenbach, Ellicott, Langen, Eders., M. and M., Woolsey, Keil; undecided, Farrar. For an interesting discussion of the point, see Bynaeus, i. 443.

[2] See Alford and Keil, *in loco*.

may be, that in this are references to two distinct ordinances in the age to come — that of the paschal supper for the Jews, and of the Lord's supper for the Church.

Did the Lord partake of the consecrated bread and wine? This is a point which the accounts of the Evangelists do not enable us to decide. It was answered affirmatively by many of the earlier interpreters: Jerome, Augustine, Chrysostom, and others. (See Langen, 188.)

EVENING FOLLOWING THURSDAY, THE 14TH NISAN, 10–12 P. M. 6TH APRIL.

After the supper Peter makes protestations of fidelity, but the Lord announces to him that before the cock shall crow he shall deny Him. He teaches the disciples of the perils that await them, and they bring to Him two swords. He proceeds to address to them words of encouragement, and answers questions of Thomas and Philip. He adds the promise of the Comforter, and calling upon them to arise and depart with Him, He continues His address to them as they stand around Him, and ends with a prayer.	LUKE xxii. 31–38. JOHN xiii. 36–38. JOHN xiv. 1–31. JOHN xv., xvi., xvii.

Matthew and Mark narrate the Lord's announcement to Peter that he would deny Him, as if it took place after they had left the supper room, and were upon their way to the Mount of Olives; Luke and John, as taking place before they had left the room. Hence, some suppose that the announcement was made before they left it, and was renewed by the way; and that His declaration respecting the crowing of the cock was twice spoken: once in the room of the supper, as recorded by Luke and John, and once after they had left it, as recorded by Matthew and Mark.[1] Others, however, who agree with these that Jesus twice uttered the prediction respecting the denials of Peter, would identify Matthew, Mark, and Luke; but the last not narrating in chronological order. (See Edersheim, ii. 534, who seems to say that John and the Synoptists all refer to the same warning, and that on the way to Gethsemane.) This identification is defended on internal grounds, and especially that the Lord's words to Peter, as given by Luke, " When thou art converted, strengthen thy brethren," seem plainly to point to His words respecting all the apostles, as given by Matthew and Mark, " All ye shall be

---

[1] Meyer, Alford, Oosterzee, Farrar, Riddle, Langen.

offended because of me this night." [1]   That the prediction respecting Peter's denials was twice spoken, first at the paschal supper and then as they went to Gethsemane (so Lightfoot, Patritius, Townsend), is intrinsically probable, and wholly in accordance with Peter's character.   Jesus had said (John xiii. 33) that
He must go whither His disciples could not follow Him.   This
leads Peter to ask whither He was going, and why he could not
now follow Him; and he adds: "I will lay down my life for
thy sake."   Now the Lord declares to him that ere the cock
crow, he shall deny Him thrice.   (Keil thinks this warning of
Peter was put by John in the supper room, because it could not
well be inserted later between chapters xvii. and xviii.)   Later,
perhaps as they were approaching the garden of Gethsemane,
Jesus, addressing them as a body, declares that "they all shall
be offended in Him this night" (Matt. xxvi. 31).   This leads
Peter to repeat his protestations of fidelity, and to affirm that
though all others should be offended, yet he would not.   The
Lord therefore repeats, and more emphatically: "Verily I say
unto thee, this day, even in this night, before the cock crow
twice, thou shalt deny me thrice" (Mark xiv. 30).

According to some, the Lord three times predicted Peter's
denials, once as given by John, once by Luke, and once by
Matthew and Mark.[2]   On the other hand, some make but one
prediction, which John and Luke relate rightly as at the supper,
and Matthew and Mark by retrospection.[3]   Others still think it
rightly placed by Matthew and Mark while on the way to Gethsemane.[4]

The words the "cock shall not crow," may be understood
as referring, not to a literal cock, but to that watch of the night
known as the "cock-crowing" (see Mark xiii. 35), or the third
watch, that from 12–3 A. M.   "Within the time of cock crowing," says Lightfoot, "the short space of time between the first
and second crowing."   This would be equivalent to saying
before early dawn thou shalt deny me.   But the Lord seems to
include the actual crowing of the cock, as the event shows (Mark

---

[1] See Bynaeus, ii. 9.
[2] So Augustine, Greswell, Grenville, Sadler.
[3] Newcome, Robinson, Riggenbach, Godet, Nebe.
[4] So substantially Patritius.

xiv. 66–72). The second crowing was probably about 3 A. M. That Mark should say, "Before the cock crow twice thou shalt deny me thrice," while the other Evangelists say, "Before the cock crow thou shalt deny me thrice," makes no real discrepancy. The latter speak generally of the cock-crowing as a period of time within which the three denials should take place; Mark more accurately says, that during this period the cock should not crow twice ere the denials were made.[1] The assertion that no cocks were permitted at Jerusalem has no basis.[2]

The allusion to the swords is found only in Luke. Some, as Stier and Edersheim, make this incident to have taken place on the way to Gethsemane, and just before the entrance into it. As, however, it seems to be directly connected with the words spoken to Peter, it may have occurred in the supper room.[3]

After thus warning His disciples of the twofold danger from invisible temptation and external violence, and encouraging them to trust in Him, and giving them the promise of the Comforter, He offers His farewell prayer, the hymn is sung—the second part of the Hallel, Psalms cxv.–cxviii., or, as some say, Psalm cxxxvi. — and the paschal solemnity is ended. We may, however, connect this hymn with His words (John xiv. 31), "Arise, let us go hence," or place it before the discourse. (So Eders., Farrar.)

There is much difference of opinion as the place where these discourses of the Lord were made. Those who deny this supper in John (xiii. 2) to have been the paschal supper, but make it one previous at Bethany, place its close at xiv. 31, when Jesus arose to go to Jerusalem. Bynaeus finds three distinct discourses: the first, John xiii., at the supper on the evening of Wednesday preceding the paschal supper; the second, John xiv., on Thursday just before Jesus left Bethany to go to Jerusalem to the paschal supper; the third, John xv., xvi., xvii., on the night following the paschal supper.

But those who make the supper in John the paschal supper, agree that the Lord's words from xiii. 31 to xiv. 31 were spoken in the upper room ; the question is as to chapters xv., xvi., and

---

[1] See Friedlieb, Archäol., 79; Greswell, iii. 211.

[2] See Alford on Matt. xxvi. 34. "It is certain that there were cocks at Jerusalem as well as at other places." Lightfoot; Eders., ii. 537, note.

[3] So Da Costa, Ebrard, Oosterzee, Farrar, Godet.

xvii. Many understand the words "Arise, let us go hence," as
showing that He then left the upper room to go to Gethsemane,
and that the following discourse and the prayer were on the
way.   But to this there are some obvious objections.   After His
words, "Arise, let us go hence," no change of place is mentioned
till the prayer is ended.   Whether the statement of John xviii.
1, "When Jesus had spoken these words, He went forth over the
brook Cedron," refers to His departure from the upper room, or
departure from the city, is in dispute.   But if to the former, it
is not probable that His discourse was spoken while they were
walking, and still less His prayer.   Godet thinks of some "retired spot on the slope which descends into the valley of the
Cedron."   Westcott makes this discourse and prayer to have
been spoken in the temple.   (See *contra*, Eders., ii. 528, note.)
The more general belief is that the Lord arose from the table
with the apostles, but remained in the room, and all standing,
He continued His discourse, and ended it with the prayer.[1]

NIGHT FOLLOWING THURSDAY, 14TH NISAN, 6TH APRIL.

After His prayer is ended, Jesus goes with His disciples over the brook Cedron (Kidron) to the garden of Gethsemane, where He awaits the coming of Judas.   This
apostate, after leaving the supper room, had gone to the
priests, and with them made arrangement for the immediate arrest of the Lord.   Coming to the garden, Jesus takes
with Him Peter and James and John, and retires with them
to a secluded spot.   Here He begins to be heavy with sorrow, and, leaving the three, goes alone to pray.   Returning, He finds them asleep.   Leaving them, He again prays
and in His agony sweats a bloody sweat, but is strengthened by an angel   Again returning to the three disciples,
He finds them asleep.   He goes a third time and prays,
and returning, bids them sleep on, but soon announces
the approach of Judas.

JOHN xviii. 1, 2.
MATT. xxvi. 30–36.
LUKE xxii. 39.
MARK xiv. 26–32.
JOHN xviii. 3.

MATT. xxvi. 37–46.
MARK xiv. 33–42.
LUKE xxii. 40–46.

The hour when Jesus left the supper room to go to Gethsemane cannot be exactly determined.   Lichtenstein (411) puts
it at midnight: first, because usually at this hour the supper was
ended; second, because if He had left earlier, there would have

---

[1] So Meyer, Stier, Alford, Norton, Tholuck, Ellicott, Luthardt, Edersheim, Weiss;
that it was spoken on the way, Langen, Lange, Da Costa, Ebrard, Patritius, Godet.

been too great delay at Gethsemane. Greswell puts it between eleven and twelve o'clock; Morrison at nine or ten; Fairbairn at eight or nine; Jarvis at eight. Supposing the paschal supper to have commenced soon after 6 P. M. or sundown, the several incidents of the feast and the Lord's discourse and prayer must have occupied them till near midnight. The only datum of time bearing on it is the crowing of the cock (Mark xiv. 68, 72), and this gives no definite result.

The traditional site of the upper room where the paschal supper was eaten — the Cœnaculum — is on the western hill generally known as Mt. Zion, and near the traditional house of Caiaphas. It is a room in the mosque known as Neby Daud, and is described by Robinson (i. 241) as " a large, dreary room of stone, fifty or sixty feet long by some thirty in width. At the east end is a small niche in the wall, which the Christians use at certain seasons as an altar, and celebrate mass." The building in which it is, was formerly a Christian Church, and is of very high antiquity, and was early held to be the place where the apostles were assembled at Pentecost when the Holy Ghost descended upon them. As it is probable that they were assembled in the same room where the Lord's supper was instituted, the tradition, at least as regards the site, seems quite credible. It is said by Epiphanius (A. D. 450) that this building escaped destruction by Titus, and was used by the Christians after their return to Jerusalem from Pella. Another tradition, however, put the Cœnaculum on the side of the Mount of Olives near the Church of the Virgin Mary. Barclay objects to the traditional site on the ground that when Peter and John (Luke xxii. 10) entered the city from Bethany to prepare for the paschal supper, they would necessarily have gone a long way before meeting the man bearing the pitcher of water, and prefers the northeastern brow of Mt. Zion and nearer Gethsemane; and Greswell supposes it to have been in the eastern part of the city. Wherever it was, it could have been but a little distance from the garden.[1] We cannot be far wrong if we suppose the Lord to have reached Gethsemane about midnight.

---

[1] As to the traditional claims of the " Upper Room," see Williams, H. C., ii. 507; Survey of Western Pal., 419.

Gethsemane, "valley of oil," or "oil press," to which the
Lord went, was a place He was accustomed to visit (John xviii.
2), and a little way out of the city. The designation χωρίον,
means a place enclosed — a farm. It is not mentioned by John
as Gethsemane, but as "a garden." Luke speaks only of His
going to the Mount of Olives. It seems to have been an olive
orchard, and not connected with any private residence. If, however, this was a private garden, still, as at the feasts all the houses
and gardens were thrown open to the public, Jesus could visit it
at this time without hindrance or attracting to Himself any
special attention. Greswell hints that the family of Lazarus
might have had possessions there, and Meyer infers that its owner
must have been friendly to Jesus. From a comparison of
Luke xxi. 37 with xxii. 39, it appears that the Lord had spent
some part of the previous nights there, perhaps alone in prayer.

Whether the site of the modern Gethsemane is to be identified with the ancient garden is questioned, as the Evangelists do
not say on what part of the Mount of Olives it lay. It is first
mentioned by Eusebius as at the Mount of Olives, and afterward more definitely by Jerome as at the foot of the Mount.[1]
Several of the most recent inquirers are disposed to deny the
identification. Thomson (ii. 483) says: "The position is too near
the city, and so close to what must have always been the great
thoroughfare eastward, that our Lord would scarcely have
selected it for retirement on that dangerous and dismal night."
He finds a better site several hundred yards to the northeast on
the Mount of Olives. Weiss (iii. 320) remarks: "The name
applies to a remote part of the mountain where an oil press was
situated, most likely entirely forsaken, or at least unemployed."
Barclay (63) thinks it evident that the present enclosure, from
its narrow dimensions, can occupy only in part the site of the
ancient garden, and finds a better position higher up in the valley. Stanley (415) is undecided. But whether the present garden occupies precisely the old site or not, it is certain that it
must be near it. It lies a little east of the valley of the Kidron,
at the intersection of two paths, both leading in different directions over the Mount of Olives. Descending from St. Stephen's

---

[1] Robinson. i. 235.

gate into the valley and crossing a bridge, it is easily reached, being distant but nine or ten rods from the bridge. Formerly, it was unenclosed, but recently the Latins have built a high wall around it. There are within eight venerable olive trees, undoubtedly of great age, their trunks much decayed, but their branches flourishing. "The most venerable of their race on the face of the earth," says Stanley, "their gnarled trunks and scanty foliage will always be regarded as the most affecting of the sacred memorials in or about Jerusalem." The Greeks, envious of the Latins, have recently enclosed a piece of ground a little north beside the Virgin's tomb, and contend that this is the true garden.[1]

The words of Jesus at the paschal supper (John xiii. 27), "That thou doest, do quickly,"[2] forced Judas to do at once what he had apparently not designed to do till the feast was over. Perhaps he feared that if the arrest was not made the same night, Jesus would the next day leave the city. Of the movements of Judas after he left the supper, none of the Evangelists give us an account till he reappears at the garden of Gethsemane ; but we can readily picture them to ourselves in their outline. Going immediately to Caiaphas, or to some other leading member of the Sanhedrin, he informs him where Jesus is, and announces that he is ready to fulfill his compact and at once to make the arrest. It was not, as we have seen, the intention to arrest Him during the feast lest there should be a popular tumult (Matt. xxvi. 5); but now that an opportunity offered of seizing Him secretly at dead of night when all were asleep or engaged at the paschal meal, and therefore without danger of interference or uproar, His enemies could not hesitate. Once in their hands, the rest was easy. A hasty trial, a prejudged condemnation, an immediate execution, and the hated Prophet of Galilee was forever removed out of their way. All, perhaps, might be done by the hour of morning prayer and sacrifice.[3] With great despatch all the necessary arrangements are made. Some soldiers the Sanhedrin had under its own direction, the guards of the temple com-

---

[1] Porter, i. 177; Baedeker, 216.

[2] It is a strange fancy of Greswell that those words were spoken to Satan who had entered into Judas.

[3] Lichtenstein, 414.

manded by "the captains of the temple," or, as translated by
Campbell, "officers of the temple guard;"[1] and to these they added
some of their own servants armed with staves.   But they must
be attended by Roman soldiers in case a disturbance should
arise; and to this end Pilate was persuaded to place at their
command the cohort, or a part of it, under its captain, $\chi\iota\lambda\iota\alpha\rho\chi o\varsigma$,
that during the feast was stationed at Fort Antonia for the
preservation of order.[2]   Some of the chief priests and elders
were also themselves to be present, to direct the proceedings,
and if necessary, to control the people.[3]   The soldiers, or some
portion of them, were to be provided with lanterns and torches,
probably to search the garden if any attempt was made to escape.
That at this time the moon was at the full, presents no objection.
"They would," says Hackett (140), "need lanterns and torches,
even in a clear night and under a brilliant moon, because the
western side of Olivet abounds in deserted tombs and caves."
It is possible that they thought to surprise Him asleep.   It was
agreed that Judas should precede the others, and, approaching
Him in a friendly way, kiss Him, and thus make Him known.
This indicates that no resistance was anticipated.

Of the events at Gethsemane prior to the arrival of Judas,
John says nothing.   Luke is brief, and, omitting the choice of
the three apostles to accompany Jesus, mentions but one prayer.
On the other hand, he alone mentions the bloody sweat and the
presence of the angel (xxii. 40–46).   In Matthew and Mark we
find the fullest details.

Whether all the apostles entered the garden does not appear;
but if so, all except Peter, James, and John, remained near the
entrance.   How long time He was with the three in the recesses
of the garden can but be conjectured, for the words given by
Matthew (xxvi. 40), "What, could ye not watch with me one
hour?" do not imply, as said by Greswell, that this was the
time actually occupied in His prayer, but are a proverbial expres-

---

[1] Luke xxii. 52, probably a police force; Joseph., War, vi. 5. 13; Eders., Temple
Services, 119.

[2] John xviii. 3 and 12. See Meyer, *in loco*. Nebe (268) thinks that this was not
done by Pilate, but by the chiliarch on his own responsibility. Bäumlein questions
whether any Roman soldiers were present. The point, what part Pilate had in the
arrest, will be examined later.

[3] Luke xxii. 52.   Lichtenstein, 415.

sion denoting a brief interval.   As Luke alone mentions the
appearing of the angel, it is not certain where this should find
place in Matthew's account.   Some place it between the first
and second prayer to strengthen Him for that more terrible
struggle to come when He sweat drops of blood.[1]   Others
make the agony and bloody sweat to have taken place before the
appearance of the angel, and to have been its occasion, although
narrated after it.   That the grief and heaviness were greatest
during the first prayer, may be inferred from Matthew and Mark.
The language of Luke does not permit us to think of sweat
falling in large, heavy drops like blood, but of sweat mingled
with blood.[2]

The Lord's words to the three apostles after His last return
to them (Matt. xxvi. 45; so Mark), "Sleep on now and take
your rest," are understood by some as giving them permission
and opportunity to sleep, because the hour of His agony was past
and the need of their help.   "The obvious objection to this
explanation is that in the same breath He tells them to awake;
but even this is not unnatural, if taken as a sort of after-thought
suggested by the sight or sound of the approaching enemy."[3]
Others understand them as ironically spoken.[4]   Others still, as
interrogatively: "Sleep ye on still and take ye your rest?"[5]
The first explanation is to be preferred.   "The former words,"
says Ellicott, "were rather in the accents of a pensive contemplation — the latter in the tones of exhortation and command."
It was the sudden appearance of Judas and his band that caused
the words, "Rise, let us be going; behold, he is at hand that
doth betray me," and explain their apparent abruptness.[6]
Hackett (254) connects them with the local position of the garden from which Jesus could survey at a glance the entire length
of the eastern wall and the slope of the hill toward the valley.

---

[1] Meyer, Alford, Keil.

[2] Meyer, Alford, DeWette.   For cases having points of similarity, see Stroud on
Death of Christ, 85, and note iii.   By W. and H., verses 43 and 44 in Luke xxii. are
bracketed.

[3] Alexander. See Lichtenstein, 414.   [4] Calvin, Campbell, Meyer.

[5] Greswell, iii. 194; Robinson, Har., 151.   The former would refer Luke xxii. 45,
not to the three disciples, but to the eight whom He found also asleep near the entrance
of the garden.   There seems no basis for this.

[6] See Mark xiv. 41: "It is enough, the hour is come," i. e., "Ye have slept
enough."

" It is not improbable that His watchful eyes at that moment caught sight of Judas and his accomplices as they issued from one of the eastern gates, or turned round the northern or southern corner of the walls in order to descend into the valley."

Night following Thursday, the 14th Nisan, 6th April.

Upon the arrival of Judas and those with him, Jesus, accompanied by the apostles, goes forth from the garden to meet him. Judas, coming forward before the others, kisses Him as a sign to them. Addressing Judas with the words, " Betrayest thou the Son of man with a kiss," He advances to the multitude and demands of them whom they seek. At their reply, " Jesus of Nazareth," He answers, " I am He," and they go backward and fall to the ground. Again He asks the same question, and receives the same reply. He now requests that the apostles may go free. As they proceed to take and bind Him, Peter smites a servant of the high priest, but the Lord heals the wound. Beholding their Master in the power of His enemies, all the apostles forsake Him and flee, and also a young man who had followed Him. He reproaches the multitude that they had come to arrest Him as a thief.

John xviii. 3–12.
Matt. xxvi. 47–56.
Mark xiv. 43–52.
Luke xxii. 47, 48.

Luke xxii. 49–53.

The time spent in the garden was probably more than an hour, so that, if they entered it an hour before midnight, it was about midnight when Judas came.[1] Some suppose that Judas with his band must first have gone to the room of the supper, and then, not finding the Lord, to the garden (so Stroud, Edersheim). The Lord seems to have met him near the entrance of the garden, whether without it or within it, is not certain. " He went forth " (John xviii. 4); "out of the garden " (Meyer); "out of the circle of the disciples " (Lange); "from the shade of the trees into the moonlight " (Alford); "from the bottom of the garden to the front part of it " (Tholuck). The matter is unimportant. According to his arrangement with the priests, Judas, seeing the Lord standing with the disciples, leaves those that accompanied him a little behind, and coming forward salutes Him with the usual salutation, and kisses Him. To this Jesus replies, " Friend, wherefore art thou come ? " (R. V., " Friend, do that for which

---

[1] Jones, Notes, 331, makes the arrest to have been about 10 P. M., and Jesus taken to Caiaphas about 11 P. M; Stroud, the arrest at 11; McClellan about midnight.

thou art come," Matt. xxvi. 50). "Betrayest thou the Son of
man with a kiss?" (Luke xxii. 48). Appalled at these words,
Judas steps backward, and Jesus goes toward the multitude,
who were watching what was taking place, and who, beholding
Him advance, await His approach. It may be that Judas had
advanced so far before his companions that he was not seen by
them to kiss the Lord, and that they were still awaiting the
sign. He asks, "Whom seek ye?" They reply, "Jesus of
Nazareth." His words, "I am He," spoken with the majesty that
became the Son of God, so overawed them that they went backward and fell to the ground. After a like question and reply,
He requests them to let the apostles go free, thus implying His
own willingness to be taken; and they, thus emboldened, now
lay hands upon Him. At this moment Peter draws his sword
and smites one of the band. Jesus orders him to put up his
sword, and declares that He gives Himself up to them voluntarily, and that, if He needed help, His Father would send Him
legions of angels. The healing of the servant's ear is mentioned
only by Luke (xxii. 51). He now addresses a few words to the
chief priests and captains and elders, who had probably to this
time been standing behind the soldiers, and now came forward;
and, as He finished, the apostles, seeing Him wholly in the
power of His enemies, forsook Him and fled. It does not appear that there was any design to arrest them. If their Master
was removed out of the way, the Sanhedrin doubtless thought
that they would soon sink into obscurity. There was no attempt
to seize them, and in the darkness and confusion they could
easily escape. Peter and John, however, continued waiting near
by, watching the progress of events. The incident of the young
man "having a linen cloth cast about his naked body," is
mentioned only by Mark (xiv. 51, 52). From the linen cloth
or cloak, Lightfoot infers that he was a religious ascetic, and
not a disciple of Jesus, but a casual looker-on. Lichtenstein
(395) and many make him to have been the Evangelist Mark
himself, and son of the man at whose house Jesus ate the
paschal supper, and thus having a personal interest in the narrative; others, John; others, James the Just.[1]

---

[1] See Alexander, *in loco*. The matter is elaborately discussed by Bynaeus, ii. 228;
Edersheim, ii. 545, speaks as if it were Mark without doubt.

The circumstances connected with the arrest are put by some in another order, in which the incidents narrated by John (xviii. 4–9), the going forth of Jesus to the multitude, His questions to them, and their prostration, all took place before Judas approached Him to kiss Him.[1] According to Stier (vii. 277), Judas was with the band, but stood irresolute as the Lord came to meet them. He with the others fell to the ground, but, reviving, went forward to give the kiss. But why give the kiss to make Jesus known, when He already avowedly stood before them ? It was not needed as a sign. Stier affirms that it was given in "the devilish spirit to maintain his consistency and redeem his word." This may be so, but the order before given is more probable.[2]

FRIDAY MORNING, 15TH NISAN, 7TH APRIL.

From the garden Jesus is taken first to the house of	JOHN xviii. 13–15.
Annas, and after a brief delay here, to the palace	
of Caiaphas, the high priest; Peter and John follow-	MATT. xxvi. 57, 58.
ing Him. Here, while the council is assembling, He	MARK xiv. 53, 54.
is subjected to a preliminary examination by Caiaphas	LUKE xxii. 54, 55.
respecting His disciples and doctrine. The council	JOHN xviii. 19–24.
having assembled, He is put on trial. As the wit-	MATT. xxvi. 59–66.
nesses disagree and no charge can be proved against	MARK xiv. 55–64.
Him, He is adjured by Caiaphas to tell whether He	
be the Christ. Upon His confession He is condemned	MATT. xxvi. 69–75.
as guilty of blasphemy. During this period, Peter,	MARK xiv. 66–72.
who had followed Him with John to the high priest's	LUKE xxii. 56–62.
palace, there denies Him, and, reminded of His words	JOHN xviii. 15–18.
by the crowing of the cock, goes out to weep.	JOHN xviii. 25–27.

The general order of events immediately following the arrest is plain: 1. The Lord is led to Annas.   2. He is sent by Annas to Caiaphas the high priest.   3. He is brought before the Sanhedrin, tried and condemned.   4. During this period Peter three times denies the Lord. But there are some points of controversy: 1. Before whom, Annas or Caiaphas, was the first examination held ?   2. What was the nature of this examination? 3. The competence of the court and the legality of the trial. 4. When and where did the denials of Peter take place?

1. *Before whom, Annas or Caiaphas, was the first examination held ?* It is said by Matthew (xxvi. 57) that after the Lord's arrest "they

---

[1] So Robinson, Alford, Stier.
[2] So Lichtenstein, Kraft, Ebrard, Luthardt, Meyer, Patritius.

led Him away to Caiaphas the high priest." Mark and Luke say only that He was led to the high priest, without naming him. John (xviii. 13) alone mentions that "He was led to Annas first," and was afterward sent by him to Caiaphas, and from Caiaphas was taken to the prætorium or hall of judgment (verse 28). This Evangelist mentions no hearing before the Sanhedrin unless it be this one conducted by the high priest (verses 19–23). At first view, it seems that Caiaphas, not Annas, must be meant (verse 19: "The high priest asked," etc.). The ground assigned by John for taking Him to Annas is that he "was father-in-law to Caiaphas, which was the high priest that same year." Caiaphas is again called the high priest, verse 24, and it would seem that the palace of the high priest to which John and Peter went following the Lord, must have been that of Caiaphas, and that the informal examination that then took place, was by him; and this was the understanding of the translators of the A. V., for they translate verse 24, "Now Annas had sent Him bound unto Caiaphas the high priest." If this rendering be kept, it would show that this sending was before the examination mentioned (verses 19–23), and that this examination was by Caiaphas.

But it is said that verse 24 cannot be rendered "had sent" ἀπέστειλεν — it must be rendered as in the R. V., "sent;" "Annas sent Him bound." If so understood, the examination was by Annas, and before he sent the Lord to Caiaphas. But this is a point upon which the grammarians differ,[1] and one which we are not called upon to discuss. Many look upon verse 24 in John's narrative as parenthetical. Thus it is said by Edersheim: "It is an intercalated notice, referring to what had been previously recorded in verses 15–23;" and by Greswell: "A notice parenthetically inserted." In this case nothing is told us of the interview between Annas and the Lord; all that is recorded is the informal examination in the house of Caiaphas.[2]

If, then, as said by Winer, the meaning of this statement "cannot be decided on grammatical grounds," we must seek help by considering the attendant circumstances, and first those connected with the person and residence of Annas.

---

[1] Winer, Gram., trans. 275, leaves the point undecided; so Buttmann, New Test. Gram., 173. In favor of rendering "had sent," De Wette, Tholuck, Robinson, Greswell, Norton, Edersheim, Krafft, Gardiner; for the rendering "sent," Meyer, Godet, Luthardt, Ellicott, Westcott, Riddle, Nebe; for a full argument on the aorist here defending its use as pluperfect, see Gardiner in *Journal of Bib. Lit.*, June 1886, 45 ff.; also Bäumlein, Keil, *in loco; contra*, Meyer, *in loco*, Dwight, additional note to Godet.

[2] For this solution, beside the older harmonists and commentators, Lightfoot, Lardner, Bynaeus, Grotius; of the later, Robinson, Greswell, Krafft, De Costa, Norton, Friedlieb, Bäumlein, Edersheim, Langen.

Why was the Lord taken to Annas? It is often said that he was the president or vice-president of the Sanhedrin [1] and so had a legal right to examine Him. But John (xviii. 13) seems to assign the real cause when he says that he was father-in-law to Caiaphas (so Ellicott, 333, note). It is apparent from Josephus (Antiq., xx. 9. 1), for his name occurs in the Gospels only here and in Luke iii. 2, that he was a man of very great influence; and probably may have been in fact, though not in name, the ecclesiastical head of the nation. It is in this personal reputation and authority rather than in any official position, that we find the explanation of the fact that the Lord was taken to him first. As the former high priest, as father-in-law of the present high priest, as an experienced and able counsellor, and deeply interested in this matter, a wish on his part to see privately so noted a man, aside from other reasons, would sufficiently explain why the Lord was led before him (Weiss, iii. 333). But if He was examined by him, Annas is called "the high priest," for "the high priest asked Jesus of His disciples." It seems scarcely possible that the Evangelist should make such repeated mention of the high priesthood of Caiaphas, emphasizing his official position, and yet should put the only examination of the Lord he mentions before Annas, whose only claim to this high dignity was that he was father-in-law of the high priest. And this is the more remarkable since John evidently regarded Caiaphas (see verse 14) as the Lord's chief and most determined enemy.

The assertion of many, that Luke, who does not mention his name, intends to designate Annas as the high priest (xxii. 54) has no sufficient basis. That he does (iii. 2) speak of both Annas and Caiaphas as high priests, and in Acts (iv. 6) names Caiaphas without any official title but calls Annas the high priest, does not show that Annas is here meant. There is no question that Caiaphas was the legal and acting high priest. As such he is designated by Matthew and Mark, and as such he takes the lead in all the judicial proceedings against Jesus. Of these facts Luke could not be ignorant. He himself names Caiaphas high priest. The presumption is therefore very strong that he alludes to him here, and that all he relates (verses 54–65) was in his palace.

As the place of Annas' residence to which the Lord was taken, whether the same as that of Caiaphas or separate, makes an important element in our enquiry, we must examine it.

There is a tradition that Annas had a house on the Mount of Olives near the booths or bazaars under the "Two Cedars." It is said by Lightfoot (x. 20) that "there were two cedars on Mt. Olivet, and

---

[1] See earlier discussion, page 142, and Keim, iii. 322; Wies., Beiträge, 205.

under one of these were four shops where all things needful for
purification were found," but he does not connect them with Annas.
(See his map of the city, where the two cedars and the booths are
shown.)   In another place he speaks of the Sanhedrin as removed
from the room Gazith to the shops.   It is said by Derenbourg (200,
note 13): "These shops were probably owned by the priests, and
at this time belonged to the friends of Annas."   That Annas had
a house here, and that Jesus was led to him after His arrest, is said by
Stapfer.   (See also Westcott on John xviii. 15.)   Another tradition
makes Annas to have had a house on the "Hill of Evil Counsel,"
where it is said the Jews met to take counsel how to destroy Jesus;
and here Jesus was taken.   But Robinson (i. 276) thinks that this
name given to the hill does not go back later than the ending of
the 15th century.   Following the tradition that Annas had a house
on this hill, Barclay (84) makes Jesus to have been taken to him
there, and then taken to the palace of Caiaphas on Mt. Zion.   But
the tradition which places the palace of Annas on Mt. Zion, has
much more in its favor, and to this quarter of the city we conclude
that the Lord was led from Gethsemane.   Whether Annas and Caia
phas had each a palace here, is in question.   One tradition points
out the ruins of the country house of Caiaphas on the Hill of Evil
Counsel; and another puts it where now stands the Armenian Monastery; and not far removed was the house of Annas, perhaps, as said
by Edersheim, on the slope between the upper city and the Tyropœon.

But did the high priest at this time have an official residence?
This is often said.   Thus Ellicott speaks of " a common official residence," and Godet of " the sacerdotal palace."   (See also Wies., Beiträge, 209.)   But no distinct mention of any such official residence is
found, though Josephus (War, ii. 17. 6) speaks of the burning of
the high priest's house.   According to Stroud (187), this palace
was within the precincts of the temple, and included the hall of
judgment where the Sanhedrin had its sessions, but he cites no
authorities.

The view that Annas and Caiaphas, being near relatives, had a
common residence, is an old one; there is nothing intrinsically improbable in it and it is now accepted by many.   It is modified by
McClellan (Har., 603), who supposes that Annas may have been "present at the palace of Caiaphas, and occupying for the occasion a separate official chamber, whence he sent Jesus to the official chamber of
Caiaphas," and finds an illustration in the judges of the several courts
in Westminster Hall having their special official rooms.   So in this
case, the palace was that of the high priest, and thither Jesus
was taken and brought before Annas, who was awaiting Him, and

who had a preliminary examination in one room while the members of the Sanhedrin were assembling in another. Some say that Caiaphas was with Annas and took the leading part in the examination. (So M. and M.) Still it must be admitted that the statement that He was taken to Annas first and then sent by him to Caiaphas, seems to imply more than a mere transference from one room to another in the same palace. Perhaps, however, an argument may be found for this view in the statement that Annas sent Him "bound" unto Caiaphas. Having been bound at the time of His arrest (John xviii. 12), it might appear that He was not unbound during that examination, which then must have been a very brief one, the object of the bonds being to prevent His escape while passing to the place of trial. For this reason, He was unbound when before the court, and bound again when taken to Pilate (Matt. xxvii. 2).

Another view of the matter is preferred by some: that Jesus was led to the palace of Annas and that Caiaphas was there, and, as the high priest, conducted the examination mentioned by John; and that Jesus was sent after it by Annas to the house of Caiaphas, where the Sanhedrists were assembling.

The bearing of the denials of Peter on the point before us may be briefly noticed. The first denial, at least, must have been in the house where the first examination was held; if this was the house of Annas, Peter must have followed the Lord thither. That the second and third denials were in the same house or court, is plain from the mention of the fire kindled there (John xviii. 18). But Matthew (xxvi. 58) seems clearly to say that Peter followed Jesus to the palace of Caiaphas where the scribes and elders were assembled, and that here in its court the denials of Peter were made. Some find here an irreconcilable discrepancy between Matthew and John (Meyer, Bleek).

We have thus two suppositions. 1st. That Annas and Caiaphas had a common palace. In this case, both might have been present at the examination; or which is in effect the same, that Annas was at the palace of Caiaphas waiting for the Lord's arrest. But whether the questions were asked by Caiaphas as the high priest, or by Annas who is so called, is not determined.

2d. That Annas and Caiaphas had separate palaces, that Jesus was first taken to Annas but not examined by him, and was sent to the palace of Caiaphas, and that here the examination mentioned by John took place. In this case the statement in verse 24 is supplementary. The obvious objection to this is that it seems to make the mention of the taking to Annas superfluous, as nothing is related of the interview. But it is a little detail which a writer might naturally mention for the sake of completeness; or it may be to show that all were united in their hostility to the Lord. It certainly presents no greater difficulty than the abrupt manner in which this Evangelist passes from the examination, supposing it to have been by Annas, to the next statement (verse 28): "Then led they Jesus from Caiaphas unto the hall of judgment." But in whatever point of view we regard it, the position of verse 24 is peculiar. Some would place it after verse 13 (so Luther quoted in Meyer), but for this there is no authority; some find the key to its meaning in the word "bound," as referring us back to verses 22 and 23. Annas had sent Him to Caiaphas bound, yet Caiaphas, the high priest, permits Him thus helpless to be smitten in his presence. Looking upon the matter historically, the most probable arrangement is that the Lord, though taken to the palace of Annas first, (if examined by him, which is not unlikely, no record of it is given,) was after a short interval sent to Caiaphas, in whose palace the examination took place.

2. *The nature of this first examination.* Are we to identify this with that before the council in Matt. xxvi. 59? This is said by some, but the statement of John shows that this examination had no judicial character; there was no formal accusation, no witnesses, no sentence pronounced. There is nothing to indicate that Jesus was now before the Sanhedrin charged with a definite crime, and the questions asked seemed designed to find some matter of accusation.

We conclude then that this examination was one preliminary to the trial; and this is generally accepted.

3. *The trial before the Sanhedrin.* This is given only by the Synoptists, John's account, as we have seen, being that only of the preliminary examination. In considering the legality of the trial several points are before us.

a. The competency of the court. As to this, no reasonable doubt can exist. It is said by Schürer (ii. 1. 185) that it was "the supreme native court, which here, as almost everywhere else, the Romans had allowed to continue as before, only imposing certain restrictions with regard to competency. . . . It was the final court of appeal for questions connected with the Mosaic law. . . . It also enjoyed a considerable amount of criminal jurisdiction." Among the offenses of which it took cognizance, were false claims to prophetic inspiration, and blasphemy. It also had charge of police matters, and had its own officers to make arrests (John vii. 32; Acts iv. 1–3; see Edersheim ii. 553). Several instances are mentioned in the Acts of the Apostles where the disciples were arraigned before it: iv. 5–21; v. 17–40; vi. 12–15; xxiii. 1–10. Although its origin cannot easily be traced, it was at this time the recognized tribunal for the trial of all the more important offenses.[1]   That usually the trials were fair and the judgments equitable, there seems no good reason to doubt.

While the Sanhedrin had power to try those charged with capital offenses, it had no power to execute the sentence of death.   "It was only in cases in which such sentence of death was pronounced, that the judgment required to be ratified by the authority of the procurator" (Schürer).   It is generally agreed that from the time Judæa became a Roman province, or from the deposition of Archelaus (759) the authority to punish capitally, the *jus gladii*, had been taken away from the Jewish tribunals.   Lightfoot (on Matt. xxvi. 3) gives as a tradition of the Talmudists: "Forty years before the temple was destroyed, judgment in capital cases was taken away from Israel."   But this limitation to forty years has clearly no basis.   It seems to have been the custom of the Romans to take into their own hands, in conquered provinces, the power of life and death, as one of the principal attributes of sovereignty.[2]   That the Sanhedrin lost this power by its own remissness and not by any act of the Romans, as affirmed by Lightfoot from the Talmudists, is wholly improbable.[3]

It has been inferred by some from Pilate's words to the Jews (John xix. 6), "Take ye Him and crucify Him," that the right to inflict capital punishment in ecclesiastical cases, though not in civil, was still continued to them.[4]   Bynaeus (iii. 10) affirms that the Jews had had judgment in capital cases other than that of treason, but that from fear of the people they charged the Lord with this offense in order to throw the odium of His execution upon Pilate.   But these words seem to have been spoken in bitter irony.[5]   Crucifixion was not a Jewish punishment, nor could they inflict it.   Krafft (142) explains their language (John xviii. 30), "If He were not a malefactor, we would not have delivered Him up unto thee," as meaning that He was guilty of a civil offense; as if they had said, "Were this man a spiritual offender, we would have punished Him ourselves."   They therefore accused Him of civil crime in order to throw the responsibility of His death upon Pilate.   But against this is the fact that Pilate refused to punish Him for any such offense, and that the Jews were at last obliged to charge Him with violation of ecclesiastical law (John xix. 7).   It is certain that if they had had power to punish Him upon this ground, he would at once have given

---

[1] Friedlieb, Archäol., 20; Winer, ii. 552.

[2] See Dupin, Jesus devant Caïphe et Pilate.   Paris, 1855, p. 88.

[3] See Winer, ii. 553, note 1; Friedlieb, Archäol., 97.

[4] So A. Clarke, Krafft.

[5] Meyer, *in loco*.   "Is He to be crucified?   Then it shall be by yourselves, and **not** by me."   M. and M.

the case into their hands and thus thrown off all responsibility from himself. Their words (xviii. 31), "It is not lawful for us to put any man to death," seem plainly to cover the whole ground and to embrace ecclesiastical as well as civil cases.[1] The view supported by some,[2] that the Jews had authority to put Jesus to death, but did not dare exercise it because of the holiness of the day, and yet did not dare retain Him in prison lest it should provoke insurrection, and so sought Pilate's help, seems without any good basis.

It thus appears that all capital offenses must be reserved to the cognizance of the procurator. The Sanhedrin could try and convict, but must obtain his assent ere the sentence could be executed. These reserved cases Pilate seems to have been in the habit of hearing when he went up from Cæsarea to Jerusalem at the feasts. The case of Jesus, then, must necessarily come before him, and he could confirm or set aside their verdict as he pleased. "It appears," says Lardner, "from the sequel, that Pilate was the supreme judge in this case and the master of the event. For he gave the case a fresh hearing, asked the Jews what accusation they had brought, examined Jesus, and when he had done so, told them that he found in Him no fault at all. Thus his conduct is full proof that he was the judge, and that they were only prosecutors and accusers."

b. The legality of the procedure. It cannot be denied that in some important points the court did not observe its own rules. These were violated both as regards the time and the place. No session could be held at night, but "they spent the night in judging on a capital cause, which is expressly forbid by their own canon" (Light. on Matt. xxvii. 1); and the regular place of meeting was in the hall Gazith connected with the temple (Light., "Prospect of the Temple", chapter xxii.). But more important violations were that no formal accusation was presented, and no accuser appeared; that no witnesses appeared for the Lord, and that the witnesses against Him were not shown to be trustworthy; that He Himself was put under oath;[3] and that the sentence was immediately carried into execution, the usual delay of twenty-four hours not being granted. That the legal forms were not observed, is not only said by Christians but admitted by some of the Jews. Thus Jost (quoted in Edersheim, ii. 553) calls the condemnation "a private murder, committed by burning enemies, not the sentence of a regularly constituted Sanhedrin." In fact, He had long

---

[1] As to the death of Stephen (Acts vii. 58), and its bearings on this point, see Meyer and Lechler *in loco*, who maintain that it was an act of violence, and illegal; so Schürer; *contra*, Alexander, *in loco*; Winer, ii. 553, note 2.

[2] Early by Augustine; see Godwyn, Moses and Aaron, 200.

[3] See Friedlieb, Archäol., 87; Dupin, 75; Keim, iii. 327 ff.

been prejudged and His death predetermined. Almost from the beginning of His ministry, spies had been sent to watch His actions; and afterward it was agreed that if any man did confess that He was Christ, he should be put out of the synagogue (John ix. 22). After the resurrection of Lazarus, it was determined in council by the advice of Caiaphas that He should be put to death, and that on the ground of the public welfare, without regard to His guilt or innocence (John xi. 47–53). After His public entry into Jerusalem, several attempts were made to entangle Him in His talk; then a consultation was held how they might take Him by subtlety and kill Him; then one of His apostles was bribed to betray Him; and at last He was arrested at dead of night. The abuse which He suffered both before and after the trial, and in the very presence of His judges, sufficiently shows how bitter and cruel was their enmity toward Him.

  c. The nature of the accusation. It was very difficult for the rulers to find any offense recognized as such by the Roman governor, for which the Lord could be condemned to death. As He said at His examination before the high priest, He had spoken openly to the world in the temple and the synagogue, He had said nothing in secret, so that there was no want of witnesses; but there was nothing that answered their purpose till two testified of His words spoken at the first passover (John ii. 19): "Destroy this temple, and in three days I will raise it up." By perverting His language, this was made a boast or a threat; but if deserving of any punishment, certainly not worthy of death; and even here the witnesses did not agree. Some more serious offense must be found, and this must be found in His Messianic claims. That Jesus claimed to be the predicted Messiah, and that His disciples believed on Him as such, was well-known. But that the mere claim to be the Messiah, if proved false, was regarded by the Jews as blasphemy and a capital offense, is very questionable; still if so, there was the difficulty in finding sufficient proof against Him. In no instance recorded, except that of the Samaritan woman (John iv. 26), did He avow Himself to be the Christ when other than His disciples were present. Nor did He permit evil spirits to proclaim Him as the Messiah (Mark i. 34). To the direct question of the Jews (John x. 24), He answered by referring them to His works. He permitted the apostles to confess their faith in Him as the Christ (Matt. xvi. 16), but He gave them strict command that they should tell it to no man (verse 20). Probably no two witnesses could be found outside of the ranks of the disciples, who had ever heard out of His own lips an avowal of His Messiahship. Had, then, such an avowal been blasphemy, they could not on this ground have condemned Him for want of proof.

  22*

What grounds of accusation did His acts give? That in several points He had disregarded the Pharisaic traditions was not denied. He had broken the Sabbath according to their construction of the law, by the healing of the sick on that day, and perhaps in other ways; He had assumed the right to forgive sins; He had declared Himself the Lord of the Sabbath; He had cleansed the temple, and spoken very severe words against the ecclesiastical rulers and the popular leaders. But we may doubt whether if these were all, He would have been found worthy of death.[1]

It has been said that the Jews found cause to charge Jesus with blasphemy in that He had wrought miracles in His own name. "He had performed many miracles, but never in any other name than His own."[2] It is said that He had thus violated the law (Deut. xviii. 20). "He that shall speak in the name of other gods, even that prophet shall die"; for if to prophesy in the name of another god deserved death, equally so to perform any miracle or supernatural work in his name. But it may well be questioned whether, on this ground, He could have been tried for blasphemy. If He did not work His miracles expressly in the name of Jehovah, yet He ever affirmed that the power was not in Himself, but from God. (Compare John v. 19, viii. 18.) Nor was He ever understood to work them by virtue of His own deity. Beholding what He did, the multitudes "marvelled and glorified God who had given such power unto men" (Matt. ix. 8). And at His final entry into Jerusalem the cry of the people was, "Blessed is He that cometh in the name of the Lord."

We conclude, then, that upon no ground could the Jews, through their witnesses, convict Him of any ecclesiastical offense punishable with death. Neither for His Messianic claims, nor for the works by which He attested them, nor as a false prophet, could He be legally convicted of blasphemy. His violations of the Sabbath were not such as they could punish with severity, if at all. He had not denied the authority of the law, He had not spoken against Jehovah. If He had disturbed the public peace, punishment of this offense properly belonged to the Romans. Thus, upon the rule which He had Himself laid down (John xviii. 21), "Ask them which heard me what I have said unto them," He could not have been convicted. Only by His own testimony was He brought within the scope of the law. He was at last condemned upon His confession that He was the Christ

---

[1] In John v. 16, where it is said, "The Jews sought to slay Him because He had done these things on the Sabbath day," the clause "sought to slay Him," is omitted by Tischendorf. So Alford, Meyer, W. and H., and R. V.

[2] Greenleaf, Test. of Evangelists, 524.

and the Son of God. This fact is very remarkable, and demands our attentive consideration.

d. Ground of condemnation. A Jewish writer, Salvador, in his "Histoire des Institutions de Moïse,"[1] commenting upon the trial of Jesus, attempts to show that He was tried fairly, and condemned legally. He spoke of Himself, says this writer, as God, and His disciples repeated it. This was shocking blasphemy in the eyes of the citizens. It was this, not His prophetic claims, which excited the people against Him. The law permitted them to acknowledge prophets, but nothing more. In answer to Caiaphas, He admits that He is the Son of God, this expression including the idea of God Himself. "The Sanhedrin deliberates. The question already raised among the people was this: Has Jesus become God? But the senate having adjudged that Jesus had profaned the name of God by usurping it to Himself, a mere citizen, applied to Him the law of blasphemy (Deut. xiii., and xviii. 20), according to which every prophet, even he who works miracles, must be punished when he speaks of a God unknown to the Jews and their fathers; and the capital sentence was pronounced."

Had the accusation against Jesus, as asserted by Salvador, had respect simply to His assertion that He was the Son of God, and had He been condemned upon this ground only; however great the blindness and guilt in not recognizing His divine character, it could not be said that the court acted illegally. Such an assertion from the lips of any mere man was blasphemous. If a false prophet deserved to die, how much more he who made himself equal with God! Was it for this that He was, in fact, condemned? When nothing worthy of death could be proved against Him by the witnesses, Caiaphas adjured Him by the living God, "Tell us whether thou be the Christ, the Son of God."[2] We cannot certainly determine how these two expressions, "the Christ," and "the Son of God," were connected in the mind of Caiaphas. It may be that he regarded them as of substantially the same meaning, though it may be questioned how far the title, Son of God, was one of the customary titles of the Messiah at this time. Still, it had been so often and openly applied to Jesus, that we cannot well suppose Caiaphas ignorant of it. At the time of His baptism, John the Baptist testified of His Divine Sonship (John i. 34): "I saw and bare record that this is the Son of God." Very soon after (verse 49), Nathanael thus avows his faith: "Rabbi, thou

---

[1] Cited by Greenleaf, Test., 529, and by Dupin, Refutation, 41.

[2] Matt. xxvi. 63. According to Mark, "Art thou the Christ, the Son of the Blessed?" This adjuration, according to Jewish custom, was equivalent to putting the Lord under oath. Friedlieb, Archäol., 91.

art the Son of God; thou art the King of Israel." Often was He thus addressed by evil spirits whom He cast out (Matt. viii. 29; Mark iii. 11, v. 7; Luke iv. 41, viii. 28). After the stilling of the tempest (Matt. xiv. 33), those in the ship said, "Of a truth thou art the Son of God." So was He addressed by Martha (John xi. 27): "I believe that thou art the Christ, the Son of God." At His death the centurion and guard said (Mark xv. 39), "Truly this was the (a) Son of God." Only in one instance, however, did Jesus directly claim for Himself this title (John ix. 35–37), although He often indirectly applied it to Himself. (So John xi. 4.) In like manner He repeatedly speaks of God as His Father (John v. 17).

Granting that this phrase, "Son of God," was currently applied to men of great wisdom and piety, still, as Salvador admits, it could not have been so used by Caiaphas. If it did not, in its ordinary usage, imply participation of the Divine nature, it nevertheless was in this act of adjuration and was designed to be, a designation that distinguished the Lord from all other men.

Perhaps Caiaphas, in his adjuration, purposely selected both titles, that in this way the Lord's own conceptions of His Messianic dignity might be drawn out, and the way opened for further questions. The answer of Jesus, "Thou hast said," was an express affirmation, as if He had said, "I am," and was regarded as blasphemy. It could have been so only as it implied equality with God, or an assumption of the power and authority that belonged to Jehovah alone. That the Jews so understood it, is plain from their language (John xix. 7) to Pilate afterward. When they learned that in His teaching He presented Himself as one with the Father, or "made Himself equal with God" (John v. 18), this was a flagrant transgression of the law and a capital offense. The first of the ten commandments was, "Thou shalt have no other gods before me," and for a man to make himself God, the equal of Jehovah, was a violation of this command, and a crime of the deepest dye. It was both blasphemy and treason, and hence the attempt of the Jews to kill Him upon the spot. A few months later they "murmured at Him because He said, I am the Bread which came down from Heaven" (John vi. 41). When, a little later, He said, "Before Abraham was, I am" (viii. 58), thus implying a divine pre-existence, they took up stones to stone Him; and when afterward (x. 30) He still more plainly affirmed, "I and my Father are one," they again sought to stone Him. They expressly declared, "We stone thee for blasphemy, and because that thou, being a man, makest thyself God."

4. *The Denials of Peter.* Let us now consider more fully the three denials of Peter. After the arrest, he, with "another disciple," fol-

lowed Jesus to the high priest's palace. It is disputed who this
other disciple was. Most regard it as a modest designation of John
himself; others, of some unknown disciple. A. Clarke approves
Grotius' conjecture that it was the person at whose house Jesus
had supped. Some have thought of Judas. This disciple, being
known unto the high priest, was permitted to enter with those who
were leading Jesus, but Peter was shut out. Perceiving this, he
turned back and persuaded the woman that kept the door to admit
Peter also. They seem then, or soon after, to have separated, as
no mention is afterward made of the other disciple. Either before
or soon after Peter's entrance, the officer and soldiers made a fire of
coals in the court.

To understand the details that follow, it is necessary to have in
mind the ordinary construction of oriental houses, which is thus described by Robinson:[1] "An oriental house is usually built around a
quadrangular interior court, into which there is a passage (sometimes
arched) through the front part of the house, closed next the street by
a heavy folding gate with a smaller wicket for single persons, kept by
a porter. In the text the interior court, often paved and flagged,
and open to the sky, is the αὐλή, (translated in A. V., 'palace,' 'hall,'
and 'court,' but in R. V., uniformly 'court') where the attendants
made a fire; and the passage beneath the front of the house, from the
street to this court, is the προαύλιον (Mark xiv. 68) or πυλών (Matt. xxvi.
71), both translated 'porch.' The place where Jesus stood before
the high priest may have been an open room or place of audience on
the ground floor in the rear or on one side of the court; such rooms,
open in front, being customary." In Smith's Bible Dictionary (i. 838),
the writer speaks of "an apartment called *makad*, open in front to
the court, with two or more arches and a railing, and a pillar to support the wall above. It was in a chamber of this kind, probably one
of the largest size to be found in a palace, that our Lord was arraigned before the high priest at the time when the denial of Him by
St. Peter took place." That the trial of Jesus actually occurred in
such an interior apartment seems plain from Matt. xxvi. 69, where
Peter is spoken of as sitting "without in the palace," or court,
ἔξω ἐν τῇ αὐλῇ, implying that the Lord and His judges were in an
inner room.[2] Mark (xiv. 66) speaks of Peter as "beneath in the
palace," ἐν τῇ αὐλῇ κάτω, "in the court below." "Not in the lower
story of the house or palace," says Alexander, "as the English version seems to mean, but in the open space around which it was
built, and which was lower than the floor of the surrounding
rooms."

---

[1] Har., 225.
[2] See Meyer, *in loco*.

The questions connected with Peter's denials, respect place, time, and persons. For convenient inspection, we give them in tabular form:

FIRST DENIAL.

	MATTHEW.	MARK.	LUKE.	JOHN.
Questioner.......	Maid servant.	Maid servant.	A certain maid.	Portress.
Time	Indefinite.	Indefinite.	Indefinite.	Soon after entering.
Place...........	Court.	By fire in court.	By fire in court.	Court.
Question.........	"Thou also wast with Jesus of Galilee."	"Thou also wast with Jesus of Nazareth."	"This man was also with Him."	"Art thou not also one of this man's disciples?"
Denial...........	"I know not what thou sayest."	"I know not, neither understand I, what thou sayest."	"Woman, I know Him not."	"I am not."

SECOND DENIAL.

	MATTHEW.	MARK.	LUKE.	JOHN.
Questioner.......	Another maid.	The maid.	A man.	They.
Time	Indefinite.	Indefinite.	After a little while.	Indefinite.
Place...........	Porch.	Porch.	Indefinite.	By the fire.
Question	"This was also with Jesus of Nazareth."	"This is one of them."	"Thou art also of them."	"Art not thou also one of His disciples?"
Denial...........	With an oath, "I do not know the man."	He denied it again.	"Man, I am not."	"I am not."

THIRD DENIAL.

	MATTHEW.	MARK.	LUKE.	JOHN.
Questioner.......	They that stood by.	They that stood by.	A man.	A servant of the high priest, kinsman of Malchus.
Time	After a while.	A little after.	About the space of an hour after.	Indefinite.
Place...........	Indefinite.	Indefinite.	Indefinite.	Indefinite.
Question.........	"Surely thou art also one of them, for thy speech betrayeth thee."	"Surely thou art one of them, for thou art a Galilæan, and thy speech agreeth thereto."	"Of a truth this fellow also was with Him, for he is a Galilæan."	"Did I not see thee in the garden with Him?"
Denial...........	With cursing and swearing, "I know not the man."	"I know not the man of whom you speak."	"Man, I know not what thou sayest."	Peter then denied again.

The points of place and time are closely connected with some points already discussed. If the Lord was examined in the court of Annas and then taken to the house of Caiaphas, the first denial was in the court of Annas, and probably also the second, and the third only in

that of Caiaphas.   To this change of place there is a strong objection
in the fact of the fire, which indicates one and the same court.   If
Annas and Caiaphas had the same court, this objection, indeed, does
not hold, as there was no change of place.   But if, as seems most
probable, the examination was before Caiaphas, not Annas, all took
place in his court.

The exact relations in which the denials of Peter stand in order
of time to the examination and trial of the Lord, it is impossible to
determine.   Probably the first denial and perhaps, also, the second —
for there seems to have been but a short interval between them (Luke
xxii. 58) — may have been during the preliminary examination before
Caiaphas, or at least before the assembling of the Sanhedrin; and
the third about an hour later, during the trial or at its close.   The
incident recorded by Luke (xxii. 61), that immediately after the third
denial, as the cock crew, the Lord turned and looked upon Peter, is
supposed by some to show that Jesus was now passing from one
apartment to another, and as He passed, turned and looked upon Peter
who was standing near by.   But if so, when was this?   Those who
put the preliminary examination in the house of Annas, and Peter's denials there, make this the departure to Caiaphas after the examination
(Godet); others, the change from the apartment in Caiaphas' palace
where He had been examined, to that in which He was to be tried;
others, His departure after the trial from Caiaphas to Pilate.   But it is
not necessary to suppose any change of place on the part of the Lord.
As we have seen, the Sanhedrin probably assembled in a large room
directly connected with the court and open in front, and therefore
what was said in the one could, with more or less distinctness, be
heard in the other.   There is, then, no difficulty in believing that
Jesus may have heard all the denials of Peter; and that now, as he
denied Him for the third time, and the cock crew, He turned Himself
to the court and looked upon the conscience-stricken apostle.   Meyer,
indeed, finds it psychologically impossible that he should have made
these denials in the presence of Jesus; but in fact, Peter was not
in His presence, though not far removed.   Still, the probability is
that this third denial was when the trial was over and the Lord was
brought from the inner room into the court.

A second question respects the persons.   In regard to the first
denial there are no special difficulties.   How soon after Peter entered
the court he was addressed by the damsel who kept the door, or por-
tress, does not appear.   It is probable that, as her attention had been
specially drawn to him when he was admitted as a friend of John,
she watched him as he stood by the fire; and that something in his
appearance or conduct may have confirmed her suspicions that he was

a disciple.   The attention of all who heard her must now have been directed to Peter, but no one seems to have joined her in her accusation.

In regard to the second denial, there are several apparent discrepancies both as to the persons and the place.   The former are described as "another maid," "the (same) maid," "another person," "they." But in the several narratives it is plain that it is not deemed important to specify who addressed Peter; the important point is his denials.   The matter may very naturally be thus arranged: The damsel who first accused him, silenced for the time but not satisfied with his denial, speaks to another maid servant and points out Peter to her as one whom she knew or believed to be a disciple.   Seeing him soon after in the porch or fore-court, for, in the agitation of his spirit he cannot keep still, she renews the charge that he is a disciple, and the other maid repeats it.   Others, hearing the women, also join with them, perhaps dimly remembering his person, or now noting something peculiar in his manner.   That, under the circumstances and in the excitement of the moment, such an accusation, once raised, should be echoed by many, is what we should expect.   During the confusion of this questioning, Peter returns again to the fire in the interior court where most were standing, and there repeats with an oath his denial.   There is no necessity for transposing, with Ellicott, the first and second denials as given by John.

The second denial, so energetically made, seems to have finally silenced the women, and there is no repetition of the charge for about the space of an hour.   During this interval, Peter, perhaps the better to allay suspicion, joins in the conversation, and is recognized as a Galilæan by his manner of speech.   As most of the disciples of Jesus were Galilæans, this again draws attention to him.   Perhaps the kinsman of Malchus, who had been with the multitude and had seen him in the garden, and now remembers his person, begins the outcry and the bystanders join with him; and the more that Peter's very denials betray his Galilæan birth.   The charge, thus repeated by so many, and upon such apparently good grounds, threatens immediate danger, and Peter therefore denies it with the utmost vehemence, with oaths and cursings.[1]

We have no datum to determine at what hour of the night these denials took place, except we find it in the cock-crowings.   Mark

---

[1] For a recent discussion of these denials, see McClellan, Har., 494. He thinks that we cannot limit the acts of denial to three, and finds six; three in the court by the fire, and three in the porch.   To the objection that the Lord foretold a threefold denial, he answers that "thrice" is to be taken in an indefinite sense. See Gardiner Har., *in loco;* Nebe, ii. 353,

(xiv. 68) relates that after the first denial the cock crew. All the Evangelists mention the third denial in connection with the second cock-crowing. Greswell (iii. 216) makes the first cock-crowing to have been about 2 A. M., and the second, about 3 A. M.[1] But we do not know whether this second cock-crowing was at the end of the first examination, or during the formal trial, or at its close, and to determine when the Sanhedrin began its session. We cannot, however, well place it later than 2 A. M. How long it continued we shall presently see.

We may thus give the order of events:

1. The Lord and His apostles leave the upper room an hour before midnight, and go to Gethsemane.

2. The arrest in Gethsemane about midnight or a little after.

3. He is taken to Annas, but no examination before him is recorded.

4. He is soon taken to Caiaphas, and here is a brief preliminary examination, mentioned only by John, and after it followed the abuse by one of the high priest's officers.

5. The Sanhedrin assembles at one or two in the morning in the palace of Caiaphas, and the Lord is formally tried and condemned, and then abused by the members (Matt. xxvi. 67).

6. The Sanhedrin, after a temporary adjournment, reassembles at break of day to determine how to bring Jesus before Pilate; and at this time His confession is repeated, but without a formal trial. This hearing only in Luke (xxii. 66).

7. The Lord is taken to Pilate in the early morning.

FRIDAY MORNING, 15TH NISAN, 7TH APRIL, 783. A. D. 30.

After the Sanhedrin had pronounced Him guilty of blasphemy, and so worthy of death, it suspends its session to meet at break of day. During this interval Jesus remains in the high priest's palace, exposed to all the ridicule and insults of His enemies, who spit upon Him, and smite Him. As soon as it is day the Sanhedrin again assembles, and after hearing His confession that He is the Christ, formally adjudges Him to death. Binding Him, they led Him away to the Roman governor Pontius Pilate, that he may execute the sentence. Judas Iscariot, learning the issue of the trial, and that Jesus is about to be put to death, returns the money the chief priests have given him, and goes and hangs himself.

MATT. xxvi. 67, 68.
MARK xiv. 65.
LUKE xxii. 63–65.
MATT. xxvii. 1, 2.
MARK xv. 1.
LUKE xxii. 66–71.
LUKE xxiii. 1.

MATT. xxvii. 3–10.
ACTS i. 18,19.

---

[1] So, in substance, Wieseler, 406; Lichtenstein, 422; McClellan.

Condemned to death as a blasphemer, Jesus was now given up by the council to the abuse of His captors and of the crowd; and cruel personal violence was added to most contemptuous speech.   Salvador (*Jésus-Christ et sa Doctrine*) denies that the council would have permitted Him to be so treated in its presence; but it is to be remembered that most of its members cherished the most bitter and vindictive feelings against Him, and in their fierce fanaticism thought that no mercy should be shown to one guilty of such a crime. (Compare Acts xxiii. 2.)   According to Matthew, the judges themselves seem to have taken part in this abuse; but Luke speaks only of those that held Jesus.

It has been inferred from Matt. xxvii. 1 and Mark xv. 1, that there was a second and later judicial session of the Sanhedrin than that at which Jesus was tried.[1]   Others suppose that the Sanhedrin continued its session after the trial proper had ended, perhaps with a brief recess, having as the special subject of consultation how the sentence pronounced against Jesus could be carried into effect.[2]   The language of these two Evangelists is not decisive as to the point.   That which most implies a new and distinct session is the designation of time; in Matthew: "When the morning was come, πρωΐας δὲ γενομένης, all the chief priests," etc.; in Mark: "And straightway in the morning," εὐθέως ἐπὶ τὸ πρωί, etc.   This allusion to the fact that it was morning, seems to have some special significance, and may refer to the fact that capital cases could not be legally tried in the night; and hence a morning session was necessary.   "Capital cases were only to be handled by day."[3]   This is affirmed by Salvador (quoted by Greenleaf): "One thing is certain, that the council met again on the morning of the next day, or of the day after, as the law requires, to confirm or to annul the sentence; it was confirmed "   Neither Matthew nor Mark states that the place of session had been changed, though perhaps their language may intimate a meeting more largely attended.[4]

---

[1] Greswell, iii. 202; Friedlieb, 326; Godet.

[2] Meyer, Ellicott, Lichtenstein.

[3] Lightfoot; see Friedlieb, Archäol., 95.

[4] Compare Mark xiv. 53 with xv. 1, in the latter case, " the whole council " being expressly mentioned.

Our decision as to a second and distinct session of the Sanhedrin will mainly depend upon the place we give to the account
in Luke xxii. 66–71. Is this examination of Jesus identical
with that first session of Matt. xxvi. 57–68, and of Mark xiv.
53–65 ?[1] Against this identity are some strong objections:
1st. The mention of time by Luke: "As soon as it was day."
This corresponds well to the time of the morning session of Matthew and Mark, but not to the time when Jesus was first led before the Sanhedrin, which must have been two or three hours
before day. 2d. The place of meeting: "They led Him into their
council," ἀνήγαγον αὐτὸν εἰς τὸ συνέδριον ἑαυτῶν. This is rendered
by some: "They led Him up into their council chamber," or the
place where they usually held their sessions.[2] Whether this council
chamber was the room Gazith at the east corner of the court of
the temple, is not certain. Lightfoot (on Matt. xxvi. 3) conjectures
that the Sanhedrin was driven from this its accustomed seat half
a year or thereabout before the death of Christ. But if this
were so, still the "*Tabernæ*," where it established its sessions,
were shops near the gate Shusan, and so connected with the
temple. They went up to that room where they usually met.[3]
3d The dissimilarity of the proceedings, as stated by Luke,
which shows that this was no formal trial. There is here no
mention of witnesses — no charges brought to be proved against
Him. He is simply asked to tell them if He is the Christ (" If
thou art the Christ, tell us," R. V.); and this seems plainly to
point to the result of the former session. Then, having confessed Himself to be the Christ, the Son of God, He was condemned to death for blasphemy. It was only necessary now
that He repeat this confession, and hence this question is put
directly to Him: "Art thou the Christ? tell us." His reply,
" If I tell you, ye will not believe; and if I also ask you, ye will
not answer me, nor let me go," points backward to his former
confession. To His reply they only answer by asking, "Art

---

[1] So Meyer, Alford, Lichtenstein, Ebrard, Keil.

[2] See Meyer. *in loco;* Rob., Lex., Art. συνέδριον: here "as including the place of
meeting; the Sanhedrin as sitting in its hall." So Keil, McClellan.

[3] So Kraft, Greswell. See, however, against this, John xviii. 28, which implies
that Jesus was led, not from the temple, but from the palace of Caiaphas to Pilate. This
does not disprove the fact of a second session of the Sanhedrin, but shows that it was
held at the same place as the first.

thou then the Son of God?" The renewed avowal that He is the Son of God, heard by them all from His own lips, opens the way for His immediate delivery into Pilate's hands.[1] 4th. The position which Luke gives (xxii. 63–65) to the insults and abuse heaped upon Jesus. There can be no doubt that they are the same mentioned by Matthew and Mark as occurring immediately after the sentence had been first pronounced.

From all this it is a probable, though not a certain conclusion, that Luke (xxii. 66–71) refers to the same meeting of the Sanhedrin mentioned by Matthew (xxvii. 1) and Mark (xv. 1), and relates, in part, what then took place. (Alford thinks that Luke has confused things, and relates as happening at the second session what really happened at the first.) This meeting was, then, a morning session convened to ratify formally what had been done before with haste and informality. The circumstances under which its members had been earlier convened at the palace of Caiaphas, sufficiently show that the legal forms, which they were so scrupulous in observing, had not been complied with. The law forbidding capital trials in the night had been broken; the place of session was unusual, if not illegal; perhaps the attendance, so early after midnight, had not been full. On these accounts it was expedient that a more regular and legal sitting should be held as early in the morning as was possible. At this nothing need be done but to hear the confession of Jesus, to pronounce sentence, and to consult in what manner it could best be carried into effect; for, although they had condemned Him, they had no power to execute the sentence. To put Jesus to death, they must have at least the assent of Pilate. Their plans for obtaining this will appear as we proceed. Being again bound, He was led early in the morning before Pilate.

There are two points connected with Judas that are in dispute: 1. His return of the money paid him for his treachery and the subsequent use of it; 2. The manner of his death.

1. As soon as Judas saw that the Lord was condemned by the Sanhedrin, probably beholding Him as they led Him away to Pilate, he repented bitterly of his treachery. Taking the money, the price of his crime, he carried it back to the chief

---

[1] See Stier, vii. 336; Greswell, iii. 204.

priests and elders, confessing his sin in betraying innocent blood.
It is not necessary to suppose them all assembled together; some
acted for the rest.   It is not said where he found them, whether
at the palace of Caiaphas, or at their own council chamber, or at
some other chamber in the temple.   If they were at the temple
we have a ready explanation of the fact that " he cast down the
pieces of silver in the temple and departed." [1]   That part of the
temple in which he cast them, is defined as ἐν τῷ ναῷ, which,
according to the uniform usage of the term in the Gospels, cannot mean any thing else than the inner court or holy place, and
only open to the priests. [1]   Into this it was not lawful for him to
enter, but he could approach the entrance and cast the silver
within; or, perhaps in his remorse and despair forcing his way
into the holy place, he cast it down at the feet of the priests,
who, it may be, were there preparing to offer the morning
sacrifice.

Probably the money which had been paid to Judas had
been taken from the treasury of the temple, and the priests and
elders, unwilling to return to it the price of blood, determined to
buy a field to bury strangers in.   Peter (Acts i. 18) speaks as if
Judas had himself bought it: " Now this man purchased a field
with the reward of iniquity."   Perhaps he may be here understood as speaking rhetorically, and as meaning only to say that
the field was bought, not by Judas in person but with his
money, the wages of his iniquity. [2]   If so, the actual purchase of
the field was doubtless made after the Lord's crucifixion, as the
time of the priests and elders was too much occupied upon that
day to attend to such a transaction; and Matthew narrates it as
taking place before the crucifixion, in order to finish all that
pertained to Judas.   Others make Judas to have purchased a
field before his death with part of the money he had received,
and in this field to have hanged himself; in this case, his death was
probably not till some period after the crucifixion.   Some say that
the priests after his death, with the remainder of the money, purchased another, [3] and thus there were two fields, both called " the

---

[1] See Greswell, iii. 219.

[2] Alexander, *in loco*; Meyer on Acts i. 18.   Trench *Synonyms, sub voce.*

[3] See Greswell, iii. 220; Smith's Bib. Dict., i. 15.

field of blood," Aceldama, but for different reasons: one as bought with the price of blood, the other as the place where Judas hanged himself.   It is said that " ecclesiastical tradition appears from the earliest times to have pointed out two distinct though not unvarying spots as referred to in the two accounts."   Early travellers mention Aceldama as distinct from the spot where Judas hanged himself.[1]   Maundrell also (468) mentions two Aceldamas, one on the west side of the valley of Hinnom, and another on the east side of the valley of Jehoshaphat, not far distant from Siloa.   To the latter Saewulf (42) refers as at the foot of Mount Olivet, a little south of Gethsemane.   That two fields are referred to by the Evangelists, is doubtful, and the former solution of the discrepancy is to be preferred.

"The field of blood " is still pointed out in the eastern part of the valley of Hinnom.   " The tradition which fixes it upon this spot reaches back to the age of Jerome, and it is mentioned by almost every visitor of the Holy City from that time to the present day.   The field or plat is not now marked by any boundary to distinguish it from the rest of the hillside."[2]   Hackett[3] observes: " Tradition has placed it on the Hill of Evil Counsel.   It may have been in that quarter, at least, for the field belonged originally to a potter, and argillaceous clay is still found in the neighborhood.   A workman in a pottery which I visited at Jerusalem, said that all their clay was obtained from the hill over the valley of Hinnom."   A charnel house now in ruins, built over a cave in whose deep pit are a few bones much decayed, is still shown.   Some would identify it with the tomb of Ananus mentioned by Josephus.[4]

2. The manner of his death.   It is said by Matthew that, after he had cast down the pieces of silver into the temple, he departed and went and hanged himself.   It is not said whither he went, and, so far as here stated, the place of his death may have been away from the city.   Some question has been raised as to the meaning of the term ἀπήγξατο — "hanged himself."   Grotius and others understand it of a natural death, but one brought about by agony of conscience and remorse.   But the great majority of interpreters understand it of a death by hanging

---

[1] So Maundeville, Early Trav., 175.   [3] Ill. Scrip., 267. See Baed., 230.
[2] Robinson, i. 354.   [4] War, v. 12. 2. So Barclay.

In the Vulgate : *Abiens laqueo se suspendit.* (Lightfoot insists that
he was strangled by the devil.)   But how is this statement to be
reconciled with that of Peter (Acts i. 18), that, "falling headlong, he burst asunder in the midst — καὶ πρηνὴς γενόμενος
ἐλάκησε μέσος — and all his bowels gushed out ? "   De Quincey [1]
finds here only a figurative statement that "he came to utter
and unmitigated ruin," and died of a "broken heart."   But the
language is obviously to be taken in its literal sense;[2] and the
bursting asunder of Judas may readily have happened after he
had hung himself.   Such a thing as the breaking of a cord or a
beam or bough of a tree is not unusual; or, at the moment when
the body was about to be taken down, it may by accident or
carelessness have fallen.   Hackett,[3] referring to a suggestion
that he may have hung himself upon a tree overhanging the
valley of Hinnom, says: "For myself, I felt, as I stood in the
valley and looked up to the rocky terraces which hang over it,
that the proposed explanation was a perfectly natural one.   I
was more than ever satisfied with it."   He found the precipice,
by measurement, to be from twenty-five to forty feet in height,
with olive trees growing near the edges and a rocky pavement
at the bottom, so that a person who fell from above would probably be crushed and mangled as well as killed. [4]

Meyer finds proof that Matthew, in his statement that Judas
"hanged himself," and Luke, in his report of Peter's statement
that he "burst asunder," followed different traditions, in the fact
that as self-murder was very unusual among the Jews, Peter
could not have passed it by in silence.   But, as the falling and
bursting asunder were subsequent to the hanging, and presupposed it; and as the event had taken place but a few days before,
and was well known to all present, there was no necessity that
he should give all the details; especially as his purpose was to
admonish the apostles by this fearful judgment to use all caution
in the nomination of his successor.

Matthew refers to the purchase of the field as the fulfillment

---

[1] Essay upon Judas Iscariot.
[2] Meyer, *in loco.*   [3] Ill. Scrip., 266.
[4] As to the various traditional accounts of Judas' death, see Hofmann's *Leben
Jesu*, 333. Bynaeus (ii. 431) gives a full statement of the various opinions up to his day.
Arculf (*Early Travels*, 4), A. D. 700, speaks of being shown the large fig tree from the top
of which Judas suspended himself.

of a prediction of Jeremy the prophet.   Many recent writers find here an error of reference, the passage being found in Zechariah (xi. 12, 13).   For the solutions we must refer to the commentators.   "The simplest explanation," says Riddle, "is that the name 'Jeremiah' is applied to the whole book of the prophets, since the Jews placed that prophet first."

Our purpose does not lead us to inquire into the motives that impelled Judas to betray his Lord.   The theory, however, advocated by many,[1] that, sharing the general Jewish expectations as to the Messianic kingdom, and fully believing Jesus to be the Messiah, he had no intention of imperilling His life, but wished only to arouse Him to direct and positive action, cannot be sustained.   If, knowing the supernatural powers of Jesus, he had no fears that He could suffer evil from the hands of His enemies, and delivered Him into the power of the Jewish authorities in order that He might be forced to assert His Messianic claims, why should he bargain with them for thirty pieces of silver? He could in many ways have accomplished this end, without taking the attitude of a traitor.   The statements of the Evangelists about his covenant with the chief priests, his conduct at the arrest, his return of the money, the words of Peter respecting him, and especially the words of the Lord, "Good were it for that man if he had never been born," conclusively show that he sinned, not through a mere error of judgment while at heart hoping to advance the interests of his Master, but with deliberate perfidy, designing to compass His ruin.[2]

FRIDAY MORNING, 15TH NISAN, 7TH APRIL, 783. A. D. 30.

The members of the Sanhedrin who lead Jesus to Pilate refuse to enter the judgment hall lest they be defiled; and thereupon he comes out to them and asks the nature of the accusation.   They charge Him with being a malefactor, and Pilate directs them to take Him and judge Him themselves.   As they cannot inflict a capital punishment, they bring the charge of sedition; and Pilate, reentering the judgment hall and calling Jesus, examines Him as to His Messianic claims. Satisfied that He is inno-

JOHN xviii. 28–33.

LUKE xxiii. 2–4.
MARK xv. 2.
JOHN xviii. 33–38.
MATT. xxvii. 11.

[1] De Quincey, Whately.
[2] See Winer, i. 635; Ebrard, 524; Christian Review, July, 1855; Langen, 44.

cent, Pilate goes out and affirms that he finds no fault in Him. The Jews renewing their accusations, to which Jesus makes no reply, aud mentioning Galilee, Pilate sends Him to Herod, who was then at Jerusalem; but Jesus refuses to answer his questions, and is sent back to Pilate. The latter now resorts to another expedient. He seats himself upon the judgment seat, and, calling the chief priests and elders, declares to them that neither himself nor Herod has found any fault in Him. According to custom, he will release Him. But the multitude beginning to cry that he should release Barabbas not Jesus, he leaves it to their choice. During the interval while the people are making their choice, his wife sends to him a message of warning. The people, persuaded by the priest and elders, reject Jesus and choose Barabbas, and Pilate in vain makes several efforts to change their decision. At last he gives orders that Jesus be scourged previous to crucifixion. This is done by the soldiers with mockery and abuse; and Pilate, going forth, again takes Jesus and presents Him to the people. The Jews continue to demand His death, but upon the ground that He made Himself the Son of God. Terrified at this new charge, Pilate again takes Jesus into the hall to question Him but receives no answer. Pilate still strives earnestly to save Him, but is met by the cry that he is Cæsar's enemy. Yielding to fear, he ascends the tribunal, and, calling for water, washes his hands in token of his own innocence, and then gives directions that He be taken away and crucified. As He comes forth, he presents Him to them as their King. They cry " Crucify Him, Crucify Him,,' and He is led away to the place of crucifixion.

MATT. xxvii. 12–14.
MARK xv. 3–5.
LUKE xxiii. 5–12.

MATT. xxvii. 15–18.
MARK xv. 6–10.
LUKE xxiii. 13–17.

JOHN xviii. 39, 40.

MATT. xxvii. 19.

MATT. xxvii. 20–23.
MARK xv. 11–14.
LUKE xxiii. 18–25.
MATT. xxvii. 26–30.
MARK xv. 15–19.
JOHN xix. 1–4.
JOHN xix. 5–12.

MATT. xxvii. 24–25.

JOHN xix. 13–16.

The time when the Lord was taken before Pilate cannot be exactly defined. There are two sources of information; Roman usage, and the statements of the Evangelists. As a rule, the Roman courts did not open before sunrise, nor was judgment pronounced till after six o'clock A. M. The Evangelists give only general notices of the time: Matthew, "when the morning was come"; Mark, "And straightway in the morning"; John, "and it was early." All use the same designation of time, πρωΐα or πρωΐ, which may include all the time from 3 to 6 A. M. In this indefiniteness much room is given to difference of opinion. Lichtenstein and M. and M. put the leading of the Lord to Pilate soon after 3 o'clock; but most later — Ewald, an hour before sunrise; McClellan, Jones, a little before sunrise; Farrar, later, about 7. Those who put it before sunrise, suppose that

Pilate, having been told that a noted prisoner would be brought before him, took his judicial seat before the usual hour.

It is not easily determined whether the Prætorium or judgment hall, to which Jesus was taken, was in the palace of Herod the Great, and then occupied by Pilate, or in the fortress Antonia, or in a palace near it. That the Roman governors sometimes used Herod's palace as headquarters, appears from Josephus, where Florus is said to have done so; and afterward mention is made of his leading out the troops from the royal residence[1]. The palace of Herod at Cæsarea was used in like manner (Acts xxiii. 35). The palace at Jerusalem was situated on the north side of Mount Sion, and was a magnificent building of marble, with which, according to Josephus, the temple itself bore no comparison.[2] It is to be distinguished from the palace of Solomon, which was lower down on the side of the mount, and near the temple, and where Agrippa afterward built.[3] That it was used by Pilate when he visited Jerusalem is very probable.[4] Those who place the judgment hall at the fortress Antonia refer in proof to John xix. 13, where it is said that Pilate "sat down in the judgment seat, in a place that is called the Pavement, but in the Hebrew, Gabbatha."[5] This Pavement is supposed to have been between the fortress Antonia and the western portico of the temple, and identical with that mentioned by Josephus.[6] Pilate was thus sitting upon the highest point of the large temple area, where what he did was plainly visible to all present. But the fact that the outer court of the temple was "paved throughout"[7] does by no means show that Pilate here erected his tribunal. Lightfoot (*in loco*) argues at some length to show that this Pavement was the room Gazith in the temple, where the Sanhedrin sat, and that as the Jews would not go to Pilate's judgment hall, he went to theirs. But Greswell observes that "to suppose that the tribunal of Pilate could have been placed in any court of the temple, either would be palpably

1 War, ii. 14. 8; ii. 15. 5.
2 War, i. 21. 1; v. 4. 4.
3 Josephus, Antiq., viii. 5. 2; xx. 8. 11.
4 So Meyer, Winer, Alford, Friedlieb, Lewin. Ewald (v. 14) supposes this palace to have been reserved for the use of Herod's heirs, when they came to the capital.
5 Wieseler, 407; T. G. Lex., Gabbatha.
6 War, vi. 1. 8; and vi. 3. 2.
7 Josephus, War, v. 5. 2.

absurd." We must then conclude, that this **Pavement** was a movable one, like that which Suetonius mentions when he says that Julius Cæsar took with him pieces of marble ready fitted that they might be laid down at any place, and the judgment seat be placed upon them; or, which is more probable, that it was the open paved space before the palace of Herod. (So Riehm, 624.) The latter view is confirmed by Josephus,[1] for Florus, when he had fixed his quarters in the palace, erected his tribunal in front of it, and there gathered the chief men of the city before him. The judge seems to have been at liberty to place his tribunal where he pleased, and Pilate on one occasion did so in the great circus.[2] We consider it then most probable that all the judicial proceedings before Pilate were at the palace of Herod upon Mount Sion.[3]

Pilate, being informed that members of the Sanhedrin had brought a criminal before him, and of their unwillingness to enter the palace, goes out to meet them. The ground of their unwillingness has been already considered. It was plainly the purpose of the priests and elders to obtain at once from Pilate a confirmation of their sentence, without stating the grounds upon which He had been condemned; but this plan was wholly baffled by his question: "What accusation bring ye against this man?' Whether Pilate asked this question from a sense of justice, not thinking it right to condemn any man to death without knowing his offense; or whether he already knew who the prisoner was, and that He had been condemned upon ecclesiastical grounds, we cannot determine. We can scarce doubt, however, that he had some knowledge of Jesus, of His teaching, works, and character. Without troubling himself about ecclesiastical questions, he would closely watch all popular movements; and he could not overlook a man who had excited so much of public attention. If, as is most probable, he was in Jerusalem at the time of the Lord's public entry, he must have heard how He was

---

[1] War, ii. 14. 8. See T. G. Lex., where it is denied to be portable.

[2] Josephus, War, ii. 9. 3.

[3] Winer, ii. 29; Greswell, iii. 225; Tobler, Top., i. 222. Many, however, place the judgment hall in the castle Antonia; so Williams, Barclay, Godet, M. and M. Langen thinks that Pilate was at this time at Antonia, though the Procurators sometimes occupied Herod's palace. The point is of interest only in its bearings on the site of the sepulchre, and the direction of the Via Dolorosa.

hailed by the multitude as King of the Jews; and the fact that he placed a part of the Roman cohort at the disposal of the priests when about to arrest Him, shows that they must have communicated to him their design. Some, however, think that Pilate would not have asked them the question about the nature of His offense, if he had the evening before placed his soldiers at their service to aid in the arrest. (See Bäumlein on John xviii. 3.) It is possible that this was the act of the commander of the cohort without the knowledge of Pilate. But, however this may have been, it is plain that he was by no means disposed to be a mere tool in the hands of the priests and elders to execute their revengeful plans. Vexed at his question, they reply, almost contemptuously: "If He were not a malefactor, we would not have delivered Him up unto thee." It is as if they had said: 'We have tried Him, and found Him to be a malefactor; there is no need of any further judicial examination. Rely upon us that He is guilty, and give us without more delay the power to punish Him.'

It is not certain what force is to be given to the word, "malefactor,"[1] but apparently His accusers design to designate Jesus as one who had broken the civil laws, and therefore was amenable to the civil tribunals. By the use of this general term they conceal the nature of His offense, which was purely ecclesiastical. They had condemned Him for blasphemy. But for this Pilate would not put Him to death — probably he would not entertain the case at all; and, as they knew not what other crime to lay to His charge, they present Him as a malefactor. This vague and artful reply displeases Pilate, who is, beside, touched by the cool effrontery of the council in demanding that he shall, without examination, ratify their sentence; and he answers tartly: "Take ye Him and judge Him according to your law." It is as if He had said: If you can judge, you can also execute; but if I execute, I shall also judge. This answer forces them to confess that they have no power to put Him to death; and shows them that, if they would accomplish their purpose, they must bring some direct and definite charge, and one of which Pilate would take cognizance. They therefore now begin

---

[1] Κακὸν ποιῶν, Tischendorf, Alford, W. and H.

to accuse him of perverting the nation, of forbidding to give tribute to Cæsar, and of saying that He Himself was Christ, a king (Luke xxiii. 2). These were very serious accusations, be-cause directly affecting Roman authority, and such as Pilate was bound to hear and judge.

Up to this time the accusers of Jesus and Pilate had been standing without the Prætorium. According to Roman law, the examination might take place within the Prætorium, but the sentence must be pronounced in public without. Entering it, Pilate calls Jesus and demands of Him, " Art thou the King of the Jews ? " The Synoptists give simply this reply: " Thou sayest," or " I am "; but John relates the reply in full, in which Jesus describes the nature of His kingdom (xviii. 33–38). The effect of this conversation upon Pilate was very great. He saw at once that Jesus was no vulgar inciter of sedition, no ambitious demagogue or fanatical zealot, and that the kingdom of which He avowed Himself to be the king, was one of truth and not of force. At worst, He was only a religious enthusiast, from whose pretensions Cæsar could have nothing to fear; and he determines to save Him, if possible, from the hands of His enemies. Taking Jesus with Him, he goes out and declares to them that he finds no fault in Him. This, probably unexpected, exculpation on his part only makes them " the more fierce," and they renew the charge that He stirreth up the people throughout all Judæa and Galilee, and even to Jerusalem (Luke xxiii. 5). Mark (xv. 3) says: " And the chief priests accused Him of many things." Galilee may have been thus mentioned because the Galilæans were prone to sedition. To all these accusations Jesus answers nothing, so that His silence makes even Pilate to marvel. The incidental mention of Galilee suggests to the governor that he might relieve himself from responsibility by sending Him to Herod Antipas, who was then in the city, and unto whose jurisdiction, as a Galilæan, Jesus rightfully belonged. He accordingly sends Him to Herod, and hopes that he is now quit of the matter; or, if Herod should decline jurisdiction, that he would express some opinion as to his guilt or innocence. The chief priests and scribes follow Him, that they may renew their accusations before the new judge.

By Herod the Lord was gladly received, as he had long
desired to see Him, and hoped that He would now work some
miracle before him.   But to all the king's questions He an
swered nothing, nor did He reply to the accusations of His
enemies.   Angry at His continued silence, and doubtless interpreting it as a sign of contempt, Herod and his soldiers mock
Him with pretended homage, and, clothing Him in a gorgeous
robe, send Him back to Pilate.[1]   His return so attired was a
very intelligible sign to Pilate that Herod, who from his position
must have known His history, had no knowledge of any seditious
practices in Galilee, and regarded Him as a harmless man,
whose Messianic pretensions were rather to be ridiculed than
severely punished.   This sending of Jesus by Pilate to Herod
was understood by the latter, and probably designed by the
former, as a mark of respect and good-will; and was the means
of restoring friendship between them, which had been broken,
perhaps by some question of conflicting jurisdiction.[2]   Where
Herod took up his residence when in the city, is not known.   If
Pilate occupied the fortress Antonia, Herod would doubtless occupy his father's palace.   It is not probable that both occupied
the latter together, as some suppose.[3]   Possibly he now made his
abode at the old palace of the Maccabees.[4]   In either case, the
distance was not great, and but little time was spent in going to
and returning from Herod.

After Jesus was brought back to Pilate, the latter calls
together "the chief priests and the rulers and the people"
(Luke xxiii. 13).   He now designs to pronounce Him innocent
and end the trial, and therefore seats himself upon his judgment
seat (Matt. xxvii. 19).   There was a custom that at this feast a
prisoner chosen by the people should be released from punishment.   As to the origin of this custom, nothing definite is known.
From the language of the Synoptists — κατὰ ἑορτήν — it has

---

[1] Some would make this a white robe, such as candidates for office were accustomed
to wear, and chieftains when they went into battle. Thus robed, He appeared as a can-
didate for the honor of the king of the Jews. So Friedlieb, Archäol., 109; Langen;
Riggenbach makes it the white vestment of the priest; contra, Meyer; in Vulgate, veste
alba.

[2] Some would trace the origin of this quarrel to the incident mentioned by Luke
xiii. 1. See Greswell, iii. 26.

[3] Lichtenstein, 432.

[4] Josephus, Antiq., xx. 8. 11.

been inferred that at each of the feasts a prisoner was released.
John, however, confines it to the Passover, and it might have
had some special reference to the release of the people from
Egyptian bondage.　No traces of it are to be found in later Jewish writings.　It may possibly have been established by the
Romans as a matter of policy, but more probably it was of Jewish origin and continued by the Roman governors.[2]　Whether
Pilate had this custom in mind when he took his seat upon the
tribunal, is not certain; but his words (Luke xxiii. 16) strongly
imply this, as does also the fact that he had gathered the people
together with the chief priests and rulers.　Ascending the tribunal, he formally declares that, having examined Jesus, he had
found no fault in Him, neither had Herod, to whom he had
sent Him; and after chastising Him he will therefore release
Him.　It seems from the scope of the narrative that he intended
to chastise Jesus, thus to propitiate the priests, and then to release Him under the custom without further consulting the people.　In this way, apparently, Pilate thought to satisfy all: the
people, by releasing Him; the priests and elders, by chastising
Him; and himself, by delivering Him from death.　But he satisfied none.　The people, reminded of their claim, began to
clamor for it; but they did not demand that Jesus should be released.　To satisfy the priests and rulers His chastisement was
far too light a punishment.　The cry is raised, "Away with this
man, and release unto us Barabbas."　Pilate, who knew how well
affected the people at large had been to Jesus, cannot believe
that they will reject Him and choose Barabbas; and he therefore
accepts the alternative, and leaves them to elect between the two.

Of this Barabbas, son of Abbas, little is known.　According
to some authorities, the true reading (Matt. xxvii. 16, 17) is
Jesus Barabbas.[3]　From the statements of the Evangelists respecting him, it appears that he was one of that numerous and
constantly growing party who detested the Roman rule, and
who afterward gained such notoriety as the Zealots.　In company with others, he had stirred up an insurrection in the city,
and had committed murder (Mark xv. 7; Luke xxiii. 19).　John

---

[1] Friedlieb, Archäol., 110.

[2] Winer, ii. 202; Hofmann, 360.

[3] So Meyer, Ewald; and formerly, Tischendorf; *contra*, Alford, W. and H.

speaks of him as a robber also; but this crime was too common
to attract much attention or bring upon its perpetrator much
odium. Josephus,[1] speaking of Florus, says that "he did all
but proclaim throughout the country that every one was at liberty to rob, provided he might share in the plunder." It is remarkable that Barabbas was confessedly guilty of the very crime
with which the priests and rulers had falsely charged Jesus —
that of sedition; and no plainer proof of their hypocrisy could
be given to the watchful Pilate than their efforts to release the
former and to condemn the latter. And this result it was easy for
them to effect; for the tide of popular feeling ran very strong in
favor of national independence, and one who had risen up against
the Romans and had shed blood in the attempt, was deemed
rather a hero and a patriot than a murderer. On the other
hand, Jesus, so far from encouraging the rising enmity to
Roman rule, had always inculcated obedience and submission —
teachings ever unpalatable to a subject nation. It is probable,
too, that most of those present were citizens of Jerusalem
rather than pilgrims from other parts of the land; and, if
there were some from Galilee, that they did not dare, in opposition to the rulers, to express openly their wishes.

While waiting for the people to come to a decision, he receives the message from his wife mentioned by Matthew (xxvii. 19).
Nothing is known of her but her name, which tradition gives as
Procla, or Claudia Procula.[2] This dream was generally regarded
by the fathers as supernatural, and by most ascribed to God, but
by some to Satan who wished to hinder the Lord's death.[3] This
message would naturally tend to make Pilate more anxious to
release "that just man," even if he did not ascribe to the dream
a divine origin.[4]

The Synoptists agree that Pilate made three several attempts
to persuade the people to release Jesus, though the order of the
attempts is not the same in all. The events may be thus
arranged: Pilate presents to the people the two, Jesus and

---

[1] War, ii. 14. 2.

[2] Winer, ii. 262; Hofmann, 340.   [3] See Jones, Notes, 359.

[4] Lewin (129) finds in this circumstance a proof that the locality was Pilate's ordinary residence, the palace of Herod; and that the charge against Jesus was brought at so
early an hour that he was aroused from his slumbers to hear it.

Barabbas, between whom they are to choose.   A little interval follows, during which he receives his wife's message.   He now formally asks the people whom they wished to have released (Matt. xxvii. 21; Mark xv. 9; Luke xxiii. 16-18).   They answer, Barabbas.   Pilate, hoping that by changing the form of the question he could obtain an answer more in accordance with his wishes, says: " What shall I do then with Jesus which is called Christ ?" (Matt. xxvii. 22; Mark xv. 12.   Luke xxiii. 20 does not give the question; but the answer shows that it must have been the same as in Matthew and Mark.)   To this they reply, " Let Him be crucified."   Alexander (on Mark xv. 13) suggests that the cry " Crucify Him" arose from the fact that, as Barabbas by the Roman law would have been crucified, Jesus should now stand in his stead and bear his punishment.   Bynaeus (iii. 118) explains it on the ground that crucifixion was the usual punishment of sedition, of which He was accused.   But we can scarce doubt that it was first raised by the Sanhedrists, who through this punishment would both gratify their own hatred and better cast the responsibility of His death on the Romans.   Pilate now sees that not only do the people reject Jesus, but that they insist upon the most severe and ignominious punishment. He had proposed chastisement; they call for crucifixion.   He had not anticipated this, and will reason with them.   He therefore asks: " Why, what evil hath He done?" (Matt. xxvii. 23; Mark xv. 14).   Luke (xxiii. 22) adds: " I have found no cause of death in Him, I will therefore chastise Him and let Him go." This judicial declaration of His innocence and attempt to substitute the milder punishment, only cause the people to cry out the louder, " Let Him be crucified."

John (xviii. 39, 40) sums up the narrative very briefly, and gives no details.   He omits the sending to Herod and states only the result of the popular choice.

The great and rapid change in public feeling in regard to Jesus which four or five days had brought, would appear incredible did we not find many analogous cases in history.   The thoughtlessness and fickleness that characterize a populace are proverbial.   Besides, we here find special causes in operation to bring about this change.   The multitude that shouted " **Hosanna**

to the Son of David " on the day of His triumphal entry, doubtless expected that He would immediately assert His kingly
claims, and take a position before the public corresponding to
His high dignity. But so far from this, He reappears the next
day, not as a prince but as a teacher; He does nothing answering to their expectations; He passes much of His time in seclusion at Bethany, and the excitement of His entry dies away.
Still, He has a powerful hold on the popular mind as a prophet
and worker of miracles; and this is recognized by the rulers in
the manner in which they effect His arrest, and the haste with
which they press on the trial. But He puts forth no miraculous
power against His enemies; He offers no resistance; He is
insulted and grossly abused, and complains not. How were
they mistaken in thinking that He could be the Messiah, and
fulfill the national hopes, and overcome the resolute Roman !
But it was His conviction as a blasphemer that turned the heart
of the people against Him. The chief priests, the elders, the
scribes, all those in whom they trusted and who guided public
opinion, were busy in declaring that He had blasphemed in the
presence of the whole Sanhedrin. He assumed to be something
more than the Messiah whom they expected — to be even the
Son of God. All His teachings, all His miracles are straightway forgotten. He is a blasphemer, He must die.

It may be also, as has been said, that most of those that
cried "Crucify Him" were citizens of Jerusalem who, under
the influence of the hierarchy, had never been well inclined
toward Him, and who do not seem to have joined in the hosannas and rejoicings upon the day of His entry.

From the Synoptists it would appear that, after the failure
of the attempts to induce the multitude to release Jesus, Pilate,
despairing of success, washed his hands before the people, and
then gave Him up to be scourged and crucified (Matt. xxvii. 26;
Mark xv. 15). Luke (xvii. 16) gives Pilate's words: "I will
therefore chastise Him and release Him," but says nothing of
any scourging. (It is in question what is meant by "chastise "
here — παιδεύω. Some say it is equivalent to scourge; so T.
G. Lex.; but Meyer says: "what kind of chastisement is left
indefinite." Verse 17 is omitted by W. and H. and Tisch.) But

John (xix. 4–12) relates other and apparently subsequent attempts to save Him, placing them after and in connection with the scourging. Was He, then, twice scourged? This is affirmed by some who regard the scourging of John (xix. 1–3) as designed to gratify the elders and priests, and to excite popular compassion;[1] but that mentioned by the Synoptists as the scourging usually inflicted before crucifixion. But this is improbable (so Luthardt). That scourging generally preceded the crucifixion appears from Josephus.[2] This scourging was excessively severe, the leathern thongs being often loaded with lead or iron, and cutting through the flesh even to the bone, so that some died under it.[3] But the Lord having been once scourged, there seems no reason why it should be repeated, nor is it likely that Pilate would have permitted it if he could have prevented it.

If, then, Jesus was scourged but once, and the accounts of the Synoptists and of John refer to the same event, why did Pilate now permit it? Was it that finding himself unable to save Jesus, and having no further expedient, he gives up the struggle, and sends him away to be scourged as preliminary to His death?[4] Or did he permit it hoping that through the milder punishment he might awaken pity, and thus rescue Him from death?[5] It is not easy to decide as to Pilate's motives. He had early offered to chastise Jesus and then release Him; but this the multitude refused, and demanded His crucifixion. It does not, then, seem probable that He could hope that the mere sight of Jesus suffering this punishment could so awaken their pity as to change their determination.[6] And why, if this were his purpose, should Jesus be taken into the common hall, or Prætorium, and be subjected to the insults and mockery of the soldiers? We infer then, that Pilate, having yielded to the priests and rulers, sent Him to be scourged as preliminary to His crucifixion, which was done by the soldiers in their usual

---

[1] So Bleek, Bruckner in DeWette, Nebe, ii. 80.

[2] War, ii. 14. 9, and v. 11. 1. See Winer, i. 677; Friedlieb, Arch., 114.

[3] As to flagellation among the Jews, see Ainsworth on Deut. xxv. 1–3.

[4] Bynaeus, Stier, Krafft, Ellicott.

[5] Meyer, Sepp, Alford, Jones, Tholuck, Godet.

[6] It is not certain whether He was scourged in the Prætorium in the court, or without it and in front of it, where the tribunal was placed. The words of Matthew and Mark imply the latter; so Meyer, Lange. But if He was scourged but once, it would seem from John xix. 4 that it was done in the Prætorium; so Bynaeus.

cruel way; and that, beholding Him bloody from the scourge, clothed with the purple robe, and wearing the crown of thorns, his own compassion was awakened and he resolved to make one last effort to deliver Him from death. He therefore leads Him forth, and after an emphatic declaration for the third time that he finds no fault in Him, presents Him to the people, saying, "Behold the man." He hoped that the sight of one so meek, so helpless, so wretched, would touch the hearts of all as it had touched his own. Stier gives rightly the meaning of his words: "Is this man a king? an insurgent? a man to be feared, or dangerous? How innocent and how miserable! Is it not enough?" It is probable, as said by Jones, that as He wore the crown of thorns and purple robe, so He also bore in His hand the reed. But nothing could touch the hearts of His embittered enemies. As they saw Him, the chief priests and officers raised anew the cry, "Crucify Him, crucify Him." It is not said that the people at large joined in it; and perhaps for a time, through fear or pity, they were silent.

Angry at the implacable determination of the rulers that Jesus should be crucified, Pilate tauntingly responds to the cry, "Take ye Him and crucify Him, for I find no fault in Him." Lardner (i. 54) paraphrases these words: "You must crucify Him then yourselves, if you can commit such a villany, for I cannot. He appears to me innocent, as I have told you already, and I have now punished Him as much as He deserves." (Godet, ii. 374.) The Jews now perceived that Pilate, knowing that the charge of sedition was baseless, and deeply sympathizing with Jesus, would not put Him to death; and were compelled to return to the original charge of blasphemy upon which he was condemned. " We have a law and by our law He ought to die, because He made Himself the Son of God." This gives a new turn to the accusation; they had charged Him with saying that He was Christ a King, but here is far more (Godet). This mention of the fact that Jesus made Himself the Son of God, had a power over Pilate who now heard of it for the first time, which the Jews little anticipated. Was then his prisoner, whose appearance, words, and conduct had so strangely and so deeply interested him, a divine being? Full of fear he returns to the

judgment hall and commands Jesus to be brought, and demands,
"Whence art thou?" His silence at first, and still more His
answer afterward, confirmed Pilate in his determination to release
Him, and he may probably have taken some open step toward it.
But the rulers will not thus give up their victim. They begin
to threaten that if he release Him he thereby shows that he is
Cæsar's enemy, and that they will accuse him before the emperor.
Pilate now perceives the danger of his position. Such an accusation he must, at any cost, avoid. His administration would
not, in many respects, bear a close scrutiny; and the slightest
suspicion that he had shown favor to a claimant of the Jewish
throne, falling into the ear of the jealous and irritable Tiberius,
would have endangered, not only his office but his life. Such
peril he could not meet. The shrewd elders and priests, who
knew the selfish weakness of his character, pressed their advantage, and Pilate dared do no more. Jesus must be crucified.
He now prepares to give final sentence. But he will first clear
himself of the guilt of shedding innocent blood. He takes water
and washes his hands before all, to show that he is clean.[1]
"Then answered all the people, His blood be on us and on our
children." At this moment, about to give sentence, Pilate could
not give up the poor satisfaction of mocking the Jews in what
he knew well to be a most tender point — their Messianic hopes.
He cries out, "Behold your king." His contemptuous words
only bring back the fierce response, "Away with Him; crucify
Him." Still more bitterly he repeats, "Shall I crucify your
king?" The answer of the chief priests, for the people are not
said to have joined in it, "We have no king but Cæsar," was an
open renunciation of their allegiance to Jehovah and of the covenant which He had made with the house of David (2 Sam. vii.
12). Thus had the Jews been led, step by step, not only to
reject their Messiah, to prefer a robber and murderer before Him,
to insist mercilessly that He should be put to a most shameful
death, but even to accept and openly proclaim the Roman emperor as their king. This was the culminating point of national
apostasy.

---

[1] Many place this after the words of the Jews, "We have no king but Cæsar"
(John xix. 15); so Stier. Some before the scourging of Jesus; so Jones.

Some points presented by the narrative demand further con-sideration. Brief reasons have been given for supposing that Jesus was scourged but once. Some, however, would make the scourging mentioned by John (xix. 1) a kind of judicial torture, or *quaestio per tormenta*, for the purpose of forcing a confession if the prisoner were really guilty. To this torture by scourging, it is said, Pilate subjected Jesus, not that he had any doubt of His innocence, but that if no confession of guilt were extorted, he might have stronger grounds for setting Him free.[1] Torture was customary with the Romans (Acts xxii. 24), and was practised by Herod the Great.[2] But that Pilate should now have recourse to it, when he himself knew Jesus to be innocent, merely that he might say to the Jews that He had made no confession, is most improbable. Sepp (vi. 241) supposes that the soldiers regarded the scourging as intended to extort a confession, and acted accordingly though Pilate had other designs.

The person to be scourged was bound to a low pillar that, bending over, the blows might be better inflicted. The pillar to which the Lord was bound is mentioned by Jerome and Bede and others.[3] There is now shown in the church of the Holy Sepulchre a fragment of a porphyry column called the Column of the Flagellation, and a rival column is preserved at Rome. (See Baed., 198; Williams, H. C., ii. 207.)

The traditional site in the Via Dolorosa of the place where Pilate presented Jesus to the people, or the Arch of the *Ecce Homo*, has been recently defended by Saulcy (ii. 291) who says that this arched gate was connected with a wall of Pilate's palace, and answered the purpose of a gallery or tribune when the governor wished to address the people. (See Rob., iii. 171, 220.) We know that Pilate brought Jesus out, and seated him-self upon the platform or tribune — βῆμα — (John xix. 13), which was situated in the pavement, and there, for the second time, showed Him to the people. Some have understood it that he placed the Lord upon the tribune as if in mockery; most reject this. (For its position see Nebe, ii. 150.)

---

[1] Hug, cited by Tholuck; Bucher, 777; Kirchen, Lex., vi. 271; Friedlieb, 331, see, however, *contra*, his Archäol., 116; Nebe, ii. 111.

[2] See Josephus, Antiq. xvi. 10. 3. and 4.

[3] Hofmann, 365.

The form of Pilate's sentence is not given. The customary
form was, *Ibis ad crucem.* Friedlieb (Arch., 125) gives a sentence pretended by Adrichomius to be genuine, but rightly rejects it. Another sentence, said to have been found in Aquila
in Italy, has been often printed. Another was found at the
same place a few years since.[1] Both are obvious fabrications.

It has been much disputed whether Pilate transmitted to the
emperor at Rome any account of Christ's trial and death. In
itself this is intrinsically probable, for it seems to have been the
custom of governors of provinces to send thither records of the
more important events occurring during their administration.
Thus Philo speaks of the "acts," (*acta*,) transmitted to Caligula
from Alexandria. That Pilate did send such records, appears
from Justin Martyr's address to the Emperor Pius, in which he
appeals to them as proving Christ's miracles and sufferings.
Tertullian, in his Apology, also appeals to them. Eusebius, in
his history (ii. 2), relates, upon the authority of Tertullian, that
Tiberius, receiving these acts of Pilate containing an account of
the Lord's resurrection and of His miracles, proposed to the senate that He should be ranked among the gods. If, however,
Pilate really sent such an account, we obtain from it no additional particulars respecting the trial and death of the Lord.
No writer gives any quotation from it, from which it may be
inferred that none, even of those who refer to it, had ever seen
it ; and it is said by Schürer to have no historical value. (See
Leyrer in Herzog, xi. 665.) The supposition that Pilate's records
had been destroyed by the senate or emperor before the time of
Constantine, in order to remove this proof of Christianity, is not
very probable.[2]

Some have attempted to cast additional light upon the evangelical narratives by referring to the Apocryphal Gospel of Nicodemus, in the first part of which an account is given of the trial,
death, burial, and resurrection of the Lord. But from it very
little of value can be drawn.[3]

That we may keep before us the order of events from the time the
Lord was brought before Pilate to His departure to the place of cru-

---

[1] See both given by Hofmann, 360--369.

[2] See Jones, Canon N. Test. ii. 330; Pearson on Creed, art. 4; Jarvis, 375.

[3] See Tischendorf's Pilati Circa Christum Judicium, Lipsiae, 1855; Hofmann, 334.

cifixion, we may note the following subdivisions of time. 1. From the bringing to Pilate to the sending to Herod. 2. While with Herod. 3. After the return from Herod till the scourging and presentation to the people as Ecce Homo. 4. To the final sentence.

1. (*a*) Jesus is presented before Pilate by the rulers as a malefactor. He refers the case back to them: "Take ye Him and judge Him according to your law." (*b*) They bring the more specific charge of sedition. Pilate now examines the Lord, and is convinced that it is not true, and so declares to the Jews. (*c*) They renew more loudly the charge of sedition, and speak of Galilee. Pilate determines to send Him to Herod.

2. (*a*) The Lord is sent to Herod. The chief priests and scribes follow and vehemently accuse Him. He refuses to answer. (*b*) He is mocked by Herod and the soldiers, and sent back to Pilate.

3. (*a*) On His return, Pilate calls together the chief priests and rulers and the people that he may declare Him innocent; but they are more vehement against Him. (*b*) He prepares to release Jesus according to the custom of the feast. The multitude chose Barabbas and cry, Crucify Jesus. (*c*) Message of his wife. (*d*) He orders Jesus to be scourged and presents Him to the people: "Behold the man," hoping to awaken their compassion.

4. (*a*) The chief priests and officers renew their cries to crucify Him. (*b*) Pilate refuses and bids them crucify Him. They renew the charge, adding that He made Himself the Son of God. (*c*) Pilate examines Jesus anew, and again seeks to release Him. (*d*) The rulers threaten to accuse Pilate before the emperor. (*e*) Pilate is afraid, and yields to their demands. (*f*) He takes water and washes his hands. (*g*) He gives Jesus up to be crucified.

FRIDAY, 15TH NISAN, 7TH APRIL, 783. A. D. 30.

Delivered by Pilate into the hands of soldiers, He is led without the city to a place called Golgotha, bearing His cross. Being exhausted under the burden, the soldiers compel Simon of Cyrene, whom they meet, to bear it with Jesus. To some women following Him and weeping, He speaks words of admonition, and foretells the judgments about to come upon Jerusalem. After He has been affixed to the cross, they give Him wine mingled with gall, but He will not drink. Two malefactors are crucified with Him, one on the right hand and one on the left. As they are nailing Him to the cross, He prays to His Father to forgive them. The inscription placed over His head displeases the Jews,

JOHN xix. 16-22.
MATT. xxvii. 31-33.
MARK xv. 20-26.

LUKE xxiii. 26-33.

MATT. xxvii. 33-38
MARK xv. 27, 28.

LUKE xxiii. 34.

but Pilate refuses to change it. The soldiers who keep   JOHN xix. 23-4.
watch at the foot of the cross, divide His garments
among themselves.

After the chief priests had declared that they "had no king
but Cæsar," Pilate delivered Jesus to them, " and they took Him
and led Him away " (John xix. 16). But this they did through
the soldiers of the governor, as said by the Synoptists. Mark
mentions that "they led Him out to crucify Him." The place
of crucifixion was outside the city. (The Holy City, like the
camp of old, must not be defiled with blood, Num. xv. 35; so
Naboth, 1 Kings xxi. 13, and Stephen, Acts vii. 58, were stoned
without.) With Jesus two malefactors were led (Luke xxiii. 32).
As they also were crucified, it must have been by command of
the governor. Why he took this occasion we are not told; most
probably they had been previously sentenced. Nebe (ii. 191)
ascribes it to a purpose on Pilate's part to mock the Messianic
expectation of the Jews, the nation being represented by the two
malefactors, and their Messiah between them.

Some controverted points as to the time and the manner
of the crucifixion here meet us. We will consider them in
their order. The place will be considered later in connection
with the burial.

The time of the crucifixion. If the Sanhedrin held its second
session at day-break, or a little before sunrise, as the statements of
the Evangelists lead us to suppose, the events subsequent down to
the crucifixion, must have occupied several hours. The time when
Jesus was led to the hall of judgment is noted by John (xviii. 28),
" and it was early " — ἦν δὲ πρωί. If this denote the fourth watch of
the night, it was from 3–6 A. M. The usual hour for opening judicial
proceedings among the Romans, according to Friedlieb, was 9 A. M.,
but according to Nebe (ii. 27), much earlier, at sunrise, if necessary;
and probably Pilate now a little anticipated the time. The crucifixion itself was at some point during the interval from nine to twelve.
It was, according to John (xix. 14), "about the sixth hour " —
ὥρα δὲ ὡσεὶ ἕκτη — (ὥρα ἦν ὡς ἕκτη, Tisch., W. and H.) when Pilate sat
down in the judgment seat to pronounce final sentence. But this
seems in direct opposition to Mark (xv. 25), "And it was the third
hour, and they crucified Him." Against John's statement is that
also of all the Synoptists, that there was darkness from the sixth hour
over all the land till the ninth hour (Matt. xxvii. 45; Mark xv. 33;

Luke xxiii. 44). This darkness did not begin till Jesus had been for some time nailed to the cross.

Many efforts have been made to harmonize this discrepancy.[1] That change of punctuation which places a period at the word "prepa-ration" (in John xix. 14), and joins "of the passover" with "hour," making it to read, "And it was the preparation, and about the sixth hour of the passover," has been already spoken of in another connec-tion. (Licht., after Hofmann.) It is forced and untenable. Some would change "sixth" into "third," regarding the former as an error of copyists,[2] and thus bring John into harmony with Mark. But all the weight of authority is in favor of the present reading.[3] Light-foot finds a solution in his interpretation of Mark, who does not say, "it was the third hour *when* they crucified Him," but "it was the third hour *and* they crucified Him." This notes that the fathers of the Sanhedrin should have been present at the third hour in the temple, offering their thank offerings: "When the third hour now was, and was passed, yet they omitted not to prosecute His conviction." This is wholly unsatisfactory. Some would make the "preparation" of John (xix. 14): "It was the preparation — $\pi a \rho a \sigma \kappa \epsilon \nu \dot{\eta}$ — of the pass-over," to denote not the whole day, but that part of it immediately preceding the Sabbath, or from 3–6 P. M. Thus John's meaning would be, it was the sixth hour before the commencement of the preparation, or about 9 A. M., which would agree with Mark. Oth-ers would read it, "about the sixth hour, or noon, the preparation time of Passover day commenced." Both these constructions are arbitrary. Some would make the term hour — $\check{\omega} \rho a$ — to be used by John in a large sense. The day of twelve hours, it is said, was di-vided into four equal periods, and to each of these periods was the term "hour" applied. Thus the first period was from 6–9 A. M., the second, from 9–12, the third, from 12–3 P. M., the fourth from 3–6. During the period from 9–12 A. M. the condemnation and cruci-fixion of the Lord took place. Mark speaks of the third hour, or beginning of the second period, including the time from 9 to 10 A. M. ; John of the sixth hour, or end of that period, including the time from 11 to 12 A. M.[4] Both agree that in the interval from 9–12 the Lord was condemned and crucified. Hengstenberg *in loco* says:

---

[1] For a full account of early opinions, see Bynaeus, iii. 178.

[2] Bynaeus; Robinson, Har., 261, Luthardt, Bloomfield. Farrar speaks of this as "a possible solution," but Riddle thinks such an error unlikely: "No recent editor accepts the reading." See Langen, 329.

[3] Tischendorf, Alford, Greswell, Wieseler, Meyer, but see W. and H. Ap.

[4] It is said by Jones (iv. 41): "The sixth hour was deemed to continue till 9 A. M." and by Grotius on Matt. xxviii. 45, that whatever was done between the third and sixth hour, might be referred to the beginning or end. So Campbell, Krafft.

" The sentence of Pilate and the leading away to crucifixion, fill in the middle between the third and sixth hours, that is, about half an hour after ten." Ellicott says: " The crucifixion was somewhere between the two broad divisions of the third and sixth hours." But we cannot regard this meaning of the term hour as warranted.[1]

Many affirm that John reckons the hours according to the Roman mode, from midnight; and if so, the sixth hour would be 6 A. M. But there is much dispute as to the Roman mode of computation. It is said by many that the Romans had no such reckoning from midnight (so Farrar), but the better opinion is that the Romans used both modes, from midnight and from sunrise. (See Wieseler, Syn. 410; Beiträge, 252; see page 159 for other references.) It is thus possible that John may have reckoned from midnight in this case, though we have seen reason to think that in other cases he reckons from sunrise. If Pilate counted the hours from midnight, and if there was a fixed hour for the opening of his court, it is very probable that this hour was the sixth, and that the Evangelist here followed this mode of computation. The objections are made that all the events narrated by the Evangelists from the first session of the Sanhedrin to the condemnation, could not have taken place by 6 A. M., and that the interval from 6 to 9 is too long for the preparation necessary after the condemnation for the crucifixion; and these objections seem well taken. But we are to remember that our exact divisions of time were unknown to the ancients;[2] and that in our ignorance of the circumstances, we can here have no accurate measure of the time consumed; and also, that John says it was "about the sixth hour," which shows that he does not mean to give an exact note of the time.

We conclude, then, that John may have reckoned the hours from midnight, the sixth hour when Pilate sat down on the judgment seat, extending from 6 to 7 A. M.; the subsequent preparations for the crucifixion, and the time occupied in going to the cross, may well have brought the act of nailing to the cross about nine o'clock, as said by Mark. But if John reckoned, like the Synoptists, from sunrise, then we must suppose an error in his text (Nebe), or in that of Mark (Caspari), or find a discrepancy which we know not how to reconcile.

We give the following arrangements:

Ewald: The Lord was brought to Pilate an hour before sunrise,

---

[1] See T. G. Lex., *sub voce*. Robinson, Greek Lex.: " With a numeral, marking the hour of the day as counted from sunrise."

[2] See Pauly, Real Encyc., ii. 1017, art. Dies.

the sentence was pronounced at 6 A. M., and the crucifixion took place at 9 A. M.

Edersheim: The process before Pilate began at 6.30 A. M., and occupied two hours; the Lord reached Golgotha about 9.

Caspari: The Lord was taken before Pilate about 6 A. M.; the proceedings in the Prætorium lasted till near noon; the crucifixion was about 12 M., the Lord hanging on the cross only three hours.

To the place of crucifixion Jesus was conducted by the soldiers, Pilate not having lictors to whom such duty specially belonged. It is said by John (xix. 17): "And He bearing His cross, went forth." (R. V. "He went out, bearing the cross for Himself.") Luke (xxiii. 26) adds the incident "that they laid hold upon one Simon a Cyrenian, . . . and on him they laid the cross, that he might bear it after Jesus." It is often said that the cross was first borne by the Lord alone according to custom, but fainting under the burden, it was put upon Simon. It is plain from Matthew (xxvii. 32) that the procession met Simon as they passed out of the gate of the city and he was entering in, and so that the Lord bore the cross alone to this point. Whether He bore the whole cross or only a part of it — the cross-beam or *patibulum* — is in dispute. It is said by Zoeckler [1] (93) and Nebe (ii. 168) that He bore the whole cross; by others, as Keim, that He bore only the lighter transom. The data for a judgment are very scanty, but the belief of the early church was that the whole cross was put on the Lord; and this is shown in the early paintings, and in such expressions as " to bear the cross," *ferre crucem, in crucem tollere*, which refer to it as complete and set up (Luke xiv. 27; see Meyer on Matt. xxvii. 32, note). It is nowhere said that He fell under the burden; this is an inference and a very probable one, and the painters so represented it. The weight of the cross is estimated by Vigouroux at 70–75 kilograms; we may say about 150 lbs. It is doubted by some whether it was the Roman custom for all criminals to bear their own crosses, and whether the two malefactors did; if they did, we do not know whether they went in the same procession with the Lord. This is said by Sepp, they went before Him.

Of this Simon who bore the cross, little is known except that

---

[1] *The Cross of Christ* (Trans., 1877).

he was a Cyrenian and the father of Alexander and Rufus (Mark xv. 21). Many suppose him a slave from the fact, that while so many Jews must have been present, they were passed by, and he was seized upon to perform this degrading office.[1] The reason, however, of his selection may simply have been that, chancing to be close at hand when Jesus sank down from weariness, they compelled him to assist. Others suppose him to have been a disciple, and on that account selected; but this fact could scarcely have been known to the soldiers. That he subsequently became a disciple is more probable. Following the Lord upon the way to the place of crucifixion was "a great company of people and of women, which also bewailed and lamented Him" (Luke xxiii. 27). These women seem to have been not those only who followed Him from Galilee, but were in great part those of the city or the country adjacent, who had seen Him or heard Him, and now sympathized with Him, and whom He addresses as the "Daughters of Jerusalem."

The Via Dolorosa. The way along which the Lord passed from the hall of judgment to the place of crucifixion is traditionally known as the *Via Dolorosa.*[2] Its course depends on the position we give to the two termini, about both of which there is uncertainty. Assuming that He was crucified near the present Holy Sepulchre, if the Prætorium was at Herod's palace, the way ran north; if at Antonia, it ran southwest (see cut); the distance being about the same in both cases, and is estimated in the Speakers' Commentary (Matt. xxvii. 31) as less than one-third of a mile.

It is said by Vigouroux (Le Nouveau Testament) who puts the Prætorium at Antonia, that the length of the way was from 500–600 metres; an old measurement made it 1,321 steps. Of the way from Herod's palace tradition says nothing, but makes frequent mention of the way from Antonia. But it is said by Robinson (iii. 170) that the first allusion to the present Via Dolorosa he had found, was in the 14th century, and that in the 12th we know that no street in Jerusalem bore this name. Sepp (vi. 305), who puts the Prætorium at Herod's palace, supposes the Lord to have passed through the

---

[1] So Meyer, Sepp.

[2] For a minute account of the Lord's progress from the judgment hall to the cross, along the Via Dolorosa, and the traditionary incidents, see Hofmann, 371. And for full details as to the traditional stations along this way, see Tobler, Top., i. 262, etc. If the place of crucifixion was north of the Damascus gate, we are still uncertain as to the point from whence the way began. Sepp, *Kritische Beiträge*, 60.

Gennath or garden gate, and thence to Golgotha; and Edersheim (ii. 586), "through the gate in the first wall, and so into the busy quarter of Acra." All traces of the Lord's route have been long obliterated by the changes through which the city has passed. **Col. Wilson** (Bib. Ed., iv. 278) remarks that "the Armenian gardens

Traditional Way

Holy
Sepulchre

Antonia

Herod's Palace

THE VIA DOLOROSA OR DOLOROUS WAY.

are from forty to fifty feet above those of Herod's palace, and that the present Via Dolorosa is about the same height above the pavements of the ancient street."

The Crucifixion. This was a punishment used by the Greeks, Romans, Egyptians, and many other nations, but not by the Jews. It was, indeed, permitted by the law to hang a man on a tree, but only after he had been put to death (Deut. xxi. 22, 23). Upon this, Maimonides, quoted by Ainsworth, remarks: "After they are stoned to death, they fasten a piece of timber in the earth and out of it there crosseth a piece of wood; then they tie both his hands one to another, and hang them near unto the setting of the sun." The form of the cross might be varied. Sometimes it was in the shape of the letter **X**, this was called *crux decussata.* Sometimes it was in the shape of the letter **T**, this was called *crux commissa.* Sometimes it was in the form following: **✝**, this was called *crux immissa.* These designations seem to have been invented by Lipsius (*De Cruce,* i. vii.). The *crux decussata* is better known as St. Andrew's cross; the *crux commissa,* as the Egyptian, or St. Anthony's, or the Greek cross; the *crux immissa* as the Latin cross. According to Zoeckler (65) **neither** the *crux decussata* nor *commissa* can be shown to be a Roman instrument of punishment. Tradition affirms that the cross on which the Lord suffered was the Latin cross; and early painters have so represented it, and this is generally accepted.[1] The upright post or beam was by no means lofty, generally only so high as to raise the person a few inches from the ground. It is uncertain whether the cross was placed in the ground before the victim was nailed to it, or after; but the former is most probable.[2] Midway upon it was a little projection, *sedile*, upon which the person sat, that the whole weight of the body might not fall upon the arms and they thus be torn from the nails. The arms were sometimes tied with cords, perhaps to prevent this pressure upon the nails, or that the nailing might be the more easily effected. The head was not fastened. Whether the feet were generally nailed, has been much disputed.[3] That the Lord's feet were thus nailed may be inferred from Luke xxiv. 39, 40. Appearing to the Eleven upon the evening following His resurrection, He said to them: "Behold my hands and my feet that it is I Myself; handle me and see, for a spirit hath not flesh and bones as ye see me have. And when He had thus spoken, He showed them His hands and His feet." This showing of the hands and feet could not be simply to convince them that His body was a real body and not a mere phantasm; but was also intended to convince them of His identity. "It is I Myself, and in proof of this, look at the prints of the nails remaining in my hands and my feet." John (xx. 20) says, "He showed unto them His hands and His side." From both narratives, it follows that He showed them the wounds in His hands, His side, and His feet. That, at His second appearing to the Eleven, He spake to Thomas only of His hands and His side, is to be explained as giving all the proof that that skeptical apostle had demanded (verse 25). Alford gives a little different explanation: "He probably does not name the feet, merely because the hands and side would more naturally offer themselves to his examination than the feet to which he must stoop." That the feet of the Lord were nailed, has been the current view of commentators.[4] But it has been questioned whether

---

[1] Hofmann, 372. See Bynaeus (iii. 225), and Didron's *Christian Iconography* (Trans. i. 374) for a discussion of the various forms of the cross; also, *History of our Lord*, Jameson and Eastlake, ii. 320; Nebe, ii. 169.

[2] Friedlieb, Arch., 142; Greswell, iii. 245; Zoeckler, 412; Edersheim, ii. 589, is undecided.

[3] In neg., see Paulus (Handbuch, iii. 669), who discusses this point at great length; Winer, i. 678; in aff., Friedlieb, 144; Meyer on Matt. xxvii. 35, who says "that the feet were usually nailed, and that the case of Jesus was no exception to the general rule, may be regarded as beyond doubt."

[4] Tholuck, Stier, Lange, Ebrard, Ewald, Olshausen.

the feet were separately nailed, or one nail was used for both. According to Hofmann, most of the painters have represented the feet as lying one over the other and both pierced by the same nail.[1] Didron (Christian Iconography) observes: "Previous to the thirteenth century, Christ was attached to the cross by three or four nails indifferently. After the thirteenth century, the practice of putting only three nails was definitely in the ascendant." On the other hand, early tradition speaks of four nails, and it is said by Vigouroux that all the Greek painters have four.[2] It is possible that the crown of thorns remained upon His head, as represented by the painters. Matthew and Mark, who both speak of taking off the purple robe, say nothing of the soldiers removing the crown of thorns.[3]

Both Matthew (xxvii. 34) and Mark (xv. 23) speak of a potion given to the Lord (that mentioned in Luke xxiii. 36 was later), and some find a contradiction between them, the first speaking of "vinegar mingled with gall," the last of "wine mingled with myrrh." According to W. and H. and Tisch., we should read οἶνον — wine — in Matthew, and thus the difference in their statements is only the mention by one of gall, by the other of myrrh. It is insisted by Meyer that these two terms cannot be interchanged. If this view be taken, we may distinguish the two, as is done by Townsend and Jones; the first, wine mingled with gall, offered Him in derision, which He tasted but refused; the second, an intoxicating draught which He also refused. The object in offering the last seems to have been to stupefy the sufferer, so that the pain might not be so acutely felt, and this was usually given before the nailing to the cross. This, however, was a Jewish, not a Roman custom, though now permitted by the Romans.[4] Lightfoot (on Matt. xxvii. 34) quotes from the Rabbins: "To those that were to be executed they gave a grain of myrrh infused in wine to drink, that their understanding might be disturbed or they lose their senses, as it is said, 'Give strong drink to them that are ready to die, and wine to them that are of sorrowful heart.'" This mixture the Lord tasted, but, knowing its purpose, would not drink it. He would not permit the clearness of His mind to be thus disturbed, and, in the full possession of consciousness, would endure all the agonies of the cross. It is said that this potion was prepared by

---

[1] See, however, Friedlieb, Archäol., 145 note; Langen, 317.

[2] See Winer, i. 678; Sepp, vi. 333; Ellicott, 353; Zoeckler, 416.

[3] See History of Our Lord, ii. 101: On His way to Calvary, He is generally represented in Art as with the crown of thorns on His head, but on the cross, often without it.

[4] Friedlieb, Archäol., 140.

benevolent women of Jerusalem, and brought to those condemned to this punishment.

In this view of the matter, there were two potions offered to the Lord before He was nailed to the cross; one of wine and gall, offered, as said by Lightfoot, "for greater mockage and out of rancor"; this He tasted but would not drink; and one of wine and myrrh, which He did not take because of its stupefying effect. Others, however, think that Matthew and Mark refer to the same potion, "myrrh" and "gall" being general terms for bitter substances, and put here for the whole class. (So Alexander; Keil, "the same drink with different name.")

The Inscription. It was customary with the Romans to affix to the cross an inscription or superscription — *titulus*, τίτλος, αἰτία, ἐπιγραφή — giving the name of the criminal and the nature of his crime. Whether, written upon a tablet, it was borne before the criminal, or hung upon his neck, or was attached to the cross, is uncertain; but, on reaching the place of execution, it was set up over his head. As this inscription is differently given by the Evangelists, it has been conjectured that it was differently written in the Greek, Latin, and Hebrew.[1] Pilate, who as judge prepared the inscription, took occasion to gratify his scorn of the Jews who had so thwarted him; and his short and decisive answer, when he was requested by them to change it, "What I have written, I have written," shows the bitterness of his resentment. Greswell and Edersheim suppose this request may have been made before the arrival at Calvary, but probably it was after the cross was set up. It seems to have been a formal request, probably made at the Prætorium by the chief priests in a body.

We give the superscription in a tabular form:

Matt. xxvii. 37.	Mark xv. 26.	Luke xxiii. 38.	John xix. 19.
This is Jesus The KING OF THE JEWS.	The KING OF THE JEWS.	This is The KING OF THE JEWS.	Jesus of Nazareth The KING OF THE JEWS.

The designation of the offense is the same in all the Evangelists, — "The King of the Jews"; the words before it are merely introductory or explanatory, and might have been wholly omitted, as by Mark, without leaving less clear the nature of the offense or the person of the offender. Probably Pilate wrote it in Latin, the official tongue; and then himself or another translated it into Hebrew, the

---

[1] Pearson on The Creed, Art. 4. Langen, 323.

language of the land; and into Greek, which was very generally spoken, especially by the Jews from other countries.[1] That Pilate was justified in setting up this inscription is shown in the fact that this was the accusation of the rulers (Luke xxiii. 2), and the ground on which he had condemned Him.

From the silence of the Evangelists as to any inscriptions over the malefactors, it cannot be inferred that there were none. It is said that it was by these that the Empress Helena (326 A. D.) was first able to distinguish the cross of the Lord.

The two Malefactors. With Jesus were crucified two malefactors, of whom we know nothing, but who may have been companions of Barabbas.[2] One early tradition makes them to have been two robbers, named Titus and Dumachus, whom Jesus met in Egypt; and it is said that He then predicted that both should be crucified with Him.[3] Another tradition gives their names as Gestas and Dysmas. It is probable that both were Jews, and certainly the penitent one, as appears from his request to the Lord. Some have conjectured that he had been earlier one of His followers, but had fallen away. The Lord's position between the two was probably directed by Pilate to spite the priests and to cast contempt on their Messianic hopes; but it may have been done by the soldiers; it is not likely that the priests directed in the matter. Greswell (iii. 246), from John xix. 32, 33, conjectures that the crosses of the two malefactors looked to the west, but that of Jesus to the east. Tradition makes His to have looked to the west.[4]

The prayer, "Father, forgive them, for they know not what they do," given only by Luke (xxiii. 34), was probably spoken while the soldiers were nailing Him to the cross, or immediately after. It doubtless embraced all who took part in His crucifixion — not only the soldiers, who were compelled to obey the orders given them, but the Jewish priests and elders, and the Roman governor — all who had caused His sufferings.

The garments of the crucified belonged to the soldiers as their spoil. After the four appointed to this duty had divided His garments, they sat down to watch the crosses.

---

[1] See Merivale. Rom. Hist., iv. 392; McClel., 506; Jones, 409.

[2] As to the abundance of thieves and robbers at this time and its causes, see Lightfoot on Matt. xxvii. 38.　　　　　[3] Hofmann, 176.

[4] Hofmann, 376.

FRIDAY, 15TH NISAN, 7TH APRIL, 783. A. D. 30.

While hanging upon the cross, the multitudes, as they pass by, revile and deride Him. In this mockery the high priests and scribes and elders, and even the two malefactors, join. From the cross, beholding His mother standing near by with John, He commends him to her as her son, and her to him as his mother; and John takes her to his own house. Darkness now overspreads the land from the sixth to the ninth hour, and during this period He suffers in silence. Afterward drink is given Him, and after He has drunk He commends His spirit to God, and dies. At this moment the veil of the temple is rent, the earth shakes, the rocks are rent, and graves opened. The centurion bears witness that He was the Son of God, and the multitude return smiting their breasts.	MATT. xxvii. 39–44. MARK xv. 29–32. LUKE xxiii. 35–43. JOHN xix. 25–27. MATT. xxvii. 45–56. MARK xv. 33–41. LUKE xxiii. 44–49. JOHN xix. 28–30.

The place of crucifixion being near the city, and great multitudes being gathered at the feast, it was natural that crowds should come to look upon Him, whom all knew by reputation, and many in person. From the time of the crucifixion to the time when the darkness began, sufficient time elapsed to allow His enemies, who hastened to the spot, to behold Him upon the cross. Matthew (xxvii. 39–44) divides those who reviled Him into three classes: the passers-by; the chief priests, elders, and scribes; and the malefactors. (So Mark xv. 29–32.) Luke says, that "the rulers with the people derided Him," which implies that the rulers began the mockery. He adds that "the soldiers also mocked Him, coming to Him, and offering Him vinegar." Some, as Stier, would identify this with the offer to Him of the mixed wine as He was about to be nailed to the cross; some, as Lichtenstein, to the giving of the vinegar just before His death. Most probably, however, it is to be distinguished from these, and refers to something done a little before the darkness began; perhaps, as the soldiers were eating their dinner near the cross.[1] The vinegar was doubtless the sour wine, or *posca*, which they usually drank. Their offers were in derision, no wine being actually given. It is called by Meyer, "a mocking offer, not an actual giving to drink."

---

[1] Greswell, Alford. Keil regards it as a summary statement of the mockings to which He was subject.

It is not certain whether both of the malefactors reviled the Lord, or but one.   Matthew and Mark speak of both; Luke, of but one.   According to some, both joined at first in the general derision; but, beholding the godlike patience and forbearance of Jesus, and knowing on what grounds He was condemned, one repented, and began to reprove his more wicked companion.[1] The obvious objection, however, to this is, that the first act of one so converted could scarcely be to reprove in another what he had but a few moments before been guilty of himself.   This, perhaps, is more plausible than sound.   Most, after Augustine, suppose that Matthew and Mark speak in general terms of them as a class of the persons that joined in deriding Jesus, but without meaning to say that both actually derided Him.[2]   At what time the words were spoken by the Lord to the penitent thief, we are not told.   Most place them before His words to His mother and to John (John xix. 25–27).[3]   They were thus the second words spoken from the cross.

We cannot determine whether the mother of Jesus, or any of the women that followed Him from Galilee, or any of the apostles, was present at the time when He was nailed to the cross; but if not there, some of them soon after came, doubtless hoping to comfort Him by their presence.   For a time, they would naturally stand at a distance till the first outbreaks of anger and mockery were past, and His chief enemies, satiated with the spectacle, had withdrawn.   The statement of the Synoptists (Matt. xxvii. 55, 56; Mark xv. 40, 41; Luke xxiii. 49), that His acquaintance, and the women that followed Him from Galilee, stood afar off, seems to refer to a later period, and after the darkness; perhaps, to the moment of His death.   The incident narrated by John of the commendation of the Virgin mother to him, may thus have been a little before the darkness began; and after this the disciples, terrified by it and by the signs that attended His death, may not have dared to approach the cross. Krafft, however (150), supposes that it was after the darkness

---

[1] So early, many; recently, Lange.

[2] Ebrard, Da Costa, Lichtenstein, Edersheim.   Meyer finds two traditions; and Alford, that Matthew and Mark report more generally and less accurately than Luke. For a statement of opinions, see Bynaeus, iii. 367.

[3] Ebrard, Stier, Da Costa, Greswell.

that His mother and John, with the other women, approached Him, and that the Synoptists refer to an earlier period.

According to many, John at once took Mary to his home, or to the house he was occupying during the feast; for it does not appear otherwise that he had any house in Jerusalem of his own.[1] A confirmation of this is found in the fact that the Synoptists do not mention her name among those that beheld afar off at the hour of His death. It has, therefore, been inferred that Jesus, in his compassion, would spare her the pain of seeing His dying agonies, and so provided that she be taken away.[2] But it may be questioned whether the words, "And from that hour that disciple took her unto his own house," mean any more than that ever after this she was a member of John's household, and was treated by him as a mother.[3] But if John then led Mary away from the place of crucifixion, he must afterward have returned, as he declares himself to have been an eye-witness of the piercing of the side, and the flowing out of the blood and water (xix. 35). Whether he was the only apostle present at the Lord's death, is matter of conjecture. This is supposed by Stier; but there is no good reason why others, if not daring to approach near, should not have looked on from a distance.

That the darkness, which is not mentioned by John, was no natural darkening of the sun, but a supernatural event, is recognized by all who do not wholly deny the supernatural element in the Gospel narratives. The reading in Luke xxiii. 44, 45 is in question. (For the T. R., "The sun was darkened," Tisch., W. and H., and others substitute τοῦ ἡλίου ἐκλειπόντος. R. V., "The sun's light failing." See T. G. Lex., ἐκλείπω. Meyer regards the last reading as a gloss.) But the new reading does not affect the miraculous element, as it does not explain the cause of the sun's light failing. The attempt to bring it into connection with the eclipse mentioned by Phlegon of Tralles, has been already mentioned; and that it could have been caused in such a way is disproved by the fact that it was then full moon.[4] Some, however, would connect it with the earth

---

[1] Townson, Greswell, Stier, Meyer.

[2] Bengel.

[3] Luthardt, ii. 421; Lichtenstein, 448.

[4] The attempt of Seyffarth to show that the Jews might then have kept the Passover on the 25th March, finds no defenders. See Winer, ii. 482: Langen, 342.

quake, and explain it as the deep gloom that not unfrequently precedes such convulsions of nature.[1] But this supposes that the earthquake was a mere natural event, whereas this also was plainly extraordinary. Meyer: "Not an ordinary earthquake, but a supernatural phenomenon." The darkness began at the sixth hour, or twelve M., and continued till the ninth, or three P. M. According to Caspari, the Lord was crucified at the sixth hour, and then the darkness began. Hengstenberg also makes the darkness to have begun at the time of the crucifixion, but at the third hour. Whether the darkness came gradually, and gradually ceased, is not said; many held its beginning and ending to have been sudden. The forms of expression, "over all the land," $\pi\tilde{a}\sigma a\nu$ $\tau\dot{\eta}\nu$ $\gamma\tilde{\eta}\nu$ (Matthew), "over the whole land," $\H{o}\lambda\eta\nu$ $\tau\dot{\eta}\nu$ $\gamma\tilde{\eta}\nu$ (Mark and Luke), do not determine how far the darkness extended. Many would confine it to the land of Judæa, as our version does, except in Luke where it is rendered, "over all the earth."[2] If, however, it extended beyond Judæa, the phrase "whole earth" need not be taken in its most literal sense, but is to be regarded as a general expression, embracing the countries adjacent.[3] Some, however, would extend it over all that part of the earth on which the sun was then shining.[4]

That during this period of darkness many of the bystanders should have left the place of crucifixion and returned to the city, is probable, though not stated. Stier, however, affirms: "No man dares to go away, all are laid under a spell; others, rather, are attracted to the place." But when we consider that the Lord's enemies would naturally construe the darkness as a sign of God's anger against Him, if they gave it any supernatural character, any such fear can scarce be attributed to them; nor does it appear in their subsequent conduct. That some of the spectators remained, appears from Matthew's words (xxvii. 47), that there were some standing there when He called for Elias. (See also Luke xxiii. 48.) It is probable, though not explicitly stated, that the darkness began to disperse a few

---

[1] Paulus, Handbuch, iii. 764; *contra*, Nebe, ii. 302.

[2] So Ebrard, Olshausen, A. Clark, Keil, Norton, who renders it, "over the whole country."

[3] Meyer, Lange, Nebe.

[4] So Alford, who makes the fact of the darkness at Jerusalem all that the Evangelists testify to as within their personal knowledge.

moments before the Lord's death, and that the returning light
emboldened His enemies to renew their mockeries.[1]

The cry of Jesus, "Eli, Eli, lama sabachthani"—"My God,
my God, why hast thou forsaken me?" was about the ninth
hour; either a little before the cessation of the darkness,[2] or
just after its cessation.[3] So far as appears, during the three
hours of gloom, the Lord was silent, and doubtless all were
silent around Him. But by whom were His words understood
as a call for Elias? From the similarity of sound, the Roman
soldiers might have so misunderstood Him; but it is not probable that they knew much of the current Jewish expectations
respecting Elias as the forerunner of the Messiah. Lightfoot
explains it, that the word "Eli" is not properly Syriac, and
thus was strange to the Syrian ear and deceived the standers-by.
But such a misunderstanding on the part of the Jews, whether
they were from Judæa or from other lands, is not easily credible. Some affirm that the Jews, terrified by the darkness, now
began to fear that the day of God's judgment was actually at
hand; and, in their superstitious terror, naturally interpreted
Christ's words as a call for him, the prophet whose coming was
closely connected in their minds with the great day of God.[4]
But this is not consistent with what follows. The general view,
therefore, seems to be the right one, that they were Jews, who
wilfully perverted His meaning, and made the cry of distress an
occasion of new insult and ridicule.[5]

In immediate connection with the words of the bystanders,
"this man calleth for Elias," one of them is said by Matthew
and Mark to have run, and taking a sponge and filling it with
vinegar, gives Him a drink. This act, which in the Synoptists
seems unexplained, may have followed from His words which
are recorded only by John (xix. 28), "I thirst." We may thus
arrange the events: Immediately after His exclamation, "My
God, why hast thou forsaken me?" He adds, "I thirst." One
of those present, perhaps a soldier, perhaps a spectator, moved
by a sudden feeling of compassion, prepares the vinegar or sour

---

[1] Stier, Lichtenstein.
[2] Stier, Ellicott.   [3] Greswell.
[4] Olshausen, Lange, Jones.
[5] Meyer, Alexander, Alford, Friedlieb, Ellicott, Keil.

wine, the drink of the Roman soldiers, which was at hand, and makes ready to give Him to drink. While doing this, the others call upon him to wait a little, that they may see whether Elias will come to save Him (Matt. xxvii. 49). He, however, gives Jesus the drink, and then adds, either to conceal his compassionate impulse or as ashamed of it, "Let alone, now we will wait for Elias" (Mark xv. 36). Thus the words of Matthew will be those of the spectators; those of Mark the words of the giver of the drink. John (xix. 29) omits this mockery, and merely says in general terms, "they filled a sponge with vinegar," etc. Luke's words (xxiii. 36) may be referred to earlier mockeries.[1]

After Jesus had received the vinegar, He cried out with a loud voice, "It is finished." The Evangelist adds, "And He bowed His head and gave up the ghost" (John xix. 30). Luke (xxiii. 46) narrates that "When He had cried with a loud voice, He said, Father, into Thy hands I commend my spirit: and having said this, He gave up the ghost." Matthew and Mark both mention that He cried with a loud voice, but do not relate what He said. There can be little doubt that His words given by John, "It is finished," were spoken before those given by Luke, "Father, into thy hands I commend my spirit."[2] Having taken the vinegar, which gave Him a momentary relief from His thirst, He says, feeling that the end was at hand, "It is finished." He now turns to God, and, addressing to Him His dying prayer, bows his head and dies.

The order of the words spoken by our Lord from the cross may be thus given: — Before the darkness: 1st. His prayer for His enemies. 2d. His promise to the penitent thief. 3d. His charge to His mother and to John. During the darkness: 4th. His cry of distress to God. After the darkness: 5th. His exclamation, "I thirst." 6th. His declaration, "It is finished." 7th. The final commendation of His spirit to God.[3] Ebrard would thus arrange the first three: 1st. His prayer for His ene-

---

[1] See Stier, viii. 14–18; Alexander, *in loco.* As to the kind of drink given Him, and the motive with which it was given, see various suppositions in Bynaeus, iii. 423. As to the hyssop branch on which the sponge was put, see Royle, Jour. Sac. Lit., Oct., 1849.

[2] Meyer, Stier, Da Costa, Alford; *contra*, Neander.

[3] Stier, Greswell, and many.

mies.   2d. His charge to His mother and John.   3d. His promise to the penitent thief.   Krafft's order is as follows: 1st. His
prayer for His enemies.   2d. His promise to the penitent thief.
3. His cry of distress to God.   4th. His charge to His mother
and John.   5th. His exclamation, "I thirst."   6th. "It is finished."   7th. Commendation of His spirit to God.

The quaking of the earth and the rending of the veil of the
temple and of the rocks, appear from Matthew and Mark to have
been at the same instant as His death.   Luke (xxiii. 45), who
mentions only the rending of the veil, speaks as if it took place
when the sun was darkened, but his language is general.   Meyer's interpretation of the statement that "there was a darkness
over all the earth until the ninth hour," as denoting only a partial obscuration of the sun, but that at the ninth hour it "was
darkened," and wholly disappeared from sight, and that at the
same moment the veil of the temple was rent, has little substantial in its favor.   Darkness, in which the sun was still visible,
could scarcely be so called.   The first statement, verse 44, is the
effect, the second, verse 45, the cause.[1]   Perhaps the darkness
may have deepened in intensity to near its close.   That the rending of the veil could not be ascribed to an earthquake, however
violent, is apparent.   There were two veils, one before the holy
and one before the most holy place (Exod. xxvi. 31–36).   It is
generally agreed that the latter is here meant.

The account given by Matthew only (xxvii. 52, 53), of the
opening of the graves and appearing of many bodies of the
saints, some, as Norton, have rejected as an interpolation.   There
is, however, no doubt as to the genuineness of the text.   The
graves seem to have been those in the immediate vicinity of
Jerusalem, but the Evangelist does not say this.   That those
who arose are called "saints" — ἅγιοι,— does not determine
who are meant; whether some who had died recently, perhaps
since Christ began His ministry, or some who died long before
and had been buried there, perhaps patriarchs and prophets.
Some of the early fathers affirmed that all the saints from the
beginning arose.   From the fact that they appeared to many,
the presumption is, that they had not long been dead, and thus

---

[1] Oosterzee, *in loco.*

were recognized by those to whom they appeared.   That their
resurrection was after Christ's resurrection, although the opening of their tombs was at His death, best harmonizes with the
scope of the narrative.   This, however, is questioned by Meyer,
who supposes the Evangelists to say that they came out of the
graves at His death, but did not enter the holy city till after
His resurrection;[1] after He had arisen they appeared openly,
their resurrection thus giving force and meaning to His.   But it
was the Lord's resurrection, not His death, that opened the gates
of Hades.   Dying, the rocks were rent and the doors of the
sepulchres were opened ; but, rising, He gave life to the dead.[2]
Da Costa (429) places, however, the opening of the graves also
subsequent to the resurrection.   Whether those thus raised were
raised in the immortal and incorruptible body, and soon ascended
to heaven; or whether, like others, they died again, we have no
means of determining.   The language, they "appeared unto
many," implies that they, like the Lord Himself after His resurrection, were not seen by all, but only by those to whom they
wished to manifest themselves.[3]

   The impression made upon the centurion by all the wonderful events accompanying the Lord's death was such that he
openly testified his conviction that Jesus was "The Son of God"
(Matt. and Mark).   "Certainly this was a righteous man"
(Luke).   How much these expressions may have meant, for
probably at different times he uttered both, is not clear ; but
probably knowing that He was condemned by the Jews because
He made Himself the Son of God, he meant that Jesus was
more than mere man — a demi-god (Meyer) — and was wrongly
condemned.[4]   We cannot suppose that the mystery of the Incarnation was known to him.

---

[1] So Bynaeus, Nebe.

[2] Calvin, Lightfoot, Whitby, A. Clarke, Calmet, Greswell, Krafft, Ebrard Bengel,
Alford.

[3] For early opinions, see Calmet, translated in Journal Sac. Lit. 1848, vol. i.   See
also Lardner, ix. 328; Sepp, vi. 401.

[4] The name of this centurion is given by tradition as Longinus, and that becoming
a believer, he was afterwards bishop of Cappadocia.   Hofmann, 380.

Friday, 15th Nisan, 7th April, 783.   A. D. 30.

Soon after the Lord's death, the chief priests come to   John xix. 31–37.
Pilate, requesting that the bodies may be taken down
before sunset, because the next day is the Sabbath.
Obtaining their request, the legs of the two malefactors
are broken to hasten their death; but Jesus, being found
already dead, is pierced with a spear in the side.   At this   Matt. xxvii. 57–60
time, Joseph of Arimathea goes to Pilate, and inform-   John xix. 38–42.
ing him that Jesus is already dead, asks His body   Mark xv. 42–46.
for burial; and Pilate, after satisfying himself that   Luke xxiii. 50–54.
He is actually dead, orders the body to be given him.
Aided by Nicodemus, Joseph takes the body and winding
it in linen clothes with spices, lays it in his own sepul-   Luke xxiii. 55, 56.
chre in a garden near the cross, and shuts up the sepul-
chre.   Some women beholding where He is laid, and re-
turning home, prepare spices and ointments that they   Matt. xxvii. 61.
may embalm Him after the Sabbath is past.   During   Mark xv. 47.
the Sabbath the council obtains permission from Pilate
to seal up the sepulchre, and set a watch, lest the disci-   Matt. xxvii. 62–66.
ples should steal the body.

It was the custom of the Romans to permit the body to remain on the cross till it was consumed by the birds or beasts or
wasted by corruption. (Pearson, The Creed, Art. 4.)   But it was
an express command of the law (Deut. xxi. 23), that the body
should not remain all night upon the tree, but must be taken
down and buried the same day.[1]   Aside from this command of
the law, it was probably thought desirable by the rulers that
the body of Jesus should be, as early as possible, removed from
public sight.   It is not certain whether the Jews who came to
Pilate knew that He was actually dead; but their request that
the legs of the crucified might be broken, implies that they did
not.   If so, they must have come to Pilate about three p. m., or
a little before His death.   If, however, they did know that He
was dead, as they might from the marked circumstances that attended the act of dissolution, their request had reference to the
two malefactors, who were still living; and perhaps also was designed to make the death of Jesus certain.[2]   That the natural
effect of the breaking of their legs would be to hasten death is
plain, and this was the end the Jews sought.   Usually the

[1] Josephus, War, iv. 5. 2; Josh. x. 26.
[2] So Meyer.

Romans did not in this, or any other way, hasten it; though sometimes the crucified were subjected to personal injuries, as pounding with hammers or breaking of limbs, in order to increase their sufferings. The term *crurifragium*, though literally applicable only to the breaking of the legs, and which sometimes constituted a separate punishment, seems to have been applied to various other acts which tended to increase the pain, and so to shorten life; and may have included the use of the spear (Zoeckler, 418.) The Jews did not wish to increase their sufferings, but to hasten death; and we may well suppose that the soldiers were directed, if the breaking of the legs should not prove sufficient, to use other means.[1] Whether, in addition to the breaking of the legs of the two malefactors, other violent means were used, is not certain; but the narrative does not imply it.

The object of piercing the Lord's side was not so much to cause death as to make sure that he was already dead. Which side was pierced, is not said; and the painters, as well as the commentators, have been divided in opinion; most, however, suppose the left side. This, as will be seen, has a bearing on the cause of the Lord's death. With what intent does the Evangelist mention the flowing out of the blood and the water? Does he mention it as a simple physiological fact, and in proof of the Lord's death; or as a supernatural event to which he attaches some special significance? And here some questions arise as to the nature of the Lord's death, and its physical cause.

First of all is the inquiry, whether He died as other crucified persons died, death being the natural consequence of his bodily sufferings; or whether He gave up His life by an immediate act of His own will, or by an immediate act of His Father in answer to His prayer. The latter view seems to have prevailed in the early Church, though by no means universally. (See Stroud, *Physical Cause of Christ's Death*, London, 1847.) Of recent writers, Tholuck says: "By an act of power the Redeemer actually separated His spirit from His body, and placed it, as a deposit, in His Father's keeping." Alford observes: "It was His own act, no feeling the approach of

---

[1] Friedlieb, Archäol., 164.

death, as some, not apprehending the matter, have commented, but a determined delivering up His spirit to the Father." This Stier, in like manner, says: "He dies, as the act of His will, in full vigor of life." In like way speak Greswell, Alexander, Jones, Baumgarten. If this opinion be correct, and Jesus died by His own act, it is not easy to see how it can be said that He was put to death by the Jews. His crucifixion was indeed, in the large sense the cause of His death, but the actual separation of soul and body was by His own volition; it would have come in process of time, but He anticipated it. There is the strong objection to this, that it clearly tends to the denial of His true humanity, and throws an air of unreality over all His sufferings. That which would have been suicide in another, is not to be imputed to Him who became very man for our salvavation (Heb. ii. 17). We, therefore, conclude that, though He voluntarily gave Himself to death (John x. 17, 18), and submitted to be nailed to the cross, yet that death came to Him as to the two malefactors, naturally, not supernaturally; and was the consequence of His physical sufferings aggravated by mental distress.[1]

Many, however, have found difficulty in explaining in this way the quickness of the Lord's death. He was not upon the cross, at the longest, more than six hours; while it is well known that the great majority of the crucified live at least twelve hours; many, one or two days; and some, three or four days (Langen). But there seems no valid reason why we may not attribute this speedy decease to the physical weakness caused by His previous bodily and mental sufferings, superadded to the ordinary agonies of crucifixion. That those sufferings were most intense. we know from the account given of the hour passed at Gethsemane; and that the Lord, already exhausted by His great spiritual conflicts with the power of darkness, by the excitement and fatigue of that awful night, and by the scourging inflicted upon Him, should have died so much sooner than was

---

[1] So in substance, Pearson, Bloomfield, Stroud, Ellicott. We may perhaps find the word ἐκπνέω — (Mark and Luke), "gave up the ghost,"— proof of a life gradually ebbing away, a breathing slower and slower to the end. (See Nebe, ii. 365.) The expression in John (xix. 30) that "He gave up His spirit" (R. V.) no more shows that He died by His own volition at that moment than Stephen's words (Acts vii. 17), "Lord Jesus, receive my spirit," show that he died by his free act.

usually the case, can excite no surprise. Nor do the objections
based upon the natural vigor and healthfulness of the Lord's
body, the short duration of His mental agony in the garden,
and the proof of unabated physical strength shown by the loud-
ness of voice with which He uttered His last words upon the
cross, seem of much weight.[1]

Those who regard the Lord's death as a natural event, yet
one whose quick consummation is not adequately explained by
the pains attendant upon His crucifixion, are forced to give another explanation. Of these, several have been presented.
One is that of Stroud, that the immediate physical cause was
rupture of the heart, caused by the great mental suffering He
endured (pp. 74, 143). Another attributes His death to the
piercing of the spear, but this is so directly at variance with the
narrative (John xix. 30, 33) that after receiving the vinegar
" He bowed His head and gave up the ghost," and that the
soldiers, when they came to break His legs. saw that He was
already dead, that this explanation may be at once dismissed.
But, as the explanation of Stroud, which has its chief support
in the flowing of the blood and water from the Lord's pierced
side, has found much acceptance, we must briefly consider it.

Does John here narrate a natural or a supernatural event ?
And with what purpose is it mentioned ? That he attached
some special importance to it, is apparent from his words (verse
35) which seem chiefly to refer to it, though the reference may
be to all related by him in verses 32–34. But commentators
are by no means agreed in opinion that the Evangelist regarded
it as supernatural.[2]

Let us suppose that the Evangelist regarded the flowing
of the blood and water as a natural event. Why did he mention it ? Some say, to prove the validity of the Lord's body
as against the Docetæ. (So Coleridge in Stroud: "The effusion showed the human nature. It was real blood, and not a
mere celestial ichor, as the Phantasmatists allege." So, in

---

[1] As to the pains of crucifixion, and their natural effects in destroying life, see
Richter in Friedlieb, Archäol., 155.

[2] On the one side may be mentioned Calvin who says: " *Hallucinati sunt quidam
miraculum hic fingentes;* in the same way, Clarke, Tholuck, Ebrard, Ewald, Alford;
on the other side, Lightfoot, Bengel, Greswell, Meyer, Luthardt, Godet.

substance, Alford.)   But the reality of His body had been proved in a thousand ways during His life; and if His body, sensible to touch and sight, was a phantom, so much more easily might be this seeming blood and water.   But granting that the intention of the Evangelists was to show the reality of His death, how was it thus shown?   Are proper blood and water here meant, *aqua pura et vera, sanguis purus et verus,* as said by Bengel?   No, for this would remove it into the region of the supernatural.   Have we, then, in these terms, merely a hendiadys for reddish lymph, or bloody water?   This is inadmissible.   Does the apostle then mean blood that had decomposed, and was thus resolved into crassamentum and serum, or the thick red part of the blood and the aqueous transparent part?   This is the view taken by many; and it is said that we have in this, conclusive proof not only of His death, but that He had also been some time dead, since the blood had begun to decompose.   Thus Neander says: "I must believe that John, as an eye-witness, meant to prove that Christ was really dead from the nature of the blood that flowed from the wound."

Admitting, for the moment, that the blood and water were the constituent parts of blood now decomposed, whence came they?   According to Stroud, from the pericardium, into which, through the rupture of the heart, there was a great effusion of blood, which was there decomposed.   The pericardium being pierced by the spear, it flowed in crassamentum and serum, "a full stream of clear watery liquid, intermixed with clotted blood, exactly corresponding to the clause of the sacred narrative."   Ebrard (563) supposes it to have been extravasated blood, that, flowing into some of the internal cavities of the chest, there decomposed, and these cavities being opened by the spear, the constituent parts made their escape.

Against all these explanations which are based upon the coagulation of the blood, and aside from the physiological objections to which they are open, we find an invincible difficulty in the words of the Psalmist, that God would not suffer His Holy One to see corruption ; and in the declaration of St. Peter, that "His flesh did not see corruption."   His body was not to see corruption, or, in other words, the usual processes of decay were not to commence in it. Decomposition of the blood can scarcely be considered as other than the initial step of corruption. The full separation of His soul and His body must take place ; but, after this, he "that had the power of death" had no more power over the Holy One.

The explanations of the Grüners who think the Lord not wholly dead, and of the Bartholines,[1] are free from this difficulty, since they do not affirm a coagulation of the blood. The former suppose that both pericardium and heart were pierced by the spear, and that from the former came the water, and from the latter the blood. But if it be admitted that there was a considerable quantity of water in the pericardium, it is difficult to explain in this way the flowing of the blood, since the heart of a dead person is usually emptied of its blood; or, if any remains, it would flow very slowly; and to say that Jesus was not wholly dead when pierced with the spear, is contrary to the sacred narrative. (Tholuck *in loco*.)

The second explanation, that of the Bartholines, supposes that the water and blood came from one or both of the pleural sacs. It is said that, during the sufferings of crucifixion, a bloody serum was effused in these sacs from which, when pierced by the spear, it flowed out. But aside from the fact that such an effusion of bloody serum or lymph as the narrative demands is not proved in cases of crucified persons, if indeed, in any case whatever ; there is the further objection that such bloody serum does not answer to the Evangelist's "blood and water."

The view of Stroud that the Lord died of rupture of the heart, has found some medical support.[2]

---

[1] See Stroud, 135–137.

[2] Prof. Simpson (in Hanna "The last Days of Christ," N. Y., 1864, app.) endorses it "as fundamentally correct." "In rupture of the heart, the blood escapes from the interior of the heart into the cavity of the large surrounding heart-sac or *pericardium*, which has been found in dissection to contain three or more pounds of blood accumulated in it and separated into red clots and limpid serum, or blood and water." Dr. Struthers, who agrees with Simpson, speaks of the form of death as "a new illustration of the awful agony which our Redeemer must have suffered." But, on the other hand, it is said by another physician, Biglie, that "rupture of the heart is comparatively a rare affection, and that the cases on record are limited to those advanced in life, or to such as have been laboring under some degeneration of the structure of the organ." Of those accepting Stroud's view, are Ewald, Sepp, Friedlieb. Rejecting it, are Westcott, who thinks Stroud's theory "inadequate and inconsistent with the facts"; and Luthardt, who says that "all the attempts to explain the manner of His death are useless." In this general result agree Weiss, Ellicott, Langen, and most.

We conclude, then, that the attempts to explain this phenomenon as a merely natural event, and upon physiological grounds, are by no means satisfactory, and that we must regard it as something supernatural.[1] It is not within our scope to enquire as to its special significance. It may have been a sign that the body of the Lord was not under the common law of corruption. His spirit had departed from it, and with it that vital energy which held together its constituent elements, yet disorganization and dissolution did not begin. According to Lange, it was a sign that a change in the body preparatory to the resurrection had already begun ; the power of God was already working in it to prepare it for immortality and incorruptibility. The same view is taken by Godet : " The body which sin had never tainted, moved forward to the resurrection without having to pass through dissolution."

To explain the facts that the Lord died so soon after the nailing to the cross, and yet that He still had much bodily strength, as shown in " the loud voice " with which He commended His spirit into His Father's hands,[2] can be satisfactorily done without attributing His death to the spear-thrust. He was dead before this ; this thrust was only to make sure that He was dead. To explain the speedy death, we need not say that He put an end to His life by an act of His will, or that He died of rupture of the heart caused by the mental agony He suffered. The burden that had been upon Him all the week of the Passion, His contests with His enemies, the treachery of Judas, the desertion of the apostles, the denials of Peter, the distress in Gethsemane, the scourging and abuse, the pain of the cross, the hiding of the Father's face — all these serve to show that the Lord died, as other men die, through the entire exhaustion of the vital forces. It was His last expiring effort when, summoning all His strength, He commended His spirit unto His Father.

It was in the power of governors of provinces to grant private burial to criminals when requested by friends, and this was

---

[1] It is said by Cardinal Wiseman, *Lectures*, 163, that this was " the concurrent sentiment of all antiquity "; see also, Westcott, additional note on John xix. for patristic interpretations.

[2] Luke xxiii. 46, McClellan supposes that the words " It is finished " were spoken in a loud voice, but the commendation of His spirit, in a low tone.

usually done unless they were very mean and infamous.¹ But
for the request of Joseph of Arimathæa, a member of the Sanhedrin, the Lord's body would probably have been buried in some
place appropriated to criminals, perhaps where the two malefactors were buried.   "They that were put to death by the council were not to be buried in the sepulchres of their fathers; but
two burying places were appointed by the council, one for those
slain by the sword and strangled, the other for those who were
stoned or burnt." ²   Pilate could have had no objection to granting Joseph's request, as, on the one hand, his position as a member of the Sanhedrin entitled him to a favorable hearing; and,
on the other, he was not unwilling that the innocent victim
should have an honorable burial.   That Joseph made the request at the solicitation of the disciples, as said by Weiss, is
possible, but is not intimated. (Mark xv. 45.) He gave the
body to Joseph; or, more literally, made a gift or present of the
body to him.   According to Mark xv. 44, Pilate was surprised
that He was already dead; and, calling the centurion who as being
on the spot, was aware of His death (verse 39), made inquiries
how long He had been dead.

How is this coming of Joseph related to that of the Jews
(John xix. 31) who asked that the bodies might be taken down ?
We may suppose that the Jews, who desired that all the crucified
should be taken down before the Sabbath began, came about
3 P. M., before the coming of Joseph, and were ignorant of the
Lord's death.   Joseph may have stood near the cross and heard
His last words, and thus have known of His death as soon as
it occurred. He went to Pilate "when the even was come"
(Matt. xxvii. 57), or during the interval from 3–6 P. M., and
probably very soon after His death. Going to Pilate, he informs him of it, and the latter, knowing that sufficient time has
not elapsed for the execution of the order respecting the breaking of the legs, already given, or at least for their death after
their legs were broken, is surprised. The Jews, indeed, may
have made their request after Joseph had preferred his, and
Pilate may have given the soldiers orders to make sure that

¹ Pearson, Creed, 332 ; Weiss, iii. 377.
² Lightfoot on Matt. xxviii. 58.

Jesus was really dead ere He was given up for burial; but the former order is most probable. It is not necessary to suppose that Joseph knew of the permission already given to have the bodies taken down, though he might, as Luthardt thinks, have done so.

Joseph, having received permission to take the body, is aided by his servants or by the soldiers ; and, taking it down, they wrap it in linen clothes with " myrrh and aloes about an hundred pound weight," which the latter had brought, and lay it in a new sepulchre in a garden near at hand which belonged to Joseph.[1] It has been questioned whether the spices were actually used, because of the shortness of time, but John's words are express that the spices were used. It, however, remains doubtful whether the customary embalming was then perfected. Lardner (x. 368) remarks that "all was done, as may reasonably be supposed, after the best manner, by the hands of an apothecary or confectioner, or perfumer, skilled in performing funeral rites. There must have been many such at Jerusalem." But for this there was plainly no time. Norton [2] makes the transactions of anointing and burying the body to have occupied many hours, and the dawn of the Sabbath to have appeared ere all engaged in them had left the tomb. But it is more probable that Joseph and Nicodemus were themselves able to do all that was necessary to be done, for there is no reason to suppose that the body was embalmed in any Egyptian sense of that term. " The Egyptians filled the interior of the body with spices, but the Jews, who buried on the day of decease, only wrapped the body round with spices."[3] It is probable that all they could do was finished before the Sabbath began. If, however, the body was then properly prepared for its burial, why did the women, who " beheld the sepulchre and how the body was laid," prepare additional spices and ointments ? It could not well have been as said by Weiss, from ignorance of what Nicodemus had done. We must, therefore, suppose that this further anointing was something customary;[4] or that the first was imperfect, and this there-

---

[1] It is not certain that Nicodemus came till the body had been taken from the cross.

[2] Notes, 317.

[3] Michaelis on the Resurrection, 93; Greswell, iii. 260, note.

[4] Friedlieb, Archäol., 172.

fore necessary ; or that it was a mark of love which was not satisfied till it had brought superabundance.[1]

Some find a contradiction between Mark and Luke in that
the last speaks of preparing spices and ointments on Friday
before the Sabbath began, and the first, that they were bought
after the Sabbath was past. If we admit that the same women
are meant, which is not certain, it may be that their preparations
were not completed the first day and were resumed when the
Sabbath was over.

The Lord was laid in the tomb on Friday before sunset, and
nothing further could be done by the disciples, the next day being the Sabbath when all were to rest according to the commandment.   But, although He was dead and buried, the rulers
were not at ease, and the chief priests and Pharisees came to
Pilate desiring that the door of the sepulchre might be sealed,
and a watch set, to prevent the disciples from stealing the body;
alleging, as the ground of their fear, His words, " After three
days I will rise again."   At what time this request was made, is
in question.   It is said by some that they went to Pilate on the
evening following the burial, perhaps two or three hours later,
the object being to secure the body before the darkness made
its theft possible (so McKnight, Bucher, Jones). And if they
went to the palace, they would have been ceremonially defiled
and unable to eat the peace offering of that day. But the language of Matthew: " Now on the morrow," leads us rather to
think of the morning after, but at how early an hour we cannot
tell; nor do we know where they met Pilate, whether at his palace or not.   The whole proceeding was a violation of the sanctity of the Sabbath.

Meyer regards all this account as unhistorical, chiefly for the
reason that the Pharisees could not have heard Christ's predictions respecting His resurrection; or, at least, could not have
thought them worthy of attention; and that if the disciples did not
understand or believe these predictions, much less would His
enemies.   But this by no means follows.   He had openly

---

[1] Meyer, Greswell; Alex. on Mark xvi. 1. Lange regards the first as only for the
preservation of the body, and the second as the proper anointing.   Jones affirms that, as
Joseph and Nicodemus were secret disciples, the women had no acquaintance with them
and did not know their purpose.

spoken of His death and resurrection to His disciples (Matt. xvi. 21; xvii. 22, 23). This was then unintelligible to them, because they truly believed that He was the Christ who would over-come all His enemies; and when He was actually crucified, in their grief and despair all remembrance of His promise seems to have escaped them. To the Pharisees He had spoken of the sign of the prophet Jonah as to be fulfilled in Himself (Matt. xii. 40); and now that He was dead, they must have thought of its actual fulfillment. Besides, it is scarce possible that they should not, through some of the disciples, have heard of His words respecting His resurrection spoken to them. Judas must have known what his Lord said, and may have told the priests. They were far too sagacious not to take precautions against all possible contingencies. Even if they did not believe His resurrection possible, and had no faith in His words, still it was wise to guard against the stealing of the body. But it is not certain that they did not fear that He would rise. Did they not know of the resurrection of Lazarus? and might not He who then bade the dead arise, Himself come forth? In their state of mind, to seal the stone and set the watch was a very natural precaution.

But why was not the body, when taken from the cross, at once taken charge of by the Pharisees, and not delivered into the hands of His disciples? Very likely this may have been their purpose, and the request of Joseph for the body may have been something unknown and unexpected to them ; but as it was given to him by permission of Pilate they could not interfere. It was of no importance in what sepulchre it was placed, pro-vided it was secure; and doubtless they knew that it was in the sepulchre ere they sealed the stone. When the stone was sealed, is not said, but probably sometime during the Sabbath (Matt. xxvii. 62). "The prediction of our Lord was that He would rise the third day, and till it was approaching they would give themselves no concern about His body. The absence of it from the tomb before the commencement of that day would rather falsify the prediction than show the truth of it."[1] Perhaps they relied on the sanctity of the Sabbath as a sufficient

[1] Townson, 93.

preventive against His disciples, and thought no guard necessary
till the day was past.   Perhaps they supposed at first that with
His death all cause of apprehension from His disciples had vanished, and that afterward, seeing the boldness of Joseph and
Nicodemus in the matter of His burial, they began to reflect,
and this step occurred to them.   Of course it was in itself
wholly unimportant when the stone was sealed, provided only
that the body was then there.   There is no reason to believe
that they would give any publicity to their acts, and the women
who went to the sepulchre the next morning seem to have been
ignorant of the sealing of the stone and setting of the watch.

That the account is given by Matthew only, is readily explained from the fact that he wrote specially for the Jews,
among whom the report of stealing the body had been put in
circulation.   It is omitted by Mark and Luke, who wrote for
another class of readers.[1]

We give a summary of the events recorded as having taken place
during the thirty-six hours that elapsed from the burial to the resurrection.   They are few : the purchase of spices by the women from
Galilee after the burial on Friday afternoon, and before the Sabbath
began, or before sunset; the sealing of the sepulchre and setting a
watch sometime during the Sabbath; the purchase of more spices
after the Sabbath was ended, or after sunset of Saturday.   Whether
the visit of the two Marys to see the sepulchre (Matt. xxviii. 1) is to
be put at the close of the Sabbath, or on the morning following, is
a disputed point, and we must briefly examine it.   There are two
points, the time of their visit, and its purpose.

We read, A. V. : "In the end of the Sabbath, as it began to dawn
toward the first day of the week, came " etc. ; R. V. : " Now late on
the Sabbath day, as it began to dawn toward the first day of the
week, came " etc.   The interpretation depends mainly on the force of
the words 'Οψὲ δὲ σαββάτων.[2]   Do they mean,   "After the Sabbath was
ended," the length of time after being left undefined?   Or, "Late in
the Sabbath, but before its end " ?   (As to ὀψὲ, see T. G. Lex., *sub
voce*; Winer, Gram., 203.)   If we take it in the last sense, the two
Marys came to the sepulchre just before the close of the Sabbath,—
the sunset of Saturday.   In this way it is taken by Patritius (Lib.,
iii. 546) and by McClellan (512), who remarks: " The hour specified
undoubtedly belongs to Saturday evening, not to Sunday morning."

---

[1] See Michaelis on the Resurrection, 98.

[2] As to επιφώσκω, Meyer, *in loco*.

It is said by Westcott: "Mary Magdalene and the other Mary go to view the sepulchre just before 6 P. M. on Saturday"; and Edersheim: "It must remain uncertain whether Saturday evening or early Sunday morning is meant." But it is a valid objection to Saturday evening that, if the two women came at this time to see the sepulchre, they must have returned to their home again that same evening, or have remained watching at the tomb all the night. The former is said by McClellan: "They returned to Bethany"; the latter by Chrysostom (Hom. on Matt. 89). But this night-watch is intrinsically improbable. Seeing on their arrival the guard there, they must have known that no entrance was possible so long as the guard remained. If they departed and returned again at early dawn, we must put this departure and return between verses 1 and 2 of Matthew xxviii., of which he gives no hint. But the weight of authority is in favor of the received rendering. It is said by Meyer: "We are not to suppose Saturday evening to be intended, but far on in the Saturday night, toward daybreak on Sunday."[1]

The second point is the object of the women in this early visit to the sepulchre. By Matthew it is said that they came "to see the sepulchre"; by Mark and Luke that they might anoint the body. The discrepancy is unimportant as the one was preparatory to the other.

Golgotha and the Holy Sepulchre. The Lord was crucified at a place called in the Hebrew, Golgotha, and His body was laid in a sepulchre in a garden near by. Thus two points are before us : the place of the crucifixion and of the burial; but as these were near each other, both may be embraced in one enquiry. The site of this sepulchre has been much discussed and with great learning and ingenuity, but without leading to any certain result. For many centuries the Christian Church received, without question, the traditionary tomb beneath the dome of the present church of the Holy Sepulchre, as that to which He was borne, and from which He arose. Of this belief is still the great body of Christians. But a large number of modern travellers have been led, by a personal inspection of the spot, to doubt the tradition, and have brought very cogent arguments against it. Fortunately, here, as often, it is of little importance whether the traditionary site be or be not the true one. The fact of the

---

[1] So Rob., Licht., Gardiner, and most. It is rendered by Weizsäcker: Nach Ablauf des Sabbats aber in Morgengrauen des ersten Wochentages kamen, etc. For early opinions see Maldonatus, *in loco;* for later, Nebe, *Auferstehungsgeschichte.*

Lord's resurrection is a vital one, but not whether He arose from
a tomb in the valley of Jehosaphat, or on the side of Acra.   Nor
is, as affirmed by Williams,[1] "the credit of the whole Church
for fifteen hundred years in some measure involved in its ver-
acity."   Few will so press the infallibility of the Church as to
deny the possibility of its falling into a topographical error.   The
little value attached by the apostles to the holy places appears
from the brevity with which they speak of them when they allude
to them at all.   Not to the places of His birth and of His burial
would they turn the eyes of the early Christians, but to Himself
— the ever-living One, and now the great High Priest at the
right hand of God.

But however unimportant in itself, either as confirmatory of
the Gospel narratives, or as illustrating the Lord's words, still,
as a point that has so greatly interested men, it may not be
wholly passed by.   A brief statement of the question will therefore be given, that the chief data for a judgment may be in the
reader's possession.   It naturally presents itself, first, as a question of topography ; and second, of history.

The name of the place where He was crucified was Golgotha, a
skull — κρανίον, Vul. calvaria.   "The proper writing and pronunciation of this word," says Lightfoot, " had been Golgolta, but use had
now brought it to be uttered Golgotha."   The earlier opinion was that
it was so called, either because of the tradition that Adam was buried
here, and his skull found here; or that it was the common place
of execution; but in recent times the name is generally ascribed to
its shape, as resembling a human skull.

It may be questioned whether the tradition as to Adam's being
buried here was of Jewish or Christian origin; it is, therefore, of no
value in this discussion.   (Langen, 369, thinks it to have sprung
from the Christian doctrine as to the relation of the second to the
first Adam.)   That it was the place of execution was said by Jerome:
Locum decollatorum.   (Light., iii. 164; Greswell, iii. 243; Ewald, v.
484; so Stier.)   But it is at least doubtful whether the Jews had any
one place set apart as a place of public execution; this was not the
custom of the Orientals.   (Langen, 368; Riehm, 525.   But see Edersheim, ii. 585.)   As the crucifixion of the Lord was the act of the
Romans, it is most probable that their officers selected the spot where
it should take place, taking care only that it should be without the
walls, and in some conspicuous and public place, that the sight might

---

[1] Holy City. ii. 2.

terrify others. (Bib. Lex., ii. 506; Kitto, Bib. Cyc., i. 779.) But if
there was a fixed place for public executions, and the Lord was crucified
here, would a rich man, like Joseph, have had a garden there? This
is very unlikely. We may rather suppose that the Romans, according
to their custom, took the condemned to the nearest convenient place
in the suburbs of the city. That the place of the Lord's crucifixion
was one well known, appears from the use of the article (Luke xxiii.
33): "And when they came unto the place which is called 'The
skull,' there they crucified Him." R. V. (John xix. 17: "Unto the
place called 'The place of a skull.'" That it was a hill or mount
is nowhere said; Robinson affirms that neither Eusebius, nor Cyril, nor
Jerome, nor any of the historians of the fourth or fifth century so calls
it. The application of this term to the present Golgotha will be
noted later.

But if the other derivation of Golgotha be accepted that "it was
so called because its form resembled a skull" (T. G. Lex., *sub voce*),
then the idea of elevation is conveyed — a skull-shaped hill. It is
said by Maldonatus that Cyril of Jerusalem first presented this view —
a forma monticuli humano similis capiti, but gave it up as not reconcil-
able with the topography. This derivation is now generally held.
(Reland, Bengel, Bleek, Langen, Meyer, Luthardt, Godet, Edersheim;
Farrar undecided; Stier, against.)

Since the name gives us no definite information as to the site of
Golgotha, we must ask what site best conforms to the narrative. It
must answer to the following conditions: (*a*) It must have been without the city walls (John xix. 17; Matt. xxviii. 11; Heb. xiii. 12). (*b*)
It must have been near the city (John xix. 20). (*c*) It must have been
near a rock-hewn sepulchre (John xix. 41; Matt. xxvii. 60) which
was in a garden. (*d*) It must have been near some frequented road
(Matt. xxvii. 39; Mark xv. 29).

Two inquiries arise here: 1. How far the traditional Golgotha
answers to these conditions. 2. How far any other supposed site
answers to them.

1. (*a*) The place of crucifixion was without the city walls. The
site of the church of the Holy Sepulchre is within the present city
wall, but it is admitted that the present wall is not the same as then existed, and a chief point in dispute is as to the location of that wall.
Was the site of the Holy Sepulchre within or without it? Josephus
mentions three walls. (War, v. 4. 2.) With the first built by David
and Solomon, and embracing Mount Zion, and with the last built by
Agrippa after the Lord's death, we have no concern. The question
concerns only the position of the second wall, which was standing in
our Lord's day. To determine its course, Josephus gives us as data

the two termini — the gate Gennath and the Fortress Antonia.   He states also that the wall did not run in a straight line from one of these points to the other, but was curved and encircled the northern part of the city.

The fortress Antonia, one terminus, is well known; but where was the gate Gennath, the starting point?   The name indicates that it was a gate leading to a garden outside the first wall, or at least was near one.   The north line of the first wall in which was this gate, ran in nearly a straight line from the tower of Hippicus eastward to the temple wall, a distance, according to Robinson, of some 630 yards. It is generally agreed that Hippicus is to be identified with the modern citadel, the castle of David — El Kalah — near the Jaffa gate. (Some dissent from this; Lewin says this is not Hippicus, but Phasæ-lus; Schwartz puts Hippicus far to the north; Fergusson identifies it with the present Kasr Jalud — Goliath's Castle).   Somewhere in this first wall between Hippicus and the temple area was the gate Gennath, of which no sure traces are now to be found, for the gate now so called is said by Col. Wilson to be comparatively a modern structure.   (B. E., iv. 279.)   By Robinson, it is put quite at the west end of the wall near Hippicus (so Conder, Merrill, Tobler, Wilson, and others); by Schaffter and Thrup, quite to the east near to the temple wall; and by others, at various points intermediate.   (Rob., i. 312; iii. 212; Williams, H. C., ii. 14.)

In this great diversity of opinion the exact position of the gate Gennath must be left undecided.   As to the general position of Anto-nia, the other terminus of the second wall, there is no doubt.   It was on the north of the temple area; and according to Robinson (iii. 233), it extended east and west along its northern side; but by most it is placed on the northwest corner.   (So Raumer, 389; Williams, H. C., i. 409; Merrill.)   In this discussion the matter is not important.

With this imperfect knowledge of the termini, we now ask as to the probable course of the wall.   As we have seen, it was not straight, but curved.   Can we, from the nature of the ground, its hills and valleys, judge with some probability where it must have run in order to have been a defense?   Some affirm this, but there is great diversity of judgment arising in part from the changes which many centuries have made in the whole contour of the ground, the cutting down of the hills and the filling up of the valleys; the debris in this part of the city having in many places a thickness of from forty to fifty feet. (Conder, H. B., 331.)   Col. Wilson says (B. E., iv. 278): "One of the most striking features in Jerusalem is the vast accumulation of rubbish;" and it is from this cause that so many reconstructions of the city have been proposed, sixteen at least it is said.   (See Baede-

ker, 155, for several of them.) Unable in this way to come to any
certain result as to the course of the second wall, we ask, Are there
any visible remains of it by which we can trace its course? Robinson
(iii. 190, 206, and 218) discovered in the present wall at the Damascus gate some ancient remains, which he identifies with the guard
houses of a gate of the second wall, and the identification is accepted
by Williams, DeSaulcy, Merrill, Wilson, and others. In this case,
our investigations are narrowed down to the course of the wall from
the gate Gennath to the Damascus gate. But later explorations have
made this identification doubtful. (Recov. Jer., 216.) They may
have belonged to the third wall, that of Agrippa.

Similar remains have been found in an angle of the present wall
near the Latin convent (Rob., iii. 219), which are said by Merrill to
have belonged to the second wall; others question this. Are there
other traces of the second wall? It is said by Dr. Merrill: " In 1886
I had the good fortune to discover what is unquestionably the second
wall. . . . This was ten or more feet below the surface of the
ground, and twenty feet of it were exposed; its direction was northwest to southeast. Had the southern end been extended a few yards,
it would have touched the tower of David about in the middle of the
north side; near that point must have been the gate Gennath." (Qt.
St., January, 1886; see also articles in Qt. St., April and July and
October by Conder, Schick, and Mrs. Finn.) Assuming that the remains of the wall at the Damascus gate are those of this second wall,
a line drawn in circle touching the tower of Antonia, the Damascus
gate, and the newly discovered wall, would run far to the north and
west of the Holy Sepulchre, and exclude forever its claims." In
a later communication (*Sunday School Times*, June 1, 1889), Dr.
Merrill affrms that six points of the second wall are now known,
and that the Holy Sepulchre must have been within it. But on
the other hand, some, taking the same termini, so draw its course
that the sepulchre is without it. (So Schick; see Qt. St., January,
1888, for plan of the second wall; also that for April of same year.)
In favor of the present site, it is said that a gateway and part of a
wall have been found east of the Holy Sepulchre, which are remains
of the second wall. (Friedlieb, 191; *contra*, Merrill, S. S. T., June
1, 1889.) As the matter now stands, nothing very positive can be
said as to the course of the second wall, and therefore nothing
positive as to the position of the Holy Sepulchre, whether within this
wall or without it; this, future explorations must decide.

(*b*) The second condition to be met is that Golgotha should have
been near the city (John xix. 20). Some infer from this passage that
the inscription was read from the city, but this is not warranted.

(For another reading, see R. V. margin: "The place of the city where Jesus was crucified was nigh at hand." Some press this so far as to make Golgotha within the city.)

(*c*) The third condition is, that very near the place of crucifixion was a garden in which was a rock-cut sepulchre. That this condition is fulfilled in the traditional tomb, is affirmed by some and denied by others. It is affirmed that other ancient tombs are found not far removed from the traditional one, proving the fact that an ancient Jewish burial-place existed here. It is said by Wilson (B. E., iv. 284): "To the west of the Rotunda there is a chamber containing several receptacles for bodies, similar to those seen without the city." Willis, quoting Schultz (H. City, ii. 194), speaks of "a rock-tomb formed, long before the church was built, and probably belonging to an old Jewish sepulchre of an age prior to the destruction of Jerusalem by the Romans." The tomb is known as the tomb of Joseph of Arimathæa and of Nicodemus. "The existence of these sepulchres," says Stanley (452), "proves almost to a certainty, that at some period the site of the present church must have been outside the walls of the city; and lends considerable probability to the belief that the rock excavation, which perhaps exists in part still, and certainly once existed entire, within the marble casing of the chapel of the Holy Sepulchre, was at any rate a really ancient tomb, and not, as is often rashly asserted, a modern structure intended to imitate it." (So Adler, *Der Felsendom*, Berlin, 1873.) New tombs have been found under the Coptic Convent, of which Schick gives a plan and description. (Qt. St., July, 1887.) He says, that these prove the existence of rock-hewn tombs in this vicinity before the church of the Holy Sepulchre was built; and that they also testify to the genuineness of the tombs in the Western Rotunda. On the other side, Robinson denies the antiquity of all these rock-tombs. This rock-hewn tomb of Joseph .vas in a garden (Matt. xxvii. 60; Mark xv. 46; Luke xxiii. 53; John xix. 41. As to gardens in cities and tombs in gardens, see Hamburger, i. 396.) That there were gardens in that part of the city where the Holy Sepulchre now is, finds support from the proximity of Herod's palace, and the name of the gate Gennath.

(*d*) The last condition is, that it was near some frequented road. (Matt. xxvii. 39; Mark xv. 29.) Such a place the Romans were accustomed to choose for public executions. But this does not enable us to determine in what direction from the city it ran, much less that it was a road especially travelled by the feast pilgrims.

2. If the traditional site be rejected as not answering to these conditions, what site answering to them has been presented? Certainly not

that brought forward by Mr. Fergusson, who asserts that the sepulchre was in the rock under the dome of the Mosque of Omar, and that
this building is the identical Church of the Resurrection erected by
Constantine. (See it as stated by himself in Smith's Bible Dict., i.
1018.) It has been accepted by very few and need not be considered here. Another site was suggested by Dr. Barclay on the
side of Olivet, on a spur projecting into the valley of Kidron above
Gethsemane. Dr. Thomson placed it on the west bank of the Kidron north of St. Stephen's gate; Bishop Gobat, "on the hill just
outside the walls to the northeast of Herod's gate," which Sir Charles
Wilson also prefers; and still another site is suggested at the junc-
tion of the valley of Hinnom
with the Kedron. All these
are mere conjectures resting
upon some local fitness, real or
supposed.

    The view which has attract-
ed most attention is that Golgotha is the hill lying without
the present wall a little northeast of the Damascus gate.
This is probably owing to an
early suggestion of Robinson
(i. 407), that a frequented spot
without the gate and nigh to
the city, "would only be found
upon the western or northern
side of the city on the road
leading towards Joppa or Damascus." Soon after, others
began to speak of the hill now
called by many "Skull Hill,"
by others, Grotto Hill, above the grotto of Jeremiah, and near the
Damascus gate, as a possible Golgotha; and at the present time it
has many advocates; some notice of it is therefore necessary.

    It is thus described by Principal Dawson (Modern Science in
Bible Lands): "Skull Hill was originally a part of the Moriah ridge,
extending northward from it as a short and narrow spur. It contained a continuation of the fine white limestone which underlies
the Moriah ridge. Here a quarry was opened, probably as early as
the building of Solomon's temple. The quarrying operations were
finally extended right through the hill, so as to separate the Skull
Hill entirely from the remainder. This excavation was carried from

the city walls on the one side to the grotto of Jeremiah on the other, leaving only a round knoll to represent the former extremity of the ridge, and even this undermined extensively in the grotto. From some cause the quarrying in the hill was abandoned, and the rock hollowed under ground in the great quarries under the Bezethan quarter." As to its present appearance, Conder says: "The hill is quite bare with scanty grass covering the rocky soil; not a tree or shrub exists on it. . . . The hillock is rounded on all sides but the south, where the yellow cliff is pierced by two small caves high up on the sides." Its height is about 40 feet above the surface of the ground around it. (Qt. St., April, 1883, p. 69; also Qt. St., April and October, 1885.

What are the claims of this hill to be considered as the place of the crucifixion? (*a*) Its resemblance to the shape of a skull. This is apparent, at least from some points of view, and this resemblance is heightened by two caves or hollows in it, natural or artificial, which look at a distance like eye-sockets. But this resemblance, however striking, cannot have much weight, and some part of it may result from later excavations. (*b*) It stands outside the probable course of the second wall, but whether near it depends on the course of that wall. If it ran north as high as the Damascus gate, the hill is some 100 yards outside of it, but if this wall did not extend so far north, the distance of the hill from it is proportionately increased. (*c*) It is near a frequented road. The present road to Nablous and Damascus runs south of it, but hardly so near as to answer to the narrative (Matt. xxvii. 39), which implies that those passing by were able to see or hear what was done or said at the cross. Merrill lays stress on the fact, that remains of an old Roman military road from the fortress Antonia to Cæsarea ran a little north of the hill, and infers that the place of execution would be near it.

(*d*) That a garden was near it, and in it a sepulchre. This is the most important point, since the existence of a sepulchre is permanent, but the position of a cross leaves no permanent traces. Do we find ground to believe that there was a garden near this hill and in it a sepulchre? (As to gardens north of the city, see Joseph. War, v. 2. 2.) This is said by Edersheim: " Close by were villas and gardens." Its entire summit is now covered with Moslem graves, but in our Lord's day the top of the hill, it is claimed, was given up to public executions. If so, is it probable that private gardens would have been found upon its slopes, and do we find any remains of ancient sepulchres? In the western face of this hill is a large tomb, judged by its remains to be more Jewish than Christian, and which may show that the Jews had used it before the Lord's day for burial purposes. (Merrill in Qt. St., October, 1885.) In the northwest there is a Jewish tomb with several chambers, and other sepulchres are found west of the hill. (See Schick in Zeitschrift des Pal. Verein, 9. 74; Con · der in Qt. St., 1881, 201; April, 1883. See also Qt. St., October, 1879.) But do any of these sepulchres date back to the Lord's time? This is said by Conder, who thinks that he finds in one of these, ly- ing 770 feet from the hill, the Lord's sepulchre (Qt. St., April, 1883, with plans). On the other hand, Payne (Bibliotheca Sac., Jan., 1889, 178) thinks that without doubt it is the tomb of St. Stephen, and is too far removed from the place of crucifixion, and also that it is not of the right character or date. He affirms that a rock-hewn sepul- chral chamber like that in which the Lord was laid, is no where to be found about this hill.

That there is no tradition connecting this hill with the Lord's crucifixion, all admit. That there is a present belief among the Jews of Jerusalem that this was the place of public execution — the an- cient place of stoning (Levit. xxiv. 14, Num. xv. 35) — is affirmed by Conder and Chaplin, and accepted by Edersheim (ii. 585); but Merrill admits that it is of no great antiquity and attaches little importance to it. That the proto-martyr St. Stephen was stoned here, is a tra- dition of the fifth century; but if true, it is, of course, no proof that the Lord was crucified here, or that this was the common place of execution. (As to early notices of the hill, see Lewis, 108.)

One or two points remain still to be considered. If, as said by Dawson, and generally held, the space between Jeremiah's grotto and the north city wall was, in the Lord's day, a quarry, it is not probable that a part of it would be chosen as a place of crucifixion.

And it is certain that during the many centuries since intervening, great changes must have taken place as to the shape and appearance of the hill. It is said by Payne that the present configuration is so recent as to be wholly unknown to the early Christians and church historians, and even to the whole line of pilgrims to the holy places down to mediæval times. Another and more important objection to the claims of this Hill is, that no one until a very recent date has spoken of it as the Golgotha. Had it been the place of the Lord's crucifixion and burial, the memory of it must have been preserved in tradition, since it has remained unaffected by all the devastations of the city itself. Its conspicuous position, lying without the wall, must have made it both known and accessible to all pilgrims; and Constantine could not have chosen a more obscure site without some voice being heard against it.

We conclude, then, that there is no sufficient proof that Skull or Grotto Hill was the place of the Lord's crucifixion. (This view, perhaps, suggested by Robinson, 1841, stated by Thenius, 1842, defended by Fisher Howe, "The true site of Calvary," New York, 1871, and advocated by Conder, Merrill, General Gordon, Dawson, and accepted by Edersheim, "To me this seems the most sacred and precious locality in Jerusalem," needs much additional proof to give it probability. See Lewis, The Holy Places, 108 ff. for a fair statement of the matter.)

But if there is no sufficient evidence that this hill was Golgotha, still this does not show that the traditional site is the true one. We therefore ask, What do history and tradition tell us of the places of the crucifixion and burial? For convenience' sake, let us divide the time embraced in our inquiry into three periods: From the Lord's death to the destruction of the city by Titus, 70 A. D.; from this destruction to its overthrow by Hadrian, 136 A. D.; from this overthrow to the pilgrimage of Helena, 326 A. D.

1. 30–70 A. D.   It is certain that the places of crucifixion and burial were known, not only to the disciples, but to the priests and rulers and to many of the inhabitants of the city. It is in the highest degree improbable that they could have been forgotten by any who were witnesses of the Lord's death, or knew of His resurrection. As the apostles, according to a commonly received tradition, continued for a number of years after this at Jerusalem, there could be no doubt that each site was accurately known to them and their followers. Besides, the Evangelists, writing from twenty to fifty years after His death, mention distinctly Golgotha and the garden. Down to the destruction of Jerusalem by Titus, A. D. 70, there can be no question that these places were well known. During the siege of the city, most or all of the Jewish Christians retired to Pella, but they seem soon to have returned. Was the city so destroyed that the former site of the sepulchre could not be recognized? This is not claimed by any one. Robinson (i. 366) speaks of it as "a destruction terrible, but not total." We conclude, then, that the site was known to the Jewish Christians after the destruction of Jerusalem by Titus.

2. 70–136 A. D.   What is known of the Holy Sepulchre during this period? It is unquestioned that there was during it a Christian church, standing, as some say, on the site of the Coenaculum — the "upper room" of the last supper; and it is most improbable, therefore, that knowledge of the places of the crucifixion and the tomb should have been lost. Whether pilgrimages began before the end of this period, may be questioned; and whether up to the destruction by Hadrian the sepulchre had been marked by any monument,

does not appear. This is possible, though we cannot believe, as assumed by Chateaubriand, that a church was erected upon it.

3. 136–326 A. D. That the city was not wholly destroyed by Hadrian, and that the work of rebuilding began immediately after the close of the war, is historically proved. It became in many respects a new city, taking the name of Aelia Capitolina, by which it was generally known for many years. It was in this period that the Jewish Christian Church at Jerusalem first elected a Gentile bishop; and Eusebius gives a list of his successors, twenty-three in number, down to the time of Constantine. Although the general character of the new city was heathen through the bringing in of new citizens, yet this must have served to intensify the regard of the Christians for their sacred places. To this we must add the interest kept alive by the visits of pilgrims, for it is well established, that pilgrimages to the holy sites were not unfrequent in the second century, and they were still more frequent in the next.

But however strong the probability that the sepulchre was known, yet in point of fact, for this period of about 190 years, we hear nothing of it except what we learn from a statement of Eusebius (Vita Const., iii. 26), that impious men had erected over it a temple to the goddess Venus, first covering it with earth to conceal it and to get a better foundation. It is not clear whether the temple was built by Hadrian, or by some enemies at a later period. Jerome (395 A. D.) speaks of a statue of Venus which stood upon the spot, and ascribes it to Hadrian. This temple to Venus, taken in connection with a temple to Jupiter built by Hadrian upon the temple area, and his placing there an equestrian statue of himself, seems clearly to show his purpose to dishonor both Jews and Christians in their representative sacred places — the Temple Mount and the Hill of Golgotha. But if a temple was built over the sepulchre, and a statue of Venus placed where the cross stood, this would indeed serve to hinder the Christians of the city from gathering there, and pilgrims from visiting there, but it would not give over to forgetfulness the holy places; rather it would tend to keep them in memory.

If the early Christians knew the places of the crucifixion and the resurrection, can we believe that they would soon forget them? It is obvious that no other places could be so deeply interesting to them, and none, in the nature of the case, would be so generally known and so firmly impressed on the memory. Few perhaps, knew of the birthplace of the Lord, for His connection with Bethlehem was transient, and it was many years before the attention of the disciples in general was turned to it. The same may be said of the place of His ascension; only the eleven were with Him, and there was nothing monumental to mark the exact spot of His ascent; but all Jerusalem and multitudes from Galilee knew where were the cross and sepulchre. And besides the great publicity of His death and burial and resurrection, the supernatural character of the events attending them made it impossible that they could be easily forgotten. The cross was soon taken down, but the sepulchre remained its own witness. The fact of His resurrection being made the central truth in the Apostolic preaching (Acts iv. 2), every circumstance connected with it was thus kept before the public mind. It must be admitted that no such regard was at first paid to the sacred places as in later times; the hope of the Lord's speedy return in glory making the disciples comparatively indifferent to the local associations of His earthly life. Their faces were turned to the future rather than to the past; and to this we must ascribe the fact that the site of the resurrection was for many years, so far as we know, distinguished by no monument. But this is very far from entire forgetfulness of the place itself.

But does not the language of Eusebius (Life of Constantine, iii. 25, 26) imply, that Constantine learned the site of the sepulchre by immediate revelation from God, and that, therefore, it could not have been previously known?

We may make two suppositions :— 1. That through the several overthrows of the city and the devastations attending them, the tomb was so far obliterated that all memory of it was lost; and that when the temple of Venus was built, whether in Hadrian's time or after, it was built without any knowledge of, or reference to, the tomb. In this case, its discovery by Constantine may well have been ascribed by Eusebius to a supernatural revelation.

2. That the tomb, perhaps hidden under the earth, survived these devastations, and that the site of it was known when the temple of Venus was built, and that this temple was placed over it with the intent to hide it from all eyes, and cause it to be forgotten. But this would certainly help to keep it in memory; and we may therefore believe that Constantine was not ignorant of its site, and needed no special divine guidance when he ordered the temple to be destroyed.

Taking all the data into account, it seems most reasonable to accept the last supposition. Doubtless, the intent of those who built the temple of Venus on that spot, was to show their aversion to the Christian faith; and their expectation was that the new sect, built upon the great delusion or imposture of the resurrection of its founder, would soon cease to exist; and that to hide the sepulchre from all eyes was a means to that end. But for the continued existence of the little church at Jerusalem, and its growing faith in the Risen One, this forgetfulness would doubtless have been the result.

On the contrary, the sight of the heathen temple served, in fact, to preserve alive the remembrance of the place of His resurrection. This best explains the action of Constantine, who, if he had had no knowledge of the real site, and now made a selection from among the possible places, would not have chosen one so central, and so far within the then existing western wall. Some good reason must have existed for connecting it locally with the temple of Venus. The divine impulse which Eusebius ascribes to him, was not the knowledge where the sepulchre was to be found, but the desire to build there a church in honor of the Lord. Prof. Lewis (100) thinks that Constantine "built on a site which he fully believed to be that of our Lord's burial, and that he had knowledge to guide him as to its correctness." It is said by Lewin: "In the days of Constantine not the least doubt was entertained where the sepulchre was situated; but the only hesitation was, whether, by removing the temple, the sepulchre itself could be recovered."

It is to be borne in mind that "the Invention of the cross," or its discovery by the Empress Helena (326 A. D.), stands in no historical relation to the discovery of the site of the sepulchre.[1] Besides the intrinsic objections, the silence of Eusebius in regard to the invention seems conclusive against it, since he was well disposed to believe such an account. (Giesseler, ii. 37, note.) We can trace the constantly growing legendary character of the narrative: at first the Lord's cross was distinguished from those of the two malefactors by the title Pilate had attached to it; then through the ordeal of healing a sick person; then through the greater miracle of recalling a dead person to life. (See Zoeckler, *The Cross of Christ*, 146.) That Helena may have found some pieces of timber and iron belonging to some former structure, and which she believed to be part of the cross, is suggested by Prof. Willis (128), and is very probable.

The late explorations show that the traditional Golgotha was elevated above the ground around it; that it was not a high hill is shown by the way in which Epiphanius speaks of it, comparing it disparagingly with the hill of Zion and the Mount of Olives (Qt. St., April, 1880). Robinson ascribes the origin of the term "mount" to the fact that the rock of Golgotha was left in the midst of the large open court, formerly the garden. According to Willis, the rock of Calvary was part of a little swell of the ground forming a somewhat abrupt brow on the west and south sides. "This would afford a convenient spot for the place of public execution. For the south-

---

[1] See Winer, i. 437, note 6. Isaac Taylor (Ancient Christianity, ii. 277) argues more forcibly than fairly that the whole was a stupendous fraud.

western brow of the rock has just sufficient elevation to raise the wretched sufferers above the gazing crowd that would naturally arrange itself below and upon the sloping ridge opposite." [1] Recent explorations show a rising of the rock as we go north to the holy sepulchre. " From these and other neighboring observations it is clear that the Church of the Holy Sepulchre stands on a hilltop, and that the ground falls rapidly south of it," and there is a sharp descent of some forty feet to the north (Qt. St., April, 1880, page 79.)

In concluding this brief statement, it may be added that, as the topographical argument now stands, it is indecisive. Further excavations and researches may, however, wholly change the aspect of the question. The historical argument in its favor has not yet been set aside. Modern opinions are about equally divided. While most of the Roman Catholic and Greek writers defend its genuineness, some deny it; and on the other hand, many Protestants defend it. [2]

---

[1] See Furrer in Bib. Lex., *sub voce.*

[2] Among those not already cited who deny it, may be mentioned: Wilson, Barclay, Bonar, Stewart, Arnold, Meyer, Ewald, Edersheim. Among those who defend it: Tischendorf, Olin, Prime, Lange, Alford, Friedlieb, Lewin, Caspari, Langen, Furrer. Among those who are undecided: Ritter, Raumer, Winer, Bartlett, Stanley, Ellicott.

PART VIII.

THE RESURRECTION OF THE LORD.

Before entering upon the details of the narratives of the
resurrection, it will be well to ask from what point of view are
these narratives to be regarded. Were they intended to be to their
readers proofs of the resurrection? This is often said, and in a
certain sense is true. But the Evangelists wrote for believers,
that, as said by Luke, they might "know the certainty concerning the things wherein they were instructed," or, as in the margin, "were taught by word of mouth" (R. V.). The fact of the
resurrection was one of those "most surely believed"; one of
the first truths taught in the churches (1 Cor. xv. 3). On whose
testimony did this belief rest? Primarily, on that of the apostles
whom God had called to be official witnesses (Acts i. 22; x. 41;)
secondarily, on that of all who had seen Him after He rose from
the dead (Acts xiii. 31).

Writing, after so many years, of this great and then everywhere received fact, which had its own special witnesses, and
had become an essential article of Christian faith, the Evangelists
did not take upon themselves the work of proving it to their
readers by cumulative testimony; for, if this had been their purpose, they would carefully have cited all the eye-witnesses of
whom they had any knowledge. But evidently they do not do
this. Each of them passes by in silence some of the strongest
proofs; not from ignorance, which in the cases of Matthew and
John was impossible, and very improbable in the cases of Mark
and Luke. Their object, was quite another; and to show this,
we must note some points that have often been overlooked.

(*a*) The distinction between the act of resurrection and the

(589)

subsequent manifestations of the Risen One. The resurrection itself no eye beheld; His disciples knew it only as a fact accomplished. How could it be proved? The proof of the empty tomb, the grave clothes and the napkin, the testimony of the angels — all this was not wholly convincing, and the disciples continued to doubt. He Himself must be seen alive; this alone was a testimony not to be doubted. It is the death of a man that must be proved; of his birth his existence is the conclusive and continuous proof. So was it with the Lord. His resurrection was His second birth, the beginning of a new and higher and permanent form of life.

(b) The possibility of ever new manifestations. As the Risen One He could at any time manifest Himself to men, either in person to their senses, or through the works done by men in His name and by His power. As a living man need not be ever referring to baptismal registers to prove the fact of his birth, but is his own witness, so the living Lord was not dependent upon the Evangelic records to prove that He is risen; if they had never been written, the fact of His resurrection remained the same, and consequently the same permanent power of proof. As this testimony in its very nature could be repeated at His pleasure, it could not, therefore, be limited by the Evangelists to certain given times and places. It could not be summed up as completed and incapable of addition.

But, when we speak of the Lord as risen, we enter into a new region; we meet the phenomena of resurrection life, whose laws are wholly unknown to us. So far as we know, none could see Him in this new condition of being but those to whom He was pleased to manifest Himself. The risen Lazarus could not hide himself from the senses of men, not so the risen Lord. The amount of sensible evidence to His resurrection through His visible presence or the touching of His body, was, therefore, wholly in His own power.

(c) The object of these manifestations. The Lord's first step was to convince His disciples that He was, indeed, risen — a true man, not a phantasm, or ghost, — that through resurrection He had become "the beginning of the new creation," "the heavenly man." In Him the disciples should see the noblest

type of humanity — humanity no longer under the law of sin and
death, but immortal, incorruptible, and having all fullness of
life.   Not till the apostles came to look upon Him as in a condition of being in which He was to abide, in perfected and immortal manhood, could they shake off the fear that ever marks all
intercourse with the disembodied, and attain to that calmness
and repose of spirit which would enable them to receive His instructions as to their future work.

(*d*) The continuity and progressive nature of the Lord's redemption work.   As He Himself was the same Person before
and after His resurrection, though under differing conditions of
humanity, so His work was the same though in differing stages.
And as the apostles had been His helpers in the first stage, so
should they be also in the second.   Their old relation to Him as
His apostles was not changed, and yet it must be renewed, and
they be instructed and endowed by Him for the new form of
their labors.   Thus it was necessary, first of all, that the Lord
convince the apostles of the reality and of the nature of His
resurrection, and thus enable Him to establish the new relations
between them and Himself as the Risen One, — relations which
were to continue during the whole time of His absence in heaven.
He must first bring them to such measure of faith in Him as
the Living One, that He could proceed to teach them respecting
His future work by them after His departure.   When this was
done, He could give the apostles their commission to be His witnesses to the world, and then ascend to God, and send down
upon them His Spirit.   The period of the forty days was, therefore, filled with sensible manifestations of the Lord, not merely
as proofs that He was risen, but also that they might know Him
in the new and heavenly sphere of His activity, and have faith
in Him as personally teaching and guiding them after He ascended out of their sight.

Turning now to the narratives of the resurrection, we notice
in them two chief elements.   1. The attempts of the Lord to
convince the apostles that He had risen and had entered into a
new and higher condition of manhood.   2. His teachings and
directions given them with reference to their future work, when
they were so convinced.

Before His death He had directed them to go to Galilee, and there they should see Him; but it is plain that they had never understood what He had said to them of His resurrection, and therefore they did not leave the city after His burial. They saw others perform the last rites of love; loving women anointed His body as others did their dead, and left it at rest in the sepulchre to wait for the resurrection at the last day. The apostles continuing in Jerusalem, it was therefore necessary, first of all, to prove to them there that He was risen. They saw that the stone was rolled away, but this human hands might have done; they saw that His body was not in the sepulchre, but His enemies might have taken it away; the folded grave clothes gave no certainty. He gives them through the women the testimony of angels, but even this does not remove doubt; He must manifest Himself again and again till faith is assured; this He does now to one, now to another. Four or five times He appears on the day of His resurrection, the last time to the Eleven, and gives them the strongest sensible proofs of the reality of His bodily presence. Still, there is one apostle unbelieving, and therefore the Eleven cannot yet go to Galilee; he must be convinced, and therefore a week later the Lord appears again to them, and the doubting Thomas believes. Now, all can return to Galilee, and there He manifests Himself to them, and to the great body of His disciples, all doubtless meeting Him according to His special direction.

When the apostles were thus not merely convinced of the fact of His resurrection, but had learned in some degree its significance, and been brought into such knowledge of Him as the Risen One that He could teach them respecting their future work, they could receive their commission to act as His apostles in making Him known to the world, as One who was dead but now alive again. Recognizing His new relations to them, they were prepared to fulfill their new duties.

Thus we see that to prove the fact of the resurrection by citing all possible witnesses, was by no means the chief end of the Evangelists. His resurrection was the beginning of a new and higher stage of the Lord's redemptive work, and it was essential that His disciples, and especially His apostles, should be convinced

of this by His personal manifestations to them, and thus be prepared to be His witnesses (Acts x. 41; xiii. 31), whose testimony
the world should believe.   But the object of the Evangelists was
to show, each from his own point of view, how the Lord first
by repeated revelations of Himself brought the apostles to such
faith in Him as Risen, that He could instruct them during the
forty days of His stay on earth, and carry on His new work by
them after His departure.

We are not, then, to expect in the Evangelists any full and
orderly statement of the manifestations of the Risen One, as
proofs of His resurrection.   No one of them designs to give
anything like a complete summary of the evidence to establish
it.   Of course, every appearance mentioned is a proof ; every
one who saw Him became a witness.   But the purpose of their
narratives is not only to show the fact of His resurrection, but
also what means He employed to assure them that He had risen in
true though glorified manhood, the gradual growth of their faith,
and the nature of the work He commissioned His Church to do.

In our examination of the Evangelic narratives, we must bear
in mind that the purpose of God did not include a manifestation
of the Lord after He rose from the dead to the world at large,
or to His own covenant people as such, but to those only who had
believed on Him.   And among these the apostles were to be His
special witnesses, and therefore, to them would He give the
strongest proofs (Acts i. 22; x. 41).   Nor was it His purpose
to appear to them in Jerusalem, or even in Judæa, but in Galilee,
whence most of His disciples came.   This last point claims our
attention.

We shall fail to understand the accounts of the resurrection
if we do not give due place to the Lord's words spoken after the
paschal supper.   It is said by Matthew (xxvi. 30–32): "They
went out into the Mount of Olives.   Then saith Jesus unto them,
All ye shall be offended because of me this night, for it is written, I will smite the Shepherd, and the sheep of the flock shall
be scattered abroad.   But after I am risen again, I will go before
you into Galilee."   (So in almost the same words in Mark xiv.
26–28; but they are not given in Luke or John.)   It is evident that the Lord here directs the apostles, who alone were

then with Him, to go to Galilee, promising to meet them
there (In the angelic message, Matt. xxvii. 7: "There shall ye
see Him"; in His own message, verse 10: "There shall they see
Me"). Had they had faith in His words, the apostles, beholding
the Shepherd smitten, would have left Jerusalem after His
resurrection and returned to Galilee, and there have awaited His
appearance. But their faith failed them. They saw Him dead
and buried, nothing remained but to disperse and go to their distant homes, their work being ended. The risen Lord finds all
the disciples lingering around the sepulchre, some bringing spices
to anoint His body; and He has pity on them, and especially on
the women who have given Him such proofs of their love. By
them will He send messages to His apostles, who did not come to
the sepulchre, and seemed to have lost all faith; He will remind
them of His final direction to them to go to Galilee, if in this
way He can re-awaken their faith. To this end, He commissions certain angels to speak to the women, and lest the
angelic messages may terrify and bewilder them, He will even
Himself appear to them and renew His direction.

But all this was in vain. The testimony of the women was
not believed. It is said by Luke (xxiv. 11): "Their words
seemed to them as idle tales, and they believed them not."
(That John believed at his visit to the sepulchre, xx. 8, that
He had risen, is almost certain; but if so, he was but one of the
apostles.) Jesus appears to two of the disciples going to Emmaus,
that they may testify of Him unto the Eleven; and at last He
appears to Peter; and then to the assembled apostles, and to
others with them. But even this personal appearance does not
convince them all, and lead them to do as He had directed them,
and go into Galilee. They linger another week in Jerusalem,
perhaps visiting often the garden, hoping again to meet Him
there; and it was not till His second appearance to the Eleven,
that they were willing to leave the city and go to Galilee.

Thus we see that a distinction is to be taken between the
Judæan and Galilæan appearances after His resurrection. It
was not in Judæa, not in the Holy City where He was crucified,
that He would manifest Himself as the Risen One; His appearances there were simply to convince the disciples, especially

the apostles, of the reality of His resurrection, and prepare them for His further communications to them. In Jerusalem He must die, from the Mount of Olives He must ascend, but in Galilee He would gather around Him those who had there seen His work, and heard His words, and believed.

It is apparent that the Evangelists do not avowedly discriminate these two elements — the first appearances of the Lord, whose object was to show the apostles that He had risen, and the later, which were to give them instruction and guidance for the future — yet they do this in fact (Acts i. 3). Thus Matthew mentions the appearance of the angels to the women in Jerusalem, and afterward the appearance of the Lord to them; all this was to assure them that He was risen; His later appearance to the Eleven in the mountain in Galilee was to give them their apostolic commission. Mark mentions the appearance of the angels to the women, and the message given them (xvi. 1–8); and in the Appendix (verses 9–18) three appearances of the Lord are mentioned — one to Mary Magdalene, one to the two disciples, and one to the Eleven at meat, all in Jerusalem. The first two appearances did not effect belief, and therefore when He appeared to the Eleven, He upbraided them because they believed not them which had seen Him after He was risen.

John mentions the appearance to Mary Magdalene, and afterwards two appearances to the Eleven in Jerusalem. The object in all these was plainly to beget faith in Him as preparatory to His further directions and teaching in Galilee. His appearance at a later time to several at the Sea of Tiberias was not to prove His resurrection, for all knew that it was the Lord, but to instruct them, especially Peter, in regard to their future relations to Him. Luke mentions only the appearances in Judæa — the appearance of the angels to the women, and the Lord's appearance to the two at Emmaus, and incidentally that to Peter; and then that to the Eleven when He ate before them. Having thus proved that He had really arisen, He teaches them what the Scriptures had foretold of His death and resurrection, and of the preaching of the Gospel by them to all nations.

SUNDAY, 17TH NISAN, 9TH APRIL, A. D. 30.

As the day begins to dawn there is a great earthquake; and an angel of the Lord, descending, rolls away the stone from the door of the sepulchre and sits upon it. For fear of him, the soldiers become as dead men. Immediately after come Mary Magdalene and other women, to anoint the body. As they approach the sepulchre, Mary Magdalene, beholding the stone rolled away, and supposing that the body has been removed by the Jews, runs to find Peter and John to inform them. The other women proceed to the sepulchre, and there meet an angel (or angels) who tells them of the Lord's resurrection, and gives them a message to the disciples.	MATT. xxviii. 2-4.
	MATT. xxviii. 1.
	MARK xvi. 1.
	LUKE xxiv. 1.
	JOHN xx. 1, 2.
	MARK xvi. 2-8.
	LUKE xxiv. 2-8.
	MATT. xxviii. 5-8.
Soon after they have departed, Peter and John, who have heard the story of Mary Magdalene, come in haste to see what has occurred; and Mary follows them. Entering the sepulchre, they find it empty, and the grave clothes lying in order, and John then believes. They leave the tomb to return, but Mary remains behind weeping. Looking into the sepulchre, she sees two angels, and immediately after, the Lord appears to her and gives her a message to bear to the disciples; and soon after, gives another message to some of the other women. The accounts of the women seem to the disciples as idle tales, and are not believed. Upon the return of the soldiers from the sepulchre into the city, the priests and elders, learning what had taken place, bribe them to spread the report that the disciples had stolen the body away.	JOHN xx. 3-10.
	LUKE xxiv. 12 & 24
	JOHN xx. 11-18.
	MATT. xxviii. 9, 10.
	MARK xvi. 9-11.
	LUKE xxiv. 9-11.
	MATT. xxviii. 11-15.

The number of the Lord's appearances after the resurrection during the forty days following, or to His ascension, as given by the Evangelists, is generally said to be nine. Of these, five were on the day of the resurrection, one on the Sunday following, two at some later period, and one when He ascended. As regards place, five were in Jerusalem, one in Emmaus, two in Galilee, and one on the Mount of Olives. If to these we add that to James, mentioned only by St. Paul (1 Cor. xv. 7), which was probably at Jerusalem, we have ten recorded appearances. We may well believe that these were not all, the language in Acts i. 3, R. V. : "Appearing unto them by the space of forty days, and speaking the things concerning the kingdom of God," clearly implying that the Lord met the apostles often for instruction.

To deal with the many intricate details which the Lord's appearances present, it will be well to examine each appearance by itself, taking them in the order of their occurrence.

I. The appearances on the day of the resurrection. These were five in number: 1. To Mary Magdalene. 2. To the other women. 3. To the two disciples at Emmaus. 4. To Peter. 5. To the Eleven at evening. If we identify that to Mary Magdalene with that to the other women, we have four; if we also identify that to Peter with that to the two at Emmaus, as Lightfoot, we have only three.[1]

1. Thus the first point before us is, Were there one or two appearances of the Lord to the women, and if two, to whom were they made? But before we can determine this, there are some preliminary questions to be considered: the number of the women who came to the sepulchre; whether all came together, or in two or more parties; the times of their arrival; and the several angelic appearances and messages.

(a) The number of the women. We know that a considerable number came from Galilee, some of whose names are mentioned: Mary Magdalene, Mary mother of James, Salome, Joanna, Susanna, and "many others" (Mark xv. 41). Some of these came to anoint the Lord's body as early as possible on the morning after the Sabbath (Luke xxiv. 1). Of these, John (xx. 1) mentions Mary Magdalene only; Matt. (xxviii. 1) mentions Mary Magdalene and "the other Mary"; Mark (xvi. 1), Mary Magdalene, Mary mother of James, and Salome; Luke (xxiii. 55): "The women which came with Him from Galilee;" and of these are mentioned by name (xxiv. 10), Mary Magdalene, Joanna, and Mary mother of James. (Susanna is not mentioned in the accounts of the crucifixion.) Thus there were five and more women; how many more is conjecture.

(b) Did these women come to the sepulchre together, or in distinct parties, and at successive times? John mentions Mary Magdalene only, but it is generally agreed that her words : "We know not," etc., imply that one, or more, were with her. Matthew mentions two; Mark, three; do they thus exclude all others? This is said by McClellan (514). But the more reasonable view is that no one of the Evangelists designs to enumerate all who came early to the sepulchre; they mention only those who took a leading part, or whose presence had to them some special significance. How many women came, who they were, whence they came, whether singly or in groups, circumstances important indeed in a court of justice, were to them minor matters.

---

[1] An appearance to the Virgin Mary, and that the first of all, is affirmed by Maldonatus, a Lapide, and others, but has no other basis than a desire to honor her.

All agree in this, that the Lord first appeared to some women, but they use great freedom in the arrangement of the details.   As we have seen, they are not designing to prove the fact of the resurrection by heaping up evidence, but are illustrating the manner in which the Lord manifested Himself, the gradual steps of the manifestation, and the difficulty in awakening belief.   We are not then to regard the mention of one or two or more women by name as necessarily exclusive of others.   Nor does it prove that they came to the sepulchre in so many distinct groups.   All may have reached it together, or nearly so; the Evangelists, for reasons connected with their narratives, making prominent one or more.   But, on the other hand, there is no intrinsic improbability in supposing that there were two or more distinct parties. That they lodged in different parts of the city, perhaps some in Bethany, and so came from different quarters, is not unlikely, and if so, they would arrive at the sepulchre at successive times.[1]   But the fact of successive parties does not decide the question as to one or two appearances of the Lord to them.

(c) The time of their arrival at the sepulchre.   Our examination of Matthew xxviii. 1, has shown us that as regards the time of arrival at the sepulchre, he is in accord with the other Evangelists. Luke (xxiv. 1) marks the time as "on the first day of the week, very early in the morning" (in R. V., "at early dawn"); John (xx. 1) as "early, when it was yet dark."   But Mark (xvi. 2) has two designations of the time: "very early in the morning" — λίαν πρωΐ — and "at the rising of the sun" — ἀνατείλαντος τοῦ ἡλίου — (in R. V., "when the sun was risen"; in Vul. *orto jam sole;* see W. and H. in margin). Assuming that the rendering in R. V. is right — "When the sun was risen," — are the two designations of time inconsistent?   As "early" — πρωΐ — is used of the fourth watch, 3 to 6 A. M., "very early" would indicate the first part of this period.   As we cannot suppose the Evangelist would contradict himself in the same sentence, we must conclude that he speaks of the sunrise, not as its appearing above the horizon but as bringing in the day, the illumination heralding its coming, or, as said by Ellicott, "a general definition of the time" (so Rob., see however Caspari, 239, who maintains that the aorist participle should have been translated, "when the sun was about to rise, *sole orituro*).   If this be inadmissible, we may say with Greswell (iii. 283) and others, that "very early" may be understood of

---

[1] That, as said in Speaker's Com., Zebedee had a house in Jerusalem near the gate Gennath, and near the sepulchre, and that from this his wife Salome and Mary Magdalene and the other Mary started, while Joanna, wife of Herod's steward, started with others from the Hasmonean palace on Mt. Zion, more remote, has very slight traditional basis.

the time when the women first set out, and "when the sun had risen,"
of the time when they reached the sepulchre.

In this discussion as to the time of their arrival, it is necessary to
keep in mind that at this season of the year the sun rose about half-
past five, and it began to be light enough to discern objects at least
half an hour earlier.[1]

As we cannot suppose that the women would leave their homes
till the day began to break, and yet would endeavor to reach the sepulchre as early as possible, we may place the earliest arrival, that of
Mary Magdalene, at about 5 A. M. (so Westcott; McClellan, the first
arrival at 4.45 A. M.). The only discrepancy as to time of arrival is
found in the statements of Mark and John. According to the former
the sun had arisen; according to the latter, it was yet dark — σκοτία.
But this is an indefinite expression, and if strictly taken, is inconsistent with the fact that Mary Magdalene saw that the stone had
been rolled away, and this apparently while yet at some distance.

(d) *The angelic appearances to the women, and the number of the
angels.* According to John, Mary Magdalene, seeing that the stone
was rolled away, did not go to the sepulchre or see any angel, but ran
immediately to tell Peter and John; on her return she saw two angels.
According to Matthew, the two Marys saw an angel who spake to
them and gave them a message to the disciples. According to Mark,
the two Marys and Salome entered into the sepulchre, and saw there an
angel who gave them a message. According to Luke, all the women
saw that the stone was rolled away, and entering the sepulchre, saw
two angels who addressed them. We thus conclude that there were
three appearances of the angels to the women.

The discrepancies as to the number of the angels seen are of
small importance. We know so little of the modes of angelic existence, how they who are ordinarily invisible can make themselves
visible, what parts were here severally assigned to them, and of the
grounds of their action, that it is wholly impossible for us to say how
many may have been present at this time within or around the sepulchre. Doubtless the angelic guards were there watching over the
body of their Lord all the time it was in the tomb. As said by
Lessing: "They appeared, not always one and the same, not always
the same two; sometimes this one appeared, sometimes that; sometimes

---

[1] The following, kindly furnished by Prof. Luther of Trinity College, will be found
of value: "I make sun's declination on the morning of April 9, A. D. 30, 7° 27' 7''; time
of sunrise, 5h. 37m. 24s. apparent time; 5h. 39m. 12s. meantime; twilight begins at
4h. 28m. approximately." See in McClellan, 526, a less accurate statement. Robinson
(iii. 35) speaks of breakfasting in Northern Palestine "by the dim mingled light of the
grey dawn and the pale moon, and at 5.10 we were again on our way."

in this place, sometimes in that; sometimes alone, sometimes in company; sometimes they said this, sometimes they said that." Matthew and Mark each speak of one angel; in the first, he meets the women without the sepulchre, and invites them to enter: "Come, see the place where the Lord lay"; in the last, he meets them within the sepulchre, and says to them, "Behold, the place where they laid Him." It is impossible for us to say whether the same angel is meant by the two Evangelists. Luke mentions two angels seen by the women, standing within the sepulchre; and John, that Mary Magdalene saw "two angels in white sitting, the one at the head, the other at the feet, where the body of Jesus had lain."

(e) *The messages given by the angels.* Matthew mentions one, that to the two Marys: "Go quickly and tell His disciples that He is risen from the dead; and, behold, He goeth before you into Galilee, there shall ye see Him"; and adds, to emphasize the certainty of this, "Lo, I have told you." The message in Mark is almost the same: "Go your way, tell His disciples and Peter that He goeth before you into Galilee, there shall ye see Him, as He said unto you." In Luke no message is given, but the women are reminded that the Lord, while yet in Galilee, had foretold His crucifixion and resurrection. In John, nothing is said of any message given to Mary Magdalene; the two angels simply ask her, "Woman, why weepest thou?" Thus the Lord sent by the angels through the women apparently but one message to His disciples — the direction to go into Galilee. The Lord's own message through the women (Matt. xxviii. 10) was a repetition of this; that to Mary Magdalene was of another character.

We may now consider the point whether there were one or two appearances of the Lord to the women.

The real ground of the difficulties which some find in regard to these appearances lies in this : that the Evangelists use the liberty which is given to all chroniclers or historians, to speak of things as happening to one or two which in fact happened to more, and as happening to several, when in fact they happened but to one. When Mark says that "Jesus went into the borders of Tyre and Sidon, and entered into a house, and would that no man should know it," no one supposes that He was absolutely alone; we know from other sources, and from Mark himself, that the Twelve were with Him. When John says that Mary Magdalene came to the sepulchre, saying nothing of others, this does not show that she came alone. The same is true of the other Evangelists The mention of the two Marys by Matthew, and of them and Salome by Mark, does not show that no others were with them, or compel us to say that there were two distinct parties coming at different times.   Whether, when Matthew speaks of the Lord's appearing to the two Marys, he is speaking of the same appearance which John mentions when Mary Magdalene only is named, must be determined by an examination of the details and attendant circumstances.

We now proceed to ask whether the appearance of the Lord in Matthew (xxviii. 9, 10) is to be identified with that in John (xx. 14) and Mark (xvi. 9).   Before comparing them, each account must be considered.

According to Matthew, the two Marys, as they approached the sepulchre, saw an angel sitting upon the stone that had been rolled back from the door.   Were they witnesses of the earthquake and of what followed?   This is said by Meyer, Alford, and others.   But the rendering: "There was a great earthquake," does not show that this was after the arrival of the women.[1]   It is the more general belief that the earthquake was earlier, and that the stone had been rolled away before they came.   Whether the women saw the soldiers lying as dead men before the angel, or whether they had already gone into the city, is in question.   Some understand the angels' words "Fear not ye," addressed to the women, as marking a contrast between them and the terror-stricken keepers.   His presence sitting upon the stone, was the proof that the stone had not been rolled away by the earthquake or by human hands.   It was a sign to prove how vain it was to shut and seal and guard what the Lord would open.

The connection between the descent of the angel and rolling away of the stone, and of the resurrection of the Lord, is not defined.   It was the general opinion of the fathers, that He rose and left the tomb before the stone was rolled away; the object of this act by the angel being, not to give the Lord a way of exit, but to open the way for the women to enter.   There is no indication that the soldiers saw Jesus as He left the sepulchre, and their terror is expressly ascribed to the sight of the angel.

Whether by the "earthquake," σεισμὸς, we are to understand a literal earthquake, has been questioned.   Some would refer it to the confusion or commotion which the sudden appearance of the angel made among the soldiers keeping watch; others to the shock made by the rolling away of the stone, which was very great; others to a tempest, or tempest and earthquake.[2]   If, however, it was a literal

---

[1] It is said by Canon Cook: "The aorist declares the fact, not the time of its occurrence"; and by Riddle: "The aorists have their usual force, but it does not follow that the events succeeded the arrival of the women."   See Winer, Gram., Trans., 275.

[2] The word means literally "a shaking" without defining the cause.   See Matt. viii. 24, where it is rendered "tempest;" compare Heb. xii. 26, 27, and Matt. xxi. 10.

earthquake, it is doubtful whether it was felt throughout the city, for such an event, taken in connection with what occurred at the crucifixion, could scarce have passed unnoticed by the disciples. "The first earthquake," says Stier, "extended all over Jerusalem to the temple and graves; the second only moves the stone in Joseph's garden, and scares the guards away." [1]

After announcing to the women that the Lord is not in the sepulchre, but is risen as He said, the angel invites them to come and see the place where He lay, and then gives them the message to the disciples. "And they departed quickly from the tomb with fear and great joy, and ran to bring His disciples word. And behold Jesus met them, saying, 'All hail,' and they came and took hold of His feet and worshipped Him. Then saith Jesus unto them, Fear not, go tell my brethren that they depart into Galilee, and there shall they see Me."

We turn to the account of John (xx. 1–12). Mary Magdalene alone is mentioned, but that she was unaccompanied is not probable, the hour being so early; and incidental proof that others were with her is found in the use of the plural (verse 2) : " We know not where they have laid Him." (Compare verse 13, where the singular is used ; so Norton, Luthardt, Stier, Godet, M. and M.) The sepulchre, whether it was on the traditional site or elsewhere, was probably excavated in a rocky ridge, and its entrance or door visible at some distance. Mary Magdalene, who saw no more than that the stone was rolled away, naturally supposed that the body had been taken away, and leaving those with her ran to find Peter and John. Whether the two apostles lodged together, we do not know. (The inference drawn from the repetition of the preposition, "She cometh to Simon Peter,

---

[1] As to the construction of Jewish tombs in the Lord's time, reference must be made to those who have written of them. It is sufficient to say here that the best informed divide the rock-cut tomb into two classes — *Kokim* tombs and *Loculus* tombs. In the former, the body is laid in a tunnel cut at right angles with the face of the rock, the head being at the further end, and the feet at its entrance. This was the earlier form, the loculus tomb is later. In this the body lay parallel with the side of the chamber in a cavity or recess. That the tomb in which the Lord lay was of this kind, appears from the fact that Mary Magdalene saw the angels sitting one at His head, another at His feet, a thing impossible in a kokim tomb. The tombs were closed in several ways, but the rolling stone was most in use at this time. This stone is described as round, generally about three feet in diameter and one foot in thickness, with an average weight of 600 pounds. Running in an inclined groove, it was difficult to move it back, and the shock of an earthquake could hardly have done this. That the tomb in the garden was thus closed, there is little reason to doubt. See Conder, Qt. St., 1869, p. 31, etc., also Qt. St., 1876 and 1877; Tobler, Qt. St., 1875, 1878.

and to the other disciple," that she found them in separate places — so Bengel and others — is not certain.) Peter and John, hearing the words of Mary, immediately run to the sepulchre, and enter it to find only the grave clothes and napkin ; no angel is seen. They depart, and Mary Magdalene, who must have followed them although her return is not mentioned, and now stood by the sepulchre, stooping down looked into it and saw two angels, who addressed her, asking why she wept. She turned back, and then she saw the Lord, who addressed her and gave her a message to bear to His brethren.

Comparing the accounts of Matthew and John, do they refer to the same appearance ? Was Mary Magdalene alone, or were others with her when she saw the Lord? That she was alone, is the impression which the whole narrative makes upon us. Every circumstance indicates this ; the Lord addresses her alone : " Woman, why weepest thou ? " He calls her by name, " Mary "; (contrast this with His salutation to the women : " All hail.") And it is confirmed by Mark's words (xvi. 9): " He appeared first to Mary Magdalene." It is said that these words do not mean that His first appearance, absolutely speaking, was to her, but that the first of the appearances related by Mark was to her. Thus Robinson: " Mark mentions three and only three appearances of the Lord; of these three, that to Mary Magdalene takes place first." But the larger part of the commentators understand Mark's words as referring to His first appearance to any one after His resurrection, and as showing that Mary Magdalene was alone (see Riddle's note, Har. 270).

We are led to the same result by considering the Lord's words to Mary Magdalene, and the message He gave her. It is not in our province to interpret the words, " Touch me not, for I am not yet ascended to my Father," but the message He gave her — " Go to my brethren and say unto them, I ascend unto my Father and your Father, and to my God and your God." — must be regarded in its relations to the time and purpose for which it was given. It was not like that in Matthew (xxviii. 10), a direction to go to Galilee. What was its significance ? It is said by Townson, that it was a voucher to the apostles that Mary Magdalene had actually seen Him, for He had spoken these very

words to them on the evening before His death (John xiv. 12
28, xvi. 16, 17). Hearing them now repeated from her lips,
they could not doubt that He had appeared to her. Admitting
that the message might thus serve as a voucher, this does not
fully explain its meaning. The Lord seems here to intend
to recall to the minds of the apostles His last discourse to
them in its chief themes — His departure to the Father, the
sending of the Comforter, and their work as His witnesses
during His absence. Thus, He encourages them to enter upon
their new work, and to look to Him, as risen and about to go
into heaven to be with the Father who loved Him, who also is
their Father; and with God, who has all power and can ever
uphold His servants. Greater works than He had done should
His servants do, because He ascends unto the Father. Thus
they were taught that His death did not dissolve their apostolic
relation to Him; with His resurrection their true apostolic activity was to begin. It is not congruous with the spirit of this
message that the Lord should immediately after direct Mary
Magdalene to go and tell His brethren to go into Galilee. It
would more fitly be given to other messengers.

Thus comparing the several accounts of the Evangelists, we
conclude that the Lord appeared first to Mary Magdalene alone,
and afterward to other women; and that His two messages in
Matthew and John are not to be identified as given to the same
persons.[1]

If we accept two appearances of the Lord to the women, one
to Mary Magdalene alone, and one to other women, in what relations of time, place, and persons do the two stand to each other?

As to time. We have already seen reason to believe that
the appearance to Mary Magdalene was the first. But some who
accept two appearances invert this order. Thus Robinson puts
the first appearance to the other women while Mary Magdalene
was going to call Peter and John. But we thus encounter the
difficulty that the women first reported a vision of angels (Luke

---

[1] Opinions whether there were one or two appearances of the Lord to the women,
are very evenly divided. For one appearance: Lightfoot, Lardner, Bengel, Godet, Bäum-
lein, Caspari, Da Costa, Lichtenstein, Ebrard, Greswell, Krafft, Tischendorf, Wieseler,
Tholuck, Weitbrecht; undecided, Edersheim. For two appearances: West, Newcome,
Olshausen, Stier, Robinson, Patritius, Friedlieb, Riddle, Gardiner, Ellicott, Geikie,
McClellan, Farrar, Lange, Sepp, Riggenbach, Stroud.

xxiv. 23), which shows that at this time they had not seen the
Lord.   The order of Giekie, who puts a very little interval of
time between the two appearances, is open to the same objection.
According to him, while Mary Magdalene runs to call Peter and
John, the other women remain in the garden till she returns, and
while the Lord is yet speaking with her, they approach and worship at His feet, and receive His message.   Greswell puts the
appearance to the other women a week after that to Mary Magdalene.   In this he stands alone.   As bearing on this point of
time, we must keep in mind the fact already referred to, that
the first report from the sepulchre was that of a vision of angels;
this was all that was known by the two disciples when they left
Jerusalem for Emmaus.   This vision must have been some time
before any one saw the Lord; and some women must, therefore,
have been at the sepulchre, and returned to the city and told
the disciples there of that vision before Mary Magdalene could
have brought to them her joyful tidings.

   As to the place.   Mary Magdalene saw the Lord in the garden and near the sepulchre; where did He meet the other
women?   It is said by Matthew (xxviii. 8, 9) that after seeing
the angels in the sepulchre, they left it, "and did run to bring
His disciples word.   And as they went to tell His disciples, behold, Jesus met them."   (In R. V., "And as they went to tell
His disciples," is omitted.)   It is impossible to judge from this
account whether He met them in the garden or without it; but
as the garden could not well have been a large one, we may
suppose it was without it.   On the other hand, the place of His
manifestation could not well have been in a street of a crowded
city.   It is not improbable that they were lodging outside the
city walls, and that He met them at some secluded part of the
road.

   As to the persons.   That Mary Magdalene did not go alone to the
sepulchre, is most probable.   Who were with her?   Was the other
Mary only?   Were there two, the other Mary and Salome? Were all
the Galilæan women with her?   The most probable supposition is,
that most of these women, (for there were others whose names are not
mentioned,) went to the sepulchre, either to help in anointing the
body or to look upon the place where He was lying.   It is not likely
that all went together, for probably they lodged in several different

places, but as all would go early, they would all arrive at nearly the
same time. It is easily credible that Mary Magdalene, the other
Mary, and Salome may have gone together and reached the sepulchre
first. This group may have been divided into two by the going of
Mary Magdalene to call Peter and John. In this case the two remaining women enter the sepulchre, see the angels, receive a message, and
return back to the disciples in the city. Did another party of
women, of whom the name of Joanna only is given, come to the tomb
while they and Mary Magdalene were absent? There is nothing incredible in this, and some affirm it. If so, it must have been to them
that the vision of angels recorded by Luke (xxiv. 4) was given.
According to this arrangement, we have: 1st, the vision of angels
given to the other Mary and Salome (Matt.); 2d, that given to Joanna
and those with her (Luke); 3d, that to Mary Magdalene on her return
to the tomb (John). All three were before the appearance of the
Lord to Mary Magdalene. To which of the groups, the second or
third, did the Lord afterward appear? If to the second — the other
Mary and Salome — it must have been after their return from delivering the message given them by the angel, since otherwise they,
having seen Him, would have announced His resurrection. If to
the third — Joanna and those with her — it could not have been long
after His appearance to Mary Magdalene.

On the supposition of two appearances of the Lord to the women,
several divisions of the persons have been made to show to whom He
appeared the second time. We may thus classify them:

1. To all the women together except Mary Magdalene. (So
Gardiner, Lex., Stroud, Westcott, Riddle, Farrar, Ellicott.)

2. To all including Mary Magdalene. (So Newcome.)

3. To the other Mary and Salome. (So West, Stier, Grenville,
Friedlieb.)

4. To the three — the other Mary, Salome, and Mary Magdalene.
(So Townson.)

5. To the two, the other Mary and Mary Magdalene. (So McClel.)

6. To Joanna and her party, or to all excepting the two Marys and
Salome.

Thus according to three of the above divisions, Mary Magdalene
twice saw the Lord, once alone and once in company with others.
It is said by a Lapide on Matthew (xxviii. 9) that this was held by
St. Chrysostom, Jerome, and others of the fathers.

We have not space to give the various arrangements based upon
the above classification. It will be readily seen that many variations
of the order will arise if we suppose the women to have arrived at

the tomb together, or in two or more groups. Thus Gardiner makes but one party, and supposes that while Mary Magdalene went to Peter and John, the rest entered the sepulchre and saw the angel and received his message, but were then divided into two groups — some being so terrified that they say nothing to any one (Mark), the others bear the message to the apostles, and subsequently return; and it is on this return that the Lord appears to them. On the other hand, Riddle makes two parties — the two Marys and Salome who come first to the sepulchre, and while Mary Magdalene goes to find Peter and John, the other two enter the tomb, see the angel, hear the message, and go back to meet the other women. In the meantime, Mary Magdalene sees the Lord, and returns to the city to give His message. Her two companions going to the city, meet the other women on their way to the sepulchre; returning with them, they see the two angels, and on their way back to the city they see the Lord. McClellan thinks that there were two parties; the first to reach the tomb were Joanna and those with her; a little later came the two Marys and Salome; by agreement, the last party goes to find Peter and John, the others remaining at the tomb. Peter and John visit the tomb and go back to the city, and then all the women enter it, see the angels, receive a message and depart, some going to Bethany and some to the apostles in the city. Peter goes a second time to the tomb with John and Mary Magdalene; the two apostles return to the city, and then Mary Magdalene sees the Lord, and returns to give His message to the disciples. After this she visits the tomb again with the other Mary, and on the way the Lord meets them. Thus Mary Magdalene saw Him twice.

A point not yet noticed demands attention. Did Peter twice visit the sepulchre? We know that he visited it with John; as Luke (xxiv. 12) does not speak of John, not a few have said that Luke mentions a second visit of Peter alone. The cause of this visit, it is said, was the message given him by Mary Magdalene after she saw the Lord (so Jones); but McClellan makes the cause of the second visit the message of the angel by the women, and thinks that he was accompanied by John and Mary Magdalene; it was after this second visit that she saw the Lord. But most identify the two accounts (so Keil, Friedlieb, Nebe, Gardiner).[1]

This examination of the several narratives shows us how many of the data are wanting which are necessary to enable us to form a reg-

---

[1] The genuineness of this verse (xxiv. 12) has been questioned. It is omitted by Tisch. and bracketed by W. and H.; Gardiner retains it, but thinks "it may have slipped from its proper place." It is retained by Meyer, Keil, Riddle. Friedlieb.

ular, harmonious, and complete history of this eventful morning. Each of the Evangelists gives us some particulars which the others omit, but no one of them aims to give us a full and connected account. To a superficial examination there seem many discrepancies, not to say contradictions, but a thorough investigation shows that the points of real difference are very few, and that in several ways even these differences may be removed. While thus we cannot say of any order which we can frame, that it is certain, we can say of several that they are probable; and if they cannot be proved, neither can they be disproved. This is sufficient for him who finds in the moral character of the Gospels the highest vouchers for their historic truth.

To bring before the reader some of the many possible arrangements of these events, and to show what the special difficulties in the way of the harmonists are, we select the following. It will be noted that the point which chiefly determines the order, is whether Jesus appeared once or twice to the women. We begin with those who affirm only one appearance.

I. *Lightfoot.* 1. Earthquake and resurrection of Christ. 2. Visit of Mary Magdalene and other women to the tomb, which they reach just as the sun is up. They are told of His resurrection by the angels, and go back to the disciples. 3. Peter and John go to the sepulchre followed by Mary Magdalene. They return and she remains. 4. Christ appears to her and she takes Him for the gardener. She afterward embraces His feet, kissing them. Thus Matthew (xxviii. 9) and John (xx. 14) refer to the same appearance.

Lardner. 1. The women with Mary Magdalene go to the sepulchre and find it empty. 2. Mary, with others, goes to the apostles Peter and John. 3. They come to the tomb and then return home. 4. Mary Magdalene and the others follow the two apostles back to the tomb, and remain there after Peter and John are gone. 5. Jesus appears to them all there. 6. Mary Magdalene and the others go and announce all to the disciples. Here, also, the appearance to Mary Magdalene mentioned by John, and that to the two Marys mentioned by Matthew, are made the same.

Da Costa. 1. The two Marys, Joanna, Salome, and others, start before daybreak for the sepulchre, and find the stone rolled away. 2. Mary Magdalene runs to find Peter and John. 3. The other women enter the sepulchre, see the angels, receive their message, and return to the disciples. 4. Peter and John visit the sepulchre and depart home. 5. Mary Magdalene, who had followed them, sees first the angels and then the Lord, and returns to the disciples. Here the Lord appears to Mary Magdalene only.

Ebrard. 1. Mary Magdalene visits the sepulchre early while it is yet dark. She finds the stone rolled away, and runs to find Peter and John. 2. Mary, mother of James, Joanna, Salome, and other women, go to anoint the body, and looking into the tomb, see an angel who gives them a message. They depart, but dare not report to any one what has occurred. 3. Peter and John come to the grave and return home. 4. Mary Magdalene, who had followed them, sees two angels, and then the Lord. She returns and tells the disciples. Here there is one appearance only — that to Mary Magdalene.

II. Arrangements affirming two appearances of the Lord to the women:

Townson. 1. The two Marys and Salome go to the tomb, and while they are on the way the angel descends and rolls away the stone. They reach it at the rising of the sun. 2. Mary Magdalene goes for Peter and John. 3. The other Mary and Salome enter the porch of the sepulchre, see an angel, receive his message, and depart in great fear. 4. Peter and John come and visit the tomb. 5. Mary Magdalene returns and sees first the angels and then the Lord. 6. Mary Magdalene departing, falls in with the other Mary and Salome, and to them together Jesus appears the second time. 7. Joanna and her party now come, and, entering the tomb, see two angels. They return, and confirm to the disciples what the other women had already reported. 8. Peter goes a second time to the sepulchre, and finds only the clothes. 9. The two disciples set out for Emmaus. 10. The Lord appears to Peter. Here are made two successive appearances to Mary Magdalene: first, when alone; second, to her in company with the other Mary.

Newcome. 1. The two Marys, Salome, Joanna, and others, go to the sepulchre, and, finding the stone removed, enter the tomb. Two angels appear to them, and one gives them a message. 2. They return to Jerusalem, and Mary Magdalene communicates the message to Peter and John, and the other women to the other disciples. 3. Peter and John go to the sepulchre and return. 4. The two disciples, having heard the report of the women and of Peter and John, depart for Emmaus. 5. Mary Magdalene and the other women follow Peter and John to the tomb. She, arriving before them, or following after them, sees the angels and afterward the Lord. 6. She joins the other women who were near by, and, as they are returning to Jerusalem, Jesus meets them. 7. He appears to Peter. 8. He appears to the two at Emmaus. Here Mary Magdalene alone first sees the Lord, and afterward she sees Him the second time in company with others.

Lange. 1. The two Marys and Salome go to the grave. Another party — Joanna and others with her — was to follow with the spices

26*

and ointments. The former see the stone rolled away, and Mary Magdalene runs to find Peter and John. 2. The other Mary and Salome approach and see one angel sitting upon the stone, and afterward another within the sepulchre who gives them a message, and they depart. 3. Peter and John visit the sepulchre and return. 4. Mary Magdalene sees two angels and then the Lord. 5. Jesus appears to the other Mary and Salome on their way to the disciples. 6. These two fall in with Joanna and her party, and together return to the sepulchre and see two angels. 7. He appears to the two disciples. 8. He appears to Peter. Here the Lord appears first to Mary Magdalene, then to the other Mary and Salome.

Robinson. 1. The two Marys, Joanna, and Salome, and others, go to the sepulchre to embalm the body, and find the stone rolled away. 2. Mary Magdalene runs to find Peter and John. 3. The other women see two angels in the tomb, who give them a message to the disciples, and they depart. 4. Jesus meets them on the way and renews the message. 5. Peter and John come to the sepulchre and return home. 6. Mary Magdalene sees the two angels and then the Lord. 7. Jesus appears to Peter. 8. He appears to the two going to Emmaus. Here the Lord first appears to the other women, and then to Mary Magdalene.

Westcott.— 1. (5 A. M.) Mary Magdalene with others goes to the sepulchre. She leaves them and goes to find Peter and John. 2. (5.30 A. M.) The other women go to the sepulchre, see an angel, and receive a message and return to the city. 3. (6 A. M.) Another party — Joanna and those with her — go to the sepulchre and see two angels. 4. (6.30 A. M.) Peter and John reach the sepulchre and return. 5. Mary Magdalene returning, sees two angels and the Lord. 6. He appears to the other women as they are coming back to the sepulchre.

Greswell, as has been already observed, makes a second appearance to the women — the other Mary and Salome — but puts it on the following Sunday, a week later.

Let us now attempt to frame a continuous narrative from the accounts of the several Evangelists. Very early in the morning the women from Galilee to the number of five or more, who had been present at the crucifixion and burial, start for the sepulchre to anoint the body, probably coming from different parts of the city, or perhaps from without it. Perhaps Mary Magdalene alone, or with the other Mary and Salome, may have a little preceded the others. They knew, for some at least were eye-wit nesses, that a great stone had been rolled to the door of the sepulchre, and it was therefore a question with them how they could roll it away. But they did not know of the sealing of the stone and the setting of the watch which took place after the Sabbath had begun. As they approach the sepulchre, they see that the stone is rolled away; and Mary Magdalene, who naturally inferred that the Jews had removed the body, in deep excitement runs to inform the two chief apostles, Peter and John, of this fact. The other women continue to approach the sepulchre. That the angel was not now sitting upon the stone and visible to them, and that the guards were not lying as dead men before the door, seem most probable, as otherwise their fears would have deterred them from advancing. Seeing nothing, they enter the sepulchre. An angel now appears to them, and, after bidding them not be afraid, shows them the empty niche where the body was laid, and proceeds to announce to them that He is risen, and will meet the disciples in Galilee, as He had said to them while He was with them. Greatly agitated by what they had seen and heard, fear contending with joy, they leave the sepulchre and return to the city.

Soon after their departure, but how soon is uncertain, as we do not know where Mary Magdalene found Peter and John, the two apostles come running with all speed to determine the truth of her account. John, who reaches the tomb first, only looks in, but Peter enters, and is followed by John. The body is gone; but, examining carefully, they see the grave clothes arranged in order, and the napkin lying by itself. John is convinced by all that he sees that the Lord is indeed risen; but Peter only marvels. They seem to have departed very quickly again, perhaps to inform the other disciples that the body was truly gone; or perhaps they were afraid lest they should be found by the Lord's enemies at the tomb. Mary Magdalene, who had followed them back to the sepulchre, did not depart with them, but remained standing without, weeping. It is plain from the whole narrative that she was under the power of the most intense grief, believing that the body of her Lord had been borne away by His enemies. While weeping she stoops down to look in, as if a faint hope still lingered that she should see Him there, and sees two angels sitting, one at the head and one at the feet, where the body had lain. Unlike the other women, who had been greatly terrified at the angelic apparition, she seems scarce to have noticed them; and to their question, "Woman, why weepest thou ?" she answers in words showing how wholly her heart was filled with her one great sorrow. Lifting her head, for she was now looking into the tomb, and turning back, she sees Jesus, but does not recognize Him. He addresses her with the inquiry, "Woman, why weepest thou?" Supposing Him to be the gardener, probably because it was natural that he should be there, and thinking that he might possibly have taken away the body, she addresses Him in words full of passionate earnestness. The Lord's reply, "Mary," spoken in His own familiar voice, recalls her to herself. She recognizes Him, and, prostrating herself, would hold Him by the feet to worship Him. He forbids her to touch Him, and gives her a message to His brethren. She departs and tells the disciples, but they believe not. A little after this, the Lord appears to the two women who had been to the city, and who were probably accompanied by others, and permits them to worship Him, and gives to them a message.

Thus we find most probable that there were three visions of angels, the first to the two women, the second to Mary Magdalene, the third to the other women; and two appearances of the Lord, that to Mary Magdalene, and that to the other women returning to the tomb; all closely following each other. As yet, these supernatural manifestations were vouchsafed only to the women. Peter and John saw at the sepulchre neither angels nor the Lord. They found, indeed, the sepulchre open and the body gone; but the fact that He had risen, rested solely on the testimony of the women. Perhaps the fact that He had not appeared to any of the apostles, had something to do with the incredulity of the latter, for it was natural to suppose that He would first manifest Himself to them (Mark xvi. 11).

Rumors that the sepulchre was empty must have become current among the disciples early in the day, and probably most or all of them, or at least of the apostles, visited it, though we have no record of their visits.

The historical accuracy of the account of the bribing of the soldiers by the chief priests and elders, has been often questioned,[1] but on insufficient grounds.   The number constituting the watch is not mentioned; some say two, some four; the latter number appears oftenest in Art.   The watch came into the city, report-ing to the chief priests, to whom they were responsible, what had taken place at the sepulchre.   The priests, who took counsel with the elders, may have believed this or may not, but they doubtless ascertained to their own satisfaction that the body was actually gone.   What should they do?   Should they report the statement of the soldiers to their commander?   But to what end? since all the facts of the affair must thus necessarily come to the ears of Pilate, and become more generally known.   As it could not be concealed that the body was gone, some plausible explanation must be given.   What could answer the purpose so well as to admit this fact, and say that the disciples had done what they attempted to guard against when they set the watch — had stolen away the body?   But this, if openly said, the soldiers would naturally contradict as exposing them to military punish-ment, and the priests would therefore gently hint it rather than expressly affirm it; and in this way it would spread among the people as a rumor, and gradually gain credence.   To guard against any denial on the part of the soldiers, these must be bribed to admit that the story set afloat by the priests was true.   They would not affirm the absurdity that they knew what the disciples were doing while they were sleeping; but would merely keep silence as to what they had actually seen, and not deny that they might have been asleep, and that the theft of the body might possibly have occurred.   Of course this report thus secretely circulated would soon become cur-rent, and by most of the Jews be believed.[2]   Whether it ever reached the ears of Pilate, we do not know; probably he very soon left Jerusalem for Caesarea, but if it did, he might be bribed to pass their offense by in silence.   Very probably, he was not much displeased at the disappearance of the body, or grieved at the discomfiture of the priests and Pharisees.

---

[1] See Meyer, *in loco.*

[2] See the excellent observations of Jones, Notes, 483.

SUNDAY, 17TH NISAN, 9TH APRIL, 783.   A. D. 30.

Early in the afternoon two of the disciples leave Jerusalem for Emmaus. As they go, Jesus joins Himself to
them, and converses with them till they reach the village.
At their urgent request He sits down to eat with them,
and as He is breaking the bread, their eyes, which were
holden that they should not know Him, are opened, but
He immediately vanishes out of their sight.   They return
at once to Jerusalem, and find the Eleven and others gathered together, who meet them with the announcement
that the Lord is indeed risen and has appeared to Simon.
But the account of the two disciples that they had
also seen Him at Emmaus, is disbelieved. While yet
speaking together, Jesus Himself stands in the midst of
them, although the doors are shut, and salutes them.   He
convinces them of the reality of His bodily presence by
showing them His hands and His feet, and by eating before them.   He breathes upon them, and gives them the
power to remit sins, and opens their understanding to
understand the Scriptures.

LUKE xxiv. 13–32.
MARK xvi. 12.

LUKE xxiv. 33.
MARK xvi. 13, 14.
LUKE xxiv. 34, 35
1 COR. xv. 5.

LUKE xxiv. 36–48.
JOHN xx. 19–23.

The name of one of the disciples going to Emmaus was
Cleopas (Luke xxiv. 18).   Many identify him with Cleophas,
Clopas, or Alphæus, the husband of Mary (John xix. 25).   It is
most probable that he was a different person.   (So Meyer, Keil.)
The name of the other disciple is not given.   Lightfoot supposes him to have been Peter himself; it was early a very
common opinion that he was Luke, the narrative seeming to be
that of one present, and that the Evangelist through modesty
did not mention his own name.   Wieseler (431), who makes
Cleopas to have been Alphæus, makes the other the apostle
James, his son ; and this the appearance mentioned by St. Paul
(1 Cor. xv. 7).   Another early tradition calls him Simon.   It was
formerly said by some that the two mentioned in Mark xvi. 12,
whose names are not given, were different persons, but this is
not now held by any.

The place to which the two went was Emmaus.   Josephus
mentions three places of this name; one on the Lake of Galilee near Tiberias (War, iv. 1. 3), another sixty furlongs from
Jerusalem, where eight hundred Roman soldiers were colonized
(War, vii. 6. 6); and still another, a city mentioned in connection with Gophna (Antiq., xiv. 11. 2; War, iii. 3. 5), and after-

wards known as Emmaus Nicopolis. (See Winer, ii. 325.) The distance he gives of the second of these places from Jerusalem coincides exactly with that of Luke (xxiv. 13). But there is some question as to the right reading in Josephus, whether thirty or sixty stadia; the last is generally accepted. (See T. G. Lex., *sub voce.*)

We have three data in Luke for identifying Emmaus — its name, its distance from Jerusalem, and its designation as "a village " — κώμη. The name is defined by Josephus (War, iv. 1. 3), speaking of the town near Tiberias as "signifying warm water — θέρμα — the name being derived from a warm spring which rises there, possessing sanative properties." This warm spring still exists, and is the same mentioned in Joshua (xix. 35), and called Hammath. But it does not appear that there were ever any warm springs at the other two places spoken of by Josephus. The name Emmaus, therefore, does not of itself show that there were hot springs at each place so called; it might be given to a place where were springs affording water for baths, whether cold or artificially heated. That the Emmaus Nicopolis of Josephus had any hot spring does not appear, though there was one there with medicinal properties (in T. G. Lex., erroneously said "noted for its hot springs"; Lightfoot, x. 298; Hamburger, ii. 172; for present conditions Baedeker, 138). Nor are there now hot springs anywhere in the neighborhood of Jerusalem, or indeed, in Judæa, whatever may have been the case formerly. Baths, warm and cold, were found in all the large cities. We may, therefore, conclude that the name Emmaus was sometimes applied to places where were springs, hot or cold, and with or without baths. Thus the name gives only this much of positive result, that the Emmaus which we seek must have been at some place where were springs and an abundance of water, and probably baths.

The second datum is its distance from Jerusalem — sixty furlongs. The oldest and most prominent claimant is Emmaus Nicopolis, which lies in the plain of Judah about twenty miles west from Jerusalem, a village a little to the left of the road from Ramleh, and now called Amwas (Rob. ii. 265 and iii. 347). The claim is supported by Robinson, mainly on the ground that it is the traditional site: "For thirteen centuries did the interpretation current in the whole Church regard the Emmaus of the New Testament as identical with Nicopolis." But tradition, to which Robinson is not usually so deferential, cannot overcome the intrinsic difficulties lying in its remoteness from Jerusalem. To do this, he must deny the genuineness of the received reading in Luke of sixty furlongs, and maintain that the reading found in some manuscripts of one hundred and sixty furlongs, is the true one. This correction of the text is accepted by few. But if we accept it, it would take some five or six hours to go from Jerusalem to Emmaus, and if the two disciples left the city at twelve M., they would not have reached the village till near six P. M. Allowing that only a very brief time was spent in preparation for the evening meal, and that after it they returned with all haste, they could not have reached Jerusalem till near midnight. Considering the habits of the Orientals, it is very improbable that on their return they found the disciples assembled together at that hour, nor is it likely that the Lord would have chosen it to make His first appearance to them. We have, moreover, some marks of the time when the two met the disciples. Mark (xvi. 14) says: "He appeared unto the Eleven as they sat at meat." John (xx. 19) says that when He appeared to the Eleven it was evening — ὀψία — and this was probably "the first evening," which began at three P. M. and ended at sunset. As the sun at this season set soon after six o'clock, and there is but a short twilight, the two from Emmaus, on arriving at Jerusalem, probably found the disciples at their evening meal, or soon after it. All this shows that the two must have reached Jerusalem at least early in the evening, and that Emmaus must have been within easy reach of the city.

The third datum is the designation by Luke of Emmaus as a "village"; but Emmaus Nicopolis was "a city," a large and important place, not a village.

Upon these grounds, we must believe that the Emmaus of Luke cannot be placed at a greater distance than he has placed it — sixty furlongs, and was not Emmaus N. Robinson himself was earlier of this opinion (Bib. Sacra., 1845, 181), and said that the distance of Emmaus Nicopolis was too great for the disciples to have returned the same evening, and concluded: "We must therefore abide by the usual reading." (See the note in Bonar's "Land of Promise," Index, 537. Most reject the claims of Emmaus Nicopolis, Meyer, Godet, Keil, Edersheim.)

Setting aside Emmaus Nicopolis, there are three other places which have their advocates. The first of these is a village called El Kubeibeh, lying northwest from Jerusalem, and on the road to Lydda. Its distance from the city, as measured by the German architect Schick, is very nearly sixty furlongs, though others make it a little more. It has in its favor a tradition dating from the crusades, or perhaps earlier. Baedeker (142) speaks of it as having many ruins, and a beautiful situation. There is a fountain, but not very copious, and no traces of any baths. But Robinson finds no tradition earlier than the fourteenth century, and denies that there are any grounds in its favor but its distance from Jerusalem.

The second is Kulonieh, a village a little northwest of Jerusalem on the road to Joppa. Its name is derived by some from the Latin Colonia. If this be the derivation, it answers to the statement of Josephus respecting the colonization at Emmaus of the Roman soldiers. The distance, however, does not correspond with Luke's statement, for it is less than sixty furlongs from Jerusalem. (Edersheim, ii. 638, says forty-five furlongs; Conder, Qt. St., 1885, 348, only thirty-five furlongs.) A good spring is found there, and it was, and still is, a place of pleasure resort for the inhabitants of Jerusalem. Some advocates of this site connect it with a Motsa mentioned in the Talmud and identified with Kulonieh, whence willows were brought to Jerusalem for the feast of Tabernacles. (So Caspari, 242; Conder, Tentwork, 25.) Edersheim (ii. 639) rejects this on the ground that Kulonieh was northwest of Jerusalem, while Motsa was south of it. He accepts a view presented in Qt. St., (1881, 237) that puts Emmaus between Kulonieh and Kubeibeh. "Between these places is Beit Mizza, or Hammoza, which I regard as the real Emmaus. It would be nearly fifty-five or about sixty furlongs, sufficiently near to Kolonieh (Colonia) to account for the name, since the colony would extend up the valley, and sufficiently near to Kubeibeh to account for the tradition, that this was the Emmaus of the crusaders.'' (See Qt. St., 1881, 274, and 1884, 247. In favor of identifying Kulonieh with Emmaus, Sepp, Caspari, Woolf in Riehm, Henderson, Oosterzee, Godet; *contra*, Rob. iii. 158.)

A third claimant is found in Khamasa, where some ruins were found by Capt. Conder, not far from the Roman road which passes by Solomon's pools south of Jerusalem. "Ancient rock-cut sepulchres and a causeway mark the site as being one of considerable antiquity, and its vicinity is still remarkable for its fine supply of spring water" (Qt. St., 1879, 107). Khamasa is eight miles southwest of Jerusalem according to Conder, but others make the distance nine to ten miles. As this identification is said to be given up by Conder who first presented it, it need not be further discussed. (But it still appears in his "Hard Book," 1882.)

There is still another claimant in Urtas, a valley a little eastward of the main road from Bethlehem to Hebron, and about a mile from the pools of Solomon at El Burak, and probably the Etam of the Old Testament. (Rob., iii. 273.) Its claims were first presented by Mrs. Finn (Qt. St., 1883, 53), who for ten years had made diligent personal search all around Jerusalem to find the true Emmaus. Its claims rest upon its distance from Jerusalem, about sixty furlongs; the existence there of Roman baths; and its name of Latin origin — Urtas — a corruption of *hortus*, a garden; all these pointing to its identification with the second Emmaus of Josephus. It has a large and noble fountain, and by this the valley is watered and not from Solomon's pools. Tristram (B. P., 70) says: "The valley is now a blooming garden, and many most interesting proofs of its wealth have been exhumed, especially a beautiful set of marble baths built after the Jewish fashion, with rich carving in the Egyptian style." These Mrs. Finn supposes to have been Roman baths, and to point to a residence there of the discharged Roman soldiers mentioned by Josephus. Here is plenty of water, and remains of baths, such as are not found elsewhere in the vicinity of Jerusalem. The Arabic name Hammam, which, according to Conder, is used of any bath, hot or cold, was applied to these remains by the natives, and would well answer to the name

Emmaus. But that this name was the old one, and that it was later changed by the Roman soldiers from Emmaus to Hortus and corrupted into Urtas, is only a probable conjecture.

As the evidence now is, the choice seems to lie between Kubeibeh and Urtas. Both would satisfy the conditions as to distance, and both have springs. In favor of Kubeibeh is a tradition, though of late date, and its proximity to Kulonieh; in favor of Urtas, its name, and its baths, and the possible remains of an old fortification. The question can be settled only by further local examination, and we must for the present regard the site of Emmaus as an unsolved problem.

The time when the two disciples left Jerusalem is not mentioned, but it was probably about noon or soon after. At the time of their departure they had heard of the appearance of the angels to the women, and of the visit of Peter and John to the sepulchre, but not of any appearance of the Lord (Luke xxiv. 22–24). As the distance was only some eight miles, they may have reached Emmaus a good while before sundown, but it is to be remembered that the Lord gave them much instruction by the way (verse 27), making it probable that they went slowly.

When the Lord met the two, He was not recognized by them. Luke says (verse 16): "Their eyes were holden that they should not know Him." This some have thought discrepant with Mark's statement (xvi. 12) that "He appeared in another form — $\dot{\epsilon}\nu\ \dot{\epsilon}\tau\dot{\epsilon}\rho\alpha\ \mu o\rho\phi\hat{\eta}$ — unto two of them." The latter expression may refer to His previous appearance to Mary Magdalene by whom He had been mistaken for the gardener,[1] or to another form than that before the resurrection. That His bodily aspect was in many points after the resurrection unlike what it had been before, we cannot doubt, though it is impossible for us to tell wherein those distinctions consisted. (See John xxi. 4.) Still the language of Luke implies that there was no such change as to forbid His recognition; and that, in this case, except the eyes of the disciples had been specially holden, they would have known Him. As said by Alexander: "Luke gives the cause, Mark the effect." "Their eyes were opened and they knew Him, and He vanished out of their sight" (Luke xxiv. 31).[2] Rising up the same hour,

---

[1] So Lardner.

[2] The explanation of the failure of the disciples to recognize the Lord during the forty days, would demand an enquiry into the nature of the resurrection body which would be foreign to our purpose. But the explanation which assumes a process of bodily glorification, and so a progressive change of appearance (Meyer, Godet, Edersheim), has

they returned to Jerusalem, reaching it probably early in the evening, joy at again beholding their Lord adding wings to their feet, and find the Eleven [1] as they sat at meat.   The place where the apostles were assembled was in all probability the same in which they had eaten the paschal supper, and to which they returned from the Mount of Olives after the Ascension.

First appearance of the Eleven.   Before we consider the memorable events of this evening, some preliminary points must be discussed. Is this appearance to the Eleven, as narrated in Luke, the same as that in John xx. 19 and in Mark xvi. 14?   This is generally held, but it will be well to examine each account and compare them.

It is plain from John's words: "Then the same day at evening, being the first day of the week, . . . came Jesus," etc., that this was the Easter evening.   Luke's statements of the time are equally clear.   But Mark's designation of time (xvi. 14) is wholly indefinite, "Afterward — ὕστερον — He appeared unto the Eleven."   Some, therefore, refer this statement to the second appearance to the Eleven (John xx. 26); others hold that Mark sums up in a general way the events which John distinguishes as on two successive Sundays.   Two circumstances, however, in Mark's narrative give a note of the time; one, that they "sat at meat," the meal being then probably over. John does not mention this circumstance, nor Luke, though it is implied in the Lord's question, "Have ye here any meat?"   Another note of time is the Lord's reproof which, as we shall see, fits better to the first than to the second appearance, a week later.   But on the other hand, there are some discrepancies between Mark and Luke as to the reception of the testimony of the two disciples from Emmaus. Mark says (verse 13): "And they went and told it unto the residue,

---

very little in its favor.   If this means, as it seems to do, that the material body of the resurrection gradually lost its material element, and became at last a spiritual, *i. e.* immaterial body, this is contrary to all the teaching of the Church.   The common belief is expressed by Leo: *Resurrectio Domini non finis carnis, sed commutatio fuit, nec virtutis augmento consumpta substantia est.*   Wholly without any ground in the narratives is Godet's attempt to explain the Lord's sudden disappearance from the two at Emmaus — "He vanished out of their sight" — by saying that the body was now partially glorified, and so "obeyed more freely than before the will of the spirit."   The ground taken by some, as Rothe, that the Lord's body at the resurrection had no material element, and that from time to time, in order to manifest Himself, He took a body as a man might put on a garment, need only be mentioned.   (Nebe, Auferstehungsgeschichte, 136.) The assumption that His glorified body as such, was invisible, cannot be granted.   (2 Peter i. 16: "We were eye witnesses of His majesty.")   But it may be said as in the Speaker's Com.: "Recognition, in all cases of appearance between the resurrection and the ascension, depended on the spiritual state of the witnesses and upon His own will."

[1] Strictly speaking, only ten of the apostles were there.   It is a fancy of Caspari's that Matthew was not present, having already gone into Galilee.

neither believed they them." Luke says (verses 33–35) that, when the two found the apostles, they were met with the joyful cry: "The Lord is risen indeed, and hath appeared to Simon." These words seem to declare their firm belief that He had risen.

But before considering this supposed disagreement between Mark and Luke, we must ask how is this statement in Luke to be reconciled with the statement immediately following, that, when Jesus actually stood in the midst of them and spake to them, "they were terrified and affrighted, and supposed that they had seen a spirit?" it is not surprising that in their agitated state of mind they should at one moment have believed, and at another have disbelieved. As said by Bengel: *Credebant sed mox recurrebat suspicio et ipsa incredulitas.* Here two circumstances are to be taken into account: first, that when the Lord met the two disciples on their way, there was nothing in His appearance or manner to suggest a supernatural person. He was a man like themselves, an ordinary traveller; and it was not till after a long conversation that they knew Him in the breaking of bread. But His appearance to the Eleven was sudden; the doors were closed. How found He admittance? When He earlier appeared to the apostles walking upon the sea in the night (Matt. xiv. 25, 26), "they were troubled, saying, It is a spirit, and they cried out for fear." It is not strange, therefore, that now sudden doubts should arise in their hearts as to the reality of His resurrection. Did they indeed see Him or only His ghost?

Another circumstance is to be taken into account. The two disciples reported that He had been with them on their walk to Emmaus, perhaps joining them soon after leaving Jerusalem, and leaving them only at evening, and yet He had also been seen by Peter in the city. Here were seemingly contradictory accounts. Ignorant of the properties of His resurrection body, and the power of sudden transition from place to place, they might say that if He was with the two at Emmaus at the time they said, He could not have appeared to Peter in Jerusalem, and that the appearances, therefore, were not true bodily appearances, but phantasmal.

We do not, then, find anything inconsistent in the two statements of Luke. The events of the day had convinced all the disciples that the Lord had left the sepulchre, and was near them in some form, nor did they question Peter's witness; but had He really risen, or, were they now seeing an apparition? It was to convince them of the reality of His resurrection that He said to them: "Handle me and see," and afterward called for food and ate before them.

Returning now to the statement of Mark (xvi. 13) that the two disciples told of the Lord's appearance to them "unto the residue, neither believed they them"; it is in question whether in "the residue" the apostles are included.   Jones denies this, but most include them.   If so, the unbelief and hardness of heart in Mark which the Lord reproved, are the same as the doubts and fears in Luke; the accounts are consistent.

We may here ask in what chronological relations did the appearance to Simon Peter (Luke xxiv. 34) stand to that to the two disciples?   Some place it before (so Jones, Godet); some after (Eders., McClel., Rob., and most).   It was most probably a little after the two left Emmaus on their return, as it was generally known to the disciples when they reached the city.   Some have connected this appearance to Peter with a second visit to the sepulchre (Luke xxiv. 12), following the tidings of Mary Magdalene that she had seen the Lord in the garden; and if Peter saw Him at this time, it was before He appeared to the two.   But there are two questions here; the first as to the text.   Tischendorf omits verse 12, W. and H. bracket it; but others, Godet, Meyer, Keil, would retain it, and it is kept in R. V.   But accepting it, does it show that Peter went a second time alone to the tomb, or is it a summary mention of the earlier visit of Peter and John?   The last seems most probable, and is most in harmony with the generality of the language in the account preceding.

Turning to the account in John (xx. 19), we find it in some points like that in Luke, but in some, unlike.   They have in common the proof that the Lord gave of His real bodily presence, by showing the disciples His hands and His side,[1] but John omits the eating before them.   Luke does not speak of the shut door, but implies it in the fear that fell on them when they saw Him standing among them. John says that the disciples were glad when they saw the Lord, but this must refer to the time when He had convinced them that it was He Himself, not a spectre.   But all do not identify the account in Luke with that in John as the appearance of the Lord on Easter evening; some saying that he has generalized the accounts of John, embracing the first and second appearances; and others, that he speaks of the second meeting only (John xx. 26).   The last is maintained in the Speaker's Commentary.   The grounds of this will be considered in speaking of the ascension.

What is peculiar to John is the renewed commission to His apostles, the imparting of the Holy Ghost, and the authority to remit and retain sins.   Of this act of the Lord, and of the accompanying words

---

[1] In Luke xxiv., verse 40 is omitted by Tisch. and bracketed by W. and H., but its omission is of no importance as to the point before us.

in their theological bearing, we are not called to speak, but they are of importance to us as a renewal of the apostolic commission. As in His last prayer (John xvii. 18), He said of the apostles: "As Thou hast sent Me into the world, even so have I also sent them into the world," so here addressing them He says: "As my Father hath sent Me, even so send I you." Thus they learned that His death and resurrection made no change in their official relation to Him; that they were still His apostles, and with a new commission, and a ministry yet to be fulfilled. To fulfill this ministry they must receive the Holy Ghost. The significance of His breathing upon them, whether as a means for the giving of the Spirit, or as significant of His new life and a proof of His resurrection, belongs to the commentators. The power to remit and to retain sins clearly looked forward to a holy church, and implied such close communion with Him, though absent, that their acts were truly His acts.

We may here sum up the significance of these several appearances on the day of the resurrection.

The fact that the Lord was risen was shown by the empty sepulchre, and by the word of the angels: "He is not here; for He is risen, as he said. Come, see the place where the Lord lay." But into what condition of being had He entered? Was His body real or only phantasmal? What were His relations to His disciples? What was He about to do? All was in their minds vague, confused, uncertain. His first step therefore was to convince them that His resurrection was but a new form of His manhood. He was the same Jesus; His old relations to them were unchanged. His work was to go on, the apostles were to continue to be His helpers, the continuity of His Person and of His work was unbroken.

It is from this point of view that His words and acts on Easter Sunday are to be regarded. All tended to establish such community between the Lord as the First born from the dead and the disciples that they should see in Him the same Teacher and Master as of old,— One who, though risen, was still carrying on the work He had begun before His death, and who would fulfill all His promises to them. Thus by degrees the resurrection was seen to be only a new step in the one purpose of redemption, and with joy, not with fear, should they wait in Galilee for His appearing.

SUNDAY, 24TH NISAN, 16TH APRIL, 783. A. D. 30.

After eight days Jesus again appears to the assembled JOHN xx. 26–29. apostles, Thomas, who had been before absent, now being with them. By showing him the prints of the nails and of the spear, as he has demanded, and desiring him to touch JOHN xx. 24, 25.

them, the Lord convinces him of the reality of His resurrection; and Thomas acknowledges Him as his Lord and
his God.

A week passed away, and the apostles were still lingering in
Jerusalem. Why was this? Some say, because they were
waiting for the expiration of the paschal feast, which lasted seven
days. But Lightfoot says, that although on the first day no one
was permitted to exceed the limits of a Sabbath day's journey
and on the second, no one might go home because of "the appearance before the Lord," which then took place, yet on the
third, one might go if necessary. It is said by Stier that the Lord's
direction to go to Galilee presupposed their tarrying through
the feast. This is not at all probable; but even if so, the
feast was now ended, yet they remained. The cause of their
delay to go to Galilee was probably the unbelief of Thomas,
who was not present at the Lord's first appearing, and who
refused to believe the testimony of others, and demanded the
proof of both sight and touch. Possibly there were others of
the disciples yet in doubt, and unwilling to leave the city, but
probably most of those from Galilee had gone back to their
homes.

How the apostles spent the week, we are not told; but probably
they often visited the garden, and may have assembled every evening
in the accustomed place in the hope that He would appear again to
them. But why did not those who believed go to Galilee? Because
they had now learned that their witness to the Lord's resurrection
and their work for Him must be done by them as one body, as an
apostolic college, and they must, therefore, continue together. If
Thomas was still unbelieving, thus preventing any united action, they
must wait the Lord's further direction before taking any new step.
It thus became necessary that He should manifest Himself again to
the assembled apostles at Jerusalem, that Thomas might be convinced
and the apostolic unity be maintained. (See Edersheim, ii. 646.)

The place where the Lord met the Eleven was in all probability
the same where He met them before, and this is generally accepted.[1]
The hour was doubtless also in the evening, though this is not said.
He suddenly appeared among them, the door being shut as before,
and renewed the salutation: "Peace be unto you."

---

[1] Caspari is an exception. According to him the apostles left Jerusalem for Galilee immediately after the paschal season, and this manifestation took place at Capernaum
or Bethsaida, and is the same as that mentioned by Mark xvi. 14, 15.

Thomas was now with them.   Why he was not present at their first meeting, we are not told; most say that, being naturally skeptical, he disbelieved the reports of the other disciples.   This may be, but that he was not wanting in love or courage is shown in the matter of Laz-arus (John xi. 16).   The proof which the Lord gave him that it was He Himself now standing among them, was of the character that He had before given the ten — the evidence of his senses.   Whether Thomas actually put his finger into the print of the nails, and his hand into His side, is in question.   It was affirmed by Calvin and others, and apparently by Ellicott (403, note), but most deny it.   (So Meyer, Luthardt, Edersheim; see Nebe, Auferstehungsgeschichte, 228.)   It is said by Hengstenberg that it was the Lord's knowledge of Thomas's words and their repetition (verse 27), which was the con-vincing proof to him that the Lord was really before him; others more probably ascribe his conviction to the impression which the Lord's whole appearance made upon him.   The words of reproof addressed to Thomas: "Because thou hast seen Me thou hast be-lieved," were in their measure applicable to the other apostles, for they had refused at first to listen to the testimony of the women, and were not convinced of the reality of His resurrection till He gave them sensible evidence.

The point whether the appearance to the Twelve mentioned by Paul (1 Cor. xv. 5) was either of those already spoken of, or that upon the day of His ascension, will soon be considered.   This was the sixth and last of the earlier Judæan appearances.   The apostles now go to Galilee to meet their Lord there.

APRIL — MAY, 783.   A. D. 30.

The apostles having returned to Galilee, the Lord appears to some of them while engaged in fishing upon the lake.   The miracle of the great draught of fishes is repeated, and He feeds the seven with fish and bread. After they have eaten, He commands Peter three times to feed His sheep, and signifies his future death and the protracted life of John.   **JOHN xxi. 1-23.**

After this, He appears upon a mountain to a great body of disciples, and commands that the Gospel be preached and disciples baptized throughout the world.   **MATT. xxviii. 16-20.** **1 COR. xv. 6.** **MARK xvi. 15-18.**

How long after the Lord's second appearance to the assem-bled apostles they remained in Jerusalem, we are not told.   It is said by Hengstenberg that they went to Galilee the next day; this is probable.   It is also probable that they continued to-

gether, and went to the same place on the sea of Galilee, which
we may believe to have been Capernaum.   Six persons are
mentioned as going to fish with Peter, of these five were of the
apostles, their names being given.   Were the other two apostles?
(Some affirm this; so Lightfoot, who thinks them to have been
Andrew and Philip, in this followed by Hengstenberg and others ; *contra*, Meyer, Godet, Nebe.)   It is a point which we have
not data to decide.   That He appeared to these seven and not to
the eleven apostles, seems to indicate some symbolical meaning
lying under this number.   (As to the many points of resem
blance which this miracle has to that at the beginning of the
Lord's Galilæan ministry, see Trench, who also refers approv
ingly to Augustine's symbolical interpretations.)

This first appearance in Galilee after His resurrection, leads us to
contrast it with the Lord's earlier appearances in Judæa.   The object
of the latter was, as we have seen, to prove to the disciples the reality
of His resurrection as preparatory to His further instructions; and
this had now been done.   They were in Galilee waiting for His coming to them.   That the seven in the ship did not at first recognize
Him standing on the shore several hundred feet distant — "They
knew not that it was Jesus" (compare xx. 14) — may have been
owing in part to the distance, and perhaps to the indistinct morning
light, but more to His changed appearance.   But so soon as He is
recognized, and it is John who first recognized Him, He is again
their Lord as of old, and proceeds to give them food — it is not said
whether He Himself ate of it — and then holds a conversation with
Peter, the purpose of which is to renew his commission to feed His
flock.   He also intimates to him the manner of his death, and answers
his questions respecting the future of John (verses 18–22).   It was
now understood by Peter, and doubtless by them all, that their real
apostolic work was about to begin under His guidance, who, though
absent, would direct them when and where to cast the net.

It is said by John (xxi. 14) that "this is now the third time that
Jesus showed Himself to His disciples, after that He was risen from
the dead."   It is generally understood that the Evangelist here
speaks of manifestations made "to the circle of disciples, not to individual persons" (Meyer; so most).   It is said by Dwight that
"'third' refers to the third appearance recorded in this Gospel before
a company of the apostles."   It is clear that in his three-fold enumeration John refers to the apostles as constituting the most important
class of the disciples, although in each case he speaks of an appear-

ance to the disciples — μαθηταί — not to the apostles.   Caspari thinks
'third" refers to the third appearance of which John was a witness.

It is said by Meyer and others that these three appearances cannot
be made to harmonize with the statements of Paul (1 Cor. xv. 5, 6).   It
will be necessary therefore, at this point, to examine the apostle's
words.

The appearances mentioned by St. Paul.   Does he design to give a
chronological outline of all the appearances he knew of ?   (So Steinmeyer; *contra*, Wieseler.)   His words are: "He was seen of Cephas;
then of the Twelve; after that, He was seen of above five hundred
brethren at once;   .   .   .   after that He was seen of James; then of
all the apostles; and last of all, He was seen of me also."   Thus, excluding the last as out of our present enquiry, Paul mentions five
appearances.   The first, that to Cephas — Peter — has been already
spoken of, being mentioned by Luke (xxiv. 34).   Is the second, that
to the Twelve, to be identified with that on Easter evening, or with
that a week after, or with that just before the ascension ?   Or is it
an appearance not mentioned by the Evangelists ?   There is no good
reason why it is not to be regarded as the same as that on Easter evening (so Lightfoot, McClellan, Stroud, Rob., Westcott; but Gardiner
identifies it with that on the second Sunday evening).   The use of
the term "Twelve" here decides nothing, since this is the designation of the apostolic college, whether all were present or not.

The third appearance, that to the five hundred brethren, is not
mentioned by the Evangelists; whether it is to be identified with that
to the Eleven at the mountain in Galilee (Matt. xxviii. 16) will be
soon considered.

The fourth appearance mentioned by Paul is that to James; of
this also the Evangelists say nothing.   When and where was it ?   If
the apostle follows the chronological order, it was after that to the five
hundred; but it may have been either in Galilee or in Judæa.   What
James was this ?   Some say the apostle James, the brother of John (so
Steinmeyer), but most, James the brother of the Lord.   (So Estius,
in loco : Porro doctorum omnium sententia est ; Bp. Lightfoot, Gal., 260;
Meyer.)   If to the last, it is most probable that the Lord appeared to
him in Galilee where he dwelt with his brothers, and soon after He
Himself went to Galilee.   It is generally believed that this appearance to James was the means of convincing him and his brothers that
Jesus was the Messiah, as all appear in the upper room after His
ascension (Acts i. 14). [1]

---

[1] As to the apocryphal story in "The Gospel according to the Hebrews," it is rejected by Estius and most.   See Hofmann, 393.

The fifth appearance was to "all the apostles." This is usually identified with that mentioned in Acts i. 6, when He led them out to the Mount of Olives. But why say "all the apostles" rather than "The Twelve"? Some say that here a secondary class of Apostles is included (so Bp. Lightfoot, Meyer); others that a contrast is put between James as one of the apostles and all of them taken collectively, or between James as not an apostle and the apostolic college.

That St. Paul mentions these appearances in the order of time, is probable, the adverbial particles indicating this (so Meyer; *contra*, Wieseler); though a long interval elapses between the last appearance to the apostles and that to himself. That he mentioned all the appearances he knew of, is scarcely possible, though the principle of selection is not clear; he doubtless selected them with reference to the peculiar circumstances of the Corinthian Christians.

Returning now to the assertion of Meyer, that John and Paul contradict each other, we ask wherein the contradiction lies? That each mentions appearances not mentioned by the other is plain; that either of them professes to mention them all, is not said, or implied.

The only appearance of the Lord in Galilee mentioned by Matthew is that to the eleven disciples (xxviii. 16). Is this the same as the appearance to the five hundred? This is generally affirmed, but on differing grounds. Some find a proof that there were others beside the apostles present, in Matthew's words, "some doubted" (so Rob.). They think that none of the Eleven, to whom the Lord had said, "Receive ye the Holy Ghost," remembering the past appearances of the Lord to them, and that they were now gathered expressly to meet Him, could have been among these doubters. If not, others must have been there; and as most of His Galilæan disciples had not seen Him since His resurrection, it would not be surprising if some among them should doubt. To this may be added, as confirmatory, the fact that the Lord's direction by the angel to the women to go into Galilee was general, embracing all the disciples. Thus it is made possible that five hundred were now present; though some limit them to the Seventy. But this proof is not at all conclusive. Matthew's words seem clearly to state that some of the apostles doubted (so Meyer, Keil, Nebe; for early opinions, see Maldonatus *in loco*). The grounds of this doubt will be considered later. The fact of their doubting does not, however, show that the five hundred disciples were not there with the Eleven. (This is held by many, Lightfoot, Norton, Ebrard, Stier, Alford, Ellicott, Nebe).

But is it probable that the commission (verses 19, 20) would be given to the apostles in the presence of all? or are we to regard the commission as given to all? If given to the apostles, as the leaders and representatives of the church, as held by most, there seems a propriety in commissioning them in the presence of all the disciples. But some affirm that these words of Matthew do not refer to any special commission, or were spoken on a single occasion, but are a very brief summary of the Lord's teachings during all the forty days; and others, who hold that they were spoken to the apostles only, think them spoken in Jerusalem or on the Mount of Olives, just before the ascension. (So Maldonatus, a Lapide.) But if this view be held, it excludes the presence of the five hundred; for it is not possible that such a gathering could have taken place at Jerusalem and not have been disturbed by the Pharisees and rulers.

It has been said by some that the five hundred assembled in Jerusalem the week following the resurrection, thus distinguishing this appearance to them from the later appearance to the Eleven, which was in Galilee (so Dwight, in Godet, ii. 537). This is in all respects improbable.

The mountain in Galilee where the apostles met the Lord according to His appointment, is not named. It was, doubtless, one of those near the lake of Galilee; some have said the mount where the sermon was delivered (Matt. v. 1); others, that where He was transfigured (Matt. xvii. 1); others, that where He chose the Twelve (Mark iii. 13); or, possibly, that on the east side of the lake where He fed the five thousand (John vi. 13).[1]

When the Lord made the appointment for this meeting, we are not told. It may be that in His direction before His death to go to Galilee this mount was mentioned, but more probably it was not till later at one of His appearances to the Eleven. Wherever the five hundred were gathered, both the time and the place must have been definitely known, and the notice have been early and widely given.

If some of the apostles doubted, of what did they doubt? Whether they should offer to Him worship?[2] It is not indeed anywhere said that He had before been worshipped by them; and now something new and divine in His aspect may have impelled them to the act (see Matt. xxviii. 9, John xx. 23). But their doubts could

---

[1] It was a tradition current during the middle ages that it was the northern peak of the Mount of Olives, which had the name of Galilee. It is spoken of by Maundeville, A. D. 1322 (Early Travels, 177), as "Mount Galilee where the apostles assembled when Mary Magdalene came and told them of Christ's ascension." This tradition has recently been defended by Hofmann (Leben Jesu, 395), but is wholly untenable. There is no mention in the New Testament or in Josephus of any mountain called Galilee; only the province is so called. Ewald, Jahrbuch, 1856, 196; Nebe, Auferstehungsgeschichte, 340.

[2] So Wetstein, quoted in Meyer; De Wette, Lange.

scarce refer to this. Did they doubt of His personal identity?
Some have thought that He was so far from them that all could not
at first distinctly see Him; others refer their doubts to the changed
appearance of His body, either as already glorified, or as in an intermediate condition, midway between the earthly and heavenly.
Some, as Newcome, would translate it "had doubted," and refer it
to the earlier doubts of the apostles. "Some had doubted before;
but all were now convinced." Grammatical accuracy forbids this.

THURSDAY, MAY 18TH, 783. A. D. 30.

After the meeting upon the mountain in Galilee, the apostles return to Jerusalem. Upon the fortieth day after His resurrection, Jesus gathers the Eleven at the Mount of Olives, and, leading them toward Bethany, ascends to heaven. While they are gazing after Him, two men stand by them, and remind them that He is to return. The apostles go back to Jerusalem, and there wait for the promised baptism of the Holy Spirit. After Pentecost they begin their labors.	LUKE xxiv. 49. ACTS i. 1–3. ACTS i. 4–8. LUKE xxiv. 50, 51. MARK xvi. 19. ACTS i. 9–12. LUKE xxiv. 52, 53. MARK xvi. 20.

At what time the apostles returned to Jerusalem we are not
told, but we may believe that it was only a very short time before
the ascension. That Luke in his statement (Acts i. 3), that
Jesus "showed Himself alive after His passion by many infalli-
ble proofs, being seen of [the apostles] forty days, and speaking
of the things pertaining to the kingdom of God," includes more
interviews than are specifically recorded by any of the Evangelists, cannot well be doubted; and that these interviews occurred
in Galilee before the apostles went up to Jerusalem, not in Jerusalem, is almost certain. In favor of Galilee it may be said, that
here the apostles were at home and among friends, and that
amidst the scenes of His former teachings His present words
would come with double power and meaning; while in Jerusalem they would be among His enemies, and in a state of dis-
quietude, if not of positive fear. We may, then, suppose that it
was near the fortieth day ere they went up to Jerusalem. That
they went in obedience to some special direction, is probable,
and not simply to be present at the feast of Pentecost, which was
more than ten days later; but that they knew for what end He
had gathered them there, may be doubted. Indeed it is probable
that so far from supposing that He was then about to depart from

them into heaven, they rather hoped and expected that He was about to reveal Himself in glory, and to commence His reign. That the mother of Jesus and the other women left Jerusalem and went to Galilee, and were with the five hundred, is almost certain; and that they returned to Jerusalem with the apostles, appears from the mention of them as with the apostles in the upper chamber immediately after the ascension (Acts i. 14). Probably they were accompanied on their return by His brethren.

It is from the statements of Luke in his Gospel (xxiv. 50, 51), and in the Acts (i. 4–12), that we learn the details of the Lord's departure into heaven. In the latter (verse 4) we read: "And being assembled together with them, He commanded them that they should not depart from Jerusalem, but wait for the promise of the Father, which, saith He, ye have heard of Me. For John truly baptized with water, but ye shall be baptized with the Holy Ghost not many days hence. When they therefore were come together, they asked of Him," etc. Are two different assemblings here spoken of?[1] This seems most probable, tho two expressions "being assembled together with them," and, "when they therefore were come together," clearly pointing to two distinct and successive occasions.[2] But there need have been no long interval between them; they may have been on two successive days, or even one in the morning and the other in the afternoon of the same day. The place of their assembling was not improbably the upper room of the paschal supper.

As Luke alone of the Evangelists mentions the place of the Ascension, we must turn to his statements. He says in his Gospel (xxiv. 50): "And He led them out as far as to Bethany"—ἕως εἰς Βηθανίαν; in the Acts of the Apostles (i. 12): "Then returned they unto Jerusalem from the mount called Olivet, which is from Jerusalem a sabbath day's journey." The topographical objection to the traditional site of the ascension is, that it is but about half a mile from the city wall; and if Jesus was separated from the disciples here, He did not lead them out as far as to Bethany. There is also another objection, in the fact of its publicity, being in full view from the city. But if we construe the statement, "as far as to Bethany," to mean the village of Bethany, we, on the other hand, make Luke inconsistent with him-

---

[1] As to the right rendering in verse 4, there is question. In the margin of our version, for "being assembled" is put, "eating together with them"; this is accepted by Meyer; in Vul. *convescens.* The R. V. retains "being assembled."

[2] So Olshausen; Hackett, Com. on Acts, *in loco;* Cook, and others; *contra,* Alford, and Gloag, Com. on Acts.

self, since this is a mile below the summit of Olivet, and much more than a sabbath day's journey. But the now generally accepted text of Luke in the Gospel does not say that "the Lord led them out as far as to Bethany," but, "He led them out till they were over against Bethany," R. V. — πρὸς Βηθανίαν — Tisch., W. and H. It is remarked by Riddle (Har. 272) that "this reading has relieved us of an apparent contradiction between Luke's statements here and in Acts i. 12." It is therefore unnecessary to repeat here the several solutions formerly given. It was near Bethany or in its vicinity that the Ascension took place. That the "Mount of Olives" is a general designation embracing the eastern as well as the western slopes, is apparent from various passages in the Evangelists. We have, then, to seek a site somewhere upon the mount, in the neighborhood of Bethany, and distant about a sabbath day's journey from Jerusalem.[1] Such a site Barclay thinks he finds in a hill which overhangs Bethany, which lies about five hundred yards below. This hill is a mile from St. Stephen's gate, and within a hundred yards of the direct footpath from Bethany to Jerusalem. It is said by McGarvey (210): "About half a mile southeast of the principal summit is a rounded knoll, nearly of the same height, connected to the mount by a narrow, depressed ledge, with a steep descent on the eastern side. Bethany lies immediately under this knoll on its eastern slope." However it may be with these particular spots, there is little doubt that from some one of the heights a little below the summit of Olivet, that look to the east and overhang the village of Bethany, He ascended to sit at the right hand of His Father.

The supposed exact spot of the Ascension upon the Mount of Olives has been preserved by tradition, of which Robinson (ii. 253) speaks as "one of the very earliest traditions on record," and "which certainly existed in the third century long before the visit of Helena." It is certain that Helena, mother of Constantine, erected a church upon the summit, and probably near the present site; though Stanley (448) claims that she did not mean to honor the scene of the Ascension itself, but a cave in which, according to Eusebius, Jesus initiated His disciples into His secret mysteries. "There is, in fact, no proof from Eusebius that any tradition pointed out the scene of the Ascension."[2]

---

[1] The mountain at its base and lower slopes, is within a few rods of the city. "The mean distance," says Barclay (59), "of that portion of its summit opposite the city is about half a mile. But by the nearest pathway it is 918 yards from St. Stephen's gate to the Church of the Ascension; by the longer footpath, 1,310 yards; and by the main camel road, is perhaps a little farther."

[2] For a history of the mount and a description of the present Church of the Ascension, see Baed., 218, who says: "In the center of the chapel, which is octagonal in shape with a small dome, is the spot where Christ is said to have ascended. It belongs to the

As to the rock within the present chapel, which has been pointed out to pilgrims since the seventh century as bearing the imprint of the Lord's footsteps, Stanley says, "There is nothing but a simple cavity in the rock, with no more resemblance to a human foot than to anything else."

The traditional site is defended by Williams (Holy City, ii. 240). The northern peak of the ridges began to be known in the 16th century as *viri Galilaei*, because it was said that "the two men in white" stood here and addressed the apostles : "Ye men of Galilee, why stand ye gazing up into heaven" ?

The ascension itself is mentioned only by Mark and Luke; how are we to account for the silence of Matthew and John?   Not of course from ignorance, or because they disparaged its importance; but because it was the natural sequence of the resurrection, and therefore needed no special mention.   The Lord had often spoken of His departure to the Father, and explained to the apostles its necessity. Except He ascended into Heaven, He could not send upon them the Holy Ghost; and without His presence they could not do their work, nor the Church be gathered.   His departure, therefore, was a step onward, and one essential to the accomplishment of the divine purpose in the establishment of the Messianic kingdom.   Besides, as He had appeared to them for brief intervals during the forty days and again disappeared, His personal absence for a longer but an indefinite period did not seem to them as an event, like the resurrection, to be recorded, with all fullness of detail.   We are also to remember that none then believed that His absence would be long, but looked upon his reappearing as possible at any hour.   Thus placing ourselves in the position of the early Christians, we are not surprised that two of the Evangelists pass the ascension over without mention.   It was the natural sequence of the resurrection, it had been foretold, they had become familiar during the forty days with His sudden appearings and disappearings, they looked to see Him speedily appear again; it might, therefore, be passed over, or if mentioned, only briefly.   This brief mention is all that we find in the Gospels of Mark and Luke. It is only in the Acts of the Apostles that Luke enters more into detail, evidently regarding the ascension as the beginning of the Lord's heavenly activity, and therefore, as having its right place as introductory to the work of the apostles.   The Gospels end with the end of the Lord's work on the earth; any mention of the ascension was not demanded.

Moslems, who also regard it as sacred, but Christians are permitted to celebrate mass in it on certain days."   See also Smith's Bib. Dict., Art., Mount of Olives.

But we have still to consider the manner in which Mark and Luke seem to connect the ascension with the resurrection, as if taking place the same day. And we will first examine the language of Mark (xvi. 14–20). Two points here meet us: *a*, the time of the appearance (verse 14); *b*, the time when the words (verses 15–18) were spoken.

a. That this appearance was on the evening of the day of the resurrection, and the same as that mentioned by John (xx. 19), has been already shown. It is hardly credible that the Lord who on that evening showed himself to the Eleven, would at any later period have upbraided them with their unbelief and hardness of heart in not believing those who had seen him.

b. Were the words (vs. 15–18) — the command to go into all the world and preach the gospel, and the promise of the signs to follow — spoken at this supper or later?

From the connection in which His words stand, it would seem that they were spoken to the Eleven as they sat at meat on the evening of the day of the resurrection, and that immediately after He ascended into heaven. This, however, is wholly irreconcilable with the statements of Luke in the Acts; and it is also intrinsically improbable that upon the occasion of His first meeting with the apostles after He had risen, and while their minds were in so great excitement, He should give them this commission.

It is affirmed by some, as Meyer and Alford, that Mark, intending to relate what took place at one and the same time, brings together here by mistake what really took place on several distinct occasions. He supposed that the Lord spake these words to the Eleven on the evening of the day He rose, and the same evening ascended to heaven. But the same rule of interpretation seems also to show that He was received up from the room in which they were eating, and that the Eleven, going immediately forth from this room, began at once to preach the Gospel. Of course, if this were so, the writer, whether Mark or some one else, could have known nothing of the several appearances of Jesus during the forty days, of the ascension from Bethany, or of the ten days' waiting for the Spirit ere the disciples began to preach. The supposition of such ignorance on his part itself presents a greater difficulty than that it is intended to remove.

We give some of the solutions that have been proposed:

1st. That which takes Mark's narrative as strictly chronological. The Lord's words were spoken to the Eleven on the evening of the day of the resurrection, and His ascension immediately followed. This is affirmed by those who, as Kinkel and Jones, maintain that He repeatedly ascended to heaven; and, indeed, that He departed thither after each appearance to His disciples. The ascension on the fortieth day (Acts i. 9) was the last, and as such was visible, and marked with especial solemnity.[1] This view of several ascensions may remove some difficulties, but involves others greater, both historical and dogmatic.

2d. That which makes Jesus to have spoken these words to the Eleven on the evening of the day of the resurrection, but defers the Ascension itself to the fortieth day following. In this case the phrase, μετὰ τὸ λαλῆσαι, "After the Lord had spoken to them" (verse 19), is not to be confined to the few words just recorded, but embraces His discourses in general, down to the time He ascended.

3d. That which places His interview with the Eleven on the evening of the day of the resurrection (verse 14), but the words following upon some subsequent occasion, perhaps upon the mount in Galilee; and the ascension at a still later period.

4th. That which makes this interview with the Eleven to have been after the return of Jesus and the disciples from Galilee to Jerusalem, and immediately before the ascension at Bethany. (See Acts, i. 4.)

The obvious and natural interpretation of Mark's narrative is this: The Evangelist, wishing to give in the briefest way the substance of the Lord's missionary commission to the Church, with its accompanying promises, connects it with a meeting of the eleven apostles, which, for reasons already given, was probably on the evening of the day of the resurrection. All the instructions of the forty days upon this point are summed up in these few words. In the same concise way it is said, that after the Lord had spoken to them, or after He had finished His instructions, He was received up. To press this brevity as indicating ignorance on his part of the real order of events, is hypercritical.

Substantially the same difficulties meet us in the narrative of Luke as in that of Mark. In his Gospel (xxiv. 33–51), he seems to represent the ascension as taking place the evening after Jesus rose from the dead. The Lord meets the Eleven and others as they were gathered together, and after convincing them that He was really risen by eating before them and discoursing to them, He leads them out to Bethany, and blessing them, is carried up into heaven.

We have already seen that this appearance of the Lord in Luke when He ate before them, is the same as the appearance in John (xx.

---

[1] See Kinkel, Studien u. Krit., 1841, translated in Bib. Sacra, Feb., 1844. Jones, (Notes, 480): "He was, during the forty days, ordinarily an inhabitant of the heavenly world." See *contra*, Robinson, in Bib. Sacra, May, 1845.

19.) It was on the evening of the day of the resurrection that the
two returned from Emmaus and found the Eleven gathered together,
and then the Lord appeared to them.

Our second inquiry is as to the time when the words (verses
44–48) were spoken. This is not certain. Some, regarding them as
spoken at one time, would put them in immediate connection with
what precedes; others refer them to a later period — to the second
interview with the Eleven after eight days, or to the meeting upon
the mount in Galilee, or to the day of the ascension; others affirm
that the Evangelist gives here a summary of Jesus' teachings during
the forty days; giving especial prominence to His teaching respecting
the fulfillment of prophecy in His death, and in its further fulfillment through the preaching of the Gospel to all nations. Whether
the opening their understanding to understand the scriptures refers
to some special act (John xx. 22), or to a gradual process of spiritual
illumination, is in question.

We have seen that Luke in his statements in the Gospel and in
the Acts is consistent as to the place of the ascension, is he consistent
also as to the time? Before comparing them as to this point, we
must examine the text of the Gospel. Tischendorf, in verse 51, omits
"and was carried into heaven," and in verse 52: "and they worshipped
Him." (They are bracketed by W. and H., but retained in the R. V.)
If omitted, we read: "And it came to pass, while He blessed them,
He was parted from them, and they returned to Jerusalem with
great joy." This very brief mention here is wholly in keeping with
Luke's intention to speak more fully in his later treatise.

The question now arises whether this Evangelist in the Acts of
the Apostles contradicts anything he has said in his Gospel. This is
affirmed by Meyer. According to him, there were two traditions, one
of which represented the Lord as ascending upon the day of the resurrection; the other, after forty days. In his Gospel, Luke follows the
former; in the Acts, the latter. With Meyer, Alford agrees. "Luke,
at the time of writing his Gospel, was not aware of any Galilæan appearances of the Lord, nor indeed of any later than this one. That
he corrects this in Acts i., shows him to have become acquainted with
some other sources of information, not however, perhaps, including
the Galilæan appearances." All this is arbitrary conjecture. There
is not the slightest hint that the Evangelist wished to correct in the
later account an error in the earlier. Had he made so gross a mistake,
common honesty toward his readers would have demanded an explicit
statement of it, and a retraction; for how otherwise could Theophilus
or any of his readers, know which account to believe? On the contrary, he says that his former treatise embraced all that Jesus did and

taught " until the day in which He was taken up," " being seen of
the apostles forty days." This is a plain averment that in his Gospel
he placed the ascension on the fortieth day, although he did not
there give any specific designation of time.[1]

Those who, like Jones, make the Lord to have often ascended,
refer these accounts of Luke to different events. In the Gospel, he
speaks of the ascension on the evening following the resurrection;
in Acts, of the last ascension. And as the time, so the place was
different; the former ascension being from Bethany, the latter from
the summit of the Mount of Olives.[2] But Luke's language in his
Gospel, plainly shows that he cannot speak of an ascension upon
the evening of the day when Jesus arose. The day was far spent
when He was with the two disciples at Emmaus, and they had still
to return to Jerusalem, and probably were some time with the Eleven,
ere He joined them. Hours may have passed in convincing them of
His actual resurrection, and in discoursing to them. It must, therefore, have been late in the evening ere He led them out to Bethany,
and the ascension itself must have been in the dead of night. This
is intrinsically improbable, not to say incredible. It may have been
at sunset or in the early evening.

We may now sum up the general results of our investigations.

The forty days, or five weeks and five days, beginning Easter
Sunday, April 9th, and ending Thursday, May 18th, may be
divided into three periods. 1st. That in Judæa from Easter
Sunday to the departure into Galilee. 2d. That in Galilee. 3d.
That after the return to Jerusalem to the ascension.

During the first period, from Easter Sunday till the Sunday
following inclusive, there were six appearances, five on Easter
Sunday: (*a*) to Mary Magdalene; (*b*) to the other women; (*c*) to
the two at Emmaus; (*d*) to Peter; (*e*) to the Eleven; on the next
Sunday (*f*) to the Eleven. That the Lord may have appeared
to His mother on Easter day or during the week, is probable,
but not recorded.

During the second period, after the arrival in Galilee, there
were two, probably three, recorded appearances: (*a*) to the seven
at the Sea of Tiberias; (*b*) to the five hundred, the Eleven being
present; (*c*) to James.

---

[1] See Ebrard, 596.

[2] In this way Jones (515) explains the statement of Barnabas, that the Lord ascended on the eighth day. The final ascension was on the 5th day of the week, or Thursday, that to which Barnabas refers was on the 8th or first day of the week, and the very
day on which he arose. See Hefele, Patrum Apostolicorum Opera. 42; Nebe, 381.

During the third period, after the return to Jerusalem to the ascension — some two days — there were two appearances: (*a*) to the apostles first assembling somewhere in the city; (*b*) to them in the city to lead them out to Bethany.

The length of each of these periods can only approximately be given. 1. In Jerusalem, and including time of journey to Galilee, twelve days. 2. In Galilee, twenty-three days. 3. Journey from Galilee to Jerusalem and in the city, five days. In regard to those utterances of the Lord during the forty days the time and place of which are in dispute, we give a brief classification of opinions.

1 (Matt. xxviii. 18–20). (*a*) In Galilee to the Eleven alone; (*b*) to the Eleven and five hundred; (*c*) in Jerusalem before or at His ascension ; (*d*) a summary of all the Galilæan teachings.

2 (Mark xvi. 15–18). (*a*) In Jerusalem on the evening of Easter day; (*b*) on evening of second Sunday; (*c*) just before or at His ascension; (*d*) spoken at same time with Matt. xxviii. 18–20.

3 (Luke xxiv. 44–48). 1. All spoken at one time. (*a*) On evening of Easter day; (*b*) in Jerusalem after return from Galilee. 2. Spoken at different times. (*a*) Some parts on day of the ascension; (*b*) other parts earlier during the forty days; (*c*) a summary of all His teachings to His ascension; (*d*) some parts spoken on day of ascension, other parts earlier during the forty days. That the command (verse 49) to tarry in the city of Jerusalem was spoken after they had returned thither from Galilee, and is identical with the command Acts i. 4, needs no proof.

Thus comparing the several Evangelists, we find that the Lord during the forty days first manifested Himself to His disciples in Judæa, and going thence to Galilee, returned again to Judæa to ascend to God. So far as we can learn, it was not His purpose to have shown Himself to them in Jerusalem, for He had commanded them to go into Galilee, and there they should see Him. But their unbelief in His words respecting His resurrection, made it necessary that He should manifest Himself to them there; yet even after they had seen Him, the unbelief of one seems to have detained them some days in Jerusalem. As in Galilee He had gathered His disciples, so here **He appoints a**

place of general meeting.   But He cannot ascend to His Father
from Galilee.   As He went up to Jerusalem to die, He now goes
up thither again, that from the Mount of Olives overlooking the
Holy City and the temple, He may ascend to His Father's right
hand to receive the kingdom; to enter on His work of intercession; to send the Holy Ghost for the gathering and forming of
His church; and to await the hour when His feet shall stand
again upon the Mount, and His enemies shall be made His foot-
stool, and the rejected and crucified One shall be King over all
the earth.

"Ye men of Galilee, why stand ye gazing up into heaven?
This same Jesus which is taken up from you into heaven, shall
so come in like manner as ye have seen Him go into heaven."

APPENDIX.

I. The Miracles of the Gospels.
PREPARED BY MR. E. E. NOURSE.

In the Gospels there are, if I mistake not, fifty-seven distinct miraculous occurrences noted.

The above enumeration does not include such events as have a more or less supernatural character, but which cannot be classed as miraculous. I mean such events as Mary's psalm of praise, the words of Zacharias at the baptism of John, the utterances of Simeon and Anna — all of which were inspired in a greater or less degree by the Holy Spirit. The mission of the wise men, the warnings given to Joseph in a dream, the temptation of Christ, the impulse of John the Baptist to preach, his knowledge of Christ — all these are more or less extraordinary and supernatural in character, but are not to be called miraculous.

Of the fifty-seven events of the Gospel history which we have called miraculous, five are events connected with the Saviour's birth and infancy. They are:

1. Angel appears to Zacharias. Luke i.
2. Angel appears to Mary. Luke i.
3. Loosening of Zacharias' tongue, etc. Luke i.
4. Angel appears to Joseph. Matt. i.
5. Angel appears to shepherds. Luke ii.

Of the remaining fifty-two, there are two which were performed without any direct volition of the Saviour, that is by God Himself. They are:

1. The baptism of Christ by the Holy Spirit at the Jordan. Matt. iii. 16.
2. The miracles at the crucifixion — rending of the vail of the temple, opening of graves, etc. Matt. xxvii., xxviii.

The fifty we now have left, are capable of still further subdivision. Twelve of these fifty were events which were miraculous in their nature, actings of the Father upon the Son, or appearances of the Son or of angels after His resurrection, but were not wrought, like healings, upon others. They are:

1. The transfiguration of Christ.   Matt. **xvii**.
2. The resurrection of Christ.   Matt. xxviii.
3. The angels at the sepulchre.   Matt. xxviii.
4. Jesus appears to the women.   Matt. xxviii.
5. Jesus appears to Mary Magdalene.   Mark **xvi**.
6. Jesus appears to Peter.   Luke xxiv.
7. Jesus appears to two disciples.   Luke xxiv.
8. Jesus appears to ten disciples (Thomas being absent).   **John xx.**
9. Jesus appears to eleven disciples.   John xx.
10. Jesus appears on mountain in Galilee.   Matt. xxviii.
11. Jesus appears to seven disciples in Galilee.   John xxi.
12. Ascension.   Mark xvi.

We have left now thirty-eight events which may be called miracles of Our Lord.   About two of them there may be more or less dispute, viz.: (1) The falling backward of the band of men who came to arrest Jesus in the garden (John xviii. 4); and (2) the fire of coals, etc., noticed by the disciples on the shore of the sea of Galilee, when Jesus appears to seven of them at that place.   See John xxi.   As to the remaining thirty-six we think there is no dispute.   They may be found classified in the helps in the Teachers' Bible.

The following occurred at Capernaum:
1. Healing of demoniac.   Mark i.
2. Healing of Peter's mother-in-law and many others.   **Matt. viii.**
3. Healing of paralytic.   Matt. ix.
4. Healing of centurion's servant.   Matt. viii.
5. Raising of Jairus' daughter.   Matt. ix.
6. Healing of two blind men.   Matt. ix.
7. Healing of the dumb spirit.   Matt. ix.
8. Stater in the fish's mouth.   Matt. xvii.
9. Healing of woman with bloody issue.   **Matt. ix.**

In Galilee (place not certain) occurred
1. Healing of a leper.   Matt. viii.
2. Healing of withered hand.   Matt. **xii.**
3. Healing of demoniac.   Matt. xii.

On, or in the immediate vicinity of, the sea of **Galilee, occurred**
1. Miraculous draught of fishes.   Luke v.
2. Stilling of tempest.   Matt. viii.
3. Feeding of five thousand.   Matt. **xiv.**
4. Walking on water.   Matt. xiv.
5. Draught of fishes.   John xxi.

In Jerusalem, or near it, occurred
1. Healing of man at pool of Bethesda.   **John v.**
2. Healing of a blind man.   John ix. and **x.**

3. Withering of fig tree. Matt. xxi.
4. Healing of Malchus' ear (Gethsemane). Luke **xxii.**

In the Decapolis occurred

1. Healing of deaf and dumb (and many). Mark **vii.**
2. Feeding of four thousand. Matt. xv.

The following places witnessed the performance of one **miracle** each:

1. Cana (see below) — Water into wine. John ii.
2. Nain — Son of widow raised. Luke vii.
3. Gadara — Legion of devils cast out. Matt. viii.
4. Region of Tyre and Sidon — Daughter of **woman** healed. Matt. xv.
5. Bethsaida Julias — Blind man. Mark viii.
6. Samaria — Ten lepers. Luke xvii.
7. Bethany — Raising of Lazarus. John **xi.**
8. Jericho — Two blind men. Matt. xx.
9. Nazareth — Miraculous escape of Jesus. Luke **iv.**
10. Caesarea Philippi — Healing of demoniac. Matt. **xvii.**

'n the Peræan region probably occurred

1. Healing of an infirm woman. Luke xiii.
2. Healing of man with dropsy. Luke xiv.

Cana and Capernaum have each an almost equal right to claim the miracle of the healing of the nobleman's son. The word was spoken at Cana, the cure took place at Capernaum. John iv.

If we give this to Capernaum it can claim ten miracles.

If I mistake not, six of our Lord's miracles were performed on a Sabbath. They are

1. Healing of demoniac (Mark i.) in a synagogue.
2. Healing of man in Jerusalem at Bethesda. John v.
3. Healing of withered hand, Galilee (Matt. xii.), in a synagogue.
4. Healing of blind man in Jerusalem (John ix.) near the temple.
5. Healing of an infirm woman, Peræa (Luke xiii.), in a synagogue.
6. Healing of a man with dropsy, Peræa (Luke xiv.), in house of a Pharisee.

There were apparently only three miracles performed in a synagogue.

To the above we subjoin the following note on the Galilæan miracles, prepared by Prof. Barbour.

The fourteen recorded miracles of the southern Galilæan ministry (period from John's imprisonment to his death) would seem, from the way in which they fall naturally into pairs, to be carefully selected samples from a much larger number. The twelve given by St. Luke (chs. iv.–viii.) thus group themselves.

(a) Two wrought on nature: Fishes (animate), Tempest (inanimate).

(b) Ten wrought on man, as follows:

1. Two demoniacs: unclean spirit, legion.

2. Two (chronic) impurity: general, leprosy; local, issue.

3. Two (chronic) helplessness: general, palsy; local, withered hand.

4. Two (acute) severe cases: great fever, point of death (inflammatory rheumatism).

5. Two dead: girl just dead; the widow's son about to be buried.

To which add the pair given by Matthew — two cases of organic defect: blind, dumb.

II. ABRIDGED GENEALOGY OF THE HERODIAN FAMILY.

PREPARED BY PROF. BARBOUR.

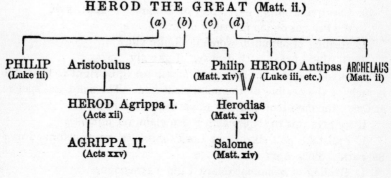

HEROD THE GREAT (Matt. ii.)

(a) *(b)* *(c)* *(d)*

PHILIP (Luke iii)   Aristobulus   Philip (Matt. xiv)   HEROD Antipas (Luke iii, etc.)   ARCHELAUS (Matt. ii)

HEROD Agrippa I. (Acts xii)   Herodias (Matt. xiv)

AGRIPPA II. (Acts xxv)   Salome (Matt. xiv)

Four of the wives of Herod the Great
{
(a) Cleopatra.
(b) Mariamne, granddau. of Hyrcanus.
(c) Mariamne, dau. of Simon.
(d) Malthace.
}

Rulers in CAPITALS.

III. The book, "Gospel Difficulties, or the Displaced Section of St. Luke," by J. J. Halcombe, London, 1886, has not been referred to because it seems incredible that such a displacement could have taken place, and yet no hint of it be found in any ancient manuscript or author. But in many respects the book is worthy of an examination.

GENERAL INDEX.

CHRONOLOGICAL INDEX.

PASSAGES OF SCRIPTURE REFERRED TO IN THE HISTORY.

DATE DUE

10/24			
FEB 18 '82			
MAR 4 '82			
MAR 26 '82			

YLORD   PRINTED IN U.S A